Samuel Fallows

The American Manual and Patriot's Handbook

Vol. 1

Samuel Fallows

The American Manual and Patriot's Handbook
Vol. 1

ISBN/EAN: 9783337308179

Printed in Europe, USA, Canada, Australia, Japan

Cover: Foto ©Suzi / pixelio.de

More available books at **www.hansebooks.com**

THE
AMERICAN MANUAL

AND

PATRIOT'S HANDBOOK,

——BY——

THE RT. REV. SAMUEL FALLOWS, A. M., D. D.,

Author of "*Liberty and Union,*" "*Synonyms and Antonyms,*" "*The Home Beyond,*" "*The Progressive Supplemental Dictionary,*" *Etc., Etc.*

CHICAGO:
T. S. DENISON.
1888.

INDEX.

A.

A Compendious History of the United States	17 - 24
Adams, John	28 - 29
Adams, John Quincy	36 - 37
Adams, Samuel	72
Aggregate Banking Capital and Deposits in the United States	244
Agriculture, Department of	190, 214
Allen, Ethan	72
America and England,—Hon. Thos. A. Hendricks	320 - 321
America, Meaning of	289
American Union and Constitution, The,—Judge Elliot	305
America's Highest Mountain	287
America's Lucky Day	281
Amounts expended for pensions	242
Analysis of the Constitution of the United States	177 - 178
Appointments by the President	188 - 190
Armstrong, *Biography of*	72
Army, The United States	206
Arnold, Benedict	72
Arthur, Chester A.	66 - 67
Articles of Confederation	150 - 155
Ashe, John, *Biography of*	72
Atkinson, Henry	72
Attorney-General	231
A Young Hero	289

B.

Bainbridge, William	72
Banner, The Star Spangled	308
Barney, Commodore, *Biography of*	72
Brooks, John A., *Life of*	418
Brown, Jacob, *Biography of*	72

Brown, Major, *Biography of* 72
Brown's, John, Origin of the Song of 287
Buchanan, James . . . . 54 - 55
Burr, Aaron, *Biography of* 72
Butler, Zebulon, *Biography of* 72

C.

Candidates, Presidential 308
Cane, A Historical 314
Cession of the Northwest Territory . . . . 315 - 317
Chandler, John 74
Christian Commission, The United States,—Rev. J. O. Foster . . . . 254 - 264
Clark, George Rogers, *Biography of* 74
Clay, Green, *Biography of* 74
Clay, Henry, *Biography of* 74
Cleveland, Grover, *Life of* . . . . 68, 69 - 410
Climate of the United States, The 224
Clinton, James, *Biography of* 74
Coffee, Gen. John, *Biography of* 74
Coins of the United States . . . . 252 - 253
Commission, The United States Christian,—Rev. J. O. Foster, A. M. D. D. . . 254 - 264
Committees, Republican and Democratic National . . . . 342 - 343
Composition, A Unique 286
Confederate Relics 309
Confederation, The 131
Confederation, Articles of . . . . 135 - 155
Confederation of the Original States 135
Congress, Length of Sessions . . . . 235 - 235
Constitution of the United States . . . . 162 - 169
Constitution of the United States, Amendments to the . . . . 169 - 176
Constitution of the United States, Analysis of the . . . . 177 - 178
Constitution of the United States, Comments on the,—Justice Samuel Miller . . 179 - 184
Constitution, the American Union and,—Judge Elliot 305
Construction, Railway 389
Conventions, National 389
Cowdrey, Robt. H., *Life of* 420

D.

Dates of the birth and death of our Presidents	241
Day, America's Lucky	286
Dearborn, Henry, *Biography*	74
Decatur, Stephen, *Biography*	74
Declaration *of Independence*, Fac-simile of signatures to the	147 - 148
Declaration of Independence in a New Light, The	297 - 302
Declaration of Independence, The	142 - 148
Declaration of Independence, The Mecklenburg—Hon. Jno. M. Bright	137 - 141
Department, Agriculture	190, 214
" Executive	185 - 187
" Interior	189, 212 - 213
" Justice	190, 219
" Legislative	191 - 195
" Navy	189, 209 - 211
" Post-office	190, 213 - 215
" State	188, 196 - 199
" Treasury	188, 200 - 202
" War	189, 203 - 208
Diplomatic and Consular Offices	220
Doric Organ of Yankee	288
Dues, A Congressional	285

E.

Educational, *Statistics, etc*	249 - 250
Election Laws of different States	241 - 242
Elections, History of Presidential	238 - 240
Electorial Vote, Legislature, etc	241 - 242
England and America,—Hon. Thos. Hendricks	320 - 321
Evacuation of New York, The	290
Executive Department, The	185 - 187
Expenditures in the District of Columbia	251

F.

Facsimile of the Signatures of the Declaration of Independence . . . . 147 - 148
Federal Vessels Captured or destroyed by Confederate "Cruisers" 242
Figure, A Historic 284
Fillmore, Millard . . . . 50 - 51
First blood of the Revolution 296
First and last things of the Civil War . . . . 265 - 273
Fisk, Clinton B., *Life of* . . . . 413 - 417
Flag, The President's 291
Fulton, Robert, *Biography of* 74

G.

Gaines, Edmund P., *Biography of* 74
Garfield, James A., *Life of* . . . . 64 - 65
Gates, Horatio, *Biography of* 74
Gold and Silver produced in the United States from 1845 to 1886 inclusive 251
Governmental Instructor . . . . 130 - 135
Grant, Ulysses S., *Life of* . . . . 60 - 61
Green, Nathaniel, *Biography of* 74

H.

Hancock, John, *Biography of* 74
Harrison, Benjamin, *Life of* . . . . 399 - 408
Harrison, Wm. Henry, *Biography of* . . . . 42 - 43
Hayes, Rutherford B., *Life of* . . . . 62 - 63
Henry, Patrick, *Biography of* 74
Hero, A Young 289
Heroes of the Revolution and War of 1812 . . . . 72 - 81
Heroic Figure, A 284
Historical Cane, A 314
Historical Notes . . . . 126 - 129
Historical Trees 293
History of Political Conventions, Brief . . . . 344 - 346
History of Presidential Elections . . . . 238 - 240
History of the Civil War must not be Ignored—The Rt. Rev. Dr. Sam'l Fallows . . . . 318 - 319

History of the United States, A Compendious............................ 17 - 24
History, Population, etc., of the States and Territories........................ 244 - 245
History, Tariff of the United States,—Henry J. Philpott, Esq.............. 421 -423
House of Representatives... 193
Howard, John Eager, *Biography of*... 76
Hull, Isaac, *Biography of*... 76
Hull, William, *Biography of*.. 76

I.

Immigration for 1887... 292
Independence, Declaration of.. 142 - 148
Independence, The Mecklenburg Declaration of,—Hon. John M. Bright........ 137 - 141
Instructor, Governmental... 130 - 135
Interior Department.. 189, 212 - 214
Izard, George, *Biography of*.. 76

J.

Jackson, Andrew, *Life of*... 38 - 39
Jay, John, *Biography of*.. 76
Jefferson, Thomas, *Life of*... 30 - 31
Jesup, Thomas S., *Biography of*.. 76
Johnson, Andrew, *Life of*.. 58 - 59
Jones, John Paul, *Biography of*... 76
Judiciary... 190
Justice, Department of... 190, 219

K.

Kearney, Stephen W., *Biography of*.. 76

L.

Lady who rejected Washington's hand, The................................... 283
La Fayette, Marquis de, *Biography of*..................................... 76
Land-office, The original... 287
Land we live in, The.. 306
Lawrence, James, *Biography of*.. 76
Lee, Charles, *Biography of*... 76

Lee, Henry, *Biography of* 78
Lee, Richard Henry, *Biography of* 76
Legal Holidays of the States 307
Legislative Department . . . . .191 - 195
Legislature, Electoral Votes, etc, ...242 - 243
Length of Sessions of Congress from 1789 to 1888 . . . . .233 - 234
Liberty 132
Lincoln, Abraham, *Life of* . . . . 56 - 57
Lincoln, Benjamin, *Biography of* 78
Lives of Democratic Candidates . . . . .410 - 412
  "   " Industrial Reform Candidates 420
  "   " Prohibition Candidates .413 - 418
  "   " Republican Candidates .399 - 409
  "   " Union Labor Candidates 420
  "   " United Labor Candidates 420
  "   " Woman's Rights Candidates 418
  "   " the Presidents . . . . 25 - 69
Lockwood, Belva A., *Life of* 418
Losses of the Government for every administration from 1789 to 1876 222

II.

Macomb, Alexander, *Biography of* 78
Madison, James, *Life of* . . . . 32 - 33
Mather, Cotton and Salem Witchcraft . . . . .303 - 304
McClellan's letter of acceptance . . . . .328 - 329
McDonough, Thomas 76
Meaning of America 289
Mecklenburg Declaration of Independence, The,—Hon. Jno. M. Bright . . . . .137 - 141
Mercer, Hugh, *Biography of* 78
Mifflin, Thomas, *Biography of* 78
Monarchist, Van Buren a 285
Monroe, James, *Life of* . . . . 34 - 35
Montgomery, Richard 78
Morgan, Daniel, *Biography of* 78
Morton, Levi P., *Life of* . . . . .408 - 409

Moultrie, William, *Biography of* 78
Mountain, America's highest 287

N.

Names of the States,—Hamilton B. Staples . . . . 274 - 280
National Conventions 389
Nativity of soldiers in our Civil War 389
Navy Department . . . . 189, 209 - 211
Newspapers and Periodicals in the United States, 1870—1880 250
New York, The Evacuation of 290
Nolan, Philip,—Edward Everett Hale . . . . 312 - 313
Notes, Historical . . . . 126 - 129

O.

Offenses for which States Disfranchise . . . . 332 - 333
Officers, Diplomatic and Consular 220
Ordinance of 1787 . . . . 156 - 161
Origin of the Song of "John Brown's Body" 287
Origin of Yankee Doodle 288
Otis, James, *Biography of* 78

P.

Patent-Office Business 243
Pensions, Amount expended for 242
Pickens, Andrew 78
Pierce, Franklin, *Life of* . . . . 52 - 53
Pike, Zebulon M., *Biography of* 78
Platforms from 1860 to 1888, Political . . . . 348 - 396
Polk, James K., *Life of* . . . . 46 - 47
Population, History, etc., of the States and Territories . . . . 244 - 245
Population of the principal cities of the United States . . . . 247 - 248
Population of the United States by Races in 1870 and 1880 . . . . 246 - 247
Population, Our Foreign,—The Rev. Geo. C. Lorimer, D. D. . . . . 322 - 327
Porter, Commodore David, *Biography of* 78
Postal Rates in 1792 311
Postmaster-General 232
Post-office Department 190, 215
Prayer of Cardinal James Gibbons 310
Prescott, William, *Biography of* 78
Presidency, The 281
President, Appointments by the . . . . 188 - 190

Presidential Candidates..398
Presidential Tickets for 1888...................................398
President's Cabinet, The..187
President's Flag, The...291
Presidents, Lives of the.................................... 25 - 79
Presidents, The dates of birth and death of our.................241
Presidents, The..283
President, The, (Executive Department).........................185
Prohibition, The Republican and Democratic Parties on..... 336 - 341
Property Rights of Wives.................................. 294 - 296
Public Debt of the United States...............................243
Putnam, Gen., *Biography of*....................................78

Q.

Qualifications required for suffrage in each of the 38 States... 330 - 331

R.

Railway Construction...389
Redfield, *Life of*...420
Relics, Confederate..309
Religious Denominations of the U. S. Statistics........... 221 - 222
Representatives, House of......................................193
Representatives, Speakers of the House of................. 236 - 237
Republicanism, The Wedge of....................................288
Revolution, First blood of the.................................296
Revolution, Heroes of the War of 1812 and of the.......... 72 - 81
Rutledge, John, *Biography of*..................................78

S.

Salaries of officers and clerks, etc., in the Executive offices...187
Salem Witchcraft and Cotton Mather........................ 303 - 304
Schuyler, Richard, *Biography of*...............................80
Scott, Winfield, *Biography of*.................................80
Secretaries of Interior..232
    "   " Navy...230
    "   " State..226
    "   " Treasury...228
    "   " War..230
Senate, The..191
Shelby, Isaac, *Biography of*...................................80
Smith, Samuel, *Biography of*...................................80
Soldiers in the Civil War, Nativity of.........................398
Speakers of the House of Representatives.................. 236 - 237

State Department..188, 196 - 199
States, Confederation of the original... 135 - 136
States, Legal Holidays of the...307
States, Names of the.. 274 - 280
Statesmen, Titles of...398
Statistics of Religious Denominations in the United States.................... 221 - 222
Star Spangled Banner, The..308
Steuben, Baron, *Biography of*.. 80
Stirling, Wm. A., *Biography of*.. 80
Streeter, A. J., *Life of*..420
Sullivan, John, *Biography of*.. 80
Sumpter, Thomas, *Biography of*... 80
Supreme Court of the United States.. 223 - 224
Survey, United States Coast...219

T.

Tariff History of the United States, Henry J. Philpott, Esq................ 421 - 423
Taylor, Zachary.. 48 - 49
Territory, Cession of the Northwest.. 315 - 317
Texas, The oldest structure in..289
Thomas, Gen., *Biography of*.. 80
Thomson, Charles, *Biography of*.. 80
Thurman, Allen G., *Life of*.. 412 - 413
Tickets, Presidential for 1888..397
Titles of our Statesmen...398
Treasury Department..188, 200 - 202
Trees, Historical...293
Twiggs, David E., *Biography of*.. 80
Tyler, John, *Life of*... 44 - 45

U.

Union, The Existence of the,—A. Hamilton................................... 160 - 161
United States, A Compendious History of the................................ 17 - 24
United States, Analysis of the Constitution of the........................ 177 - 178
United States Christian Commission, Rev. J. O. Foster, A. M. B. D.......... 254 - 264
United States, Comment on the Constitution of the,—Justice S. F. Miller... 179 - 184
United States, Constitution of the.. 162 - 176
United States Patent-office Business..243
United States Survey..219

V.

Van Buren, a Monarchist 285
Van Buren, Martin . . . . 40 - 41
Vessels captured or destroyed by Confederate "Cruisers" 242
Vessels captured or destroyed for violation of the blockade or in battle from May 1861 to May 1865 242
Vote, Legislatures, electoral 242

W.

War Department . . . . 189, 203 - 208
War, First and Last things of the Civil . . . . 265 - 273
War, History of Civil, must not be ignored,— Rt. Rev. Samuel Fallows, D. D. . . 318 - 319
War, Nativity of Soldiers in our Civil 398
Warren, Joseph, *Biography of* 80
Washington, George, *Life of* . . . . 26 - 27
Washington's hand, The Lady who rejected 283
Washington, Wm., *Biography of* 80
Widows of the Revolutionary Soldiers 292
Wives, Property Rights of 294

Y.

Yankee Doodle, Origin of 288

A PRESIDENTIAL INAUGURATION.

A COMPENDIOUS HISTORY OF THE UNITED STATES.

PERIODS.

1 Aboriginal. 2 Period of Discovery. 3 Colonial Period. 4 Revolutionary Period. 5 National Period.

1. Aboriginal Period.

The time from the first peopling of America to its discovery by Columbus A. D. 1492.

2. The Period of Discovery.

The time from 1492 to 1607 A. D.

3. The Colonial Period.

The time from 1607 to 1775 A. D.

4. The Revolutionary Period.

The time from 1775 to 1789.

5. The National Period.

From the organization of the Government under the Constitution, to the present time.

THE ABORIGINAL PERIOD.

The Indians were called such because of their supposed origin. They were called Indians because it was thought by Columbus that he had discovered India. Nothing is known of their origin, although some have supposed they were descended from the Israelites. The Indians inhabiting the greater part of that portion east of the Mississippi were the Algonquins. The Huron and Iroquois lived around the shores of Lake Erie and Ontario. South of the Algonquins were the Cherokees and the Mobilian Nations. The Mobilian Nation embraced the Yamasees, Creeks, Seminoles, Choctaws and Chickasaws. The tribes west of the Mississippi River were the Dakotas, Comanches, Shoshones and the Aztecs. Among the tribes of the present are the Choctaws, Cherokees, Creeks and Chickasaws in the Indian Territory.

THE PERIOD OF DISCOVERY.

The western continent was discovered by Herjulfson, an Icelander, in the year 986 A. D. The actual discovery of America was made by Lief Erickson, a Greenlander, about 1000 later, and during the twelfth, thirteenth and fourteenth centuries other voyages were made to this continent, but without result.

In the year 1492, Christopher Columbus, a Genoese

under the patronage of **Ferdinand**, King of Spain, sailed from the port of Palos, and landed on the Island which he named **San Salvador**. This navigator made three more voyages to the new land, but beyond its discovery little was done to render it of much value to Europe.

The first ones to discover the Continent of America proper, were **John Cabot**, a Venetian, and his son **Sebastian**, who, sailing under English colors, in 1497 reached the coast of North America and explored it from what is now New England to Labrador. The Greater Antilles were occupied and settled by the **Spaniards**, from whence they sent out many expeditions to the main land.

SUMMARY OF SPANISH EXPEDITIONS.

Ojeda, 1510, settled Darien ; from which place.
Balboa, 1513, started and discovered the Pacific.
Ponce de Leon, 1512, discovered Florida.
Cordova, 1517, discovered Yucatan.
Grijalva, 1518, explored Mexico.
Cortez, 1519-21, conquered Mexico.
De Soto, Governor of Cuba, landed in Florida, and going north and west discovered the Mississippi, 1539.
Melendez, attempted to settle Florida, where, 1565, he founded St. Augustine, the oldest city in the U. S.

In the meantime other nations were also engaged in exploring the new world, chief among which were the **French** and **English**.

PROMINENT FRENCH EXPLORERS.

Verazani, 1524, sailed along the eastern coast from North Carolina to Newfoundland. This was made one of the grounds of the French claim during the French and Indian war.

Cartier, 1534, sailed up the St. Lawrence, and tried to form a settlement on Orleans Island, but failed; he tried it again in 1541, but again was unsuccessful.

Ribaut, 1562, tried to start a Huguenot colony at Port Royal (N. C.), but failed. Two years later,

Laudonniere, 1564, came for the same purpose, but the settlers were attacked by the Spaniards and nearly all put to death.

De Monts, 1603, obtained the grant of Acadia and settled it at Port Royal, 1605.

Champlain, 1608, founded Quebec and, 1609, discovered the lake called after him.

PROMINENT ENGLISH EXPLORERS.

Frobisher, 1576, in search of a northwesterly route to India, cruised around northern British America.

Drake, 1579, while on a plundering expedition, entered San Francisco harbor, and named the California coast New Albion.

Gilbert, 1583, took possession of Newfoundland for England, but his ship was lost on the homeward voyage and all perished.

Raleigh, 1584, received a grant of territory from Queen Elizabeth, and sent out an exploring expedition under Amidas and Barlow who named the tract they explored Virginia.

Gosnold, 1602, explored the Massachusetts coast and named Cape Cod.

NAMES GIVEN BY EXPLORERS.

Acadia, which consisted of Cape Breton Island, Nova Scotia, and New Brunswick; **Canada**, which included the tract along the St. Lawrence and great lakes; **Virginia**, the district from the St. Lawrence to Albemarle Sound; **New Spain**, or Mexico and Central America; **New France**, including Acadia, Canada, and much other territory, overlapping the English claims; **New England**, a name given later to the northern part of **Virginia**; and **New Netherland**, the name of the Dutch claim.

From these facts we find that the **claims** of the four strongest powers were:

France:—Canada and Acadia and the district north of New York Bay, besides a portion in the south called Carolina.

England:—From Labrador to Florida, extending indefinitely westward.

Spain:—The region bordering on the Gulf of Mexico including Florida.

Holland:—Between the mouth of Delaware Bay and Acadia.

THE COLONIAL PERIOD.

VIRGINIA.

In 1607, the **First Permanent English Colony** was established by the London Company in Virginia, and was called **Jamestown**.

The President of the Colonial first Council was **Wingfield**.

Captain John Smith was first a member of the Council, and afterwards President of it. He made several explorations, and was finally captured by the tribe of Indians of whom **Powhatan** was the chief. Being condemned to death, he was rescued by **Pocahontas** the chief's daughter and restored to his Colony.

In 1615, the Colonists commenced the cultivation of **tobacco** and through its means the Colony began to prosper.

In 1619, the **First Representative Assembly** ever convened in America met at Jamestown, under the name of "**Burgesses**."

In the same year **negro slavery** was introduced, and about the same time the **cultivation of cotton** was attempted.

In 1622, the Colony was nearly destroyed by an Indian war. The **Company**, much displeased with its want of success, began to quarrel. The king thereupon assumed the Government, and Virginia remained a **royal province** until the Revolutionary War.

Incited by the tyranny of **Berkely** the Colonial Governor, the people, in 1676, rose in rebellion under the leadership of **Bacon**, but were soon reduced to subjection by the Governor.

NEW YORK.

New York was the only American Colony settled by the **Dutch**, who based their claim on **Henry Hudson's** voyage up the river which bears his name.

To the territory thus claimed the name **New Netherlands** was given. Upon Manhattan Island at the mouth of the Hudson, a city was built which was named **New Amsterdam**.

In 1664, the country fell into the hands of the English, and the name of the town, and the whole region was changed to **New York** in honor of the **Duke of York**, brother of Charles II.

MASSACHUSETTS.
The Plymouth Colony.

The first attempt at settlement in this region was made in 1607, but it proved a failure.

The **first successful settlement** was made in 1620 by a body of **Pilgrims**, and the name Plymouth was given to it. They experienced great suffering during the first year, and but for the friendly aid of the Indians the colony would have proved a failure.

The **Plymouth Colony** remained independent for seventy two years, when it was united with the **Massachusetts Bay Colony** by order of the king.

The Massachusetts Bay Colony.

In 1628, a grant was obtained by several **Puritans** from the Council for New England, stretching from Boston Harbor to the Merrimack, in which a settlement called **Salem** was established. In the following year **Charlestown** was founded, and in 1630 a large number of **Puritans** settled at Boston. These and other settlements in the same grant received the name **Massachusetts Bay Colony**.

In 1668 the **Navigation Act** was seriously resisted in Boston, because it greatly interfered with the New England Colonies. As a punishment, the colony was deprived of its Charter, and **Sir Edmund Andros** sent over as Royal Governor. The colony remained a royal province until the Revolution.

NEW HAMPSHIRE.

In 1622, **Gorges** and **Mason** received a grant of land from the Council for New England north of that given to the Pilgrims, to which the name New Hampshire was given by **Captain John Mason**, because he had been governor of Hampshire, England. The first settlements were made near Portsmouth in 1623, and shortly after, in the same year, at Dover.

Three times the Colony joined Massachusetts and

as many times became separated. Finally, in 1741, it became independent and remained so until 1776.

CONNECTICUT.

Connecticut was settled by people from Massachusetts. In 1635, the settlements of **Windsor** and **Saybrook** were established on the Connecticut River. In 1636, **Hartford** and **Wethersfield** were settled. The four settlements above mentioned were called the **Connecticut Colony**. Its government was democratic, all the governing officers being chosen by the people. The colony of **New Haven** was founded in 1638 by settlers from England, and remained separate until 1662, when it became a part of the Connecticut Colony.

RHODE ISLAND.

In 1635, **Roger Williams** being driven from the colony of Massachusetts Bay on account of his religious views, finally settled on the Pawtucket River in 1636, with a few comrades. The settlement he named **Providence**. Soon after, he was joined by others who had also suffered for their religious beliefs, and in 1639, **Newport** was settled.

After some difficulties with the Massachusetts Colony regarding the proprietorship of the district, in 1644 **Roger Williams** succeeded in obtaining a Charter. This colony like all the others in New England, was under the rule of Andros while he was in power.

MARYLAND.

In 1632, a tract of land lying north of the Potomac River was obtained by **Lord Baltimore** for the purpose of affording a refuge for Catholics. The charter gave the people the right to choose their own form of government and to make their own laws; it was the **first charter** to allow that right. The first settlement was **St. Mary's** in 1634. Baltimore was founded in 1730.

The **Toleration Act** was passed by the Colonial Legislature in 1649, which provided that all who came to the colony should be permitted to enjoy their religious opinions unmolested.

The government remained in the family of **Lord Baltimore** till 1691, when a Royal Governor was appointed; but in 1715 the grant was given to the fourth **Lord Baltimore**, and it continued under rule of the family until 1776.

PENNSYLVANIA.

In 1681 **William Penn**, a Quaker, received from Charles II., a grant of territory extending without limit from the Delaware River westward, and in the following year obtained from the **Duke of York** that part of the Duke's grant which forms the present State of Delaware. **Penn's** intention was to found a colony for persecuted Quakers.

1683 **Philadelphia** was founded, and by the purchase of the territory from the Indians, all trouble with them was averted.

DELAWARE.

The colonists who had settled in the territory which Penn obtained from the **Duke of York**, became dissatisfied with the general government, and wished to govern themselves. In 1703 Penn allowed them to form a separate government, but they remained under his governorship, and that of his heirs after his death.

Pennsylvania and Delaware were the only two colonies which at sometime, did not become royal provinces. They remained under the control of the Penn family until the Revolution.

NEW JERSEY.

The territory of New Jersey originally formed part of New Netherlands. When this district passed into the hands of the **Duke of York**, he ceded the southern part to Sir **George Carteret** and **Lord Berkely**, and the name New Jersey was given to it.

In 1664 Elizabethtown was founded by the English. In 1674 Berkely sold his right to two Quakers, and New Jersey was divided into East and West Jersey—Carteret retaining the eastern part, the Quakers holding the western.

William Penn and others bought out Carteret's right in 1682, and the territory became wholly a Quaker region.

NORTH AND SOUTH CAROLINA.

A large tract of land lying south of the Loudon Company's grant was given to **Lord Clarendon** and others in 1663. They named it Carolina after the king.

In 1664, a settlement was made called the Albemarle Colony. The next year Wilmington was founded and received the name of Clarendon Colony. Charleston was founded in 1680.

King George II. assumed the government in 1729, and Carolina was divided into two Colonies, **North and South Carolina**, each under its own governor, and so remained until the Revolution.

GEORGIA.

King George II. gave a large portion of South Carolina to James Oglethorpe in 1732, to which the name Georgia was given in honor of the king. Oglethorpe's idea was to afford a home for the oppressed and the poor. In 1713 he founded Savannah. On account of the dissatisfaction of the colonists Georgia was made a royal province in 1752.

This was the last founded of the thirteen colonies.

THE UNION OF THE THIRTEEN COLONIES.

The first step toward the union was made in 1643. "Massachusetts Bay," "New Haven," and "Connecticut," formed a league for the purpose of defence against the Indians, French, and Dutch, which was called The United Colonies of New England.

INTER COLONIAL WARS.

The colonies were involved in four wars called respectively **King William's War, Queen Anne's War, King George's War**, and the **French and Indian War**.

KING WILLIAM'S WAR.

The reign of **James II.**, who succeeded **Charles II.**, was very unpopular, resulting finally in his being driven from the throne. He fled from France, and the **French Government** taking up his cause, declared war against **England**, 1639. War between the French and English at once followed. It was fought chiefly in **New York, New Hampshire**, and **Acadia**. The French, aided by the Indians, burned Schenectady, N. Y., and destroyed many small settlements. The **English** captured **Port Royal**, Acadia, which was given back by the **TREATY OF RYSWICK**, which closed the war, in 1697.

QUEEN ANNE'S WAR.

Peace lasted but **five years**. In 1701 a war regarding the **Spanish Succession** broke out in Europe, and, as one result, **QUEEN ANNE** declared war against France in 1702. The war lasted eleven years. Again **New Hampshire** and **Massachusetts** suffered, and again **Port Royal** was captured. The **TREATY OF UTRECHT** ended the war in 1713, this time giving **Acadia** to Great Britain.

KING GEORGE'S WAR.

This was called in Europe the **WAR OF THE AUSTRIAN SUCCESSION**, because it arose out of a dispute as to who should ascend the Austrian throne, in 1744. **Great Britain** took one side and **France** became the ally of the other. **Louisburg**, on Cape Breton Island, was captured by the **English** in 1715, but was restored to **France** by the **TREATY OF AIX-LA-CHAPELLE**, which ended the war in 1748. Louisburg became a very important point of attack in the **French** and **Indian War**.

FRENCH AND INDIAN WAR.

This war was caused by disputes in regard to territory, thereby differing from the three previous **Intercolonial Wars**, which took their rise in Europe. During the first four years the **English** were unsuccessful, chiefly as a result of poor management. The **French** acted almost entirely on the defensive, and during the last three years were gradually driven north by being forced to abandon **Louisburg** and **Forts Du Quesne, Ticonderoga, Crown Point**, and **Niagara**. They made their last great stand at **Quebec**, where **the decisive battle of the war** was fought. During the war the **French** were greatly assisted by the Indians; the **English** scarcely at all. The treaty of 1763 made **Great Britain** sole possessor of everything east of the Mississippi, even **Florida**, which later, was given back to **Spain**.

THE REVOLUTIONARY PERIOD.

Causes of the Revolution.

The French and Indian War left **Great Britain** with a largely increased debt. To pay it the Government proposed to tax the colonies. This the colonies would not agree to, because not allowed a voice in the matter. The **first tax-bill** was passed in 1764; the Stamp Act followed it in 1765. Both were repealed in 1766 owing to the determined resistance of the people. 1767 a **new tax-bill** was passed taxing tea, paint, paper, lead, and glass; repealed 1773 except so far as the tax on tea. In 1768 **General Gage** was ordered to Boston; in 1770 occurred the **Boston Massacre**, so called. 1773 **Boston Tea Party**, and, as a result, the closing of the port of Boston, and appointment of Gage as military governor of Massachusetts. Sept. 5, 1774, **First Continental Congress** met at Philadelphia. September, 1774, **Gage** fortified Boston Neck, and both sides began to prepare for war.

Important Events—1775.

The Americans had collected stores at **Concord** which Gage sent a force to destroy. This resulted in the **Battle of Lexington**, April 19, which caused the militia to gather about Boston. Gage's army was also reinforced. The **Americans** endeavored to pen the **British** in Boston by fortifying **Breed's Hill**. Result: **Battle of Bunker Hill**, June 17, British successful. In the meantime **Ticonderoga** and **Crown Point** were captured by **Arnold** and **Warner**, May 10. An expedition against **Quebec** was planned as a result. **Montgomery** captured **Montreal**, November 13, but the expedition failed to capture **Quebec** after a severe battle, December 31st. **Second Continental Congress** met May 10; they appointed **Washington** Commander-in-Chief, June 15, two days before the Battle of Bunker Hill.

Important Events—1776.

In January **Lord Howe** sent **Clinton** to attack New York. **Washington** sent Lee to head him off, and **Clinton** sailed for the south to attack Charleston. He failed in this, being repulsed at **Fort Moultrie**, June 28, and came north to Staten Island, where he joined **Howe**. March 17, **Washington** compelled **Howe** to evacuate Boston. **Howe** went to Halifax, but shortly after sailed to Staten Island to attack New York. **Washington's** troops were sent to Long Island. On August 27 the **Battle of Long Island** was fought in which the Americans were badly defeated. **Washington** withdrew his troops to New York, thence to **White Plains**, where he was defeated, and then crossed the Hudson. He abandoned Ft. Lee November 20, and **Cornwallis** pursued him across New Jersey to the Delaware. **Washington** crossed the Delaware December 8, but on Christmas night recrossed and surprised a body of Hessian soldiers at **Trenton**, capturing 1000. Congress this year passed the **Declaration of Independence** and applied to France for aid.

Important Events—1777.

The campaign divides itself into two parts: 1st. The **British operations** against Philadelphia; and 2d, **Burgoyne's Expedition**. (1) **Cornwallis** moved from Princeton to attack **Washington** at Trenton, but the latter slipped away, and getting behind **Cornwallis** defeated a British force at **Princeton**, January 3. Most of the British troops were withdrawn from New Jersey and taken to the Chesapeake to attack Philadelphia. **Washington** moved south to oppose this, and the Battle of **Chad's Ford**, on the Brandywine, was fought in defense of the city, the Americans being defeated, September 11. The **British** entered Philadelphia fifteen days after, but most of the troops were stationed at Germantown. Here **Washington** attacked them, but was defeated, October 4. To open communication the British attacked and captured **Forts Mifflin** and **Mercer**, on the Delaware, November 15 and 17. (2) **Burgoyne**, with an army of 9000 men, entered New York by way of Lake Champlain. He captured **Ticonderoga**, July 2, defeated the retreating garrison at **Hubbardton**, July 7, and proceeded against Fort Edward. This was abandoned on his approach, July 29, and **Schuyler**, the commandant, moved to Stillwater. A branch

British expedition besieged **Fort Schuyler**, but withdrew upon Arnold's approach. **Gates** superseded **Schuyler** and was attacked by the British, Sept. 19, near **Stillwater**, where an indecisive battle was fought. On October 7 another was fought and the British defeated. Finally **Burgoyne** surrendered on October 17.

Important Events—1778.

This year was marked by two important events: 1st. The **offers of peace** from Great Britain, which were rejected; and 2d. The **Treaty of Alliance** with France. Both resulted from the surrender of **Burgoyne** the year before. The British did not plan any special campaign this year. On June 18, **Philadelphia** was evacuated on account of the expected arrival of the French fleet in the Delaware. **Washington** pursued the British and the battle of **Monmouth** was fought, June 28. The French fleet arrived in July and an expedition was planned against **Gen. Pigot** in Rhode Island; **Sullivan** was to act with the fleet, A storm interfered and **Sullivan** withdrew after fighting the battle of **Quaker Hill**, Aug. 29. In July the massacre at **Wyoming**, Pa., occurred, and in November that at **Cherry Valley**, N. Y. The British then turned their attention to the south, and on Dec. 29, **Savannah**, Ga., surrendered to **Campbell**. After this the chief events occurred in the south.

Important Events—1779.

This year the seat of war was changed to the south and remained there until the end of the war. On Jan. 9, **Sunbury**, Ga., was captured, and shortly Georgia was overrun with British. **Prevost**, in command of the British, moved on **Charleston**, but abandoned the attack, and shortly defeated Lincoln, who opposed him, at **Stono Ferry**, June 20. In September, **Lincoln**, assisted by **Count D'Estaing's** fleet, endeavored to retake Savannah, but was repulsed. Though the chief events occurred in the south there was still more or less warfare in the north. An expedition against a British force on the **Penobscot** failed, and the American fleet was destroyed. **Clinton** sent **Tyron** into Conn., who burned **Norwalk** and **Fairfield**, and sacked New Haven. In central New York the Indians were severely punished for the massacres of **Wyoming** and **Cherry Valley** in 1778, at the battle of **Chemung** (Elmira), Aug. 29, by Gen. Sullivan. At sea **Paul Jones** attacked and captured two British vessels, Sept. 23.

Important Events—1780.

SOUTH: **Clinton** sailed south, captured **Charleston** May 12, overran South Carolina, and leaving **Cornwallis** in command returned to New York. Congress appointed **Gates** to raise an army in the south. This was no sooner done than the forces were attacked by **Cornwallis** and defeated, August 6, at **Camden**, S. C. (Sanders' Creek.) On Aug. 16 **Sumter** defeated a force of British at **Hanging Rock**, but two days after was attacked and his force utterly destroyed. On October 7 a detachment of Cornwallis's troops was defeated at **King's Mountain**. NORTH: In May a portion of the American army at **Morristown**, being unable to endure their suffering, mutinied, but being aided by **Robert Morris**, and appealed to by **Washington**, came again under authority. In July a French fleet arrived, but was blockaded in **Narragansett Bay** by a British fleet and rendered useless. In September, **Arnold**, who had fallen into disgrace, offered to surrender **West Point** to the British, but the plot failed, though he escaped.

Important Events—1781.

The campaign was entirely in the south this year. **Arnold** entered Virginia on a plundering expedition and burned Richmond, Jan. 5. The Pennsylvania soldiers, unable to endure further suffering, mutinied, Jan. 1, marched to get aid from Congress, but were finally pacified. **Cornwallis** still in charge in S. C. sent **Tarleton** to attack **Morgan**. Morgan defeated him at the battle of the **Cowpens**, Jan. 17. **Cornwallis** pursued **Morgan**, who was shortly joined by **Greene**, who took command. Greene retreated across N. C. into Va., where the pursuit ended. **Cornwallis** started to return, followed by **Greene**, whom he attacked at **Guilford C. H.**, March 15. **Greene** was defeated and went south to S. C. where he attacked

Rawdon at **Hobkirk's Hill**, but was defeated again, April 24. **Cornwallis** went to Wilmington, and thence to Yorktown, Va. **Washington** and the French forces attacked him there, while the French fleet closed the harbor. **Cornwallis** surrendered his army Oct. 19, 1781.

Important Events—1781-1789.

The war left the Colonies **Independent States**, but almost as independent of one another as of Great Britain. **Articles of Confederation** accepted in 1781. They did not form a strong enough government. In 1786 **Shay's Rebellion** broke out in Massachusetts, in resistance to the Government tax, requiring force of arms to subdue it. A **Convention** to frame a stronger plan of government met in Philadelphia in 1787, and in the same year drew up the **present Constitution**. This was accepted by **eleven States** by the end of 1788, and went into operation the next year, 1789.

THE NATIONAL PERIOD.

This period relates to the **Government** under the **Constitution**, and is the **most important** of all, inasmuch as our country now becomes the **United States**.

Under the **Constitution** the powers of our Government are arranged under three heads, **Legislative, Executive**, and **Judicial**.

The **Legislative** power is vested in **Congress**, composed of a **Senate** and a **House of Representatives**. The Senators are chosen for a term of six years by the Legislatures of the several States. Each State is allowed two **Senators**. The **Representatives** are elected by the people for two years only, each State being entitled to a number of Representatives **proportionate** to its population.

The **Executive** power is vested in a **President**, elected by what is called the **Electoral College**, for a term of four years.

The **Electoral College** is composed of electors, chosen by the people. Each State is entitled to as many electors as there are **Senators** and **Representatives** from that State in Congress.

The duty of the **President** is to enforce the laws of Congress in accordance with the **Constitution**. He is Commander-in-chief of the armies and navies of the United States.

The **Judicial power** of the United States is vested in a **Supreme Court** and **Inferior Courts** established by Congress.

To enable the business of the **Executive** to be better attended to, Congress established four Executive Departments, those of **War, State, Treasury** and **Law**. Later these were increased in number until now there are seven, the **Interior** and the **Post-office** being subsequently formed as the necessities of the Government demanded. The chiefs of these Departments, called **Secretarys**, (excepting the heads of the Post Office and Law departments who are respectively styled, **Post Master General** and the **Attorney General**), form the **President's Cabinet**.

The **important events** of the National Period will be found in connection with the **lives and administrations** of the Presidents of the United States.

LIVES OF THE PRESIDENTS

OF THE

UNITED STATES,

WITH

The Prominent Measures

OF

Their Administrations.

GEORGE WASHINGTON.

George Washington was born on the Potomac river, in Westmoreland county, Virginia, February 22d, 1732, and died December, 14, 1799. In 1754 he was made Lieutenant Colonel of the militia, and accompanied Braddock in his expedition against Fort Duquesne in 1755. In the same year he was made Commander-in-chief of the military forces of the Colony of Va., and in 1787 he was unanimously chosen President of the Convention that met to frame a Constitution. In early life he followed the occupation of an engineer. He was married to Mrs Martha Custis, in January, 1759. Congress unanimously elected him commander of the revolutionary forces, and he took active command July, 2, 1775, and he held supreme military control throughout the struggle for independence.

Washington was left fatherless at eleven years of age; his education was directed by his mother, a woman of strong character, who kindly, but firmly, exacted the most implicit obedience. Of her Washington learned his first lessons of self-command. His favorite amusements were of a military character: he made soldiers of his playmates; and officered all the mock parades. His inherited wealth was great, and the antiquity of his family gave him high social rank. As a President, he carefully weighed his decisions, but, his policy once settled, he pursued it with steadiness and dignity, however great might be the opposition. As an officer, he was brave, enterprising and cautious. His campaigns were rarely startling, but they were always judicious. He was capable of great endurance. Calm in defeat, sober in victory, commanding at all times but irresistible when aroused, he exercised equal authority over himself and his army. His last illness was brief, and his closing hours were marked by his usual calmness and dignity. "I die hard," he said, "but I am not afraid to go." Washington left no children. It has been beautifully said "Providence left him childless that his country might call him Father."

Administration.

Washington was inaugurated April 30, 1789, in New York, the first capital.-A great deal of labor fell upon this administration.-The country was suffering severely from the effect of the war.-At Hamilton's suggestion a plan for improving the public credit was accepted, 1790. —The capital was in that year changed to Phila.—In 1792 Washington was re-elected.— In 1793 Eli Whitney invented the cotton-gin, a machine for separating the cotton-seed from the fiber; this proved of immense importance in the country's history.—In 1794 difficulties arose with France through an endeavor of the French minister, Genet, to obtain aid from France, which was then at war with Great Britain.—In 1794 a disturbance broke out in Pennsylvania, called the Whiskey Rebellion, arising from an endeavor to resist the excise tax, which had been (1790) recommended by Hamilton as a means of obtaining funds.—In 1794 a treaty was signed with Great Britain which arranged several disputed points,—particularly the surrender of certain western territory.

GEORGE WASHINGTON.

JOHN ADAMS.

John Adams was born in Braintree, Mass., October 1735, and died in 1826. He graduated at Harvard College in 1755, and, abandoning the idea of becoming a minister of the gospel, was admitted to the bar in 1758. He was one of the delegates first sent to the Continental Congress from Massachusetts. In 1776 he was made President of the Board of War, and was sent to France as a Commissioner in 1777. He was a member of the first and second Congresses, and nominated Washington as commander-in-chief. Jefferson wrote the Declaration of Independence, but Adams secured its adoption in a three-days debate. He was a tireless worker, and had the reputation of having the clearest head and firmest heart of any man in Congress. In his position as President he lost the reputation he had gained as Congressman. His enemies accused him of being a bad judge of men; of clinging to old and unpopular notions, and of having little control over his temper. They also ridiculed his egotism, which they declared to be inordinate.

He lived, however, to see the prejudice against his administration give place to a more just estimate of his great worth and exalted integrity. As a delegate to the Constitutional Convention, he was honored as one of the fathers of the Republic. Adams and Jefferson were firm friends during the Revolution, but political strife alienated them. On their return to private life they became reconciled. They died on the same day—the fiftieth anniversary of American Independence. Adam's last words were, "Thomas Jefferson still survives." Jefferson was, however, already lying dead in his Virginia home. Thus, by the passing away of these two remarkable men, was made memorable the 4th of July, 1826.

Administration.

John Adams succeeded Washington as President. He belonged to the Federalist Party.—The event of greatest national interest in his administration was the death of Washington, on Dec. 14, 1799.—In the same year, previous to his death, war had been declared against France, and fighting had even begun at sea when a treaty of peace was made.

JOHN ADAMS.

THOMAS JEFFERSON.

Thomas Jefferson was born at Shadwell, Virginia, April 2d, 1743, and died July 4, 1826. After graduating from William and Mary College, he adopted the profession of law.

"Of all the public men who have figured in the United States," says Parton, "he was incomparably the best scholar and the most variously accomplished man." He was a bold horseman, a skillful hunter, an elegant penman, a fine violinist, a brilliant talker, a superior classical scholar, and a proficient in the modern languages. On account of his talent, he was styled "The Sage of Monticello." The immortal document, the Declaration of Independence, was, with the exception of a few words, entirely his work. He was an ardent supporter of the doctrine of State rights, and led the opposition of the Federalists. Like Washington, he was of aristocratic birth, but his principles were intensely democratic. He hated ceremonies and titles; even "Mr." was distasteful to him. These traits were the more remarkable to one of his superior birth and education, and peculiarly endeared him to the common people. Coming into power on a wave of popularity, he studiously sought to retain this favor. There were no more brilliant levees or courtly ceremonies as in the days of Washington and Adams. On his inauguration day, he rode down to Congress unattended, and leaping from his horse, hitched it, and went into the chamber dressed in plain clothes, to read his fifteen-minutes' inaugural. Some of the sentences of that short but memorable address have passed into proverbs. The unostentatious example then set by the Nation's President was wise in its effects. Soon the public debt was diminished, the army and navy reduced, and the Treasury replenished. A man of such marked character necessarily made bitter enemies, but Jefferson commanded the respect of even his opponents, while the admiration of his friends was unbounded. The last seventeen years of his life were spent at Monticello, near the place of his birth. By his profound hospitality, he had, before his death, spent his vast estates. He died poor in money but rich in honor. His last words were, "This is the fourth day of July."

Administration.

Jefferson was a candidate of the Republican party.—In 1803 he arranged with the French government for the purchase of the territory of Louisiana; this nearly doubled the area of U.S. possessions.—In 1801 a war broke out with the Barbary powers resulting from the conduct of those governments, particularly that of Tripoli, in imposing a tax on foreign merchant vessels in the Mediterranean.—It resulted in the Tripolitan government being compelled to guarantee no further cause of trouble.—In 1804 Alexander Hamilton was shot by Aaron Burr in a duel.—During the administration there were growing troubles with Great Britain on account of the treatment of American merchant vessels by British men-of-war.—These led the way to the war of 1812.—In 1808 the exportation of slaves was forbidden by law.

THOMAS JEFFERSON.

JAMES MADISON.

James Madison was born in King George county, Virginia, March 16, 1751, and died in 1836. He graduated at Princeton College in 1778, after which he studied law. In Congress in 1789 he became one of the strongest advocates of the Constitution and did much to secure its adoption. From his political principles he was obliged, though reluctantly, to oppose Washington's administration, which he did in a courteous and temperate manner. He led his party in Congress, where he remained till 1797. The next year he drafted the famous "1798-99 Resolutions," enunciating the doctrines of State Rights, which, with the accompanying "Report" in their defense, have been the great text-book of the Democratic party. He was Secretary of State to Jefferson. After his Presidential services, he retired from public station. Madison's success was not so much the result of a great natural ability as of intense application and severe accuracy. His mind was strong, clear, and well balanced, and his memory was wonderful. Like John Quincy Adams, he had laid up a great store of learning, which he used in the most skillful manner. He always exhausted the subject upon which he spoke. "When he had finished, nothing remained to be said." His private character was spotless. His manner was simple, modest, and uniformly courteous to his opponents. He enjoyed wit and humor, and told a story admirably. His sunny temper remained with him to the last. Some friends coming to visit him during his last illness, he sank smilingly back on his couch, saying, "I always talk better when I lie." It has been said of him, "It was his rare good fortune to have a whole nation for his friends."

Administration.

In 1811 two events occurred that greatly irritated the country against Great Britain: The firing on the President by the Little Belt, and the Indian war in the northwest, brought on by British agents.—In 1812, war was declared with Great Britain, July 19. The war was fought mainly in the North and at sea.—The Americans were most successful when acting on the defensive.—Towards the end the war changed to the South, but was interrupted by the treaty of peace, Dec. 24, 1814.—After the treaty the battle of New Orleans was fought, Jan. 8, 1815. —A second war with the Barbary powers took place during the administration, resulting in a final stoppage of the abuses of those governments, as far as our commerce was concerned. —In 1814 a body of opponents of the war met at Hartford and protested against it; this was called the Hartford Convention, and so injured the Federal party that it soon afterwards disappeared.

JAMES MADISON.

JAMES MONROE.

James Monroe was born in Westmoreland county, Virginia, April 28, 1758, and died in the city of New York, July 4, 1831. He filled the office of President of the United States from the year 1817 to 1825. As a soldier under General Washington he bore a brave record, and especially distinguished himself in the battles of Brandywine, Germantown, and Monmouth. Afterwards he studied law, and entered political life. Having been sent by Washington as Minister to France, he showed such marked sympathy with that country as to displease the President and his cabinet, who were just concluding a treaty with England, and wished to preserve a strictly neutral policy. He was therefore recalled. Under Jefferson, who was his warm friend, he was again sent to France in 1803, when he secured the purchase of Louisiana. He is said to have always taken particular pride in this transaction, regarding his part of it as among the most important of his public services. Soon after his inauguration as President, he visited the military posts in the north and east, with a view to thorough acquaintance with the capabilities of the country in the event of future hostilities. This tour was a great success. He wore a blue military coat of home-spun, light-colored breeches, and a cocked hat, being the undress uniform of a Revolutionary officer.

Thus was the nation reminded of his former military services. Monroe was a man more prudent than brilliant, who acted with a single eye to the welfare of the country. Jefferson said of him: "If his soul were turned inside out, not a spot could be found on it." Like that beloved friend, he died, "poor in money, but rich in honor," and like him also, he passed away on the anniversary of the Independence of the Country he served so faithfully.

Administration.

Monroe became President in 1817.—In 1817, the Seminole Indians becoming troublesome, Jackson invaded Florida and put an end to the matter.—This brought on trouble with Spain, the result of which was that Florida was purchased by the U. S. for $5,000,000 in 1821.—In 1820 Missouri asked to be admitted to the Union.—There was at once a great contest in congress as to whether it should be a free or a slave state.—This was finally terminated by the passage of a bill admitting it as a slave state, but forbidding slavery north of 36° 30' N. Lat. in any future state.—In 1820 Monroe was re-elected.—In 1822 the famous Monroe Doctrine was announced.—This was a protest against further European occupation of American territory.—There was no choice for President resulting from the election in 1824, and the duty of selecting a President fell to the House of Representatives, which elected J. Q. Adams to the office.

JAMES MONROE.

JOHN QUINCY ADAMS.

John Quincy Adams was born at Braintree, Mass., July 11, 1767, and died at Washington, February 23, 1848. He was President from 1825 to 1829.

John Q. Adams was a man of learning, of blameless reputation and unquestioned patriotism. As President he was hardly more successful than his father. This was, doubtless, owing greatly to the fierce opposition which assailed him from the friends of disappointed candidates, who at once combined to weaken his measures and prevent his re-election. Their candidate was Andrew Jackson, a man whose dashing boldness, energy and decision attracted the popular masses, and hid the more quiet virtues of Adams. To add to his perplexities, a majority of the House, and one-half of the Senate, favored the new party; and his own Vice President, John C. Calhoun, was also the candidate of the opposition, and of course committed to it. To stem such a tide was a hopeless effort. In two years Adams was returned to Congress, where he remained until his death, over sixteen years afterwards.

Ten years of public service were thus rendered after he had passed his "three-score years and ten," and so great was his ability in debate at this extreme age, that he was called "the old man eloquent." Like his father, he was a wonderful worker, and his mind was a complete store-house of facts. He lived economically, and left a large estate. He was the Congressional advocate of anti-slavery, and a bitter opponent of secret societies. His fame increased with his age, and he died a trusted and revered champion of popular rights. He was seized with paralysis while occupying his seat in Congress, after which he lingered two days in partial unconsciousness. His last words were, "This is the last of earth; I am content."

Administration.

In 1826, by a singular coincidence, John Adams and Thos. Jefferson both died on the same day, and that day the anniversary of American Independence, July 4. -The great measure of J. Q. Adams' administration was the Tariff Act of 1828, which was distasteful to the South and led to serious trouble in the next administration.

JOHN QUINCY ADAMS.

ANDREW JACKSON.

Andrew Jackson was born in Waxhaw settlement, North or South Carolina, March 15, 1767, and died at the Hermitage, near Nashville, June 8, 1845. He served as President of the United States from 1829 to 1837.

Jackson was of Scotch-Irish descent. His father died before he was born, and his mother was very poor. As a boy, Andrew was brave and impetuous, passionately fond of athletic sports, but not at all addicted to books. His life was crowded with excitement and adventure. At fourteen, being captured by the British, he was ordered to clean the commander's boots. Showing the true American spirit in his refusal, he was sent to prison with a wound on head and arm. Here he had the small-pox, which kept him ill for several months. Soon after his mother had effected his exchange, she died of ship-fever while caring for the imprisoned Americans at Charleston. Left entirely destitute, young Jackson tried various employments, but finally settled down to law, and in 1796 was elected to Congress. Jackson first distinguished himself as a military officer in the war against the Creek Indians which he made a signal victory. His dashing successes in the war of 1812 completed his reputation, and ultimately won him the Presidency. His nomination was at first received in many States with ridicule, as, whatever might be his military prowess, neither his temper nor his ability seemed to recommend him as a statesman. However, his re-election proved his popular success as a President. His chief intellectual gifts were energy and intuitive judgment. He was thoroughly honest, intensely warm-hearted, and had an instinctive horror of debts. His moral courage was as great as his physical, and his patriotism was undoubted. He died at the "Hermitage," his home near Nashville, Tennessee.

Administration.

General Jackson the candidate of the Democratic Party, was President from 1829 to 1837. His administration was marked by energy and decision.—In 1832 he vetoed the bill to recharter the U. S. Bank.—France was induced to promise the payment of $5,000,000 for damages done to our commerce, and failing to fulfill the promise was threatened with war, and speedily paid over the balance due (1833).—In 1832 South Carolina voted the Tariff Act of 1828 unconstitutional, and for that reason not binding on the people; and threaten d that the state would leave the Union if the law was enforced.—Jackson promptly put down these "Nullifiers" by force.—Two Indian wars, the Black Hawk, 1832, and the Seminole, 1835, disturbed this administration, which taken all in all was a very eventful one.

ANDREW JACKSON.

MARTIN VAN BUREN.

Martin Van Buren was born at Kinderhook, New York, December 5, 1782, and died, at the same place, July 24, 1862. He studied law and was admitted to practice in 1803, was elected President of the United States, and served four years, from 1837 to 1841. He early took an interest in politics, and in 1818 started a new organization of the Democratic party in New York, his native State, which had the power for over twenty years. In 1831 he was appointed Minister to England, whither he went in September, but when the nomination came before the Senate in December it was rejected, on the ground that he had sided with England against the United States, on certain matters, and had carried party contests and their results into foreign neogotiations. His party regarded this as an extreme political persecution, and the next year elected him to the Vice-Presidency. He thus became head of the Senate which a few months before had condemned him, and where he now performed his duties with "dignity, courtesy and impartiality."

As a President, Van Buren was the subject of much partisan censure. The Country was passing through a peculiar crisis, and his was a difficult position to fill with satisfaction to all. That he pleased his own party is proved from the fact of his re-nomination in 1840 against Harrison. In 1844 he was once more urged by his friends, but failed to get a two-thirds vote in the convention on account of his opposition to the annexation of Texas. In 1848 he became a candidate of the "Free Democracy," a new party advocating anti-slavery principles. After this he retired to his estate in Kinderhook, N.Y., where he died.

Administration.

Over-speculation in trade in Jackson's term had brought on great business troubles, ending in the panic of 1837.-To remedy this the Sub-Treasury Bill was passed, at Van Buren's desire, but it helped matters very little, and resulted in Van Buren being defeated in his second canvass for the Presidency.

MARTIN VAN BUREN.

WILLIAM HENRY HARRISON.

William Henry Harrison was born in Charles City county, Virginia, February 9th, 1773. He entered the army in 1791, after graduating from Hampden-Sydney College. After reaching the grade of Captain he resigned in 1797; was chosen delegate to Congress from the North-western Territory in 1797; appointed Governor of Indiana in 1801. and continued to 1813. He was elected President of the United States in 1840, and had scarcely entered upon the duties of his office when he died at Washington, April 4, 1841. In 1812 he distinguished himself during the war, especially in the battle of the Thames. His military reputation made him available as a Presidential candidate. His character was unimpeachable, and the chief slur cast upon him by his opponents was that he had lived in a "log cabin" with nothing to drink but "hard cider." His friends turned this to good account. The campaign was noted for immense mass-meetings, long processions, song-singing and general enthusiasm. "Hard cider" became a party watch-word, and "log cabins" a regular feature in the popular parades. He was elected by a very large majority, and great hopes were entertained of his administration. Though advanced in years, he gave promise of endurance. But "he was beset by office-seekers; he was anxious to gratify the numerous friends and supporters who flocked about him; he gave himself incessantly to public business; and at the close of the month he was on a sick bed." His illness was of eight days' duration. His last words were, "The principles of the Government, I wish them carried out. I ask nothing more."

WILLIAM HENRY HARRISON.

JOHN TYLER.

John Tyler was born in Charles City county, Virginia, March 29, 1790, and died at Richmond, Va., January 17, 1862. He studied law, and was elected to Congress in 1816, and served some five years; was elected U. S. Senator in 1827; re-elected in 1833, and was Pres. of the Peace Convention at Washington in 1861.

Mr. Tyler became President upon the death of Mr. Harrison as his constitutional successor as Vice President of the United States. John Tyler was in early life a great admirer of Henry Clay, and is said to have wept with sorrow when the Whigs in convention rejected his favorite candidate for the Presidency, and selected Harrison. He was nominated Vice President by a unanimous vote, and was a great favorite with his party. In the popular refrain, "Tippecanoe and Tyler too," the people sang praises to him as heartily as to Harrison himself. The death of Harrison and the succession of Tyler, was the first instance of the kind in our history.

Tyler's administration was not successful. He opposed the measures of his party and made free use of the veto power. His former political friends denounced him as a renegade, to which he replied that he had never professed to endorse the measures which he opposed. The feeling increased in bitterness. All his cabinet, except Webster, resigned. He was, however, nominated by a convention composed chiefly of office-holders, for the next Presidency; he accepted, but, finding no popular support, soon withdrew from the canvass. In 1861 he became the presiding officer of the Peace Convention in Washington. All efforts at reconciliation proving futile, he renounced his allegiance to the United States and followed the Confederate fortunes. He died in Richmond, where he was in attendance as a member of the Confederate Congress.

Administration.

Tyler became President on the death of Harrison. He greatly offended his party by vetoing the Bank of the U. S. bill, 1841, and thus lost the nomination in 1848. In 1842 a rebellion broke out in Rhode Island resulting from party feeling. Dorr, claiming to be governor, was the leader.— It was put down by military force and Dorr was imprisoned. In 1844 Texas applied for admission to the Union. This was at first refused, but the Democratic party, which favored its admission, being successful in the election of 1844, the bill passed next spring, and Texas became a state March 1, 1845.

JOHN TYLER.

JAMES K. POLK.

James K. Polk was born in Mecklinburg county, North Carolina, November 2, 1795, and died at Nashville, June 15, 1849. He graduated from the University of North Carolina in 1816, and studied law: was elected to Congress in 1825, and several terms subsequently; chosen speaker of the House, 1835 and 1837, and Governor of Tennessee in 1839. Mr. Polk was very unexpectedly nominated for President, in Baltimore, on the 27th day of May, 1844. He pleased his party as a candidate, and justified their fondest expectations as a man well worthy and well qualified to fill the office of Chief Magistrate of the United States, who surrounded himself with an able body of counsellors. He served as President from 1845 to 1849.

Mr. Polk was one of the most conspicious opposers of the administration of J.Q. Adams, and a warm supporter of Jackson. In 1839, having served fourteen years in Congress, he declined a re-election and was chosen Governor of Tennessee. His Presidential nomination, in connection with that of George M. Dallas, of Pennsylvania, as Vice-President, had the effect of uniting the Democratic party, which had been disturbed by dissensions between the friends and opponents of Martin Van Buren. However, the Mexican war, which in many States was strongly opposed, the enactment of a tariff based on a revenue principle instead of a protective one, and the agitation caused by the "Wilmot Proviso," all conspired to affect his popularity before the end of his term. He had, however, previously pledged himself not to be a candidate for re-election. He died about three months after his retirement from office.

Administration.

Polk was inaugurated President in 1845.—Trouble arose with Mexico about the admission and the boundary of Texas, Mexico claiming to the Nueces River, while Texas claimed to the Rio Grande.—This brought on the war (May 11, 1846). Mexico was at once invaded by three armies: one in California under Gen. Kearney; one on the Rio Grande and in what is now northern Mexico; while a third, under Gen. Scott, marched on Mexico city.—These expeditions were all successful, the United States forces winning every battle.—By the end of 1847 Mexico was conquered and the capital in Gen. Scott's hands.—20,000 men had conquered 50,000 and taken possession of a country containing more than 7,000,000 inhabitants.—The Treaty of Peace was signed at Guadaloupe Hidalgo, Feb. 2, 1848; Mexico by it acknowledged the Rio Grande as boundary and ceded California and New Mexico to the United States for $15,000,000.—In 1848 gold was discovered in California, causing much excitement, and great emigration thither.

JAMES K. POLK.

ZACHARY TAYLOR.

Zachary Taylor was born in Orange County Virginia, November 24, 1784. He entered upon the duties of President in 1849, and died at the Presidential Mansion July 9, 1850, after an illness of five days. Soon after his birth his parents moved to Kentucky. His means of education were of the scantiest kind, and until he was twenty-four years of age he worked on his father's plantation. Madison, who was a relative, and at that time Secretary of State, then secured for him an appointment in the army as lieutenant. From this time he rose by regular and rapid degrees to a major generalship. His triumphant battles at Palo Alto, Resaca de la Palma, Monterey, and Buena Vista, won him great applause. He was the popular hero of a successful war. The soldiers admiringly called him "Old Rough and Ready."

Having been offered the nomination for President, he published several letters defining his position as "a Whig but not an Ultra-whig," and declaring that he would not be a party candidate or the exponent of party doctrines. Many of the whig leaders violently opposed his nomination. Daniel Webster called him "an ignorant frontier colonel." The fact that he was a slaveholder was warmly urged against him. He knew nothing of civil affairs, and had taken so little interest in politics that he had not voted in forty years. But he was nominated and elected. His nomination caused a secession from the Whigs, resulting in the formation of the Free-soil party. He felt his want of qualifications for the position, and sometimes expressed his regret that he had accepted it; yet he maintained as President the popularity which had led to his election, and was personally one of the most esteemed who have filled that office.

ZACHARY TAYLOR.

MILLARD FILLMORE.

Millard Fillmore, being elected Vice-President to President Taylor, became his constitutional successor, and served the unexpired term from 1850 to 1853. Very exciting questions arose during his term of office: among them the slavery question, the admission of California into the Union as a free State, and the passage of the Fugitive Slave Law—providing for the return to their owners of slaves escaping to a free State. During the debate of these questions, for awhile it seemed as if the Union would be rent asunder. Mr. Fillmore treated them with dignity, if not with statesmanship, till finally conciliatory measures prevailed, and the questions were amicably settled. In every respect Mr. Fillmore discharged the duties of President as a conscientious, sensible man, thoroughly acquainted with legislative and general political principles.

President Fillmore was born in Cayuga co., New York, January 7, 1800, and died March 8, 1874. He had not a very liberal education, and, when young, served as an apprentice to the fuller's trade. In the year 1821, he was admitted to the bar and practiced law with success. From 1832 to 1840 he was a member of Congress; in 1842 he was nominated by the Whigs of New York for Governor, and was defeated; and in 1856 the Native American party run him for President, and he received only the electoral vote of Maryland.

Upon the death of President Taylor, the entire Cabinet resigned.

Administration.

On the death of General Taylor, Fillmore became President. During his administration the Omnibus Bill was passed, 1850.—This admitted California as a free state and settled a number of other questions.—It also provided for the capture of runaway slaves (Fugitive-Slave Law), a measure which caused much trouble in the North.—A Fisheries Treaty was concluded with Great Britain.—Franklin Pierce was elected President in 1852.

MILLARD FILLMORE.

FRANKLIN PIERCE.

Franklin Pierce was born at Hillsborough, New Hampshire, on the 23d of November, 1804, and died in 1869. He graduated at Bowdoin College, Maine, in 1824; studied law and was admitted to the bar in 1827. He was President from 1853 to 1857.

Mr. Pierce had barely attained the requisite legal age when he was elected to the Senate. He found there such men as Clay, Webster, Calhoun, Thomas H. Benton, and Silas Wright. Nathaniel Hawthorn says in his biography of Mr. Pierce: "With his usual tact and exquisite sense of propriety, he saw it was not the time for him to step forward prominently on this highest theatre in the land. He beheld these great combatants doing battle before the eyes of the Nation, and engrossing its whole regards. There was hardly an avenue to reputation save what was occupied by one or another of those gigantic figures." During Tyler's administration, he resigned. When the Mexican war broke out, he enlisted as a volunteer, but soon rose to the office of brigadier-general. He distinguished himself under General Scott, against whom he afterwards successfully ran for the Presidency, and upon whom, during his administration, he conferred the title of lieutenant-general. On the question of slavery, Mr. Pierce always sided with the South, and opposed anti-slavery measures in every shape. In a message to Congress in 1856, he characterized the formation of a free State government in Kansas as an act of rebellion, and justified the principles of the Kansas and Nebraska act. He, however, espoused the National cause at the opening of the civil War, and urged a cordial support of the administration at Washington.

Administration.

The Gladstone Purchase from Mexico gave us a large piece of territory (1853). In 1854 a Treaty of Commerce was concluded with Japan.—In 1858 the Kansas and Nebraska Bill was passed, though opposed by the North.—This allowed the people of those territories to choose whether they should come in as free or slave states when they applied for admission.—The South and North both sent emigrants to Kansas, where a bloody civil war began, which lasted till 1861.

FRANKLIN PIERCE.

JAMES BUCHANAN.

James Buchanan was born in Franklin county, Pennsylvania, April 13, 1791, and died at Wheatland, June 1, 1868. He was a graduate of Dickinson College and was admitted to the bar in 1812. He was President from 1857 to 1861, and was so constantly in office from 1820 up to that time that he was known by the sobriquet of "Public Functionary."

The "bachelor-President," as Mr. Buchanan was sometimes called, was sixty-six years old when he was called to the Executive chair. He had just returned to his native Country after an absence of four years as Minister to England. Previously to that he had been well known in public life as Congressman, Senator, and as Secretary of State under President Polk. As Senator in Jackson's time, he heartily supported his administration. With Van Buren, he warmly advocated the idea of an independent treasury against the opposition of Clay, Webster, and others. Under Tyler, he was urgently in favor of the annexation of Texas, thus again coming in conflict with Clay and Webster. However, he cordially agreed with them in the compromise of 1850, and urged its favor upon the people. Much was hoped from his election, as he avowed the object of his administration to be "to destroy any sectional party, whether North or South, and to restore, if possible, that National fraternal feeling between the different States that had existed during the early days of the Republic." But popular passion and sectional jealousy were too strong to yield to pleasant persuasion. When Mr. Buchanan's administration closed, the fearful conflict was close at hand. He retired to his estate in Pennsylvania, where he died.

Administration.

Buchanan was inaugurated March 4, 1857.— In 1859 John Brown seized the arsenal at Harper's Ferry, and was hung for it, an event which caused a great deal of excitement.— Lincoln, the anti-slavery candidate, was elected President in 1860, whereupon South Carolina and six other states seceded, December 1860. Five others seceded in 1861.

JAMES BUCHANAN.

ABRAHAM LINCOLN.

Abraham Lincoln was born in Hardin county, Kentucky, on the 12th day of February, 1809. He was elected President in 1860, and was re-elected in 1864, and had entered upon the duties of his office for the second time, when he was assassinated by John Wilkes Booth, April 14th 1865, and died the following day.

His father was unable to read or write. Abraham's education consisted of one year's schooling. When he was eight years old, his father moved to Indiana, the family floating down the Ohio on a raft. When nineteen years of age, the future President hired out as a hand on a flat-boat at $10 a month, and made a trip to New Orleans. On his return he accompanied the family to Illinois, driving the cattle on the journey, and on reaching their destination helped them to build a cabin and split rails to enclose the farm. He was now in succession a flat-boat hand, clerk, captain of a company of volunteers in the Black Hawk War, country store-keeper, postmaster and surveyor, yet he managed to get a knowledge of law by borrowing books at an office, before it closed at night, and returning them at its opening in the morning. On being admitted to the bar, he rapidly rose to distinction. At twenty-five he was sent to the Legislature, and was thrice re-elected. Turning his attention to politics, he soon became a leader. He was sent to Congress; he canvassed the State, haranguing the people daily on great National questions; and, in 1858, he was a candidate for Senator, a second time, against Stephen A. Douglass. The two rivals stumped the State together. The debate, unrivalled for its statesmanship, logic and wit, won for Lincoln a National reputation. He lost the election in the Legislature, as his party was in the minority. After his accession to the Presidency, his history, like Washington's, is identified with that of his Country. He was a tall, ungainly man, little versed in the refinements of society, but gifted by nature with great common sense, and everywhere known as "Honest Abe." Kind, earnest, sympathetic, faithful, democratic, he was only anxious to serve his Country. His wan, fatigued face, and his bent form, told of the cares he bore and the grief he felt.

Administration.

Lincoln was inaugurated March 4, 1861.—Fort Sumter was evacuated April 14, 1861.—Civil war ensued, lasting from 1861 to 1865, terminating in the surrender of Lee at Appomattox C.H., Va., April 9, 1865, and of Johnston at Raleigh, N. C., April 26.

ABRAHAM LINCOLN.

ANDREW JOHNSON.

Andrew Johnson was born near Raleigh, North Carolina, December 22, 1808. He was Vice-President when Abraham Lincoln was assassinated, and by his death Mr. Johnson became the constitutional President of the United States. He died in 1875, while serving as United States Senator from Tennessee.

When only ten years of age, Mr. Johnson was bound apprentice to a tailor of Raleigh. Never having been a day at school in his life, he yet determined to secure an education. From a fellow-workman he learned the alphabet, and from a friend something of spelling. Thenceforth, after working ten or twelve hours per day at his trade, he spent two or three every night in study. In 1826, he went West to seek his fortune, with true filial affection carrying with him his mother, who was dependent on his labor for support. After his marriage at Greenville, Tenn., he continued his studies under the instruction of his wife, pursuing his trade as before by day. His political life commenced with his election as alderman. He was successively chosen mayor, member of the Legislature, Presidential elector, State Senator, twice Governor, and for fifteen years United States Senator. Remaining true to the Union when his State seceded, his loyalty attracted general attention. A life-time Democrat, he was elected on the Republican ticket as Vice-President, in reward for his faithfulness. Coming into office with a Republican Congress, it is not strange that his way was hedged with difficulties, and his Presidential career a most unhappy one.

Administration.

Johnson was inaugurated April 15, 1865.—He proceeded to reorganize the South on his own plan, but presently found himself strongly opposed by Congress.—He vetoed several measures, but they were promptly repassed over his vetoes; one of these was the Tenure-of-Office Bill.—Later, Congress passed a bill settling the terms on which the seceding States might be readmitted.—This was also vetoed and repassed.—At length an attempt on Johnson's part to remove Secretary Stanton without consent of Congress led to his impeachment, which failed after a long trial.—In 1867 Alaska was purchased from Russia for $7,500,000.

ANDREW JOHNSON.

ULYSSES S. GRANT.

Ulysses S. Grant was born at Point Pleasant, Clermont county, Ohio, April 27, 1822. He was very unwilling to follow his father's trade, which was that of a tanner, and, at seventeen, an appointment was secured for him at West Point. His name having been wrongly registered, Grant vainly attempted to set the matter right, but finally accepted his "manifest destiny,", assumed the change thus forced upon him, and thenceforth signed himself "Ulysses Simpson," the latter being his mother's family name. Two years after completing his four years course as cadet, the Mexican war broke out, in which Grant conducted himself with great gallantry, receiving especial mention and promotion. In 1847 he was made first-lieutenant, captain in 1853, and in 1854 he resigned his commission, and entered the leather and saddlery business at Galena, Illinois, in 1859, where he remained until the opening of the war in 1861, when he immediately offered his services in behalf of the Union. His modesty and diffidence delayed their acceptance, and Governor Yates, of Illinois, was the first to avail himself of them. Grant finally took the field as Colonel of the Twenty-first Regiment Illinois Volunteers. In February, 1862, he was made a major-general, and commanded the armies of the South-west. On the 12th of March, 1864, he was made lieutenant-general and put in command of all the armies, and took personal direction of the military operations in Virginia, and, on the 9th of April, 1865, General Lee surrendered the Confederate armies to him, at Appomattox Court House, and hostilities were ended.

He was nominated and elected by the Republicans President of the United States in 1868, and re-elected by the same party in 1872. He died amid the regrets of the civilized world, and was borne to his last resting place by the gallant Union officers he had commanded, and the brave Confederate officers who had fought against him.

Administration.

In 1868 Grant was elected President. In 1869 the Pacific Railroad was completed, and in 1870 the 15th Amendment guaranteeing the right of suffrage to Negroes became a law. In 1873 the Court of Arbitration, to which the Alabama claims and other questions had been referred, decided nearly everything in favor of the United States, and ordered that Great Britain pay $15,000,000 to this Government.—In 1872 Grant was re-elected.—In 1876 the Centennial of American Independence was celebrated by a great international exhibition at Philadelphia.—The same year the election for President took place.—This resulted doubtfully, and the question was referred to an Electoral Commission, which decided that Gov. *Hayes*, the Republican nominee, had been elected.

U. S. GRANT.

RUTHERFORD B. HAYES.

Rutherford B. Hayes was born at Delaware, Ohio, October 4, 1822. He graduated at Kenyon College, Ohio. He commenced the practice of law in Cincinnati in his thirty-fourth year, when he received his first official position as the City Solicitor, which he held till the war broke out in 1861. Very near its opening he enlisted in the Twenty-third Ohio Volunteers, and served with the regiment till he received the command of a brigade in 1864. His first appointment was as Major, his first promotion came within less than a year, and in September of 1862 he held a commission as Lieutenant-Colonel, and was in command of his regiment, which he led into the battle of South Mountain. During the battles of the Army of the Potomac, Col. Hayes received a severe wound in the arm, but remained with his regiment to the last, and was the first officer whose command established a position at South Mountain. Two years later he had become Brigadier-General Hayes, and was elected to Congress from the second Ohio district by the Republicans. In the fall of 1866, Mr. Hayes was nominated and elected to Congress a second time by the Republicans, but Congress had held but one session, when he was nominated and elected Governor of Ohio by the same party. During his political career, he was three times elected Governor of Ohio, and twice a Member of Congress. By a reference to the "Important Events" in 1876-77, will be found the particulars of his election to the Presidency of the United States in 1877. Mr. Hayes took the oath of office on Saturday the 3d of March, and was inaugurated President of the United States, Monday the 5th of March. Pending the time of the election and before the meeting of the electoral commission, the country was greatly agitated and seemed threatened with civil war, but immediately after his inauguration quiet and confidence were restored and peace reigned throughout the United States.

Administration.

Hayes was inaugurated March 5, 1877.—In 1877 a railroad strike occurred, which resulted in considerable rioting and bloodshed.—A commission to settle the fisheries question which had arisen with Great Britain decided against the U. S. in 1877, and ordered the payment of $5,500,000 to Great Britain, for damages.—Silver money was made a legal tender for all debts by a bill passed over the President's veto early in 1878.

RUTHERFORD B. HAYES.

JAMES A. GARFIELD.

James Abram Garfield, the twentieth President of the United States, was born in Orange, Cuyahoga county, Ohio, November, 1831, and died in Elberon, New Jersey, September 19th, 1881.

Born amid a life of poverty and struggles, he acquired a good common school education; drove some months for a boat on the Ohio canal; obtained a seminary education, and further instruction at the Hiram Institute, O., and graduated at Williams College with the highest honors in 1856.

In 1857 he was elected President of the Hiram Institute. In 1859 he was elected to the Senate of Ohio.

He was appointed Colonel of the 42 Regiment of Ohio Volunteers in 1861. For his bravery and skill in defeating General Marshall at Middle Creek, January 10, 1862, he was commissioned Brigadier-General. He was made a Major-General for gallantry at Chicamauga September 19, 1863. He entered Congress as Representative in December, 1863. He was chosen United States Senator from Ohio, January 13, 1880.

He was nominated for President by the Republican National Convention in Chicago, June 8, 1880, on the thirty-sixth ballot, and was elected President in the November following. He was shot by the infamous lunatic Guiteau, July 2, 1881, and died ten weeks after, exhibiting the greatest fortitude and bravery.

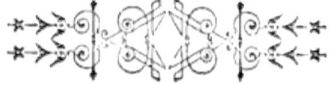

JAMES A. GARFIELD.

CHESTER A. ARTHUR.

Chester Alan Arthur, twenty-first President of the United States was born in Fairfield, Franklin County, Vermont, October 5, 1830. He was the oldest of nine children of the Rev. Wm. Arthur D. D., a Baptist clergyman and an author on antiquarian subjects, who emigrated from Ireland at the age of eighteen. Chester Arthur was graduated at Union College in 1845. In 1853 he entered the law office of Erastus D. Culver, New York City, and soon thereafter was admitted to the bar. Mr. Arthur was a firm friend of the slave and took part in defending them in several suits brought to re-enslave them after being on free soil.

In 1861 he was a Brigadier-General and acting Quartermaster-General on the staff of Governor Morgan of New York. In 1862 he was appointed Inspector-General of New York troops in the field. In 1871 he was appointed by President Grant, Collector of the port of New York. In 1880, at Chicago, he was nominated by the Republican National Convention for Vice-President. On the death of President Garfield, September 19, 1881, General Arthur succeeded to the Presidency. The general verdict upon his administration was favorable.

Administration.

The bill placing Ulysses S. Grant on the retired list of the army with full pay, May 3d, 1884.—Bureau of Annual Industry established, May 29, 1884.—Bureau of Labor Statistics established, June 28, 1884.—The bill on Chinese Immigration, July 5, 1884.—The bill on the American Merchant Marine, June 28, 1884.—The Bureau of Navigation established, October 5, 1884.—The bill on the French Spoliation Claims, January 20, 1885.—The bill on Forfeited Land Grants approved March 2, 1885.—The bill prohibiting Foreign Contract Labor, March 2, 1885.—The bill prohibiting the unlawful occupancy of Public Lands, February 25, 1885.—The bill on the Chinese Indemnity Fund, March 3, 1885.—The reduction of letter postage from three to two cents, March, 1883.—The making of the unit of weight one ounce instead of half an ounce, March, 1885.

CHESTER A. ARTHUR.

GROVER CLEVELAND.

Grover Cleveland, twenty-second President of the United States, was born in Caldwell, Essex county, New Jersey, March 18, 1837. On the paternal side he is of English origin.

He was educated at a seminary taught by his father at Fayettville, near Syracuse, New York. At the age of seventeen he was assistant teacher in the New York Institution for the blind, in New York City. He was admitted to the bar in Buffalo, N. Y. in 1859. He served as Assistant District Attorney of Erie County for three years from January 1, 1863.

He was the Democratic candidate for District Attorney of Erie County in 1865, but was defeated.

In the Autumn of 1881 he was elected Mayor of Buffalo by a majority of 3,530, the largest ever given to a candidate in that city.

He became known as the "Veto Mayor" for checking what he deemed unwise, illegal or extravagant expenditure of the public money.

On September 22, 1882, he was nominated by the Democratic State Convention at Syracuse for Governor and was elected the November following by a large majority.

He was nominated for President by the Democratic National Convention at Chicago, July 10, 1884, and was elected President in the following November. On the 8th of July, 1888, he was unanimously re-nominated for President, at St. Louis, by the Democratic National Convention.

Administration.

Removal from office of persons for "offensive partisanship," March 13, 1885.—Proclamation to remove from the Oklahoma country, in the Indian Territory, all white intruders, August 10, 1885.—Bill regulating the Presidential succession, January, 19, 1886.

GROVER CLEVELAND.

CLARA BARTON.

Heroes of the Revolution and the War of 1812.

Samuel Adams was born in Boston in 1722. He was one of the signers of the declaration of Independence; was afterwards Governor of Massachusetts, and died in 1803. It is also believed that he was one of the leaders of the patriots in the Boston massacre, March 5, 1770.

Ethan Allen was a colonel in the patriot army. He was born in Litchfield county, Conn. He attacked the English at Montreal, was defeated, taken prisoner, and sent to England in irons. He was never engaged in active military service after his capture. He died in Vermont in 1799, and his remains lie in a cemetery two miles from Burlington.

General Armstrong was born in Pennsylvania in 1758; served in the War of the Revolution; was Secretary of the State of Pennsylvania; Minister to France in 1804; Secretary of War in 1813, and died in Duchess county, N. Y., in 1843.

Benedict Arnold was a native of Norwich, Conn., where he was born in January, 1740. He fought nobly for freedom until 1778, when his passions got the better of his judgment and conscience, and he became a traitor and joined the British army. He went to England after the war, and died in London, June 14, 1801.

John Ashe was born in England in 1721, and came to America when a child. He was engaged in the Regulator war in North Carolina in 1771, and was a general in the Continental army. He died of small-pox in 1781.

Henry Atkinson was a native of South Carolina and entered the army as a captain in 1808. He was retained in the army after the War of 1812, was made adjutant-general, and finally appointed to the command of the Western Army. He died in Jefferson Barracks, in June, 1842.

William Bainbridge (Commodore) was born in New Jersey in 1774. He was the captain of a merchant vessel at the age of 19, and entered the naval service in 1798. He was distinguished during the War of 1812, and died in 1833.

Commodore Barney was born in Baltimore in 1759. He entered the naval service of the Revolution in 1775, and was active during the whole war. He bore the American flag to the French National Convention in 1796, and entered the French service. He returned to America in 1800, and took part in the War of 1812, and died at Pittsburg in 1818.

Jacob Brown was born in Pennsylvania in 1775. He engaged in his Country's service in 1813, and soon became distinguished. He was made major-general in 1814. He was Commander-in-chief of the United States army in 1821, and held that rank and office when he died, in 1838.

Major Brown was born in Massachusetts in 1788; was in the War of 1812, and was promoted to major in 1843. He was wounded in the Mexican War by the bursting of bomshell, and died on the 9th of May, 1846. He was 58 years of age.

Aaron Burr was born in New Jersey in 1756. In his twentieth year he joined the Continental army, and accompanied Arnold in his expedition against Quebec. Ill health compelled him to leave the army in 1779, and he became a distinguished lawyer and an active public man. He died on Staten Island, N. Y., in 1836.

Zebulon Butler was born in Connecticut in 1731. Served in the Revolution as a colonel, and died in

THE AMERICAN MANUAL.

Wyoming in 1795.

John Chandler was a native of Massachusetts, and served as a general in the War of 1812. Some years after the War he was a United States Senator from Maine. He died at Augusta, in that State, in 1844.

Arthur St. Clair was a native of Scotland, and came to America in May, 1755. He served under Wolfe, and when the Revolution broke out he entered the American army. He served as a general during the War, and died in 1818 at the age of 84.

George Rogers Clarke was a native of Virginia, and was born in 1752. He was one of the most accomplished and useful officers of the Western pioneers during the Revolution. He died near Louisville, Ky., in 1848.

Green Clay was born in Virginia in 1756, and was made a brigadier of Kentucky volunteers early in 1813. He commanded at Fort Meigs, in 1813. He died in 1526.

Henry Clay was born in Virginia in 1772. He became a lawyer at Richmond, and at the age of 21 he established himself in his profession at Lexington, Ky. He first appeared in Congress, as Senator, in 1806, and from that period his life was chiefly devoted to the public service. He died in Washington City, while United States Senator, in 1852.

General John Coffee was a native of Virginia. He did good service in the War of 1812, and in subsequent campaigns among the Indians. He died in 1834.

James Clinton was born in Ulster county, N. Y., in 1736. He was a captain in the French and Indian War, and an active general in the Revolutionary army. He died in 1812.

Henry Dearborn was an officer of the Revolution, and, in the war of 1812, was appointed major-general and Commander-in chief of the armies. He was born in New Hampshire. He returned to private life in 1815, and died at Roxbury, near Boston, in 1829, at the age of 78 years.

Stephen Decatur was born in Maryland in 1779. He entered the navy at the age of 19. After his last cruise in the Mediterranean he superintended the building of gunboats. He rose to the rank of commodore, and during the War of 1812 he was distinguished for his skill and bravery. He afterward humbled the Barbary powers, and after returning home he was killed in a duel with Commodore Barron, in March, 1820.

Robert Fulton, the inventor and discoverer of steam navigation, was born in Pennsylvania, and was a student of West, the great painter, for several years. He had more genius for mechanics than for the fine arts, and he turned his efforts in that direction. He died in 1815, soon after launching a steamship-of-war, at the age of 50 years.

Edmund P. Gaines was born in Virginia in 1777. He entered the army in 1799, and rose gradually until he was made major-general for his gallantry at Fort Erie in 1814. He remained in the army until his death, in 1849.

Horatio Gates was a native of England, and was educated for military life. He was the first adjutant-general in the Continental army, and was made major-general in 1776. He retired to his estate in Virginia at the close of the War, and finally took up his abode in New York, where he died in 1806 at the age of 78 years.

Nathaniel Greene was born of Quaker parents, in Rhode Island, in 1840, was an anchorsmith, and was pursuing his trade when the Revolution broke out. He hastened to Boston after the skirmish at Lexington, and from that time until the close of the War he was one of the most useful generals in the army. He died near Savannah in 1786, and was buried in a vault in that city. His sepulchre can not be identified.

John Hancock was born at Quincy, Mass., in 1737. He was an early and popular opponent of British power, and was chosen the second President of Congress. He was afterwards Governor of Massachusetts, and died in 1793.

Patrick Henry was born in Hanover county, Virginia, in 1736. He appeared suddenly in public life when almost thirty years of age. He was an active public man during the Revolution, was Governor of Virginia, and died in 1799.

John Eager Howard, of the Maryland line, was born in Baltimore county in 1752. He went into military service at the commencement of the War. He was a colonel, and was in all the principal battles of the Revolution; was chosen Governor of Maryland in 1778, and was afterward a United States Senator. He died in 1827.

William Hull was born in Connecticut in 1753. He rose to the rank of major in the Continental army. Though severely censured for his surrender of Detroit in 1812, he was a good man, and distinguished for his bravery. He was appointed Governor of the Michigan Territory in 1805. After the close of his unfortunate campaign he never appeared in public life. He died, near Boston, in 1825.

Isaac Hull was made a lieutenant in the navy in 1798, and in 1812 was commodore, in command of the United States frigate, Constitution. He died in Philadelphia in February, 1843.

George Izard was born in South Carolina in 1777. He was a general, and made military life his profession. After the War he left the army. He was Governor of Arkansas Territory in 1825, and died at Little Rock, Ark., in 1828.

John Jay was a descendant of a Huguenot family, and was born in the city of New York in 1745. He was early in the ranks of patriots, and rendered very important services during the Revolution. He retired from public life in 1801, and died in 1829, at the age of 84 years. His residence was at Bedford, Westchester county, N. Y.

Thomas S. Jesup was born in Virginia in 1778. He was a brave and useful officer during the War of 1812, and was retained in the army. He was breveted major-general in 1828, and was succeeded in command in Florida by Col. Zachary Taylor in 1838. He died in Washington City.

John Paul Jones was born in Scotland in 1747, and came to Virginia in boyhood. He entered the American navy in 1775, and served as commodore during the War. He was an intrepid and daring officer. He was afterwards rear-admiral in the Russian service. He died in Paris in 1782.

Baron de Kalb was a native of Alsace, a German province ceded to France. He had been in America as a secret French agent, about fifteen years before. He came to America with Lafayette in 1777, and Congress commissioned him a Major-General. He died of wounds received at the battle of Camden in 1780.

Stephen W. Kearney was a native of New Jersey. He was a gallant soldier in the war of 1812. He was breveted a brigadier in 1846, and major-general in December the same year, for gallant conduct in the Mexican War. He died at Vera Cruz, in October, 1848, at the age of 54 years.

Marquis de La Fayette was born in France in 1757. He was an active patriot during the Revolution, and contributed men and money to the patriot cause. He was commissioned major-general by the Continental Congress July 31, 1777. He died in France in 1834, at the age of 77.

James Lawrence was a native of New Jersey, and received a midshipman's warrant at the age of 16. He is remembered by every American as the author of those brave words: "Don't give up the ship." On this occasion he was wounded while commanding the United States frigate Chesapeake, and the engagement took place in 1814. He died four days after receiving the wound, at the age of 31 years.

Charles Lee was born in Wales in 1731. He was a brave officer in the British army. He settled in Virginia in 1773, and was one of the first brigadiers of the Continental army. He was arrested and tried by a court-martial for disobedience of orders and disrespect to Washington at the battle of Monmouth. He was found guilty, and was suspended from command for one year. He never entered the army again, and died in obscurity in Philadelphia in 1782.

Richard Henry Lee was born in Westmoreland county, Virginia, in 1732. He was much in public life, signed the Declaration of Independence, was a U. S. Senator, and died in 1794.

Henry Lee was born in Virginia in 1756. He entered the military service as a captain of a Virginia company in 1776, and in 1777 joined the Continental army. At the head of a legion, as a colonel, he performed extraordinary services during the War, especially in the South. He was afterward Governor of Virginia, and a member of Congress. He died in 1818.

Benjamin Lincoln was born in Massachusetts in 1733. He was a farmer. He joined the Continental army in 1779, and rose rapidly to the position of major-general. He died in 1810.

Alexander Macomb was born in Detroit in 1782, and entered the army at the age of 17 years. He was made a brigadier in 1814. In 1835 he was commander-in-chief of the armies of the United States, and died in 1841.

Thomas McDonough was a native of Delaware, and a commodore in the navy. He was 28 years of age at the time of the engagement at Plattsburg. The State of New York gave him one thousand acres of land on Plattsburg Bay for his services. He died in 1822 at the age of 39 years.

General McDougal was born in Scotland, and came to America in early childhood. He rose to the rank of major-general, was a New York State Senator, and died in 1786.

Hugh Mercer, a general in the Continental army, was killed at the battle of Princeton. He was a native of Scotland, and was practicing medicine at Fredericksburg, Va., when the Revolution broke out. He was 56 years of age when he died.

Thomas Mifflin was born in Philadelphia in 1744. He was a Quaker, but joined the patriot army in 1775, and rapidly rose to the rank of major-general. He was a member of Congress after the War, and also Governor of Pennsylvania. He died in January, 1800.

Richard Montgomery was born in Ireland in 1737. He was with Wolfe at Quebec, in 1759; afterward married and settled in the State of New York. He was a general in the patriot army, and was killed at the battle of Quebec, in 1775.

Daniel Morgan was born in New Jersey in 1736, and was in the humble sphere of a wagoner when called to the field. He had been a soldier under Braddock, and joined Washington at Cambridge in 1775, and became a general. He was a farmer in Virginia after the War, where he died in 1802.

William Moultrie was born in South Carolina in 1730, and died in 1805. He was a general in the Revolution, and an active officer until made prisoner in 1780, when for two years he was not allowed to bear arms.

James Otis was born at Barnstable, Mass., 1725. He was the leader of the Revolutionary party in Massachusetts at the beginning. He was wounded by a British official in 1769, and never entirely recovered. He was killed by lightning in 1772.

Andrew Pickens was born in Pennsylvania in 1739, and served as a general in the Revolution. In childhood he went to South Carolina, and was one of the first in the field for liberty. He died in 1617.

Zebulon M. Pike was born in 1779. While pressing toward the capture of York (Toronto), in 1813, the powder magazine of the fort blew up, and General Pike was mortally wounded. He was carried on board the flagship of Commodore Chauncey, where he died, with the captured British flag under his head, at the age of 34 years.

Commodore David Porter was among the most distinguished of the American naval commanders. He was a resident Minister of the United States in Turkey, and died near Constantinople, in March, 1843.

William Prescott was born at Groton, Mass.; was a colonel at the battle of Bunker Hill, and served under Gates until the surrender of Burgoyne, when he left the army. He died in 1795.

General Putnam was born at Salem, Mass., in 1718. He was a very useful officer during the French and Indian War, and was in active service in the Continental army, commencing with the battle of Bunker Hill until 1779, when bodily infirmity compelled him to retire. He died in 1790 at the age of 72.

John Rutledge was born in Ireland, and came to South Carolina when a child, and was Governor of that State in 1780. After the Revolutionary War he

was made a judge of the Supreme Court of the United States, and also Chief Justice of South Carolina. He died in 1800.

Richard Schuyler was born in Albany, N. Y., in 1733, and died in 1804. He was a captain under Sir William Johnson, and was in active public service until the Revolution. He was a general in the patriot army, and was a legislator after the War.

Winfield Scott was born in Virginia in 1786. He was admitted to law practice at the age of 21 years. He joined the army in 1808, was made lieutenant-colonel in 1812, and passed through the War that ensued with great honor to himself and his company. He was brevetted major general in 1814, and was made general-in-chief of the army in 1841. His success in Mexico greatly added to his laurels, and he was considered one of the greatest captains of the age. He was made lieutenant-general in 1855. He died May 29, 1866, at West Point, aged 80 years.

Isaac Shelby was born in Maryland in 1750. He entered military life in 1774, and went to Kentucky as a land surveyor in 1775. He engaged in the War of the Revolution, and was distinguished in the battle of King's Mountain, in October, 1780. He was made Governor of Kentucky in 1792, and soon afterward retired to private life, from which he was drawn in 1813. He died in 1826.

Samuel Smith, the commander of Fort Mifflin in 1777, was born in Pennsylvania in 1752. He entered the Revolutionary army in 1776; served as a general in command when Ross attacked Baltimore in 1814; afterward represented Baltimore in Congress, and died in April, 1839.

Baron Steuben came to America in 1777, and joined the Continental army at Valley Forge. He was a veteran from the armies of Frederick the Great, of Prussia. He was made Inspector General of the American army. He died in the interior of New York in 1795.

William Alexander Stirling was a descendant of the Scotch Earl of Stirling. He was born in the city of New York in 1726. He became attached to the patriot cause and served as a faithful officer during the War. He was made prisoner at the battle of Long Island. He died in 1783.

John Sullivan was born in Maine in 1740. He was a delegate to the first Continental Congress in 1774, and was one of the first eight brigadiers in the Continental army. He resigned his commission of general in 1779; was afterward member of Congress and Governor of New Hampshire, and died in 1795.

Thomas Sumter was a native of South Carolina and was early in the field. Ill health compelled him to leave the army just before the close of the War in 1781. He was afterward Congressman and died on the high hills of Santee, S. C. in 1832, at 98 years of age.

General Thomas was a native of Plymouth, Mass., and was one of the first eight brigadiers appointed by Congress in 1775. He died with the small-pox in 1776, at Chambly, in Canada.

Charles Thomson was born in Ireland in 1730, and came to America when he was only eleven years of age. He settled in Pennsylvania, and was Secretary of Congress perpetually from 1774 until the adoption of the Federal Constitution, and the organization of the new government in 1789. He died in 1824 at the age of 94.

David E. Twiggs was born in Georgia in 1790. He was a major at the close of the War of 1812, and was retained in the army. He was brevetted major-general after the battle of Monterey, and for his gallantry there he received a gift of a sword from Congress.

Joseph Warren was born at Roxbury, Mass., in 1740. He was killed by a musket ball at the battle of Bunker Hill, while retreating, and was buried where he fell, near the redoubt. The tall Bunker Hill monument stands on the very spot where he fell, commemorates his death, as well as the patriotism of his countrymen. He was a physician, and was 35 years of age when he died. His remains now rest in St. Paul's Church, Boston. A statue to his honor was inaugurated on the 17th of June, 1857.

William Washington, a relative of the General, was born in Stafford county, Va. He entered the army under Mercer, and greatly distinguished himself at the south as a commander of a corps of cavalry.

Taken prisoner at the battle of Eutaw Springs, he remained a captive until the close of the war, and died in Charleston in 1810. In a personal combat with the British Colonel Tarleton, at the battle of Cowpens, Washington wounded his antagonist in the hand. Some months afterward, Tarleton said, sneeringly, to Mrs. Willie Jones, a witty American lady, "that Colonel Washington, I am told, is illiterate, and cannot write his own name." "Ah! Colonel," said Mrs. Jones, "you ought to know better, for you hear evidence that he can make his mark." At another time he expressed a desire to see Colonel Washington. Mrs. Jones' sister instantly replied, "Had you looked behind at the Cowpens, you might have had that pleasure."

Anthony Wayne was born in Pennsylvania in 1745. He was a professional surveyor, then a provincial legislator, and became a soldier in 1775. He was very active during the whole War, and was successful in subduing the Indians in the Ohio country in 1795. He died on his way home, at Erie, Pa., near the close of 1796.

Daniel Webster was born in Salisbury, New Hampshire, in 1782. He was admitted to the bar in Boston in 1805. He commenced his political career in Congress in 1818. He was in public employment a greater portion of the remainder of his life, and was the most distinguished statesman of his time. He died at Marshfield, Mass., in October, 1852.

General Wilkinson was born in Maryland in 1757, and studied medicine. He joined the Continental army at Cambridge, in 1775, and continued in service during the War. He died near the city of Mexico, in 1825, at the age of 68 years.

James Winchester was born in Maryland in 1756. He was made a brigadier in 1812; resigned his commission in 1815, and died in Tennessee in 1826.

John Ellis Wool (General) was a native of New York. He entered the army in 1812, and soon rose to the rank of lieutenant-colonel, for gallant conduct on Queenstown Heights, in 1812. He was breveted brigadier in 1845, and for gallant conduct at Buena Vista, in 1847, was breveted major-general.

William J. Worth (General) was born in Columbia county, New York, in 1794; was a gallant soldier during the War of 1812; was retained in the army, and for his gallantry at Monterey, during the Mexican War, he was made a major-general, by brevet, and received the gift of a sword from Congress. He was of great service during the whole war with Mexico. He died in Texas, in May, 1849.

RECORD
—OF—
IMPORTANT EVENTS.

1857.

Jan. 4. The **Lecompton Constitution** is rejected by Kansas.

Feb. 12. $300,000 is donated by George Peabody, to establish a free literary and scientific Institute at Baltimore.

JAMES BUCHANAN.

March 4. James Buchanan is inaugurated President, and John C. Breckinridge Vice-President.

Dec. 8. The **Death** of Father Theobald Matthew, aged 67, occurs.

1858.

Feb. 14. The **Mormons** in an engagement at Eco Cannains are defeated by the United States army.

March 28. Nicaragua places herself under the protection of the United States.

May 11. Minnesota is admitted as a State.

July. The remains of President Monroe are removed from New York City to Richmond, Virginia.

GOV. WISE.

Aug. 5. Atlantic telegraph cable is laid, President Buchanan's message to Queen Victoria was sent on the 16th, but cable proves a failure.

1859.

Feb. 14. Oregon is admitted as a State.

Oct. 16. John Brown, fifteen white men and five negroes, seized Harper's Ferry Arsenal.

Oct. 17. The armory captured by Colonel (afterward the Rebel General) Lee. One marine and twelve of Brown's men killed. Brown and four men taken prisoners.

Oct. The death of J. Y. Slidell, U. S. Minister to France, occurs at Paris.

Nov. Gen. Scott is sent to protect American interests in San Juan.

Nov. 28. Death of Washington Irving, the American novelist and historical writer.

Dec. 2. John Brown and two negroes hung, under the authority of Gov. Wise.

April 23. The Democratic National Convention assembles at Charleston, S. C.

April 30. The Cincinnati Platform rejected by the National Democratic Convention, and, upon the adopting of a platform, the Southern delegates secede.

May 4. The National Democratic Convention adjourns until June 18.

May 16. The National Republican Convention assembles at Chicago.

HANNIBAL HAMLIN.

1860.

Feb. 1. Pennington, of New Jersey, is elected Speaker of the House of Representatives.

March 10. Stevens and Hazlitt hung at Charlestown, Va.

March 27. Japanese Embassy, the first to leave Japan, arrived at San Francisco.

JOHN C. BRECKINRIDGE.

May 18. The Republican Convention nominates Abraham Lincoln, of Illinois, for President, and Hannibal Hamlin, of Maine, for Vice-President.

May 19. The Constitutional Union Convention, at Baltimore, nominates John Bell for President, and Edward Everett for Vice-President.

June 23. The National Democratic Convention meets at Baltimore, and nominates

Douglas and Johnson; the seceders also meet, and nominate Breckinridge and Lane.

Nov. 6. Abraham Lincoln of Illinois, and Hannibal Hamlin, of Maine, are elected President and Vice-President of the United States. Lincoln and Hamlin, 108 electoral votes; Bell and Everett, 39; Breckinridge and Lane, 72; Douglas and Johnson, 12.

Nov. 7. The news of Mr. Lincoln's election received at Charleston, South Carolina, with cheers for a Southern Confederacy,

the right of the general government to coerce a seceding State.

Dec. 10. Howell Cobb, Secretary of the Treasury, resigns. Senator Clay, of Alabama, also resigns.

Dec. 14. Lewis Cass, Secretary of State resigned because the President would not send reinforcements South.

Dec. 18. The "Crittenden Compromise," settling the difference between the North and the South, is rejected by the United States.

ROBERT TOOMBS.

A. H. STEPHENS.

Nov. 9. An attempt is made to seize the arms at Fort Moultrie.

Nov. 18. Major Anderson is sent to Fort Moultrie to relieve Colonel Gardner.

Dec. 1. The Great Rebellion. Florida Legislature ordered the election of a convention. Great secession meeting in Memphis.

Dec. 3. Congress Meets. The President denies the right of a State to secede, and asserts

Dec. 26. General Anderson evacuates Fort Moultrie, Charleston, and occupies Fort Sumter.

Dec. 20. South Carolina secedes from the Union.

Dec. 30. President Buchanan declines to receive any delegates from South Carolina.

Deaths this Year. The death of Samuel G. Goodrich, "Peter Parley," author, aged 67 years, occurs.

1861.

Jan. 4. **Fort Morgan,** Mobile Harbor, seized by State troops.

Jan. 5. **The Star of the West** chartered and sent to Fort Sumter to reinforce Major Anderson.

Jan. 8. **Forts Johnson and Caswell,** N. C., seized by the rebels. Secretary Thompson resigns from the Interior Department.

Jan. 12. **The Pensacola Navy Yard** seized by rebels, and the cutter " Lewis Cass " seized at New Orleans.

Jan. 14. **The Senators** from Mississippi withdraw from Congress.

Jan. 17. **Batteries** commanding the Mississippi erected at Vicksburg.

Jan. 19. **Georgia Secedes.** Fort Neale, at Little Washington, N. C., captured by the rebels.

Jan. 20. **The fort** at Ship Island captured by the rebels.

ROBERT B. RHETT OF SOUTH CAROLINA.

COL. ELLSWORTH.

Jan. 9. **Mississippi Secedes.** The first gun of the rebellion fired; the forts on Morris Island fire on the "Star of the West," and she puts to sea.

Jan. 10. **Florida Secedes.**

Jan. 11. **Alabama Secedes.** U. S. Arsenal at Baton Rouge, Forts Philip and Jackson, below New Orleans, and Fort Pickens, on Lake Ponchartrain, seized by Louisiana.

Jan. 21. **The Alabama** delegation in Congress leave.

Jan. 23. **Georgia** members of Congress resign, among them Robert Toombs.

Jan. 24. **The United States** arsenal at Augusta, Georgia, is seized by the Confederate State troops.

Jan. 26. **The Louisiana Legislature** passed secession ordinance by a vote of 113 to 17.

Feb. 1. Texas Convention passed an ordinance of secession. Mint and Custom House at New Orleans seized.

Feb. 4. Delegates from the seceded States met at Montgomery, Alabama, to organize a Confederate government.

Peace Congress met at Washington.

Feb. 8. The United States arsenal at Little Rock surrenders to Arkansas.

Feb. 9. Jefferson Davis and A. H. Stephens are elected Provisional President and Vice-President of the Southern Confederacy.

Feb. 10. Fort Kearney, Kansas, is seized by the Confederates.

Feb. 21. Jeff. Davis appointed his Cabinet—Toombs, Sec. State; Memminger, Treasury, and L. P. Walker, War.

Feb 22. President Lincoln's night journey from Harrisburg to Washington, in order to prevent an anticipated outrage in Baltimore.

Feb. 23. Gen. Twiggs surrendered Government property in Texas valued at $1,200,000 to the Confederacy.

"PARSON" BROWNLOW.

GEN. M'CLELLAN.

Feb. 11. President Lincoln started for Washington.

Feb. 13. Electoral vote counted; Lincoln and Hamlin officially declared elected.

Feb. 18. Jefferson Davis inaugurated President of the Confederate States of America. Twiggs surrenders the military posts in Texas.

Feb. 25. News received of the surrender and treason of Major General Twiggs in Texas.

Feb. 26. Capt. Hill refused to surrender Fort Brown, Texas.

March 1. Gen. Twiggs is expelled from the army.

March 4. The inauguration of President Lincoln takes place.

THE AMERICAN MANUAL.

The State Convention declared Texas out of the Union.

March 5. Gen. Beauregard took command of the troops of Charleston.

March 6. Fort Brown on the Rio Grande, was surrendered by special agreement. The Federal troops evacuated the fort and sailed for Key West and Tortugas.

March 28. Vote of Louisiana on secession made public. For secession, 20,448; against, 17,926.

The steamer Atlantic sailed from New York with troops and supplies.

April 12. Bombardment of Fort Sumter was commenced by the Confederates.

April 13. The bombardment of Fort Sumter was continued; Gen. Wigfall coming with a flag of truce, arrangements were made for evacuating the fort.

April 14. Major Anderson and his men sailed for New York.

GEN. BUTLER.

March 30. Mississippi Convention ratified the Confederate Constitution by a vote of 78 to 70.

April 3. South Carolina Convention ratified the Confederate Constitution by a vote of 114 to 16.

April 7. All intercourse between Fort Sumter and Charleston stopped by order of Beauregard.

GEN. M'DOWELL.

April 15. The President issues a proclamation commanding all persons in arms against the United States to disperse within twenty days. He also called for 75,000 volunteers. The New York Legislature authorizes the raising of $3,000,000 for their equipment and support.

April 16. The Governors of Kentucky, Virginia, Tennessee, and Missouri refuse to furnish troops under the President's proclamation. 32,-

000 men are called for by the Confederate Government.

April 17. Virginia Convention adopted secession ordinance.

Jefferson Davis issued proclamation offering to all who wished to engage in privateering, letters of marque and reprisal.

April 18. Lieut. Jones destroys U. S. arsenal at Harper's Ferry to prevent its falling into the hands of the enemy. The first troops to enter Washington for its defense were 400 sol-

MAJ. WINTHROP.

diers of the 25th Penn. Regiment, under Col. Cope.

April 19. Steamer Star of the West seized by Confederates at Indianola, Texas.

Attack on 6th Massachusetts Regiment in Baltimore.

President Lincoln issued a proclamation by which ports of South Carolina, Florida, Georgia, Mississippi, Louisiana and Texas are declared to be in a state of blockade.

April 20. The Confederates seize the U. S arsenal at Liberty, Mo.

Confederates seize Norfolk Navy Yard.

The 4th Massachusetts Regiment arrive at Fortress Monroe.

April 21. Federal Government takes possession of the Philadelphia & Baltimore Railroad.

Harper's Ferry arsenal was burned by its garrison.

GEN. FREMONT.

April 22. Confederate troops seize U. S. arsenal at Fayetteville, N. C. The arsenal at Napoleon is seized by Arkansas.

April 24. The Confederates under Senator Boland seize Fort Smith, Ark.

April 25. Maj. Sibley surrenders 440 U. S. troops to the Confederate Colonel Van Dorn, at Salaria, Texas.

Virginia is proclaimed a member of the Southern Confederacy by Governor Letcher

April 27. Virginia and North Carolina included in the blockade.

All Officers of the Army were required to take the oath of allegiance.

April 29. The Maryland House of Delegates voted against secession, 63 to 13.

May 1. North Carolina Legislature passed a bill calling a State Convention to meet on the 20th of May.

May 6. Tennessee secedes. Tennessee Legislature passes a secession ordinance to be submitted to the people.

May 9. Lieut. Col. Reeve and 313 men surrender to Van Dorn, at San Antonio, Texas.

May 10. Gen. Lyon captures Frost's brigade at St. Louis, Mo.

The **rebel schooner** Atwater captured off Apalachicola.

Gen. Lee assumes command of the rebel army of Virginia.

GEN. DIX.

GEN. LYON.

The **Legislature** of Tennessee passed an act in secret session by which the Governor is authorized to form a league with the Southern Confederacy.

President Lincoln called for 42,000 three years' volunteers; 22,000 troops for the regular army, and 18,000 seamen.

May 4. The Department of Ohio, comprising the States of Ohio, Indiana and Illinois, put under command of Gen. McClellan.

May 11. Blockade of Charleston, S. C.

May 13. Queen Victoria issues proclamation of neutrality.

May 16. General Scott fortifies Arlington Heights.

May 17. Rebels fortify Harper's Ferry.

May 18. General Butler assigned to the command of the Military Department of Virginia, created, comprising Eastern Virginia.

North and South Carolina, with headquarters at Fortress Monroe.

May 19. Engagement between Sewall's Point Battery and four gunboats.

May 20. North Carolina secedes.

Governor Magoffin proclaims the neutrality of Kentucky.

May 21. Tennessee seceded.

May 22. Fortifications of Ship Island destroyed to keep them from the enemy.

May 24. Thirteen thousand troops crossed the Potomac into Virginia. Alexandria occupied by Federal troops.

Col. Ellsworth shot by Jackson at Alexandria, Va.; the murderer was instantly killed.

GEN. PIKE.

Arlington Heights occupied by Union troops.

Gen. Butler declared slaves contraband of war.

May 25. Federal troops destroy bridges on the Alexandria and Leesburg Railroad.

Ellsworth's funeral in Washington.

May 26. Alexandria put under martial law. The port of New Orleans blockaded by the sloop-of-war Brooklyn. All postal service in the seceded States suspended.

May 27. Mississippi River blockaded.

Gen. McDowell took command at Washington.

Mobile blockaded.

May 28. Gen. Butler captures Newport News.

June 1. Lieut. Tompkins, with forty-seven men, attacks the Confederates at Fairfax Court House.

GEN. PEMBERTON.

The steamers Freeborn and Anacosta engaged the batteries at Aequia Creek the second time.

June 3. Hon. S. A. Douglas died in Chicago. Born at Brandon, Vt., April 23, 1813.

Gen. Beauregard assumes command of the Confederate forces at Manassas Junction, Va.

June 10. Battle of Big Bethel. Major Winthrop, a brilliant scholar, a graduate of Harvard, killed.

Neutrality in the American conflict is proclaimed by Napoleon III.

June 14. Confederates evacuate Harper's Ferry, after destroying all available property.

June 15. Brig Perry arrived at New York with the privateer Savannah.

June 17. Wheeling Convention unanimously declare Western Virginia independent of the Confederate portion of the State.

GEN. HOWARD.

June 20. Gen. McClellan assumes command in person of the army in Western Virginia.

June 23. Forty eight locomotives belonging to the Baltimore & Ohio Railroad, valued at $4,000,000, destroyed by the Confederates.

June 26. The Wheeling Government of West Virginia was acknowledged by the President.

June 29. The Confederate privateer Sumter escaped from New Orleans.

July 1. First War Loan of the United States Government, $250,000,000, is made.

July 4. Congress meets in extra session.

July 6. The Western Department, consisting of the State of Illinois and the States and Territories west of the Mississippi, and east of the Rocky Mountains, was put under command of Gen. J. C. Fremont, with headquarters at St. Louis.

JOHN SLIDELL.

July 11. J. M. Mason and R. M. Hunter, of Virginia; T. L. Clingman and Thomas Bragg, of North Carolina; L. T. Wigfall and J. U. Hemphill, of Texas; C. B. Mitchell and W. K. Sebastian, of Arkansas, and A. O. S. Nicholson, of Tennessee, were expelled from the United States Senate.

July 13. The Federals under Col. Lowe were defeated.

President Lincoln is authorized to call out the militia, and accept the services of 500,000 men.

July 18. Gen. John A. Dix placed in command of the Department of Maryland; headquarters at Baltimore.

July 19. Gen. Banks supersedes Gen. Patterson.

July 20. The Confederate Congress meets at Richmond.

Aug. 6. The extra session of Congress closes.

Aug. 7. The Confederates destroyed the village of Hampton, Virginia.

Aug. 10. Gen. Lyon killed at Wilson Creek, Mo.

Aug. 12. President Lincoln appointed the 30th of September as a fast day.

GOV. RAMSEY.

July 22. Gen. McClellan takes command of the Army of the Potomac.

Three-months volunteers begin to return home.

Aug. 1. The Confederates retreat from Harper's Ferry to Leesburg.

Aug. 3. Congress passed the Confiscation bill, and bill for raising $20,000,000 by direct taxation.

GOV. YATE .

Aug. 14. Gen. Fremont declares martial law in St. Louis.

Aug. 16. Gen. Wool takes command at Fortress Monroe.

President Lincoln interdicts all commercial relations with the seceded States.

Sept. 1. The Confederates were defeated at Booneville.

Sept. 6. Gen. Grant enters Paducah, Ky.

Sept. 11. President Lincoln modifies Gen. Fremont's emancipation proclamation.

Sept. 18. The Provost Marshal closes the

Maryland Legislature and sends the secession members to Fort McHenry.

Sept. 21. John C. Breckinridge departs from Frankfort, Ky., and joins the Confederates.

Oct. 7. The Confederate iron-clad steamer Merrimac makes its first appearance within sight of Fortress Monroe.

Oct. 11. Confederate steamer Theodore escapes from Charleston, S. C., with Mason and Slidell on board.

GEN. SHERIDAN.

Oct. 29. The second naval expedition, consisting of 80 vessels and 15,000 men, sails from Fortress Monroe. The naval force under Commodore Dupont; the land forces under Gen. Sherman.

Nov. 1. Gen. Scott resigns as commander-in-chief of the armies of the United States. Gen. McClellan appointed in his place.

Nov. 2. Gen. Hunter supersedes Gen. Fremont in the command of the Western Department.

The Confederate schooner, Bermuda, runs the blockade at Savannah.

Nov. 11. Gen. Halleck takes command of the Western Department.

Nov. 18. Confederate Congress meets.

COM. DUPONT.

Nov. 21. The privateer Royal Yacht was captured by the U. S. vessel Santee, off Galveston, Texas.

Nov. 27. Gen. McClellan directs the observance of the Sabbath in all the camps of the U. S. army.

Nov. 30. Lord Lyons, the British minister at Washington, was instructed from Earl Russell to leave America within seven days, unless the United States government consent to the unconditional liberation of Messrs. Mason and Slidell.

Jefferson Davis was elected President of the Confederate States.

Dec. 3. **Congress** meets.

Dec. 4. **John C. Breckinridge** expelled from the United States Senate.

Dec. 9. **The Confederate Congress** passes a bill by which Kentucky is admitted into the Southern Confederacy.

Feb. 3. **The** Federal government decided that the crews of the captured privateers were to be considered as prisoners of war.

Feb. 6. **Commodore Foote** with 7 gunboats, attacked Fort Henry on the Tennessee River. An unconditional surrender was made by the Confederate commander, General Tilghman.

LORD LYONS.

SIMON CAMERON.

Dec. 23. Troops sent to Canada by the British government as a precaution against possible aggression by the U. S.

Dec. 30. Cash payments were suspended by the New York banks.

1862.

Jan. 1. **Mason** and **Slidell** leave Fort Warren for England in the British steamer Rinaldo.

Jan. 11. **Simon Cameron** resigns his position as Secretary of War. E. M. Stanton is appointed in his place.

Feb. 8. **Gen. Burnside** captures six forts on Roanoke Island.

Feb. 10. **Elizabeth City**, N. C., surrendered to Gen. Burnside.

Feb. 13. **Gen. Curtis** takes possession of Springfield, Mo.

Feb. 14. **Com. Foote** attacked Fort Donelson with the gunboats, and was compelled to withdraw.

Feb. 21. **The Federals** were defeated at Fort Craig, New Mexico, by the Texans.

Feb. 22. **Jefferson Davis** inaugurated President, and A. H. Stephens Vice-President, of the Southern Confederacy.

Feb. 24. The Union troops occupied Nashville, Tenn.

Feb. 27. Columbus was evacuated by the Confederates.

March 1. Two Union gunboats and a Confederate battery have a fight at Pittsburgh Landing.

March 11. Gen. McClellan takes command of the Army of the Potomac; Gen. Fremont, of the Mountain Department; Gen. Halleck, of the Department of the Mississippi.

March 12. Com. Dupont takes possession of Jacksonville, Fla.

April 11. Gen. Mitchell occupies Huntsville, Ala., taking 200 prisoners, 15 locomotives, and a large number of cars.

EDWIN M. STANTON.

GEN. BURNSIDE.

March 4. Andrew Johnson was appointed military governor of Tennessee.

Pike's Opera House, Cincinnati, burned.

March 6. President Lincoln proposed a plan of pecuniary assistance for the emancipation of the slaves in any States adopting an abolition policy.

March 9. Battle between the Confederate iron-clad, Merrimac, and the Federal floating battery, Monitor; the former compelled to retire.

Congress passed a bill abolishing slavery in the District of Columbia.

April 28. Forts Jackson and St. Philip surrender.

May 3. The Confederates evacuate Yorktown, Jamestown, and Mulberry and Gloucester islands, leaving ammunition, camp equipage, and 100 guns behind.

May 9. The Confederates evacuated Pensacola, and destroyed the Navy Yard.

May 10. **The Federal** forces took possession of Norfolk, Va., Gosport Navy Yard destroyed by the Confederates. Gunboat fight on the Mississippi, near Fort Wright; the Confederates were repulsed, losing two vessels.

May 11. **The Confederates** blow up their iron-clad Merrimac, to prevent its capture by the United States forces.

May 12. **Natchez, Miss.**, surrendered to Com. Farragut.

GOV. O. P. MORTON.

May 17. **Confederates** driven across the Chickahominy, at Bottom Bridge.

May 18. **Gen. Cox** engages the Confederate General Humphrey Marshall, at Princeton, Va.

May 20. **Confederates** evacuated Corinth, Miss.

Corinth taken.

June 6. After a naval battle, Memphis surrendered to the Union troops.

June 9. **The United States Senate** decree the abolition of slavery in all the Territories of the Union.

June 17. **Col. Fitch** destroyed a Confederate battery at St. Charles, Ark.

June 18. **Union** troops occupy Cumberland Gap.

June 26. **General Pope** assigned to the command of the Army of Virginia. The Con-

HUMPHREY MARSHALL.

federates under Gen. Robert E. Lee attacked McClellan's right wing at Mechanicsville. Battle undecided.

July 1. **President Lincoln** calls for 300,000 additional volunteers.

July 11. **Gen. Halleck** appointed commander of all the land forces of the United States.

July 17. **President Lincoln** sanctions a bill confiscating the property and emancipating the slaves of all persons who shall continue in arms against the Union for 60 days.

July 19. **Severe** skirmish at Memphis, Tennessee; Union loss, 6 killed and 32 wounded.

July 21. **John S. Phelps** appointed military Governor of Arkansas.

Aug. 3. **Gen. Halleck** orders Gen. McClellan to evacuate the Peninsula of Virginia.

Aug. 4. **The Secretary of War** orders a draft of 300,000 men.

Aug. 5. **Gen. Robert McCook** murdered by

Aug. 25. **Confederates** made an unsuccessful attack at Fort Donelson.

Sept. 2. **Gen. McClellan** appointed to the command of the troops for the defense of Washington.

Sept. 5. **Confederates** begin crossing the Potomac into Maryland.

Sept. 7. **Gen. Banks** is assigned to the command of the fortifications in and around Wash-

GENERAL LEE.

GEN. HALLECK.

the Confederates while wounded, and riding in an ambulance. The Confederate General J. C. Breckinridge made an unsuccessful attack on Baton Rouge, La.

Aug. 7. **Col. Canby** engages the Confederate General Sibley at Fort Filmore, N. M.

Aug. 16. **Gen. McClellan** evacuates Harrison's Landing.

Aug. 19. **Gen. Wright** placed in command of the Department of the Ohio.

ington. General McClellan takes the field at the head of the Army of the Potomac.

Cumberland Gap evacuated by the Federals.

Sept. 18. **The Confederates** recrossed the Potomac into Virginia, having been in Maryland two weeks. Evacuated Harper's Ferry.

President Lincoln's Emancipation Proclamation issued.

Sept. 25. **Habeas corpus** suspended by the United States Government.

Sept. 29. Gen. Nelson was shot by Gen. Jeff C. Davis, at Louisville, Ky.

Oct. 18. The Confederate Gen. Morgan occupies Lexington, Ky.

Oct. 19. The Confederate Gen. Forrest defeated near Gallatin, Tenn.

Oct. 22. Confederate salt works in Florida destroyed.

Oct. 30. Gen. Rosecrans assumes command of the Army of the Cumberland.

Dec. 6. Gen. Banks' Expedition sails for New Orleans.

Dec. 7. The Confederates were defeated with heavy loss.

Dec. 11. The City of Fredericksburg bombarded by the Union troops, under cover of which they crossed the Rappahannock.

Dec. 13. Gen. Thomas Francis Meagher engages in the battle of Fredericksburg.

GEN. FORREST.

GEN. MEAGHER.

Gen. Mitchell dies at Port Royal, S. C.

Nov. 5. Gen. McClellan relieved of the command of the Army of the Potomac, and Gen. Burnside succeeds him.

Nov. 16. President Lincoln enjoins on the United States forces the orderly observance of the Sabbath.

Nov. 22. The Political State prisoners released.

Dec. 14. Gen Banks supersedes Gen. Butler at New Orleans.

Dec. 16. Gen. Burnside's army removed to the north side of the Rappahannock.

Dec. 17. The Union troops occupy Baton Rouge, La.

Dec. 19. The Confederates recapture Holly Springs, Miss., taking the garrison prisoners.

Dec. 23. The **Confederates** repulsed by Gen. Sigel at Dumphries, Va.

Dec. 28. Second Attack on Vicksburg. The Federals drive the Confederates from the first and second lines of defense and advance to within two and a half miles of Vicksburg.

Gen. Blunt entered Van Buren, Ark., capturing four steamboats laden with provisions.

Dec. 29. The **Confederates** attack Gen.

GEN. SIDLEY.

Sherman with their whole force, and drive him back to the first line of defense.

Dec. 31. Battle of Murfreesboro, or Stone River. The Union army numbers 45,000 men under Gen. Rosecrans.

Deaths in the United States in 1862. Cornelius C. Felton, scholar and critic, President of Harvard University, aged 55 years. Theodore Frelinghuysen, statesman, aged 75 years.

The **Westfield** destroyed to keep it from falling into the hands of the enemy. Commodore Renshaw perishes with his vessel.

President Lincoln publishes a proclamation confirming his manifesto of Sept. 22, 1862, and declares all the slaves in the Confederate States free, and under the military protection of the United States.

1863.

Jan. 3. On the **night of** Jan. 3, the rebels commence their retreat from Murfreesboro.

GEN. SIGEL.

The Federal army withdraws from before Vicksburg.

Jan. 28. Gen. Burnside relieved of the command of the Army of the Potomac, and Gen Hooker appointed in his place.

Gens. Sumner and Franklin relieved from duty in the Army of the Potomac.

Feb. 2. The **Federal ram Queen** of the

West ran the blockade at Vicksburg, but was captured a few days after by the Confederates.

The negro brigade take Jacksonville, Florida.

Major General Burnside appointed to command the Department of the Ohio.

May 1. Gen. Carter, with 5,000 men attacked the Confederate forces at Monticello, under Pegram, and drove them from the field.

Battle of Fort Gibson. Gen. Grant defeated Gen. Bowen.

GEN. HOOKER.

May 2. On the morning of the 17th of April, 1863, the 6th and 7th Illinois cavalry, 900 strong, under command of Col. Grierson, of the 6th Illinois, set out from Lagrange, Tenn., marched through the center of Mississippi, destroying as they went railroads, bridges and stores of all kinds belonging to the Confederates, in immense quantities. They reached Baton Rouge, La., on the evening of the 2d of May.

They had traveled nearly 800 miles in 16 days. At several points the enemy made great attempts to capture them, but failed. They brought into Baton Rouge over 1,000 horses and a large number of cattle; 500 negroes followed them.

May 8. Col. Streight's command of 1,700 men were captured by Forest's cavalry, two miles from Cedar Bluff Ga., after severe fighting.

COL. GRIERSON.

The Confederate General, Van Dorn, killed by Dr. Peters in Manny county, Tenn.

May 9. Col. Jacobs routed a guerilla force near Horse Shoe Bend on the Cumberland River.

May 10. The Confederate General, Stonewall (Thos. J.) Jackson, died at Richmond, Va., of wounds and pneumonia.

May 12. Gen. McPherson attacks Raymond, Miss.

May 18. Investment of Vicksburg by the Federals under Gen. Grant and Admiral Porter.

May 25. Confederate navy yard destroyed at Yazoo City.

May 27. Gen. Banks commences the siege of the forts at Port Hudson, Miss.

June 1. Gen. Hunter removed from the command of the Department of the South Gen. Gilmore succeeds him.

GEN. "STONEWALL" JACKSON.

June 17 Federal cavalry under Col. Kilpatrick encountered Gen. Fitzhugh Lee's cavalry brigade near Aldie, Va.

June 21. Gen. McClernard removed by Grant, and Gen. Ord succeeds him.

June 26. Rear Admiral Foote died in New York City.

June 29. Gen. Hooker relieved of his command of the Army of the Potomac at his own request. Gen. Meade succeeds him.

Rosecrans drives Bragg from Tullahoma.

July 8. Major General Gardner surrendered.

July 13-16. Riots take place in New York, Boston, and other Union cities, in consequence of the enforcement of a conscription decree.

July 13, 14, 15. Draft Riots in New York City. Mobs have possession of the city for three days. Offices where the draft was going on were demolished, and the buildings were burned. Several negroes were murdered. The

GEN. KILPATRICK.

colored orphan asylum on Fifth Avenue was pillaged and burnt down. Several persons were killed during the prevalence of the riot. The city paid above $1,500,000 as indemnity for losses that occurred during the riot.

July 22 Chattanooga was shelled by Col. Wilder of Rosecrans' advance,

July 23. Eight Hundred men of Gen. Spinola's brigade utterly routed twice their number of Georgia and North Carolina troops at Manassas Gap.

Kentucky again invaded. Kit Carson, with a part of the first New Mexico regiment, defeats the Navajoe Indians in a severe fight beyond Fort Canby.

Aug. 7. President Lincoln rejects the demand for the suppression of the conscription in the State of New York.

property destroyed; 191 persons were killed, many of whom were helpless women and children; 581 were wounded, many of them mortally. About 80 of the murderers were killed.

Sept. 4. Burnside occupies Knoxville, Tenn.

Sept. 9. General Crittenden's division of Rosecrans' army enters Chattanooga.

Sept. 10. Gen. Steele takes possession of Little Rock, Ark.

REAR ADMIRAL FOOTE.

Aug. 17. Lieut. Col. Phillips attacked the Confederate forces at Grenada, Miss., under command of Gen. Slimmer, and drove them from the place.

Aug 20 The town of Lawrence, Kan., was surprised in the middle of the night by 300 guerillas under the leadership of Quantrell. The town was set on fire and 182 buildings burned to the ground, and $2,000,000 worth of

GEN. MEADE.

Sept. 15. President Lincoln suspends the Habeas Corpus act.

Oct. 9. Wheeler's Confederate cavalry was defeated with considerable loss at Farmington, Tennessee, and again near Shelbyville.

Oct. 20. The Departments of the Cumberland and Mississippi consolidated and placed under the command of General Grant.

Gen. Rosecrans removed, and Gen. Thompson appointed in his place.

Nov. 5. **Brownsville**, Texas, captured.

Nov. 25. **The Confederate** army under Bragg defeated near Chattanooga.

Nov. **The First** Fenian convention assembled at Chicago. According to tradition the Fenians or Finians were a national militia established in Ireland by Fin or Fionn, the son of Cumhal.

Dec. 4. **Gen. Longstreet** commences the siege of Knoxville, Nov. 17.

Feb. 22. A skirmish between Union troops and the Confederates under Gen. Mosby.

March 8. **Gen. Grant** formally presented by the President with his commission as Lieut. General, and on the 12th assigned to the command of the armies of the United States.

April 12. **General Forrest** captures Fort Pillow, and immediately after commences an indiscriminate massacre of our wounded soldiers,

GEN. BRAGG.

1864.

Feb. 1. **President Lincoln** orders a draft for 500,000 men.

Feb. 9. A large number of prisoners, including Col. Streight, escape from Libby Prison, Richmond.

Feb. 15. **Gen. W. T. Sherman** with his troops arrives at Meridian, Miss., on his great raid into the heart of the enemy's country.

GEN. MOSBY.

both colored and white, not excepting women and children who had taken refuge in the fort.

April 23. **The Governors** of Ohio, Illinois, Iowa, Wisconsin, and Indiana offer to raise for the general Government 85,000 men for one hundred days.

April 26. **Government** accepts services of one-hundred day men, and appropriates $20,000,000 for their payment.

May 5. Draft ordered in Massachusetts, New Jersey, Ohio, Minnesota, Kentucky and Maryland.

Gen. Butler lands on the south side of the James.

May 8. Sherman occupies Dalton.

May 16. Nathaniel Hawthorne, American novelist, died, aged 55 years.

May 23. Confederates forced to evacuate their fortifications near Spottsylvania C. H.

June 12 Gen. Hancock drives the Confederates from Bottom Bridge at the point of the bayonet.

June 14. Gen. Leonidas Polk killed at Pine Mountain, Ga.

June 30. Secretary Chase resigns, and Hon. Wm. Fessenden was appointed to fill the vacancy.

July 5. The Confederates under Early invaded Maryland.

GEN. SHERMAN.

John Morgan enters Kentucky with 4,000 men.

May 27. Grant crosses the Pamunkey, and occupies Hanovertown.

May 30. Gen. Grant reaches Mechanicsville.

June 8. Abraham Lincoln and Andrew Johnson nominated for President and Vice-President.

GEN. POLK.

July 22. Gen. McPherson killed at the battle of Atlanta.

July 30. A mine containing six tons of powder, under a Confederate fort at Petersburg, explodes, destroying the fort and garrison.

Chambersburg, Pa., burned by the Confederates.

Aug. 5. Commodore Farragut's fleet passes Forts Morgan and Gaines. The Confederate ram Tennessee is captured, and several other vessels destroyed. Shortly after Fort Gaines surrenders, and Fort Powell is evacuated.

Aug. 18. The Weldon Railroad is seized by Gen. Grant.

Aug. 23. Fort Morgan surrenders.

Sept. 2. The Federal troops take possession of Atlanta.

Sept. 7. The Confederate General John Morgan killed near Greenville, Tennessee.

Oct. 31. Union troops recapture Plymouth, N. C.

Nov. 8. The Presidential election takes place. Lincoln and Johnson receive 212, McClellan and Pendleton twenty-one electoral votes.

McClellan resigns his command in the army.

GEN. MACPHERSON.

Sept. 16. Engagement between Gens. Gregg and Kantz, and Confederate General Wade Hampton.

Sept. 28. Gen. Grant advanced his lines on the north side of the James River to within seven miles of Richmond. The Confederates under General Sterling Price invade Missouri.

Oct. 7. The pirate vessel Florida captured by the United States steamship Wachusett.

DAVID G. FARRAGUT.

Nov. 16. General Sherman leaves Atlanta and begins his great march to the Atlantic.

Dec. 29. Hood's army crosses the Tennessee River, thus ending the Tennessee campaign.

1865.

Jan. 3. Massachusetts ratified the Constitutional amendment.

Jan. 8. General Butler removed from the

command of the Army of the James. He was succeeded by Gen. Ord.

Jan. 15. **Edward Everett**, American Statesman and distinguished orator, dies, aged 71 years.

Jan. 20. **Confederates** evacuate Corinth.

Jan. 27. **Confederate** incendiaries set fire to the city of Savannah.

Feb. 1. **Congress** abolishes slavery in the United States.

Illinois ratifies the Constitutional amendment.

GEN. WADE HAMPTON.

Feb. 2. Maryland, Michigan, New York and Rhode Island ratify the Constitutional amendment.

Feb. 4. Illinois black laws are repealed.

Feb. 7. Maine ratifies the Constitutional amendment.

Feb. 12. **Gen. Sherman** occupies Branchville, S. C.

Feb. 13. **Indiana** ratifies the Constitutional amendment.

Feb. 17. Louisiana ratifies the Constitutional amendment.

Gen. Sherman's victorious columns enter Columbia, S. C., and burn the city.

Feb. 16. **Gen. Lee** assumes supreme command of the Confederate armies, and recommends arming of the blacks.

Charleston, S. C., evacuated, and taken possession of by Gen. Gilmore. Six thousand bales of cotton destroyed. Ammunition stored in the railroad depot explodes, and many lives

STERLING PRICE.

were lost. Gen. Gilmore hoists the U. S. flag over Fort Sumter.

Feb. 10. Fort Anderson, N. C., is taken.

Feb. 21. **Wisconsin ratifies** the Constitutional amendment. Fort Armstrong, N. C., taken.

Feb. 22. **Confederate** Congress decrees that the slaves shall be armed.

Feb. 23. **Raleigh, N. C.**, was captured. Governor Vance captured.

March 4. **Inauguration** of Abraham Lincoln and Andrew Johnson as President and Vice-President of the United States.

Gen. Sherman occupies Fayetteville, N. C.

March 13. Gen. **Schofield** occupies Kingston.

March 16. Confederate Gen. Hardee was defeated at Averysboro, N. C.

March 17. Confederate Congress adjourns "sine die."

ANDREW JOHNSON.

March 19. Confederate Gen. Johnson defeated at Bentonville, N. C.

March 25. Confederates attack Gen. Grant, and are severely defeated.

April 3. Richmond taken.

April 8. Surrender of Gen. Lee and his whole army at Appomattox Court House, Va.

April 12. The Union flag hoisted at Fort Sumter.

April 13. Drafting and recruiting stopped.

April 14. President Lincoln shot by J. Wilkes Booth in Ford's Theater, Washington; Mr. Seward and his son wounded.

April 15. Death of President Lincoln. Vice-President Johnson sworn in as President of the United States.

April 26. Gen. Johnson surrenders.

April 27. Booth, the murderer of President Lincoln, mortally wounded and captured.

DR. BELLOWS.

May 4. General Dick Taylor surrenders.

May 10. Jefferson Davis captured at Irwinville, 75 miles southwest of Macon, Ga., by the 4th Michigan cavalry, under Col. Pritchard, of Gen. Wilson's command; also his wife, mother, Postmaster-General Regan, Col. Harrison, private secretary, Col. Johnson, and other military characters.

May 19. **Confederate** Gov. Watts, of Alabama, was arrested.

May 21. **Confederate** Gov. Letcher, of Virginia, is arrested.

May 24. **Grand Review** of Gen. Sherman's army occurs at Washington.

Jefferson Davis indicted for treason.

May 26. **Kirby Smith** surrenders. The last armed Confederate organization succumbs.

STEPHEN A. DOUGLAS.

May 31. Confederate Gen. Hood and staff surrender.

June 22. President Johnson rescinded order requiring passports from all travelers entering the United States, and opened Southern ports.

July 7. Execution of Payne, Atzerott, Harold, and Mrs. Surratt, for complicity in the assassination of President Lincoln.

Oct. 11. Pardon of Alexander Stephens and other Southern officials.

Nov. 9. **Confederate** privateer Shenandoah surrendered at Liverpool, having destroyed about 30 vessels; crew released.

Nov. 10. Execution of Wirz, the Confederate prison keeper, for cruelty to Union prisoners.

1866.

Jan. 28. Hon. Thomas Chandler died.

Feb. 19. President vetoed Freedmen's Bureau bill. This bill required the Government to take care of the emancipated slaves and destitute whites of the South.

JOHN ROSS.

March 14. Jared Sparks, historian, dies.

March 27. President Johnson vetoed Civil Rights bill. This bill guaranteed the same rights to the negro, in every particular, as those enjoyed by the white man.

April 2. President Johnson issued a proclamation declaring that the insurrection which heretofore existed in the States of Georgia,

South Carolina, North Carolina, Virginia, Tennessee, Alabama, Louisiana, Arkansas, Mississippi and Florida, is at an end, and henceforth to be so regarded.

April 9. Civil Rights Bill was passed over the President's veto.

April 12. Hon. Daniel S. Dickinson dies.

May 16. President Johnson vetoed the admission of Colorado as a State.

GIDEON WELLES.

May 29. Death of General Winfield Scott, aged 80 years.

June 7. President Johnson issued a proclamation against the Fenian movement in the United States.

Fenians from the United States made a raid into Canada.

June 17. Hon. Lewis Cass dies.

July 13-27. The Atlantic Telegraph is successfully laid between Great Britain and America.

July 16. Freedmen's Bureau bill became a law.

July 30. Major-General Lysander Cutler dies.

Aug. 14. National Union Convention assembles in Philadelphia wigwam.

Sept. 1. Southern Unionists Convention assembles in Philadelphia.

Sept. 7. Matthias W. Baldwin, pioneer in American locomotives, dies.

GEN. PLEASONTON.

Oct. 13. "Prince" John Van Buren, son of Martin, dies.

Dec. 13. Congress passes a bill giving negroes the right to vote in the District of Columbia.

Dec. 26. Major-General Samuel R. Curtis dies.

1867.

Jan. 9. Virginia rejected the Fourteenth Amendment. This amendment guaranteed civil rights to all, regardless of race or color.

Jan. 10. Congress passed a bill providing for "universal suffrage" in the Territories.

Jan. 29. The bill to admit Nebraska is vetoed by President Johnson.

Feb. 6. Delaware and Louisiana rejected Constitutional amendment.

May 9. General strike of working men throughout the States.

May 13. Jefferson Davis was admitted to bail at Richmond, Va.

June 3. Gen. Sheridan removed Gen. Welles, of Louisiana, and on the 6th appointed B. F. Flanders, Governor.

July 11. Reciprocity treaty between the United States and the Hawaiian Islands.

GEN. MITCHELL.

CASSIUS M. CLAY.

Feb. 8. Nebraska is admitted as a State.

Feb. 25. Tenure of Office bill was passed over President's veto. This bill makes the consent of the Senate necessary before the President can remove any person from a civil office.

Feb. 30. It was announced at Washington that Russia cedes Alaska to the United States.

May 3. Eight-hour riots in Chicago.

July 24. New York State Constitutional Convention rejects the proposition of woman suffrage.

July 30. General Sheridan removed Governor Throckmorton, of Texas.

Aug. 5. Secretary Stanton was requested by the President to resign, but refused.

Aug. 12. Stanton is suspended, and Gen. Grant is appointed Secretary of War *ad interim*.

Aug. 17. General Sheridan was relieved at New Orleans.

Aug. 16. National Labor Congress met at Chicago.
Sept. 8. President issued amnesty proclamation.
Sept. 30. Negro riots in Savannah, Ga.
Oct. 3. Whisky riot in Philadelphia.
Nov. 2. General Sherman announces Indian war to be at an end.
Nov. 14. Denmark concluded a treaty by which the islands of St. Thomas, San Juan, and Santa Cruz were ceded and sold to the United States.
Nov. 22. Jefferson Davis returned to Richmond, Va.
Dec. 7. Resolution of Judiciary Committee to impeach President Johnson was voted down in the House—102 to 57.

1868.

Jan. 2. Governor Flanders of Louisiana resigns, and Joshua Baker is appointed his successor by Gen. Hancock.

Jan. 6. Congress Met. The President is censured in the House for removing General Sheridan.
Gen. Meade assumes command of the third military district, consisting of Alabama, Georgia and Florida.
House of Representatives passes a bill making eight hours a day's work for Government laborers.

Jan. 10. Secretary Seward announced to the House that 21 States had ratified the 14th article of the amendment to the Constitution.
Jan. 11. The Chinese Government appointed Anson Burlingame, formerly United States Minister in Pekin, its special envoy to all the treaty powers, at a salary of $10,000.
Jan. 13. The United States House of Representatives passes a bill declaring that five members shall constitute a quorum of the Su-

JOHN CALDWELL CALHOUN.

JOSEPH HOOKER.

preme Court, and that a concurrence of two-thirds of all the members shall be necessary to a decision adverse to the validity of any law passed by Congress.

The Senate reinstated Stanton.

Jan. 14. **The Virginia Constitutional** Convention declares that Virginia shall forever remain in the Union, and that slavery is forever abolished in the State.

GOV. CURTIN.

General Grant vacated War Office in favor of Secretary Stanton.

Jan. 15. **Gen. Pope** was assigned to the command of the Department of the Lakes with headquarters at Detroit.

Jan. 24. Fifty thousand American breech-loading rifles were ordered by the Spanish Minister of War.

Jan. 29. **The President** instructs Gen. Grant in writing, not to obey any orders from the War Department, unless authorized by himself.

Feb. 5. **Congress** passed a bill authorizing the Secretary of War to employ counsel to defend Generals or other persons intrusted with reconstruction in cases brought against them for their acts under the reconstruction laws.

Thermometer 51 degrees below zero in Wisconsin.

Feb. 13. **Another attempt** is made to impeach President Johnson.

J. P. BENJAMIN.

Feb. 18. **Senate** bill is passed for the reduction of the army.

Feb. 21. **The President** ordered the removal of Secretary Stanton from the war office, and authorized Gen. Thomas to act as Secretary of War *ad interim*. Stanton decided to retain personal possession of the office until action in the matter be taken by the Senate. The Senate disapproved the action of the President, declaring it to be unconstitutional.

Feb. 22. **Adjutant-General Thomas** arrested for violation of the tenure of office bill on complaint of Secretary Stanton. He is released on $10,000 bail.

Feb. 23. Conclusion of a treaty between the North German Confederation and the United States, concerning the nationality of persons emigrating from one of the two countries to the other.

J. A. ANDREWS.

Feb. 24. The United States House of Representatives resolve by a vote of 126 to 47, that "Andrew Johnson, President of the United States, be impeached of high crimes and misdemeanors." The President sends a message to the Senate vindicating his position.

Feb. 25. The Committee of the House appoints Boutwell, Stevens, Bingham and Wilson, a sub-committee to take evidence and prepare articles of impeachment.

The Florida Convention adopts the new Constitution.

The House informs the Senate and presents their action in regard to the impeachment of President Johnson.

Governor Ward of New Jersey, vetoes resolution of Legislature withdrawing ratification of Fourteenth Amendment.

Feb. 26. Gen. L. Thomas discharged from arrest and began a suit against Secretary Stanton for false imprisonment and malicious prosecution, setting his damages at $150,000.

T. J. PORTER.

An amendatory reconstruction bill passes Congress, providing that any election in the Southern States should be decided by a majority of the votes actually cast.

March 2. The Senate adopts a code of procedure for an impeachment trial.

The House adopts nine articles of impeachment, and appoints seven managers of the impeachment trial.

March 5. New Jersey Senate passes over Gov. Ward's veto as to amendment; the lower House does the same.

March 6. President Johnson was summoned to appear before the courts of impeachment, on the 18th of March.

March 12. The House passes the bill to abolish the tax on manufacturers.

Trial of Jeff Davis is postponed until April 14th.

ment opens for the trial of President Johnson. The President filed his answer to the articles of impeachment. His counsel asks for further delay.

March 26. The Senate passes the Habeas Corpus appeal bill over the President's veto. They also ratify the treaty with the North German Confederation, recognizing the rights of naturalized citizens.

C. F. ADAMS.

COM. GOLDSBOROUGH.

March 13. The President asks forty days' time to prepare his answer to the articles of impeachment. The Senate extends the time till March 23.

March 18. The House passes the bill providing that in case of the death or removal of the Chief-Justice, the senior Associate Justice of the Supreme Court shall perform the duties of Chief-Justice.

March 23. The High Court of Impeach-

March 27. The House passes the Supreme Court bill over the President's veto.

March 28. A new indictment is found against Jeff Davis by the United States Grand Jury at Richmond.

March 30. G. A. Ashburn, a member of the Constitutional Convention, was assassinated at Columbus, Ga.

Gen. B. F. Butler of Massachusetts, opens in

the Court of Impeachment, the prosecution on the part of the managers.

April 2. **North German Parliament** passes the neutralization treaty with the United States.

April 4. The case for the prosecution in the Court of Impeachment is closed.

General Schofield appoints Henry H. Wells Governor of Virginia.

April 6. **Michigan** votes against negro suffrage.

JOHN TYLER.

April 9. The counsel for President Johnson opens the argument for the defense in the Court of Impeachment.

April 20. **Evidence** in the impeachment case closed.

April 23. **Charles Dickens** left the United States.

April 24. A treaty of peace was concluded with the Sioux Indians.

May 6. **Argument** in the impeachment trial was closed.

May 21. **U. S. Grant** was nominated by the Republicans at Chicago as candidate for President, and Schuyler Colfax for Vice-President.

May 22. **Arrival of** Chinese Embassy in New York.

May 26. **Impeachment** trial concluded, and the President found not guilty.

May 30. **The Grand Army** of the Republic decorated with flowers the graves of the Union soldiers in the cemeteries throughout the country.

G. P. T. BEAUREGARD.

June 1. **Ex-President** James Buchanan died.

June 3. **Trial of** Jeff Davis again postponed till November.

June 4 **Ex-President Buchanan** buried at Wheatland, Penn.

June 10. **The Senate** passes a bill for the admission of the Southern States with only five negative votes.

June 12. Reverdy Johnson confirmed as Minister to England.

June 16. Governor, Humphreys, of Mississippi, removed by Gen. McDowell, Gen. Ames appointed military governor in his stead.

June 19. The House passes the Senate bill giving thanks to Secretary Stanton.

June 20. The House passes the bill for the admission of Arkansas over the President's veto without debate.

June 22. King of Belgium reviewed United States squadron under Farragut off Ostend.

June 24. The Senate ratifies the Chinese treaty. The House passes a bill for the immediate reorganization of the States of Virginia, Mississippi and Texas.

June 25. The Freedmen's Bureau bill passed over the President's vote.

July 4. President Johnson issues a proclamation of general amnesty and pardon to all engaged in the late rebellion except those already indicted for treason or other felony.

July 21. Congress passes a resolution declaring the 14th article ratified. The Senate passes a resolution appealing to the Turkish government in behalf of the Cretans.

Aug. 1. General Jeff C. Davis is assigned to the command of the military district of Alaska.

JERE S. BLACK.

GEN. MEIGS.

Sept. 18. Gen. Hindman was assassinated at Helena, Arkansas.

Oct. 7. Death of Gen. Adam J. Slemmer occurs at Fort Laramie.

James Hind, member of Congress from Arkansas, is assassinated.

Nov. 3. Iowa and Minnesota vote in favor of negro suffrage, and Missouri against it.

Nov. 23. Gen. Howard issues an order for the discontinuance of the Freedmen's Bureau after January 1, except the educational department, and the collection of money due to soldiers.

Dec. 25. President Johnson issues a universal amnesty proclamation.

Dec. 20. Mosby Clark, a revolutionary soldier, died at Richmond, Va., at the advanced age of 121 years.

Dec. 31. General Sheridan captures the Indian chiefs, Santanta and Lone Wolf.

GEN. HANCOCK.

The house passes the bill repealing an act prohibiting the organization of militia in all the reconstructed States except Georgia; also a resolution allowing women in the government employ the wages of men for the same work.

The Senate denounces the views of President Johnson on the national debt; also passes a resolution disapproving the President's financial recommendations.

The Secretary of the Navy accepts the transfer of League Island by the city of Philadelphia to the Government for a navy yard.

1869.

Feb. 20. Martial law is declared in Tennessee.

Feb. 22-26. Congress passed Fifteenth Amendment. Kansas was the first State (Feb. 27), to ratify it, though imperfectly, and Delaware the first to reject it.

L. WALLACE.

March 25. Pennsylvania ratified Fifteenth Amendment.

April 13. Senate rejected Alabama treaty with Great Britain.

May 13. Woman Suffrage Convention in New York city.

May 19. President Grant proclaimed that there be no reduction in Government laborers' wages because of reduction of hours.

June 18. Hon. Henry J. Raymond, of *N. Y. Times*, dies.

July 13. Completion of Atlantic cable from Brest to St. Pierre; thence to Duxbury, Mass.
Aug 16. National Labor Convention, Philadelphia.
Sept. 1. National Temperance Convention, Chicago.
Sept. 8. Hon. William Pitt Fessenden dies.
Sept. 10. Hon. John Bell dies.
Sept. 16. Hon. John Minor Botts dies.

Dec. 24. Hon. Edwin M. Stanton died.

1870.

Jan. 26. Virginia is re-admitted into the Union.
Feb. 9. U. S. Signal Bureau established by Act of Congress.
Feb. 17. Mississippi was re-admitted into the Union.

GEN. PICKETT.

REVERDY JOHNSON.

Sept. 24. Black Friday So named on account of the losses on gold speculations, etc.
Oct. 8. Virginia ratifies Fourteenth and Fifteenth Amendments.
Ex-President Franklin Pierce died.
Nov. 4. George Peabody died.
Nov. 6. Admiral Charles Stewart dies.
Nov. 24. National Woman-suffrage Convention, Cleveland, Ohio; Henry Ward Beecher was chosen President.

Feb. 23. Hon. Anson Burlingame dies.
March 28. Major-General George H. Thomas died.
March 29. Texas is re-admitted to representation in Congress, thus completing the work of reconstruction.
March 30. President Grant announced the adoption of the Fifteenth Amendment.
July 12. Admiral John A. Dahlgren died.
Aug. 14. Admiral David G. Farragut died.

Aug. 15. National Labor Congress, Cincinnati.

Aug. 22. President Grant issued a proclamation enjoining neutrality as to war between France and Prussia.

Aug. 23. Irish National Congress convenes, Cincinnati.

Oct. 4. Second Southern Commercial convention, Cincinnati.

1871.

Jan. 20. Motion to strike out the word "male" in the section of the Fourteenth Amendment giving the elective franchise to all male citizens, was defeated in the House of Representatives; vote, 55 to 117.

Jan. 26. The income tax was repealed.

Feb. 22. Arrival in New York of the British members of the Joint High Commission.

March 24. President Grant, by proclamation orders certain bands of armed men in South Carolina to disperse within thirty days.

April 26. The United States Supreme Court decides that the general government cannot tax the salaries of State officials.

June 17. The ratification of the treaty of Washington was exchanged in London.

June 24. Corner stone of the Capitol was laid in Albany.

July 4. President Grant proclaimed the complete ratification of the Treaty of Washington.

July 12. Orangemen riot. On the occasion of a procession of Protestant Orangemen in New York, they were attacked by the Roman Catholic Irish. Threats of assault having been given the Orangemen were protected by the military. Stones, pistols, and guns, being discharged at the militia, several were killed and wounded, when an order was given to the soldiers to fire on the rioters. Five soldiers and about a hundred rioters were killed.

July 30. The Westfield Horror. The steamer's boiler explodes; 40 persons killed outright, and 63 injured—subsequently died.

Sept. 27. Chief Justice McKean, of Utah, decided against Mormons serving as grand jurors in Federal courts.

Oct. 2. Brigham Young was arrested by the United States Marshal for Mormon proclivities.

Oct. 3. Daniel H. Wells, Mayor of Salt Lake City, and a Mormon bishop, is arrested by the United States Marshal for Mormon proclivities.

Oct. 7. The first of the great fires in Chicago breaks out; loss, $300,000.

Oct. 8. The great fire by which Chicago was desolated broke out at 10 o'clock at night; loss $190,526,000.

The great forest fires: Peshtigo, Wisconsin, destroyed by fire, 600 of its inhabitants perish; Manistee, Williamsonville, Menckaunee, Marinette, and Brussels, Wis., burned; a number of inhabitants perish.

Oct. 9. The great Chicago fire continued to rage and destroy.

Oct. 12. President Grant summoned the Ku-Klux-Klan of South Carolina to disband and deliver up their arms and ammunition.

Oct. 17. President Grant suspended the writ of habeas corpus in nine counties of South Carolina.

Oct. 24. Riot in Los Angeles, Cal.; a mob attacks the Chinese quarter, and captures and hangs eighteen Chinamen.

Oct. 26. A warrant is issued for the arrest of Wm. M. Tweed, James H. Ingersoll, A. J. Garvey, and E. A. Woodward at the suit of Attorney-General Chamberlain.

Oct. 27. Wm. M. Tweed arrested and bailed.

Nov. 19. Grand Duke Alexis, son of the Czar of Russia, arrived in New York.

Nov. 21. Grand Duke Alexis was formally received by President Grant.

1872.

Jan. 2. Brigham Young returned to Salt Lake City and surrendered to an indictment for the murder of Richard Yates; bail is refused, and he is ordered into the custody of the law officers.

Feb. 10. The Grand Jury of the Court of General Sessions of New York City present indictments against Mayor A. O. Hall, R. B. Connelly, Wm. M. Tweed, Nathaniel Sands, and others.

Feb. 29. **The Japanese** Embassy arrived in Washington.

March 4. President Grant received the Japanese Embassy.

April 10. Philip Klingon Smith, of Lincoln county, Nevada, a former Mormon bishop, charges the Mormons with the "Mountain Meadow Massacre" of immigrants in 1857, and exonerated the Indians.

April 15. The counsel of the U. S. and the English arbitrators on the Alabama claims met in Geneva, Switzerland. The "cases" were exchanged, and the British Consul presented a protest against the claims for indirect damages.

The British authorities at Kingston, Jamaica, seize the American steamer Edgar Stuart as a Cuban privateer.

May 29. Canadian authorities seize the American fishing schooner, Enola C., for violating the fishery laws.

June 6. The United States Minister at Madrid demands the release of Dr. Houard.

June 15. The members of the Tribunal of Arbitration assemble in Geneva, Switzerland, and organize; after a short session, the tribunal adjourns until the 17th inst.

June 17. The World's Peace Jubilee opens in Boston.

June 18. Mexican soldiers at Matamoras fire on and arrest the American occupants of a pleasure boat on the Rio Grande, between that city and Brownsville, Texas.

The Canadian cutter, Stella Marie, seizes the American fishing schooner, James Bliss, for violating the fishery laws; the American flag is insulted by being turned Union down under the Dominion flag on the captured vessel.

June 20. The bodies of Confederate soldiers killed and buried at Gettysburg, were removed and conducted through Richmond, Va., in mournful procession.

July 7. The Cuban privateer, Pioneer, was captured by the U. S. Revenue cutter, Moccasin, off Newport, R. I., and brought into that port.

Aug. 3. The Cuban privateer, Pioneer, is formally seized by the U. S. Marshal at Newport, R. I., for violation of the neutrality laws.

Aug. 19. Judge G. G. Barnard, of the Supreme Court, found guilty by the Court of Impeachment, at Albany, of high crimes and misdemeanors, removed from the bench, and declared ineligible ever to hold office in the state.

Aug. 20. Prince Philip, of Coburg-Gotha, arrives in New York city to join his brother, the Duke of Saxe.

Dr. Houard arrived in New York City from Cadiz, Spain.

Sept. 7. The Cuban steamer Virginius escapes from the blockade of the Spanish war vessels at Puerto Cabello, Venezuela.

Sept. 14. The Geneva, Switzerland, Tribunal of Arbitration on the Alabama claims awards $16,250,000 to the United States.

Oct. 22. The Emperor William, of Germany, communicates his decision on the San Juan dispute to the representatives of England and the United States. It approves the claims of the United States Government.

Nov. 9. The greatest fire that ever raged in Boston breaks out early this evening, and continues all night.

Nov. 10. The great fire in Boston is got under control about 3 P. M., after having burned over an area of 200 acres, in the business center of the city; again at about 12 P. M., the flames appear near the place of origin of the first fire, and spread rapidly to buildings that had escaped them, before; an explosion of gas produced this second conflagration.

Nov. 20. Henry M. Stanley, the discoverer of Livingstone, arrives in New York from England.

Nov. 22. The Erie Railroad Co. begins an action against Jay Gould for the recovery of $9,726,551; Gould is arrested, but immediately after bailed in $1,000,000.

Dec. 17. Jay Gould restores $9,000,000 worth of property to the E. R. R. Co., for the sake of peace.

Dec. 26. Great storm throughout the country and along the coast; many shipping disasters result.

1873.

March 4. Second inauguration of President Grant.

March 30. Wreck of the White Star steamship Atlantic, off the coast of Halifax; 700 lives lost.

April 11. Gen. Canby and Rev. Dr. Thomas treacherously murdered by the Modocs on the lava beds.

April 18. Attack on the Modoc lava beds. Second battle with the Modocs.

April 27. The Modocs surprise and destroy a detachment of troops.

May 10. The Modocs evacuate the lava beds.

May 20. Surrender of Hot-Creeks and Modocs to Gen. Davis.

May 22. Gen. McKenzie's excursion into Mexico.

May 30. The great Boston fire No. 2.

June 1. Modoc Jack's surrender.

June 17. Indians attack the Northern Pacific surveying party; four Indians killed.

June 27. The work of laying the new Atlantic cable completed.

Aug. 11. Sanguinary battle occurs between the Pawnees and Sioux in the Republican Valley; reported.

Sept. 9. The settlement of the Geneva award was consummated.

Sept. 18. Failures occur on Wall street, New York—Jay Cooke & Co., and others.

Oct. 3. Execution of the Modocs, Capt. Jack, Scouchin, Boston Charley, and Black Jim, for the murder of Gen. Canby and Rev. Dr. Thomas, at Fort Klamath, Oregon.

First business session of the Evangelical Alliance held.

Oct. 4. Capt. Buddington and ten other survivors of the Polaris expedition, arrive in New York by the steamship City of Antwerp.

1874.

Wm. M. Tweed sentenced to twelve years' imprisonment, and to pay a fine of $12,500.

May 16. The Mill River Reservoir disaster near Northampton, Mass. Fearful loss of life.

July 1. Abduction of Charley Ross at Germantown, Pa.

Oct. 5. First annual meeting of the Episcopal Church Congress of the United States.

1875.

June 17. The Bunker Hill Centennial Celebration.

Nov. 22. Hon. Henry Wilson, Vice President of the United States, dies at Washington, D. C., aged 64 years.

Dec. 4. Escape of Wm. M. Tweed.

Dec. 11. The Dynamite explosion at Bremerhaven; 60 persons killed; the steamship Mosel injured and detained.

1876.

Jan 1. On Staten Island the Rev. Henry Boehm, the venerable patriarch of the Methodist church, dies, aged one hundred and one years.

Jan. 9. In South Boston, Dr. Samuel Gridley Howe, the distinguished philanthropist, dies, aged 74 years.

Feb. 11. The Centennial Appropriation bill was passed by the Senate. The President, on the 16th, signed the bill with a quill from the wing of an American eagle shot near Mount Hope, Oregon.

Feb. 15. The historic elm, above 200 years old, on Boston Common, was blown down by a high wind Tuesday evening.

April 15. Arrival of Dom Pedro, Emperor of

Brazil, at New York.

April 18. President Grant vetoed the bill passed by Congress, reducing his successor's salary to $25,000 per annum.

May 10. Opening of Centennial Exposition at Philadelphia.

June 16. The National Republican Convention at Cincinnati, nominated Governor Rutherford B. Hayes of Ohio, for President of the United States, and the Hon. William A. Wheeler, of New York, for Vice-President.

June 25. Gen. Custer's force was overpowered and annihilated. Gen. Custer, his two brothers and nephew, were killed. Not one of the command escaped. Col. Reno's force was surrounded and sustained severe losses, but was finally rescued by Gen. Gibbons' command. The entire loss was 261 killed and 50 wounded.

June 27. The Democratic National Convention met at St. Louis, and on the 28th of June, nominated Governor Samuel J. Tilden, of New York, for President, and Hon. Thomas A. Hendricks, of Indiana, for Vice-President.

July 16. Congress unanimously passed the Senate joint resolution for the completion of the Washington Monument.

July 26. Argument of the Belknap impeachment case closed. The result was a failure to convict.

August 1. President Grant issued a proclamation declaring Colorado to be a State of the Union.

Aug. 11. The first wire stretched across East River for the great suspension bridge, to connect New York and Brooklyn.

Sept. 24. Hell Gate, or the mine under Hallett's Point Reef, Astoria, Long Island, was exploded by General Newton.

Nov. 7. Election of President of the United States.

Nov. 10. Closing of the great Centennial Exhibition, Philadelphia.

Dec. 5. First cremation in the United States was performed at Washington, Pa. It was the body of Baron De Palm, who was born in Augsburg, Southern Germany, in the year 1809.

Dec. 29. Terrible railroad accident at Ashtabula, Ohio, over 100 lives lost. Among them, P. P. Bliss, the singer, and wife.

1877.

The monopoly of sewing machines expired this year, reducing the prices of these machines to about one-half their original cost.

The last of the troops that were left in the South, the result of the rebellion, were withdrawn this year from all the Southern States, and thus, virtually, these States became free for the first time since the rebellion.

Jan. 4. Cornelius Vanderbilt died at his residence in New York City, aged 83 years. He was the richest man in the United States, his wealth being estimated at $80,000,000.

Jan. 17. House of Representatives ordered the arrest of the Louisiana Returning Board for refusing to furnish papers to the investigating committee in relation to the Presidential election in Louisiana.

Jan. 18. The Congressional joint committee reported to both Houses in the shape of a bill, a plan for counting the electoral vote.

Jan. 25. Senate passed the Electoral bill. Yeas 47; nays 17.

Jan. 26. The House passed the Electoral bill by a vote of 191 to 96.

Jan. 30. The Senate and House each elected five members to serve on the Electoral Commission as follows: Senators Edmunds, Morton, Frelinghuysen, Thurman and Bayard, and Representatives Payne, Hunton, Abbott, Garfield and Hoar.

Jan. 31. The four United States Associate Justices to serve on the Electoral Tribunal—Clifford, Miller, Field and Strong, chose as the fifth member of the Tribunal Justice Joseph P. Bradley. Colorado declared a State.

March 2. The Electoral count finished, and Hayes and Wheeler declared President and Vice-President of the United States by a vote of 8 to 7.

March 5. President Hayes and Vice-President Wheeler inaugurated.

March 23. Execution of John D. Lee, Mormon Bishop, convicted of being the main instigator in the Mountain Meadows massacre in 1857.

April 2. The southwestern portion of Chicago was covered with water to the extent of nearly seven miles square.

April 11. The Southern hotel, one of the largest and finest in St. Louis, destroyed by fire. Fourteen lives lost.

July 16. The firemen and brakemen of the freight trains on the Baltimore & Ohio R'y at Baltimore, Md., struck on account of reduction of wages.

July 20. The strikes on the Baltimore and Ohio and Pennsylvania Railroads continue, and a strike took place on the Erie Railway, stopping all trains.

July 22. The railroad strikers continue their riotous work at Pittsburgh.

July 26. Rioting took place in Chicago, Ill., the police and troops fighting the mob nearly all day. Fifteen persons were known to have been killed, and many wounded.

Aug. 11. A battle between Gen. Gibbons' command and the Nez Perces Indians, on the Big Hole River, M. T., Aug. 9. Among the killed were Captain Wm. Logan, and Lieut. James H. Bradley.

Aug. 16. The Centenary of the battle of Benningtou, Vt., was celebrated.

Aug. 29. Brigham Young died at Salt Lake City. He had nineteen wives, and was considered worth $6,000,000.

1878.

Nov. 21. Payment of fisheries award under protest by Minister Welsh in London.

Dec. 11. Discovery of rich silver miles, Leadville, Col.

1879.

Jan. 1. Specie payments resumed.

1880.

June 8. James A. Garfield nominated for President, and Chester A. Arthur for Vice-President, by the Republican National Convention in Chicago.

June 24. Winfield Scott Hancock nominated for President, and W. H. English for Vice-President by the Democrat National Convention in Cincinnati.

Nov. 2. James A. Garfield and Chester A. Arthur elected President and Vice-President, receiving 214 of the 369 electoral votes.

1881.

July 2. President Garfield shot by Charles J. Guiteau.

Sept. 19. President Garfield dies.

1882.

June 30. Charles J. Guiteau, assassin of President Garfield, hung.

1883.

Feb. 9. Wm. E. Dodge, philanthropist, died, New York, aged 78 years.

April 14. Peter Cooper, founder of Cooper Institute, died, aged 92.

May 24. The Brooklyn Bridge formally opened.

Oct. 15. The U. S. Supreme Court set aside the Civil Rights Act as unconstitutional.

1884.

Feb. 2. Wendell Phillips died, aged 73.

March. 3. Validity of the Legal Tender Act reaffirmed by the U. S. Supreme Court.

June 2. Blaine and Logan nominated for President and Vice-President by the Republican National Convention in Chicago.

July 10. Democratic National Convention nominated Cleveland and Hendricks for President and Vice-President at Chicago.

July 24. The Prohibitionists at Pittsburgh nominated Gov. J. P. St. John for President.

Sept. 13. Robert Hoe, inventor of the Hoe press, died in New York, aged 70.

Nov. 4. Cleveland and Hendricks elected.

1885.

Jan. 1. The Washington Monument dedicated at Washington, D. C. Schuyler Colfax died at Mankato, Minn., aged 62.

March 4. Grover Cleveland inaugurated President.

July 23. Gen. U. S. Grant died at Mt. McGregor, N. Y., aged 65 years.

Aug. 8. Gen. Grant buried, New York.

Oct. 29. Gen. Geo. B. McClellan died at Orange, N. J.

Nov. 25. Vice-President Hendricks died at Indianapolis, Ind., aged 66.

1886.

Feb. 9. Gen. W. S. Hancock died at Governor's Island, N. Y., aged 62.

Feb. 12. Ex-Governor Horatio Seymour died at Utica, N. Y., aged 76.

May 4. Anarchist riots in Chicago.

June 26. Hon. David Davis died at Bloomington, Ill., aged 71.

Aug. 14. Hon. Samuel J. Tilden died at Greystone, N. Y., aged 72.

Dec. 27. Gen. John A. Logan died, aged 61.

1887.

Jan. 11. Bill creating Department of Agriculture and Labor passed by the National House of Representatives.

Jan. 14. The U. S. Senate passed the Inter-State Commerce Bill.

Feb. 4. President Cleveland signs the Inter-State Commerce Bill.

Feb. 5. Terrible R. R. accident near White River Junction, Vt. Forty-six persons killed and many injured.

March 8. Rev. Henry Ward Beecher dies.

March 31. John G. Saxe, humorous poet, dies.

May 9. The American Exhibition formally opened in London, England.

May 19. The steamers Celtic and Britannic, of the White Star Line, collide near Sandy Hook.

June 4. Ex-Vice-President Wheeler died at Malone, N. Y., aged 68.

Aug. 10. Fearful R. R. accident near Chatworth, Ill. More than 100 killed and 300 injured.

August 28. Ute Indian War in Colorado at an end.

Oct. 29. Propeller Vernon lost near Manitowoc Wis. Fifty lives lost.

Nov. 11. Anarchists Spies, Parsons, Fischer, and Engle executed at Chicago.

Dec. 24. Daniel J. Manning, ex-Secretary of the U. S. Treasury, died at Albany, N. Y., aged 56.

JOHN A. LOGAN.

HISTORICAL NOTES.

THE Constitution of the United States was adopted in 1789. It was framed by delegates from twelve of the "thirteen" states which declared themselves independent of the Government of Great Britain, in 1776. A Convention was called by the Continental Congress for the purpose of framing a Constitution, and all the states sent delegates except Rhode Island.

The American Colonies were planted along the Atlantic coast under various climates from the rugged north to the sunny south. They were not settled by an entirely homogeneous race, there being Dutch, (Hollanders) Swedes, and persons of other nationalities as well as English among the immigrants. The English settlers differed widely in religious and political views, and in the motives which prompted them to seek a new country. The Colonies were also originally organized and governed in three different modes, known as "Charter," "Proprietary" and "Royal" or "Provincial,, governments.

These diversities, however, were advantageous in the end, as giving rise to a diversity of ideas, experiences and pursuits; and did not prevent the rise and development of a common nationality. Common dangers, hardships and interests, suggested, at a very early period, the necessity of some bond of union, and of some common government.

In 1643, the four Colonies of Plymouth, Massachusetts, New Haven and Connecticut, formed a league under the title of the United Colonies of New England. This confederation had its Congress of Delegates from each of these Colonies, and continued forty years.

In 1754, commissioners representing New Hampshire, Massachusetts, Rhode Island, Connecticut, New York and Maryland met at Albany, and resolved that a union of all the Colonies was necessary, and recommended a plan of Federal Government.

In 1765, a Convention of Delegates representing nine of the Colonies met in New York, and drew up a document on the subject of taxation, known as a "Declaration of the Rights and Grievances of the Colonies." This may be regarded as the First Colonial Congress of signal importance.

In 1774, the Second Colonial Congress assembled in Philadelphia, being composed of delegates from all the Colonies, except Georgia. This was the great Congress of the Revolution. It assembled again in May, 1775, (Georgia being then represented), and after watching anxiously the progress of the Revolutionary struggle for more than a year, it assumed the responsibility of severing the connection between the Thirteen Colonies and the Government of Great Britain, by the memorable Declaration of Independence, adopted on the 4th of July, 1776.

This step of course involved the adoption of some settled plan of general government for the Colonies in place of the one thus cast off, and deliberations upon this subject were coeval with the Declaration of Independence. A committee appointed for the purpose reported a scheme of government for the "United States of America"—which the Colonies had now become—known as the "Articles of Confederation." After considerable discussion, at different sessions, the scheme was agreed to by the Continental Congress, in November, 1777.

The Articles were immediately sent to the several States for their consideration and adoption. Delays and objections arose, in some of the States, and as the form of government proposed could not go into operation until the consent of all the States was obtained, the Confederation was not established till March, 1781, when the consent of Maryland, the last of the States, was finally given.

Scarcely however had this confederation of the States taken effect, when its weakness and defect as a frame of government began to be seen. When we remember that the leading political sentiment of the colonies for a whole generation had been a feeling of jealousy and a sense of resistance in regard to external government, we shall not wonder that they framed a General Government for themselves of very little force or efficiency. It was devised in time of war, and met many of its exigencies, but was very poorly adapted to a time of peace.

It will assist us in understanding and appreciating the Constitution, afterwards adopted, and the reasons for its adoption, if we note the limited and inoperative powers conferred by the Articles of Confederation upon the Continental Congress as the depository and executor of the functions of a General Government for the States: Congress could make treaties, but could not enforce their observance; it could appoint embassadors, but could not provide for their salaries or expenses; it could borrow money, but was not empowered to pay it; it could coin money, but could not import bullion for the purpose; it could declare war, and determine how many troops were necessary to carry it on, but could not raise the troops. It could not legislate directly upon persons and could only recommend the States what action to take; it could punish no one for a breach of neglect of its own enactments; it could levy no taxes and collect no revenue. In short, it could merely recommend what should be done, but was entirely without power to enforce any law or recommendation; and it was soon found that it was in vain to expect that thirteen different States would voluntarily accede to mere recommendations, with any sufficient degree of readiness or unanimity. Efforts were made, without success, to prove an enlargement of the powers of Congress, and it soon became apparent that the Confederation must dissolve from its own weakness, unless a more efficient government were substituted in its place.

In 1785, Commissioners from Maryland and Virginia met to regulate the navigation of waters common to both States, and feeling the want of suitable power to act, recommended a Convention of a larger scope. In 1786, the Legislature of Virginia therefore proposed a general Convention of Commissioners from the States, to consider matters of general interest. Commissioners were appointed, in five States, who met at Annapolis and drew up a report to be laid before the Continental Congress. In this report it was advised that a General Convention of Delegates should meet and revise the Articles of Confederation.

In February, 1787, Congress acted upon the recommendation and called a Convention to meet in Philadelphia in May following. All the States were represented except Rhode Island. After a long deliberation, attended with much difference of opinion, a Constitution was adopted, and Congress was recommended to lay it before the several States, in Conventions to be held for that purpose, that it might be considered and ratified. This was done; Conventions were held in all the States but Rhode Island, and after warm discussions, the Constitution was ratified by all the States except Rhode Island and North Carolina.

As it required the assent of only nine of the States to give effect to the Constitution, Congress, having been informed of the ratification by twelve of the States, took measures, in September, 1788, to put the new form of Government into operation. The first President and Vice President were chosen, and the first Congress, under the Constitution, assembled in

New York, on the 4th of March, 1789, for the transaction of business.

Although the Constitution was thus happily ratified, and had become the fundamental law of the land, it was not satisfactory to a large body of the people. The old jealousy of the powers of a general or central Government continued, and it was loudly demanded that the Constitution should embrace a Bill of Rights. Hence, at the first session of Congress under the Constitution, twelve different Amendments were proposed, ten of which were ratified by three-fourths of the States, and became a part of the Constitution from and after the 15th of December, 1791. Most of these amendments were intended to allay the fears of the people that the General Government might encroach upon their individual rights and liberties.

The Eleventh Article of Amendment took effect in 1798, the Twelfth in 1804, the Thirteenth in 1865, the Fourteenth in 1868, the Fifteenth and last in 1870.

GOVERNMENT.

The necessity of government is furnished in man's **social** and **moral** nature. As a reasonable and dependent being, he is fitted for **society** and **law**. **Law** is a rule of **action**. Government is the embodiment, the defender, and the enforcer of law.

RIGHTS.

A **right** is either a **just** claim or a **just** and **lawful** claim.

Rights are **political** and **civil**.

Political rights are those which belong to the citizen in his relation to government.

Civil rights are those which are not political and which are often termed **natural** or **inalienable** rights.

They include:
I. **Absolute rights** and
II. Relative rights.

1. Absolute civil rights are those which man possesses as an individual, in his relation as a member of society to other members of society.

Two classes of these rights are often termed **personal rights**, or **the rights of persons**.

They embrace:

I. The **Rights of Personal Security**.—The right from injury to **life, body, health, reputation**.

II. **The Rights of Personal Liberty**.—The right to go where one chooses.

The other two classes of absolute rights are:

I. The **Right of Private Property**.—The right to acquire property and enjoy it, without molestation.

(2.) **Religious Rights**.—The rights of men to worship God according to the dictates of their own consciences.

II. **Relative Civil Rights** are those which men possess in relation to particular persons or classes. These are either **Public** or **Private**. **Public Civil Rights** are those man possesses in his relations to the government (except the right to participate in it). It includes the right of the government and its officers to our respect and obedience.

Private Civil Rights embrace those in relation of

(1.) Husband and Wife.
(2.) Parent and child.
(3.) Guardian and ward.
(4.) Employer and employed.

THE AMERICAN MANUAL.

HON. E. B. WASHBURN.

LIBERTY.

Liberty is the freedom man possesses to enjoy his rights.

It embraces:
(a.) **Natural Liberty.**
(b.) **Political Liberty.**
(c.) **Civil Liberty.**
(d.) **Religious Liberty.**

LAW.

Law.—The object of Law is to defend and secure man in the enjoyment of his right.

It includes:
1. **Political Law.**
2. **Civil** or **Municipal Law.**

The **Moral Law** prescribes man's duties to his fellow man and to God. It is contained in the Ten Commandments, to love God with all our hearts, and our neighbor as ourselves. It is **broader** and more comprehensive than Political or Civil Law.

DIFFERENT FORMS OF GOVERNMENT.

I. **Patriarchal.**—In the early stages of the world.
II. **Theocratical.**—The direct government of the Jews by Jehovah.
III. **Monarchical.**—The government by a King, Emperor or Prince. This may be
  (a.) **Absolute,** when all the power rests in the one governing, or
  (b.) **Limited,** when the power of the monarch is abridged by law, legislative bodies, or other power.

A **Monarchy** may be either
  (a.) **Hereditary,** as when it passes from father to son, or from a monarch to his successor, or
  (b.) **Elective.**—When on the death of a monarch his successor is chosen by an election. (Rare).

IV. **Aristocratical.**—When the government is administered by a few persons distinguished by birth, rank, wealth, etc.

V. **Democratical** or **Republican.**—When the government is administered by the people. This may be
  (a.) **Pure Democracy.**—When the people meet in one body to make laws and appoint officers, or
  (b.) **A Republican** or **Representative Democracy,** often called a **Commonwealth**; when the people through **delegates** or **representatives** enact laws and choose officers.

OUR NATIONAL GOVERNMENT.

The Government of the United States.

There have been three stages in the **Government** of our country; the **Colonial** Government, the **Confederation** and the **National Government**.

The **Colonial Governments** were the governments of the different colonies when the inhabitants were British subjects.

There were originally *three* different *forms* of government in the colonies, viz: **The Charter,** the **Proprietary,** and **Royal Governments.** The Charter Governments were confined to New England; the middle and southern colonies were divided between the Proprietary or Royal Governments.

The **Charter Governments** were composed of a Governor, Deputy-governor, and Assistants, *elected by the people*; these, with the freemen, i. e., citizens of the colony, were to compose the "**General Courts,**" which were authorized to appoint such officers, and make such laws and ordinances for the welfare of the colony as to them might seem meet. These first forms of government in New England contained the same principles as, and were doubtless the origin of, our Republican system.

The **Proprietary Governments** were those of Maryland, Pennsylvania, the Carolinas and Jersey. Part of these soon became Royal Governments. In the Proprietary governments, the power of appointing officers and making laws rested in the proprietors, by the advice and assent, generally, of the freemen. In some of them, as in the Carolinas, singular irregularities were found. In all, great confusion took place.

In the **Royal Governments,** which were New York, Virginia, Georgia and Delaware, the Governor and Council were appointed by the *crown*; and the people elected *representatives* to the Colonial legislature. The Governor had a **negative** in both houses of the

SENATOR GEORGE F. EDMUNDS.

legislature; and most of the officers were appointed by the king.

The colonists had no representatives in Parliament, and when an obnoxious act was passed by that body, laying duties on all tea, glass, paper, etc., imported into the colonies, the American people resisted it justly, claiming there should be no **taxation** without **representation**. Their petition for a repeal of the unjust proceeding being of no avail, they resisted the tax. Troops were sent to enforce it. The colonies began to arm to meet them. On the 4th of July, 1776, the Declaration of Independence was made by the delegates from the several colonies, which was followed by a war of several years, resulting in their complete separation from the throne of Great Britain.

Under the Colonial Governments several efforts were made to effect a **union** of the colonies in whole or in part.

I. **Articles of Confederation** were made in **1643** between the colonies of Massachusetts, Connecticut and New Haven, which was expressly declared to be a *league*, under the name of the **United Colonies of New England**. This league declared:

1st. That each colony shall have *peculiar jurisdiction and government within its own limits*.

2d. That the quotas of men and money were to be furnished in *proportion to the population*, for which purpose a *census* was to be taken from time to time of such as were able to bear arms.

3d. That to manage such matters as concerned the whole confederation, a congress of two commissioners from each colony should meet annually, with power to weigh and determine all affairs of *war and peace, leagues*, aids, charges, and whatever else were proper concomitants of a confederation offensive and defensive; and that to determine any question, three fourths of these commissioners must agree, or the matter is to be referred to the general courts.

4th. That these commissioners may choose a president; but that such president has no power over the business or proceedings.

5th. That neither of the colonies should engage in any war without consent of the general commissioners

6th. That if any of the confederates should *break* any of these articles, or otherwise injure any of the other confederates, then such breach should be *considered* and *ordered* by the commissioners of the *other colonies*.

II. **A Congress of Commissioners**, representing New Hampshire, Massachusetts, Rhode Island, Connecticut, New York, Pennsylvania, and Maryland, was held at Albany in 1754. This convention unanimously resolved that a **union** of the colonies was necessary for their preservation. They proposed a general plan of federal government, which provided,

1. That the general government should be *administered* by a president-general appointed by the crown, and a grand council chosen by the representatives of the people in their general assemblies.

2. That the council should be chosen every three years, and shall meet once each year.

3. That the assent of the President be necessary to all acts of the council, and that it is his duty to see them executed.

4. That the President and council may hold treaties, make peace, and declare war with the several Indian tribes.

5. That for these purposes they have power to levy and collect such duties, imposts and taxes as to them shall seem just.

This plan was not adopted.

THE CONFEDERATION.

In the year 1774 the colonies united in the plan of a Congress to consult on the common good, and to resist the claims of the English Parliament. It was to be composed of delegates from the different colonies.

The Continental Congress assembled in May, 1775, which carried on the affairs of the country until the war had almost closed.

But in order to form a more efficient union, a **Confederation** of the States was formed under certain **articles** called "**Articles of Confederation and Perpetual Union** between the **States**." They were to go into effect when the assent of all the States was gained. Maryland delayed consent until March,

1781. They were therefore not effective until about two years before the revolutionary war closed.
(See articles of Confederation.)

This **Confederation** was found to be radically **defective**, having reference mainly to the condition of the country in the time of **war** instead of **peace**. It was inherently **weak**, in that it had merely a **Legislative department** and no **Executive** and **Judicial Department**. It could do but little more than **recommend** measures. It could borrow money but it had no means of raising money to pay the debts contracted. It could determine what number of troops the several States should furnish, but it could not enforce its demands. It could levy no **Taxes** or **Duties**, that power being reserved to the several States. Each State imposed such duties with foreign countries and with the other States, as it saw fit. Hence arose **discord** and **Jealousies**.

Convention of **1786.**—The Legislature of Virginia in January, 1786, proposed a convention of commissioners to take into account the subject of trade and commercial regulations. The commissioners of five States only, **New York, New Jersey, Pennsylvania, Delaware,** and **Virginia** met pursuant to the call at Annapolis, Maryland, in September, 1786. These commissioners recommended a general convention of all the States to meet in Philadelphia in May, 1787, to consider, not the regulations of commerce, but amendments to the articles of confederation to make the union of the States more effective.

Convention of **1787.**—In accordance with this recommendation, in February, 1787, Congress passed a resolution calling for a convention. All the States, except **Rhode Island**, sent delegates, who met and framed the present **Constitution** of the **United States**, and recommended Congress to submit it to the several States for their adoption.

Adoption of Constitution.—As soon as **nine** States ratified the Constitution it was to go into effect as far as those States were concerned. In July, 1788, the ninth State, **New Hampshire**, sent in its ratification. **North Carolina** and **Rhode Island** did not send their ratification until one year after the government was organized.

CONFEDERATION OF THE ORIGINAL STATES.

ON Monday, the 5th of September, 1774, there were assembled at Carpenter's Hall, in the city of Philadelphia, a number of men who had been chosen and appointed by the several colonies in North America to hold a Congress for the purpose of discussing certain grievances imputed against the mother country. This Congress resolved, on the next day, that each colony should have one vote only. On Tuesday, the 2d of United Colonies are, and of right ought to be, Free and Independent States," etc., etc.; and on Thursday, the 4th July, the whole Declaration of Independence having been agreed upon, it was publicly read to the people. Shortly after, on the 9th of September, it was resolved that the words "United Colonies" should be no longer used, and that the "United States of America" should thenceforward be the style and title of the Union. On Saturday, the 15th of November, 1777, "Articles of Confederation and Perpetual Union of the United States of America" were agreed to by the State delegates, subject to the ratification of the State legislatures severally. Eight of the States ratified these articles on the 9th July, 1778; one on the 21st July; one on the 24th July; one on the 26th November of the same year; one on the 22d February, 1779; and the last one on the 1st March, 1781. Here was a bond of union between thirteen independent States, whose delegates in Congress legislated for the general welfare, and executed certain powers so far as they were permitted by the articles aforesaid. The following are the names of the Presidents of the Continental Congress from 1774 to 1788:

Peyton Randolph, Virginia..............5th Sept., 1774.
Henry Middleton, South Carolina........22d Oct., 1774.
Peyton Randolph, Virginia..............10th May, 1775.
John Hancock, Massachusetts............24th May, 1776.
Henry Laurens, South Carolina..........1st Nov., 1777.
John Jay, New York.....................10th Dec., 1778.
Samuel Huntington, Connecticut.........28th Sept., 1779.
Thomas McKean, Delaware................10th July, 1781.

John Hanson, Maryland..................5th Nov., 1781.
Elias Boudinot, New Jersey.............4th "   1782.
Thomas Mifflin, Pennsylvania...........3d   "   1783.
Richard Henry Lee, Virginia............30th "   1784.
Nathaniel Gorham, Massachusetts........6th Jan., 1786.
Arthur St. Clair, Pennsylvania.........2d Feb., 1787.
Cyrus Griffin, Virginia................22d Jan., 1788.

The seat of government was established as follows: At Philadelphia, Pa., commencing September 5, 1774, and May 10, 1775; at Baltimore, Md., December 20, 1776; at Philadelphia, Pa., March 4, 1777; at Lancaster, Pa., September 27, 1777; at York, Pa., September 30, 1777; at Philadelphia, Pa., July 2, 1778; at Princeton, N. J., June 30, 1783; at Annapolis, Md., November 26, 1783; at Trenton, N. J., November 1, 1784; and at New York City, N. Y., January 11, 1785.

On the 4th March, 1789, the present Constitution, which had been adopted by a convention and ratified by the requisite number of States, went into operation.

THE MECKLENBURG DECLARATION OF INDEPENDENCE.

HON. JOHN M. BRIGHT, TENNESSEE.

(*May 20, 1775*)

THE news of the passage of the stamp act fell upon North Carolina like a spark into a powder magazine. The explosion of indignation shook the colony to its center, while John Ashe, speaker of the General Assembly, rung the articulate echo in the ear of Gov. Tryon: "This law will be resisted to blood and death!" When the sloop of war Diligence anchored off Cape Fear with stamped paper for the use of the colony, the brave men of Hanover and Brunswick, headed by the heroic Ashe and Waddell, prohibited the terrified captain from landing the cargo. From thence they marched to Wilmington, besieged the governor's palace, and extorted from him a pledge, and swore his stamp-master not to attempt the execution of the law. Here the king, parliament, and viceroy were all defied. Here we have an act far transcending in daring the Boston tea party, who were disguised as Indians to escape identification, while here the act was performed in open day, the parties were without disguise, and known, and it was because they were known, that the governor capitulated in his castle.

And yet the feat of tumbling the tea into Boston harbor is known to every school-boy in the land, and the last celebration of the event was held in the rotunda of the national capital.

* * * * * *

The news of the battle of Lexington resounded from Nova Scotia to Florida. It was borne by the relays of heralds, day and night, all along the coast of the Atlantic, and from the coast to the mountains, the Alleghanies shouted it to the Cumberland, awakening the settlers on Watauga, and sending the echoes far beyond the hunters of Kentucky, who, on receiving the news named their camping-ground Lexington, now the site of a flourishing city, in memory of the battle-ground which had been consecrated by the blood of the patriots. Upon receiving the news, the patriots of Mecklenburg swarmed from the "Hornet's Nest." They met in convention on the 19th, and continued their session into the 20th of May, 1775, on which day they gave to the world the Mecklenburg declaration of Independence. This declaration was not the child of a patriotic frenzy which was not expected to outlive the paroxysm which gave it birth. It was the result of profound wisdom, sagacity, and statesmanship.

With faith in God, they saw no path of escape, except that which was illuminated by the light which flashed from the patriot's sword. They saw no sovereign remedy for their direful woes, except in absolute and unconditional independence. And they were the first to reach the height of this conclusion, and the first to embody in it a high resolve upon the American continent.

In full view of the gibbets of Alamance—with a full conviction that they would have to toil up a path slippery with blood to the grandeur of independence, yet their patriotism and courage towered and expanded before the danger, and burning the bridge behind them, "they hung their banners on the outer walls." All honor to the twenty-seven noble signers of the Mecklenburg Declaration of Independence! Eulogy cannot overdraw their praise, nor admiration surpass their merit. Let each name be consecrated to Freedom, and each find a sanctuary in every patriot's heart. But some would make the disparaging insinuation that their declaration was only the expression of the prevailing sentiment at the time. The facts of history do not sustain the position. Washington "abhorred the idea of independence" when he took command of the army, and he had rolled the tide of war about one year before he was committed to the idea. Mr. Jefferson, in a letter dated 25th of August, 1775, said he would "rather be in dependence on Great Britain, properly limited, than on any other nation upon earth," but added, "rather than submit to the right of legislating for us, assumed in the British Parliament, I would lend my hand to sink the whole island in the ocean." * * * On the 8th of July, 1775, every member of the continental congress signed a petition to the king, stating that they have not "raised armies with the ambitious design of separating from Great Britain and establishing independence." Other evidence might be multiplied to the same effect. None of these had the ring of the old Mecklenburg declaration; but they show the fact that up to the 4th of July, '76, the continental war was waged for the redress of grievances, and not for independence. Thus, it is clear that the morning star of American independence first rose upon the field of Mecklenburg. * * *

(The orator here discusses the authenticity of the declaration at length, but we need not go over it with him.)

The voice of Mecklenburg now became the voice of the whole colony, and the voice of the colony soon became the voice of the united colonies, which proclaimed the united Declaration of Independence to the nations of the earth. The provincial assembly of North Carolina on the 12th of April, 1776, was first to instruct her delegates in the continental congress to "concur with the other colonies in declaring independence." Virginia, that grand old State, menaced by a similar diabolical scheme of massacre and insurrection, planned by Gov. Dunmore, next instructed her delegates to vote for independence, on the 15th of May. As remarked by an impartial writer: "No members of that body (the continental congress) brought with them credentials of a bolder stamp than the delegates of North Carolina."

THE MECKLENBURG DECLARATION OF INDEPENDENCE.

(Charlotte, North Carolina, May 20, 1775.)

There are few facts better attested in all history than the Mecklenburg Declaration of Independence.

That questions may be raised that cannot be fully answered in regard to it, matters little; for that, as any candid person must admit, may not only occur with regard to any historical fact, but with regard to any, the most recent affair even, the actors and witnesses in which are all living. Many living men have conversed with those who either participated in making the Mecklenburg declaration or were present when it was made. Well-authenticated copies of the original declaration are in existence, made by a survivor of the Mecklenburg committee into whose hands all the records passed; and if the original document itself be not forthcoming, that is well accounted for by the fact that it was burned when the house in which it was kept was destroyed by fire. Moreover, the legislature of North Carolina, years ago, when the question was first mooted, appointed a commission to inquire into the authenticity of the declaration, and this commission found fourteen survivors, respectable and intelligent, who *all* made solemn affidavit that a declaration of independence was made at Charlotte, Mecklenburg county, during the month of May, 1775, they being present, some of them members of the county committee, and seven were positive that the date was the 20th of May.

Any one who glances at the colonial history of

North Carolina will be struck with one prominent fact, and that is the impatience of her people under wrong and oppression of any kind. There is scarcely a decade in her chronicles, from the first settlement to 1776, that is not marked by a struggle against usurped or improperly exercised authority, or what the people thought to be so, which amounts, as far as regards them, to the same thing. No wonder, then, that when the greater abuses arose, the people of North Carolina were the first, or among the first, to resent them. They signalized their resistance to the stamp act by refusing to allow a sheet of the stamped paper to be landed from the ship which brought it, and they made the stamp-distributor swear that he would not attempt to exercise his office in the State. On the 23d of October, 1769, the following resolutions were unanimously adopted by the house of assembly:

That the sole right of imposing taxes on the inhabitants of North Carolina has ever been vested in the house of assembly;
That the inhabitants have the undoubted right of petitioning for a redress of grievances;
That trials for treason, committed in the colony, ought to be had here; and
That removing suspected persons, to be tried beyond the sea, is derogatory to the rights of a British subject.

The same body prepared a petition to the king containing the same sentiments.

Gov. Tryon at once dissolved the assembly.

The regulators themselves, much misunderstood and much villified, were organized as much to resist the stamp act and the other usurpations of parliament as they were the local fees and taxes illegally exacted by the State and county officers, backed by Gov. Tryon; and the battle of Alamance, fought May 16, 1771, was as much a battle for American freedom and independence as that of Lexington, which occurred four years later.

There were special reasons, too, why the declaration should be made in Mecklenburg. Gov. Tryon, having his palace in the East, at New bern, so contrived as to pit that section against the West; and from the eastern portions of the State, as being nearest to him and more directly subject to his control, he drew his forces to coerce the western and other sections of the State. Thus it happened in those turbulent and troublous times that the people of Mecklenburg county, under the lead of able and patriotic men, formed a sort of committee of safety, composed of delegates, two elected from each militia district. Col. Thomas Polk was elected chairman of the committee, with authority to call it together when he saw sufficient cause. In May, 1775, Col. Polk had learned that the then governor of North Carolina (Martin) had dissolved the house of assembly, after a session of only a few days, and that he had issued his proclamation forbidding the assembling of the provincial congress of the State. He thereupon called the committee to meet at Charlotte on the 19th of May; and on that day, accordingly, not only were the greater portion of the committee men present in the town, but large numbers of the people from all sections of the county, anxious to hear the latest news, and to learn what action the committee would take.

The committee found itself a mass-meeting, by reason of the attendance of the people, and therefore organized as a convention, with Abraham Alexander, president, and John McKnitt Alexander and Ephraim Brevard, secretaries. Soon after the actual business had been broached which caused the assemblage, a messenger arrived with a printed circular, conveying the first news of the battle of Lexington, which had occurred precisely one month before. This created the most intense wrath and excitement. Speeches were made by Rev. Hezekiah James Balch, Dr. Ephraim Brevard, and Wm. Kennon, a lawyer. These added fuel to the flames, and the cry was unanimous for separation and independence. On motion, Messrs. Balch, Brevard and Kennon were appointed a committee to prepare appropriate resolutions to express the sense of the meeting. The resolutions, however (of which Dr. Brevard is the accredited author), were not presented to the committee until next day (the twentieth), when they were unanimously adopted. It was then proposed and carried that they be read to the people from the court-house door, and Col. Thomas Polk was deputed as reader. It took but a short while to gather the multitude then in Charlotte before the court-house door to hear a document in which all were so deeply concerned. Col. Polk read in a loud, emphatic voice, and the people heard in complete and solemn silence until the reading was done. Then arose an enthusiastic shout of ratification, women and children joining with the men in the approving acclamation. The resolutions so adopted and so ratified were as follows:

Resolved, 1. That whosoever directly or indirectly abetted, or in any way, form, or manner, countenanced the unchartered and dangerous invasion of our rights, as claimed by Great Britain, is an enemy to this country, to America, and to the independent and inalienable rights of man.

Resolved, 2. That we, the citizens of Mecklenburg county, do hereby dissolve the political bonds which have connected us with the mother country, and hereby absolve ourselves from all allegiance to the British crown, and adjure all political connection, contract, or association with that nation who have wantonly trampled on our rights and liberties, and inhumanly shed the blood of American patriots at Lexington.

Resolved, 3. That we do hereby declare ourselves a free and independent people; are, and of right ought to be, a sovereign and self-governing association, under the control of no power other than that of our God and the general government of the congress, to the maintenance of which independence we solemnly pledge to each other our mutual co-operation, our lives, our fortunes, and our most sacred honor.

Resolved, 4. That as we acknowledge the existence and control of no law, nor legal office, civil or military, within this country, we do hereby ordain and adopt, as a rule of life, all, each, and every of our former laws, wherein, nevertheless, the crown of Great Britain never can be considered as holding rights, privileges, immunities, or authority therein.

Resolved, 5. That it is further decreed that all, each, and every military officer in this county is hereby retained in his former command and authority, he acting conformably to these regulations. And that every member present of this delegation shall henceforth be a civil officer, viz., a justice of the peace, in the character of a committee-man, to issue process, hear and determine all matters of controversy according to said adopted laws, and to preserve peace, union, and harmony in said county; and to use every exertion to spread the love of country and fire of freedom throughout America, until a general organized government be established in this province.

Ten days afterward, on the 30th of May, the Mecklenburg committee met again at Charlotte, and adopted 20 other resolutions; but as all from the 4th to the 15th, both inclusive, merely enter into the details of the temporary government established for the county, they need not be repeated here. The remainder of these resolutions on May 30 are as follows:

CHARLOTTE, MECKLENBURG COUNTY, May 30, 1775.—This day the committee of the county met and passed the following resolves:

Whereas, By an address presented to his majesty by both houses of parliament, in February last, the American colonies are declared to be in a state of actual rebellion, we conceive that all laws and commissions confirmed by or derived from the king and parliament are annulled and vacated, and the former civil constitution of these colonies for the present wholly suspended: To provide in some degree for the exigencies of this county in the present alarming period, we deem it proper and necessary to pass the following resolves, viz.:

1. That all commissions, civil and military, heretofore granted by the crown to be exercised in these colonies, are null and void, and the constitution of each particular colony wholly suspended.

2. That the provincial congress of each province, under the direction of the great continental congress, is invested with all legislative and executive powers within their respective provinces, and that no other legislative or executive power does or can exist at this time in any of these colonies.

3. As all former laws are now suspended in this province, and the congress has not yet provided others, we judge it necessary for the better preservation of good order, to form certain rules and regulations for the internal government of this county, until laws shall be provided for us by the congress.

16. *That whatever person shall hereafter receive a commission from the crown, or attempt to exercise any such commission heretofore received, shall be deemed an enemy to this country;* and upon confirmation being made to the captain of the company in which he resides, the said company shall cause him to be apprehended and conveyed before two select men, who, upon proof of the fact, shall commit said offender to safe custody, until the next sitting of the committee, who shall deal with him as prudence may direct.

17. That any person refusing to yield obedience to the above rules shall be considered equally criminal, and liable to the same punishment as the offenders above last mentioned.

18. That these resolves be in full force and virtue until instructions from the provincial congress regulating the

jurisprudence of the province shall provide otherwise, or the legislative body of Great Britain r sign its unjust and arbitrary pretensions with regard to America.

19. That the eight militia companies of this county provide themselves with proper arms and accoutrements, and hold themselves in readiness to execute the commands and directions of the general congress of this province and this committee.

20. That the committee appoint Col. Thomas Polk and Dr. Joseph Kennedy to purchase 300 pounds of powder, 100 pounds of lead, and 1,000 flints, for the use of the militia of this county, and deposit the same in such place as the committee may hereafter direct.

Signed by order of the committee.
EPHRAIM BREVARD, Clerk of the Committee.

About these resolutions there is no dispute whatever, for they were extensively published, soon after their date, in North Carolina, South Carolina, New York, Massachusetts, etc., and were the subject of a denunciatory proclamation from Gov. Martin himself. Why these should have been published and those of the 20th of May suppressed, is easy to understand, for at that time the earlier resolutions, known as the declaration of independence, were considered generally unadvised and premature, while the later ones were fully warranted by the situation, and were, indeed, necessary to the preservation of order. It is barely possible that the two sets of resolutions were once embodied together, and that prudential or other considerations caused them to be subsequently separated. However that may be, both sets of resolutions are really declarations of independence, full and complete, with only ten days between them—the difference being that those of May 30 are more guarded than those of the 20th.

DECLARATION OF INDEPENDENCE.

IN CONGRESS, TUESDAY, JULY 4, 1776.

AGREEABLY to the order of the day, the Congress resolved itself into a committee of the whole, to take into their further consideration the Declaration; and after some time, the President resumed the chair, and Mr. Harrison reported that the Committee had agreed to a Declaration, which they desired him to report. (The committee consisted of Jefferson, Franklin, John Adams, Sherman, and R. R. Livingston.)

The Declaration, being read, was agreed to, as follows:

A DECLARATION BY THE REPRESENTATIVES OF THE UNITED STATES OF AMERICA, IN CONGRESS ASSEMBLED.

When, in the course of human events, it becomes necessary for one people to dissolve the political bands which have connected them with one another, and to assume among the powers of the earth the separate and equal station to which the laws of nature and of nature's God entitle them, a decent respect for the opinions of mankind requires that they should declare the causes which impel them to the separation.

We hold these truths to be self-evident: That all men are created equal; that they are endowed by their Creator with certain inalienable rights; that among these are life, liberty, and the pursuit of happiness. That, to secure these rights, governments are instituted among men, deriving their just powers from the consent of the governed; that, whenever any form of government becomes destructive of these ends, it is the right of the people to alter or abolish it, and to institute a new government, laying its foundation on such principles, and organizing its powers in such form, as to them shall seem most likely to effect their safety and happiness. Prudence, indeed, will dictate that governments long established should not be changed for light and transient causes; and, accordingly, all experience hath shown that mankind are more disposed to suffer, while evils are sufferable, than to right themselves by abolishing the forms to which they are accustomed. But, when a long train of abuses and usurpations, pursuing invariably the same object, evinces a design to reduce them under absolute despotism, it is their right, it is their duty, to throw off such government, and to provide new guards for their future security. Such has been the patient sufferance of these colonies, and such is now the necessity which constrains them to alter their former systems of government. The history of the present King of Great Britain is a history of repeated injuries and usurpations, all having in direct object the establishment of an absolute tyranny over these States. To prove this, let facts be submitted to a candid world:

He has refused his assent to laws the most wholesome and necessary for the public good.

He has forbidden his Governors to pass laws of immediate and pressing importance, unless suspended in their operation till his assent should be obtained; and, when so suspended, he has utterly neglected to attend to them.

He has refused to pass other laws for the accommodation of large districts of people unless those people would relinquish the right of representation in the legislature—a right inestimable to them, and formidable to tyrants only.

He has called together legislative bodies at places unusual, uncomfortable, and distant from the depository of their public records, for the sole purpose of fatiguing them into compliance with his measures.

He has dissolved representative houses repeatedly for opposing, with manly firmness, his invasions on the rights of the people.

He has refused, for a long time after such dissolutions, to cause others to be elected; whereby the legislative powers, incapable of annihilation, have returned to the people at large for their exercise, the State remaining, in the meantime, exposed to all the danger of invasion from without, and convulsions within.

He has endeavored to prevent the population of these States; for that purpose obstructing the laws for naturalization of foreigners; refusing to pass others to encourage their emigration hither, and raising the conditions of new appropriations of lands.

He has obstructed the administration of justice, by refusing his assent to laws for establishing judiciary powers.

He has made Judges dependent on his will alone for the tenure of their offices and the amount and payment of their salaries.

He has erected a multitude of new offices, and sent hither swarms of officers to harass our people, and eat out their substance.

He has kept among us, in times of peace, standing armies, without the consent of our legislature.

He has affected to render the military independent of, and superior to, the civil power.

He has combined, with others, to subject us to a jurisdiction foreign to our constitution, and unacknowledged by our laws; giving his assent to their acts of pretended legislation:

For quartering large bodies of armed troops among us;

For protecting them, by mock trial, from punishment for any murders which they should commit on the inhabitants of these States; For cutting off our trade with all parts of the world;

For imposing taxes on us without our consent;

For depriving us, in many cases, of the benefits of trial by jury;

For transporting us beyond seas to be tried for pretended offenses;

For abolishing the free system of English laws in a neighboring province, establishing therein an arbitrary government, and enlarging its boundaries, so as to render it at once an example and fit instrument for introducing the same absolute rule into these colonies;

For taking away our charters, abolishing our most valuable laws and altering, fundamentally, the powers of our governments;

For suspending our own legislature, and declaring themselves invested with power to legislate for us in all cases whatsoever.

He has abdicated government here, by declaring us out of his protection, and waging war against us.

He has plundered our seas, ravaged our coast, burnt our towns, and destroyed the lives of our people.

He is, at this time, transporting large armies of foreign mercenaries to complete the works of death, desolation and tyranny, already begun, with circumstances of cruelty and perfidy, scarcely paralleled in the most barbarous ages, and totally unworthy the head of a civilized nation.

He has constrained our fellow-citizens taken captive on the high seas, to bear arms against their country, to become the executioners of their friends and brethren, or to fall themselves by their hands.

He has excited domestic insurrections amongst us, and has endeavored to bring on the inhabitants of our frontiers the merciless Indian savages, whose known rule of warfare is an undistinguished destruction of all ages, sexes, and conditions.

In every stage of these oppressions, we have petitioned for redress in the most humble terms; our repeated petitions have been answered only by repeated injury. A prince, whose character is thus marked by every act which may define a tyrant, is unfit to be the ruler of a free people.

Nor have we been wanting in attention to our British brethren. We have warned them, from time to time, of attempts made by their legislature to extend an unwarrantable jurisdiction over us. We have reminded them of the circumstances of our emigration and settlement here. We have appealed to their native justice and magnanimity, and we have conjured them by the ties of our common kindred, to disavow these usurpations, which would inevitably interrupt our connections and correspondence. They, too, have been deaf to the voice of justice and consanguinity. We must, therefore, acquiesce in the necessity which denounces our separation, and hold them as we hold the rest of mankind, enemies in war—in peace, friends.

We, therefore, the representatives of the UNITED STATES OF AMERICA, in GENERAL CONGRESS assembled, appealing to the Supreme Judge of the World for the rectitude of our intentions, do in the name, and by the authority of the good people of these colonies, solemnly publish and declare, That these United Colonies are, and of right ought to be, FREE AND INDEPENDENT STATES; that they are absolved from all allegiance to the British crown, and that all political connections between them and the State of Great Britain is, and ought to be, totally dissolved; and that as FREE AND INDEPENDENT STATES, they have full power to levy war, conclude peace, contract alliances, establish commerce, and to do all other acts and things which INDEPENDENT STATES may of right do. And for the support of this Declaration, with a firm reliance on the protection of DIVINE PROVIDENCE, we mutually pledge to each other, our lives, our fortunes, and our sacred honor.

The foregoing Declaration was, by order of Congress, engrossed, and signed by the following members:

JOHN HANCOCK.

New Hampshire.

JOSIAH BARTLETT,
WILLIAM WHIPPLE,
MATTHEW THORNTON.

Massachusetts Bay.

SAMUEL ADAMS,
JOHN ADAMS,
ROBERT TREAT PAYNE,
ELBRIDGE GERRY.

New York.

WILLIAM FLOYD,
PHILIP LIVINGSTON,
FRANCIS LEWIS,
LEWIS MORRIS.

Connecticut.

ROGER SHERMAN,
SAMUEL HUNTINGTON,
WILLIAM WILLIAMS,
OLIVER WOLCOTT.

Rhode Island.

STEPHEN HOPKINS,

WILLIAM ELLERY.

Pennsylvania.

ROBERT MORRIS,
BENJAMIN RUSH,
BENJAMIN FRANKLIN,
JOHN MORTON,
GEORGE CLYMER,
JAMES SMITH,
GEORGE TAYLOR,
JAMES WILSON,
GEORGE ROSS.

New Jersey.

RICHARD STOCKTON,
JOHN WITHERSPOON,
FRANCIS HOPKINSON,
JOHN HART,
ABRAHAM CLARK.

Maryland.

SAMUEL CHASE,
WILLIAM PACA,
THOMAS STONE,
CHARLES CARROLL, of Carrollton.

North Carolina.

WILLIAM HOOPER,
JOSEPH HEWES,
JOHN PENN.

South Carolina.

EDWARD RUTLEDGE,
THOMAS HEYWARD, JR.,
THOMAS LYNCH, JR.,
ARTHUR MIDDLETON.

Virginia.

GEORGE WYTHE,
RICHARD HENRY LEE,
THOMAS JEFFERSON,
BENJAMIN HARRISON,
THOMAS NELSON, JR.,
FRANCIS LIGHTFOOT LEE,
CARTER BRAXTON.

Delaware.

CÆSAR RODNEY,
GEORGE READ,
THOMAS M'KEAN.

Georgia.

BUTTON GWINNETT,
LYMAN HALL,
GEORGE WALTON.

Facsimile of Signatures to Declaration of Independence.

Lewis Morris   Abra Clark   Casar   Phil Livingston
Arthur Middleton   Fras. Hopkinson   Rodney
Geo Walton   Cartery Braxton   James Wilson
Richard Henry Lee   Thos. Heyward Junr
Benjamin Rush   John Adams   Rob Morris
Lyman Hall   Joseph Hewes   Button Gwinnett
Francis Lightfoot Lee
William Ellery   Edward Rutledge   Jas. Smith

ARTICLES OF CONFEDERATION AND PERPETUAL UNION BETWEEN THE STATES.

The Articles of Confederation reported July 12, '76, and debated from day to day, and time to time, for two years, were ratified July 9, '78, by ten States; by New Jersey on the 20th of November of the same year; and by Delaware on the 23d of February following. Maryland, alone, held off two years more, acceding to them March 1, '81, and thus closing the obligation. The following are the Articles:

O all whom these Presents shall come, We, the undersigned Delegates of the States affixed to our names send greeting—Whereas, the Delegates of the United States of America, in Congress assembled, did, on the 15th day of November, in the year of our Lord, 1777, and in the Second Year of the Independence of America, agree to certain articles of Confederation and Perpetual Union between the States of New Hampshire, Massachusetts Bay, Rhode Island and Providence Plantations, Connecticut, New York, New Jersey, Pennsylvania, Delaware, Maryland, Virginia, North Carolina, South Carolina and Georgia, in the words following, viz:

"*Articles of Confederation and Perpetual Union between the States of New Hampshire, Massachusetts Bay, Rhode Island and Providence Plantations, Connecticut, New York, New Jersey, Pennsylvania, Delaware, Maryland, Virginia, North Carolina, South Carolina, and Georgia.*

ARTICLE 1. The style of this Confederacy shall be "The United States of America."

ART. 2. Each State retains its sovereignty, freedom and independence, and every power, jurisdiction, and right, which is not by this confederation expressly delegated to the United States in Congress assembled.

ART. 3. The said States hereby severally enter into a firm league of friendship with each other for their common defense, the security of their liberties, and their mutual and general welfare, binding themselves to assist each other against all force offered to, or attacks made upon them, or any of them, on account of religion, sovereignty, trade, or any other pretense whatever.

ART. 4. The better to secure and perpetuate mutual friendship and intercourse among the people of the different States in this Union, the free inhabitants of each of these States—paupers, vagabonds, and fugitives from justice excepted—shall be entitled to all privileges and immunities of free citizens in the several States; and the people of each State shall have free ingress and egress to and from any other State, and shall enjoy therein all the privileges of trade and commerce, subject to the same duties, impositions and restrictions, as the inhabitants thereof respectively, provided that such restriction shall not extend so far as to prevent the removal of property, imported into any State, to any other State of which the owner is an inhabitant; provided also, that no imposition, duties or restriction shall be laid by any State on the property of the United States, or either of them.

If any person guilty of or charged with treason, felony, or other high misdemeanor in any State, shall flee from justice, and be found in any of the United States, he shall, upon demand of the Governor, or executive power of the State from which he fled, be delivered up and removed to the State having jurisdiction of his offense.

Full faith and credit shall be given in each of these States, to the records, acts, and judicial proceedings of the courts and magistrates of every other State.

ART. 5. For the more convenient management of the general interest of the United States, Delegates shall be annually appointed in such manner as the legislature of each State shall direct, to meet in Congress on the first Monday in November, in every year, with a power reserved to each State, to recall its Delegates, or any of them, at any time within the year, and to send others in their stead, for the remainder of the year.

No State shall be represented in Congress by less than two, nor by more than seven members; and no person shall be capable of being a Delegate for more than three years in any term of six years; nor shall any person, being a Delegate, be capable of holding any office under the United States, for which he, or another for his benefit, receives any salary, fees, or emolument of any kind.

Each State shall maintain its own Delegates in any meeting of the States, and while they act as members of the Committee of the States.

In determining questions in the United States in Congress assembled, each State shall have one vote.

Freedom of speech and debate in Congress shall not be impeached or questioned in any court or place, out of Congress, and the members of Congress shall be protected in their persons from arrests and imprisonments, during the time of their going to and from, and attendance on Congress, except for treason, felony, or breach of the peace.

ART. 6. No State, without the consent of the United States in Congress assembled, shall send an embassy to, or receive an embassy from, or enter into any conference, agreement, alliance, or treaty with any King, Prince or State; nor shall any person holding office of profit or trust under the United States, or any of them, accept of any present, emolument, office or title of any kind whatever from any King, Prince, or Foreign State; nor shall the United States in Congress assembled, or any of them, grant any title of nobility.

No two or more States shall enter into any treaty, confederation or alliance whatever between them, without the consent of the United States in Congress assembled, specifying accurately the purposes for which the same is to be entered into, and how long it shall continue.

No State shall lay any imposts or duties which may interfere with any stipulations in treaties entered into by the United States in Congress assembled, with any King, Prince or State, in pursuance of any treaties already proposed by Congress, to the Courts of France and Spain.

No vessels of war shall be kept up in time of peace by any State except such number only, as shall be deemed necessary by the United States in Congress assembled, for the defense of such State, or its trade; nor shall any body of forces be kept up by any State, in time of peace, except such number only, as in the judgment of the United States in Congress assembled, shall be deemed requisite to garrison the forts necessary for the defense of such State; but every State shall always keep up a well regulated and disciplined militia, sufficiently armed and accoutred, and shall provide and have constantly ready for use, in public stores, a due number of field-pieces and tents, and a proper quantity of arms, ammunition and camp equipage.

No State shall engage in any war without the consent of the United States in Congress assembled, unless such State be actually invaded by enemies, or shall have received certain advice of a resolution being formed by some nation of Indians to invade such a State, and the danger is so imminent as not to admit of a delay, till the United States in Congress assembled can be consulted; nor shall any State grant commissions to any ships or vessels of war, nor letters of marque or reprisal, except it be after a declaration of war by the United States in Congress assembled, and then only against the Kingdom or State, and the subjects thereof, against which war has been so declared, and under such regulations as shall be established by the United States in Congress assembled, unless such State be infested by pirates, in which case vessels of war may be fitted out for that occasion, and kept so long as the danger shall continue, or until the United States in Congress assembled, shall determine otherwise.

ART. 7. When land forces are raised by any State for the common defense, all officers of or under the rank of colonel, shall be appointed by the legislature of each State respectively, by whom such forces shall be raised, or in such manner as such State shall direct, and all vacancies shall be filled up by the State which first made the appointment.

ART. 8. All charges of war, and all other expenses that shall be incurred for the common defense or general welfare, and allowed by the United States in Congress assembled, shall be defrayed out of a common treasury, which shall be supplied by the several States, in proportion to the value of all land within each State, granted to or surveyed for any person, as such land and the buildings and improvements thereon shall be estimated according to such mode as the United States in Congress assembled shall from time to time, direct and appoint. The taxes for paying that proportion shall be laid and levied by the authority and direction of the legislatures of the several States within the time agreed upon by the United States in Congress assembled.

ARTICLE 9. The United States in Congress assembled shall have the sole and exclusive right and power of determining on peace and war, except in the cases mentioned in the 6th article—of sending and receiving embassadors—entering into treaties and alliances, provided that no treaty of commerce shall be made whereby the legislative power of the respective States shall be restrained from imposing such imposts and duties on foreigners, as their own people are subjected to, or from prohibiting the exportation¹ or importation of any species of goods or commodities whatsoever—of establishing rules for deciding in all cases what captures on land or water shall be legal, and in what manner prizes taken by land or naval forces in the service of the United States shall be divided or appropriated—of granting letters of marque and reprisal in times of peace—appointing courts for the trial of piracies and felonies committed on the high seas and establishing courts for receiving and determining finally appeals in all cases of captures, provided that no member of Congress shall be appointed a judge of any of the said courts.

The United States in Congress assembled shall also be the last resort on appeal in all disputes and differences now subsisting or that hereafter may arise between two or more States concerning boundary, jurisdiction, or any other cause whatever; which authority shall always be exercised in the manner following:—Whenever the legislative or executive authority or lawful agent of any State in controversy with another shall present a petition to Congress, stating the matter in question, and praying for a hearing, notice thereof shall be given by order of Congress, to the legislative or executive authority of the other State in controversy, and a day assigned for the appearance of the parties by their lawful agents, who shall then be directed to appoint, by joint consent, commissioners or judges to constitute a court for hearing and determining the matter in question; but if they cannot agree, Congress shall name three persons out of each of the United States, and from the list of such persons each party shall alternately strike out one, the petitioners beginning, until the number shall be reduced to thirteen; and from that number not less than seven, nor more than nine names, as Congress shall direct, shall in the presence of Congress be drawn out by lot, and the persons whose names shall be so drawn or any five of them, shall be commissioners or judges, to hear and finally determine the controversy, so always as a major part of the judges who shall hear the cause shall agree in the determination; and if either party shall neglect to attend at the day appointed,* without showing reasons which Congress shall judge sufficient, or being present shall refuse to strike, the Congress shall proceed to nominate three persons out of each State, and the Secretary of Congress shall strike in behalf of such party absent or refusing; and the judgment and sentence of the court to be appointed, in the manner above prescribed, shall be final and conclusive; and if any of the parties shall refuse to submit to the authority of such court, or to appear or defend their claim or cause, the court shall, nevertheless, proceed to pronounce sentence or judgment, which shall in like manner be final and decisive, the judgment or sentence and other proceedings being in either case transmitted to Congress and lodged among the acts of Congress for the security of the parties concerned: provided that every commissioner, before he sits in judgment, shall take an oath, to be administered by one of the judges of the Supreme or Superior Court of the State where the cause shall be tried, "well and truly to hear and determine the matter in question, according to the best of his judgment, without favor, affection, or hope of reward:" provided also that no State shall be deprived of territory for the benefit of the United States.

All controversies concerning the private right of soil claimed under different grants of two or more States, whose jurisdictions as they may respect such lands, and the States which passed such grants, are adjusted; the said grants or either of them being at the same time claimed to have originated antecedent to such settlement of jurisdiction, shall, on the petition of either party to the Congress of the United States, be finally determined as near as may be in the same manner as is before prescribed for deciding disputes respecting territorial jurisdiction between different States.

The United States in Congress assembled shall also have the sole exclusive right and power of regulating the alloy and value of coin struck by their own authority, or by that of the respective States—fixing the standard of weights and measures throughout the United States - regulating the trade and managing all affairs with the Indians, not members of any of the States; provided that the legislative right of any State within its own limits be not infringed or violated—establishing or regulating post-offices from one State to another, throughout all the United States, and exacting such postage on the papers passing through the same as may be requisite to defray the expenses of the said office—appointing all officers of the land forces in the service of the United States, excepting regimental officers—appointing all the officers of the naval forces, and commissioning all officers whatever in the service of the United States—making rules for the government and regulation of the said land and naval forces, and directing their operations.

The United States in Congress assembled shall have authority to appoint a committee, to sit in the recess of Congress, to be denominated "A Committee of the States," and to consist of one delegate from each State; and to appoint such other committees and civil officers as may be necessary for managing the general affairs of the United States, under their direction—to appoint one of their number to preside; provided that no person be allowed to serve in the office of president more than one year in any term of three years—to ascertain the necessary sums of money to be raised for the service of the United States, and to appropriate and apply the same for defraying the public expenses—to borrow money, or emit bills on the credit of the United States, transmitting every half year to the respective States an account of the sums of money so borrowed or emitted—to build and equip a navy—to agree upon the number of land forces, and to make requisitions from each State for its quota, in proportion to the number of white inhabitants in such State; which requisition shall be binding; and thereupon the legislatures of each State shall appoint the regimental officers, raise the men, and clothe, arm, and equip them in a soldier-like manner, at the expense of the United States; and the officers and men so clothed, armed, and equipped, shall march to the place appointed, and within the time agreed on by the United States in Congress assembled; but if the United States in Congress assembled shall, on consideration of circumstances, judge proper that any State should not raise men, or should raise a smaller number than its quota, and that any other State should raise a greater number of men than the quota thereof, such extra number shall be raised, officered, clothed, armed, and equipped in the same manner as the quota of such State, unless the legislature of such State shall judge that such extra number cannot be safely spared out of the same; in which case they shall raise, officer, clothe, arm, and equip as many of such extra number as they judge can be safely spared. And the officers and men so clothed, armed, and equipped, shall march to the place appointed, and within the time agreed on by the United States in Congress assembled.

The United States in Congress assembled shall never engage in a war, nor grant letters of marque and reprisal in time of peace, nor enter into any treaties or alliances, nor coin money, nor regulate the value thereof, nor ascertain the sums and expenses necessary for the defense and welfare of the United States, or any of them, nor emit bills, nor borrow money on the credit of the United States, nor appropriate money, nor agree upon the number of vessels of war to be built or purchased, or the number of land or sea forces to be raised, nor appoint a commander-in-chief of the army or navy unless nine States assent to the same; nor shall a question on any other point, except for adjourning from day to day, be determined, unless by the votes of a majority of the United States in Congress assembled.

The Congress of the United States shall have power to adjourn to any time within the year, and to any place within the United States, so that no period of adjournment be for a longer duration than the space of six months, and shall publish the journal of their proceedings monthly, except such parts thereof relating to treaties, alliances, or military operations, as in their judgment require secresy; and the yeas and nays of the delegates of each State on any question shall be entered on the journal when it is desired by any delegate; and the delegates of a State, or any of them, at his or their request, shall be furnished with a transcript of the said journal, except such parts as are above excepted, to lay before the legislatures of the several States.

ARTICLE 10. The committee of the States, or any nine of them, shall be authorized to execute, in the recess of Congress, such of the powers of Congress as the United States in Congress assembled, by the consent of nine States, shall, from time to time, think expedient to vest them with; provided that no power be delegated to the said committee; for the exercise of which, by the Articles of Confederation, the voice of nine States in the Congress of the United States assembled is requisite.

ARTICLE 11. Canada, acceding to this confederation and joining in the measures of the United States, shall be admitted into, and entitled to all the advantages of this union; but no other colony shall be admitted into the same unless such admission be agreed to by nine States.

ARTICLE 12. All bills of credit emitted, moneys borrowed, and debts contracted by, or under the authority of Congress, before the assembling of the United States, in pursuance of the present confederation, shall be deemed and considered as a charge against the United States—for payment and satisfaction whereof, the said United States and the public faith are hereby solemnly pledged.

ARTICLE 13. Every State shall abide by the determinations of the United States in Congress assembled on all questions which, by this confederation, are submitted to them. And the articles of this confederation shall be inviolably observed by every State, and the union shall be perpetual; nor shall any alteration at any time hereafter be made in any of them, unless such alteration be agreed to in a Congress of the

United States, and be afterward confirmed by the legislatures of every State.

And Whereas, It hath pleased the Great Governor of the World to incline the hearts of the legislatures we respectively represent in Congress, to approve of and to authorize us to ratify the said Articles of Confederation and perpetual union: Know Ye that we, the undersigned delegates, by virtue of the power and authority to us given for that purpose, do, by these presents, in the name and in behalf of our respective constituents, fully and entirely ratify and confirm each and every of the said Articles of Confederation and perpetual Union, and all and singular the matters and things therein contained. And we do further solemnly plight and engage the faith of our respective constituents, that they shall abide by the determinations of the United States in Congress assembled on all questions which, by the said confederation, are submitted to them. And that the articles thereof shall be inviolably observed by the States we respectively represent, and that the union shall be perpetual. In witness whereof we have hereunto set our hands in Congress. Done at Philadelphia, in the State of Pennsylvania, the 9th day of July, in the year of our Lord 1778, and in the 3d year of the Independence of America.

ORDINANCE OF 1787.

IN CONGRESS, JULY 13, 1787.

An Ordinance for the Government of the Territory of the United States, Northwest of the River Ohio.

Be it ordained, by the United States in Congress assembled, that the said Territory, for the purpose of temporary government, be one district; subject, however, to be divided into two districts, as future circumstances may, in the opinion of Congress, make it expedient.

Be it ordained, by the authority aforesaid, that the estates both of resident and non-resident proprietors in the said Territory, dying intestate, shall descend to, and be distributed among their children, and the descendants of a deceased child in equal parts: the descendants of a deceased child or grandchild, to take the share of their deceased parent, in equal parts, among them, and where there shall be no children or descendants, then in equal parts to the next of kin, in equal degree; and among collaterals, the children of a deceased brother or sister of the intestate shall have, in equal parts, among them, their deceased parent's share; and there shall in no case be a distinction between kindred of the whole and half blood; saving in all cases to the widow of the intestate her third part of the real estate for life, and one-third part of the personal estate; and this law relative to descents and dower shall remain in full force until altered by the Legislature of the district. And until the Governor and judges shall adopt laws as hereinafter mentioned, estates in the said territory may be devised or bequeathed by wills in writing, signed and sealed by him or her, in whom the estate may be (being of full age), and attested by three witnesses; and real estates may be conveyed by lease or release, or bargain and sale, signed, sealed, and delivered by the person, being of full age, in whom the estate may, and attested by two witnesses, provided such wills be duly proved, and such conveyances be acknowledged, or the execution thereof duly proved, and be recorded within one year after proper magistrates, courts and registers shall be appointed for that purpose, and personal property may be transferred by delivery, saving, however, to the French and Canadian inhabitants, and other settlers of the Kaskaskias, Saint Vincents, and the neighboring villages, who have heretofore professed themselves citizens of Virginia, their laws and customs now in force among them, relative to descent and conveyance of property.

Be it ordained, by the authority aforesaid, that there shall be appointed, from time to time, by Congress, a Governor, whose commission shall continue in force for the term of three years, unless sooner revoked by Congress; he shall reside in the district and have a freehold estate therein, in one thousand acres of land, while in the exercise of his office. There shall be appointed, from time to time, by Congress, a Secretary, whose commission shall continue in force for four years, unless sooner revoked; he shall reside therein, and have a freehold estate therein, in five hundred acres of land, while in the exercise of his office; it shall be his duty to keep and preserve the acts and laws passed by the Legislature, and the public records of the district, and the proceedings of the Governor in his executive department, and transmit authentic copies of such acts and proceedings, every six months, to the Secretary of Congress. There shall also be appointed a court, to consist of three judges, any two of whom to form a court, which shall have a common law jurisdiction, and reside in the district, and have each therein a freehold estate in five hundred acres of land, while in the exercise of their offices; and their commissions shall continue in force during good behavior.

The Governor and judges, or a majority of them, shall adopt and publish in the district such laws of the original States, criminal and civil, as may be necessary, and best suited to the circumstances of the district, and report them to Congress, from time to time, which laws shall be in force in the district until the organization of the General Assembly therein, unless disapproved by Congress; but afterward, the Legislature shall have authority to alter them as they shall think fit.

The Governor, for the time being, shall be commander-in-chief of the militia, appoint and commission all officers in the same, below the rank of general officers. All general officers shall be appointed and commissioned by Congress.

Previous to the organization of the General Assembly, the Governor shall appoint such magistrates and other civil officers in each county or township, as he shall find necessary for the preservation of the peace and good order in the same. After the General Assembly shall be organized, the powers and duties of magistrates and other civil officers shall be regulated and defined by the said Assembly; but all magistrates and other civil officers, not herein otherwise directed, shall, during the continuance of this temporary government, be appointed by the Governor.

For the prevention of crimes and injuries, the laws to be adopted or made, shall have force in all parts of the district, and for the execution of process, criminal and civil, the Governor shall make proper divisions thereof; and shall proceed, from time to time, as circumstances may require, to lay out the parts of the district in which the Indian titles shall have been extinguished, into counties and townships, subject, however, to such alterations as may hereafter be made by the Legislature.

So soon as there shall be five thousand free male inhabitants, of full age, in the district, upon giving proof thereof to the Governor, they shall receive authority, with time and place, to elect representatives from their counties or townships, to represent them in the General Assembly; *Provided*, That for every five hundred free male inhabitants there shall be one representative, and so on progressively with the number of free male inhabitants, shall the right of representation increase, until the number of representatives shall amount to twenty-five, after which the number and proportion of representatives shall be regulated by the Legislature; *Provided*, That no person be eligible or qualified to act as a representative, unless he shall have been a citizen of one of the United States three years and be a resident in the district, or unless he shall have resided in the district three years, and in either case shall likewise hold in his own right, in fee simple, two hundred acres of land within the same; *Provided*, also, that a freehold in fifty acres of land in the district, having been a citizen of one of the States, and being resident in the district, or the like freehold and two years' residence in the district, shall be necessary to qualify a man as an elector of a representative.

The representative thus elected, shall serve for the term of two years, and in case of the death of a representative, or removal from office, the Governor shall issue a writ to the county or township for which he was a member, to elect another in his stead, to serve for the residue of the term.

The General Assembly, or Legislature, shall consist of the Governor, Legislative Council, and a House of Representatives. The Legislative Council shall consist of five members, to continue in office five years, unless sooner removed by Congress, any three of whom to be a quorum; and the members of the Council shall be nominated and appointed in the following manner, to wit: As soon as representatives shall be elected, the Governor shall appoint a time and place for them to meet together, and, when met, they shall nominate ten persons, residents in the district and each possessed of a freehold in five hundred acres of land, and return their names to Congress, five of whom Congress shall appoint and commission to serve as aforesaid; and whenever a vacancy shall happen in the Council, by death or removal from office, the House of Representatives shall nominate two persons qualified as aforesaid, for each vacancy, and return their names to Congress, one of whom Congress shall appoint and commission for the residue of the term; and every five years, four months at least before the expiration of the time of service of the Council, the said House shall nominate ten persons qualified as aforesaid, and return their names to Congress, five of whom Congress shall appoint and commission to serve as members of the Council five years, unless sooner removed. And the Governor, Legislative Council, and House of Representatives, shall have authority to make laws in all cases for the good government of the district, not repugnant to the principles and articles in this ordinance established and declared. And all bills having passed by a majority in the House, and by a majority in the Council, shall be referred to the Governor for his assent; but no bill or legislative act whatever, shall be of any force without his assent. The Governor shall have power to convene, prorogue, and dissolve the assembly, when in his opinion it shall be expedient.

The Governor, Judges, Legislative Council, Secretary, and such other officers as Congress shall appoint in the district, shall take an oath or affirmation of fidelity, and of office—the Governor before the President of Congress, and all other officers before the Governor. As soon as a Legislature shall be formed in the District, the Council and House, assembled in one room, shall have authority, by joint ballot, to elect a delegate to Congress, who shall have a seat in Congress, with the right of debating, but not of voting, during this temporary government.

And for extending the fundamental principles of civil and religious liberty, which form the basis whereon these republics, their laws and constitutions, are elected; *to fix and establish those principles as the basis of all laws, constitutions, and governments, which* FOREVER *hereafter shall be formed in the said Territory;* to provide also for the establishment of States, and for their admission to a share in the Federal Council on an equal footing with the original States, at as early periods as may be consistent with the general interest:

It is hereby ordained and declared, by the authority aforesaid, that the following articles shall be considered as articles of compact between the original States and the people and States in the said Territory, and forever remain unalterable, unless by common consent; viz.:

ARTICLE I. No person, demeaning himself in a peaceable and orderly manner, shall ever be molested on account of his mode of worship or religious sentiments in the said Territory.

ART. II. The inhabitants of the said Territory shall always be entitled to the benefit of the writ of *habeas corpus* and of the trial by jury; of a proportionate representation of the people in the Legislature, and of judicial proceedings according to the course of the common law; all persons shall be bailable unless for capital offenses, where the proof shall be evident, or the presumption great; all fines shall be moderate, and no cruel or unusual punishments shall be inflicted; no man shall be deprived of his liberty or property but by the judgment of his peers or the law of the land; and should the public exigencies make it necessary for the common preservation to take any person's property, or to demand his particular services, full compensation shall be made for the same; and, in the just preservation of rights and property, it is understood and declared, that no law ought ever to be made, or have force in the said territory, that shall, in any manner whatever, interfere with or affect private contracts or engagements, *bona fide*, and, without fraud, previously formed.

ART. III. Religion, morality, and knowledge being necessary to good government and the happiness of mankind, schools and the means of education shall forever be encouraged. The utmost good faith shall always be observed toward the Indians; their lands and property shall never be taken from them without their consent; and in their property, rights, and liberty, they never shall be invaded or disturbed, unless in just and lawful wars authorized by Congress; but laws founded in justice and humanity shall, from time to time, be made, for preventing wrongs being done to them, and for preserving peace and friendship with them.

ART. IV. The said Territory, and the States which may be formed therein, shall forever remain a part of this Confederacy of the United States of America, subject to the Articles of Confederation,* and to such alterations therein as shall be constitutionally made; and to all the acts and ordinances of the United States in Congress assembled, conformable thereto. The inhabitants and settlers in the said Territory shall be subject to pay a part of the Federal debts contracted, or to be contracted, and a proportional part of the expenses of government, to be apportioned on them by Congress, according to the same common rule and measure by which apportionments thereof shall be made on the other States; and the taxes for paying their proportion shall be laid and levied by the authority and direction of the Legislatures of the District, or Districts, or new States, as in the original States, within the time agreed upon by the United States in Congress assembled. The Legislatures of those Districts, or new States,

* This ordinance was drawn up before the Constitution was formed.

shall never interfere with the primary disposal of the soil by the United States in Congress assembled, nor with any regulations Congress may find necessary for securing the title in such soil to the *bona fide* purchasers. No tax shall be imposed on lands the property of the United States; and in no case shall non-resident proprietors be taxed higher than residents. The navigable waters leading into the Mississippi and St. Lawrence, and the carrying places between the same, shall be common highways, and forever free, as well to the inhabitants of the said Territory as to the citizens of the United States, and those of any other States that may be admitted into the confederacy, without any tax, impost, or duty therefor.

ART. V. There shall be formed in the said Territory not less than three, nor more than five States; and the boundaries of the States, as soon as Virginia shall alter her act of session and consent to the same, shall become fixed and established as follows, to wit: The Western State shall be bounded by the Mississippi, the Ohio, and Wabash Rivers; a direct line drawn from the Wabash and Post Vincents due north to the territorial line between the United States and Canada, and by the said territorial line to the Lake of the Woods and Mississippi. The Middle State shall be bounded by the said direct line, the Wabash from Post Vincents to the Ohio, by the Ohio, by direct line drawn due north from the mouth of the Great Miami to the said territorial line, and by said territorial line. The Eastern State shall be bounded by the last mentioned direct line, the Ohio, Pennsylvania, and the said territorial line; *Provided*, however, and it is further understood and declared, that the boundaries of these three States shall be subject so far to be altered, and, if Congress shall hereafter find it expedient, they shall have authority to form one or two States in that part of the said Territory which lies north of an east and west line drawn through the southerly bend or extreme of Lake Michigan; and whenever any of the said States shall have sixty thousand fre-

inhabitants therein, such States shall be admitted, by their delegates, into the Congress of the United States, on an equal footing with the original States in all respects whatsoever ; and shall be at liberty to form a permanent constitution and State government ; *Provided*, the constitution and government so to be formed shall be republican, and in conformity to the principles contained in these articles ; and, so far as it can be consistent with the general interest of the confederacy, such admission shall be allowed at an earlier period, and when there may be a less number of free inhabitants in the State than sixty thousand.

ART. VI. There shall be neither slavery nor involuntary servitude in the said Territory, otherwise than in the punishment of crimes whereof the party shall have been duly convicted ; *Provided*, always, that any person escaping into the same, from whom labor or service is lawfully claimed in any of the original States, such fugitive may be lawfully reclaimed and conveyed to the person claiming his or her labor or service as aforesaid.

THE EXISTENCE OF THE UNION

*ON the existence of the Union, depends the safety and welfare of the parts of which it is composed; the fate of an empire, in many respects, the most interesting in the world. Among the most formidable obstacles which the new Constitution will have to encounter, we may reckon the perverted ambition of men, who will either hope to aggrandize themselves by the confusions of their country, or will flatter themselves with fairer prospects of elevation from the subdivision of the empire into several partial confederacies, than from its Union under one Government. * * * * * The vigor of Government is essential to the security of liberty."*

CONSTITUTION OF THE UNITED STATES OF AMERICA.*

We, the People of the United States, in Order to form a more perfect Union, establish Justice, insure domestic Tranquility, provide for the common defence, promote the general Welfare, and secure the Blessings of Liberty to ourselves and our Posterity, do ordain and establish this Constitution for the United States of America.

ARTICLE I.

SECTION 1. All legislative Powers herein granted shall be vested in a Congress of the United States, which shall consist of a Senate and *House of Representatives.*

SECTION 2. The House of Representatives shall *be composed* of Members chosen every second Year by the people of the several States, and the Electors in each State shall have the Qualifications requisite for Electors of the most numerous Branch of the State Legislature.

No person shall be a Representative who shall not have *attained to* the Age of twenty-five Years, and been seven Years a Citizen of the *United States,* and who shall not, when elected, be an Inhabitant of that State in which he shall be chosen.

Representative and *direct Taxes* shall be apportioned among the several States which may be included within this Union, according to their respective Numbers, which shall be determined by adding to the whole Number of free Persons, including those bound to Service for a Term of Years, and excluding Indians not taxed, three-fifths of all other Persons. The actual Enumeration shall be made within three Years after the first meeting of the Congress of the United States, and within every subsequent Term of ten Years, in such Manner as they shall by Law direct. The Number of Representatives shall not exceed one for every thirty Thousand but each State shall have at Least one Representative; and until such enumeration shall be made, the State of New Hampshire shall *be entitled* to chuse three, Massachusetts eight, Rhode Island and Providence Plantations one, Connecticut five, New York six, New Jersey four, Pennsylvania eight, Delaware one, Maryland six, Virginia ten, North Carolina five, South Carolina five, and Georgia three.

When vacancies happen in the Representation from any State, the Executive Authority thereof shall issue Writs of Election to fill such Vacancies.

The House of Representatives shall chuse their Speaker and other Officers; and shall have the sole Power of Impeachment.

SECTION 3. The Senate of the United States shall be composed of two Senators from each State, chosen by the Legislature thereof, for six Years; and each Senator shall have one Vote.

Immediately after they shall be assembled in Consequence of the first Election, they shall be divided as equally as may be into three Classes. The Seats of the Senators of the first Class shall be vacated at the Expiration of the second Year, of the second Class at the Expiration of the fourth Year, and of the third Class at the Expiration of the sixth Year, so that one-third may be chosen every second Year; and if Vacancies happen by Resignation, or otherwise, during the Recess of the Legislature of any State, the Executive thereof may make temporary Appointments until the next Meeting of the Legislature, which shall then fill such Vacancies.

No Person shall be a Senator who shall not have *attained to* the Age of thirty Years, and been nine Years a Citizen of the United States, and who shall not, when elected, be *an Inhabitant* of that State for which he shall be chosen.

The *Vice-President* of the United States shall be President of the Senate, but shall have no Vote, unless they be equally divided.

The Senate shall chuse their other Officers, and also a President *pro tempore*, in the Absence of the Vice President, or when he shall exercise the Office of President of the United States.

The Senate shall have the sole Power to try all Impeachments. When sitting for that purpose, they shall be on Oath or Affirmation. When the President of the United States is tried, the Chief Justice shall preside: And no Person shall be convicted without the Concurrence of two thirds of the Members present.

Judgment in Cases of Impeachment shall not extend further than to removal from Office, and disqualification to hold and enjoy any Office of honor, Trust or Profit under the United States; but the Party convicted shall nevertheless be liable and subject to Indictment, Trial, Judgment, and Punishment, according to Law.

SECTION 4. The Times, Places and Manner of holding Elections for *Senators and Representatives*, shall be prescribed in each State by the Legislature thereof; but the Congress may at time by Law make or alter such Regulations, except as to the Places of chusing Senators.

The Congress shall assemble at least once in every Year, and such meeting shall be on the first Monday in December, unless they shall by Law appoint a different Day.

SECTION 5. Each House shall be the Judge of the Elections, Returns and Qualifications of its own Members, and *a Majority* of each shall constitute a Quorum to do business; but a smaller Number may adjourn from day to day, and may be authorized to compel the Attendance of absent Members, in such Manner, and under such Penalties as each House may provide.

Each House may determine the Rules of its Proceedings, punish its Members for disorderly Behavior, and, with the Concurrence of two-thirds, expel a Member.

Each House shall keep a Journal of its Proceedings, and from time to time publish the same, excepting such Parts as may in their Judgment require Secrecy; and the Yeas and Nays of the Members of either House on any question shall, at the Desire of one-fifth of those Present, be entered on the Journal.

Neither House, during the Session of Congress, shall, without the Consent of the other, adjourn for more than three days, nor to any other Place than that in which the two Houses shall be sitting.

SECTION 6. The *Senators and Representatives* shall receive a Compensation for their Services, to be ascertained by Law, and *paid out of* the Treasury of the United States. They shall in all Cases, except Treason, Felony and Breach of the Peace, be privileged from Arrest during their Attendance at the Session of their respective Houses, and in going to and returning from the same; and for any Speech or Debate in either House, they shall not be questioned in any other Place.

No Senator or Representative shall, during the Time for which he was elected, be appointed to any civil Office under the Authority of the United States, which shall have been created, or the Emoluments whereof shall have been increased during such time; and no Person holding any Office under the United States, shall be a Member of either House during his Continuance in Office.

SECTION 7. All Bills for raising Revenue shall originate in the House of Representatives; but the Senate may propose or concur with Amendments as on other Bills.

Every Bill which shall have passed the House of Representatives and the Senate, shall, before it become a Law, be presented to the President of the United States; if he approve he shall sign it, but if not he shall return it, with his Objections to that House in which it shall have originated, who shall enter the Objections at large on their Journal, and proceed to reconsider it. If after such Reconsideration two thirds of that House shall agree to pass the Bill, it shall be sent, together with the Objections, to the other House, by which it shall likewise be reconsidered, and if approved by two-thirds of that House, it shall become a Law. But in all such Cases the Votes of both Houses shall be determined by Yeas and Nays, and the Names of the Persons *voting for and against* the Bill shall be entered on the Journal of each House respectively. If any Bill shall not be returned by the President within ten days (Sundays excepted) after it shall have been presented to him, the Same shall be a law, in like manner as if he had signed it, unless the Congress by their Adjournment prevent its Return, in which case it shall not be a Law.

Every Order, Resolution, or Vote to which the Concurrence of the *Senate and House of Representatives* may be necessary (except on a question of Adjournment) shall be presented to the President of the United States; and before the Same shall take Effect, shall be approved by him, or being disapproved by him, shall be repassed by two-thirds of the Senate and House of Representatives, according to the Rules and Limitations prescribed *in the Case* of a Bill.

SECTION 8. The Congress shall have Power:

To lay and collect Taxes, Duties, Imposts, and Excises, to pay the Debts and provide for the common Defence and general Welfare of the United States; but all Duties, Imposts and Excises shall be uniform throughout the United States;

To borrow Money on the credit of the United States;

To regulate Commerce with foreign Nations, and among the several States, and with the Indian Tribes;

To establish an uniform Rule *of Naturalization*, and uniform Laws on the subject of Bankruptcies throughout the United States;

To coin Money, regulate the Value thereof, and of foreign Coin, and fix the Standard of *Weights and Measures;*

To provide for the Punishment of counterfeiting the Securities and current Coin of the United States;

To establish Post Offices and *post Roads;*

To promote the Progress of Science and useful Arts, by securing for limited Times to Authors and Inventors the Exclusive Right to their respective Writings and Discoveries;

To constitute Tribunals inferior to the Supreme Court;

To define and punish Piracies and Felonies committed on the high Seas, and Offences against *the Law of Nations;*

To declare War, grant Letters of Marque and Reprisal, and make Rules concerning Captures on Land and Water;

To raise and support Armies, but no Appropriation of Money *to that Use* shall be for a longer Term than two Years;

To provide and maintain a Navy;

To make Rules for the Government and Regulation of the land and naval Forces;

To provide for calling forth the Militia to execute the Laws of the Union, suppress Insurrections and repel Invasions;

To provide for organizing, arming, and disciplining the Militia, and for governing such Part of them as may be employed in the Service of the United States, reserving to the States respectively, the Appointment of the Officers, and the Authority of training the Militia according to the discipline prescribed by Congress;

To exercise exclusive Legislation in all Cases whatsoever, over such District (not exceeding ten Miles square) as may, by Cession of particular States, and the Acceptance of Congress, become the Seat of the Government of the United States, and to exercise like Authority over all Places purchased by the Consent of the Legislature of the State in which the Same shall be, for the Erection of Forts, Magazines, Arsenals, dock-Yards, and other needful Buildings;—And

To make all Laws which shall be necessary and proper for carrying into Execution the foregoing Powers, and all other Powers vested by this Constitution in the Government of the United States, or in any Department or any Officer thereof.

SECTION 9. The Migration or Importation of such Persons as any of the States now existing shall think proper to admit, shall not be prohibited by the Congress prior to the Year *one thousand eight hundred and eight*, but *a* Tax or duty may be imposed on such Importation, not exceeding ten dollars for each Person.

The Privilege of the Writ *of Habeas Corpus* shall not be suspended, unless when in Cases of Rebellion or Invasion the public Safety may require it.

No Bill of Attainder or *ex po t facto Law* shall be passed.

No Capitation, or other direct, Tax shall be laid, unless in Proportion to the Census or Enumeration hereinbefore directed to be taken.

No Tax or Duty shall be laid on Articles exported from any State.

No Preference shall be given by any Regulation of Commerce or Revenue to the Ports of one State over those of another; nor shall Vessels bound to, or from, one State, be obliged to enter, clear, or pay Duties in another.

No Money shall be drawn from the Treasury, but in Consequence of Appropriations made by Law; and a regular Statement and Account of the Receipts and Expenditures of all public Money shall be published *from time to time.*

No Title of Nobility shall be granted by the United States: And no Person holding any Office of Profit or Trust under them, shall, without the Consent of the Congress, *accept of* any Present, Emolument, Office, or Title, of any kind whatever, from any King, Prince, or foreign State.

SECTION 10. No State shall *enter into* any Treaty, Alliance, or Confederation; grant Letters of Marque and Reprisal; coin Money; emit Bills of Credit; make any Thing but gold and silver Coin a Tender in Payment of Debts; pass any Bill of Attainder, ex post facto Law, or

Law impairing the Obligation of Contracts, or grant any Title of Nobility.

No State shall, without the Consent of the Congress, lay any Imposts or Duties on Imports or Exports, except what may be absolutely necessary for executing its *inspection* Laws: and the net Produce of all Duties and Imposts, laid by any State on Imports or Exports, shall be for the Uses of the Treasury of the United States; and all such Laws shall be subject to the Revision and Control of the Congress.

No State shall, without the Consent of Congress, lay any Duty of Tonnage, keep Troops, or Ships of War in time of Peace, *enter into* any Agreement or Compact with another State, or with a foreign Power, or engage in War, unless actually invaded, or in such imminent Danger as will not admit of delay.

ARTICLE II.

SECTION 1. The executive Power shall be vested in a President of the United States of America. He shall hold his Office during the Term of four Years, and, together with the Vice President chosen for the same Term, be elected, *as follows*:

Each State shall appoint, in such Manner as the Legislature thereof may direct, a Number of Electors, equal to the whole number of Senators and Representatives to which the State may *be entitled* in the Congress: but no Senator or Representative, or Person holding an Office of Trust or Profit under the United States, shall be appointed an *Elector*.

[The Electors shall meet in their respective States, and vote by Ballot for two Persons, of whom one at least shall not be *an Inhabitant* of the same State with themselves. And they shall make a List of all the Persons voted for, and of the Number of Votes for each; which List they shall sign and certify, and transmit sealed to the *Seat of the Government* of the United States, directed to the President of the Senate. The President of the Senate shall, in the Presence of the Senate and House of Representatives, open all the Certificates, and the Votes shall then be counted. The Person having the greatest Number of Votes shall be the President, if such Number be a Majority of the whole Number of Electors appointed; and if there be more than one who have such Majority, and have *an equal* Number of Votes, then the House of Representatives shall immediately chuse by Ballot one of them for President; and if no Person have a Majority, then from the five highest on the List the said House shall in like Manner chuse the President; but in chusing the President, the Votes shall be taken by States, the Representation from each State having one Vote; A quorum for this Purpose shall consist of a Member or Members from two thirds of the States, and a Majority of all the States shall be necessary to a Choice. In every Case, after the Choice of the President, the Person having the greatest Number of Votes of the Electors shall be the Vice President. *But if* there should remain two or more who have equal Votes, the Senate shall chuse from them by Ballot the *Vice President.*]

The Congress may determine the Time of chusing the Electors, and the Day on which they shall give their Votes; which Day shall be the same throughout the United States.

No Person except a natural born Citizen, or a Citizen of the United States, at the time of the Adoption of this Constitution, shall be *eligible to* the Office of President; neither shall any Person be eligible to that Office who shall not have *attained to* the Age of thirty-five Years, and been fourteen Years a Resident within the United States.

In Case of the Removal of the President from Office, or his Death, Resignation, or Inability to discharge the Powers and Duties of the said Office, the Same shall *devolve on* the Vice President, and the Congress may by Law provide for the Case of Removal, Death, Resignation, or Inability both of the President and Vice President, declaring what Officer shall then act as President, and such Officer shall act accordingly, until the Disability be removed, or a President shall be elected.

The President shall, at stated Times receive for his Services, a Compensation, which shall be neither increased nor diminished during the Period for which he shall have been elected, and he shall not receive within that Period any other Emolument from the United States, or any of them.

Before he enter on the Execution of his Office, he shall take the following Oath or Affirmation:—

"I do solemnly swear (or affirm) that I will faithfully execute the Office of President of the United States, and will to the best of my Ability, preserve, protect and defend the Constitution of the United States."

SECTION 2. The President shall be *Commander in Chief* of the Army and Navy of the United States, and of the Militia of the several States, when called into the actual Service of the United States; he may require the Opinion, in writing, of the principal Officer in each of the executive Departments, upon any Subject relating to the Duties of their respective Offices, and he shall have Power to grant Reprieves and Pardons for Offenses against the United States, except in Cases of Impeachment.

He shall have Power, by and with the Advice and Consent of the Senate, to make Treaties, provided two-thirds of the Senators present concur; and he shall nominate, and by and with the Advice and Consent of the Senate, shall appoint Ambassadors, other Public Ministers and Consuls, Judges of the Supreme Court, and all other Officers of the United States, whose Appointments are not herein otherwise provided for, and which shall be established by Law; but the Congress may by Law vest the Appointment of such inferior Officers, as they may think proper, in the President alone, in the Courts of Law, or in the Heads of Departments.

The President shall have Power to fill up all Vacancies that may happen during the Recess of the Senate, by granting Commissions which shall expire at the End of their next Session.

SECTION 3. He shall from time to time give to the Congress Information of the State of the Union, and recommend to their Consideration such Measures as he shall judge necessary and expedient; he may, on extraordinary Occasions, convene both Houses, or either of them, and in Case of Disagreement between them, with Respect to the Time of Adjournment, he may adjourn them to such Time as he shall think proper; he shall receive Ambassadors and other public Ministers; he shall take Care that the Laws be faithfully executed, and shall Commission all officers of the United States.

SECTION 4. The President, Vice-President and all civil Officers of the United States, shall be removed from Office on Impeachment for, and Conviction of, Treason, Bribery, or other high Crimes and Misdemeanors.

ARTICLE III.

SECTION 1. The judicial Power of the United States shall be vested in one Supreme Court, and in such inferior Courts as the Congress may from time to time ordain and establish. The Judges, both of the supreme and inferior Courts, shall hold their Offices during good Behavior, and shall, at stated Times, receive for their Services, a Compensation, which shall not be diminished during their Continuance in Office.

SECTION 2. The judicial Power shall *extend to* all Cases in Law and Equity, arising under this Constitution, the Laws of the United States, and Treaties made, or which shall be made, under their Authority;—to all Cases affecting Ambassadors, other public Ministers, and Consuls;—to all Cases of admiralty and maritime Jurisdiction;—to Controversies to which the United States shall be a Party;—to Controversies between two or more States;—between a State and Citizens of another State;—between Citizens of different States,—between Citizens of the same

State claiming Lands under Grants of different States, and between a State, or Citizens thereof, and foreign States, Citizens or Subjects.

In all Cases affecting Ambassadors, other public Ministers and Consuls, and those *in which* a State shall be a Party, the Supreme Court shall have original Jurisdiction. In all the other Cases before mentioned, the Supreme Court shall have *appellate Jurisdiction*, both as to Law and Fact, with such Exceptions, and under such Regulations as the Congress shall make.

The Trial of all Crimes, except in Cases of Impeachment, shall be by Jury; and such Trial shall *be held* in the State where the said Crimes shall have been committed; but when not committed within any State, the Trial shall be at such Place or Places as the Congress may by Law have directed.

SECTION 3. Treason against the *United States*, shall consist only in levying War against them, or in adhering to their Enemies, giving them Aid and Comfort. No person shall be convicted of Treason unless on the Testimony of two Witnesses to the same overt Act, or on Confession in open Court.

The Congress shall have Power to declare the Punishment of Treason, but no Attainder of Treason shall work *Corruption of Blood*, or Forfeiture except during the Life of the Person attainted.

ARTICLE IV.

SECTION 1. Full Faith and Credit shall be given in each State to the public Acts, Records, and judicial Proceedings of every other State. And the Congress may by general Laws prescribe the Manner in which such Acts, Records and Proceedings shall be proved, and the Effect thereof.

SECTION 2. The Citizens of each State shall *be entitled* to all Privileges and Immunities of Citizens of the several States.

A Person charged in any State with Treason, Felony, or other Crime, who shall flee from Justice, and be found in another State, shall on Demand of the executive Authority of the State from which he fled, be delivered up, to be removed to the State having Jurisdiction of the Crime.

No Person held *to Service or Labour* in one State, under the Laws thereof, escaping into another, shall, *in Consequence* of any Law or Regulation therein, be discharged from such *Service or Labour*, but shall be delivered up on Claim of the Party to whom such Service or Labour may be due.

SECTION 3. New States may be admitted by the Congress into this Union; but no new State shall be formed or erected within the Jurisdiction of any other State; nor any State be formed by the Junction of two or more States, or Parts of States, without the Consent of the Legislatures of the States concerned as well as of the Congress.

The Congress shall have Power to dispose of and make all needful Rules and Regulations respecting the Territory or other Property belonging to the United States; and nothing in this Constitution shall be so construed as to Prejudice any claims of the United States, or of any particular State.

SECTION 4. The United States shall guarantee to every State in this Union a Republican Form of Government, and shall protect each of them against Invasion; and on Application of the Legislature or of the Executive (when the Legislature cannot be convened) against domestic Violence.

ARTICLE V.

The Congress, whenever two thirds of both Houses shall deem it necessary, shall propose Amendments to this Constitution, or, on the Application of the Legislatures of the several States, shall call a Convention for proposing Amendments, which, in either Case, shall *be valid* to all Intents and Purposes, as Part of this Constitution, when ratified by the Legislatures of three fourths of the several States, or by Conventions in three fourths thereof, as the one or the other Mode of Ratification may be proposed by the Congress; Provided that no Amendment which may be made *prior to* the Year One thousand eight hundred and eight shall in any Manner affect the first and fourth Clauses in the Ninth Section of the first Article; and that no State, without its Consent, shall be deprived of its equal Suffrage in the Senate.

ARTICLE VI.

All Debts contracted and Engagements entered into, before the Adoption of this Constitution, shall be as *valid against* the United States under this Constitution, as under the Confederation.

This Constitution, and the Laws of the United States which shall be made in pursuance thereof; and all Treaties made, or which shall be made, under the Authority of the United States, shall be the supreme Law of the Land: and the Judges in every State shall be bound thereby, any Thing in the Constitution or Laws of any State to the Contrary notwithstanding.

The Senators and Representatives before mentioned, and the Members of the several State Legislatures, and all executive and judicial Officers, both of the United States and of the several States, shall be bound by Oath or Affirmation, to support this Constitution; but no religious Test shall ever be required as a qualification to any Office or public Trust under the United States.

ARTICLE VII.

The Ratifications of the Conventions of nine States, shall be *sufficient for the Establishment of* this Constitution between the States so ratifying the Same.

Done in Convention by the Unanimous Consent of the States present the Seventeenth Day of September in *the Year of our Lord* one thousand seven hundred and Eighty seven and of the Independence of the *United States of America* the Twelfth In witness whereof We have hereunto subscribed our Names,

GEO. WASHINGTON—
President and Deputy from Virginia.

[This edition of the Constitution of the United States has been taken from the edition published by Joseph Bartlett Burleigh LL. D. from his script imitation of the Constitution which was compared with the original in the Department of State, and also found to be correct in capitals, orthography, text, and punctuation. In every particular, as to capitals, orthography, text, and punctuation, this edition follows Dr. Burleigh's.]

AMENDMENTS TO THE CONSTITUTION OF THE UNITED STATES.

[The following amendments were proposed at the first session of the first congress of the United States, which was begun and held at the city of New York on the 4th of March, 1789, and were adopted by the requisite number of States. Laws of the U. S., vol. 1, page 82.]

[The following preamble and resolution preceded the original proposition of the amendments, and as they have been supposed by a high equity judge (8th Wendell's Reports, p. 100) to have an important bearing on the construction of those amendments, they are here inserted. They will be found in the journals of the first session of the first congress.

CONGRESS OF THE UNITED STATES.

Begun and held at the city of New York, on Wednesday, the 4th day of March, 1789.

The conventions of a number of the States having, at the time of their adopting the constitution, expressed a desire, in order to prevent misconstruction or abuse of its powers, that further declaratory and restrictive clauses should be added, and as extending the ground of public confidence in the government will best insure the beneficent ends of its institution:

Resolved, By the Senate and House of Representatives of the United States of America, in congress assembled, two-thirds of both houses concurring, that the following articles be proposed to the legislatures of the several states, as amendments to the constitution of the United States; all or any of which articles, when ratified by three-fourths of the said legislatures, to be valid to all intents and purposes, as part of the said constitution, namely:]

ARTICLE I.

Congress shall make no law respecting an establishment of religion, or prohibiting the free exercise thereof; or abridging the freedom of speech or of the press; or the right of the people peaceably to assemble, and to petition the government for a redress of grievances.

ARTICLE II.

A well regulated militia being necessary to the security of a free state, the right of the people to keep and bear arms shall not be infringed.

ARTICLE III.

No soldier shall, in time of peace, be quartered in any house without the consent of the owner, nor in time of war, but in a manner to be prescribed by law.

ARTICLE IV.

The right of the people to be secure in their persons, houses, paper and effects, against unreasonable searches and seizures, shall not be violated; and no warrants shall issue but upon probable cause, supported by oath or affirmation, and particularly describing the place to be searched, and the persons or things to be seized.

ARTICLE V.

No person shall be held to answer for a capital or otherwise infamous crime, unless on a presentment or indictment of a grand jury, except in cases arising in the land or naval forces, or in the militia, when in actual service in time of war or public danger; nor shall any person be subject for the same offense to be twice put in jeopardy of life or limb; nor shall be compelled in any criminal case, to be a witness against himself, nor be deprived of life, liberty or property, without due process of law; nor shall private property be taken for public use without just compensation.

ARTICLE VI.

In all criminal prosecutions, the accused shall enjoy the right to a speedy and public trial, by an impartial jury of the state and district wherein the crime shall have been committed, which district shall have been previously ascertained by law; and to be informed of the nature and cause of the accusation; to be confronted with the witnesses against him; to have compulsory process for obtaining witnesses in his favor, and to have the assistance of counsel for his defense.

ARTICLE VII.

In suits at common law, where the value in controversy shall exceed twenty dollars, the right of trial by jury shall be preserved; and no fact tried by a jury shall be otherwise re-examined in any court of the United States, than according to the rules of the common law.

ARTICLE VIII.

Excessive bail shall not be required, nor excessive fines imposed, nor cruel and unusual punishments inflicted.

ARTICLE IX.

The enumeration in the constitution of certain rights shall not be construed to deny or disparage others retained by the people.

ARTICLE X.

The powers not delegated to the United States by the constitution, nor prohibited to it by the states, are reserved to the states respectively, or to the people.

[The following amendment was proposed at the second session of the third congress. It is printed in the Laws of the United States, vol. 1, p. 73, as article 11.]

ARTICLE XI.

The judicial power of the United States shall not be construed to extend to any suit in law or equity, commenced or prosecuted against one of the United States by citizens of another state, or by citizens or subjects of any foreign state.

[The three following sections were proposed as amendments at the first session of the eighth congress. They are printed in the Laws of the United States as article 12.]

ARTICLE XII.

1. The electors shall meet in their respective states, and vote by ballot for president and vice-president, one of whom at least shall not be an inhabitant of the same state with themselves. They shall name in their ballots the person voted for as president, and in distinct ballots the person voted for as vice-president; and they shall make distinct lists of all persons voted for as president, and of all persons voted for as vice-president, and of the number of votes for each; which lists they shall sign and certify, and transmit sealed to the seat of the government of the United States, directed to the president of the senate. The president of the senate shall, in the presence of the senate and house of representatives, open all the certificates, and the votes shall then be counted. The person having the greatest number of votes for president shall be the president, if such number be a majority of the whole number of electors appointed; and if no person have such majority, then from the persons having the highest numbers, not exceeding three, on the list of those voted for as president, the house of representatives shall choose immediately, by ballot, the president. But in choosing the president, the votes shall be taken by states, the representation from each state having one vote; a quorum for this purpose shall consist of a member or members from two-thirds of the states, and a majority of all the states shall be necessary to a choice. And if the house of representatives shall not choose a president, whenever the right of choice shall devolve upon them, before the fourth day of March next following, then the vice president shall act as president, as in the case of the death or other constitutional disability of the president.

2. The person having the greatest number of votes as vice-president shall be the vice-president, if such number be a majority of the whole number of electors appointed, and if no person have a majority, then from the two highest numbers on the list the senate shall choose the vice-president. A quorum for the purpose shall consist of two-thirds of the whole number of senators, and a majority of the whole number shall be necessary to a choice.

3. But no person constitutionally ineligible to the office of president shall be eligible to that of vice-president of the United States.

ARTICLE XIII.

SECTION 1.

Neither slavery nor involuntary servitude, except as a punishment for crime, whereof the party shall have been duly convicted, shall exist within the United States, or any place subject to their jurisdiction.

SECTION 2.

Congress shall have power to enforce this article by appropriate legislation.

The following is the certificate of the secretary of state of the United States, announcing the ratification of the foregoing article:

WILLIAM H. SEWARD, *Secretary of State of the United States:*

To ALL TO WHOM THESE PRESENTS MAY COME, GREETING:

Know Ye, That, whereas the congress of the United States, on the first of February last, passed a resolution, which is in the words following, namely: "A Resolution submitting to the legislatures of the several states a proposition to amend the constitution of the United States.

"*Resolved*, By the senate and house of representatives of the United States of America in congress assembled (two-thirds of both houses concurring), that the following article be proposed to the legislatures of the several states as an amendment to the constitution of the United States, which, when ratified by three-fourths of said legislatures, shall be valid, to all intents and purposes, as a part of the said constitution, namely:"

(See Article XIII, above.)

And whereas it appears from official documents on file in this department, that the amendment to the constitution of the United States proposed as aforesaid, has been ratified by the legislatures of the States of Illinois, Rhode Island, Michigan, Maryland, New York, West Virginia, Maine, Kansas, Massachusetts, Pennsylvania, Virginia, Ohio, Missouri, Nevada, Indiana, Louisiana, Minnesota, Wisconsin, Vermont, Tennessee, Arkansas, Connecticut, New Hampshire, South Carolina, Alabama, North Carolina and Georgia; in all twenty-seven states.

And whereas, the whole number of states in the United States is thirty-six; and whereas, the before specially-named states, whose legislatures have ratified the said proposed amendment, constitute three-fourths of the whole number of states in the United States:

Now, therefore, be it known, that I, WILLIAM H. SEWARD, Secretary of State of the United States, by virtue and in pursuance of the second section of the act of congress, approved the twentieth of April, eighteen hundred and eighteen, entitled, "An act to provide for the publication of the laws of the United States, and for other purposes," do hereby certify, that the amendment aforesaid has become valid, to all intents and purposes, as a part of the constitution of the United States.

In testimony whereof, I have hereunto set my hand, and caused the seal of the department of state to be affixed.

Done at the city of Washington, this eighteenth day of December, in the year of our Lord one thousand eight hundred and sixty-five, and of the Independence of the United States of America the ninetieth.

[L. S.]

WILLIAM H. SEWARD,
Secretary of State.

ARTICLE XIV.

SECTION 1.

All persons born or naturalized in the United States, and subject to the jurisdiction thereof, are citizens of the United States and of the state wherein they reside. No state shall make or enforce any law which shall abridge the privileges or immunities of citizens of the United States; nor shall any state deprive any person of life, liberty or property, without due process of law, nor deny to any person within its jurisdiction the equal protection of the laws.

SECTION 2.

Representatives shall be apportioned among the several states according to their respective numbers, counting the whole number of persons in each state, excluding Indians not taxed. But when the right to vote at any election for the choice of electors for president and vice-president of the United States, representatives in congress, the executive and judicial officers of a state, or the members of the legislature thereof, is denied to any of the male inhabitants of such state, being twenty-one years of age, and citizens of the United States, or in any way abridged, except for participation in rebellion or other crime, the basis of representation therein shall be reduced in the proportion which the number of such male citizens shall bear to the whole number of male citizens twenty-one years of age in such state.

SECTION 3.

No person shall be a senator or representative in congress, or elector of president and vice-president, or hold any office, civil or military, under the United States, or under any state, who, having previously taken an oath as a member of congress, or as an officer of the United States, or as a member of any state legislature, or as an executive or judicial officer of any state, to support the constitution of the United States, shall have engaged in insurrection or rebellion against the same, or given aid or comfort to the enemies thereof. But congress may, by a vote of two-thirds of each house, remove such disability.

SECTION 4.

The validity of the public debt of the United States authorized by law, including debts incurred for payment of pensions and bounties for services in suppressing insurrection or rebellion, shall not be questioned. But neither the United States nor any state shall assume or pay any debt or obligation incurred in aid of insurrection or rebellion against the United States, or any claim for the loss or emancipation of any slave; but all such debts, obligations, and claims shall be held illegal and void.

SECTION 5.

The congress shall have power to enforce, by appropriate legislation, the provisions of this article.

The following are the certificates of the secretary of state of the United States, announcing the ratification of the foregoing article:

WILLIAM H. SEWARD, *Secretary of State of the United States:*

TO ALL TO WHOM THESE PRESENTS MAY COME, GREETING:

WHEREAS, the congress of the United States, on or about the sixteenth of June, in the year one thousand eight hundred and sixty-six, passed a resolution, which is in the words and figures following, to wit:

"Joint Resolution proposing an Amendment to the Constitution of the United States.

"*Be it Resolved*, By the senate and house of representatives of the United States of America in congress assembled (two-thirds of both houses concurring), That the following article be proposed to the legislatures of the several states as an amendment to the constitution of the United States, which, when ratified by three-fourths of said legislatures, shall be valid as part of the constitution, namely:"

(See Article XIV, above.)

And whereas, by the second section of the act of congress, approved the twentieth of April, one thousand eight hundred and eighteen, entitled "An act to provide for the publication of the laws of the United States, and for other purposes," it is made the duty of the secretary of state forthwith to cause any amendment to the constitution of the United States, which has been adopted according to the provisions of the said Constitution, to be published in the newspapers authorized to promulgate the laws, with his certificate specifying the states by which the same may have been adopted, and that the same has become valid, to all intents and purposes, as a part of the constitution of the United States:

And whereas, neither the act just quoted from, nor any other law, expressly or by conclusive implication, authorizes the secretary of state to determine and decide doubtful questions as to the authenticity of the organization of state legislatures, or as to the power of any state legislature to recall a previous act or resolution of ratification of any amendment proposed to the constitution:

And whereas, it appears from official documents on file in this department, that the amendment to the constitution of the United States, proposed as aforesaid, has been ratified by the legislatures of the states of Connecticut, New Hampshire, Tennessee, New Jersey, Oregon, Vermont, New York, Ohio, Illinois, West Virginia, Kansas, Maine, Nevada, Missouri, Indiana, Minnesota, Rhode Island, Wisconsin, Pennsylvania, Michigan, Massachusetts, Nebraska, and Iowa;

And whereas, it further appears from documents on file in this department, that the amendment to the constitution of the United States, proposed as aforesaid, has also been ratified by newly constituted and newly established bodies, avowing themselves to be, and acting as, the legislatures, respectively, of the states of Arkansas, Florida, North Carolina, Louisiana, South Carolina, and Alabama;

And whereas, it further appears, from official documents on file in this department, that the legislatures of two of the states first above enumerated, to wit: Ohio and New Jersey, have since passed resolutions, respectively, withdrawing the consent of each of said states to the aforesaid amendment;

And whereas, it is deemed a matter of doubt and uncertainty whether such resolutions are not irregular, invalid, and, therefore, ineffectual for withdrawing the consent of the said two states, or of either of them, to the aforesaid amendment;

And whereas, the whole number of states in the United States is thirty-seven, to wit: New Hampshire, Massachusetts, Rhode Island, Connecticut, New York, New Jersey, Pennsylvania, Delaware, Maryland, Virginia, North Carolina, South Carolina, Georgia, Vermont, Kentucky, Tennessee, Ohio, Louisiana, Indiana, Mississippi, Illinois, Alabama, Maine, Missouri, Arkansas, Michigan, Florida, Texas, Iowa, Wisconsin, Minnesota, California, Oregon, Kansas, West Virginia, Nevada and Nebraska;

And whereas, the twenty-three states first above named, whose legislatures have ratified the said proposed amendment, and the six states next after named, as having ratified the said proposed amendment by newly constituted and established bodies, together constitute three-fourths of the whole number of states in the United States:

Now, therefore, be it known, that I, WILLIAM H. SEWARD, secretary of state of the United States, by virtue and in pursuance of the second section of the act of congress, approved the twentieth of April, eighteen hundred and eighteen, hereinbefore cited, do hereby certify, that, if the resolutions of the legislatures of Ohio and New Jersey, ratifying the aforesaid amendment, are to be deemed as remaining of full force and effect, notwithstanding the subsequent resolutions of the legislatures of those states, which purport to withdraw the consent of said states from such ratification, then the aforesaid amendment has been ratified in the manner hereinbefore mentioned, and so has become valid, to all intents and purposes, as a part of the constitution of the United States.

In testimony whereof, I have hereunto set my hand, and caused the seal of the department of state to be affixed.

Done at the city of Washington, the twentieth day of July, in the year of our Lord one thousand eight hundred and sixty-eight, and of the Independence of the United States of America the ninety-third.

[L. S.]

WILLIAM H. SEWARD,
Secretary of State.

WILLIAM H. SEWARD, *Secretary of State of the United States:*

TO ALL TO WHOM THESE PRESENTS MAY COME, GREETING:

WHEREAS, by an act of congress, passed on the twentieth of April, one thousand eight hundred and eighteen, entitled "An act to provide for the publication of the laws of the United States, and for other purposes," it is declared that, whenever official notice shall have been received at the department of state that any amendment which heretofore has been and hereafter may be proposed to the constitution of the United States has been adopted according to the provisions of the constitution, it shall be the duty of the said secretary of state, forthwith, to cause the said amendment to be published in the newspapers authorized to promulgate the laws, with his certificate, specifying the states by which the same may have been adopted, and that the same has become valid, to all intents and purposes, as a part of the constitution of the United States.

And whereas, the congress of the United States, on or about the sixteenth day of June, one thousand eight hundred and sixty-six, submitted to the legislatures of the several states a proposed amendment to the constitution, in the following words, to wit:

"Joint Resolution proposing an Amendment to the Constitution of the United States.

"*Be it Resolved,* By the senate and house of representatives of the United States of America, in congress assembled (two-thirds of both houses concurring), That the following article be proposed to the legislatures of the several states as an amendment to the constitution of the United States, which, when ratified by three-fourths of said legislatures, shall be valid as part of the constitution, namely:"

(See Article XIV, above.)

And whereas, the senate and house of representatives of the congress of the United States, on the twenty-first day of July, one thousand eight hundred and sixty-eight, adopted and transmitted to the department of state a concurrent resolution, which concurrent resolution is in the words and figures following, to wit:

"IN SENATE OF THE UNITED STATES,
"*July* 21, 1868.

"WHEREAS, the legislatures of the states of Connecticut, Tennessee, New Jersey, Oregon, Vermont, West Virginia, Kansas, Missouri, Indiana, Ohio, Illinois, Minnesota, New York, Wisconsin, Pennsylvania, Rhode Island, Michigan, Nevada, New Hampshire, Massachusetts, Nebraska, Maine, Iowa, Arkansas, Florida, North Carolina, Alabama, South Carolina and Louisiana, being three-fourths and more of the several states of the Union, have ratified the fourteenth article of amendment to the constitution of the United States, duly proposed by two-thirds of each house of the thirty-ninth congress; therefore,

Resolved, By the senate (the house of representatives concurring), That said fourteenth article is hereby declared to be a part of the constitution of the United States, and it shall be duly promulgated as such, by the secretary of state.

"Attest: GEO. C. GORHAM, *Secretary.*"

"IN THE HOUSE OF REPRESENTATIVES,
July 21, 1868.

"*Resolved,* That the house of representatives concur in the foregoing concurrent resolution of the senate, 'declaring the ratification of the fourteenth article of amendment of the constitution of the United States.'

"Attest: EDWD. McPHERSON, *Clerk.*"

And whereas, official notice has been received at the department of late that the legislatures of the several states next hereinafter named, have, at the times respectively herein mentioned, taken the proceedings hereinafter recited, upon or in relation to the ratification of the said proposed amendment, called article fourteenth, namely: The legislature of Connecticut ratified the amendment June 30th, 1866; the legislature of New Hampshire ratified it July 7th, 1866; the legislature of Tennessee ratified it July 19th, 1866; the legislature of New Jersey ratified it September 11th, 1866, and the legislature of the same state passed a resolution in April, 1868, to withdraw its consent to it; the legislature of Oregon ratified it September 19th, 1866; the legislature of Texas rejected it November 1st, 1866; the legislature of Vermont ratified it on or previous to November 9th, 1866; the legislature of Georgia rejected it November 13th, 1866; and the leg's-lature of the same state ratified it July 21st, 1868; the legislature of North Carolina rejected it December 4th, 1866, and the legislature of the same state ratified it July 4th, 1868; the legislature of South Carolina rejected it December 20th, 1866, and the legislature of the same state ratified it July 9th, 1868; the legislature of Virginia rejected it January 9th, 1867; the legislature of Kentucky rejected it January 10th, 1867; the legislature of New York ratified it January 10th, 1867; the legislature of Ohio ratified it January 11th, 1867, and the legislature of the same state passed a resolution in January, 1868, to withdraw its consent to it; the legislature of Illinois ratified it January 15th, 1867; the legislature of West Virginia ratified it January 16th, 1867; the legislature of Kansas ratified it January 18th, 1867; the legislature of Maine ratified it January 19th, 1867; the legislature of Nevada ratified it January 22d, 1867; the legislature of Missouri ratified it on or previous to January 26th, 1867; the legislature of Indiana ratified it January 26th, 1867; the legislature of Minnesota ratified it February 1st, 1867; the legislature of Rhode Island ratified it February 7th, 1867; the legislature of Delaware rejected it February 7th, 1867; the legislature of Wisconsin ratified it February 13th, 1867; the legislature of Pennsylvania ratified it February 13th, 1867; the legislature of Michigan ratified it February 15th, 1867; the legislature of Massachusetts ratified it March 20th, 1867; the legislature of Maryland rejected it March 23d, 1867; the legislature of Nebraska ratified it June 15th, 1867; the legislature of Iowa ratified it April 3d, 1868; the legislature of Arkansas ratified it April 6th, 1868; the legislature of Florida ratified it June 9th, 1868; the legislature of Louisiana ratified it July 9th, 1868; and the legislature of Alabama ratified it July 13th, 1868.

Now, therefore, be it known, that I, WILLIAM H. SEWARD, secretary of state of the United States, in execution of the aforesaid act, and of the aforesaid concurrent resolution of the 21st of July, 1868, and in conformance thereto, do hereby direct the said proposed amendment to the constitution of the United States to be published in the newspapers authorized to promulgate the laws of the United States, and I do hereby certify, that the said proposed amendment has been adopted in the manner hereinbefore mentioned by the states specified in the said concurrent resolution, namely: The States of Connecticut, New Hampshire, Tennessee, New Jersey, Oregon, Vermont, New York, Ohio, Illinois, West Virginia, Kansas, Maine, Nevada, Missouri, Indiana, Minnesota, Rhode Island, Wisconsin, Pennsylvania, Michigan, Massachusetts, Nebraska, Iowa, Arkansas, Florida, North Carolina, Louisiana, South Carolina, Alabama, and also by the legislature of the State of Georgia, the States thus specified being more than three-fourths of the States of the United States.

And I do further certify, that the said amendment has become valid to all intents and purposes, as a part of the Constitution of the United States.

In testimony whereof, I have hereunto set my hand, and caused the seal of the department of state to be affixed.

Done at the city of Washington, this twenty-eighth day of July, in the year of our Lord one thousand eight hundred and sixty-eight, and of the

[L. S.] Independence of the United States of America the ninety-third.

WILLIAM H. SEWARD,
Secretary of State.

ARTICLE XV.

SECTION 1.

The right of citizens of the United States to vote shall not be denied or abridged by the United States or by any state on account of race, color, or previous condition of servitude.

SECTION 2.

The congress shall have power to enforce this article by appropriate legislation.

The following is the certificate of the secretary of state of the United States, announcing the ratification of the foregoing article:

HAMILTON FISH, *Secretary of State of the United States;*

TO ALL TO WHOM THESE PRESENTS MAY COME, GREETING:

KNOW YE, That the congress of the United States, on or about the twenty-seventh day of February, in the year one thousand eight hundred and sixty-nine, passed a resolution in the words and figures following, to wit:

"A resolution proposing an Amendment to the Constitution of the United States.

"*Resolved,* By the senate and house of representatives of the United States of America, in congress assembled (two-thirds of both houses concurring), That the following article be proposed to the legislatures of the several states as an amendment to the constitution of the United States, which, when ratified by three-fourths of said legislatures, shall be valid as part of the constitution, namely:"

(See Article XV, above.)

And, further, that it appears from official documents on file in this department, that the amendment to the constitution of the United States, proposed as aforesaid, has been ratified by the legislatures of the states of North Carolina, West Virginia, Massachusetts, Wisconsin, Maine, Louisiana, Michigan, South Carolina, Pennsylvania, Arkansas, Connecticut, Florida, Illinois, Indiana, New York, New Hampshire, Nevada, Vermont, Virginia, Alabama, Missouri, Mississippi, Ohio, Iowa, Kansas, Minnesota, Rhode Island, Nebraska, and Texas, in all, twenty-nine states;

And, further, that the states whose legislatures have so ratified the said proposed amendment constitute three-fourths of the whole number of states in the United States;

And, further, that it appears, from an official document on file in this department, that the legislature of the state of New York has since passed resolutions claiming to withdraw the said ratification of the said amendment which had been made by the legislature of that state, and of which official notice had been filed in this department;

And further, that it appears, from an official document on file in this department, that the legislature of Georgia has, by resolution, ratified the said proposed amendment:

Now, therefore, be it known, that I, HAMILTON FISH, secretary of state of the United States, by virtue and in pursuance of the second section of the act of congress approved the twentieth day of April, in the year eighteen hundred and eighteen, entitled "An act to provide for the publication of the laws of the United States, and for other purposes," do hereby certify, that the amendment aforesaid has become valid to all intents and purposes as part of the constitution of the United States.

In testimony whereof, I have hereunto set my hand, and caused the seal of the department of state to be affixed.

Done at the city of Washington, this thirtieth day of March, in the year of our Lord one thousand [L. S.] eight hundred and seventy, and of the Independence of the United States the ninety-fourth,

HAMILTON FISH.

Analysis of the Constitution of the United States.

ARTICLE I

SECTION 1. Legislative powers; in whom vested.

SEC. 2 House of Representatives, how and by whom chosen—Qualifications of a Representative—Representatives and direct taxes, how apportioned—Census—Vacancies to be filled—Power of choosing officers, and of impeachment.

SEC. 3 Senators, how and by whom chosen—How classified—State Executive to make tempoary appointments, in case, etc.—Qualifications of a Senator—President of the Senate, his right to vote—President pro tem., and other officers of the Senate, how chosen—Power to try impeachments—When President is tried, Chief Justice to preside—Sentence.

SEC. 4. Times, etc., of holding elections, how prescribed—One Session in each year.

SEC. 5. Membership—Quorum—Adjournments—Rules—Power to punish or expel—Journal—Time of adjournments limited, unless, etc.

SEC. 6. Compensation—Privileges—Disqualifications in certain cases

SEC. 7. House to originate all revenue bills—Veto—Bill may be passed by two-thirds of each house, notwithstanding, etc.—Bill not returned in ten days—Provisions as to all orders, etc., except, etc.

SEC. 8. Powers of Congress.

SEC. 9. Provision as to migration or importation of certain persons—Habeas Corpus—Bills of attainder, etc.—Taxes, how apportioned—No export duty—No commercial preferences—No money drawn from treasury, unless, etc.—No titular nobility—Officers not to receive presents, unless, etc.

SEC. 10. States prohibited from the exercise of certain powers.

ARTICLE II.

SECTION 1. President; his term of office—Electors of President; number and how appointed—Electors to vote on the same day—Qualification of President—on whom his duties devolve in case of his removal, death, etc.—President's compensation—His oath.

SEC. 2. President to be commander-in-chief—He may require opinion of, etc., and may pardon—Treaty-making power—Nomination of certain officers—When President may fill vacancies.

SEC. 3. President shall communicate to Congress—He may convene and adjourn Congress, in case, etc.; shall receive embassadors, execute laws, and commission officers.

SEC. 4. All civil offices forfeited for certain crimes.

ARTICLE III.

SECTION 1. Judicial power—Tenure—Compensation.

SEC. 2. Judicial power; to what cases it extends—Original jurisdiction of Supreme Court—Appellate—Trial by jury, except, etc.—Trial, where.

SEC. 3. Treason defined—Proof of—Punishment of.

ARTICLE IV.

SEC. 1 Each State to give credit to the public acts, etc, of every other State.

SEC. 2. Privileges of citizens of each State—Fugitives from justice to be delivered up—Persons held to service having escaped, to be delivered up.

SEC. 3. Admission of new States—Power of Congress over territory and other property

SEC. 4. Republican form of government guaranteed—Each State to be protected.

ARTICLE V.
Constitution; how amended—Proviso.
ARTICLE VI.
Certain debts, etc., adopted—Supremacy of Constitution, treaties, and laws of the United States—Oath to support Constitution, by whom taken—No religious test.
ARTICLE VII.
What ratification shall establish Constitution.
AMENDMENTS.
I. Religious establishment prohibited—Freedom of speech, of the press, and right to petition.
II. Right to keep and bear arms.
III. No soldier to be quartered in any house, unless, etc.
IV. Right of search and seizure regulated.
V. Provisions concerning prosecution, trial and punishment—Private property not to be used for public use, without, etc.
VI. Further provision respecting criminal prosecution.
VII. Right of trial by jury secured.
VIII. Excessive bail or fines and cruel punishments prohibited.
IX. Rule of construction.
X. Same subject.
XI. Same subject.
XII. Manner of choosing President and Vice President.
XIII. Slavery abolished.
XIV. Citizenship.
XV. Rights of citizens to vote.

The first **Ten Amendments** became a part of the Constitution on and after **Dec. 15, 1791.**
The **Eleventh Amendment** took effect in 1798.
The **Twelfth Amendment** in 1804.
The **Thirteenth Amendment** in 1865.
The **Fourteenth Amendment** in 1868.
The **Fifteenth** and last **Amendment** in 1870.

COMMENTS ON THE CONSTITUTION OF THE UNITED STATES.

JUSTICE SAM'L F. MILLER.
(Senior Justice, United States Supreme Court.)

HISTORY.

As soon as it became apparent to the Constitutional Convention of 1787 that the new government must be a **nation** resting for its support upon the people over whom it exercised authority, and not a **league of independent States** brought together under a compact on which each State should place its own construction, the question of the relative power of those States in the new government became a subject of serious difference. There were those in the convention who insisted that in the legislative body, where the most important powers must necessarily reside, the states should, as in the articles of confederation, stand upon a perfect equality, each State having but one vote; and this feature was finally retained in that part of the Constitution which vested in Congress the election of President, when there should be a failure to elect by the electoral college in the regular mode prescribed by that instrument.

The Composition of the Senate.

The contest in the convention became narrowed to the composition of the Senate, after it had been determined that the legislature should consist of two distinct bodies, sitting apart from each other, and voting separately. One of these was to be a popular body elected directly by the people at short intervals. The other was to be a body more limited in numbers, with longer term of office; and this, with the manner of their appointment, was designed to give stability to the policy of the government and to be in some sense a restraint upon sudden impulses of popular will.

The House of Representatives.

With regard to the popular branches of the legislature, there did not seem to be much difficulty in establishing the proposition, that in some general way each state should be represented in it in proportion to its population, and that each member of the body should vote with equal effect on all questions before it, but when it was sought by the larger and more populous States, as Virginia, Pennsylvania and Massachusetts, to apply this principle to the composition of the Senate, the resistance of the smaller States became stubborn, and they refused to yield. The feeling arising under the discussion of this subject came nearer causing the disruption of the convention than any which agitated its deliberations. It was finally settled by an agreement that every State, however small, should have two representatives in the Senate of the United States, and no State should have any more, and that no amendment of the Constitution should deprive any State of its equal suffrage without its consent. As the Senate has the same power in enacting laws as the House of Representatives, and as each State has its two votes in that body, it will be seen that the smaller States secured, when they are in a united majority, the practical power of defeating all legislation which was unacceptable to them.

The Plan Has Worked Well.

What has the experience of a century taught us on this question? It is certainly true that there have been many expressions of dissatisfaction with the operation of a principle which gives to each of the six New England States, situated compactly together, as much power in the Senate in making laws, in ratifying treaties, and in confirming or rejecting appointment to office, as is given to the great State of New York, which, both in population and wealth, exceeds all the New England States, and nearly if not quite equals them in territory.

But if we are to form an opinion from demonstrations against, or attempts to modify, this feature of the Constitution, or any future which concerns exclusively the functions of the Senate, we shall be compelled to say that the ablest of our public men, and the wisdom of the Nation, are in the main satisfied with the work of the convention on this point after a hundred years of observation. And it is believed that the existence of an important body in our system of government, not wholly the mere representative of population, has exercised a wholesome conservatism on many occasions in our history.

THE EXECUTIVE.

It was urged against our Constitution by many liberty-loving men, both in the Convention and out of it, that it conferred upon the executive, a single individual, whose election for a term of four years was carefully removed from the direct vote of the people, powers dangerous to the existence of free government. It was said that with the appointment of all the officers of the government, civil and military, the sword and the purse of the Nation in his hands, the power to prevent the enactment of laws to which he did not assent—unless they could be passed over his objection by a vote of two-thirds in each of the two legislative houses—and the actual use of this power for four years without interruption, an ambitious man of great personal popularity, could establish his power during his own life, and transmit it to his family as a perpetual dynasty. Perhaps of all objections made to important features of the Constitution this one had more plausibility, and was urged with most force. But if the century of our experience has demonstrated anything, it is the fallacy of this objection and of all the reasons urged in its support.

THE ELECTORAL COLLEGE.

The objection that the electoral college was a contrivance to remove the appointment of the President from the control of proper suffrage, was, if it had any merit, speedily overcome without any infraction of the Constitution by the democratic tendencies of the people. The electors composing the college, who it was supposed would each exercise an independent judgment in casting his vote for President, soon came to be elected themselves on distinct pledges made beforehand, that they would vote for some person designated as a popular favorite for that office. So that at the present time the electors of each State, in sending to the capital their votes for President, do but record the instruction of a majority of the citizens voting in their State. The term of four years for the Presidential office is now deemed too long for any one, while there are many who would desire that it should be made longer, say seven or ten years.

Appointment to Office.

The power of appointment to office requires the consent of the Senate to its exercise; and that body has asserted its right of refusing that assent so courageously and so freely that there can be no real fear of its successful use by the President in a manner to endanger the liberty of the country, unless the Senate itself shall be utterly corrupted. Nor can the means for such corruption be obtained from the public treasury until Congress in both branches shall become so degenerate as to consent to such use.

Nor have we had in this country any want of ambitious men, who have earnestly desired the Presidency, or having it once, have longed for the continuation of it at the end of the lawful term. And it may be said that it is almost a custom when a President has filled his office for one term acceptably, that he is to be re-elected, if his political party continues to be a popular majority. Our people have also shown the usual hero worship of successful military chieftains, and rewarded them by the election to the Presidency. In proof of this it is only necessary to mention the names of Washington, Jackson, Harrison, Taylor, and Grant. In some of them there has been no want of ambition, nor of the domineering disposition, which is often engendered by the use of military power. Yet none of these men have had more than two terms of office.

Cæsarism.

And though a few years ago one of the most largely circulated newspapers of the United States wrote in its paper day after day articles headed "Cæsarism," charging danger to the Republic from one of its greatest benefactors and military chiefs, it excited no attention but derision, and deserved no other.

No danger from the President.

There is no danger in this country from the power reposed in the Presidential office. There is, as sad experience shows, far more danger from nihilism and assassination, than from ambition in our public servants. So far have the incumbents of the Presidency, during the hundred years of its history, been from grasping, or attempting to grasp, powers not warranted by the Constitution, and so far from exercising the admitted power of that office in a despotic manner a candid student of our political history during that time cannot fail to perceive that no one of the three great departments of the government—the Legislative, the Executive, and the Judicial—has been more shorn of its just powers, or crippled in the exercise of them, than the Presidency.

In regard to the function of appointment to office—perhaps the most important of the executive duties—the spirit of the Constitution requires that the President shall exercise freely his best judgment and follow its most sincere conviction in selecting proper men.

The Purpose of the Constitution Defeated.

It is undeniable that for many years past, by the gradual growth of custom, it has come to pass that in the nomination of officers by the President, he has so far submitted to be governed by the wishes and recommendations of interested members of the two houses of Congress, that the purpose of the Constitution investing this power in him, and the right of the public to hold him personally responsible for each and every appointment he makes, is largely defeated. In other words, the great principle lying at the foundation of all free governments, that the legislative and executive departments shall be kept separate, is invaded by the participation of the members of Congress in the exercise of the appointing powers.

History teaches us in no mistaken language how often customs and practices, which were originated without lawful warrant and opposed to the sound construction of the law, have come to overload and pervert it, as commentators on the text of Holy Scriptures have established doctrines wholly at variance with its true spirit.

THE CENTRAL POINT OF CONTEST—A CONFEDERACY OR A NATION.

Without considering many minor objections made to the Constitution during the process of its formation and adoption let us proceed to that one which was the central point of contest then, and which, transferred to the question of construing that instrument, has continued to divide statesmen and politicians to the present time. The convention was divided in opinion between those who desired a strong National government, capable of sustaining itself by the exercise of suitable powers, and invested by the Constitution with such powers, and those who, regarding the articles of confederation as a basis, proposed to strengthen the General Government in a very few particulars, leaving it chiefly dependent on the action of the states themselves for its support and for the enforcement of its laws.

Let us deal tenderly with the **articles of confederation.** We should feel grateful for any instrumentality which helped us in the day of our earliest struggle. Very few are now found to say anything for these articles, yet they constituted the nominal bond which held the States together during the war of Independence. It must be confessed that the sense of common cause and a common danger probably did more to produce this united effort than other motives. But the articles served their purpose for the occasion; and though, when the pressure of imminent danger was removed they were soon discovered to be a rope of sand, let them rest in a peaceful, honorable remembrance.

Between those who favored a strong government of the Union and those who were willing to grant it but little power at the expense of the states, there were various shades of opinion; and while it was the prevailing sentiment of the convention that "the greatest interest of every true American was the consolidation of the Union" there were many who were unwilling to attain this subject by detaching the necessary powers from the States and conferring them on the National Government.

These divergent views had their effect, both in the constitutional convention and in those held for its ratification.

Compromises and Concessions.

Around this central point the contest raged, and it was only by compromises and concessions, dictated by the necessity of each yielding something for the common good—so touchingly mentioned in the letter of the convention to Congress—that the result was reached. The **patriotism** and the **love of liberty of each party** were undisputed. The anxiety for a government which would best reconcile the possession of powers essential to the State government with those necessary to the existence and efficiency of the government of the Union, was equal, and the long struggle since the adoption of the Constitution on the same line of thought, in its construction, shows how firmly these different views are imbedded in our political theories.

The Party of State Rights.

The party which came to be called the party of State rights had always dreaded that the alleged supremacy of the National power would overthrow the State governments, or control them to an extent incompatible with any useful existence. Their opponents have been equally confident that powers essential to the successful conduct of the General Government, which either expressly or by implication are conferred on it by the Constitution, were denied to it by the State Right party. The one believed in danger to the States, from the theory which construed with a free and liberal rule the grants of power to the General Government, and the other believed that such a construction of the constitution was consistent with the purpose and spirit of that instrument and essential to the perpetuity of the Nation.

The Teaching of Experience in the Civil War.

If experience can teach anything on the subject of theories of government the late civil war teaches unmistakably that those who believed the source of danger to be in the strong powers of the Federal Government were in error, and that those who believed that such powers were necessary to its safe conduct and continued existence were in the right. The attempted destruction of the Union by eleven States, which were part of it, and the apparent temporary success of the effort was undoubtedly due to the capacity of the States under the Constitution for concerted action, by organized movements, with all the machinery ready at hand to raise armies and establish a central government. And the ultimate failure of the attempt is attributed with equal clearness to the exercise of those powers of the General Government under the Constitution, which were denied to it by extreme advocates of State Rights. And that this might no longer be matter of dispute, **three new amendments to the Constitution** were adopted at the close of the struggle, which, while keeping in view the principles of our complex form of State and Federal government, and seeking to disturb the distribution of powers among them as little as consistent with the wisdom acquired by a sorrowful experience, these amendments confer additional powers on the government of the Union, and place additional restraints upon the States. May it be long before such an awful lesson is again needed to decide upon disputed questions of Constitutional law.

A Possible Danger.

It is not out of place to remark that while the pendulum of public opinion has swung with much force away from the extreme point of State Rights doctrine, there may be danger of its reaching an extreme point on the other side. In my opinion, the just and equal observance of the rights of the States, and of the **General Government**, as defined by the present Constitution, is as necessary to the permanent prosperity of the country, and to its existence for another century, as it has been for the one whose close we are now celebrating.

OUR CONSTITUTION UNIQUE.

Other nations speak of their constitutions, which are the growth of centuries of government, and the maxims of experience and the traditions of ages. Many of them deserve the veneration they receive. But a constitution, in the American sense of the word, as accepted in all the states of North and South America, means an instrument in writing, defining the powers of government, and distributing those powers among different bodies of magistrates for their more judicious exercise.

The constitution of the United States not only did this as regards a National government, but it established a federation of many states by the same instrument, in which the usual fatal defects in such unions have been corrected, with such felicity that during the 100 years of its existence the union of the states has grown stronger, and has received within that Union other States exceeding in number those of the original federation.

The First Important Written Constitution.

It is not only the first important written Constitution found in history, but is the first one which contained the principles necessary to the successful confederation of numerous powerful States. I do not forget, nor do I mean to disparage, our sister, the federal republic of Switzerland. But her continuance as an independent power in Europe is so largely due to her compact territory, her inaccessible mountains, her knowledge of the necessity of union to safety, and the policy of her powerful neighbors, which demands of each other the recognition of her rights, that she hardly forms an exception. But Switzerland stands to-day—may she ever stand—as the **oldest witness** to the capacity of a republican federation of States for sound government, for the security of freedom, and resistance to disintegrating tendencies.

Its Results Remarkable.

But when we look to the results of confederation in the Olympic Council, and the Achaian League of ancient history, and in modern times to the States of Holland and the old German Empire, we must admit that the **United States presents the most remarkable**, if not the only successful, happy, and prosperous, federated government of the world. Let us consider for a moment the evidence of this. When the Constitution was finally ratified, and Rhode Island also accepted it, the government was composed of thirteen States. It now numbers **thirty-eight**. The inhabited area of those States was found between the Alleghany Mountains and the Atlantic Ocean, a region which, when we now look over a map of the United States, seems to be but the eastern border of the great Republic. Its area now includes all the territory between the Atlantic and Pacific Oceans—a distance of over three thousand miles east and west—and between the St. Lawrence and the great lakes on the north, and the Gulf and States of Mexico on the south. Besides these thirty-eight states, the remainder of this great region is divided into 8 Territories, with an **organized government** in each, several of which are ready to be admitted into the Union as States, under a provision of the Constitution on that subject, and in accordance with the settled policy of the Nation. The Thirteen States which originally organized this government had a population believed to be, in round numbers, 3,000,000, many of whom were slaves. To-day it seems probable that 60,000,000 are embraced in the United States, in which there breathes no soul who owns any man master.

The Impoverished Condition of the Country at the Close of the Revolutionary War.

To-day I do not **hesitate** to make the **assertion**, that if you count only that which is real wealth, and not accumulated capital in the shape of evidences of debt—which is but a burden upon such property—I mean, if you count lands and houses and furniture, and horses and cattle and jewels—all that is tangible and contributes to the comfort and pleasure of life, the **United States** is to-day the **wealthiest country** upon the face of the globe, and is the only great government which is so rapidly paying off its National debt that it is besieging its creditors to accept their money not yet due, with a reasonable rebate for interest.

THREE IMPORTANT WARS.

Under the government established by this Constitution we have, in the century we are now overlooking, had three important wars, such as are always accompanied by hazardous shocks to all governments.

The War With England.

In the first of these we encountered the British Empire, the most powerful nation on the globe—a nation which had **successfully resisted Napoleon**, with all the power of Europe at his back. If we did not attain all we fought for in that contest, we displayed an energy and courage which commanded for us an honorable stand among the nations of the earth.

The War With Mexico.

In the second—the war with Mexico—while our reputation as a warlike people suffered no diminution, we made large accessions of valuable territory, out of which States have been since made members of the Union.

The Civil War.

The last war—the recent civil war—in the number of men engaged in it, in the capacity of the weapons and instruments of destruction brought into operation, and in the importance of the result to humanity at large, must be esteemed the **greatest war** that the history of the world presents. It was brought about by the attempt of eleven of the States to destroy the Union. This was resisted by the government of that Union under the powers granted to it by the Constitution.

Results of the Civil War.

Its results were the emancipation of 3,000,000 of slaves, the suppression of the attempt to dissever the Union, the resumption of an accelerated march in the growth, prosperity, and happiness of this country. It also taught the lesson of the **indestructibility of the Union**, of the wisdom of the principles on which it is founded, and it astonished the nations of the world, and inspired them with a respect which they had never before entertained for our country.

Europe to Learn a Lesson.

I venture to hope that with the earnest gaze of the wisest and ablest minds of the age turned with profound interest to the experiment of the federative system, under our American Constitution, it may suggest something to relieve the nations of Europe from burdens so heavy that if not soon removed they must crush the social fabric. Those great nations can not go on forever adding millions upon millions to their public debts, mainly for the support of permanent standing armies, while those armies make such heavy drafts upon the able-bodied men whose productive industry is necessary to the support of the people and of the government. I need not dwell on this unpleasant subject further than to say, that these standing armies are rendered necessary by the perpetual dread of war with neighboring nations.

In the principles of our Constitution by which the autonomy and domestic government of each State are preserved, while the **supremacy** of the **General Government** at once forbids war between the States, and enables it to enforce peace among them, we may discern the elements of political forces sufficient for the rescue of European civilization from this great disaster.

The Constitution Not the Sole Reason of our Growth.

Do I claim for the Constitution, whose creation we have been celebrating, the sole merit of the wonderful epitome which I have presented of the progress of this country to greatness, to prosperity, to happiness and honor? Nay, I do not; though language used by men of powerful intellect and great knowledge of history might be my justification if I did.

Mr. Bancroft.

Mr. Bancroft, the venerable historian, who has devoted a long and laborious life to a history of his country that is a monument to his genius and his learning, says of the closing hours of the Convention: "The members were awe-struck at the result of their councils, the Constitution was a nobler work than any one of them believed it possible to devise."

THE EXECUTIVE DEPARTMENT

THE PRESIDENT.

HOW CHOSEN.—Elections for President and Vice-President are held on the Tuesday next after the first Monday in November in every fourth year, at which **Electors** are chosen.

The number of Presidential Electors is equal to the whole number of Senators and Representatives in Congress.

DUTIES OF ELECTORS.—The Electors of each State must meet and give their votes on the first Wednesday in December after the election. The electors must make and sign three certifi-

THE WHITE HOUSE

cates of all the votes given by them, each of which certificates must contain two distinct lists; one of the votes for President, and the other of the votes for Vice-President; they must then seal up the certificates, and certify upon each that the lists of all the votes given are contained therein. The certificates are disposed of as follows:

The Electors in each State appoint a person to take charge of and deliver to the President of the Senate at the seat of Government, before the first Wednesday in January next ensuing, one of the certificates.

They shall forthwith forward by the postoffice to the President of the Senate at the seat of Government, one other of the certificates.

They shall forthwith cause the other of the certificates to be delivered to the judge of that district in which the electors shall assemble.

Congress shall be in session on the second Wednesday in February, succeeding every meeting of the electors, and the certificates shall then be opened, the votes counted, and the persons to fill the offices of President and Vice-President ascertained and declared, agreeable to the Constitution.

VACANCIES.—In case of removal, death, or resignation of the **President**, his powers and duties devolve upon the **Vice-President**. In case of removal, death, or resignation of both President and Vice-President, the **President of the Senate,** or if there is none, then the **Speaker of the House of Representatives,** for the time being, shall act as President until the disability is removed, or a President elected.

NOTIFICATION.—Whenever the offices of President and Vice-President both become vacant, the Secretary of State issues a notice of the election to the Executive of every State of the fact.

VACANCY.—Electors will be appointed or chosen in the several States as follows: In case the notification is made two months previous to the first Wednesday in December then next ensuing, the electors shall be appointed or chosen within **thirty-four days** preceding such first Wednesday.

If there shall not be the space of two months between the date of such notification and such first Wednesday in December, and if the term for which the President and Vice-President last in office were elected will not expire on the third day of March next ensuing, the electors shall be chosen within thirty-four days preceding the first Wednesday in December in the next year ensuing. But if there shall not be the space of two months between the date of such notification and the first Wednesday in December then next ensuing, and if the term for which the President and Vice-President last in office were elected will expire on the third day of March next ensuing, no electors are to be chosen.

TERM AND SALARY OF THE PRESIDENT.—The President holds office for four years. His salary is $50,000 a year, with free residence in the White House, and sundry perquisites pertaining thereto.

POWERS AND DUTIES OF THE PRESIDENT.—The President is Commander-in-Chief of the Army and Navy of the United States; he has power to grant pardons and reprieves for offences against the United States; he makes treaties by and with the advice and consent of the Senate; he nominates, and with the consent of the Senate, appoints all Cabinet, Diplomatic, Judicial, and Executive officers; he has power to convene Congress, or the Senate only; he communicates to Congress by message at every session, the condition of the Union, and recommends such measures as he deems expedient; he receives all Ambassadors, and other Foreign Ministers; he takes care that the laws are faithfully executed, and the public business transacted.

THE PRESIDENT'S CABINET.

The heads of the seven principal departments constitute, according to custom, the President's cabinet, which are as follows:

The **Secretary of State**, the **Secretary of the Treasury**, the **Secretary of War**, the **Secretary of the Navy**, the **Secretary of the Interior**, the **Postmaster-General**, and the **Attorney-General**.

They are appointed by the President, by and with the advice and consent of the Senate, and are removable at pleasure. Each one has in general, the appointment of the subordinate officers, clerks, employés, agents, etc., in his Department. The salary of each Cabinet officer is $8,000 a year.

SALARIES OF OFFICERS, CLERKS, AND EMPLOYES IN THE EXECUTIVE OFFICES.

Private Secretary to the President, $3,250; Assistant secretary, $2,250; two executive clerks, each $2,000; Stenographer, Steward, and one clerk, each, $1,800; Messenger and Usher, $1,200; one clerk, $1,400; one clerk and four messengers (two mounted) each, $1,200.

SALARIES OF EMPLOYES AT EXECUTIVE MANSION.

Furnace-keeper, $864; one night watchman, $900; one night usher, one day usher at Secretary's door, and two doorkeepers, each, $1,200; one day usher at President's door, $1,400.

APPOINTMENTS BY THE PRESIDENT.

STATE DEPARTMENT.

By and with the Advice and Consent of the Senate, for an Unlimited Term, or during the pleasure of the President.

The Secretary of State; the Assistant Secretaries of State; Envoys Extraordinary and Ministers Plenipotentiary; Ministers Resident; Chargés d' Affaires; Secretaries of Legation; Consuls-General; Consuls; Commercial Agents.

By the President Alone.— Interpreters and Consular Clerks.

TREASURY DEPARTMENT.

By and with the Advice and Consent of the Senate—FOR AN UNLIMITED TERM.

The Secretary of the Treasury. The Assistant Secretaries. Supervising Inspector-General of Steam Vessels. Supervising Surgeon-General of the Marine Hospital Service. First Comptroller. Second Comptroller. Commissioner of Customs. First Auditor. Second Auditor. Third Auditor. Fourth Auditor. Fifth Auditor. Sixth Auditor. Treasurer. Register. Commissioner of Internal Revenue. Deputy First Comptroller. Deputy Second Comptroller. Deputy Commissioner of Customs. Deputy First Auditor. Deputy Second Auditor. Deputy Third Auditor. Deputy Fourth Auditor. Deputy Fifth Auditor. Deputy Sixth Auditor. Assistant Treasurer. Assistant Registrar. Deputy Comptroller of the Currency. Deputy Commissioner of Internal Revenue. Superintendent of the Life-saving Service.

REVENUE MARINE SERVICE.

Captains. First Lieutenants. Second Lieutenants. Third Lieutenants. Chief Engineers.

ASSAY OFFICERS.

Superintendent, New York, New York. Assayer, New York, New York. Melter and Refiner, New York, New York. Assayer and Melter, Charlotte, North Carolina. Assayer, Boise City, Idaho. Assayer in charge, Helena, Montana. Melter, Helena, Montana.

MINT OFFICERS.

Philadelphia, Penn.—Superintendent, Assayer, Coiner, Engraver, Melter and Refiner.
San Francisco, Cal.—Superintendent, Assayer, Coiner, Melter and Refiner.
New Orleans, La.—Superintendent, Assayer, Coiner, Melter and Refiner.
Carson, Nev.—Superintendent, Assayer, Coiner, Melter, and Refiner.
Denver, Col.—Assayer in charge, Melter and Refiner.

COLLECTORS OF CUSTOMS.

Assistant Collectors of Customs. Appraisers of Customs. Collectors of Internal Revenue.

MISCELLANEOUS OFFICERS.

Examiners of Drugs. Supervising Inspectors of Steam Vessels. The members of the National Board of Health, three of whom are officers detailed from Departments.

By and with the Advice and Consent of the Senate—FOR FIVE YEARS.

Director of the Mint. Comptroller of the Currency.

By and with the Advice and Consent of the Senate—FOR FOUR YEARS.

Assistant Treasurers at Baltimore, Maryland; Boston, Massachusetts; Chicago, Illinois; Cincinnati, Ohio; New Orleans, Louisiana; New York City, New York; Philadelphia, Pennsylvania; St. Louis, Missouri; San Francisco, California.

Collectors, Surveyors, and Naval Officers of Customs.

By the President alone.

The Superintendent of the Coast and Geodetic Survey.

WAR DEPARTMENT.

By and with the Advice and Consent of the Senate—FOR LIFE OR GOOD BEHAVIOR.

The President makes Appointments of Officers of the United States Navy.

To fill vacancies in the lowest grade of Commissioned Officers in the Army, as follows:

One-fourth of the number from non-commissioned officers in the Army. The remaining vacancies not filled by the graduates from the Military Academy, are appointed from civil life.

NAVY DEPARTMENT.

By and with the Advice and Consent of the Senate—FOR FOUR YEARS.

Chiefs of seven bureaus of the Department, embracing: Yards and Docks, Equipment and Recruiting, Navigation, Ordnance, Construction and Repair, Steam Engineering, Provisions and Clothing, Medicines and Surgery. The first five officers are selected from the list of officers of the navy, not below the grade of commander. The chief of the Bureau of Construction and Repair must be a skillful naval constructor. The chief of the Bureau of Steam Engineering is appointed from the chief engineers of the navy. The chief of the Bureau of Provisions and Clothing is taken from the list of paymasters of the navy of not less than ten years' standing. The chief of the Bureau of Medicines and Surgery from the list of surgeons of the navy. These chiefs of Bureaus have the rank and pay of **commodore** while serving as such.

APPOINTMENTS IN THE UNITED STATES NAVY.

By and with the Advice and Consent of the Senate—OFFICES HELD DURING GOOD BEHAVIOR, OR UNTIL RETIRED.

All line officers on the active list, and all officers in the several **staff corps** of the navy are appointed as follows:

LINE OFFICERS.

Admiral, Vice Admiral, Rear-Admirals, Commodores, Captains, Commanders, Lieutenant-Commanders, Lieutenants, Masters, Ensigns, Midshipmen.

STAFF OFFICERS.

Medical Corps.—Medical Directors, Medical Inspectors, Surgeons, Assistant Surgeons.

Pay Corps.—Pay Directors, Pay Inspectors, Paymasters, Passed Assistant Paymasters, Assistant Paymasters.

Engineer Corps.—Chief Engineers of the three grades, viz.: Captains, Commanders, Lieutenant-Commanders, or Lieutenants; First Assistant Engineers, with rank of Lieutenants or Masters; Second Assistant Engineers, with rank of Masters or Ensigns. Chaplains. Naval Constructors and Assistant Naval Constructors. Civil Engineers and Naval Storekeepers. Professors of Mathematics.

INTERIOR DEPARTMENT.

By and with the Advice and Consent of the Senate—TERM UNLIMITED.

Secretary of the Interior. Assistant Secretary of the Interior. Architect of the Capitol Extension. Assistant Commissioner of Patents. Assistant Inspector of Gas Meters in the District of Columbia. Auditor of Railroad Accounts. Commissioner of Education. Commissioner of General Land Office. Commissioner of Indian Affairs. Commissioner of Patents. Commissioner of Pensions. Deputy Commissioner of Pensions. Director of Geological Survey. Examiners-in-Chief of Patent Office. Inspector of Gas Meters in the District of Columbia. Principal Clerk of Private Land Claims. Principal Clerk of Public Lands. Principal Clerk of Surveys. Recorder of Deeds for the District of Columbia. Recorder of General Land Office. Register of Wills for the District of Columbia. Superintendent of the Census. Supervisors of the Census.

By and with the Advice and Consent of the Senate—TERM OF FOUR YEARS.

Governors of Territories. Indian Agents. Indian Inspectors. Pension Agents. Receivers of Public Moneys. Registers of Land Offices. Secretaries of Territories. Surveyors-General.

*By and with the Advice and Consent of the Senate—
TERM OF ONE YEAR.*

Members of the Hot Spring Commission (Arkansas).
By the President.

Commissioners to Codify the Land Laws, for an unlimited term. Members of Board of Indian Commissioners, for an unlimited term. Government Directors of the Union Pacific Railroad Company, for a term of one year. Visitors to the Government Hospital for the Insane, for a term of six years.

POST-OFFICE DEPARTMENT.

By and with the Advice and Consent of the Senate.

THE POSTMASTER GENERAL,

who serves for and during the term of the President who appoints him, and for one month thereupon, thus differing from the terms of the other cabinet officers.

*By and with the Advice and Consent of the Senate—
TERM UNLIMITED.*

First, Second, and Third Assistant Postmasters-General.

*By and with the Advice and Consent of the Senate—
TERM OF FOUR YEARS, UNLESS SOONER REMOVED.*

The Postmaster at New York City.

Postmasters of the **first, second,** and **third** classes.

The commissions of all Postmasters appointed by the President, by and with the advice and consent of the Senate, are made out and recorded in the Post-Office Department, and are under the seal of the Department, and countersigned by the Postmaster-General.

DEPARTMENT OF JUSTICE.

*By and with the Advice and Consent of the Senate—
TERM UNLIMITED.*

The Attorney-General of the United States. Assistant Attorneys-General, of which there are three. Solicitor-General. Examiner of Claims in the Department of State. Solicitor of Internal Revenue. Solicitor of the Treasury. Assistant Solicitor of the Treasury.

DEPARTMENT OF AGRICULTURE.

*By and with the Advice and Consent of the Senate—
TERM UNLIMITED.*

The Commissioner of Agriculture.

JUDICIARY.

By and with the Advice and Consent of the Senate—TO HOLD THEIR OFFICES DURING GOOD BEHAVIOR.

The Chief-Justice and the Associate Justices of the Supreme Court of the United States. Circuit Judges of the United States. District Judges of the United States. Chief-Justice and Judges of the Court of Claims. Chief-Justice, and Associate Justices of the Supreme Court of the District of Columbia.

*By and with the Advice and Consent of the Senate—
TERM OF FOUR YEARS.*

Chief-Justice and Associate Justices of the Supreme Courts of the Territories. District Attorneys of the United States. Marshals of the United States Courts. Attorneys of the United States in the Territories. Marshals of the United States in the Territories.

Legislative Department

HIS Department consists of a **Senate** and **House of Representatives**.

Two Senators represent each State, and there being now thirty-eight States, the Senate is composed of seventy-six Senators.

THE SENATE.

Time and Manner of Electing Senators.

The Legislature of each State which is chosen next preceding the expiration of the time for which any Senator was elected, on the second Tuesday after meeting, proceeds to elect a Senator. A viva voce vote is taken in each House of the Legislature, and the name of the person receiving a majority of the whole number of votes cast, is entered on the journal.

At twelve o'clock, next day, the members of each house convene in joint assembly, and if the same person has received a majority of votes in both houses he is declared elected. But if not, the joint assembly proceeds to choose, and the person receiving a majority of all the votes, a majority of all the members elected to both houses being present and voting, is elected.

If on the first day no election is made, the joint assembly meets on each succeeding day, and must take at least one vote until a Senator is elected.

Principal Officers of the Senate.

A President (the Vice-President of the United States, or a Senator, elected President *pro tem*), a Secretary, a Chief Clerk, a Sergeant at Arms, and a Chaplain.

COMPENSATION.

Senators, each	$5,000
Secretary	4,896
Chief Clerk	3,000
5 Principal Clerks	2,592
Librarian	2,220
Assistant Librarian	1,800
6 Clerks in Secretary's office	2,220
5 Clerks in Secretary's office	2,100
Stationery Keeper	2,102
Assistant	1,800
2 Messengers, each	1,571
1 Special Policeman	1,296
4 Laborers in Secretary's office	720
Chaplain of Senate	980
Secretary to Vice-President	2,102
Sergeant-at-Arms and Doorkeeper	4,320
Clerk to the Sergeant-at-Arms	2,100
Assistant Doorkeeper	2,592
Acting Assistant Doorkeeper	$2,592
3 Acting Assistant Doorkeepers, each	1,500
Postmaster to the Senate	2,250
Assistant Postmaster and Mail Carrier	2,088
4 Mail Carriers, each	1,200
Messenger to the Vice President's room	1,440
Clerk to Committee on Appropriations	2,500
Assistant Clerk on Appropriations	1,700
Clerk of Printing Records	2,220

HALL OF REPRESENTATIVES, WASHINGTON.

THE AMERICAN MANUAL. 193

Clerk to Committee on [...]	2,220
Clerk to Committee on Claims	2,220
Clerk to Committee on Commerce	2,220
Clerk to Committee on the Judiciary	2,220
Clerk to Committee on Private Land Claims	2,220
Clerk to Committee on Naval Affairs	2,220
Clerk to Committee on Pensions	2,220
Clerk to Committee on Military Affairs	2,220
Clerk to Committee on Post-Offices and Post-Roads	2,220
Clerk to Committee on District of Columbia	2,220
Clerk to Joint Committee on the Library	2,220
Clerk to Committee on the Census	2,220
Superintendent Document Room	2,100
2 Assistants in Document Room, each	1,440
1 Page in Document Room	720
Superintendent of Folding Room	2,100
1 Assistant in Folding Room	1,200
24 Messengers (Assistant Doorkeepers), each	1,440
1 Messenger to Committee on Appropriations	1,440
Messenger in charge of Store Room	1,200
Messenger in Official Reporter's Room	1,200
Chief Engineer	2,100
Assistant Engineers, each	1,440
Firemen, each	1,095
Laborers in Engineer's Department, each	720
Telegraph Operators	1,200
25 Clerks to Committees during Sessions, each at $6 per diem	
14 Pages for the Senate Chamber,	
7 Riding Pages, and	
1 Page for the Office of the Secretary, at the rate of $2.50 per day, each, when employed	
2 Folders, at $3 per day, each, when employed	
Conductor of the Elevator	1,200
8 Skilled Laborers, each	1,000
3 Laborers, each	720
12 Laborers during Sessions, at the rate of, each	720
1 Laborer in Charge of Private Passage	840
1 Female Attendant in Charge of Ladies' Retiring Room	720
Reporters of Debates, paying own Assistants	25,000

HOUSE OF REPRESENTATIVES.

The House of Representatives consists of two hundred and ninety-three Representatives and eight Delegates, apportioned among the States and Territories as follows: Maine, 5; New Hampshire, 3; Vermont, 3; Massachusetts, 12; Rhode Island, 2; Connecticut, 4; New York, 34; New Jersey, 7; Pennsylvania, 27; Delaware, 1; Maryland, 6; Virginia, 9; North Carolina, 8; South Carolina, 7; Georgia, 9; Alabama, 8; Mississippi 7; Louisiana, 6; Ohio, 20; Kentucky, 10; Tennessee, 10; Indiana, 13; Illinois, 20; Missouri, 15; Arkansas, 5; Michigan, 11; Florida, 2; Texas, 11; Iowa, 9; Wisconsin 9; California, 6; Minnesota, 5; Oregon, 1; Kansas, 7; West Virginia, 4; Nevada, 1; Nebraska, 3; Colorado, [...]; and one Delegate from each of the following Territories—Arizona, Dakota, Idaho, Montana, New Mexico, Utah, Washington, and Wyoming.

Time and Manner of Election.

Representatives in Congress are elected by ballot in districts composed of contiguous territory. The day for electing Congressmen is the Tuesday next after the first Monday in November every second year. Delegates from the Territories are elected by a majority of the votes of the qualified voters of the Territories, respectively. They have seats in the house with the right of debating, but not of voting.

Officers.

A Speaker, a Clerk of the House, a Chief Clerk, a Chaplain.

COMPENSATION.

Speaker	$8,000
Representatives and Delegates	5,000
Clerk of House	4,500
Chief Clerk	3,000
Journal Clerk	3,000
2 Reading Clerks	3,000
Tally Clerk	3,000
Printing Clerk	2,500
5 Clerks, Disbursing, File, Printing, Enrolling, each	2,250
Assistant to Chief Clerk	2,000
Assistant Disbursing Clerk	2,000
Resolution and Petition Clerk	2,000
Newspaper Clerk	2,000
Superintendent of Document Room	2,000
Index Clerk	2,000
Librarian	1,800
Distributing Clerk	1,500
Stationery Clerk	1,500
Chaplain	900
Document Clerk	1,440
Upholsterer	1,440
Locksmith	1,440
2 Assistant Librarians, each	1,440
1 Book-keeper	1,600
4 Clerks, each	1,600
Clerk to Committee on Claims	2,000
Clerk to Committee on Public Lands	2,000
Clerk to Committee on War Claims	2,000
Clerk to Committee on Invalid Pensions	2,000
Clerk to Committee on Judiciary	2,000
Clerk to Committee on District of Columbia	2,000
Clerk to Committee on Appropriations	2,500
Clerk to Committee on Ways and Means	2,500
Sergeant-at-Arms of the House	4,000
Clerk to Sergeant-at-Arms of the House	2,000
Paying Teller for Sergeant-at-Arms [...]	

THE SENATE CHAMBER.

THE AMERICAN MANUAL.   195

House.. 2,000
Messenger for Sergeant-at-Arms of the House. 1,000
2 Messengers to Committee on Appropriations..... 1,000
Assistant Clerk to Committee on Appropriations. 1,600
Assistant Clerk to Committee on War Claims... 1,600
Private Secretary to the Speaker............... 1,800
Clerk at Speaker's Table....................... 1,500
Clerk to the Speaker........................... 1,400
Assistant Clerk to Committee on Ways and
  Means....................................... 1,200
3 Messengers to Committee on Ways and Means... 1,000
13 Messengers on "Soldiers' Roll," provided said
  Messengers served in the Union Army, and
  Postmaster................................... 1,500
First Assistant Postmaster..................... 1,600
8 Messengers, each............................. 1,200
1 Messengers during the Session, at the rate of. 900
1 Laborer — Bath-Room.......................... 725
21 Laborers, each.............................. 725
1 Telegraph Operator........................... 725
10 Messengers, each............................ 1,600
10 Laborers during the Session, at the rate of,
  each.. 720
1 Laborer...................................... 840
2 Laborers, each............................... 600
8 Laborers, "Cloak-Room men," each, per month
  during the Session........................... 50
1 Female Attendant, Ladies' Retiring-Room...... 700
  Superintendent of Folding-Room............... 2,000
1 Clerk in Folding-Room........................ 1,800
2 Clerks in Folding-Room....................... 1,200
  Superintendent of Document Room.............. 3,000
  Chief Assistant in Document Room............. 2,000
  Document File Clerk.......................... 1,400
2 Stenographers for Committees, each........... 5,000

5 Official Reporters of the Proceedings and Debates of the House, each..................... 5,000
  Compiler of the General Index of the Journals
  of Congress.................................. 2,500
32 Clerks to Committees, during the Session, $ per
  day, each
1 Journal Clerk for preparing Digest of the Rules, 1,000
20 Pages, when employed, per day, each, $2.50.
1 Foreman of Folding-Room..................... 1,200
13 Folders, each............................... 720
13 Folders, each............................... 600
4 Folders, each................................ 840
1 Messenger.................................... 1,200
1 Folder in Sealing-Room....................... 1,200
1 Page.. 50
1 Laborer....................................... 100
1 Laborer....................................... 60
1 Page, per month............................... 60
1 Doorkeeper.................................... 2,500
1 Assistant Doorkeeper.......................... 2,000
1 Clerk for Doorkeeper.......................... 1,200
  Janitor....................................... 1,200
  Chief Engineer................................ 1,700
2 Assistant Engineers, each.................... 1,200
1 Electrician................................... 1,150
1 Laborer....................................... 840
1 Fireman, each................................. 900
2 Messengers in the House Library, per day, $3.50.

Capitol Police.

1 Captain.......................................$1,600
3 Lieutenants, each............................ 1,230
21 Privates, each.............................. 1,100
8 Watchmen, each............................... 900

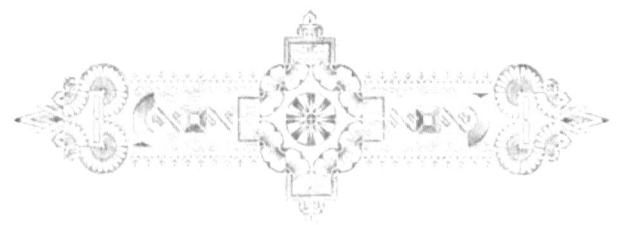

DEPARTMENT OF STATE.

ORGANIZATION.—This Department, established July 27, 1789, was originally styled the Department of Foreign Affairs, the principal officer being called the Secretary for the Department of Foreign Affairs, but its name was changed by an act of Congress, Sept. 15, 1789, to the Department of State.

The principal officer by that act was called **The Secretary of State.**

POWERS AND DUTIES OF SECRETARY OF STATE.—The Secretary of State conducts all correspondence and issues instructions to the public ministers and consuls from the United States, negotiates with public ministers from foreign states or princes, and has charge, under the direction of the President, of all matters pertaining to foreign affairs.

He takes charge of the seal of the United States, and of the seal of the Department of State. It is his duty to affix the seal of the United States to all civil commissions (except for revenue officers), for officers of the United States appointed by the President, by and with the advice and consent of the Senate, or by the President alone.

The originals of all bills, orders, and resolutions of the Senate and House of Representatives are received and preserved by this Department. It is the duty of the Secretary to promulgate and publish the laws, amendments to the Constitution of the United States, and to make known commercial information communicated by diplomatic and consular officers.

It is the duty of the Secretary of State to procure from time to time such of the statutes of the several States as may not be in his office.

He must, within ten days after the commencement of each regular session of Congress, lay before that body a statement containing an abstract of all returns made to him pursuant to law by collectors of the different ports of the seamen registered by them, together with an account of such impressments and detentions as may appear by the protest of the masters of vessels to have taken place.

He must annually lay before Congress the following **reports**:

I.—A statement, in a compendious form, of all such changes and modifications in the commercial systems of other nations, whether by treaties, duties on imports and exports, or other regulations, as shall have been communicated to the Department, including information contained in official publications of other Governments, which he may deem of sufficient importance.

II.—A synopsis of so much of the information which may have been communicated to him by diplomatic and consular officers, during the preceding year, as he may deem valuable for public information.

THE CHIEF CLERK.—The Chief Clerk has general supervision of the clerks, and of the business of the Department.

THE FOUR BUREAUS OF THE DEPARTMENT are the following, with the business pertaining to each:

NEW STATE DEPARTMENT.

The **Diplomatic Bureau** has charge of all correspondence between the Department and other diplomatic agents of the United States abroad, and those of foreign powers accredited to this government.

The **Consular Bureau** has charge of the correspondence, etc. between the department and the consuls, and commercial agents of the United States.

CABINET CHAMBER.

The Bureau of Rolls, Indices, and Archives, has charge of the enrolled acts and resolutions of Congress, as they are received from the President; prepares authenticated copies thereof; superintends their publication, and that of treaties; attends to their distribution, and that of all documents and publications in regard to which this duty is assigned to the department; writing and answering all letters connected therewith; answering calls of the principal officers for correspondence; and has charge of all Indian treaties, and business relating thereto.

The Bureau of Accounts has charge of all matters connected with accounts relating to any fund disbursed by the department; indemnity fund and bonds; care of building and property.

BRANCHES OR DIVISIONS.

STATISTICAL DIVISION.—The Clerk of this Division has the administration of the collection, analyzing, publication, and distribution of commercial information.

AUTHENTICATIONS.—The Clerk of Authentications has charge of the seals of the United States and of the department, and prepares and attaches certificates to papers presented for authentication; receives and accounts for the fees; and records all letters from the department, other than the diplomatic and consular.

PARDONS AND COMMISSIONS.—The Clerk of Pardons and Commissions prepares and records pardons and remissions, and registers and files the papers on which they are founded, and attends to applications for office.

TRANSLATIONS.—The Translator furnishes such translations as the department may require by the Secretary, Assistant Secretary, or Chief Clerk, and records the commissions of consuls and vice-consuls, when not in English, upon which exequaturs are issued

LIBRARIANS.—The Librarian has the custody of the rolls, treaties, etc., the promulgation of the laws, the care and superintendence of the library and public documents, the care of the Revolutionary archives and archives of international commissions.

Salaries and Pay of the Officers and Employes of the Department of State.

Secretary, $8,000. Three Assistant Secretaries, each, $3,500. Chief Clerk, $2,500. Translator and four Chiefs of Bureaus, each $2,100. Eleven Clerks, each, $1,800. Four clerks, each, $1,600. Two Clerks, each, $1,400. Ten Clerks, each, $1,200. Two Clerks, each, $1,000. Ten Clerks, each, $900. Engineer, $1,200. Assistant Engineer, $1,000. Two Superintendents of Watch, each, $1,000. Six Watchmen, Six Firemen, Assistant Messenger, Elevator Tender, each, $720. Twelve Laborers, each, $660. Ten Charwomen, each, $180. A small number of extra clerks, messengers, and laborers are employed from time to time.

APPOINTMENTS BY THE SECRETARY OF STATE.

UNLIMITED TERM.

Chief clerks, chiefs of bureaus, translator, clerks of the several bureaus, messengers, watchmen, laborers, and other employes of the Department.

Vice-consuls-general, vice-consuls, deputy consuls-general, vice-commercial agents, deputy consular and consular agents, on its are required under regulations prescribed by the President of the United States, to the Secretary of State, or the nomination of the principal consular officers, approved by him, and on receipt of their commissions, qualify according to law.

… AMERICAN MANUAL.

TREASURY DEPARTMENT.

Office of the Secretary, including eight regular divisions; besides the Chief Clerk's Office, the office of the Custodian of the building; and Special Agents' Division; the Secret Service, and the Division of Captured and Abandoned Property, Lands, etc.; Bureau of Engraving and Printing; Bureau of the Mint; Office of the Supervising Architect; Supervising Inspector-General of Steam Vessels; Office of the Superintendent of the Life-Saving Service; Office of the Lighthouse Board, Supervising Surgeon-General of Marine Hospitals; First Comptroller; Second Comptroller; Commissioner of Customs; First Auditor, Second Auditor, Third Auditor, Fourth Auditor, Fifth Auditor, Sixth Auditor; Treasurer; Register; Comptroller of the Currency; Commissioner of Internal Revenue; Coast Survey.

DUTIES OF THE SECRETARY.

The Secretary prepares plans for the improvement and management of the revenue, and for the support of the public credit. He prescribes the forms of keeping and rendering all accounts; grants all warrants for moneys to be issued from the Treasury in pursuance of appropriations made by Congress; reports to the Senate and House, in person or in writing, information required by them appertaining to his office, and performs all duties relative to the finances that he shall be directed to perform.

The Secretary orders the collection, the deposit, the transfer, the safe-keeping, and the disbursement of the revenue; and directs the auditing and settling the accounts, respectively.

Secretary's Office.—The Secretary of the Treasury is charged with the general supervision of the fiscal transactions of the government, and the execution of the laws concerning commerce and navigation; the survey of the coast; the lighthouse establishment; the marine hospitals of the United States, and the construction of certain public buildings for custom-house and other purposes.

The First Comptroller prescribes the mode of keeping and rendering accounts for the civil and diplomatic service, as well as the public lands, and revises and certifies the balances arising thereon.

The Second Comptroller prescribes the mode of keeping and rendering the accounts of the army, navy, and Indian departments of the public service, and revises and certifies the balances arising thereon.

The Commissioner of the Customs prescribes the mode of keeping and rendering the accounts of the customs, revenue, and disbursement, and for the building and repairing custom-houses, etc., and revises and certifies the balances arising thereon.

The First Auditor receives and adjusts the accounts of the customs, revenue and disbursements, appropriations, and expenditures on account of the civil list, and under private acts of Congress, and reports the balances to the Commissioner of the Customs and the First Comptroller respectively, for their decision thereon.

The Second Auditor receives and adjusts all accounts relating to the pay, clothing and recruiting of the army, as well as the armories, arsenals, and ordnance, and all accounts relating to the Indian department, and reports the balances to the Second Comptroller for his decision thereon.

The Third Auditor receives and adjusts all accounts for subsistence of the army, fortifications, military academy, military roads, and the quartermaster's department, pensions, and claims arising from military services previous to 1816, and for horses and other property lost in the military service, and reports the balances to the Second Comptroller for his decision thereon.

The Fourth Auditor adjusts all accounts for the service of the Navy Department, and reports the balances to the Second Comptroller for his decision thereon.

The Fifth Auditor adjusts all accounts for diplomatic and similar services performed under the direction of the State department, and reports the balances to the First Comptroller for his decision thereon.

The Sixth Auditor adjusts all accounts arising from the service of the Postoffice Department. His decisions are final, unless an appeal is taken within twelve months to the First Comptroller. He superintends the collection of all debts due the Postoffice Department, and all penalties imposed on postmasters and mail contractors for failing to do their duty. He directs suits and legal proceedings, civil and criminal, and takes legal measures to enforce the prompt payment of money due to the department; instructing attorneys, marshals, and clerks relative thereto; and receives returns from each term of the United States Courts of the condition and progress of such suits and legal proceedings, has charge of all lands and other property assigned to the United States in payment of debts due to the Postoffice Department, and has power to sell and dispose of the same for the benefit of the United States.

The Treasurer receives and keeps the moneys of the United States in his own office, and that of the depositories, and pays out the same upon warrants drawn by the Secretary of the Treasury, countersigned by the First Comptroller, and upon warrants drawn by the Postmaster-General, and countersigned by the Sixth Auditor, and recorded by the Register. He also holds public moneys advanced by warrant to disbursing officers, and pays out the same upon their checks.

The **Register** keeps the accounts of public receipts and expenditures; receives the returns, and makes out the official statement of commerce and navigation of the United States; and receives from the First Comptroller and Commissioner of Customs all accounts and vouchers decided by them, and is charged by law with their safekeeping.

The **Solicitor** superintends all civil suits commenced by the United States (*except those arising in the Postoffice Department*), and instructs the United States attorneys, marshals and clerks in all matters relating to them, and their results. He receives returns from each term of the United States Courts, showing the progress and condition of such suits; has charge of all lands and other property assigned to the United States in payment of debts (*except those assigned in payment of debts due to the Postoffice Department*), and has power to sell and dispose of the same for the benefit of the United States.

The **Lighthouse Board**.—The Secretary of the Treasury is *ex officio* president of the board. It directs the building and repairing of lighthouses, light-vessels, buoys, and beacons, contracts for supplies of oil, etc.

United States Coast Survey.—The coast survey officer is charged with the superintendence of the survey of the coast of the United States, and its superintendent is the superintendent of weights and measures.

The **Comptroller of the Currency** has charge of everything connected with the issue of money.

The **Commissioner of Internal Revenue** has charge of all matters connected with the Tax Laws.

The **Supervising Architect** has charge of the construction of public buildings.

The **Special Commissioner of Revenue** is required by law to investigate the sources of national revenue, the best methods of collecting revenue, the administration of existing revenue laws, and the relation of foreign trade to domestic industry.

PAY OF EMPLOYES IN THE OFFICE OF THE SECRETARY OF THE TREASURY.

Force in Secretary's Office.—Chief clerk (of the Department), $3,000; chief of Division of Warrants, etc., chief of Division of Customs, each, $2,750; 6 chiefs of division, 2 disbursing clerks, each, $2,500; assistant chief of division of Warrants, $2,400; 2 assistant chiefs of Division, $2,100; 6 assistant chiefs of Division, stenographer to the Secretary, $2,000; 192 clerks, from $900 to $1,900; 14 messengers and assistants, from $720 to $840; 2 conductors of elevators, each, $720; 43 laborers, each, $660; 2 lieutenants, each, $900; 58 watchmen, each, $720; 1 engineer, $1,400; 1 assistant engineer, $1,000; 1 machinist and gas-fitter, 1 storekeeper, captain of the watch, $1,200; 6 firemen, each, $720; 75 charwomen or cleaners, each, $180.

Internal Revenue Bureau.—Commissioner, $6,000; deputy, $3,200; 2 chiefs of Division, $2,500; 5 chiefs of Division, $2,250; stenographer, $1,800; 169 clerks, from $900 to $1,800; 4 messengers, $720; 10 laborers, $660. About 30 clerks and 6 messengers are employed temporarily, and paid at rates varying from $720 to $2,100 per year.

Treasury of the United States.—Treasurer, $6,000; assistant treasurer, cashier, $3,600; assistant, $3,200; superintendent National Bank Agency, $3,500; chief clerk, 5 chiefs of division, 2 bookkeepers, 4 tellers, $2,500; 2 assistants, $2,400; 2 assistants, $2,250; assistant, $2,000; 221 clerks, from $900 to $1,800; 7 messengers, $840; 10 assistants, $720; 33 laborers, from $240 to $660.

Registry of the Treasury.—Register, $1,000; assistant, $2,250; 5 chiefs of Division, disbursing clerk, $2,000; 113 clerks, from $900 to $1,800; messenger, $840; 4 assistants, $720; 7 laborers, $660.

Accounting Offices.—2 comptrollers, $5,000; 2 deputies, $2,700; commissioner of customs, $3,000; 7 deputies, $2,250; 6 auditors, $3,600; 18 chiefs of division, from $2,200 to $2,100; 1 disbursing clerk, $2,000; 693 clerks, from $900 to $1,800; 11 messengers, from $840 to $840; 56 laborers, male and female, from $180 to $660.

Bureau of the Mint.—Director, $1,500; examiner, $2,500; computer, $2,200; 3 clerks, from $1,100 to $1,800; translator, $1,400; copyist, $900; messenger, $720; laborer, $660.

Bureau of National Currency.—Comptroller of currency, $5,000; deputy, $2,800; 3 chiefs of division, $2,200; superintendent of currency, teller, 2 bookkeepers, head clerk, $2,000; 70 clerks, from $900 to $1,800; stenographer, $1,700; messenger, $840; 3 assistants, $720; 2 watchmen, $720; 3 laborers, $660.

PAY OF OFFICERS AND EMPLOYES IN THE DIFFERENT DIVISIONS OF THE TREASURY DEPARTMENT.

Bureau of Printing and Engraving.—Chief, $4,500; Assistant, $2,250; Accountant, $2,000; Stenographer, $600; 7 Clerks, from $1,000 to $1,200; 3 Copyists, each, $720; 4 Messengers, each, $720; 4 Laborers, each, $700. Large numbers of engravers, plate-printers, skilled and unskilled workmen and workwomen, etc., are employed by the day or piece, permanently or temporarily, at wages varying from $1 to $7, the whole force sometimes reaching nearly to one thousand.

Construction Bureau.—Supervising Architect, $4,500; Assistant, $2,250; Photographer, $2,250; 8 Clerks from $900 to $2,000; Messenger, $720. About 20 civil engineers, architects, draughtsmen, computers, clerks, messengers, etc., are also steadily employed in this office, and paid by the day at rates yielding from $900 to $3,600 per year.

Bureau of Statistics.—Chief, $2,400; 25 Clerks from $900 to $2,000; 5 Copyists, each, $900; Messenger, $840;

Laborer, $600, Laborer, $480. Experts are temporarily employed by this bureau to furnish statistics relative to internal and foreign commerce.

Light-House Bureau.—Chief Clerk, $2,400; 22 Clerks from $900 to $1,800; 2 Messengers, each, $720; Laborer, $480. A few engineers and draughtsmen are employed, and paid by the month from $1,200 to $2,400 per annum.

MISCELLANEOUS.

Coast and Geodetic Survey.—Superintendent, $6,000; Assistant, $4,200; Consulting Geometer, $4,000; Disbursing Agent, $2,500. There are generally employed upward of 50 so-called assistants, with salaries varying from $3,750 to $1,100, and about 100 clerks, computers, draughtsmen, printers, engravers, etc., at compensations varying from $2,000 per year down to $1.50 per day.

Revenue Marine Service.—34 Captains, each, $2,500; 35 First Lieutenants, 23 Chief Engineers, each, $1,800; 31 Second Lieutenants, 15 Assistants, each $1,500; 22 Third Lieutenants, each, $1,800; 12 Cadets, each, $500; 27 Assistants, each, $1,200.

Life Saving Service.—General Superintendent, $4,000; Assistant, $2,500; Accountant, $1,800; 5 Clerks from $900 to $1,200; Messenger, $720; Superintendent of Construction, $2,000; 12 Assistants, each, per month from $75 to $100; 11 District Superintendents, each from $1,000 to $1,800; Assistant, $600; 170 Keepers, each, $400; 1,400 Surfmen, per month, each, $40.

National Board of Health.—7 Members of Board, per day, each $10; Chief Clerk, $2,500; 5 Clerks, from $1,200 to $1,800; Messenger, per month, $50; Assistant, per month, $75; Laborer, per day, $1.25; 12 Inspectors, each, per day, $10; 2 Inspectors, each per month, from $250 to $500. The force is variable, both as to numbers and pay.

Marine Hospital Service.—Supervising Surgeon General, $4,000; 95 medical officers, with salaries ranging from $4,000 down to $100 per year; about 10 clerks at headquarters, with the usual clerical salaries paid at Washington, and about 130 stewards, nurses, and other employes, paid at rates ranging from $720 to $100 per year.

Steamboat Inspecting Service.—Supervising Inspector-General, $3,500; 12 Supervising Inspectors, $3,000; 40 Inspectors of Hulls, each, from $800 to $2,500; 51 Inspectors of Boilers, each, from $800 to $2,500; 9 clerks, each, from $900 to $1,200.

Internal Revenue Agencies.—Supervising Agent, per day, $12; 31 Agents, each, per day, from $6 to $8.

National Bank Examiners.—This force is variable in number and compensation, the banks examined paying the fees for examination, and the examiners being chosen by the Comptroller of the Currency at will.

Secret Service.—Chief, $2,500. The force is variable, but usually consists of about 50 detectives and a few clerks, paid at various rates according to time employed and service rendered. The leading duty is suppression of counterfeiting.

Special Agencies of Customs.—28 Special Agents, each, per day from $6 to $8; 4 Seal-Island Agents in Alaska, each, from $2,100 to $3,050. Each seal-island agent is allowed $600 per year for traveling to and from Alaska; 2 Isthmus Inspectors, $2,500.

APPOINTMENTS.

By the Secretary of the Treasury.

Chief Clerk, Disbursing Clerks, Chiefs of Divisions, Chief of the Bureau of Engraving and Printing, Assistant Superintendent Life-Saving Service, Assistant Chief of the Bureau of Engraving and Printing, Supervising Architect, Assistant Supervising Architect, Chief Clerk, Clerks of the several classes, fourth, third, second, first, $1,000 and $800.

⇒ WAR DEPARTMENT. ⇐

The Secretary of War has charge of all the duties connected with the army of the United States, fortifications, etc., receives commissions, directs the movement of troops, superintends their pensions, forts, clothing, arms and equipments, and ordnance, and conducts works of military engineering.

The following bureaus are attached to this department:

Commanding General's Office.—The Commanding General has charge of the arrangement of the military forces, the superintendence of the recruiting service, and the discipline of the army. He is to see that the laws and regulations of the army are enforced. The office is at Washington, and is called the Headquarters of the army.

Adjutant-General's Office.—In this office are kept all the records which refer to the *personnel* of the army, pay-roll, etc., and all military commissions are made out. All orders which emanate from Headquarters, or the War Department proper, pass through this office, and the annual returns from the army are received by it.

The Quartermaster-General's Office provides … … transportation for the army, and has charge of the barracks and the national cemeteries.

The Paymaster-General's Office has charge of the disbursements to the regular army and the Military Academy.

The Commissary-General's Office provides subsistence stores for the troops and military forts.

The Ordnance Bureau has charge of the ordnance stores, and the various arsenals and armories.

The Engineer's Office has charge of the military defenses of the country, the improvement of rivers, the surveys relating thereto, and the care of the Military Academy.

Surgeon-General's Office.—All matters connected with medicine and surgery, the management of the sick and wounded, and the hospitals, are under the control of this office.

Topographical Bureau.—This bureau has charge of all topographical operations and surveys for military purposes, and for purposes of internal improvement, and of all maps, drawings, and documents relating to those duties.

The Bureau of Refugees, Freedmen, and Abandoned Lands, the Bureau of Military Justice, the Inspector-General's Office, and the Signal Corps of the Army are also connected with the War Department.

SALARIES AND COMPENSATION OF OFFICERS AND EMPLOYES IN THE VARIOUS DIVISIONS OF THE WAR DEPARTMENT.

Chief clerk, $2,750; disbursing clerk, 7 chief clerks of bureaus, $2,000; 105 clerks, from $1,200 to $1,800; draughtsmen, $1,800; architect, foreman of printing $2,000; engineers, $1,400; 505 clerks, from $600 to $1,200; engineers, pressmen, $1,200; compositors, $1,000; messenger, $500; 13 messengers, watchmen and firemen $720; cyclometers, $660; scrub women $180.

There is, in addition to the above force, a large number of officers and employes of various grades, consisting of about 92 national cemeteries, pay, from $720 to $900 per year, with residence; about 185 officers and … serving in the Signal Corps, from $12 to $100 per month, with allowances; about 115 private physicians employed at Washington and various army posts, at a compensation of $100 per month, with quarters; and about 105 hospital stewards, with pay of from $20 to $23 per month, with rations, quarters, fuel, and clothing; about 70 postmaster clerks, at $15 per year; about 600 employes of all sorts at arsenals and armories, of 150 clerks, superintendents, and other employes, at a rate from $50 to $200 per month, also 6,000 moving the arms and its supplies by land and water, and taking care of it, barracks, storehouses, and buildings; a large force of clerks, draughtsmen and engineers, skilled workmen, etc., employed at various offices of the public buildings, grounds, and works at the seat of government and elsewhere, under charge of the Engineer Bureau, including forts and river and harbor improvements; about 150 other employes engaged upon the army, education, supplies.

ADJUTANT-GENERAL'S OFFICE.

Officers of the Army.

The Adjutant-General, with rank of brigadier-general, 1 assistant adjutant-general, with rank of colonel, 1 assistant adjutants-general, with rank of major, receiving army pay.

Enlisted Men.

78 enlisted men (general service), serving as clerks, 60 enlisted men (general service), serving as messengers and watchmen.

NOTE.—The pay and allowances per annum of enlisted men serving in the Adjutant-General's Office, and other branches of the War Department, as clerks and messengers, amount as follows:

	CLERKS		MESSENGERS
	Sergeants.	Privates.	
Pay	$1,055.45	$1,007.15	$997.50
Clothing	17.78	17.01	1.01
Total	$1,093.01	$1,094.11	$998.50

The above amounts are paid during the first and second years of service. During the third year each grade r

THE AMERICAN MANUAL.

GENERAL P. H. SHERIDAN.

PAY OF THE ARMY OF THE UNITED STATES.

...es $72 additional; fourth year, $84; and 6th year, $96. For each year of a second enlistment, for a period of five years, each grade receives $60 additional; for a third enlistment of five years, $72; and for a fourth enlistment of five years, $84; and $12 a year additional to $84 for every succeeding enlistment.

OFFICE OF INSPECTOR-GENERAL.

Inspector-General, with rank of brigadier general, 1 assistant inspector-general, with rank of colonel, receiving army pay.

BUREAU OF MILITARY JUSTICE.

Judge-Advocate-General, with rank of brigadier-general, 2 judge-advocates, with rank of major, receiving army pay.

PAYMASTER-GENERAL'S OFFICE.
Army Officers.

Paymaster-General, with rank of brigadier general, 4 paymasters, with rank of major, receiving army pay.

SURGEON-GENERAL'S OFFICE.
Army Officers.

Surgeon-General, with rank of brigadier-general, 1 assistant surgeon-general, with rank of colonel, 1 chief medical purveyor, with rank of colonel, 3 surgeons, with rank of major, 1 assistant surgeon, with rank of captain, receiving army pay.

OFFICE OF CHIEF OF ORDNANCE.
Army Officers.

Chief of Ordnance, with rank of brigadier-general, 1 major of ordnance, receiving army pay.

SIGNAL OFFICE AND SERVICE.
Army Officers.

Chief Signal Officer, with rank of brigadier-general, 1 first lieutenant of artillery, 1 first lieutenant of cavalry, 1 first lieutenant of infantry, receiving army pay.

Enlisted Men.

150 sergeants, 30 corporals, and 320 privates, receiving pay as in adjutant-general's office.

QUARTERMASTER'S DEPARTMENT.
Army Officers.

Quartermaster-General, with rank of brigadier-general, 1 assistant quartermaster-general, with rank of colonel, 2 deputy quartermasters-general, with rank of lieutenant-colonel, 1 quartermaster, with rank of major, 1 assistant quartermaster, with rank of captain (mounted), receiving army pay.

*The maximum pay of colonels is limited to $4,500, and of lieutenant-colonels to $4,000.

COMMISSARY GENERAL.

Army Officers.

Commissary-General of Subsistence, with rank of brigadier-general, 2 commissaries of subsistence, with rank of major of cavalry, 1 commissary of subsistence, with rank of captain of cavalry, receiving army pay.

OFFICE OF CHIEF OF ENGINEERS OF THE ARMY.

Army Officers.

Chief of Engineers, with rank of brigadier-general, 1 lieutenant-colonel of engineers, 1 major of engineers, 1 captain, receiving army pay.

THE UNITED STATES ARMY.

The Army of the United States consists of the following:
One general.
One lieutenant-general.
Three major-generals.
Six brigadier-generals.
Five regiments of artillery.
Ten regiments of cavalry.
Twenty-five regiments of infantry.
An Adjutant-General's Department.
An Inspector-General's Department.
A Quartermaster's Department.
A corps of engineers.
A battalion of engineer soldiers.
An Ordnance Department.
The enlisted men of the Ordnance Department.
The Medical Department.
The hospital stewards of the Medical Department.
A Pay Department.
A chief signal officer.
A Bureau of Military Justice.
Eight judge-advocates.
Thirty post chaplains.
Four regimental chaplains.
An ordnance sergeant and an hospital steward for each military post.
One band stationed at the Military Academy.
A force of Indian scouts, not exceeding 1,000.
The officers of the army on the retired list.
The professors and corps of cadets at the United States Military Academy at West Point.
The offices of general and lieutenant-general expire with the present incumbent.

GENERAL PROVISIONS.

No person who has served in any capacity in the military, naval, or civil service of the so-called Confederate States or of either of the States in insurrection during the Rebellion of 1861, can be appointed to any position in the Army of the United States.

All officers who served during the Rebellion as volunteers in the Army of the United States, honorably mustered out of the service, are entitled to wear the official title, and upon occasions of ceremony to wear the uniform of the highest grade they held, by brevet or other commissions, in the volunteer service.

The use by officers of private soldiers as servants is prohibited by law.

Four women to each company are allowed as laundresses.

RETIREMENT.

An officer who has served thirty years may, on his own application, in the discretion of the President, be placed on the retired list. One who has served forty-five years, or is sixty-two years old, may be retired from active service in the discretion of the President. He must be retired when sixty-three years old.

ARTICLES OF WAR.

The army is governed by what are called Articles of War, one hundred and twenty-eight in number, prescribed by act of Congress. They are read to every enlisted man at the time of his enlistment, and must be read to every regiment **once in six months.** Every officer must subscribe to these rules and articles before entering on duty.

QUARTERS, FUEL, AND FORAGE ALLOWED TO ARMY OFFICERS.

By act of June 18, 1878, all allowance or commutation for fuel was prohibited, but wood is furnished at $4 per cord, out of the pay of officers. Forage is furnished only in kind, and only to officers actually in the field or west of the Mississippi, on the basis of five horses for the General of the army, four for the Lieutenant-General, three each for a major or brigadier-general, and two each for a colonel, lieutenant-colonel, major, mounted captain or lieutenant, adjutant, and regimental quartermaster. Quarters are furnished on the following basis: General (commutation for quarters), $125 per month; lieutenant-general, $70 per month; major-general, six rooms; brigadier-general or colonel, five rooms; lieutenant-colonel or major, four rooms; captain or chaplain, three rooms; and first or second lieutenant, two rooms—all of which may be commuted at $10 per room per month.

NOTE.—The law provides that no allowances shall be made to officers in addition to their pay, except quarters and forage furnished in kind.

Mileage at the rate of eight cents per mile is allowed for travel under orders.

The pay of cadets at the U. S. Military Academy, West Point, was placed at $540 per annum, by Act of

Aug. 7, 1876, instead of $500 and one ration per diem (equivalent to $600.50), by former laws.

The pay of privates runs from $156 ($13 a month and rations) for first two years, to $21 a month after twenty years' service.

A retired chaplain receives three-fourths of the pay (salary and increase) of his rank (captain, not mounted).

The officer in charge of the public buildings and grounds (Washington) has, while so serving, the rank, pay, and emoluments of a colonel.

The aides-de-camp to the general, selected by him from the army, have, while so serving, the rank and pay of colonel.

The aides-de-camp and military secretary to the lieutenant-general, selected by him from the army, have, while so serving, the rank and pay of lieutenant-colonel.

Officers of the army and of volunteers, assigned to duty which requires them to be mounted, shall, during the time they are employed on such duty, receive the pay, emoluments, and allowances of cavalry officers of the same grade, respectively.

REMARKS.

Mileage, at the rate of eight cents per mile, is allowed to officer for travel under orders. Regulations governing the subject of mileage are contained, entire, in General Orders No. 17, Adjutant-General's Office, series of 1876.

Commutation of quarters, to be paid by Pay Department, as follows: General, $125 per month; lieutenant-general, $70 per month; all other grades not to exceed $10 per month per room. General Orders No. 37 and 16, Adjutant-General's Office, series of 1878.

FORAGE FOR HORSES.

Forage for horses is allowed to officers as follows: General, for five; lieutenant-general, for four; major-general, for three; brigadier-general, for three; colonel, lieutenant-colonel, major, captain, and lieutenant (mounted); adjutant, regimental quartermaster, chaplain, and storekeeper, each for two horses. Forage is now issued only to those officers on duty at posts west of the Mississippi River.

PAY OF OFFICERS AND CADETS AT THE MILITARY ACADEMY.

Superintendent, pay of colonel; commandant of cadets, pay of lieutenant-colonel; adjutant, pay of regimental adjutant; Quartermaster and commissary of the battalion of cadets, pay of his grade in the army; treasurer, pay of his grade in the army; surgeon, pay of his grade in the

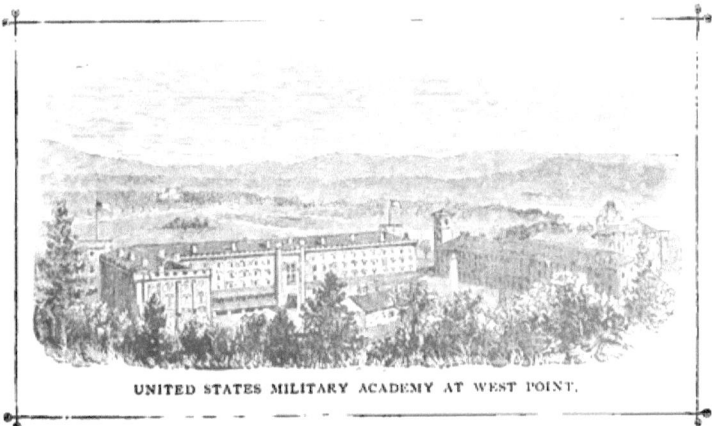

UNITED STATES MILITARY ACADEMY AT WEST POINT.

army, assistant surgeon, pay of his grade in the army; professor, of more than ten years' service at the Academy, pay of colonel; professor, of less than ten years' service, pay of lieutenant-colonel; assistant professor, pay of captain, mounted; senior assistant instructor of tactics, pay of captain, mounted; assistant instructor of tactics, commanding a company of cadets, pay of captain, mounted; acting assistant professor, pay of his grade in the army; acting assistant instructor of tactics, pay of his grade in the army; instructors of ordnance and science of gunnery, and of practical engineering, pay of major; sword-master, $1,500 per annum; cadet, $540 per annum.

PAY OF ENLISTED MEN.

Enlisted men receive from $13 to $18 per month, according to the time served in the army, with clothes and rations; non-commissioned officers, from $17 to $31, with clothes and rations.

APPOINTMENTS MADE BY THE SECRETARY OF WAR FOR AN UNLIMITED TERM, OR DURING HIS PLEASURE.

Agent for collection of Confederate records.
Anatomist, Surgeon-General's office.
Chief clerk of department.
Chief clerks of bureaus and divisions.
Clerks of the several grades in all the bureaus.
Copyists.
Disbursing clerks.
Draughtsmen.
Engineers.
Firemen.
Laborers.
Messengers.
Superintendents of buildings.
Watchmen.
Superintendents of National cemeteries.

ORDNANCE STATIONS.

Ordnance Office, Washington, D. C.
Ordnance Board, New York, N. Y.
Ordnance Agency, New York, N. Y.
The Proving Ground, Sandy Hook, N. J.
The Department of Ordnance and Gunnery at the Military Academy, West Point, N. Y.
Saint Louis Powder Depot, Jefferson Barracks, Mo.
National Armory, Springfield, Mass.
Augusta Arsenal, Augusta, Ga.
Benicia Arsenal, Benicia, Cal.
Fort Monroe Arsenal, Fort Monroe, Va.
Fort Union Arsenal, Fort Union, N. M.
Frankford Arsenal, Philadelphia, Pa.
Indianapolis Arsenal, Indianapolis, Ind.
Kennebec Arsenal, Augusta, Me.
New York Arsenal, New York, N. Y.
Pikesville Arsenal, Pikesville, Md.
Rock Island Arsenal, Rock Island, Ill.
San Antonio Arsenal, San Antonio, Texas.
Vancouver Arsenal, Vancouver, Washington Ty.
Washington Arsenal, Washington, D. C.
Watertown Arsenal, Watertown, N. Y.
Watervliet Arsenal, West Troy, N. Y.

UNITED STATES MILITARY ACADEMY.

The United States Military Academy at West Point was founded by Act of March 16, 1802, constituting the corps of engineers of the army a military academy, with fifty students or cadets, who were to receive instruction under the senior engineer officer, as superintendent. Later acts established professorships of mathematics, engineering, philosophy, etc., and made the academy a military body, subject to the rules and articles of war. In 1812 a permanent superintendent was appointed, and a year later an annual Board of Visitors was provided for, to be named by the President, the Speaker of the House, and the President of the Senate. In 1843 the present system of the appointment of cadets was instituted, which assigns one cadet to each Congressional District and Territory in the Union, to be named by the Representative in Congress for the time being, and ten appointments at large, specially conferred by the President of the United States. The number of students is thus limited to 312. A large proportion of those appointed fail to pass the examination, and many others to complete the course; the proportion being stated at fully one half hitherto. The course of instruction requires four years, and is largely mathematical and professional. The discipline is very strict, even more so than in the army, and the enforcement of penalties for offences is inflexible rather than severe. The whole number of graduates from 1802 to 1877 was about 2,700, of whom 1,200 are deceased and about 1,500 living. Of those surviving, 800 are still in the army, and about 700 out of service.

Appointees to the Military Academy must be between 17 and 22 years of age, at least five feet in height, and free from infirmity, and able to pass a careful examination in various branches of knowledge. Each cadet admitted must bind himself to serve the United States eight years from the time of admission to the academy. The pay of cadets, formerly fifty dollars per month and rations, was fixed at $540 per year, with no allowance for rations, by the act of 1870. The aggregate amount of money appropriated by the United States for the Military Academy from 1802 to 1877, inclusive, was $11,306,128, being an average of about $149,049 annually. The number of actual members of the academy, by the official register of June, 1881, was 192.

NAVY DEPARTMENT.

Secretary's Office. The Secretary of the Navy has charge of everything connected with the naval establishment, and the execution of all laws relating thereto under the general direction of the President. All instructions to commanders of squadrons and commanders of vessels, all orders to officers, commissions of officers, both in the navy and marine corps; appointments of commissioned and warrant officers, and orders for the enlistment and discharge of seamen, emanate from the Secretary's office. All the duties of the different bureaus are performed under the authority of the Secretary, and their orders are considered as emanating from him. He has a general superintendence of the marine corps, and all the orders of the commandant of that corps are approved by him. The chief of this Bureau has the rank of Commodore, navy pay.

The **Bureau of Navy Yards and Docks** has charge of all the navy yards, docks and wharves, buildings, and machinery in navy yards, and everything immediately connected with them. It is also charged with the management of the Naval Asylum.

The **Bureau of Navigation** has charge of the Naval Observatory and Hydrographical Office. It furnishes vessels with maps, charts, chronometers, etc., together with such books as are allowed to ships of war. The Naval Academy, Naval Observatory, and Nautical Almanac are attached to this bureau. The chief of this bureau has the rank of Commodore, navy pay.

The **Bureau of Ordnance** has charge of all ordnance and ordnance stores, the manufacture or purchase of cannon, guns, powder, shot, shells, etc., and the equipment of vessels of war, with everything connected therewith. Chief of Bureau, with rank of Commodore, navy pay.

The **Bureau of Construction and Repair** has charge of the building and repair of all vessels of war and purchase of material. Chief of Bureau, Chief Constructor, with rank of Commodore, navy pay.

The **Bureau of Equipment and Recruiting** has charge of providing all vessels with their equipments, as sails, anchors, water tanks, etc.; also, charge of the recruiting service. The chief of this bureau has the rank of Commodore, navy pay.

The **Bureau of Steam Engineering** has charge of the construction, repair, etc., of the machinery of steam vessels of war. The Engineer-in-Chief superintends the construction of all marine steam engines for the navy, and, with the approval of the Secretary, decides upon plans for their construction. Chief of Bureau, Engineer-in-Chief, with rank of Commodore, navy pay.

The **Bureau of Provisions and Clothing** contracts for all provisions and clothing for the use of the navy. Chief of Bureau, Paymaster-General, with the rank of Commodore, navy pay.

The **Bureau of Medicine and Surgery** manages everything relating to medicine and medical stores, treatment of sick and wounded, and management of hospitals. Chief of Bureau, Surgeon-General, with rank of Commodore, navy pay.

PAY OF OFFICERS AND EMPLOYES OF THE NAVY DEPARTMENT

Chief clerk, $2,500; disbursing clerk and superintendent, $2,100; 15 chief clerks of bureaus, $1,800; 4 draughtsmen, $1,800; 25 clerks from $1,000 to $1,600; stenographer and draughtsman, $1,600; 1 engineer, $1,200; 1 assistant engineer, $1,000; 11 messengers from $720 to $840; 3 firemen and 9 watchmen, $720; 14 laborers, $660; 8 charwomen, $180.

NAVAL OBSERVATORY.

1 Clerk, $1,600; 3 civilian astronomers, 1 instrument maker, $1,500; keeper of grounds, per month, $50; 3 watchmen, per month, $60; 1 messenger, 1 porter, per month, $53.22.

HYDROGRAPHIC OFFICE.

1 Clerk, per month, $120; 12 draughtsmen, per month, from $50 to $191.66; 2 writers, 1 painter of charts, per month, $75; 1 file clerk, per month, $60; 6 laborers, per month, from $30 to $55; 2 printers, per day, $4; 5 engravers, per day, from $3 to $4.

NAUTICAL ALMANAC OFFICE.

7 computers, $1,200 to $1,600; messenger, $720.

The remaining civil force of the Navy Department consists of a large number of clerks, draughtsmen, mechanical foremen, and skilled and unskilled operatives at the several yards and stations of the navy. Admissions of civilians to the commissioned force are restricted to naval cadets, cadet-engineers, assistant engineers, second lieutenants of marines, assistant surgeons, assistant paymasters, chaplains, and naval constructors, and to professors of mathematics, for the scientific branches of the service. Boatswains, gunners, sailmakers and carpenters, are also taken from civil life.

APPOINTMENTS BY THE SECRETARY OF THE NAVY.

For an Unlimited Term, or during his pleasure.

Assistant astronomers, Naval Observatory.
Chief clerk of the Department.
Chief clerks of the bureaus.
Clerks of the several grades.

Computed in Hydrographic Office.
Disbursing clerk.
Draughtsmen.
Engravers.
Instrument-makers, Nautical Almanac Office
Laborers.
Messengers and assistant messengers
Porters.
Printers, Hydrographic Office.
Stenographer.
Watchmen.
Writers, Hydrographic Office.

NAVAL ACADEMY, ANNAPOLIS, MARYLAND.

Professors of drawing, languages, physics, chemistry, etc., the secretary, boxing-masters, clerks, and other officers, servants, and employes, by the Secretary of the Navy, on the recommendation of the superintendent thereof.

PAY TABLE OF THE NAVY.

	At Sea.	On Shore Duty.	On leave or waiting Orders.
Admiral	$13,000	$13,000	$13,000
Vice-Admiral	9,000	8,000	6,000
Rear-Admiral	6,000	5,000	4,000
Commodores	5,000	4,000	3,000
Captains	4,500	3,500	2,800
Commanders	3,500	3,000	2,300
Lieutenant-Commander—			
First four years after date of commission	2,800	2,400	2,000
After four years from date of commission	3,000	2,600	2,200
Lieutenants—			
First five years	2,400	2,200	1,600
After five years	2,600	2,200	1,800
Masters—			
First five years	1,800	1,500	1,200
After five years	2,000	1,700	1,400
Ensigns—			
First five years	1,200	1,000	800
After five years	1,400	1,200	1,000
Midshipmen	1,000	800	600
Cadet Midshipmen	500	500	500
Mates	900	700	500
Medical and Pay Directors and Medical and Pay Inspectors and Chief Engineers, having the same rank at sea	4,400		
Fleet Surgeons, Fleet Paymasters, and Fleet Engineers	4,400		
Surgeons, Paymasters, and Chief Engineers—			
First five years after date of commission	2,800	2,400	2,000
Second five years	3,200	2,800	2,400
Third five years	3,500	3,200	2,600
Fourth five years	3,700	3,600	2,800
After twenty years	4,200	4,000	3,000
Passed Assistant Surgeons, Passed Assistant Paymasters, and Passed Assistant Engineers—			
First five years after date of appointment	2,000	1,800	1,500
After five years	2,200	2,000	1,700
Assistant Surgeons, Assistant Paymasters, and Assistant Engineers—			
First five years after date of appointment	1,700	1,400	1,000
After five years	1,900	1,600	1,200
Chaplains—			
First five years	2,500	2,000	1,600
After five years	2,800	2,300	1,900
Boatswains, Gunners, Carpenters and Sailmakers—			
First three years	1,200	800	700
Second three years	1,300	1,000	800
Third three years	1,400	1,300	900
Fourth three years	1,600	1,300	1,000
After twelve years	1,800	1,600	1,200
Cadet Engineers (after examination)	1,000	800	600

	On shore duty.	On leave or waiting orders.
Naval Constructors—		
First five years	$3,200	$2,200
Second five years	3,400	2,400
Third five years	3,700	2,700
Fourth five years	4,000	3,000
After twenty years	4,200	3,200
Assistant Naval Constructors—		
First four years	2,000	1,500
Second four years	2,200	1,700
After eight years	2,600	1,900
Secretary to Admiral and Vice-Admiral		$2,500
Secretaries to Commanders of Squadrons		2,000
Secretary to Naval Academy		1,800
Clerks to Commanders of Squadrons and Vessels		750
First Clerks to Commandants of Navy Yards		1,500
Second Clerks to Commandants of Navy Yards		1,200
Clerk, Mare Island Navy Yard		1,800
Clerk to Commandants Naval Stations		1,500
Clerks to Paymasters at Navy Yards—		
Boston, New York, Philadelphia and Washington		1,600
Mare Island		1,800
Kittery, Norfolk, and Pensacola		1,400
At other Stations		1,300

The pay of seamen is $23 ½, and of ordinary seamen $210 per annum.

NOTE.—The navy ration is commuted at 30 cents per day. The navy spirit ration was totally abolished July 1, 1870.

Navy officers are retired after forty years' service, on their own application; and they are retired in any case after 62 years of age, with some exceptions. The compensation of retired officers is 75 per cent. of the active pay of the same rank, or 50 per cent. (according to the causes of retirement.)

THE UNITED STATES NAVAL ACADEMY AT ANNAPOLIS.

The United States Naval Academy was opened October 10, 1845, and the credit of its foundation is attributed to Hon. George Bancroft, the Secretary of the Navy under President Polk. The course of instruction, designed to train midshipmen for the navy, at first occupied five years, of which three were passed at sea. Various changes have been made in the course of instruction, which was made seven years in 1850, four years in 1851, and six years (the two last of which are spent at sea) March 3, 1871, where it now remains. The Naval Academy, first located at Annapolis, Maryland, was removed to Newport, R. I., in May, 1861, but re-established at Annapolis in September, 1865, where it now is, occupying lands formerly known as Fort Severn. The academy is under the direct care and supervision of the Navy Department. There are to be allowed in the academy one cadet-midshipman for every member or delegate in the House of Representatives, appointed at his nomination, one for the District of Columbia, and ten appointed at large by the President. The number of appointments which can be made is limited by law to twenty-five each year, named by the Secretary of the Navy after competitive examination, the cadets being from 14 to 18 years of age. The successful candidates become students of the academy, and receive the pay of cadet-midshipmen, $500 per annum. Besides the cadet-midshipmen, 25 cadet engineers may be appointed each year, from 16 to 20 years of age, on competitive examination involving a higher standard of knowledge. The course for cadet-engineers is four years at the academy, and two additional years at sea. All cadets who graduate are appointed assistant engineers in the navy as fast as vacancies occur. The course of instruction is thorough, involving a close pursuit of mathematics, steam engineering, physics, mechanics, seamanship, ordnance, history, law, etc. The whole number of students in 1881 was: Cadet-midshipmen, 161; cadet-engineers, 100; total, 261. The graduating classes of 1881 numbered 72 cadet-midshipmen, and 24 cadet-engineers.

UNITED STATES NAVAL HOSPITALS.

The sum of $50,000 is appropriated yearly for Naval Hospitals at Portsmouth, New Hampshire; Chelsea, Massachusetts; Brooklyn, New York; Philadelphia, Pennsylvania; Annapolis, Maryland; Washington, District of Columbia; Norfolk, Virginia; Pensacola, Florida; Mare Island, California; Yokohama, Japan.

DEPARTMENT OF THE INTERIOR.

This department was established by an act of Congress, approved March 3, 1849. To its supervision and management are committed the following branches of the public service:

1st. **The Public Lands.**—Its head is the Commissioner of the General Land Office. The Land Bureau is charged with the survey, management, and sale of the public domain, the revision of Virginia military bounty-land claims, and the issuing of scrip in lieu thereof.

2d. **Pensions.**—The Commissioner of this bureau is charged with the examination and adjudication of all claims arising under the various and numerous laws passed by Congress, granting bounty land or pensions for the military or naval service in the revolutionary or subsequent wars.

3d. **The Indian Office** has charge of all matters connected with the Indians.

4th. **The Patent Office** is charged with the performance of all "acts and things touching and respecting the granting and issuing of patents for new and useful discoveries, inventions, and improvements."

The Department of the Interior has, besides, the supervision of the accounts of the United States marshals and attorneys, and of the clerks of the United States Courts, and the management of the lead and other mines of the United States, the duty of taking and returning the censuses of the United States, and the management of the affairs of public institutions in the District of Columbia.

OUR PUBLIC LAND SYSTEM.

The public lands of the United States which are still undisposed of and open to settlement, lie in nineteen States and eight Territories. In each case, except Ohio, Indiana, Illinois, the Indian Territory and Alaska, land offices are established, in charge of an officer known as Register of the Land Office, where the records of all surveyed lands are kept, and all applications concerning lands in each district are filed, and inquiries answered. The public lands are divided into two great classes. The one class have a dollar and a quarter an acre designated as the minimum price, and the other, two dollars and a half an acre, the latter being the alternate sections, reserved by the United States in land grants to railroads, etc. Titles to these lands may be acquired by private entry or location under the homestead, pre-emption, and timber culture laws, or, as to some classes, by purchase for cash, in the case of lands which may be purchased at private sale, or such as have not been reserved under any law. Such tracts are sold on application to the Land Register, who issues a certificate of purchase; the receiver giving a receipt for the money paid, subject to the issue of a patent, or complete title if the proceedings are found regular, by the Commissioner of the General Land Office, at Washington.

Entries under land warrants (given mostly for military services under acts of Congress) have fallen off very largely by the absorption of such warrants, there having been no military bounty land warrants provided for on account of services in the late war.

Entries under the pre-emption law are restricted to heads of families, or citizens over twenty-one, who may settle upon any quarter-section (or 160 acres), and have the right of prior claim to purchase on complying with certain regulations.

The homestead laws give the right to one hundred and sixty acres of a dollar-and-a-quarter lands, or to eighty acres of two-dollar-and-a-half lands, to any citizen or applicant for citizenship over twenty-one who will actually settle upon and cultivate the land. This privilege extends only to the surveyed lands, and the title is perfected by the issue of a patent after five years of actual settlement. The only charges in the case of homestead entries are fees and commissions, varying from a minimum of $7 to a maximum of $34 for the whole tract entered, according to the size, value, or place of record.

Another large class of free entries of public lands is that provided for under the timber culture acts of 1873-'78. The purpose of these laws is to promote the growth of forest trees on the public lands. They give the right to any settler who has cultivated for two years as much as five acres in trees to an eighty-acre homestead, or, if ten acres, to a homestead of one hundred and sixty acres, and a free patent for his land is given him at the end of three years, instead of five. The limitation of the homestead laws to one hundred and sixty acres for each settler is extended in the case of timber culture, so as to grant as many quarter sections of one hundred and sixty acres each as have been improved by the culture, for ten years, of forty acres of timber thereon; but the quarter-sections must not lie immediately contiguous. The fees and commissions in timber culture entries vary from $13 to $18 for the tract.

UNITED STATES LAND OFFICES.

Alabama—Huntsville, Montgomery.
Arkansas—Little Rock, Camden, Harrison, Dardanelle.
Arizona Territory—Prescott, Florence.
California—San Francisco, Marysville, Humboldt, Stockton, Visalia, Sacramento, Los Angeles, Shasta, Susanville, Bodie.
Colorado—Denver City, Leadville, Central City, Pueblo, Del Norte, Lake City.
Dakota Territory—Mitchell, Watertown, Fargo, Yankton, Bismarck, Deadwood, Grand Forks, Aberdeen.
Florida—Gainesville.
Idaho Territory—Boise City, Lewiston, Oxford.
Iowa—Des Moines.

Kansas—Topeka, Salina, Independence, Wichita, Kirwin, Concordia, Larned, Wa-Keeny.
Louisiana—New Orleans, Natchitoches.
Michigan—Detroit, East Saginaw, Reed City, Marquette.
Minnesota—Taylor's Falls, St. Cloud, Duluth, Fergus Falls, Worthington, Crookston, Benson, Tracy, Redwood Falls.
Mississippi—Jackson.
Missouri—Boonville, Ironton, Springfield.
Montana Territory—Helena, Bozeman, Miles City.
Nebraska—Norfolk, Beatrice, Lincoln, Niobrara, Grand Island, North Platte, Bloomington, Neligh.
Nevada—Carson City, Eureka.
New Mexico Territory—Santa Fe, La Mesilla.
Oregon—Oregon City, Roseburg, Le Grand, Lake View, The Dalles.
Utah Territory—Salt Lake City.
Washington Territory—Olympia, Vancouver, Walla Walla, Colfax, Yakima.
Wisconsin—Menasha, Falls of St. Croix, Wausau, La Crosse, Bayfield, Eau Claire.
Wyoming Territory—Cheyenne, Evanston.

BUREAU OF INDIAN AFFAIRS.

Congress, by act of July 9, 1832, authorized the President to appoint a Commissioner of Indian Affairs, to have the direction and management of all matters arising out of Indian relations, subject to the Revision of the Secretary of War (now Secretary of the Interior).

The duties of the Bureau are administered by the Commissioner, Chief Clerk, and assistants at Washington, and by a number of superintendents, agents, farmers, schoolteachers, and other appointees in the Indian country.

The estimated number of Indians is about three hundred thousand, spreading from Lake Superior to the Pacific Ocean. Those east of the Mississippi, with few exceptions, are on reservations; so also are the tribes in Kansas north of the Arkansas, and those located between the western border of Arkansas and the country known as the "leased lands."

PATENT OFFICE.

The Constitution, Art. 1, Sec. 8, confers upon Congress the power to promote the progress of science and useful arts, by securing for limited times to authors and inventors the exclusive right to their writings and discoveries. The rights of the latter class are secured by letters patent issued from the Patent Office in accordance with acts of Congress. The office as now organized was established by act of July 4, 1836.

The building erected under the authority of that act it one of the most imposing in the city of Washington. It extends over two entire blocks, and is used for storing and preserving models, as well as for offices for the Commissioner, clerks, and examiners.

PATENT OFFICE LIBRARY.

The library of the Patent Office has vastly grown in importance within the last few years. It is not only needed and used as an absolute necessity by the examiners in the performance of their duties, but it is now much consulted by inventors and those engaged in their interest. It is not an uncommon thing for persons to come from distant parts of the United States to consult books which can only be found in the Patent Office. The collection is now one of the best technical libraries in the world.

PAY OF OFFICERS, EMPLOYES, ETC., IN THE DIFFERENT DIVISIONS OF THE INTERIOR DEPARTMENT.

Assistant secretary, $3,500; chief clerk, $2,700; law clerk, $2,250; 6 chiefs of division, $2,000; 3 law clerks, $2,000; superintendent of documents, $1,720; stenographer, $1,800; captain of watch, $1,000; 5 government directors Union Pacific Railroad, honorary; director of geological survey, $6,000; superintendent of census, $5,000; chief clerk of census, $2,000.

Patent Office.—Commissioner of patents, $4,500; assistant commissioner of patents, $3,000; chief clerk of patents, $2,250; 3 chief examiners, $3,000; examiner of interferences, $2,500; examiner of trademarks, $2,400; 88 examiners of patents, from $1,100 to $2,400; finance clerk of patents, librarian of patents, $2,000; machinist of patents, $1,700; 3 draughtsmen of patents, $1,200; commissioner of land office, $4,000; chief clerk, recorder, law clerk, $2,000; 3 principal clerks, public lands, $1,800; draughtsman, land office, $1,600; assistant, $1,400; secretary, to sign land patents, $1,500.

Pension Office.—Commissioner of pensions, $4,000; deputy commissioner of pensions, $2,400; medical referee of pensions, $2,250; chief clerk of pensions, $2,000; auditor of railroad accounts $3,600; bookkeeper of railroad accounts, $2,400; assistant, $2,000; railroad engineer, $2,400.

Bureau of Indian Affairs.—Commissioner of Indian affairs, $3,600; chief clerk of Indian affairs, $2,000; stenographer, $1,200.

Bureau of Education.—Commissioner of education, $3,000; chief clerk of education, $1,800; statistician of education, $1,800; translator of education, $1,600.

Employes, etc., in General.—633 department clerks, from $900 to $1,800; messenger, $840; 10 attendants in model-room, $800; 76 laborers, from $480 to $660; 2 engineers, skilled workmen, $1,200; 2 assistant engineers, $1,000; 6 firemen, 42 watchmen; 33 messengers, $720.

This department employs a considerable force of temporary clerks, draughtsmen, etc.; also three Indian inspectors at $3,000, two special agents for Indian service at $2,000, three entomologists at $3,000, temporarily, and a considerable number of geologists and other skilled and unskilled persons on the geological surveys, at varying rates of pay.

DEPARTMENT OF AGRICULTURE.

The Department of Agriculture was established by an act of Congress, approved May 15, 1862. The act provides that the department shall be located at the seat of government of the United States, and that its designs and duties shall be to acquire and to diffuse among the people of the United States, useful information on subjects connected with agriculture, in the most general and comprehensive sense of that word, and to procure, propagate, and distribute among the people new and valuable seeds and plants.

The chief executive officer is the "Commissioner of Agriculture," who holds his office by a tenure similar to that of other civil officers appointed by the President. The Commissioner is to acquire and preserve in his department all information concerning agriculture which he can obtain by means of books and correspondence, and by practical and scientific experiments (accurate records of which experiments shall be kept in his office), by the collection of statistics, and by any other appropriate means within his power; to collect, as he may be able, new seeds and plants; to test, by cultivation, the value of such of them as may require such tests; to propagate such as may be worthy of propagation, and to distribute them among agriculturists. He annually makes a general report in writing of his acts to the President and to Congress, and he also makes special reports on particular subjects whenever required to do so by the President or either house of Congress, or whenever he thinks the subject in his charge requires it. He directs and superintends the expenditure of all money appropriated by Congress to the department, and renders accounts thereof.

The chief clerk, in the necessary absence of the Commissioner, or whenever the office becomes vacant, performs the duties of the office. The Commissioner, under the provisions of Congress, appoints and employs chemists, botanists, entomologists, and other persons skilled in the natural sciences pertaining to agriculture.

PAY OF OFFICERS AND EMPLOYES IN THE DEPARTMENT OF AGRICULTURE.

Commissioner of agriculture, $3,500; chief clerk, superintendent of gardens, entomologist, statistician, $2,000; chemist, $3,000; 2 assistants, $2,200 and $1,800; superintendent of seed division, botanist, microscopist, $1,800; 17 clerks, from $1,000 to $1,800; superintendent folding room, engineer, $1,200; lady superintendent seed-room, $850.

A small number of extra clerks, and of copyists, mechanics, laborers, and occasional experts are employed.

PATENT OFFICE.

POST-OFFICE DEPARTMENT.

THE POSTMASTER-GENERAL.

The Postmaster-General has the direction and management of the Postoffice Department. He appoints all officers and employés of the Department, except the three Assistants Postmaster-General, who are appointed by the President, by and with the advice and consent of the Senate; appoints all postmasters whose compensation does not exceed one thousand dollars; makes postal treaties with foreign governments, by and with the advice and consent of the President; awards and executes contracts, and directs the management of the domestic and foreign mail service.

THE FIRST ASSISTANT POSTMASTER-GENERAL.

The First Assistant Postmaster-General has charge of the Appointment Office, which includes five divisions, viz.:

Appointment Division.—The duty of preparing all cases for the establishment, discontinuance, and change of name or site of postoffices, and for the appointment of all postmasters, agents, postal clerks, mail messengers, and department employes, and attending to all correspondence consequent thereto.

Bond Division.—The duty of receiving and recording appointments; sending out papers for postmasters and their assistants to qualify; receiving, entering, and filing their bonds and oaths, and issuing the commissions for postmasters.

Salary and Allowance Division.—The duty of readjusting the salaries of postmasters, and the consideration of allowances for rent, fuel, light, clerk-hire, and other expenditures.

Free Delivery.—The duty of preparing cases for the inauguration of the system in cities, the appointment of letter-carriers, and the general supervision of the system.

Blank Agency Division.—The duty of sending out the blanks, wrapping-paper and twine, letter-balances, and canceling-stamps to offices entitled to receive the same

THE SECOND ASSISTANT POSTMASTER GENERAL.

The Second Assistant Postmaster-General has charge of the Contract Office, mail equipments, etc., including the following three divisions:

Contract Division.—The arrangement of the mail service of the United States, and placing the same under contract, embracing all correspondence and proceedings respecting the frequency of trips, mode of conveyance, and times of departures and arrivals on all the routes, the course of the mails between the different sections of the country, the points of mail distribution, and the regulations for the government of the domestic mail service. It prepares the advertisements for mail proposals, receives the bids, and has charge of the annual and occasional mail lettings, and the adjustment and execution of the contracts. All applications for the establishment or alteration

UNITED STATES POST OFFICE.

of mail arrangements, and for mail messengers, should be sent to this office. All claims should be submitted to it for transportation service not under contract. From this office all postmasters at the end of routes receive the statement of mail arrangements prescribed for the respective routes. It reports weekly to the Auditor all contracts executed, and all orders affecting the accounts for mail transportation; prepares the statistical exhibits of the mail service, and the reports to Congress of the mail lettings, giving a statement of each bid; also of the contracts made, the new service originated, the curtailments ordered, and the additional allowances granted within the year.

Inspection Division.—The duty of receiving and examining the registers of the arrivals and departures of the mails, certificates of the service of route agents, and reports of mail failures; noting the delinquencies of contractors, and preparing cases thereon for the action of the Postmaster-General; furnishing blanks for mail registers, reports of mail failures, and other duties which may be necessary to secure a faithful and exact performance of all mail service.

Mail Equipment Division.—The issuing of mail locks and keys, mail pouches and sacks, and the construction of mail-bag catchers.

THE THIRD ASSISTANT POSTMASTER GENERAL.

The Third Assistant Postmaster-General has charge of the Finance Office, etc., embracing the following four divisions:

Division of Finance.—The duty of issuing drafts and warrants in payment of balances reported by the Auditor to be due to mail contractors or other persons; the superintendence of the collection of revenue at depository, draft, and depositing offices, and the accounts between the Department and the Treasurer and Assistant Treasurers and special designated depositories of the United States. This division receives all accounts, monthly or quarterly, of the depository and draft offices, and certificates of deposit from depositing offices.

Division of Postage Stamps and Stamped Envelopes.—The issuing of postage-stamps, stamped envelopes, newspaper-wrappers and postal cards; also the surplying of postmasters with envelopes for their official use, and registered-package envelopes and seals.

Division of Registered Letters.—The duty of preparing instructions for the guidance of postmasters relative to registered letters, and all correspondence connected therewith; also the compilation of statistics as to the transactions of the business.

Division of Dead Letters.—The examination and return to the writers of dead letters and all correspondence relating thereto.

The Superintendent of Foreign Mails has charge of all foreign postal arrangements, and the supervision of the ocean mail steamship service.

The Superintendent of the Money Order System has the general supervision and control of the postal money order system throughout the United States, and the supervision of the international money order correspondence with foreign countries.

PAY OF OFFICERS AND EMPLOYES OF THE POST OFFICE DEPARTMENT.

Postoffice Department.—3 assistant postmasters-general, $4,500; chief clerk, 4 chiefs of bureaus, chief of division, $2,000; 3 chief clerks of division, law clerk, topographer, $2,250; 20 clerks, 1 stenographer, $1,800; 65 clerks, $1,600; 51 clerks, $1,400; 75 clerks, 1 carpenter, $1,200; 14 clerks, $1,000; 61 clerks, $900; superintendent of free delivery, disbursing clerk, $2,100; superintendent of foreign mails, superintendent of money order service, $3,000; engineer, $1,40 ; assistant, $900; fireman and blacksmith, $900; fireman and steam-fitter, $720; assistant carpenter, captain of watch $1,000; 15 watchmen, 11 messengers, $720; 35 laborers, $600; 3 female laborers, $180.

Inspection Service.—9 inspectors, $2,500; 9 inspectors, $1,600 and $5 per day for expenses; 6 inspectors, $1,600 and $4 per day for expenses; 18 inspectors, $1,500 and $4 per day for expenses; 7 inspectors, $1,200 and $4 per day for expenses; 4 inspectors, $1,400 and $4 per day for expenses; inspector, $1,400; inspector, $1,200.

Railway Mail Service.—General superintendent, $3,500; 9 assistants, $2,500; assistant superintendent, $1,600 and $5 per day for expenses; assistant superintendent, $1,600 and $4 per day for expenses; assistant superintendent, $1,500 and $4 per day for expenses; assistant superintendent, $1,200 and $5 per day for expenses; assistant superintendent, $1,200 and $4 per day for expenses; 72 route agents, $1,000; 3 route agents, $950; 49 route agents, $970; 85 route agents, $910; 26 route agents, $920; 894 route agents, $900; 41 railway postal clerks, $1,400; 356 railway postal clerks, $1,300; 443 postal clerks, $1,150; 178 railway postal clerks, $1,000; 62 railway postal clerks, $900.

Supply Service.—3 distributing agents for stamped envelopes, postage stamps, and postal cards, $2,500; 15 clerks, $1,000 to $1,800; delete clerk, $1,800.

In addition to the above there are at present some 130 local mail agents, with salaries from $100 to $1,800 per year, and a larger amount of mail route messengers, with salaries from $100 to $880 per year. Besides these are the mail contractors, 5,600 or 5,700 in number.

UNITED STATES POSTAL REGULATIONS.

First-Class Mail Matter.—LETTERS.—This class includes letters and anything of which the Postmaster cannot ascertain the contents without destroying the wrapper, or anything unsealed which may be wholly or partly in writing, except manuscript for publication accompanied by proof-sheets. Postage, 3 cents each half ounce, or for each fraction above half an ounce. On local or drop letters, at free delivery offices, 2 cents. At offices where no free delivery by carriers, 1 cent.

Postal cards, 1 cent. Postal cards and letters go to Canada same as in United States.

Registered letters, 10 cents in addition to the proper postage.

The Postoffice Department or its revenue is not by law liable for the loss of any registered or other mail matter.

Second Class.—REGULAR PUBLICATIONS.—This class includes all newspapers, periodicals, or matter exclusively in print and regularly issued at stated periods from a known office of publication or news agency. Postage, 2 cents a pound or fraction thereof.

Third Class.—MISCELLANEOUS PRINTED MATTER.—Mailable matter of the third class includes books, transient newspapers and periodicals, circulars, and other matter wholly in print (not of the second class), proof-sheets, corrected proof-sheets, and manuscript copy accompanying the same; and postage shall be paid at the rate of 1 cent for each two ounces or fractional part thereof, and shall fully be prepaid by postage stamps affixed to said matter.

Upon matter of the third class, or upon the wrapper inclosing the same, the sender may write his own name or address thereon, with the word "from" above and preceding the same, and in either case may make simple marks intended to design a word or passage of the text to which it is desired to call attention. There may be placed upon the cover or blank leaves of any book, or of any printed matter of the third class, a simple manuscript dedication or inscription that does not partake of the nature of a personal correspondence. Address, date, and signature may be written in printed circulars; but bills, statements, and other commercial papers, partly in writing, must be prepaid at letter rates.

All packages of matter of the third class must be so wrapped or enveloped that their contents may be readily and thoroughly examined by postmasters without destroying the wrappers.

Matter of the third class inclosed in sealed envelopes, notched at the ends or sides, or with the corners cut off, cannot be mailed except at letter postage rates.

Packages of matter of this class may weigh not exceeding four pounds, except in case of single books weighing in excess of that amount.

"Printed matter" is defined to be the reproduction upon paper, by any process except that of handwriting, of any words, letters, characters, figures, or images, or of any combination thereof, not having the character of an actual and personal correspondence. This includes photographs and matter produced by the hektograph or electric pen.

Fourth Class.—MERCHANDISE, SAMPLES, ETC.—Mailable matter of the fourth class includes all matter not embraced in the first, second, or third class, which is not in its form or nature liable to destroy, deface, or otherwise damage the contents of the mail-bag, or harm the person of any one engaged in the postal service.

All matter of the fourth class is subject to a postage charge at the rate of 1 cent an ounce or fraction thereof, to be prepaid by stamps affixed.

Upon any package of matter of the fourth class the sender may write or print his own name and address, preceded by the word "from," and there may also be written or printed the number and names of the articles inclosed; and the sender thereof may write upon, or attach to any such article, by tag or label, a single mark, number, name, or letter, for purpose of identification only.

All packages of matter of the fourth class must be so wrapped or enveloped that their contents may be readily and thoroughly examined by postmasters without destroying the wrappers; but seeds or other articles liable, from their form or nature, to loss or damage unless specially protected, may be inclosed in unsealed bags or boxes which can readily be opened for examination of the contents, and re-closed; or sealed bags made of material sufficiently *transparent* to show the contents clearly without opening, may be used for such matters.

Packages of matter of this class may weigh not exceeding four pounds.

Miscellaneous.—Newspapers to persons not subscribers from office of publication, or from one person to another, to be prepaid by stamps—one cent for two ounces or fraction thereof.

One or more newspapers may be inclosed in the same package and sent at the same rate.

Letters can be forwarded from one postoffice to another (as in the case of removal, etc.) at the request of the party addressed, without extra charge. "Return letters" are also sent back to the writers, free, on expiration of days named in request.

All letters not claimed in one month from their receipt, or returned to writer, are forwarded to the Dead Letter Office.

No packages forwarded in mails weighing over four pounds, except single books weighing in excess thereof.

To inclose or conceal a letter or written matter in a newspaper, magazine, or other print, subjects the entire package to letter postage, and the sender to a fine of $10.

All communications from private citizens to Government officers, and to members of Congress, are required to be prepaid by stamps.

Foreign Postage.—Letters at 5 cents per half ounce, prepayment optional (postal cards, 2 cents each), and printed matter and samples, 1 cent per 2 ounces to all countries belonging to the "Universal Postal Union," which embraces all parts of Europe and the colonies of the principal European powers; also Mexico, Cuba, Ecuador, Brazil, Uruguay, Venezuela, Argentine Republic, Chili, Peru, Japan, Hong Kong, Egypt, Liberia, Hayti, Newfoundland, Canada, and other places of less importance. (Postage to Canada is 3 cents per half ounce for letters, and 1 cent per 2 ounces for printed matter.)

APPOINTMENTS BY THE POSTMASTER GENERAL.

For an Unlimited Term.

Appointment Clerk, Assistant Attorney-General for Postoffice Department, carpenters, chief clerk to the Postmaster-General, chief clerks to Assistant Postmasters-General, chief clerk to Superintendent of Foreign Mails, chief clerk to Superintendent of Money Order System, Chief of Division of Dead Letters, Chief of Division of Inspection, Chief of Division of Mail Depredations, Chief of Division of Postage Stamps, Chief of Special Agents, clerks (fourth, third, second, first classes —$1,000 and $900 classes), disbursing clerk and superintendent of the building, engineers, firemen, fireman and blacksmith, fireman and steam-fitter, laborers (male and female), low clerk.

Letter-Carriers.—Letter-carriers are appointed by the Postmaster-General, on the nomination and recommendation of the local postmaster.

Local Mail Agents.—By the Postmaster-General, on the nomination of the local postmaster; Messengers, postmasters of the fourth class, railway postal clerks, route agents, special agents, stenographer to the Postmaster-General, superintendent of the Blank Agency, assistant superintendents of the Blank Agency, superintendent of free delivery, superintendent of money order system, superintendent of railway mail service, topographer, watchmen. Clerks and other employes in postoffices are appointed by the postmasters.

Superintendents of Mails.—Clerks in Postoffices of the first and second classes to superintend the distribution of the mail, are appointed by the Postmaster-General, on the nomination of the General Superintendent of the Railway Mail Service.

THE JUDICIAL DEPARTMENT.

UNITED STATES SUPREME COURT.

The Supreme Court consists of a Chief-Justice and eight Associate Justices.

A Clerk and a Marshal are appointed by the Court. The Clerk receives fees for the performance of the duties of his office, and, unlike other court clerks, there is no maximum fixed of the amount of fees to be retained by him.

The Supreme Court must hold one regular term a year, commencing on the second Monday in October, and such special terms as may be necessary.

JURISDICTION OF THE SUPREME COURT.

Exclusive jurisdiction of all controversies of a civil nature where a State is a party, except between a State and its citizens, or between a State and citizens of other States, or aliens, in which latter cases it shall have original, but not exclusive jurisdiction.

Exclusively of suits or proceedings against ambassadors or other public ministers, or their domestic servants; and original but not exclusive jurisdiction of all suits brought by ambassadors or other public ministers, or in which a consul or vice-consul is a party.

It has power to issue writs of prohibition in the District Courts when proceeding as courts of admiralty and maritime jurisdiction, and writs of mandamus in cases warranted by the principles and usages of law, to any United States courts, or to persons holding office under the United States, where a State or an ambassador or other public minister or consul or vice-consul is a party.

Appeals from the Circuit and District Courts.

UNITED STATES CIRCUIT COURTS.

The judicial districts of the United States are divided into nine circuits, as follows:

The first circuit includes the districts of Rhode Island, Massachusetts, New Hampshire, and Maine.
The second, Vermont, Connecticut, and New York.
The third, Pennsylvania, New Jersey and Delaware.
The fourth, Maryland, Virginia, West Virginia, North Carolina, and South Carolina.
The fifth, Georgia, Florida, Alabama, Mississippi, Louisiana, and Texas.
The sixth, Ohio, Michigan, Kentucky, and Tennessee.
The seventh, Indiana, Illinois, and Wisconsin.
The eighth, Nebraska, Minnesota, Iowa, Missouri, Kansas, and Arkansas.
The ninth, California, Oregon and Nevada.

ALLOTMENTS.

The Chief-Justice and Associate Justices of the Supreme Court are allotted among the circuits by an order of the Court.

For each circuit a circuit judge is appointed, with a salary of $6,000 a year.

Circuit courts are held by the circuit justice or by the circuit judge of the circuit, or by the district judge sitting alone, or by any two of the said judges sitting together.

The Chief Justice and each Justice of the Supreme Court must attend at least one term of the Circuit Court in each district of the Circuit to which he is allotted during every two years.

A clerk is appointed for each Circuit Court by the Circuit Judge.

SALARIES OF OFFICERS, ETC., OF THE JUDICIAL DEPARTMENT.

Supreme Court.—Chief-justice, $10,500; eight associates, $10,000; clerk (estimated emoluments), $25,000; reporter, about $1,000; marshal, $3,500; clerks, messengers, bailiffs, etc., at varying rates.

Court of Claims.—Chief-Justice, $1,500; 4 associates, $1,500; clerk, $3,000; assistant, $2,000; bailiffs, messengers, etc.

Supreme Court of District of Columbia.—Chief-justice, $4,500; 5 associates, $4,000; clerk, district attorney, marshal, register of wills, fees; deputy clerks and marshals, bailiffs, attendants, etc., in varying number and rate, from $2,500 to $500 per year.

DEPARTMENT OF JUSTICE.

The ordinary business of this office may be classified under the following heads:

1. Official opinions on the current business of the government, as called for by the President, by any head of department, or by the Solicitor of the Treasury.
2. Examination of the titles of all land purchased, as the sites of arsenals, custom-houses, lighthouses, and all other public works of the United States.
3. Applications for pardons in all cases of conviction in the courts of the United States.
4. Application for appointment in all the judicial and legal business of the government.
5. The conduct and argument of all suits in the Supreme Court of the United States in which the government is concerned.
6. The supervision of all other suits arising in any of the departments, when referred by the head thereof to the Attorney General.

To these ordinary heads of the business of the office is added at the present time the direction of all appeals on land claims in California.

PAY OF OFFICERS AND EMPLOYES IN THE DEPARTMENT OF JUSTICE.

Solicitor-general, $7,000; 3 assistant attorneys-general, $5,000; solicitor of the treasury, solicitor of internal revenue, $4,500; assistant attorney-general for postoffice department, $4,000; examiner of claims in department of state, $3,500; law clerk, $2,700; chief clerk, $2,200; 9 clerks, from $1,200 to $2,000; stenographer, $1,800; telegraph operator, $1,000; 5 copyists, $900; 2 messengers, 2 watchmen, $720; 2 laborers, $660.

UNITED STATES MINT.

The Constitution (*article 1, section 8*) gives Congress the sole power to coin money, and regulate the value thereof. The act of April 2, 1792, provided that a mint for the purpose of national coinage should be established and carried on at the seat of government of the United States, which was then at Philadelphia. Subsequent acts continued the mint at the same place temporarily, until by act of May 19, 1828, its location was permanently fixed in that city.

The officers of the mint are—a Director, a Treasurer, an Assayer, a Melter and Refiner, a Chief Coiner, and an Engraver. These officers are appointed by the President of the United States, by and with the advice and consent of the Senate.

The Director has the control and management of the mint, the superintendence of the officers and persons employed, and the general regulation and supervision of the several branches.

The Treasurer receives all moneys for the use of support of the mint, and all bullion brought to the mint for coinage; he has the custody of the same, except while legally in the hands of other officers; and on the warrant of the director, he pays all moneys due by the mint, and delivers all coins struck at the mint to the persons to whom they are legally payable.

The Assayer assays all metals used in coinage, and all coins, whenever required by the operations of the mint, or instructed by the Director.

The Melter and Refiner conducts the operations necessary to form ingots of standard silver and gold suitable for the Chief Coiner.

The Chief Coiner conducts the operations necessary to form coins from the ingots, etc., delivered to him for the purpose.

The Engraver prepares and engraves with the legal device and inscription all the dies used in the coinage of the mint and its branches.

Besides the mint at Philadelphia, Congress has, from time to time, established branches and an Assay Office at the following places:

At New Orleans, for the coinage of gold and silver .... March 3, 1835
At Charlotte, North Carolina, for the coinage of gold only .... March 3, 1835
At Dahlonega, Georgia, for gold only .... March 3, 1835
At San Francisco, California, for gold and silver .... July 3, 1852
At Denver, Colorado Territory, for gold and silver .... April 21, 1862
At Carson City, Nevada, for gold and silver .... March 3, 1863
At New York City, an Assay Office for the receipt, melting, refining, parting, and assaying of gold and silver bullion and foreign coin, and for casting the same into bars, ingots, or disks ...... March 3, 1853
At Dallas City, Oregon, for gold and silver .. July 4, 1864

UNITED STATES COAST SURVEY.

The coast survey has for its object the production of accurate charts of the coasts and harbors of the United States. With a shore line, including bays and islands, and exclusive of Alaska, of more than 25,000 miles in length, and with a commerce extending to all parts of the world, and rapidly increasing, the importance to this country of this branch of the public service will be readily appreciated.

The work was commenced on the Eastern or Atlantic

coast in 1822, under the superintendence of Professor F. R. Hassler, and after his death in 1843, was continued under the superintendence of late Professor Alexander D. Bache, and extended to the Gulf of Mexico. On the acquisition of California, the Pacific coast was included in the survey, and since the treaty with Russia, by which Alaska was brought under the Government of the United States, the survey has been extended to that Territory. The whole work is under the administrative direction of the Treasury Department. Upon the superintendent devolves the duty of planning its operations, for the scientific accuracy of which he is responsible. The corps of assistants is composed of three classes—civilians, and army and navy officers. The work is divided into three branches—the geodetic survey accurately determines the relative positions on the surface of the earth of a great number of prominent points, by a system of triangulation and observation of the true meridian lines, and of latitude and longitude. The positions fixed by the triangulation form the groundwork of the topographic survey, which delineates the shore-line of the coasts, bays, and rivers; the shape and heights of the hills; the position of the roads, houses, woods, marshes, and fields—in short, all noteworthy features of the country. The hydrographic survey, based upon the points and shore-lines furnished by the triangulation and topography, delineates the hidden configuration of the sea bottom, discovers channels, shoals, and rocks, assigns their true position, and shows the depth of water and character of the bottom over the whole extent of the chart.

The observations made in the progress of the survey are arranged and published with illustrative plates, topographic maps, and hydrographic charts.

FREEDMAN'S BUREAU.

The Bureau of Refugees, Freedmen, and Abandoned Lands was established March 3, 1865, and attached to the War Department. By its terms the law was limited to one year after the close of the rebellion. On the 16th day of July, A. D. 1866, the law was amended and continued in force for two years, and again, on the 25th of July, 1868, an act was passed continuing the educational department of the Bureau, and the collections and payments of money due soldiers and sailors or their heirs, until otherwise ordered by Congress, but the other operations of the Bureau were to be withdrawn from the reconstructed States on the 1st of January, 1869.

Major-General O. O. Howard was appointed Commissioner of the Bureau on the 12th of May, 1865, and entered upon his duties on the 15th. Ten assistant commissioners were appointed in the different States embraced under the Bureau. With one exception, these were officers in the army, who were changed from time to time as changes were made in the different military departments.

The Bureau was organized with four departments, embracing that of *Lands*, *Records*, *Financial Affairs*, and the *Medical Department*. The *Claim Division* was subsequently organized under the head of the Land Department.

The Bureau at first had supervision of farming property only, but the orders issued under the act by the President on the 2d day of July, 1865, and by the Secretary of the Treasury soon after, placed the Bureau in charge of all real property which had been abandoned, captured, or confiscated, including building lots in cities and towns, as well as plantations and farms.

As soon as possible after its organization, the Land Division proceeded to ascertain as accurately as possible the amount and character of the property committed to its charge

DIPLOMATIC AND CONSULAR OFFICERS.

Diplomatic and consular officers must not be absent from their posts more than ten days in one year, without leave obtained from the President, and then only for sixty days, not including the time spent in the round journey if the officer visits his home.

The pay of a diplomatic or consular officer is calculated from the time when he begins to receive his instructions; but not more than thirty days time is allowed to this business, and he must take the most direct route to his station. On his return home, time is allowed for the return journey by the most direct route, unless he has resigned, or been recalled, because of official misconduct.

Allowances for clerical service are made to a considerable number of the larger consulates.

The thirteen consular clerks hold office during good behavior after appointment.

The consular offices compensated only by fees, are usually sought and filled by persons who desire to hold the offices and live at the stations for purposes of business, health, or pleasure, and not for the emoluments of the offices themselves.

DIPLOMATIC SERVICE.

Ministers to France, Germany, Great Britain and Russia	$17,500
Ministers to Austria, Brazil, China, Italy, Japan, Mexico, and Spain	12,000
Ministers to Central America, Chili and Peru	10,000
Ministers to Argentine Confederation, Belgium, Colombia, Hawaiian Islands, Hayti, Netherlands, Sweden, Turkey, and Venezuela	$7,500
Ministers to Bolivia, Denmark, Paraguay, Portugal, and Switzerland	5,000
Minister to Liberia	4,000
Secretary and Interpreter of Legation at Pekin	5,000
Secretary of Legation at Constantinople	3,000
Secretaries of Legation at Paris, Berlin, London, and St. Petersburg	2,625
Secretary of Legation at Yeddo	2,500
Interpreter at Yeddo	2,500
Second Secretaries at Paris, Berlin, and London	2,000

Secretaries of Legation at Madrid, Mexico, Rio de
  Janeiro, Rome, and Vienna. 1,800

CONSULAR SERVICE.

CONSULS NOT PERMITTED TO TRADE.

Havana, Liverpool, London, Paris, Rio de Janeiro $6,000
Calcutta and Shanghai.............................. 5,000
Melbourne 4,500
Berlin, Bucharest, Cairo, Hong-Kong, Honolulu,
  Montreal 4,000
Amoy, Callao, Canton, Chin-Kiang, Foo-Chow,
  Hankow, Ningpo, and Tien-Tsin 3,500
Aspinwall, Bangkok, Bradford, Buenos Ayres, De-
  merara, Frankfort, Glasgow, Havre, Liege,
  Manchester, Matanzas, Nagasaki, Osaka,
  Panama, Rome, Tangiers, Tripoli, Tunis, Val-
  paraiso, Vera Cruz, Vienna 3,000
Antwerp, Belfast, Birmingham, Bordeaux, Bremen,
  Brussels, Cienfuegos, Dresden, Hamburg,
  Lyons, Marseilles, Santiago de Cuba, Saint
  Thomas, Sheffield, Singapore, Tonstall 2,500
Acapulco, Barmen, Basle, Beirut, Cardiff, Chem-
  nitz, Coatzacoalcos, Cologne, Cork, Dublin, Dun-
  dee, Halifax, Hamilton, Kingston, Leeds, Leip-
  sic, Leith, Lisbon, Matamoras, Mexico City,
  Montevideo, Nassau, Nuremberg, Odessa, Per-
  nambuco, Port Louis, Prague, Rotterdam, St.
  John, St. Petersburg, San Juan, Smyrna, Sonne-
  berg, Funchal, Toronto, Trieste, Zurich, ... 2,000
Amsterdam, Auckland, Barbadoes, Barcelona,
  Bahia, Bermuda, Bristol, Cadiz, Carthagena,
  Charlottetown, Clifton, Copenhagen, Corfu,
  Florence, Fort Erie, Funchal, Geneva, Genoa,
  Gibraltar, Goderich, Jerusalem, Kingston
  (Canada), Laguayra, Leghorn, Lucca, Malta,
  Malaga, Mannheim, Martinique, Messina, Mu-
  nich, Naples, Newcastle, Nice, Palermo, Pic-
  tou, Port Sarnia, Port Stanley, Prescott, Que-
  bec, St. Helena, St. John's (N. B.), San
  Domingo, Stuttgart, Tampico, Vevey, Wind-
  sor, Winnipeg. 1,500

CONSULS PERMITTED TO TRADE.

Apia, Batavia, Cape Haytien, Ceylon, Guyaquil,
  Gaspé Basin, Guatemala, Honduras, Nantes, Para,
  Rio Grande do Sul, Sabanilla, Santiago, Tahiti,
  Tamatave, Utilla, Venice, Windsor (Nova
  Scotia), Zanzibar 1,000

CONSULS AND COMMERCIAL AGENTS PERMITTED TO TRADE, AND COMPENSATED ONLY BY FEES COLLECTED.

Algiers, Alicante, Annapolis, Antigua, Archangel,
  Barmen, Bathurst, Belize, Bergen, Bogota,
  Bombay, Breslau, Brunswick, Buena Ventura,
  Cameroons, Carrara, Castellamare, Carthagena,

Chihuahua, Christiania, Ciudad Bolivar, Colo-
nia, Coquimbo, Cordoba, Corunna, Crefeld,
Curacoa, Denia, Falmouth, Galatz, Garrucha,
Geestemünd, Ghent, Guttenburg, Grand Bassa,
Guerrero, Guadaloupe, Gudericks, Helsing-
fors, Hobart-Town, Iloilo, Iquique, Lambaye-
que, La Paz, La Rochelle, La Union, London-
derry, Malta, Manila, Manzanillo, Mazatlan,
Maracaibo, Medellin, Merida, Milo, Milan,
Miraflores, Monterey, Moscow, Nuevo Cheung,
Nottingham, Nuevo Laredo, Oporto, Ottawa,
Padang, Pago Pago, Paramaribo, Paso del
Norte, Patras, Pesth, Piedras Negras, Ply-
mouth, Ponce, Port Stanley, Presidio, Norte,
Puerto Cabello, Rheims, Rio Hacha, Rosario,
Ruatan, Sagua la Grande, St. Barthelemy,
St. Christopher, St. Gall, St. George's, St.
Helen's, St. John's, St. Marc, St. Martin, St.
Pierre, Soutano, San Andres, San Blas, San
Jose, San Juan del Sur, Santa Martha, Santand-
er, Santos, Sierra Leone, Sonsonate, Stan-
bridge, Stockholm, Sydney, Teneriffe, Tehuan-
tepec, Trinidad, Victoria, Warsaw, Zacatecas.

MISCELLANEOUS.

13 Consular Clerks........................ $1,000
Interpreter at Shanghai.................. 2,000
Interpreter at Foo-Chow, Kanagawa, and Tien-
  Tsin 1,500
Interpreters at Amoy, Canton, Hankow, and
  Hong-Kong 750
22 Interpreters in China, Japan, Siam, and Turkey 500
8 Marshals of Consular Courts in China, Japan,
  and Turkey........................Fees and 1,000
Dispatch Agent at New York............... 1,000
Dispatch Agent at London................. 2,000

Statistics of Religious Denominations in the United States.

Roman Catholic............................... 6,367,330
Baptist...................................... 2,133,044
Methodist.................................... 1,742,177
M. E. South..................................   823,361
Lutheran.....................................   73,871
Presbyterian.................................   578,671
Christian....................................   572,413
Congregational...............................   334,710
Protestant Episcopal.........................   344,757
United Brethren..............................   155,434
Reformed Church (not U. S.)..................   223,720
United Evangelical...........................   140,000
Presbyterian South...........................   120,028
Protestant Methodist.........................   115,502
Cumberland Presbyterian......................   111,857
Mormon   108,952
Evangelical Association......................   90,000

The Brethren	10,006
United Presbyterian	80,237
Reformed Church in America	78,916
Freewill Baptists	76,703
Friends	67,640
Second Adventist	63,500
Anti-Mission Baptist	40,000
Universalist	37,045
Church of God	20,224
Wesleyan Methodist	17,847
Moravian	16,115
Seventh Day Adventist	14,734
Jews	13,683
Free Methodist	12,123
Adventist	11,100
Reformed Episcopal	10,459
Seventh Day Baptist	8,600
Reformed Presbyterian	6,020
New Jerusalem	4,734
Primitive Methodist	3,170
New Mennonite	2,000
American Communities	1,838
Shaker	2,450
Independent Methodist	2,103
Six Principle Baptist	2,070

LOSSES OF THE GOVERNMENT FOR EVERY ADMINISTRATION FROM 1789 TO 1876.

The following table exhibits the losses of the Government through frauds, carelessness, and from all causes, and the amount of loss on each thousand dollars, for every administration from the beginning of the government till the end of President Grant's administration, as follows:

	Period of service.	Total Losses.	Loss on $1,000.		Period of service.	Total Losses.	Loss on $1,000.
Washington	8 years.	$ 250,070	$ 2.22	Polk	4 years.	$1,732,851	$ 4.08
Adams	4 "	438,411	2.50	Taylor	1 "	1,814,400	4.19
Jefferson	8 "	603,467	2.75	Fillmore	3 "		
Madison	8 "	2,191,600	4.16	Pierce	4 "	2,167,982	3.56
Monroe	8 "	3,230,787	8.58	Buchanan	4 "	2,659,107	3.81
Adams	4 "	884,374	4.30	Lincoln	4 "	7,200,984	76
Jackson	8 "	3,761,111	7.52	Johnson	4 "	1,610,500	57
Van Buren	4 "	3,343,702	11.71	Grant	8 "	2,810,102	44
Harrison	}14 "	1,535,003	6.40	Total		$30,108,605	$1.20
Tyler							

SUPREME COURT OF THE UNITED STATES.

Chief-Justices.		Associate Justices.	State Whence Appointed.	Term of Service.	No.	Born.	Died.
1 John Jay†...........			New York.......	1789-1795	6	1745	1829
	1	John Rutledge†......	South Carolina...	1790-1791	2	1739	1800
	2	William Cushing.....	Massachusetts...	1789-1810	21	1733	1810
	3	James Wilson.......	Pennsylvania.....	1789-1798	9	1742	1798
	4	John Blair†.........	Virginia..........	1790-1796	7	1732	1800
	5	Robert H. Harrison..	Maryland.........	1789-1790	1	1745	1790
	6	James Iredell.......	North Carolina..	1790-1799	9	1751	1799
	7	Thomas Johnson †...	Maryland.........	1791-1793	2	1732	1819
	8	William Patterson...	New Jersey......	1793-1806	13	1745	1806
2 John Rutledge.‡.....		....	South Carolina...	1795-1795	...	1739	1800
	9	Salmon P. Chase.....	Maryland.........	1796-1811	15	1741	1811
3 Oliver Ellsworth†...		....	Connecticut......	1796-1799	5	1745	1807
	10	Bushrod Washington.	Virginia..........	1798-1829	31	1762	1829
	11	Alfred Moore†.......	North Carolina...	1799-1804	5	1755	1810
4 John Marshall.......		....	Virginia..........	1801-1835	34	1755	1835
	12	William Johnson.....	South Carolina...	1804-1834	30	1771	1834
	13	Brockh't Livingston..	New York.........	1806-1823	17	1757	1823
	14	Thomas Todd........	Kentucky........	1807-1826	19	1765	1826
	15	Joseph Story........	Massachusetts...	1811-1845	34	1779	1845
	16	Gabriel Duvall......	Maryland.........	1811-1836	25	1752	1844
	17	Smith Thompson....	New York.........	1823-1843	20	1767	1843
	18	Robert Trimble......	Kentucky........	1826-1828	2	1777	1829
	19	John McLean........	Ohio.............	1829-1861	32	1785	1861
	20	Henry Baldwin......	Pennsylvania....	1830-1846	16	1779	1846
	21	James M. Wayne§..	Georgia..........	1835-1867	32	1790	1867
5 Roger B. Taney.....		....	Maryland.........	1836-1864	28	1777	1864
	22	Philip P. Barbour....	Virginia..........	1836-1841	5	1783	1841
	23	John Catron........	Tennessee.......	1837-1865	28	1786	1865
	24	John McKinley......	Alabama.........	1837-1852	15	1780	1852
	25	Peter V. Daniel.....	Virginia..........	1841-1860	19	1785	1860
	26	Samuel Nelson.†...	New York.........	1845-1872	27	1792	1873
	27	Levi Woodbury.....	New Hampshire..	1845-1851	6	1789	1851
	28	Robert C. Grier†...	Pennsylvania....	1846-1870	24	1794	1870
	29	Benjamin R. Curtis†.	Massachusetts...	1851-1857	6	1809	1874
	30	John A. Campbell†..	Alabama.........	1853-1861	8	1811	....
	31	Nathan Clifford.....	Maine............	1858-....	..	1803	....
	32	Noah H. Swayne....	Ohio.............	1861-....	..	1804	....
	33	Samuel F. Miller.....	Iowa.............	1862-....	..	1816	....
	34	David Davis†.......	Illinois...........	1862-1877	15	1815	....
	35	Stephen J. Field.....	California........	1863-....	..	1816	....
6 Salmon P. Chase....		....	Ohio.............	1864-1873	9	1808	1873
	36	William Strong†.....	Pennsylvania....	1870-1880	10	1808	....
	37	Joseph P. Bradley...	New Jersey......	1870-....	..	1813	....
	38	Ward Hunt..........	New York.........	1872-....	..	1811	....
7 Morrison R. Waite..		....	Ohio.............	1874-....	14	1816	....
	39	John M. Harlan.....	Kentucky........	1877-....	..	1833	....
	40	William B. Woods...	Georgia..........	1880-....	..	1824	1887

SUPREME COURT OF THE UNITED STATES.—Concluded.

			41	Stanley Matthews	32	Ohio	1881-...		1824	
			42	Horace Gray	31	Massachusetts	1881-...		1828	
			43	Samuel Blatchford	38	New York	1882-...		1820	
			44	Lucius Q. C. Lamar	40	Mississippi	1888-...		1825	
§	Melville W. Fuller					Illinois	1888-...		1833	

* The figures before the names of the Associate Justices indicate the order of their appointment. The numbers following refer to the same numbers in the first column, and show the vacancy filled by each appointment.
† Resigned.
‡ Presided one term of the Court; appointment not confirmed by the Senate.
§ The Supreme Court, at its first session in 1790, consisted of a Chief Justice and five Associates. The number of Associate Justices was increased to six in 1807, by the appointment of Thomas Todd; increased to eight in 1837, by the appointment of John Catron and John McKinley; increased to nine in 1863, by the appointment of Stephen J. Field; decreased to eight on the death of John Catron in 1855; decreased to seven on the death of James M. Wayne, in 1867; and again increased to eight in 1870.

THE CLIMATE OF THE UNITED STATES.

State or Territory.	Place of Observation.	Mean annual temperature, degrees	State or Territory.	Place of Observation.	Mean annual temperature, degrees
Alabama	Mobile	66	Mississippi	Jackson	64
Alaska	Sitka	40	Missouri	St. Louis	55
Arizona	Tucson	69	Montana	Helena	44
Arkansas	Little Rock	63	Nebraska	Omaha	49
California	San Francisco	55	Nevada	Cape Winfield Scott	50
Colorado	Denver	48	New Hampshire	Concord	46
Connecticut	Hartford	50	New Jersey	Trenton	53
Dakota	Fort Randall	47	New Mexico	Santa Fe	50
Delaware	Wilmington	54	New York	Albany	48
District Columbia	Washington	55	North Carolina	Raleigh	59
Florida	Jacksonville	69	Ohio	Columbus	53
Georgia	Atlanta	58	Oregon	Portland	53
Idaho	Fort Boise	52	Pennsylvania	Harrisburg	54
Illinois	Springfield	50	Rhode Island	Providence	48
Indiana	Indianapolis	51	South Carolina	Columbia	62
Indian Territory	Fort Gibson	60	Tennessee	Nashville	58
Iowa	Des Moines	48	Texas	Austin	67
Kansas	Leavenworth	54	Utah	Salt Lake City	52
Kentucky	Louisville	54	Vermont	Montpelier	43
Louisiana	New Orleans	69	Virginia	Richmond	57
Maine	Augusta	45	Washington Ter.	Steilacoom	51
Maryland	Baltimore	55	West Virginia	Romney	52
Massachusetts	Boston	48	Wisconsin	Madison	45
Michigan	Detroit	47	Wyoming	Fort Bridger	41
Minnesota	St. Paul	42			

THE LATE CHIEF JUSTICE MORRISON R. WAITE.

SECRETARIES OF STATE.

Term	No.	NAME.	APPOINTED.	Term	No.	NAME.	APPOINTED.
1	1	Thomas Jefferson	Sept. 26, 1789	14a		Daniel Webster	April 6, 1841
2		Thomas Jefferson	March 4, 1793		15	Hugh S. Legare	May 9, 1843
	2	Edmund Randolph	January 2, 1794		16	Abel P. Upshur	July 24, 1843
	3	Timothy Pickering	Dec. 10, 1795		17	John C. Calhoun	March 6, 1844
3		Timothy Pickering	March 4, 1797	15	18	James Buchanan	March 6, 1845
	4	John Marshall	May 13, 1800	16	19	John M. Clayton	March 7, 1849
4	5	James Madison	March 5, 1801	16a		Daniel Webster	July 22, 1850
5		James Madison	March 4, 1805		20	Edward Everett	Nov. 6, 1852
6	6	Robert Smith	March 6, 1809	17	21	William L. Marcy	March 7, 1853
	7	James Monroe	April 2, 1811	18	22	Lewis Cass	March 6, 1857
7		James Monroe	March 4, 1813		23	Jeremiah S Black	Dec. 17, 1860
8	8	John Quincy Adams	March 5, 1817	19	24	William H. Seward	March 5, 1861
9		John Quincy Adams	March 5, 1821	20		William H. Seward	March 4, 1865
10	9	Henry Clay	March 7, 1825	20a		William H. Seward	April 15, 1865
11	10	Martin Van Buren	March 6, 1829		25	Elihu B. Washburne	March 5, 1869
	11	Edward Livingston	May 24, 1831	21	26	Hamilton Fish	March 11, 1869
12	12	Louis McLane	May 29, 1833	22		Hamilton Fish	March 4, 1873
	13	John Forsyth	June 27, 1834	23	27	William M. Evarts	March 12, 1877
13		John Forsyth	March 4, 1837	24	28	James G. Blaine	March 5, 1881
14	14	Daniel Webster	March 5, 1841	24a	29	F. T. Frelinghuysen	Dec. 12, 1881
				25	30	Thomas F. Bayard	March 6, 1885

The larger figures mark the Presidential term in which each Cabinet Officer held his appointment.

THE AMERICAN MANUAL.

JAMES G. BLAINE.

SECRETARIES OF THE TREASURY.

Term	No.	Name.	Appointed.	Term	No.	Name.	Appointed
1	1	Alexander Hamilton	Sept. 11, 1789	14a		Thomas Ewing	April 2, 1841
2		"	March 4, 1793		15	Walter Forward	Sept. 13, 1841
	2	Oliver Wolcott	Feb. 2, 1795		16	John C. Spencer	March 3, 1843
3		"	March 4, 1797		17	George M. Bibb	June 15, 1844
	3	Samuel Dexter	Jan. 1, 1801	15	18	Robert J. Walker	March 6, 1845
4	4	Albert Gallatin	May 14, 1801	16	19	William M. Meredith	March 8, 1849
5		" "	March 4, 1805	16a	20	Thomas Corwin	July 21, 1850
6		" "	March 4, 1813	17	21	James Guthrie	March 7, 1853
7	5	George W. Campbell	Feb. 9, 1814	18	22	Howell Cobb	March 6, 1857
	6	Alexander J. Dallas	Oct. 6, 1814		23	Philip F. Thomas	Dec. 12, 1860
	7	William H. Crawford	Oct. 22, 1816		24	John A. Dix	Jan. 11, 1861
8		" " "	March 5, 1817	19	25	Salmon P. Chase	March 7, 1861
9		" " "	March 5, 1821		26	William Pitt Fessenden	July 1, 1864
10	8	Richard Rush	March 7, 1825	20	27	Hugh McCulloch	March 7, 1865
11	9	Samuel D. Ingham	March 6, 1829	20		" "	April 15, 1863
	10	Louis McLane	Aug. 2, 1831	21	28	George S. Boutwell	March 11, 1869
12	11	William J. Duane	May 29, 1833	22	29	William A. Richardson	March 17, 1873
	12	Roger B. Taney	Sept. 23, 1833		30	Benjamin H. Bristow	June 4, 1874
	13	Levi Woodbury	June 27, 1834		31	Lot M. Morrill	July 7, 1876
13		" "	March 4, 1837	23	32	John Sherman	March 8, 1877
14	14	Thomas Ewing	March 5, 1841				

Secretaries of the Treasury.—Term 24, No. 33, William Windom, appointed March 5, 1881; Term 24a, No. 34, Charles J. Folger, appointed October 27, 1881; No. 35, Walter Q. Gresham, appointed September 24, 1884; No. 36, Hugh McCulloch, appointed October 28, 1884; Term 25, No. 37, Daniel Manning, appointed March 6, 1885; No. 38, Charles S. Fairchild, April 1, 1887.

GENERAL MEADE'S HEADQUARTERS AT GETTYSBURG.

THE AMERICAN MANUAL

HON. JOHN SHERMAN.

SECRETARIES OF WAR.

1	1	Henry Knox............	Sept. 12, 1781	11a	John Bell...........	April 6, 1841
2		" "	March 4, 1793	19	John C. Spencer........	Oct. 12, 1841
	2	Timothy Pickering......	Jan. 2, 1795	20	James M. Porter........	March 8, 1843
	3	James McHenry.........	Jan. 27, 1796	21	William Wilkins........	Feb. 15, 1844
3		" "	March 4, 1797	15 22	William L. Marcy........	March 6, 1845
	4	Samuel Dexter........	May 13, 1800	16 23	George W. Crawford.....	March 8, 1849
	5	Roger Griswold.......	Feb. 3, 1801	162 24	Charles M. Conrad......	Aug. 15, 1850
4	6	Henry Dearborn.......	March 5, 1801	17 25	Jefferson Davis........	March 5, 1853
5		" "	March 4, 1805	18 26	John B. Floyd.........	March 6, 1857
6	7	William Eustis........	March 7, 1809	27	Joseph Holt...........	Jan. 18, 1861
	8	John Armstrong.......	Jan. 14, 1813	19 28	Simon Cameron........	March 5, 1861
7		" "	March 4, 1813	29	Edwin M. Stanton......	Jan. 15, 1852
	9	James Monroe........	Sept. 27, 1814	20	" "	March 4, 1865
	10	William H. Crawford..	August 1, 1815	20a	" "	April 15, 1865
8	11	George Graham.......	ad interim.		U. S. Grant, ad interim.	Aug. 12, 1867
	12	John C. Calhoun......	Oct. 8, 1817		L. Thomas, " "	Feb. 21, 1868
9		" "	March 5, 1821	30	John M. Schofield......	May 28, 1868
10	13	James Barbour........	March 7, 1825	31	John A. Rawlins.......	March 11, 1869
	14	Peter B. Porter.......	May 23, 1828	32	William W. Belknap....	Oct. 25, 1869
11	15	John H. Eaton........	March 9, 1829	22	" "	March 4, 1873
	16	Lewis Cass...........	August 1, 1831	33	Alphonso Taft.........	March 8, 1876
12		" "	March 4, 1833	34	James D. Cameron.....	May 22, 1870
13	17	Joe R. Poinsett.......	March 7, 1837	28 35	George W. McCrary....	March 12, 1877
14	18	John Bell............	March 5, 1841		Alexander Ramsey.....	Dec. 10, 1879

Secretaries of War.—Term 24, No. 28, Robert T. Lincoln, appointed March 5, 1881; Term 25, No. 30, William C Endicott, appointed March 6, 1885.

NOTE.—William T. Sherman was Secretary of War from September 9, 1869, to October 25, 1869.

SECRETARIES OF THE NAVY.

3	1	Benjamin Stoddert....	May 21, 1798	14a	George E. Badger.....	April 6, 1841
4		" "	March 4, 1801	14	Abel P. Upshur........	Sept. 13, 1841
	2	Robert Smith..........	July 1, 1801	15	David Henshaw.......	July 24, 1843
5	3	J. Crowninshield.......	March 3, 1805	16	Thomas W. Gilmer....	Feb. 15, 1844
6	4	Paul Hamilton........	March 7, 1809	17	John Y. Mason........	March 14, 1844
	5	William Jones........	Jan. 12, 1813	15 18	George Bancroft.......	March 10, 1845
7		" "	March 4, 1813		John Y. Mason........	Sept. 9, 1846
	6	B. W. Crowninshield...	Dec. 19, 1814	16 19	William B. Preston....	March 8, 1849
8		" "	March 4, 1817	16a 20	William A. Graham....	July 22, 1850
	7	Smith Thompson.......	Nov. 9, 1818	21	John P. Kennedy......	July 22, 1852
9		" "	March 5, 1821	22	James C. Dobbin......	March 7, 1853
	8	Samuel L. Southard...	Sept. 16, 1823	18 23	Isaac Toucey..........	March 6, 1857
10		" "	March 4, 1825	19 24	Gid on Welles........	March 5, 1861
11	9	John Branch..........	March 9, 1829	20	" "	March 4, 1865
	10	Levi Woodbury.......	May 23, 1831	20a	" "	April 15, 1865
12		" "	March 4, 1833	21 25	Adolph E. Borie......	March 5, 1869
	11	Mahlon Dickerson.....	June 30, 1834	26	George M. Robeson.....	June 25, 1869
13		" "	March 4, 1837		" "	March 4, 1873
	12	James K. Paulding....	June 25, 1838	21 27	Richard W. Thompson...	March 12, 1877
14	13	George E. Badger.....	March 5, 1841	28	Nathan Goff Jr........	Jan. 6, 1881

Secretaries of the Navy.—Term 24, No. 28, William H. Hunt, appointed March 5, 1881; Term 24a, No. 29, William E. Chandler, appointed April 1, 1882; Term 25, No. 30, William C. Whitney, appointed March 6, 1885.

ATTORNEYS-GENERAL.

1	1	Edmund Randolph	Sept. 29, 1789		18	Hugh S. Legare	Sept. 13, 1841
2		" "	March 4, 1793		19	John Nelson	July 1, 1843
	2	William Bradford	Jan. 27, 1794	15	20	John Y. Mason	March 6, 1845
	3	Charles Lee	Dec. 10, 1795		21	Nathan Clifford	Oct. 17, 1846
3		" "	March 4, 1797		22	Isaac Toucey	June 21, 1848
	4	Theophilus Parsons	Feb. 20, 1801	16	23	Reverdy Johnson	March 8, 1849
4	5	Levi Lincoln	March 5, 1801	16a		John J. Crittenden	July 2, 1850
5	6	Robert Smith	March 3, 1805	17	24	Caleb Cushing	March 7, 1855
	7	John Breckinridge	Aug. 7, 1805	11	25	Jeremiah S. Black	March 6, 1857
	8	Cæsar A. Rodney	Jan. 28, 1807		26	Edwin M. Stanton	Dec. 20, 1860
6		" "	March 4, 1809	19	27	Edward Bates	March 5, 1861
	9	William Pinckney	Dec. 11, 1811			T. J. Coffey, *ad interim*	June 22, 1863
7		" "	March 4, 1813		28	James Speed	Dec. 2, 1864
	10	Richard Rush	Feb. 10, 1814	20		" "	March 4, 1865
8		" "	March 4, 1817	20a		" "	April 15, 1865
	11	William Wirt	Nov. 13, 1817		29	Henry Stanberry	July 23, 1866
9		" "	March 5, 1821		30	William M. Evarts	July 15, 1868
10		" "	March 4, 1825	21	31	E. Rockwood Hoar	March 8, 1869
11	12	John M. Berrien	March 9, 1829		32	Amos T. Akerman	June 23, 1870
	13	Roger B. Taney	July 20, 1831		33	George H. Williams	Dec. 14, 1871
13		" "	March 4, 1833	22		" "	March 4, 1873
	14	Benjamin F. Butler	Nov. 15, 1833		34	Edwards Pierrepont	April 26, 1875
13		" "	March 4, 1837		35	Alphonso Taft	May 22, 1876
	15	Felix Grundy	July 5, 1838	23	36	Charles Devens	March 12, 1877
	16	Henry D. Gilpin	Jan. 11, 1840	24	37	Wayne McVeagh	March 5, 1881
14	17	John J. Crittenden	March 5, 1841	24a	38	Benjamin H. Brewster	Dec. 16, 1881
14a		" "	April 6, 1841				

Attorney-General.—Term 25, No. 39, Augustus H. Garland, appointed March 6, 1885.

SECRETARIES OF THE INTERIOR.

Term	No.	Name.	Appointed.	Term	No.	Name.	Appointed.
16	1	Thomas Ewing	March 8, 1849	21	9	Jacob D. Cox	March 5, 1869
16a	2	Alexander H. H. Stewart	Sept. 12, 1850		10	Columbus Delano	Nov. 1, 1870
17	3	Robert McClelland	March 7, 1853	22	" "	March 4, 1873
18	4	Jacob Thompson	March 6, 1857		11	Zachariah Chandler	Oct. 19, 1875
19	5	Caleb B. Smith	March 5, 1861	23	12	Carl Schurz	March 12, 1877
	6	John P. Usher	Jan. 8, 1863		13	Samuel J. Kirkwood	March 5, 1881
20	"	" "	March 4, 1865	24a	14	Henry M. Teller	April 6, 1882
20a		" "	April 15, 1865	25	15	Lucius Q. C. Lamar	March 6, 1885
	7	James Harlan	May 15, 1865		16	William F. Vilas	Jan. 16, 1888
	8	O. H. Browning	July 27, 1866				

POSTMASTERS-GENERAL.

1	1	Sam'l Osgood	Sept. 26, 1789	10	12	Cave Johnson	March 6, 1845
	2	Timothy Pickering	Aug. 12, 1791	11	13	Jacob Collamer	March 8, 1849
2		" "	March 4, 1793	16a	14	Nathan K. Hall	July 23, 1850
	3	Joseph Habersham	Feb. 25, 1795		15	Samuel D. Hubbard	Aug. 31, 1852
3		" "	March 4, 1797	17	16	James Campbell	March 5, 1853
4		" "	March 4, 1801	18	17	Aaron V. Brown	March 6, 1857
	4	Gideon Granger	Nov. 28, 1801		18	Joseph Holt	March 14, 1859
5		" "	March 4, 1805		19	Horatio King	Feb. 12, 1861
6		" "	March 4, 1809	19	20	Montgomery Blair	March 5, 1861
7	5	Return J. Meigs, Jr.	March 17, 1814		21	William Dennison	Sept. 24, 1864
8		" "	March 4, 1817	20		" "	March 4, 1865
9		" "	March 5, 1821	20a		" "	April 15, 1865
	6	John McLean	June 26, 1823		22	Alexander W. Randall	July 25, 1866
10		" "	March 4, 1825	21	23	John A. J. Creswell	March 5, 1869
11	7	William T. Barry	March 9, 1829	22		" "	March 4, 1873
12		" "	March 4, 1833		24	Marshall Jewell	Aug. 24, 1874
	8	Amos Kendall	May 1, 1835		25	James N. Tyner	July 12, 1876
13		" "	March 4, 1837	23	26	David McK. Key	March 12, 1877
	9	John M. Niles	May 5, 1840		27	Horace Maynard	June 2, 1880
14	10	Francis Granger	March 6, 1841	24	28	Thomas L. James	March 5, 1881
14a		" "	April 6, 1841	24a	29	Timothy O. Howe	Dec. 20, 1881
	11	Charles A. Wickliffe	Sept. 13, 1841				

Postmasters-General.—No. 11, Walter Q. Gresham, appointed April 3, 1883; No. 32, Frank Hatton, appointed October 14, 1884; Term 25, No. 33, William F. Vilas, appointed March 6, 1885; No. 34, Don M. Dickinson, appointed January 16, 1888.

LENGTH OF SESSIONS OF CONGRESS, 1789-1888.

No. of Congress.	No. of Session.	Time of Session.
1st	1st	March 4, 1789—Sept. 29, 1789
	2d	Jan. 4, 1790—Aug. 12, 1790
	3d	Dec. 6, 1790—March 3, 1791
2d	1st	Oct. 24, 1791—May 8, 1792
	2d	Nov. 5, 1792—March 2, 1793
3d	1st	Dec. 2, 1793—June 9, 1794
	2d	Nov. 5, 1794—March 3, 1795
4th	1st	Dec. 7, 1795—June 1, 1796
	2d	Dec. 5, 1796—March 3, 1797
5th	1st	May 14, 1797—July 10, 1797
	2d	Nov. 13, 1797—July 16, 1798
	3d	Dec. 3, 1798—March 3, 1799
6th	1st	Dec. 2, 1799—May 14, 1800
	2d	Nov. 17, 1800—March 3, 1801
7th	1st	Dec. 7, 1801—May 3, 1802
	2d	Dec. 6, 1802—March 3, 1803
8th	1st	Oct. 17, 1803—March 27, 1804
	2d	Nov. 5, 1804—March 3, 1805
9th	1st	Dec. 2, 1805—April 21, 1806
	2d	Dec. 1, 1806—March 3, 1807
10th	1st	Oct. 26, 1807—April 25, 1808
	2d	Nov. 7, 1808—March 3, 1809
11th	1st	May 22, 1809—June 28, 1809
	2d	Nov. 27, 1809—May 1, 1810
	3d	Dec. 3, 1810—March 3, 1811
12th	1st	Nov. 4, 1811—July 6, 1812
	2d	Nov. 2, 1812—March 3, 1813
13th	1st	May 24, 1813—Aug. 2, 1813
	2d	Dec. 6, 1813—April 18, 1814
	3d	Sept. 19, 1814—March 3, 1815
14th	1st	Dec. 4, 1815—April 30, 1816
	2d	Dec. 2, 1816—March 3, 1817
15th	1st	Dec. 1, 1817—April 20, 1818
	2d	Nov. 16, 1818—March 3, 1819
16th	1st	Dec. 6, 1819—May 15, 1820
	2d	Nov. 13, 1820—March 3, 1821
17th	1st	Dec. 3, 1821—May 8, 1822
	2d	Dec. 2, 1822—March 3, 1823
18th	1st	Dec. 1, 1823—May 27, 1824
	2d	Dec. 6, 1824—March 3, 1825
19th	1st	Dec. 5, 1825—May 22, 1826
	2d	Dec. 4, 1826—March 3, 1827
20th	1st	Dec. 3, 1827—May 26, 1828
	2d	Dec. 1, 1828—March 3, 1829
21st	1st	Dec. 7, 1829—May 31, 1830
	2d	Dec. 6, 1830—March 3, 1831
22d	1st	Dec. 5, 1831—July 16, 1832
	2d	Dec. 3, 1832—March 3, 1833
23d	1st	Dec. 2, 1833—June 30, 1834
	2d	Dec. 1, 1834—March 3, 1835
24th	1st	Dec. 7, 1835—July 4, 1836
	2d	Dec. 5, 1836—March 3, 1837
25th	1st	Sept. 4, 1837—Oct. 16, 1837
	2d	Dec. 4, 1837—July 9, 1838
	3d	Dec. 3, 1838—March 3, 1839
26th	1st	Dec. 2, 1839—July 21, 1840
	2d	Dec. 7, 1840—March 3, 1841
27th	1st	May 31, 1841—Sept. 13, 1841
	2d	Dec. 6, 1841—Aug. 31, 1842
	3d	Dec. 5, 1842—March 3, 1843
28th	1st	Dec. 4, 1843—June 17, 1844
	2d	Dec. 2, 1844—March 3, 1845
29th	1st	Dec. 1, 1845—Aug. 10, 1846
	2d	Dec. 7, 1846—March 3, 1847
30th	1st	Dec. 6, 1847—Aug. 14, 1848
	2d	Dec. 4, 1848—March 3, 1849
31st	1st	Dec. 3, 1849—Sept. 30, 1850
	2d	Dec. 2, 1850—March 3, 1851
32d	1st	Dec. 1, 1851—Aug. 31, 1852
	2d	Dec. 6, 1852—March 3, 1853
33d	1st	Dec. 5, 1853—Aug. 7, 1854
	2d	Dec. 4, 1854—March 3, 1855
34th	1st	Dec. 3, 1855—Aug. 18, 1856
	2d	Aug. 21, 1856—Aug. 30, 1856
	3d	Dec. 1, 1856—March 3, 1857
35th	1st	Dec. 7, 1857—June 14, 1858
	2d	Dec. 6, 1858—March 3, 1859
36th	1st	Dec. 5, 1859—June 25, 1860
	2d	Dec. 3, 1860—March 3, 1861
37th	1st	July 4, 1861—Aug. 6, 1861
	2d	Dec. 2, 1861—July 17, 1862
	3d	Dec. 1, 1862—March 3, 1863
38th	1st	Dec. 7, 1863—July 4, 1864
	2d	Dec. 5, 1864—March 3, 1865
39th	1st	Dec. 4, 1865—July 28, 1866
	2d	Dec. 3, 1866—March 3, 1867
40th	1st	March 4, 1867—March 30, 1867
	"	July 3, 1867—July 20, 1867
	"	Nov. 21, 1867—Dec. 2, 1867
	2d	Dec. 2, 1867—July 27, 1868
	3d	Dec. 7, 1868—March 4, 1869

234   THE AMERICAN MANUAL.

41st ..... { 1st .... March 4, 1869—April 23, 1869
             2d .... Dec. 6, 1869—July 15, 1870
             3d .... Dec. 5, 1870—March 4, 1871

42d ...... { 1st .... March 4, 1871—April 20, 1871
             2d .... Dec. 4, 1871—June 10, 1872
             3d .... Dec. 2, 1872—March 4, 1873

43d ...... { 1st .... Dec. 1, 1873—June 23, 1874
             2d .... Dec. 7, 1874—March 4, 1875

44th ..... { 1st .... Dec. 6, 1875—Aug. 15, 1876
             2d .... Dec. 4, 1876—March 4, 1877

45th ..... { 1st .... Oct. 15, 1877—Dec. 3, 1877
             2d .... Dec. 3, 1877—June 20, 1878
             3d .... Dec. 2, 1878—March 4, 1879

46th ..... { 1st .... March 18, 1879—July 1, 1879
             2d .... Dec. 1, 1879—June 16, 1880
             3d .... Dec. 6, 1880—March 4, 1882

47th ..... { 1st .... Dec. 5, 1881—Aug. 8, 1882
             2d .... Dec. 4, 1882—Mar. 4, 1883

48th ..... { 1st .... Dec. 3, 1883—July 7, 1884
             2d .... Dec. 1, 1884—Mar. 4, 1885

49th ..... { 1st .... Dec. 7, 1885—Aug. 5, 1886
             2d .... Dec. 6, 1886—Mar. 4, 1887

50th ..... { 1st .... Dec. 5, 1887————

Note.—To determine the years covered by a given Congress, double the number of the Congress and add the product to 1789; the result will be the year in which the Congress closed. Thus the 35th Congress—70 * 1789=1859, that being the year which terminated the 35th Congress on the 4th of March. To find the number of a Congress sitting in any given year, subtract 1789 from the year; if the result is an even number, half that number will give the Congress, of which the year in question will be the closing year. If the result is an odd number, add one to it, and half the result will give the **Congress**, of which the year in question will be the first year.

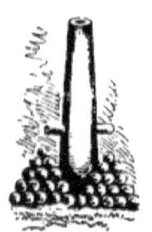

THE REV. FRANK HARDIN, D. D.

SPEAKERS OF THE HOUSE OF REPRESENTATIVES.

	Name.	State.	Congress.	Term of Service.	Born.	Died.
1	F. A. Muhlenberg...	Pennsylvania	1st Congress	April 1, 1789, to March 4, 1791	1750	1801
2	Jonathan Trumbull...	Connecticut...	2d Congress	Oct. 24, 1791, to March 4, 1793	1740	1809
	F. A. Muhlenberg...	Pennsylvania..	3d Congress	Dec. 2, 1793, to March 4, 1795	....	....
3	Jonathan Dayton.....	New Jersey...	4th Congress	Dec. 7, 1795, to March 4, 1797	1760	1824
	" "	" "	5th Congress	May 15, 1797, to March 3, 1799	....	....
4	Theodore Sedgwick..	Massachusetts..	6th Congress	Dec. 2, 1799, to March 4, 1801	1746	1813
5	Nathaniel Macon....	North Carolina.	7th Congress	Dec. 7, 1801, to March 4, 1803	1757	1837
	" "	" "	8th Congress	Oct. 17, 1803, to March 4, 1805	....	....
	" "	" "	9th Congress	Dec. 2, 1805, to March 4, 1807	....	....
6	Joseph B. Varnum...	Massachusetts	10th Congress	Oct. 26, 1807, to March 4, 1809	1750	1821
	" "	" "	11th Congress	May 22, 1809, to March 4, 1811	....	....
7	Henry Clay..........	Kentucky.....	12th Congress	Nov. 4, 1811, to March 4, 1813	1777	1852
	" "	" "	13th Congress	May 24, 1813, to Jan. 10, 1814	....	....
8	Langdon Cheves... }	S. Carolina, } 2d Session.	13th Congress	Jan 10, 1814, to March 4, 1815	1776	1857
	Henry Clay	Kentucky....	14th Congress	Dec. 4, 1815, to March 4, 1817	....	....
	" "	" "	15th Congress	Dec. 1, 1817, to March 4, 1819	....	....
	" "	" "	16th Congress	Dec. 6, 1819, to May 15, 1820	....	....
9	John W. Taylor.... }	New York... } 2d Session.	16th Congress	Nov. 15, 1820, to March 4, 1821	1784	1854
10	Philip P. Barbour,..	Virginia......	17th Congress	Dec. 4, 1821, to March 4, 1823	1783	1841
	Henry Clay	Kentucky.....	18th Congress	Dec. 1, 1823, to March 4, 1825	....	....
	John W. Taylor....	New York.....	19th Congress	Dec. 5, 1825, to March 4, 1827	....	....
11	Andrew Stevenson..	Virginia........	20th Congress	Dec. 3, 1827, to March 4, 1829	1784	1857
	" "	" "	21st Congress	Dec. 7, 1829, to March 4, 1831	.....	....
	" "	" "	22d Congress	Dec. 5, 1831, to March 4, 1833	....	....
	" "	" "	23d Congress	Dec. 2, 1833, to June 2, 1834	....	....
12	John Bell...... }	Tennessee... } 2d Session.	23d Congress	June 2, 1834, to March 4, 1835	1797	1869
13	James K. Polk......	Tennessee....	24th Congress	Dec. 7, 1835, to March 4, 1837	1795	1849
	" "	" "	25th Congress	Sept. 5, 1837, to March 4, 1839	....	....
14	Rob t M. T. Hunter..	Virginia,......	26th Congress	Dec. 16, 1839, to March 4, 1841	1809	....
15	John White........	Kentucky.....	27th Congress	May 31, 1841, to March 4, 1843	1805	1845
16	John W. Jones......	Virginia......	28th Congress	Dec. 4, 1843, to March 4, 1845	1805	1848
17	John W. Davis	Indiana.......	29th Congress	Dec. 1, 1844, to March 4, 1847	1709	1850
18	Robert C. Winthrop..	Massachusetts .	30th Congress	Dec. 6, 1847, to March 4, 1849	1809	....
19	Howell Cobb......,	Georgia........	31st Congress	Dec. 22, 1849, to March 4, 1851	1815	1868
20	Linn Boyd..........	Kentucky.....	32d Congress	Dec. 1, 1851, to March 4, 1853	1800	1859
	" "	" "	33d Congress	Dec. 5, 1853, to March 4, 1855	....	....
21	Nathaniel P. Banks..	Massachusetts..	34th Congress	Feb. 2, 1856, to March 4, 1857	1816	....
22	James L. Orr........	South Carolina.	35th Congress	Dec. 7, 1857, to March 4, 1859	1822	1873
23	Wm. Pennington....	New Jersey....	36th Congress	Feb. 1, 1860, to March 4, 1861	1796	1862
24	Galusha A. Grow....	Pennsylvania...	37th Congress	July 4, 1861, to March 4, 1863	1823	....
25	Schuyler Colfax.....	Indiana.......	38th Congress	Dec. 7, 1863, to March 4, 1865	1823	....
	" "	" "	39th Congress	Dec. 4, 1865, to March 4, 1867	....	....
	" "	" "	40th Congress	March 4, 1867, to March 4, 1869	....	....
26	James G. Blaine	Maine.........	41st Congress	March 4, 1869, to March 4, 1871	1830	....
	" "	" "	42d Congress	March 4, 1871, to March 4, 1873	....	....
	" "	" "	43d Congress	Dec. 1, 1873, to March 4, 1875	....	....

SPEAKERS OF THE HOUSE OF REPRESENTATIVES.—Continued.

27	Michael C. Kerr....	Indiana........	44th Congress	Dec. 6, 1875, to Aug. 20, 1876	1827	1876
28	Samuel J. Randall..	Pennsylvania 2d Session.	44th Congress	Dec. 4, 1876, to March 3, 1877	1828	....
	" "	Pennsylvania	45th Congress	Oct. 15, 1877, to March 1, 1879	....	....
	" "	"	46th Congress	March 18, 1879, to ———	....	....
29	J. Warren Keifer....	Ohio.........	47th Congress	Dec. 5, 1881, ——— ———	1836	....
30	John G. Carlisle,....	Kentucky.....	48th Congress	Dec. 3, 1883, to March 4, 1885.	1835	....
	" "	"	49th Congress	Dec. 7, 1885, to March 4, 1887,	....	....
			50th Congress	Dec. 5, 1887, to ——— ———	....	....

NOTE.—Speakers elected *pro tempore* are not included in the above table. The figures prefixed indicate the number of Speakers, not the sequence of their official terms.

History of Presidential Elections, Giving a Summary of Popular and Electoral Votes for President and Vice-President of the United States, 1789-1884.

Year of Elec. States, Total Elec. V.	Political Party	PRESIDENTS Candidates.	Popular.	Electoral.	V.-PRESIDENTS. Candidates.	Elect. Vote.	Year of Elec. States, Total Elec. V.	Political Party	PRESIDENTS Candidates.	Vote. Popular.	Electoral.	VICE-PRESIDENTS Candidates.	Elect. Vote.
1789 10 73		Geo. Washington John Adams John Jay R. H. Harrison John Rutledge John Hancock George Clinton S. Huntingdon John Milton James Armstrong Benj. Lincoln Edward Telfair Vacancies	69			34 9 6 4 3 2 2 1 1 1 4	1804 17 F.	R.	Thos. Jefferson C. C. Pinckney		162 14	George Clinton Rufus King	162 14
							1808 17 F.	R.	James Madison C. C. Pinckney George Clinton		122 47 6	George Clinton Rufus King John Langdon James Madison James Monroe	113 47 9 3 3
					Vacancy	1	1812 18 F.	R.	James Madison DeWitt Clinton Vacancy		128 89 1	Elbridge Gerry Jared Ingersoll	131 86
1792 15 F. 135 R.		Geo. Washington John Adams George Clinton Thos. Jefferson Aaron Burr Vacancies	132			77 50 4 1 3	1816 19 F.	R.	James Monroe Rufus King Vacancies		183 34 4	D. D. Tompkins Jno. E. Howard James Ross John Marshall Robt. G. Harper	183 22 5 4 3
1797 F. 10 R. 138 F.		John Adams Thos. Jefferson Thos. Pinckney Aaron Burr Samuel Adams Oliver Ellsworth George Clinton John Jay James Iredell Geo. Washington John Henry S. Johnson C. C. Pinckney	71 68 59 30 15 11 7 5 3 2 2 2 1				1820 24 O.	R.	James Monroe John Q. Adams		231 1	D. D. Tompkins Rich. Stockton Daniel Rodney Robt. G. Harper Richard Rush	218 8 4 1 1
					Vacancies	1	1824 R. 24 C. 261 R. R.		Andrew Jackson John Q. Adams W. H. Crawford Henry Clay	155,872 105,321 44,282 46,587	99 84 41 37	John C. Calhoun Nath. Sanford Nath. Macon A. Jackson M. Van Buren Henry Clay	182 30 24 13 9 2
1801 R. 16 R. 138 F.		Thos. Jefferson Aaron Burr John Adams C. C. Pinckney John Jay	73 73 65 64 1				1828 D 24 N R 261		Andrew Jackson John Q. Adams	647,231 509,097	178 83	J. C. Calhoun Richard Rush Wm. Smith	171 83 7

History of Presidential Elections, giving a Summary of Popular and Electoral Votes for President and Vice-President of the United States, 1789-1884.—Continued.

Year of Elect., No. of States, Total Elec. V.	Political Party	PRESIDENTS Candidates	States	Vote Popular	Electoral	VICE-PRESIDENTS Candidates	Elect. Vote	Year of Elect., No. of States, Total Elec. V.	Political Party	PRESIDENTS Candidates	States	Vote Popular	Electoral	VICE-PRESIDENTS Candidates	Elect. Vote
1832	D	Andrew Jackson	15	687,502	219	M. Van Buren	189	1864	R	Abraham Lincoln	22	2,216,067	212	A. Johnson	212
24	N R	Henry Clay	7	530,189	49	Jno. Sergeant	49	1866	D	Geo. B. McClellan	3	1,808,725	21	G. H. Pendleton	2
288		John Floyd	(		11	Henry Lee	11	314		Vacancies			81		8
	AM	William Wirt	{1	33,108	7	A. Ellmaker	7	1868	R	Ulysses S. Grant	26	3,015,071	214	S. Colfax	214
						Wm. Wilkins		1837	D	Horatio Seymour	8	2,709,613	80	F. P. Blair, Jr.	80
		Vacancies					2	317		Vacancies	3		23		23
								1872	R	Ulysses S. Grant	31	3,597,070	286	Henry Wilson	286
1836	D	M. Van Buren	15	761,549	170	R. M. Johnson	147	37	D L	Horace Greeley	6	2,834,079		B. Gratz Brown	47
26	W	W. H. Harrison			73	F. Granger	77	366	D	Charles O'Connor		29,408		Geo. W. Julian	5
294	W	Hugh L. White	2		26	John Tyler	47		T	James Black		5,608		A. H. Colquitt	5
	W	Daniel Webster	(	736,656	14	Wm. Smith	23			T. A. Hendricks				J. M. Palmer	3
	W	W. P. Mangum	)		11					B. Gratz Brown				T. E. Bramlette	1
										Chas. J. Jenkins				W. S. Groesbeck	3
1840	W	W. H. Harrison	19	1,275,017	234	John Tyler	234			David Davis				W. B. Machen	1
26	D	M. Van Buren	7	1,128,702	60	R. M. Johnson	48							N. P. Banks	1
294	L	James G. Birney		7,059						(Not Counted)			17		14
						L. W. Tazewell	11	1876	R	Ruth. B. Hayes	21	4,033,950	185	W. A. Wheeler	185
						James K. Polk	1	38	D	Samuel J. Tilden	17	4,285,585	184	T. A. Hendricks	184
								369	G	Peter Cooper		81,740			
1844	D	James K. Polk	15	1,337,243	170	Geo. M. Dallas	170		P	G. Clay Smith		9,522			
29	W	Henry Clay	11	1,299,068	105	T. Frelinghuysen	105			Scattering		2,636			
275	L	James G. Birney		62,300				1880	R	J. A. Garfield	19	4,442,950	214	C. A. Arthur	214
								38	D	W. S. Hancock	19	4,442,035	155	W. H. English	155
1848	W	Zachary Taylor	15	1,360,101	163	M. Fillmore	163	369	G	J. B. Weaver		308,507		B. J. Chambers	
30	D	Lewis Cass	15	1,220,544	127	Wm. O. Butler	127			Scattering		14,576			
290	F S	M. Van Buren		291,263		C. F. Adams									
								1884		Grover Cleveland	20	4,911,017	219	T. A. Hendricks	219
1852	D	Franklin Pierce	27	1,601,474	254	Wm. R. King	254	38		James G. Blaine	18	4,848,334	182	John A. Logan	182
31	W	Winfield Scott	4	1,386,524	42	W. A. Graham	42	401		John P. St. John		151,809		Wm. Daniel	
296	F D	John P. Hale		156,149		Geo. W. Julian				Benj. F. Butler		133,825		A. M. West	
										Scattering		11,000			
1856	D	James Buchanan	19	1,838,169	174	J. C. Breckinridge	174								
31	R	Jno. C. Fremont	11	1,341,264	114	W. L. Dayton	114								
296	A	Millard Fillmore		874,534	8	A. J. Donelson	8								
1860	R	Abraham Lincoln	17	1,866,352	180	H. Hamlin	180								
33	D	J. C. Breckinridge	11	845,763	72	Joseph Lane	72								
303	C U	John Bell	3	589,581	39	Ed. Everett	39								
	D	S. A. Douglas	2	1,375,157	12	H. V. Johnson	12								

Abbreviations—A., American; A. M., Anti-Mason; C. U., Constitutional Union; D., Democrat; D. L., Democrat Liberal; F., Federalist; F. D., Free Democrat; F. S., Free Soil; G., Greenback; I. D., Independent Democrat; L., Liberty; N. R., National Republican; O., Opposition; P., Prohibition; R., Republican; T. Temperance; W., Whig.

* Previous to the election of 1804 each elector voted for two candidates for President; the one receiving the highest number of votes, if a majority, was declared elected President; and the next highest Vice-President.

† Three States out of thirteen did not vote, viz.: New York, which had not passed an electoral law; and North Carolina and Rhode Island, which had not adopted the Constitution.

‡ There having been a tie vote, the choice devolved upon the House of Representatives. A choice was made on the thirty-sixth ballot, which was as follows: Jefferson—Georgia, Kentucky, Maryland, New Jersey, New York, North Carolina, Pennsylvania, Tennessee, Vermont, and Virginia—10 States. Burr—Connecticut, Massachusetts, New Hampshire and Rhode Island—4 States. Blank—Delaware and South Carolina—2 States.

¹) ♦ No choice having been made by the Electoral College, the choice devolved upon the House of Representatives. A choice was made on the first ballot, which was as follows: Adams—Connecticut, Illinois, Kentucky, Louisiana, Maine, Maryland, Massachusetts, Missouri, New Hampshire, New York, Ohio, Rhode Island, and Vermont—13 States. Jackson—Alabama, Indiana, Mississippi, New Jersey, Pennsylvania, South Carolina, and Tennessee—7 States. Crawford—Delaware, Georgia, North Carolina, and Virginia—4 States.

²) No candidate having received a majority of the votes of the Electoral College, the Senate elected R. M. Johnson Vice-President, who received 33 votes, Francis Granger received 16.

a) Eleven States did not vote, viz.: Alabama, Arkansas, Florida, Georgia, Louisiana, Mississippi, North Carolina, South Carolina, Tennessee, Texas, and Virginia.

b) Three States did not vote, viz: Mississippi, Texas, and Virginia.

c) Three electoral votes of Georgia cast for Horace Greeley, and the votes of Arkansas, 6, and Louisiana, 8, cast for U. S. Grant, were rejected. If all had been included in the count, the electoral vote would have been 300 for U. S. Grant and 66 for opposing candidate.

THE DATES OF THE BIRTH AND DEATH OF OUR PRESIDENTS.

Presidents.	Born.	Died.
Washington	Feb. 22, 1732	Dec. 14, 1799
Adams	Oct. 30, 1735	July 4, 1826
Jefferson	April 2, 1743	July 4, 1826
Madison	March 16, 1751	June 28, 1836
Monroe	April 28, 1758	July 4, 1831
Adams	July 11, 1767	Feb. 23, 1848
Jackson	March 15, 1767	June 8, 1845
Van Buren	Dec. 5, 1782	July 24, 1862
Harrison	Feb. 9, 1773	April 4, 1841
Tyler	March 29, 1790	Jan. 17, 1862
Polk	Nov. 2, 1795	June 15, 1849
Taylor	Nov. 24, 1784	June 9, 1850
Fillmore	Jan. 7, 1800	March 8, 1874
Pierce	Nov. 23, 1804	Oct. 8, 1869
Buchanan	April 23, 1791	June 1, 1868
Lincoln	Feb. 12, 1809	April 15, 1865
Johnson	Dec. 29, 1808	July 31, 1875
Grant	April 27, 1822	July 23, 1885
Hayes	Oct. 4, 1822	
Garfield	Nov. 19, 1831	Sept. 19, 1881
Arthur	Oct. 15, 1830	Nov. 15, 1886
Cleveland	1837	

LEGISLATURES, ELECTORAL VOTE, RATES OF INTEREST, ETC., OF STATES AND TERRITORIES.

STATES.	Legislatures. Biennially or Annually.	Term of State Representatives, Years.	Term of State Senators, Years.	Limit of Session, Days.	No. of Representatives in Congress.	No. of Electoral Votes.	When promissory notes outlaws, Years.	When open account outlaws, Years.	Legal rate of interest on contract.	Rate of Interest on contract. Per cent.
Alabama	Bie.	2	4	50	8	10	6	3	8	8
Arkansas	Bie.	2	4	60	4	6	5	3	10	6
California	Bie.	2	4	0	6	8	4	2	7	7
Colorado	Bie.	2	4		1	3	6	6		10
Connecticut	An.	1	2	N	4	6	6	6	6	6
Delaware	Bie.	2	4	N	1	3	6	3	6	6
Florida	Bie.	2	4	60	2	4	5	3	•	8
Georgia	Bie.	2	4	50	9	11	6	4	8	7
Illinois	Bie.	2	4	N	20	22	10	5	8	6
Indiana	Bie.	2	4	60	13	15	20	6	8	6
Iowa	Bie.	2	4	N	9	11	10	5	10	6
Kansas	Bie.	2	4	50	3	5	5	3	12	7
Kentucky	Bie.	2	4	60	10	12	15	2	6	6
Louisiana	Bie.	2	4	60	6	8	5	3	8	5
Maine	Bie.	2	2	N	5	7	20	6	•	6
Maryland	Bie.	2	4	90	6	8	3	3	6	6
Massachusetts	An.	1	1	N	11	13	20	6	•	6
Michigan	Bie.	2	2	N	9	11	6	6	10	7
Minnesota	Bie.	1	2	60	3	5	6	6	10	7
Mississippi	Bie.	2	4	N	6	8	6	3	10	6
Missouri	Bie.	2	4	70	13	15	10	5	10	6
Nebraska	Bie.	2	2	40	1	3	5	4	10	7
Nevada	Bie.	2	4	60	1	3	6	4	•	10
New Hampshire	Bie.	2	2	N	3	5	6	6	6	6
New Jersey	An.	1	3	N	7	9	6	6	6	6
New York	An.	1	2	N	34	36	6	6	6	6

ELECTION LAWS OF THE DIFFERENT STATES.

Length of time required in State, county and town to be a voter.

Alabama	State, 1 year; county, 3 months; ward or precinct, 30 days. *j.*
Arkansas	State, 1 year; county, 6 months; precinct or ward, 30 days. *j.*
California	State, 1 year; county, 90 days; precinct, 30 days. *h.*
Colorado	State, 6 months. Women vote at school elections. *j.*
Connecticut	State, 1 year; town, 6 months. *b e h.*
Delaware	State, 1 year; county, 1 month. *a d h.*
Florida	State, 1 year; county, 6 months.
Georgia	State, 1 year; county, 6 months. *e j.*
Illinois	State, 1 year; county, 90 days; election district, 30 days. *h.*
Indiana	State, 6 months; town, 60 days; ward or precinct, 30 days. *i d j.*
Iowa	State, 6 months; county, 60 days; town or ward, 10 days. *j.*
Kansas	State 6 months, town or ward, 30 days. *j.*
Kentucky	State, two years; county, town or city, 1 year; precinct, 60 days. *h d.*
Louisiana	State, 1 year; parish, 10 days. *h.*
Maine	State, 3 months. *h a.*
Maryland	State, 1 year; city or county, 6 months. *h.*
Massachus'ts	State, 1 year; town, 6 months; women vote at school elections. *h e a c.*
Michigan	State, 3 mos.; town or ward, 10 days. *g d j.*
Minnesota	State, 4 mos.; election dist., 10 days. *i i.*
Mississippi	State, 6 months, county, 1 month. *h.*
Missouri	State, 1 yr.; county, city or town, 60 days. *j*
Nebraska	State, 6 months; county, 40 days; ward or precinct, 10 days. *j.*
Nevada	State, 6 months; county or district, 30 dys.*h*
N. Hampshire	Town, 6 months. *b h.*
New Jersey	State, 1 year; county, 5 months. *h.*
New York	State, 1 year; county, 4 months; district town or ward, 30 days. *h.*
North Carolina	State, 1 year; county, 30 days. *b j.*

LEGISLATURES, ELECTORAL VOTE, Etc.
CONCLUDED.

North Carolina.	Bie.	2	2	00	8	10	3	3	8	6
Ohio	An.	2	2	N	20	21	15	6	8	6
Oregon	Bie.	2	4	10	1	1	6	6	12	10
Pennsylvania	Bie.	2	1	N	27	30	6	6	6	6
Rhode Island	An.	1	1	N	2	4	6	6	6	6
South Carolina	An.	2	4	N	5	7	6	6	7	7
Tennessee	Bie.	2	3	75	10	12	6	6	6	6
Texas	Bie.	2	4	10	6	8	4	2	12	8
Vermont	Bie.	2	2	N	3	5	14	6	6	6
Virginia	Bie.	2	4	90	0	11	5	5	6	6
West Virginia	Bie.	2	4	15	3	5	10	5	6	6
Wisconsin	Bie.	1	2	N	8	10	6	6	10	7
TERRITORIES.										
Arizona	Bie.			00	2	2				
Dakota	Bie.			00	2	2				
Idaho	Bie.			00	2	2				
Montana	Bie.			00	2	2	$1 a day and 20 mileage.			
New Mexico	Bie.			00	2	2				
Utah	Bie.			00	2	2				
Washington	Bie.			00	2	2				
Wyoming	Bie.			00	2	2				

(Bie., An.) Biennially or Annually. (N.) None. (*) Any rate.
Each State has two Senators.

AMOUNT EXPENDED FOR PENSIONS.

The amount of money expended each year since 1856 for pensions is as follows:

1856	$1,206,229	1872	28,533,402
1857	1,310,380	1873	29,359,120
1858	1,219,768	1874	29,038,414
1859	1,222,222	1875	29,456,216
1860	1,106,802	1876	28,257,395
1861	1,031,500	1877	27,963,752
1862	852,170	1878	27,137,019
1863	1,078,514	1879	35,121,482
1864	4,985,473	1880	56,777,174
1865	16,347,021	1881	50,059,279
1866	15,605,510	1882	61,345,194
1867	20,936,551	1883	66,012,574
1868	24,782,485	1884	55,429,228
1869	28,176,621	1885	56,102,267
1870	$28,340,202	1886	63,404,864
1871	31,443,801	1887	75,029,102
		Total	974,714,166

ELECTION LAWS OF THE DIFFERENT STATES.
CONCLUDED.

Ohio........ { State, 1 year; county, 30 days; town, village or ward, 20 days. *h.*
Oregon........ State, 6 mos.; county or district, 90 days. *j.*
Pennsylvania... State, 1 year; election district, 2 mos. *c h.*
Rhode Island.. State, 1 year; town or city, 6 months. *b h*
South Carolina. State, 1 year; county, 60 days. *h.*
Tennessee..... State, 1 year; county, 6 months. *f h d.*
Texas.... { State, 1 year; county or election district, 6 months. *a d f.*
Vermont....... State, 1 year; town, 3 months. *h d.*
Virginia....... State, 1 yr; county, city or town, 6 mos. *h a*
West Virginia.. State, 1 year; county, 30 days. *h a.*
Wisconsin..... State, 1 year. *a f.*

(*a*) Paupers not allowed to vote. (*b*) Property qualifications required. (*c*) Voters must have paid their taxes. (*d*) No registration required. (*e*) Must be able to read and write. (*f*) Must pay poll-tax. (*g*) Foreigners must be residents of the State two years and six months. (*h*) Foreigners must have lived in the U. S. five years and be naturalized. (*i*) Foreigners must be residents of the U. S. one year. (*j*) Foreigners can vote if they have declared their intention to become citizens.

Federal Vessels Captured or Destroyed by Confederate "Cruisers."

Ships	50	Steamboats	4
Brigs	16	Gunboats	2
Barks	8	Cutter	1
Schooners	67	Tug	1

Vessels Captured or Destroyed for Violation of the Blockade, or in Battle, from May, 1861, to May, 1865.

Schooners, 735; sloops, 155; steamers, 262; barks, 27; brigs, 30; ships, 13; ironclads and rams, 16; brigantines, 2; gunboats, 3; propellers, 4; pilot boats, 2; boats, 8; yachts, 2; tugs, 3; barkatine, 1 pungy, 1; miscellaneous, 86.

United States Patent Office Business.

Comparative Statement of the business of the office from 1837 to 1886, inclusive. From the Report of the Commissioner of Patents, Jan. 31, 1887.

Calendar Year.	Applications.	Caveats Filed.	Patents Issued.
1837	...	...	435
1838	...	...	520
1839	...	...	425
1840	765	228	475
1841	847	312	495
1842	761	391	517
1843	819	315	531
1844	1,045	380	502
1845	1,246	452	502
1846	1,272	448	619
1847	1,531	553	572
1848	1,628	607	660
1849	1,955	595	1,070
1850	2,193	602	995
1851	2,258	760	869
1852	2,639	996	1,020
1853	2,673	901	958
1854	3,324	868	1,902
1855	4,435	906	2,024
1856	4,960	1,024	2,502
1857	4,771	1,010	2,910
1858	5,364	943	3,710
1859	6,225	1,097	4,538
1860	7,653	1,084	4,819
1861	4,643	700	3,340
1862	5,038	824	3,521
1863	6,014	787	4,170
1864	6,932	1,063	5,020
1865	10,664	1,937	6,616
1866	15,269	2,723	9,450
1867	21,276	3,597	13,015
1868	20,420	3,705	13,378
1869	19,271	3,624	13,986
1870	19,171	3,273	13,321
1871	18,872	3,866	13,033
1872	18,246	3,090	13,590
1873	20,414	3,248	12,864
1874	21,602	3,181	13,599
1875	21,638	3,094	15,255
1876	21,425	2,697	17,026
1877	20,308	2,809	13,619
1878	20,260	2,755	12,935
1879	20,059	2,620	12,725
1880	23,012	2,490	13,947
1881	26,059	2,406	16,584
1882	31,522	2,553	18,267
1883	35,877	2,741	22,383
1884	35,600	2,582	20,413
1885	35,717	2,552	24,233
1886	35,688	2,513	22,308
Total	**561,911**	**81,103**	**384,309**

Public Debt of the United States, 1791-87.

Statement of Outstanding Principal of Public Debt of the United States on the 1st of January of each year from 1791 to 1842, inclusive; and on the 1st of July of each year from 1843 to 1881, inclusive.

From the Annual Report of the Secretary of the Treasury on Finances.

1791	$75,463,476.52	1841	13,594,480.73
1792	77,227,924.66	1842	20,201,226.28
1793	80,352,634.04	1843	32,742,922.00
1794	78,427,404.77	1844	23,461,652.50
1795	80,747,587.39	1845	15,925,303.01
1796	83,762,172.07	1846	15,550,202.97
1797	82,064,479.33	1847	38,826,534.77
1798	79,228,529.12	1848	47,044,862.23
1799	78,408,669.77	1849	63,061,858.69
1800	82,976,294.35	1850	63,452,773.55
1801	83,038,050.80	1851	68,304,796.02
1802	80,712,632.25	1852	66,199,341.71
1803	77,054,686.30	1853	59,803,117.70
1804	86,427,120.88	1854	42,242,222.42
1805	82,312,150.50	1855	35,586,858.56
1806	75,723,270.66	1856	31,972,537.90
1807	69,218,398.64	1857	28,699,831.85
1808	65,196,317.97	1858	44,911,881.03
1809	57,023,192.09	1859	58,496,837.88
1810	53,173,217.52	1860	64,842,287.88
1811	48,005,587.76	1861	90,580,873.72
1812	45,209,737.90	1862	524,176,412.13
1813	55,962,827.57	1863	1,119,772,138.63
1814	81,487,846.24	1864	1,815,784,370.57
1815	99,833,660.15	1865	2,680,647,869.74
1816	127,334,933.74	1866	2,773,236,173.69
1817	123,491,965.16	1867	2,678,126,103.87
1818	103,466,633.83	1868	2,611,687,851.19
1819	95,529,648.28	1869	2,588,452,213.94
1820	91,015,566.15	1870	2,480,672,427.81
1821	89,987,427.66	1871	2,353,211,332.32
1822	93,546,676.98	1872	2,253,251,328.78
1823	90,875,877.28	1873	2,234,482,993.20
1824	90,269,777.77	1874	2,251,690,468.43
1825	83,788,432.71	1875	2,232,284,531.95
1826	81,054,059.99	1876	2,180,395,067.15
1827	73,987,357.20	1877	2,205,301,392.10
1828	67,475,043.87	1878	2,256,205,892.53
1829	58,421,413.67	1879	2,349,567,482.04
1830	48,565,406.50	1880	2,120,415,370.63
1831	39,123,191.68	1881	2,069,013,569.58
1832	24,322,235.18	1882	1,918,312,994.03
1833	7,001,698.83	1883	1,884,171,728.07
1834	4,760,082.08	1884	1,830,528,923.57
1835	37,513.05	1885	1,863,964,873.14
1836	337,051.54	1886	1,775,063,013.78
1837	3,308,124.07	1887	1,657,602,592.63
1838	10,434,221.14		
1839	$3,573,343.82		
1840	5,250,875.54		

Aggregate Banking Capital and Deposits in the United States, June, 1882.

COMPARED WITH 1876, 1877, 1878, 1879 AND 1880.

From the Report of the Comptroller of the Currency, December, 1881.

Years.	National Banks.			State Banks, private bankers, etc.			Savings Banks with capital.			Savings Banks without Capital.			Total.		
	No.	Capital. Mill.	Deposits. Mill.	No.	Capital. Mill.	Deposits. Mill.	No.	Capital. Mill.	Deposits. Mill.	No.	Deposits. Mill.		No.	Capital. Mill.	Deposits. Mill.
1876	2,031	500.4	713.5	3,803	211.0	480.0	26	5.0	37.2	691	841.6		6,611	719.4	2,075.3
1877	2,078	481.0	708.2	3,799	218.9	479.5	26	4.9	38.2	676	843.2		6,579	704.5	2,120.1
1878	2,056	470.1	677.2	3,799	202.2	413.3	23	3.2	26.2	668	803.3		6,450	675.8	1,920.0
1879	2,048	455.1	713.4	3,039	107.0	197.0	20	4.2	36.1	641	717.1		6,380	656.5	1,893.5
1880	2,076	450.0	960.8	3,798	196.1	691.1	29	1.0	31.6	620	784.0		6,520	650.0	2,210.0
1881	2,115	460.2	1,130.0	4,016	205.5	627.5	36	4.2	37.6	629	862.3		6,796	670.9	2,667.3
1882*	2,308	484.0	1,111.8	4,471	251.4	771.0	42	4.0	41.5	625	892.2		7,448	717.3	2,902.6

*To November 19, 1882; after which date, the tax on bank capital and deposits being repealed, the Comptroller has no returns furnishing data for continuing this table.

HISTORY, POPULATION, ETC., OF THE STATES AND TERRITORIES.

STATES.	Year settled.	By Whom First Settled.	Where Each State was First Settled.	Area in Square Miles.	When Admitt'd to the Union.	Capital of Each State.	Population of Each State in 1880.	Term of Office of Governor.	Salary of Governor of Each State.	Pay of Members of the State Legislature.
Alabama	1711	French	Mobile	50,722	1814	Montgomery	1,262,505	2 yrs.	$4,000	$4 pr. day
Arkansas	1685	French	Arkansas Post	52,198	1836	Little Rock	802,525	2 "	3,500	6 "
California	1769	Spaniards	San Diego	188,981	1850	Sacramento	864,694	4 "	6,000	8 "
Colorado	1858	Americans	Denver	104,500	1876	Denver	194,327	2 "	3,000	"
Connecticut	1633	Americans	Windsor	4,674	1788	Hartford	622,700	2 "	2,000	300 pr. ses
Delaware	1627	Swedes and Finns	Cape Henlopen	2,120	1787	Dover	146,608	4 "	2,000	3 pr. day
Florida	1565	Spaniards	St. Augustine	59,268	1845	Tallahassee	269,493	4 "	3,500	6 "
Georgia	1733	English	Savannah	58,000	1788	Atlanta	1,542,180	2 "	4,000	4 "
Illinois	1720	French	Kaskaskia	55,410	1818	Springfield	3,077,871	4 "	6,000	5 "
Indiana	1690	French	Vincennes	33,809	1816	Indianapolis	1,978,301	4 "	6,000	6 "
Iowa	1833	Americans	Burlington	55,045	1846	Des Moines	1,624,615	2 "	4,000	550 pr. ses
Kansas	1850	Americans	Ft. Leavenw'th	81,318	1861	Topeka	996,006	2 "	3,000	3 pr. day

THE AMERICAN MANUAL. 245

State	Year	Settlers	Place	Population	Year	Capital	Pop.		Salary
Kentucky	1775	Americans	Boonsboro	37,680 1792	Frankfort	1,618,690	"	5,000 5	
Louisiana	1699	French	Iberville	41,346 1812	Baton Rouge	939,946	"	4,000 4	
Maine	1625	English	Bristol	31,779 1820	Augusta	648,936	"	1,500 150 pr. ses	
Maryland	1634	English	St. Mary's	11,184 1788	Annapolis	934,913	"	4,500 5 pr. day.	
Massachusetts	1620	English	Plymouth	7,800 1788	Boston	1,783,085	"	5,000 to pr. ses	
Michigan	1670	French	Detroit		Lansing	1,636,937	"	1,000 1 pr. day.	
Minnesota	1846	Americans	St. Paul	83,531 1857	St. Paul	780,773	"	3,000 5	"
Mississippi	1716	French	Natchez	47,356 1817	Jackson	1,131,597	"	4,000 8.00 pr. ses	
Missouri	1764	French	St. Louis	65,150 1821	Jefferson City	2,168,380	"	5,000 5 pr. day.	
Nebraska	1854	Americans		75,995 1867	Lincoln	452,402	"	2,500 1	"
Nevada	1851	Americans	Washoe	112,090 1864	Carson City	62,206	"	6,000 "	
New Hampshire	1623	English	Dover	9,280 1788	Concord	336,991	"	1,000 4	"
New Jersey	1623	Dutch and Danes	Bergen	8,130 1787	Trenton	1,131,116	"	5,000 500 pr. ses	
New York	1614	Dutch	New York City	17,000 1788	Albany	5,082,871	"	10,000 1500 "	
North Carolina	1661	English	Albemarle	50,703 1790	Raleigh	1,399,750	"	1,500 1 pr. day.	
Ohio	1788	Americans	Marietta	49,073 1803	Columbus	3,198,062	"	1,000 5	"
Oregon	1811	Americans	Astoria	95,241 1859	Salem	174,768	"	1,500 1	"
Pennsylvania	1682	English	Philadelphia	40,000 1787	Harrisburg	4,282,891	"	10,000 1000 pr ses	
Rhode Island	1636	English	Providence	1,30 1790	Prov. & N'port	276,531	"	4,000 1 pr. day.	
South Carolina	1650	English	Port Royal	29,185 1788	Columbia	995,577	"	4,500 5	"
Tennessee	1757	Americans	Ft. London	35,090 1796	Nashville	1,542,359	"	4,000 1	"
Texas	1690	Spaniards	St. Antonio	274,135 1845	Austin	1,591,749	"	4,000 5	"
Vermont	1725	Americans	Ft. Dummer	30,232 1791	Montpelier	332,281	"	1,000 1	"
Virginia	1607	English	Jamestown	40,094 1788	Richmond	1,512,385	"	5,000 510 pr. ses.	
West Virginia	1862	Americans	See Virginia	23,000 1862	Charleston	618,457	"	2,700 1 pr. day.	
Wisconsin	1669	French	Green Bay	51,924 1848	Madison	1,315,497	"	5,000 350 pr ses	
TERRITORIES.				(*)					
Arizona	1560	Spaniards		113,016 1863	Tucson	40,141	"	2,600	
Dakota	1809	Americans		190,032 1861	Yankton	134,500	"	2,600	
Idaho	1842	Americans		85,294 1863	Boise City	32,641	"	2,600	
Montana	1852	Americans		143,77 1864	Helena	39,157	"	2,600	
New Mexico	1815	Spaniards		121,300 1850	Santa Fe	118,430	"	2,600	
Utah	1847	Americans		84,476 1850	Salt Lake City	143,907	"	2,600	
Washington	1845	Americans		90,601 1853	Olympia	75,120	"	2,600	
Wyoming	1867	Americans		97,883 1868	Cheyenne	20,788	"	2,600	
Dist. Columbia		English		61 1790		177,685			
Indian Ter.				68,091 1834					
Alaska				577,390 1868	Sitka				

*Indicates the year organized.

Population of the United States, by Races, in 1870 and 1880.

From the Official Returns of the Ninth and Tenth Census.

	STATES AND TERRITORIES.	Total Populat'n 1880.	White 1880.	Colored 1880.	Chinese 1880.	Indians civ. or taxed, 1880.	White, 1870.	Colored, 1870.	Chinese 1870.	Indians civ. or taxed. 1870.
1	Alabama	1,262,505	662,185	600,103	4	213	521,384	475,510		98
2	Arizona	40,440	35,160	155	1,632	3,493	9,581	26	20	31
3	Arkansas	802,525	591,531	210,666	133	195	362,115	122,169	98	89
4	California	864,694	767,181	6,018	75,218	16,277	499,143	4,272	49,310	7,241
5	Colorado	194,327	191,126	2,435	612	154	39,221	456	7	180
6	Connecticut	622,700	610,769	11,547	129	255	527,549	9,668	2	235
7	Dakota	135,177	133,147	401	238	1,391	12,887	91		1,200
8	Delaware	146,608	120,160	26,442	11	5	102,221	22,791		
9	Dist. of Columbia	177,624	118,006	59,596	17	5	88,278	43,401		16
10	Florida	269,493	143,195	126,690	18	180	96,057	91,689		2
11	Georgia	1,542,180	816,906	725,133	17	124	638,926	515,142	1	40
12	Idaho	32,610	29,013	53	3,379	165	10,618	60	4,274	47
13	Illinois	3,077,871	3,031,151	46,308	212	140	2,511,096	28,762	1	32
14	Indiana	1,978,301	1,938,798	39,228	29	246	1,655,837	24,560		240
15	Iowa	1,624,615	1,614,600	9,516	33	466	1,188,207	5,762	3	748
16	Kansas	998,096	952,155	43,107	19	815	316,377	17,108		914
17	Kentucky	1,648,690	1,377,179	271,451	10	50	1,098,692	222,210	1	108
18	Louisiana	939,946	454,954	483,655	489	848	362,065	364,210	71	569
19	Maine	648,936	646,852	1,451	8	625	624,809	1,606	1	499
20	Maryland	934,943	724,693	210,230	5	15	605,497	175,391	2	4
21	Massachusetts	1,783,085	1,763,782	18,697	237	369	1,143,150	13,947	97	151
22	Michigan	1,636,937	1,614,570	15,100	28	7,240	1,167,282	11,849	21	4,292
23	Minnesota	780,773	776,884	1,564	25	2,300	438,257	759		690
24	Mississippi	1,131,597	479,398	650,291	51	1,857	382,896	444,201	16	809
25	Missouri	2,168,380	2,022,826	145,350	91	113	1,603,146	118,071	3	75
26	Montana	39,159	35,385	346	1,765	1,663	18,306	183	1,949	157
27	Nebraska	452,402	449,764	2,385	18	235	122,117	789		87

27	Nevada	62,265	53,556	488	5,419	2,803	78,069	357	1,152	23	
28	New Hampshire	346,991	345,429	185	23	63	317,697	580		23	
30	New Jersey	1,131,116	1,092,017	38,853	174	74	875,407	39,658	15	16	
31	New Mexico	119,565	108,721	1,015	57	9,772	90,393	174		1,300	
32	New York	5,082,871	5,016,022	65,104	987	819	4,330,210	52,081	29	439	
33	North Carolina	1,399,750	867,242	531,277	1	1,230	677,170	391,650		1,241	
34	Ohio	3,198,062	3,117,920	79,900	112	130	2,601,936	63,213	1	100	
35	Oregon	174,768	163,075	487	9,512	1,694	86,920	316	3,330	318	
36	Pennsylvania	4,282,891	4,197,016	85,535	156	184	3,189,691	65,291	14	31	
37	Rhode Island	276,531	269,939	6,488	27	77	212,219	4,980		151	
38	South Carolina	995,577	391,105	604,332	9	131	289,667	415,814	1	124	
39	Tennessee	1,542,359	1,138,831	403,151	25	352	936,119	322,331		70	
40	Texas	1,591,749	1,197,237	393,384	136	992	564,700	253,175	25	379	
41	Utah	143,963	142,423	232	501	807	86,044	118	415	179	
42	Vermont	332,286	331,218	1,057		11	319,691	921		14	
43	Virginia	1,514,565	880,858	631,616	6	85	712,089	512,841	1	229	
44	Washington	75,116	67,199	325	3,187	4,405	24,105	207	231	319	
45	W. Virginia	618,457	592,537	25,886	5	29	424,033	17,980		1	
46	Wisconsin	1,315,497	1,309,618	2,702	16	3,161	1,051,351	2,113		1,266	
47	Wyoming	20,789	19,437	298	914	140	8,726	183	141	66	
	Total United States	50,155,783	43,402,970	6,580,793	105,618	66,407	33,602,245	4,880,387	63,254	45,731	

PER CENT. OF INCREASE FROM 1870 TO 1880.

Total Population............................. 30.08 per cent. | Colored Population................... 34.67 per cent
White Population............................ 29.26 " " | Chinese Population................... 66.73 " "

NOTE.—The inhabitants of Alaska and the Indian Territory (both unorganized as yet) are not included in the above total. The census of Alaska in 1880 showed: White, 394; Creoles (issue of intermarriage between the whites and natives), 1,683; Aleuts, 1,960; Innuits, 17,188; Indians, 8,655; total, 30,178.
The Indian Territory is estimated to contain 60,000 to 75,000 inhabitants.
The Indians included in the census in each State and Territory are those reckoned as civilized, or outside of tribal organizations. Indians, not taxed, are by law excluded from the census. Estimates of their number vary widely—from 200,000 to 350,000 (the latter is estimated in the census of 1870), while the latest census or estimate of the Indian agencies, as reported in 1881 to the Commissioner of Indian Affairs, gives 246,117 Indians, excluding Alaska. The whole population of the United States exceeds 50,000,000, including Indians and Alaskans.
In the Chinese column are included 1,148 Japanese.

POPULATION OF PRINCIPAL CITIES OF THE UNITED STATES,

Having 10,000 Inhabitants and over, as Gathered from the Latest Census Returns.

Akron, Ohio,........ 16,512	Elizabeth, N. J...... 28,229	Memphis, Tenn.... 33,592	Richmond, Ind..... 12,742
Albany, N. Y...... 90,903	Erie, Pa............. 27,730	Manchester, N. H.. 32,630	Rutland, Vt......... 12,149
Allegheny, Pa..... 78,681	Elmira, N. Y........ 20,541	Mobile, Ala......... 31,205	Rome, N. Y........ 12,045
Allentown, Pa..... 18,064	East Saginaw, Mich. 19,016	Meriden, Conn..... 18,340	Rock Island, Ill.... 11,660
Alexandria, Va.... 13,658	Easton, Pa.......... 11,924	Montgomery, Ala... 16,713	St. Louis, Mo...... 350,521

248 THE AMERICAN MANUAL.

City	Pop.	City	Pop.	City	Pop.	City	Pop.
Albany, Pa.	10,7..	Eau Claire, Wis.	10,118	Macon, Ga.	14,748	San Francisco, Cal.	232,959
Amsterdam, N. Y.	11,7..	Fall River, Mass.	22,06.	Malden, Mass.	12,017	Syracuse, N. Y.	51,791
Atchison, Kans.	15,10.	Fort Wayne, Ind.	26,880	Middletown, Conn.	11,731	Scranton, Pa.	45,850
Atlanta, Ga.	11,858	Flushing, N. Y.	15,019	Muskegon, Mich.	11,262	St. Paul, Minn.	41,498
Attleboro, Mass.	11,111	Fond du Lac, Wis.	13,091	Madison, Wis.	10,355	Springfield, Mass.	33,310
Auburn, N. Y.	12,92.	Fitchburg, Mass.	12,105	Marlboro, Mass.	10,12.	St. Joseph, Mo.	32,181
Augusta, Ga.	23,02.	Fishkill, N. Y.	10,732	Newburyport, Mass.	13,537	Savannah, Ga.	30,281
Aurora, Ill.	11,825	Georgetown, D. C.	12,578	New York, N. Y.	207,59.	Salem, Mass.	27,89.
Austin, Texas	10,97.	Grand Rapids, Mich.	32,015	New Orleans, La.	216,14.	Somerville, Mass.	24,985
Baltimore, Md.	332,31.	Galveston, Texas	22,251	Newark, N. J.	136,40.	Sacramento, Cal.	21,420
Bangor, Maine	19,057	Gloucester, Mass.	19,32.	New Haven, Conn.	62,882	Salt Lake City, Utah	20,7..
Bay City, Mich.	20,693	Galesburg, Ill.	11,4..	New Bedford, Mass.	26,875	Springfield, O.	20,729
Belleville, Ill.	10,68.	Hempsted, N. Y.	18,16.	Norfolk, Va.	21,96.	San Antonio, Texas	20,961
Biddeford, Maine	12,98.	Hartford, Conn.	42,551	Norwich, Conn.	21,14.	Springfield, Ill.	19,749
Binghamton, N. Y.	17,315	Hoboken, N. J.	30,99.	Newport, Ky.	20,43.	Sandusky, O.	15,838
Bloomington, Ill.	17,18.	Harrisburg, Pa.	30,702	Newburgh, N. Y.	18,05.	Schenectady, N. Y.	13,075
Boston, Mass.	362,53.	Holyoke, Mass.	21,851	New Brunswick, N. J.	17,10.	South Bend, Ind.	13,259
Bridgeport, Conn.	29,15.	Houston, Texas	18,09.	Newton, Mass.	16,99.	San Jose, Cal.	12,597
Brockton, Mass.	13,60.	Haverhill, Mass.	18,475	New Albany, Ind.	16,42.	Steubenville, O.	12,093
Brooklyn, N. Y.	566,66.	Hyde Park, Ill.	15,710	Newport, R. I.	15,69.	Stamford, Conn.	11,09.
Buffalo, N. Y.	155,137	Hamilton, O.	12,122	New Britain, Conn.	13,97.	Shreveport, La.	11,017
Burlington, Vt.	11,365	Hannibal, Mo.	11,074	Norwalk, Conn.	13,95.	Saratoga Springs, N. Y.	10,82.
Burlington, Ia.	19,450	Indianapolis, Ind.	75,074	New Lots, N. Y.	13,68.	Saugerties, N. Y.	10,375
Brookhaven, N. Y.	11,531	Jersey City, N. J.	120,728	Nashua, N. H.	11,36.	Saginaw, Mich.	10,525
Cambridge, Mass.	52,740	Johnstown, N. Y.	10,64.	Norristown, Pa.	13,06.	Stockton, Cal.	10,28.
Camden, N. J.	41,658	Joliet, Ill.	16,145	Northampton, Mass.	12,17.	Shenandoah, Pa.	10,13.
Canton, Ohio	12,258	Jackson, Mich.	16,105	New London, Conn.	10,65.	Troy, N. Y.	56,747
Castleton, N. Y.	12,679	Jacksonville, Ill.	10,92.	North Adams, Mass.	10,19.	Toledo, O.	50,143
Cedar Rapids, Iowa	10,10.	Jeffersonville, Ind.	10,12.	Nashville, Tenn.	43,46.	Trenton, N. J.	29,910
Charleston, S. C.	49,99.	Jamaica, N. Y.	10,96.	Oakland, Cal.	34,550	Terre Haute, Ind.	26,040
Chattanooga, Tenn.	12,89.	Kansas City, Mo.	55,81.	Omaha, Neb.	30,518	Taunton, Mass.	21,21.
Chelsea, Mass.	21,785	Kingston, N. Y.	18,342	Oswego, N. Y.	21,117	Topeka, Kan.	15,45.
Chester, Pa.	14,99.	Keokuk, Iowa	12,117	Oshkosh, Wis.	15,749	Utica, N. Y.	33,91.
Chicago, Ill.	503,304	Kalamazoo, Mich.	11,93.	Orange, N. J.	13,80.	Virginia City, Nev.	13,705
Cincinnati, O.	255,708	Louisville, Ky.	123,645	Oyster Bay, N. Y.	14,07.	Vicksburg, Mass.	11,81.
Cleveland, O.	160,143	Lowell, Mass.	59,485	Ogdensburg, N. Y.	10,34.	Washington, D. C.	147,307
Columbia, S. C.	10,030	Lawrence, Mass.	39,178	Pittsburg, Pa.	156,38.	Warwick, R. I.	12,16.
Columbus, O.	51,605	Lynn, Mass.	38,28.	Providence, R. I.	104,850	Worcester, Mass.	58,295
Covington, Ky.	29,720	Lancaster, Pa.	25,705	Paterson, N. J.	50,887	Wilmington, Del.	42,49.
Cohoes, N. Y.	19,417	Lewiston, Me.	19,083	Portland, Me.	33,80.	Wheeling, W. Va.	31,26.
Council Bluffs, Ia.	18,09.	Long Island City, N. Y.	17,117	Peoria, Ill.	29,315	Wilkesbarre, Pa.	23,33.
Concord, N. H.	13,818	Lexington, Ky.	10,95.	Petersburg, Va.	21,60.	Waterviiet, N. Y.	22,22.
Cortland, N. Y.	12,60.	Leavenworth, Kan.	16,550	Poughkeepsie, N. Y.	20,20.	Waterbury, Conn.	20,270
Chicopee, Mass.	11,32.	Lynchburg, Va.	15,05.	Pawtucket, R. I.	19,03.	Williamsport, Pa.	18,93.
Chillicothe, O.	10,95.	Lafayette, Ind.	13,80.	Pittsfield, Mass.	13,397	Wilmington, N. C.	17,5..
Detroit, Mich.	116,342	Leadville, Col.	13,820	Pottsville, Pa.	13,253	Woonsocket, R. I.	16,053
Dayton, O.	38,077	La Crosse, Wis.	14,905	Portsmouth, Va.	11,388	Wallkill, N. Y.	11,183
Denver, Col.	35,030	Lincoln, R. I.	13,765	Portsmouth, O.	11,314	Woburn, Mass.	10,013
Des Moines, Ia.	22,40.	Lockport, N. Y.	13,522	Philadelphia, Pa.	846,984	Watertown, N. Y.	10,695
Dubuque, Ia.	22,254	Little Rock, Ark.	13,185	Quincy, Ill.	27,275	Weymouth, Mass.	10,57.
Dover, N. H.	11,687	Lincoln, Neb.	13,00.	Quincy, Mass.	10,820	Winona, Minn.	10,20.
Danbury, Conn.	11,69.	Los Angeles, Cal.	11,311	Rochester, N. Y.	89,363	Waltham, Mass.	11,71.
Derby, Conn.	11,649	Logansport, Ind.	11,198	Richmond, Va.	63,803	Yonkers, N. Y.	18,79.
Dallas, Texas	10,358	Lenox, N. Y.	10,249	Reading, Pa.	43,270	Youngstown, O.	15,431
Davenport, Ia.	21,834	Milwaukee, Wis.	115,578	Racine, Wis.	16,03.	York, Pa.	13,940
Evansville, Ind.	29,280	Minneapolis, Minn.	46,887	Rockford, Ill.	13,13.	Zanesville, O.	18,120

EDUCATIONAL.

Tables, Showing, According to Report of 1880, School Population, School Age, Enrollment, Attendance, Salaries of Teachers, etc., of Public Schools.

STATES AND TERRITORIES.	School Age.	School Population.	Number Enrolled in Public Schools.	Average Daily Attendance.	Average School Days in the Year.	Salaries of Teachers.	Total Expended.
Alabama	7-21	353,003		117,078		$362,593	$375,165
Arkansas	6-21	217,547	70,072			192,045	238,050
California	5-17	215,078	155,298	100,966	150	2,207,014	2,864,571
Colorado	7-21	35,596	22,117	12,018	9	180,426	395,547
Connecticut	1-16	130,235	119,591	78,121	179.02	1,011,730	1,108,375
Delaware	6-21	35,459	27,523		12.58	148,819	207,281
Florida	4-21	88,677	39,315	27,046		97,115	134,895
Georgia	6-18	343,411	236,533	145,190			471,020
Illinois	6-21	1,010,851	704,041	331,638	150	1,587,015	7,531,914
Indiana	6-21	703,558	511,283	321,659	136	3,305,010	1,891,350
Iowa	5-21	580,556	326,907	250,836	148	2,991,918	5,621,218
Kansas	5-21	310,947	231,434	137,067	107	1,088,501	1,818,187
Kentucky	6-20	515,101	258,854	193,874	102	730,800	803,690
Louisiana	6-18	276,515	66,419	45,626	118		380,320
Maine	4-21	213,680	149,582	104,113	120	667,201	917,081
Maryland	5-20	276,120	162,431	85,778	187.5	1,111,255	1,514,107
Massachusetts	5-15	307,321	306,777	233,142	177	5,195,225	5,136,731
Michigan	5-20	508,221	362,385	213,798	141	1,977,991	3,710,925
Minnesota	5-21	271,128	180,248	117,161	91	993,208	1,766,114
Mississippi	5-21	326,689	236,704	156,761	77.5	609,893	830,704
Missouri	6-20	728,454	375,571	219,134	10.00	2,212,917	3,152,178
Nebraska	5-21	142,318	92,549	100,415	109	535,398	1,137,995
Nevada	6-18	10,596	9,045	5,401	142.8	86,800	111,445
New Hampshire	5-21	171,132	64,341	48,010	105.3	415,50	585,139
New Jersey	5-18	330,685	204,961	115,191	192	1,119,175	1,925,171
New York	5-21	1,541,173	1,031,093	573,089	176	7,075,022	10,112,378
North Carolina	6-21	459,324	225,000	147,802	51	188,551	352,882
Ohio	6-21	1,041,320	717,048	476,479	150	5,007,533	7,066,913
Oregon	4-20	59,015	37,533	27,435	89.16	220,492	311,017
Pennsylvania	6-21	1,200,000	937,310	601,627	147	4,508,207	7,119,013
Rhode Island	5-15	54,371	41,780	29,245	184	405,668	544,200
South Carolina	6-16	225,128	131,072		77	287,161	321,620
Tennessee	6-21	511,962	290,141	191,461	68	597,601	744,862
Texas	8-14	230,547	180,785		157.1	733,801	781,146
Vermont	5-20	82,831	75,235	48,766	145	465,320	451,285
Virginia	5-21	555,807	220,716	128,401	113	711,755	916,109
West Virginia	6-21	210,113	142,850	91,701	99	555,473	710,891
Wisconsin	4-20	483,220	299,253	197,510	102.5	1,598,592	2,149,772
Total		16,127,105	9,600,403	5,711,188		51,555,201	79,535,501

		(1)				(3)	(4)	(5)	(6)	(7)
1	Arizona	6—21	7,148	4,212	2,847	102			61,172	
2	Dakota	5—21	12,036	8,042	3,170	58	61,318		121,483	
3	District Columbia	6—17	43,558	26,439	20,637	193	277,012		418,507	
4	Idaho	5—21		6,758			33,844		38,513	
5	Indian		(2)11,344	116,098	(4)3,044				3,186,359	
6	Montana	4—21	7,070	3,070	2,500	96			59,403	
7	New Mexico	(7)7—18	(8)29,312	(9)5,151		(6)132	(6)15,432		418,890	
8	Utah	6—18	40,072	24,326	17,178	128	103,313	1,175	132,194	1,174	1,241
9	Washington	(13)5—21	321,223	314,032	(10)6,585	287.5	(11)91,019		(12)14,379	
10	Wyoming	(13)7—21		12,091	11,287		(13)22,123		(13)22,120	
	Total		175,157	101,118	61,151		607,088		1,196,439	
	Grand Total		15,894,863	9,781,521	5,805,312		55,158,289		80,732,838	

(1) Estimated. (2) For the winter. (3) In 1879. (4) For whites; for colored, 6-16. (5) Census of 1870. (6) In 1878. (7) In 1873. (8) In 1877. (9) In 1875. (10) In the Cherokee, Choctaw and Creek Nations. (11) In the five civilized tribes. (12) For white schools only. (13) In the counties.

Number of Newspapers and Periodicals in the United States, 1870-1880.

From the Official Returns of the Ninth and Tenth Census.

	STATES AND TERRITORIES.	1870.		1878.	1879.	1880.	STATES AND TERRITORIES.	1870.		1878.	1879.	1880.
		No.	Circulation.	No. of Periodicals.	No. of Periodicals.	No. of Periodicals.		No.	Circulation.	No. of Periodicals.	No. of Periodicals.	No. of Periodicals.
1	Alabama	89	91,165	85	102	114	Montana	10	19,550	12	11	16
2	Arizona	1	280	5	9	10	Nebraska	42	31,600	113	137	179
3	Arkansas	56	29,830	63		103	Nevada	12	11,300	25	29	31
4	California	201	491,001	217	286	310	New Hampshire	51	173,919	68	71	82
5	Colorado	14	12,750	39	61	81	New Jersey	122	205,500	198	184	200
6	Connecticut	71	203,745	121	115	128	New Mexico	5	1,545	9	12	18
7	Dakota	3	1,652	21	42	67	New York	835	7,561,497	1,175	1,174	1,241
8	Delaware	17	20,860	22	20	24	North Carolina	61	64,820	104	112	121
9	Dist. of Columbia	22	81,100	28	31	39	Ohio	395	1,388,367	635	648	666
10	Florida	23	10,545	35	38	40	Oregon	35	45,750	49	57	64
11	Georgia	110	150,087	137	167	186	Pennsylvania	540	3,419,765	765	793	866
12	Idaho	6	2,750	5		11	Rhode Island	32	84,050	34	37	37
13	Illinois	505	1,722,541	627	702	863	South Carolina	55	80,000	74	76	77
14	Indiana	293	365,512	371	416	440	Tennessee	91	225,982	146	170	170
15	Iowa	233	210,630	301	354	518	Texas	112	55,250	197	239	251
16	Kansas	97	96,503	171	235	305	Utah	10	14,250	15	16	17
17	Kentucky	89	197,130	153	162	183	Vermont	47	71,390	64	70	76
18	Louisiana	92	81,165	80	95	100	Virginia	114	143,840	129	103	177
19	Maine	65	170,570	93	103	103	Washington	14	6,785	23	25	27
20	Maryland	88	235,450	112	123	138	W. Virginia	59	51,441	74	88	99
21	Massachusetts	259	1,692,124	345	361	392	Wisconsin	190	343,388	236	307	310
22	Michigan	211	253,771	291	364	418	Wyoming	6	1,950	7	11	10
23	Minnesota	95	110,778	134	180	209						
24	Mississippi	111	71,868	103	102	106	Total United States	5,871	20,842,475	8,133	9,147	10,101
25	Missouri	270	522,896	297	395	471						

ESTIMATE OF GOLD AND SILVER PRODUCED IN THE UNITED STATES, FROM 1845 TO 1886 INCLUSIVE.

(From Official Reports by the Director of the Mint of the United States.)

Year.	Gold.	Silver.	Total.	Year.	Gold.	Silver.	Total.
1845	$1,008,327	From 1845 to	$1,008,327	1868	48,000,000	12,000,000	60,000,000
1846	1,139,357	1858,	1,139,357	1869	49,500,000	12,000,000	61,500,000
1847	889,085	Estimated	889,085	1870	50,000,000	16,000,000	66,000,000
1848	10,000,000	product	10,000,000	1871	43,500,000	23,000,000	66,500,000
1849	40,000,000	$50,000 per	40,000,000	1872	36,000,000	28,750,000	64,750,000
1850	50,000,000	annum.	50,000,000	1873	36,000,000	35,750,000	71,750,000
1851	55,000,000		55,000,000	1874	34,000,000	37,324,594	70,815,594
1852	60,000,000	(The silver	60,000,000	1875	33,467,856	31,727,560	65,195,416
1853	65,000,000	mines of the	65,000,000	1876	39,929,160	38,783,016	78,712,182
1854	60,000,000	U. S. were	60,000,000	1877	46,897,390	39,793,573	86,690,963
1855	55,000,000	discovered in	55,000,000	1878	51,400,900	45,281,385	96,187,715
1856	55,000,000	1859.)	55,000,000	1879	38,899,858	40,812,132	79,711,990
1857	55,000,000		55,000,000	1880	36,000,000	48,130,000	
1858	50,000,000	$500,000	50,500,000	1881	34,700,000	43,000,000	77,700,000
1859	50,000,000	100,000	50,100,000	1882	32,500,000	46,800,000	79,300,000
1860	46,000,000	150,000	46,150,000	1883	30,000,000	46,200,000	76,200,000
1861	43,000,000	2,000,000	45,000,000	1884	30,800,000	48,800,000	79,600,000
1862	39,200,000	4,500,000	43,700,000	1885	31,801,000	51,600,000	83,401,000
1863	40,000,000	8,500,000	48,500,000	1886	34,860,000	51,321,500	86,173,500
1864	$46,100,000	$11,000,000	$57,100,000	Total 40 years	$1,748,346,501	$748,643,760	$2,472,973,974
1865	53,225,000	11,250,000	64,475,000				
1866	53,500,000	10,000,000	63,500,000				
1867	51,725,000	13,500,000	65,225,000				

Expenditures in the District of Columbia from 1790 to 1876.

The total amount of money expended by the Government in the District of Columbia for all purposes from July 16, 1790, to July 30, 1876, is $94,114,305. This sum was divided as follows:

Capitol	$17,184,691
Library of Congress*	1,575,517
White House	1,405,149
Purchase of works of art	602,569
Botanic Garden	722,813
Department of State, etc	4,089,918
Treasury Department	7,605,914
War Department	2,041,205
Navy Department	1,821,136
Post-Office Department	2,123,501
Department of Agriculture	3,171,192
Smithsonian Institution	2,305,420
Patent Office	13,107,998
Benevolent institutions	4,734,115
Penal institutions	4,118,320
Courts	78,180
Aqueduct	4,000,822
Fire Department	103,203
Canals	507,318
Bridges	2,203,510
Public grounds	1,857,557
Streets and avenues	5,075,201
Losses, reimbursement etc	1,927,203
Miscellaneous†	3,505,000

*First appropriation for Congressional Library, 1800.

†First appropriation for the support of Public Schools, 1866.

COINS OF THE UNITED STATES. AUTHORITY FOR COINING, AND CHANGES IN WEIGHT AND FINENESS.

Double-Eagle—$20.
Authorized to be coined, Act of March 3, 1849.
Weight, 516 grains; fineness, 900.
Total amount coined to June 30, 1877, $814,508,140

Eagle—$10.
Authorized to be coined, Act of April 2, 1792.
Weight, 270 grains; fineness, 916⅔.
Weight changed, Act of June 28, 1834, to 258 grains.
Fineness changed, Act of June 28, 1834, to 899.225.
Fineness changed, Act of January 18, 1837, to 900.
Total amount coined to June 30, 1877, $85,707,220

Half-Eagle—$5.
Authorized to be coined, Act of April 2, 1792.
Weight, 135 grains; fineness, 916⅔.
Weight changed, Act of June 28, 1834, to 129 grains.
Fineness changed, Act of June 28, 1834, to 899.225.
Fineness changed, Act of January 18, 1837, to 900.
Total amount coined to June 30, 1877, $50,312,575

Quarter-Eagle—$2.50.
Authorized to be coined, Act of April 2, 1792.
Weight, 67.5 grains; fineness, 916⅔.
Weight changed, Act of June 28, 1834, to 64.5 grains.
Fineness changed, Act of June 28, 1834, to 899.225.
Fineness changed, Act of January 18, 1837, to 900.
Total amount coined to June 30, 1877, $25,705,750.

Three-Dollar Piece.
Authorized to be coined, Act of February 21, 1853.
Weight, 77.4 grains; fineness, 900.
Total amount coined to June 30, 1877, $1,200,032.

One Dollar.
Authorized to be coined, Act of March 3, 1849.
Weight, 25.8 grains; fineness, 900.
Total amount coined to June 30, 1877, $19,344,438.

Silver Dollar.
Authorized to be coined, Act of April 2, 1792.
Weight, 416 grains; fineness, 892.4.
Weight changed, Act of January 18, 1837, to 412½ grains.
Fineness changed, Act of January 18, 1837, to 900.
Coinage discontinued, Act of February 12, 1873.
Total amount coined, $8,045,838.

Trade-Dollar.
Authorized to be coined, Act of February 12, 1873.
Weight, 420 grains; fineness, 900.
Total amount coined to June 30, 1877, $24,581,398

Half-Dollar.
Authorized to be coined, Act of April 2, 1792.
Weight, 208 grains; fineness, 892.4.
Weight changed, Act of January 18, 1837, to 206¼ grains.
Fineness changed, Act of January 18, 1837, to 900.
Weight changed, Act of February 21, 1853, to 192 grains.
Weight changed, Act of February 12, 1873, to 12½ grams, or 192.9 grains.
Total amount coined to June 30, 1877, $118,888,596.60

Quarter Dollar.
Authorized to be coined, Act of April 2, 1792.
Weight, 104 grains; fineness, 892.4.
Weight changed, Act of January 18, 1837, to 103⅛ grains.
Fineness changed, Act of January 18, 1837, to 900.
Weight changed, Act of February 21, 1853, to 96 grains.
Weight changed, Act of February 12, 1873, to 6¼ grams, or 96.45 grains.
Total amount coined to June 30, 1877, $31,773,171.50.

Twenty-cent Piece.
Authorized to be coined, Act of March 4, 1875.
Weight, 5 grams, or 77.16 grains; fineness, 900.
Total amount coined to June 30, 1877, $294,418.

Dime.
Authorized to be coined, Act of April 2, 1792.
Weight, 41.6 grains; fineness, 892.4.
Weight changed, Act of January 18, 1837, to 41⅝ grains.
Fineness changed, Act of January 18, 1837, to 900.
Weight changed, Act of February 21, 1853, to 38.4 grains.
Weight changed, Act of February 12, 1873, to 2½ grams, or 38.58 grains.
Total amount coined to June 30, 1877, $10,141,781.50

Half Dime.
Authorized to be coined, Act of April 2, 1792.
Weight, 20.8 grains; fineness, 892.4.
Weight changed, Act of January 18, 1837, to 20⅝ grains.
Fineness changed, Act of January 18, 1837, to 900.
Weight changed, Act of February 21, 1853, to 19.2 grains.
Coinage discontinued, Act of February 12, 1873.
Total amount coined, $4,880,219.50.

COINS OF THE UNITED STATES, AUTHORITY FOR COINING, AND CHANGES IN WEIGHT AND FINENESS.—Concluded.

Three-cent Piece.

Authorized to be coined, Act of March 3, 1851.
Weight, 12⅜ grains; fineness 750.
Weight changed, Act of March 3, 1853, to 11.52 grains.
Fineness changed, Act of March 3, 1853, to 900.
Coinage discontinued, Act of February 12, 1873.
Total amount coined, $1,281,859.20.

MINOR COINS.

Five-cent (Nickel).

Authorized to be coined, Act of May 16, 1866.
Weight, 77.16 grains, composed of 75 per cent. copper and 25 per cent. nickel.
Total amount coined to June 30, 1877, $6,773,000.

Three-cent (Nickel).

Authorized to be coined, Act of March 3, 1865.
Weight, 30 grains, composed of 75 per cent. copper and 25 per cent. nickel.
Total amount coined to June 30, 1877, $855,000.

Two-cent (Bronze).

Authorized to be coined, Act of April 22, 1864.
Weight, 96 grains, composed of 95 per cent. copper and 5 per cent. tin and zinc.
Coinage discontinued, Act of February 12, 1873.
Total amount coined, $912,020.

Cent (Copper).

Authorized to be coined, Act of April 2, 1792.
Weight, 264 grains.
Weight changed, Act of January 14, 1793, to 208 grains.
Weight changed by proclamation of the President, January 26, 1796, in conformity with Act of March 3, 1795, to 168 grains.
Coinage discontinued, Act of February 21, 1857.
Total amount coined, $1,562,887.44.

Cent (Nickel).

Authorized to be coined, Act of February 21, 1857.
Weight, 72 grains, composed of 88 per cent. copper and 12 per cent. nickel.
Coinage discontinued, Act of April 22, 1864.
Total amount coined, $2,007,720.

Cent (Bronze).

Coinage authorized, Act of April 22, 1864.
Weight, 48 grains, composed of 95 per cent. copper and 5 per cent. tin and zinc.
Total amount coined to June 30, 1877, $1,713,681.

Half-cent (Copper).

Authorized to be coined, Act of April 2, 1792.
Weight, 132 grains.
Weight changed, Act of January 14, 1793, to 104 grains.
Weight changed by proclamation of the President, January 26, 1796, in conformity with Act of March 3, 1795, to 84 grains.
Coinage discontinued, Act of February 21, 1857.
Total amount coined, $39,926.10.

Coinage of the U. S. Mints during the Fiscal Year ending June 30, 1882.

Gold Coinage..$ 89,113,147.50
Silver Coinage:—Silver Dollars...27,772,075.00
                Halves, Quarters and Dimes...................................31,313.75
Minor Coinage:—Five, Three, Two, and One Cent pieces................................644,757.75

          Total Coinage..$117,841,594.00

* A large amount of Silver Dollars, Half Dollars, etc., have been coined since 1873.

THE UNITED STATES CHRISTIAN COMMISSION.

THE REV. JOHN O. FOSTER, A. M. B. D.
(The Present Secretary.)

UT of the heart of the Young Men's Christian Association, the United States Christian Commission was born. The call for such an organization was issued Oct. 28th, 1861, and signed by George H. Stuart, John Vannamaker, James Grant, John Sexton and George Cookman. The first meeting was held in the Bible House, N. Y., Nov. 14th, 1861, at 3 P.M., and fifteen cities were represented. The Commission was soon organized and two days afterwards, Nov. 16, issued the notices of its object, the "spiritual good of the soldiers in the army, intellectual improvement and social and physical comforts." President Lincoln, Simon Cameron and George B. McClellan the commanding General of the U. S. army, each heartily approved of the object, and Dec. 17, 1861, the Executive Committee, appointed by the meeting, elected George H. Stuart, President during "its existence."

The "Address to the Public" was issued Jan. 13, 1862. The first Delegate was the Rev. George Bringhurst, of Philadelphia, and the second was (said to be) the Rev. George J. Mingins, D. D., now of New York.

The first few months of its existence the office was moved four times, and for lack of means, seemed to be an itinerant concern destined to a speedy death. But prayers were offered in its behalf, and by and by it was laid on the hearts of the Christian People of the Nation. President Stuart converted his store in Philadelphia into a depot of supplies, his time, talents and fortune were all consecrated as a free-will offering for his Country, the suffering soldiers and their spiritual good.

Money at last began to pour in. Men were already working for the soldiers without pay and hardly receiving their expenses, while the demand for their services exceeded the supply ten fold. The Secretary of War, Edwin M. Stanton, issued an order saying: "Every facility consistent with the exigencies of the service will be afforded to the Christian Commission, for the performance of their religious and benevolent purposes in the Armies of the United States."

The duties of the Delegates were varied. Some were regular ministers who felt called to preach whenever there was an opportunity; but they were also instructed to render all temporal aid to the suffering men within their power. Others were teamsters, book keepers, shipping clerks, librarians, cooks, office men and visitors. There was also a large and excellent Delegation of physicians and surgeons, besides a score of other agencies,—all necessary for the immense work. With the agreement before him each Delegate bound himself to work under instructions of the Agent for "not less than six weeks." He went cheerfully to his work, and with memorandum book took notes of necessitous cases, reported the same,

GEORGE H. STUART.
President of Reunion of Christian and Sanitary Commissions, etc.

THE REV. J. O. FOSTER, A. M.
Secretary of Reunion of Christian and Sanitary Commissions, etc.

wrote letters to the soldiers' friends at home, "visited, instructed, distributed stores, circulated religious publications, aided Chaplains in their ministrations and influence for the spiritual and temporal welfare of the men under their care, held meetings for prayer in the field and in the hospitals, attended to the correspondence of disabled men, encouraged every right way, discountaged every vice, cheered men to duty, and above all persuaded men to become "reconciled to God."

They were further instructed to aid the Surgeons on the battle field in the care and removal of the wounded, giving them food and drink and everything needed to mitigate suffering and aid recovery; or if dying to point them with prayer to Jesus, and give them a Christian burial. In short, they were to do all that man could do to meet the wants of brethren "far from home and kindred."

Was it any wonder, that, under such instructions, the Delegate would do his part faithfully, and that from thousands of altars prayers went up to heaven in his or her behalf? For in this work the women had a most conspicuous part. They shunned no legitimate duty, but the best of care takers and nurses, they were in the hospitals and diet kitchens; they were directing the coffee wagons and distributing needed literature; and none were more welcome by the side of the sick and suffering soldier. They confronted drunken officers, shamed them to duty, made friends out of foes, and sang, and prayed, and spoke for the Master, wherever and whenever the way was open.

And this Godly work was not done alone in the Federal Armies, for similar Relief Associations and "colporters" moved to and fro among the distressed sufferers of the Confederate Forces.

These noble men and women in both armies may not appear prominently in history, but their record is faithfully kept by Him, who said, "In as much as ye have done it unto one the least of these my brethren, ye have done it unto me." Never in the History of the World was there witnessed such stupendous benevolence as came from the sorrow wrung souls of millions during this terrible War. Homes were stripped of their comforts to supply the wants of the men in the armies, and the last dollar was sent to the loved one in the trenches, in the field or hospital, to secure a moiety of comfort, and make the sad work a little less hideous and barbarous. Despite the fearful demoralization to both armies, yet there were rifts in the clouds of darkness where the light of Christianity shone as brightly as the World has ever known.

We are indebted to Mr. Frank W. Smith for the facts and figures of the Christian Commission as exhibiting in some degree the work of the Christian Commission. We have compared them with the official report and in the main, they are correct.

There were about 5,000 Delegates commissioned. Cash raised and distributed $2,524,512. Value of stores, a multitude of articles, $2,839,445. Value of Bibles, Hymn Books, papers, magazines, etc., known as publications, $185,252. An estimation of Donations, Delegates' Services, Telegraph and Rail Road facilities granted, Offices and Rooms donated would make with the above over $6,250,000.

"Each Delegate labored, on an average, thirty-eight days, at a cost for incidental expenses of $36.10. The field service of Delegates was equal to the continuous labor of one man for five hundred and eighty years, or, with the added services of the permanent Agents, six hundred and fifty-eight years."

As items of the general wants of the soldiers, we give a few more facts. There were 58,308 sermons preached by the Delegates, 77,744 meetings held, 92,321 letters written for the sick or dying soldiers to the loved ones at home, using 7,067,000 sheets of paper and as

SCENES DURING THE CIVIL WAR.

many envelopes, and these were all given away. The stationery and stamps cost $66,342. The New York Tract Society prepared 247 distinct tracts and circulated 6,570,000 copies. The Publishers of the American Messenger issued 2,790,000 copies for the army.

The Christian Commission knew no color, whether blue or gray, white or black. The prisoner of war was waited upon with the same care as the soldier. The starving poor in captured cities received rations like those the Delegates used, and the colored refugees were fed by the same hands that ministered to the wants of the dying.

The following important paper is a fair sample of the many commendations given from time to time:

"Depot for prisoners, Johnson's Island, near Sandusky, Ohio, October 31, 1863.

The undersigned prisoners of War at Johnson's Island do hereby certify that from their personal knowledge and experience, the Delegates of the United States Christian Commission, in their Christian efforts to relieve the sick and wounded of the various battle fields, make no difference or discrimination between the contending parties, relieving alike the sufferings and wants of the Confederate and Federal, men and Officers, and we therefore sincerely trust the Authorities at Richmond and elsewhere, will treat any of the said Delegates that may fall into their hands, with the kindness justly due them, and grant them a speedy return to their Christian work."

Signed by 48 Confederate soldiers, mostly Officers.

One or two instances should appear here before we finish the sketch. Chaplain W. H. Rogers, of New York, said: "The fierce conflict which ended the nine mile Battle of the Boynton Plank Road, left the field covered with the Gray and the Blue, in about equal numbers, wounded and dying. Soon the Sanitary Commission of the Fifth Corps arrived and went to work. One of the grandest visions that ever came to my gladdened eyes was the Christian Commission Brigade. There came over that muddy road, six sleek white horses, and following them the store, or rather coffee wagon, with its kindlings all ready, and its three boilers containing tea, coffee and beef tea. Twelve Christian Commission men went to work, and soon the cries of the wounded and requests for help had some repose. Then I saw how Christianity, in the spirit of Jesus, had united the Chaplaincy, the Christian Commission and the Sanitary Commission in that supreme glory of imitating Christ in helping the needy in the extremities of life.

It is necessary to say that the Sanitary Commission handled more supplies, had more money, men and agencies than the Christian Commission. Vast volumes are in print containing the records of that Grand Movement, which had for its object, to bring needed supplies to the wounded, bury the dead, register the evidence of burials, furnish intelligence of lost ones, and in fact, do all it could for men in field and hospital and prison.

There were two great centres for gathering and distributing supplies. One in the East, another in the West. There were over three thousand tributaries in the West alone, and over thirty thousand women helped in the Western work.

The effort in the East was still larger. Great Sanitary Fairs were held, and immense sums were raised.

The two Commissions worked in harmony. The Christian Commission was largely composed of Ministers and active Christian workers, and hence their distinctive appellation. If either Commission needed anything, work or supplies and the other could grant it, it was sure to do so. The Chaplains went often to the Sanitary Commission for things they could

SCENES DURING THE CIVIL WAR.

not find temporarily in the Christian Commission. I remember two brown and bronzed men called on us one day, asking for ten barrels of pickles or saurkraut. We had none, but our requisition on the noble Sanitary men was speedily answered by an Army wagon load ordered to the front and placed under the directions of these greatly gratified Chaplains.

There is no question but that the timely aid of these vast supplies kept myriads of people from starvation. Just after the capture of Richmond, Va., April 3d, 1865, when all articles of food were consumed, the sight of the starving poor of that City was heart rending. Our Commission gave out supplies for forty days, at times over 10,000 rations a day, and the Sanitary Commission in another part of the City, was doing even more, of the same blessed work. The Government at last opened stores and sold fresh bread and meat at cost, and by and by the relief reached all the suffering ones. The total supplies of moneys, stores, medicines, transportation, publications, tents and assistance, if paid for at the regular rates, by the two Commissions would have amounted to more than $25,000,000.

We have purposely omitted the names of nearly all the prominent workers. Their records can never be written. Not a tithe is in print, though many volumes have been published. We shall only mention one name with which to close the sketch.

George H. Stuart, the Originator of the Christian Commission, has well been named, "The Great Christian Chieftain."

He threw a live soul, a business man's power, and a Christian's zeal into the spiritual and relief work. Nothing was too sacred for the good cause. A hotel dining-room filled with guests, would be called to silence while he read a telegram, and took up a subscription of thousands of dollars. Ordained by the Good Samaritan of the Skies, he entered pulpits, thrilled gathered throngs, and demanded help in the name of his Master. A poor woman in England desired to send something to the soldiers and forwarded a five pound note worth then over $25, to President Lincoln. He turned it over to Stuart saying its design was doubtless for the Christian Commission. It was held up before great audiences, sold, given back, and re-sold again and again until the poor widow's gift netted more than a hundred thousand dollars.

A piece of Jewelry "with a history" would sell for $500. Wealthy ladies threw into the collections, bracelets, diamond rings and other jewelry, for the choicest treasures were not withheld. The first year of the Christian Commission Mr. Stuart and his Assistants raised $356,000, but during the last four months $2,260,000 came in as free will offerings,

Broken in health, being a great sufferer from life long asthma, Mr. Stuart was often carried to the field, where the wounded were lying, where he gave personal directions in relief work, or led the gospel meetings. He has been so frequently before the Public as a Trustee, Chairman, Director or officer of some kind that he has really been loaded with honors for more than half a century.

The esteem of the Nation for him has been marked by Presidents calling upon him for counsel, and by a pressing invitation to take a seat in the Cabinet. All the Churches claim him as a brother beloved, and no Assembly has been under his direction but has felt itself honored by his presence.

Born April 2, 1816, God has spared him to a good old age, to see the fruits of his benevolent works.

In speaking of the Merchants' National Bank in Philadelphia, the Record of that city says of its President, Mr. Stuart. "He is a gentleman whose name has become a household word throughout our land and across the seas. Who that passed through the soulstir-

SCENES DURING THE CIVIL WAR.

ring time of the late War can forget the service that Mr. Stuart rendered his Country, as President of the United States Christian Commission, devoting his time that might have been occupied in amassing a fortune, to the needs of the sick and wounded soldiers in our Armies? President Stuart's personal career as a merchant is a conspicuous feature in the history of Philadelphia, and his name is inseparably associated with the highest ideal of commercial enterprise and business integrity."

The Work of the Christian Commission Not Done.

The Christian Commission felt that its special work was done when the War closed, hence it disbanded from the active duties of relief work. The Senate Chamber at Washington held a vast throng Jan. 1st, 1866, when the brethren said good bye.

Fifteen years passed, and no effort for a Reunion seemed to avail. The Delegates were widely scattered and yet felt the tenderest regard for one another and often expressed a wish that some one would call them together.

The Rev. John H. Vincent, D. D., answered a letter from the writer, that Chautauqua would gladly set aside a whole day to listen to the story of the War, as told by Delegates and Chaplains from both sides. The first Reunion was held at Chautauqua Aug. 7, 1880, and was an immense gathering. President Stuart presided and the enthusiasm was wonderful. The throng was so delighted that Dr. Vincent publicly invited the Second Reunion to meet there again in 1881, which was accordingly done. At this gathering the crowd was still larger, and the audience seemed as much delighted as before.

The Third Reunion was held July 5, 1882, at Lake Bluff, Ill., near Chicago. The meeting was one of remarkable interest and made a deep impression.

The Fourth Reunion was held at Ocean Grove, New Jersey, July 22-24, 1883. From the time the speakers began, to the close of the two days not a moment passed without intense interest, and Dr. Stokes, the President of the Board of Trustees, publicly invited the Reunion to come back the following year.

The Fifth Reunion was accordingly held at Ocean Grove, Aug. 1-3, 1884, and was in one respect the most remarkable gathering ever held by these good Samaritans. The Delegates were informed that General Grant was at his cottage only six miles away, at Long Branch. President Stuart directed the Secretary to invite him to a Public Reception.

In answer to the telegram, he came next day and appeared on the platform in the afternoon. The Rev. A. J. Palmer delivered one of the most telling speeches of welcome we ever heard. General Grant was assisted to the front, for he was quite lame from a fall, causing a broken tendon, and after the tumultuous greeting, waving of handkerchiefs and cheering had subsided he said.

"Ladies and Gentlemen, under the circumstances it is difficult for me to speak. An hour ago I might have made a speech, but now I am almost afraid to do so. I know, as few can, the good that these Chaplains and Members of the Commission have done—writing letters for the sick and wounded, to the friends at home, to anxious, sorrowing mothers and fathers. I have not words to express my thanks for this welcome. I appreciate"——and here his voice failed, the sentence was never finished, he sank to his chair, sobbing and weeping profusely. It was the only time the great hero was known to weep, and the vast throng was also bathed in tears. The Audience was spell bound, and for some moments silence prevailed. This was

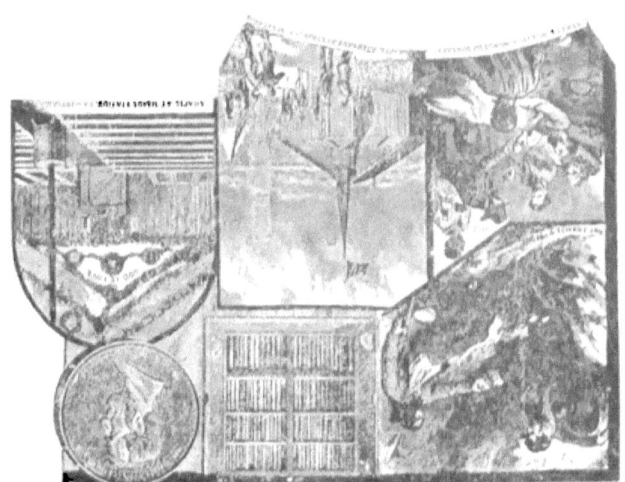

SCENES DURING THE CIVIL WAR.

General Grant's last speech before the Public.

The Sixth Reunion was held at Old Orchard, Maine, June 26-30, 1885. The Sabbath services drew an immense crowd, and the welcome and good feeling were very marked.

The Seventh Reunion was held at Valley Camp, near Pittsburg, Pa., July 29, Aug. 1, 1886.

Action was taken at this meeting for a permanent Organization by the adoption of the following order.

"The publication of the continued Organization of the United States Christian Commission (*de facto*) is hereby ordered announced in the Official Report; and that it is now ready for Relief Work at the call of the Officers."

Ocean Grove sent a pressing invitation to return there again, and the Eighth Reunion was held at that famous resort, Aug. 4-7, 1887. The attendance was simply immense and the interest for four days continued as strong as ever. Many pressing invitations came from different parts of the Country, for future meetings, and Round Lake, Saratoga Co., N. Y., was chosen for Aug. 15-20, 1888.

No great Public sorrow has called the Christian Commission to active service, thus far, but with a live organization it stands ready to respond, should occasion require.

FIRST AND LAST THINGS OF THE CIVIL WAR.

The first hostile shot of the war was fired at Fort Sumter, by Captain George S. James, of South Carolina.

The first shot fired in the defense of the Union, was fired at Fort Sumter, by Captain (General) Abner Doubleday, of New York.

Probably the first gun fired in the war was on the 16th of February, 1861, (before the attack on Sumter,) when the rebel General Ben. McCullough, captured San Antonio, Texas, and Twiggs surrendered.

The first to fire a hostile shot in the valley of the Mississippi, was battery A, 1st Illinois Light Artillery.

The first shot fired in defense of Fort Sumter, in 1861, was fired by the 1st U.S. Artillery, and the last shot fired at Appomattox Court House, was by the same Regiment.

The opening shot at the battle of Gettysburg was fired by the Confederates at 10 A. M., July 1, 1863, against Buford's picket line.

The first overt act of the war in Virginia, in its inception, was the attack on Harper's Ferry by the Confederates-simultaneous, though, in its consummation, with the capture of the navy yard at Portsmouth.

The first Confederate gun fired at the battle of Bull Run in 1861, was fired by Lieut. George S. Davidson of Lathams Battery.

A two hundred pound Parrot gun was brought to bear against Fort Sumter August 1, 1863, for the first time in the history of siege operations.

Louisiana was the first of the Seceding States that returned to her allegiance of her own free will and accord.

The first military movement of the war in the West was under the Illinois militia to Cairo. Defenses were thrown up and Gen. Prentiss was placed in command. For eight months Fort Defiance was our most Southern point.

The first successful military movement of the war took place in July, 1861, when Gen. Dix sent Gen. Lockwood into Accomac and Northampton counties, Virginia, with instructions to drive the confederates out.

The last great charge on the third day of the battle of Gettysburg was made by the confederates on the Brigade commanded by Gen. Alexander S. Webb, but the skill and bravery of Gen. Webb and the valor of his Brigade caused the repulse and route of the assailants in irretrievable confusion. Gen. Webb is now President of the College of New York.

The most remarkable instance perhaps, of a small band of heroes successfully opposing a vastly superior force, occurred at the very close of the battle of Gettysburg. "The enemy were temporarily checked," says Gen. Doubleday in his history of the battle, "by a desperate charge on their flanks made by only sixteen men under Captains Treichel and Rogers and Chaplain Newhall of Gen. McIntosh's Staff. This little band were every one killed or disabled, but they succeeded in delaying the enemy until Gen. Custer came up with the 7th Michigan Regiment.

The **Battle of Chancellorsville** was opened by an attack of Confederate skirmishers, 2 h Virginia Infantry, not the 11th as appears in Swinton's History.

The first **Secession Speech** made in the Legislature of Tennessee, was made by a man named Bennett, who afterwards joined Morgan's guerrilla band.

Gov. Letcher of Virginia, was the first man, who, as a candidate for office, openly advocated secession on the stump in Virginia.

The first Union blood shed in the war was that of a New Yorker–Daniel Hough, mortally wounded at Fort Sumter in 1861, and Col. Elmer E. Ellsworth, of the New York Fire Zouaves, shot dead at the Marshall House, Alexandria, Va.

The first to spill their blood on the breast works of the enemy at Yorktown, were the soldiers of the 40th New York Regiment, and they were the first to plant the New York State colors on the battlements of Fort Magruder.

The first innocent blood shed in the war is said to have been that of Mr. Robert E. Scott, of Fauquier Co. Va., killed by Gen. Blenker's men.

The first blood of a colored man shed in the war was that of Nicholas Biddle, of Pennsylvania. He was with the first company that passed through Baltimore in 1861, where he was wounded.

The first Confederate victim of the war, Henry S. Wyatt of N. C., was reported to have been the first, and was killed at Big Bethel. But it has been claimed in other quarters that Mr. Bailey Brown of Virginia, killed on the night of May 22, '61, was the first man. Henry St. George Tucker of the "Governors Guard," Richmond, however, died of disease contracted while on duty, twelve days before Mr. Brown was killed.

The first Cavalryman killed in the war was Jacob Erwin of Philadelphia, a member of a Company commanded by Captain Wm. H. Boyd, and was killed in a charge on the Black Horse Cavalry near Ponie Church, Va., Aug. 1861. This was the first charge of the war made by the Volunteer Cavalry.

The first to hoist the old flag over the Confederate fort at Roanoke Island, was the 51st New York Regiment, and the colors of the 51st were also the first to wave over the Capitol at Jackson, Mississippi.

The Stars and Stripes were first raised over the Capitol of the Confederate States, when the Union troops entered the City of Richmond in 1865, by Lieutenant Johnston Livingstone de Peyster, of New York.

The first flag planted on the ruins of the Confederate fort, at the explosion of the mine in front of Petersburg, July 30, 1864, was that of the 14th New York Artillery. Col. Houghton led the charge.

The only flag taken at the battle of Fair Oaks by our troops was the flag of the 22d North Carolina, captured by the 65th New York.

The first Union flag hoisted in Georgia, was the flag of the 7th Connecticut Regiment, Col. Terry, and was raised in Tybee Lighthouse.

The first Union flag found in Alabama was found nailed to a staff upon the housetop of the Hon. George W. Lane, in Huntsville.

Ohio had the most beautiful flags in the service.

The only Confederate colors taken in the battle of Chickamauga, were the colors of the 22d Alabama Regiment, and were captured by the 121st Ohio Regiment.

More bayonet wounds were inflicted upon our soldiers at the battle of Gaines Mills, than in any other battle of the war.

The **Battle of Pleasant Hill, La.**, was, probably the first time when the confederates manifested any desire to meet our soldiers in an open field fight, and particularly when they were the attacking party.

The first time an entire Confederate Brigade was driven from the field by a single Regiment, was on the third day of the battle of Gettysburg when the 1st Michigan Cavalry Regiment, engaged and defeated Hampton's Brigade.

Elk Creek was the first battle of the war fought south of the Arkansas river.

The first actual conflict of the war was in St. Louis, on the 10th of May, 1861, on the occasion of the coup d'etat of Gen. Lyons—capture of the confederate camp Jackson.

The first soldier mustered into the military service of New Jersey, at the commencement of the war, was J. Hudson Drake, of Elizabeth; and he was the first soldier to unfurl the Stars and Stripes on the soil of Virginia.

Gen. Kirby Smith, in speaking of the battle of Milliken's Bend, said: "I saw black and white men lying side by side on the ground, killed by the bayonet—the first instance, to my knowledge, in the war, where bayonets had crossed."

Gen. Meade said that the **1st Army Corps** on the first day of the battle of Gettysburg saved the position, and with it the country.

The **First Fort Taken** in the war was at Selma, Ala., and Serg't John A. Ennis was killed in taking the colors upon the ramparts.

The oldest volunteer in the war was Mr. Davis of La Porte, Indiana, eighty-four year, of age. He passed himself off for sixty-fives and with his three sons enlisted in an Illinois Regiment. He had served in the Mexican war.

The Knoxville *Whig* of January 30, 1865, said: For the first time since the war began each Southern army is held at bay by a superior or abolition force.

The battle of **Beverly Ford** June 9, '63 was the first occasion when the Cavalry of the Army of the Potomac went into action as a body.

The **Siege of Fort Sumter** in 1863 was probably the first attempt in the military history of the world, where a distant fortification was literally besieged over the heads of the garrisons of two other fortifications in direct line with the point attacked.

The only guns the Union forces lost in the battles of the Wilderness were two pieces belonging to Battery D, 1st New York Artillery.

The 56th Ohio and 34th Indiana Regiments, captured the first Battery, at the battle of Fort Gibson, which was the first victory of the Vicksburg campaign.

The youngest soldier in the army (1864)—Sergeant John Clem, 22d Michigan Regiment—twelve years of age. His home was Newark, Ohio.

Illinois was the only State in March, 1864, that had furnished all the men called for by the Government. The State had about twelve thousand to her credit above all demands.

Massachusetts furnished the first company of Sharpshooters. They were called the "Andrew Sharpshooters," and were attached to her 15th Regiment.

The first Company to respond to the call for troops in 1865, was a company of forty men from Chambersburg, Pa., commanded by Captain T. S. Stumbaugh.

The first soldier to respond to the call of duty from the State of Tennessee, was Joseph A. Cooper, who rose to the rank of Brigadier General.

The **17th New York** was the first Veteran Regiment organized in the United States.

The **102d New York Regiment** was the first to dash across the crest in the attack on Lookout Mountain, "which made them," said Gov. Geary of Pennsylvania, "the heroes of that battle."

The **16th New York Heavy Artillery** was the largest Regiment ever recruited in the United States.

The **131st New York**, are said to have saved the fortunes of the day at the battle of Winchester, September 19, 1864.

The first **volunteer Cavalry Regiment** mustered into the service was the 1st New York Mounted Rifles, and this was the last one mustered out at the close of the war.

The first **Confederate officer** killed in battle was Gen. Garnet, of Essex, Virginia.

Stonewall Jackson was the first to recognize Surgeons as non-combatants, and unconditionally entitled to exchange.

The first **Confederate officers** hung as spies during the war, were Col. Lawrence A. Williams, and Lieut. Peters.

The last **Confederate** to lay down his arms was Elias Hapner, a Tennessee guerrilla. Hapner committed murder in 1881 and was shot at Leadville, Colorado, and killed.

The first **arrest by the Confederates** for treason was that of J. W. Merriam, Collector of the Port of Georgetown, S. C., January 7, 1861.

But **one man was executed** in the Army of the Potomac up to February, 1863, for a flagrant crime, and that was a case of attempted desertion to the enemy.

The first **act of piracy in the war** was committed June 30, 1861, by Marylanders, led by Zarvona Thomas, called the "French Lady," assisted by George N. Hallins. In the expedition was a man named Martin, who kept a liquor store in Baltimore. This man, Martin, gave John Wilkes Booth, who shot the President, letters of introduction to this region of Maryland where he was a native. So here at Point Lookout in 1861 began the crime which led to the assassination in 1865.

The first **decision under the Emancipation Proclamation** was the State of Missouri against Benjamin Williams, a black man.

The first **case of emancipation** under the President's proclamation was that of three negro boys escaping from Kirby Smith's army, and appearing before Lieut. Col. Spies, Military Governor of the towns of Covington and Newport, Ky., September 23, 1862, who gave them free papers.

The term "**Contraband**" as applied to the negroes, did not originate with Ben. Butler as is generally supposed. The expression was made use of in 1863 by the Hon. George Opdyke of New York, in a published treatise on political economy.

The first **idea of raising colored Regiments**, publicly expressed, was made by Gen. Watts D. Peyster of New York, and was published in the Poughkeepsie Eagle in the winter of 1859-'60.

The first **detachment of negro troops** furnished by the State of New York was recruited at Hudson by J. M. Edwards of that place, in March, 1863. They joined the 64th Massachusetts Regiment.

The **Confederates** were the first to arm negroes. They did so at the very outset of the rebellion. They did so in Mobile before the battle of Bull Run. They did so in Louisiana before one negro had been allowed to put on a uniform of a United States soldier. They did so in Tennessee even before the State had openly seceded from the Union.

Although New Jersey was the only State which did not cast its electoral vote as a unit for Mr. Lincoln, she was the first of all States to send into the field her full quota of troops under the first three several calls from the Government.

The credit of originating the first movement for the raising of volunteers has been awarded to Gen. Butler, who issued a call for a meeting of the officers of the 6th Massachusetts Regiment to be held at Lowell, on the 21st day of January, 1861, but the records show that the honor is justly due to Captain (General) Allen Rutherford of New York City, (now of Washington.) Captain Rutherford issued a call for a meeting which was to be held at the Mercer House in New York on the 9th of January twelve days before the meeting at Lowell for the purpose of organizing for the protection of the United States and the enforcement of the laws.

The first Confederate flag captured on the battlefield, was captured by Lieut. John Coyne of the 70th New York Volunteers, the first Regiment of the Excelsior Brigade at the battle of Williamsburg on the 5th of May, 1862. The Brigade had been severely engaged most of the afternoon. A great many officers had fallen and the Brigade was sorely pressed. At this point the Confederates brought up a fresh Brigade and they were formed in line on the edge of a dense wood immediately in front of the Excelsior Brigade. Through the smoke of battle could be seen their colors advancing, until the colors of one of their Regiments was advanced within 100 yards of the 70th Regiment. Lieut. Coyne then asked for volunteers to follow him and take those Confederate colors. Sixteen brave fellows, among whom were Serg't Cook and Corporal Bateman sprang forward. It seemed only a second of time when they found themselves struggling with the Confederate Color Guard. Lieut. Coyne could not remember an incident of the struggle, except his effort to wrest the colors from the grasp of the Confederate who held them. The glare of the eyes, and the uplifted muskets, and the exclamation of **Sergt. Cook** (who was lying at his feet shot through the body), "don't let them get it back, Lieut." The brave Coyne had torn the flag from the staff and was **tying it around his body**, when the appealing words of the dying Serg't came out of that storm of lead and desperate encounter. He turned to look where his men were. All had faded away like mist. Not a man was standing, and he alone reached our lines, fainting and exhausted. This is the story of the capture of the first Confederate flag and well might Gen. Heintzelman in his letter to the Secretary of War recommending that the brave Lieutenant be promoted to Brevet-Colonel, say—"At Williamsburg with undaunted bravery and after a severe contest, he captured the colors of a **Confederate Regiment** and was mentioned by me in general orders for his gallantry.

Napoleon, Arkansas, was the first to fire on an unarmed boat in the history of the war.

The first **point at which the rebels** commenced the erection of works blockading the Mississippi river was Vicksburg.

The first **vessel of war** destroyed by a torpedo, was the iron-clad vessel "Cairo," on the Yazoo river.

The first **vessel to make a hostile demonstration** against the enemy was the "Powhattan," commanded by Admiral Porter.

The **longest pontoon bridge** ever constructed in this country was built by Co. F. 15th New York Volunteers. It extended across the Chickahominy, and was used on the occasion of McClellan's withdrawing his troops from Harrison's Landing.

Gen. McPherson was the youngest man confirmed by Congress a Brigadier General. He was thirty-one years of age.

Gen. Grant held more commissions for brave and meritorious conduct than probably any other man ever did. He had been commissioned at least thirteen times.

Col. J. J. Wilder, of the 17th Indiana Regiment, had the honor of giving the City of Chattanooga the first hostile salute it received, at the time Rosecrans marched on that city in August, 1864.

The first intimation that Gen. Grant was to take command of the Army of the Potomac, came from the New Orleans correspondent of the New York Daily News, in a letter to that paper, dated August 1, 1763.

The first instance where the regular troops were commanded by a volunteer officer was when Gen. Joseph Hayes, formerly of the 18th Massachusetts Regiment, was appointed to the command of the 1st Brigade, 2d Division of the 5th Corps.

Col. R. T. Davis, 8th New York Cavalry, killed at Beverly Ford in June, 1863, was a Mississippian, and is said to have been, up to that time, the only Cavalry officer of Southern birth, in the Union Army.

Gen. Phil Kearney was the first American officer ever decorated with the Legion of Honor by the Emperor Napoleon.

The first **West Point officer** of artillery to fall in the war was Lieut. Greble, killed at Big Bethel.

Col. Jacques of the 73d Illinois Regiment was the first man to enter the rebel entrenchments on the height of Mission Ridge. This is the Col Jacques who visited Jeff Davis in Richmond with the hope of bringing about peace.

The first **public intimation that Gen. Grant** had attempted to undermine Petersburg, Va., July 1864, came from Charles J. Browne of Petersburg, who wrote a letter on the subject to the Richmond Whig, July 16, 1864.

The first **officer to resign his position** in the United States Army for the purpose of participating in the rebellion was Wm. H. T. Walker of Georgia., who subsequently became a Major-General and was killed in battle before Atlanta, July 22, 1864.

The first **fully armed Regiment** to enter Washington when it was beleaguered by the Confederates in 1861, was the 6th Massachusetts, Col. Jones.

The **First New York Cavalry Regiment** claim to have captured more prisoners and property up to 1864, than any other Cavalry Regiment in the service. They had taken three thousand prisoners.

Battery D, 1st New York Artillery, is credited with more battles than any other in the army. In May 1864 when Gen. Meade called for the reports of all the battles the regiments and batteries had been engaged in, that they might have them inscribed on their flags, Battery D bore off the palm.

The first **Regiment to enter Yorktown**, and plant the old flag on the ramparts of the rebel forts, was the 73d New York—known as the 4th Excelsior Regiment.

The **12th New York Regiment** was the first Regiment to set foot on the soil of the Old Dominion, and the first to receive an attack after the army of invasion crossed into Virginia.

The **fortunes of the day** at the battle of the Fair Oaks, were decided by a brilliant charge of the 37th New York Volunteers, led by General Kearney.

The first of the **Monitors to see active service** was the Montauk, Captain John S. Worden, and her first service was in the attack on Fort McAllister.

The first **vessel captured** by the Confederate cruisers was the Harvey Burch. She belonged to Mr. John Brown, of New York.

The first **stoppage of navigation** was by the Confederates at Memphis, Tenn., and almost simultaneously at Napoleon and Helena, Ark.

The first **boat to descend to New Orleans** after the capture of Vicksburg, was the "Imperial."

The first **fight in the history of the world** between iron clad ships was between the Monitor and the Merrimac.

The first to suggest the **Hatteras expedition** of 1861, was Capt. R. D. Lowry, U.S.N.

The first **boat captured** by the Confederates was the steamer Ocean Belle, captured at Helena, Ark.

The first **two prisoners captured** by the army of the Potomac were taken by the 25th New York State Militia Regiment.

The first **Union prisoner** in the war was J. S. Worden, who afterwards commanded the Montauk, and subsequently commanded the "Monitor" in her fight with the "Merrimac."

The first **pardon** under the President's proclamation—he exempts Brig. E. W. Gantt of Arkansas from the penalty of treason.

The first **Union soldier** who crossed the threshold of the Libby Prison, was Capt. John Downey, of the New York Fire Zouaves.

Portsmouth, Va., was probably the first instance of an important place being confided exclusively to the care of Colored troops—1st U. S. Colored Infantry, January, 1864.

Lieut. A. S. Sanburn, of the 1st District of Columbia colored Regiment, murdered by Dr. Wright at Norfolk, Va., was probably the first officer of a colored Regiment who died in defense of the Union.

On the 7th of March, 1864, the first **negro prisoners of war** were received at Libby prison. They were James W. Corn, P. T. Lewis, R. P. Armstead and John Thomas.

Louisiana was the first State to institute the system of compensated labor.

The first **colored Provost Marshal** was Major W. O. Fiske, of the 1st Louisiana Volunteers, appointed by Gen. Banks.

The first **official recognition of negro troops** as equals by the Confederates was December, 1863, when a flag of truce borne by Major John Calhoun, a grandson of John C. Calhoun, was received at Hilton Head by Major Trowbridge of the 1st South Carolina Negro Regiment.

Senator Conness, of California, appears to have been the first man to publicly recommend that Gen. Grant be placed in command of the army of the Potomac.

The first **United States Government Bonds** were purchased by Messrs. R. S. and A. Stewart, of New York. Bond No. 1, being in possession of the late Mr. Alexander Stewart at the time of his death.

The first **meeting held in North Carolina** to oppose the action of the Confederate authorities was caused by the appointment of Major Bradford, of Virginia, to collect the taxes in that State.

Secretary Seward's letter of October 6, 1861, was the first official document laid before the people of England in which the British Government was notified that it would be held responsible for damages done by the privateer Alabama.

The first **motion made in Parliament** for an investigation into the legality of the sailing of the Alabama, Florida and other privateers, was made by Mr. J. Shaw Lefevre, Member of Reading, son of the late speaker.

Senator Sumner was the first person to urge upon President Lincoln to make public the Confiscation Proclamation.

Hon. Hiram Walbridge, of New York, was the first person to recommend to President Lincoln the importance of securing Beauport and Port Royal, S. C.

The first **case** under the Confiscation Act came up July 23d, 1863. It was that of the property of Dr. Garnett, a son-in-law of Henry A. Wise.

The first **draft** since the war of 1812, took place at Hartford, Conn., on the 10th of September, 1862.

The first **attempt at resistance to the draft** occurred in Fulton Co., Penn., about the 8th of June, 1863.

The first time the **body of a Confederate soldier** was returned to his kindred and friends with the honors of war, was on the 9th of January, 1863. It was the body of Colonel Lawton, who was wounded and captured at the battle of Fredericksburg.

The 2d **New York State Militia** (82d Vols.) is the oldest Regiment in the State of New York, and was the first to volunteer from New York for the war.

The first **Regiment** in the State of New York to offer its services to the Government, is said by Col. Adams, of the 67th, to be the Regiment he commanded.

The first **Regiment** from the State of New York to march to the defense of the Capitol was the 7th Militia Regiment.

The first **New York Regiment** raised for three years or the war was the 70th, the first Reg't. of the Excelsior Brigade, raised by Col. (now Gen.) Daniel E. Sickles.

The first **Massachusetts Regiment** furnished the first Gen. to command colored troops—Capt. Edward A. Wild, who commanded the Brigade known as "Wild's African Brigade."

The **12th Connecticut Regiment** was the first to ascend the Mississippi river after the capture of forts Phillips and Jackson.

The **5th Vermont** was the first New England regiment to enlist for three years.

The first **Hussar Regiment** raised in the country for real service in the war was organized at Trenton, N. J., by Col. Andrew J. Morrison.

Commodore Vanderbilt's name stands first on the list for magnificent donations to the United States Government. He presented the steamer "Vanderbilt," which cost $800,000.

The first contribution made by a private citizen for the defense of the Nation, was made by Col. John Jacob Astor, of New York, when he liberally furnished the means to purchase the gunboat "Yankee," which was sent to the relief of the garrison at Fort Sumter.

The National Banking Law was first suggested to the Secretary of the Treasury by the Hon. Elridge T. Spaulding, of Buffalo, N. Y.

The Treasury Note or Greenback system was first suggested by the late Mr. Silas M. Stillwell, of New York. Mr. Stillwell and not the late Secretary Chase, should have been called the "Father of Greenbacks."

The highest bid for the first Government Loan February, 1861, was made by the Bank of the Republic in New York City.

The Southern Bank of New Orleans in 1863, was the only bank North or South, that had made coin payments in full.

The last Union paper printed in the South was edited by Gen. A. B. Norton, formerly Adj. Gen. of the State of Texas. He was the only man in the South who published the inaugural message of President Lincoln.

The first time during the war that a passenger train was captured and robbed, was in February, 1864, when the Confederates captured the Baltimore express train for Wheeling. The capture was made near Kearneysville, Western Virginia.

The first printing press and type ever bought for the sole purpose of printing anti-slavery sentiments in Tennessee, arrived in Nashville, Febrnray 15, 1864.

The first time in which a balloon reconoissance was successfully made during a battle is believed to have been at the battle of Fair Oaks. Certainly the first time in which a telegraph station was established in the air to report the movements of the enemy.

The first gleam of fraternal light which beamed upon the dark feelings ruling the great contest was brought forth by a letter from the officers of the 12th Arkansas Regiment, to the officers of the 165th New York, at the time of the capture of Port Hudson in 1863.

The only representative of the Empire of China in the army of the Potomac was John Tommy, of the Excelsior Brigade (probably in the 70th New York Regiment). He was killed at Gettysburg.

The first cargo from New Orleans after the commencement of the war arrived North in June, 1862.

The first public exhibition of loyalty to the U. S. Government on the part of the citizens of Memphis, Tenn., was on the 25th of August 1863, when a grand entertainment was given to Gen. Grant.

The first soldiers cemetery dedicated during the war was dedicated by the Rev. Dr. Newman, at New Orleans, in May, 1864.

The first allusion to the subject through the press, favoring the assassination of President Lincoln, was made by —— of West Feliciana in a letter to the editor of the "Mississippian," and dated February 21, 1863.

NAMES OF THE STATES.

HAMILTON B. STAPLES.

New Hampshire.

THE origin of the name New Hampshire is very simple. The original territory, conveyed by patent of the Plymouth Company to John Mason in 1629, was named by him after Hampshire County in England.

Massachusetts.

THE life of Massachusetts as an autonomic State begins with the charter of 1691, which merged into one province the Plymouth and the Massachusetts Bay jurisdictions, and also the Province of Maine. The present name of the State is derived from the bay of that name. In fact, the word "Bay" was a part of the name of the younger colony which alone had received a charter from the crown, and was retained in the name of the new province, and afterward in the name of the State, till the constitution of 1780 went into operation. The Massachusetts Bay received its name from the Massachusetts Indians, who peopled its shores at the time of John Smith's visit in 1614. The word Massachusetts is an anglicized plural of Massachusett, meaning "at or near the great hills," "at or near the great hill country," from massa, "great," wadchu (in composition) adchu—plural wadchuash, "mountains," or "hills," and the suffix et, "at or near."

Rhode Island.

THE origin of the name of Rhode Island is quite obscure. A writer in the Providence Journal says: "Some ancient authors write the name Island of Rhodes. Some have believed that the name was to be derived from the Dutch Roode Eylandt, which signifies Red Island, and which the first Dutch explorers of the bay gave to the island. Others have written the name Rod Island. Perhaps it could also be Road Island (the island of the roadstead, or harbor island). In the early history of the State persons of the family name Rhodes are also mentioned. Could not one Mr. Rhodes have been among the first English settlers?" Mr. Schoolcraft, in his history of the Indian tribes, adopts the Dutch origin of the name. Mr. Arnold, in a note to his valuable "History of Rhode Island," says that the celebrated Dutch navigator, Adrian Block, who gave his name to Block Island, sailed into Narragansett Bay, "where he commemorated the fiery aspect of the place caused by the red clay in some portion of its shores by giving it the name of Roode Eylandt, the Red Island, and by easy transposition, Rhode Island." In support of the theory that the State was named after the island in the Mediterranean Sea we have the authority of Peterson's "History of Rhode Island." We also have the commanding authority of the public act by which the name was given.

Connecticut.

THE name Connecticut, spelled Quin-neh-tukqut signifies "land on a long tidal river." The name is so spelled in "Cotton's Vocabulary," and in the "Cambridge Records" it appears as Quinetuckquet. This explanation rests upon the authority of Dr. Trumbull.

New York.

THE territory of New York was comprised in the royal grant to the Duke of York in 1664, of all the land "from the west side of the Connecticut River to the east side of the Delaware Bay." In 1664 the Duke fitted out an expedition which took possession of New Amsterdam and the place was thereafter called New York in honor of the Duke. The same name was applied to the State. By a strange caprice of history the greatest State in the Union bears the name of the last and the most tyrannical of the Stuarts.

New Jersey.

THE State of New Jersey, granted by the **Duke of York** to **Sir George Carteret** and **Lord Berkeley** in 1664, received its name in the grant in commemoration of the brave defense of the Isle of Jersey by Carteret, its Governor, against the Parliamentary forces in the great Civil war.

Pennsylvania.

PENNSYLVANIA owes its name to its founder, **William Penn**. The name given by Penn himself was Sylvania, but King Charles II. insisted that the name of Penn should be prefixed. It is the only State in the Union named after its founder.

Delaware.

THE Counties of Newcastle, Kent, and Sussex "upon Delaware," granted by the **Duke of York** to **Penn** in 1682, were known as the territories of Pennsylvania. In 1701 Penn granted them a certain autonomy. The State was named after the bay of that name, and the bay after **Lord De-la-war**, who explored it. It has been claimed that the bay and the river were named after the Delaware Indians, who in 1660 dwelt upon their shores. This claim is unfounded. The Delaware name of the river was Lenapehittuk, meaning Lenape River.

Maryland.

MARYLAND was settled under a charter granted in 1632 by King Charles I. to **Lord Baltimore**. The State was named after **Queen Henriette Maria**. In the charter the county is called "Terra Mariete—Anglice, Maryland."

Virginia.

THE first step in the colonization of America by England was the charter granted in 1584 by Queen Elizabeth to **Sir Walter Raleigh**. Under this charter Raleigh took possession of the country west of the Roanoke, and called it **Virginia** in honor of the Virgin Queen. This is the only State in the Union whose name appears in literature associated with the royal title. Spenser dedicated the Faerie Queen to "Elizabeth, by the Grace of God, Queene of England, France, and Ireland, and of Virginia." The nearest approach to this in a public act is the order of the English Privy Council to the Virginia colony after the revolution of 1688 to proclaim **William** and **Mary** as "Lord and Lady of Virginia."

West Virginia.

THE name of West Virginia, a new State formed within the jurisdiction of Virginia, needs no separate consideration.

North Carolina and South Carolina.

NORTH Carolina and South Carolina may be considered under one head. **Allen**, in his History of Kentucky, ascribes the origin of the name Carolina to the French settlers of Port Royal, who named it after **Charles IX.**, of France. This is the popular impression, but there is reason to question its accuracy. In the charter of Carolina granted to the Lords Proprietors by **Charles II.** in 1663, the name of Carolina is recognized. More than thirty years before, **Charles I.** had granted a tract of territory south of the Chesapeake to **Sir Robert Heath**, naming it Carolina after himself. This grant became forfeited by non-user. The name, however, so given to the territory, was doubtless revived in the new charter of 1663. It would not be a pleasant reflection that two States of the Union derived their name from the King who commanded the massacre of St. Bartholomew.

Georgia.

THE name of Georgia, after **King George II.**, was by the terms of the charter conferred upon the territory granted to the company organized by **Oglethorpe** in 1732.

Maine.

MAINE owes its name to its being supposed to be the main or chief portion of the New England territory. The origin of the name is disclosed in an extract from the grant of **Charles I.** to **Sir Fernando Gorges**, in 1639, confirmatory of a patent given by the Plymouth Company in 1622, which grant the grandson of Gorges, through **John Usher**, assigned to the Massachusetts Bay Colony "all that Parte, Purparte and Porcon of the Mayne Lande of New England aforesaid, beginning att the entrance of Pascatway Harbor" (then follows the description), "all which Parte, Purparte or Porcon of the Mayne Lande and all and every the premises hereinbefore named wee doe for us, our heires and successors create and incorporate into one Province or Countie. And wee doe name, ordayne, and appoynt that the Porcon of the Mayne Lande and Premises aforesaid shall forever hereafter bee called and named The Province or Countie of Mayne."

Vermont.

THE Territory of Vermont was so named from the French words **verd mont**, "Green Mountain," the "d" being dropped in composition. The legal history of the name is a curious one. At a convention of the people held at Westminster, January 15, 1777, it was declared that the district was a State, "to be forever hereafter called, known, and distinguished by the name of **New Connecticut**, alias Vermont." The convention met by adjournment, July 2, 1777, and having in the meantime ascertained that the name of New Connecticut had already been applied to a district on the banks of the Susquehanna, it was declared that instead of New Connecticut the State should "ever be known by the name of **Vermont**." Hall, in his "Early History of Vermont," appendex No. 9, claims that the words "alias Vermont" did not belong in the name as adopted in January, and that they must have been inconsiderately added to the journal, or an early copy of it, by way of explanation after the name Vermont had been adopted in lieu of New Connecticut and afterward in transcribing, erroncously taken as a part of the original. **Mr. Hall** gives various reasons in support of this claim. In opposition to Mr. Hall's theory the words are found in Slade's "State Papers," page 70, in Williams' "History of Vermont," and in a manuscript copy of the journal of the convention, the original being lost, in the possession of **James H. Phelps**. Further, all accounts concur that the name of Vermont was given to the State by **Dr. Thomas Young**, and we find a letter of his dated April 11, 1777, addressed to "the Inhabitants of Vermont, a free and independent State," which implies that at that date the State had already received its name of Vermont, although under an alias.

Kentucky.

ALLEN, in his "History of Kentucky," says it was named "from its principal river, which is an Indian name for 'dark and bloody ground,'" Moulton, in his "History of New York," says Kentuckee signifies 'river of blood.'" In Haywood's "History of Tennessee," **Gen. Clark** is the authority for the assertion that in the Indian language Kentuke signifies "river of blood." **Ramsey**, in his "History of Tennessee," alludes to the name of Kentucky as signifying "the dark and bloody land." In Johnson's Cyclopedia the name is given as signifying "the dark and bloody ground." In opposition to all this it appears from Johnson's "Account of the Present State of the Indian Tribes of Ohio," L, page 271—that Kentucky is a Shawanoese or Shawnoese word, signifying "at the head of a river;" that the Kentucky River was in former times often used by the Shawanoese in their migrations north and south, and hence the whole country took its name. This theory of the name is quoted approvingly in Gallatin's "Synopsis of Indian Tribes." **Mr. Higginson**, in his "Young Folks' History," says the name first applied to the river means "The Long River." It lessens the weight of the authorities first cited that some of them connect the evil signification of the word with land, and some with water. It is also highly improbable that a name clothed with associations of terror should be adopted as the civic designation of a people. On the whole, it may be safely asserted that the weight of the evidence is in favor of the more peaceful origin of the name.

Tennessee.

TENNESSEE formed a part of the grant of the Carolinas. Its name is derived from its principal river, though formerly the name Tennessee did not apply to the main river, but to one of the small southerly branches thereof. There is authority for saying that the name of the river was derived from the **Village of Tunnessee**, the chief village of the Cherokee tribe, and situated on its bank. **Haywood**, in his "Natural and Aboriginal History of Tennessee," attempts to trace the origin of the name Tanasse as an Indian river name to the ancient River Taunis, and on this discovery, as well as on other similar resemblances, he founds the argument that the ancient Cherokees migrated from the western part of Asia. **Mr. Allen** claims that the name is derived from an Indian name signifying "a curved spoon;" and there is authority for still another derivation from an Indian word signifying "a bend in the river," in allusion to the course of the river. I am not aware that in either case the Indian word has been given, nor is it believed that any such word exists.

Ohio.

OHIO is named after the beautiful river, its southern boundary. From **Johnson's** "Account of the Indian Tribes," the word Ohio, as applied to the river, in the Wyandot language is **O-he-zuh**, signifying "something great." The name was called by the Senecas dwelling on the shores of Lake Erie the Oheo. **Mr. Schoolcraft** observes that the termination io in Ohio implies admiration. On the old French maps the name is sometimes "the Oehio," and sometimes "the Ovo."

Indiana.

INDIANA derived its name from one of the old ante-Revolutionary land companies which had claims in that region.

Illinois.

THE State of Illinois is named from its principal river, the Illinois. The river is named from that confederacy of Indian tribes called the **Illinois Confederacy**, which had its seat in the central part of the State. **Gallatin** gives the definition of the word "Illinois," "real men," "superior men," from the Delaware word Leno, Leni, Illin, Illini, as it is variously written. The termination ois is that by which the French softened the local inflexion when they adopted an Indian word.

Michigan.

LANMAN, in his "Red Book of Michigan," derives the name of the State from the Indian word Mich-saugyegan, signifying Lake Country. **Johnson's Cyclopædia** derives the name from the Indian words, Mitchi, Saugyegan, meaning Lake Country. I regard this as a questionable derivation. There are good reasons for supposing that the State derived its name from Lake Michigan, and not from its being nearly inclosed by lakes. If the word Michigan signifies Lake Country, why should it have been applied to the lake at all? In support of the theory that the name Michigan was descriptive, signifying "great lake," and was first given to the lake, I call attention to the fact that on the earliest maps the lake bears the name, while the peninsula, both upper and lower, bears no name whatever. Besides, the name, as applied to the lake, has a simple Indian derivation. The **Algonquin races**, at the head of which was the Chippewa tribe, dwelt on the northwestern shores of the lake. In the old Algonquin language the syllable "gan" meant lake. In the Chippewa language, "mitcha" means great.

Missouri.

THE State of Missouri was named from the river of that name, and the river itself from the Missouris, a tribe once living near its mouth, and afterwards driven into the interior. There is another theory in respect to the name of the river that is descriptive. **Col. Higginson**, in his "Young Folks' History," says Missouri means "muddy water." The Dacotahs called the Missouri Minneshoshay "muddy water," a word which might easily become Missouri. In an article on Indian migrations, by **Lewis H. Morgan**, in the North American Review, vol. cx., it is stated as a matter of tradition that the Kansas Indians were formerly established on the banks of the Mississippi, above the Missouri, and that they called the Missouri Ne-sho-ja "muddy river," a name in which the present name can be traced.

Colorado.

COLORADO is named after the great **Rio Colorado**, which rises in the Rocky Mountains and falls into the Gulf of California. The name signifies in Spanish "ruddy," "blood red," in a secondary sense "colored," in allusion to the color of its waters. The river is not within the limits of the State, and only belongs to it by some of its tributaries.

Texas.

THE State of Texas, formerly Spanish territory, then Mexican, and later an independent State, is the only State acquired by annexation. There is a conflict of opinion as to the origin of its name. Johnson's Cyclopedia, article Texas, states that "it is now proved conclusively to be of Indian derivation, the generic title of numerous tribes known to La Salle on his visit in 1685." On Seale's map, 1750, the center of the territory is occupied by Indians called the Tecas, which may be the generic title referred to. But Mr. Bryant, in his "History of the United States," Vol. II., page 518, note, says: "It is supposed that the name of Texas is from the Spanish Tejas, in allusion to the covered houses" found by La Salle on his visit in 1685. In Morphis' "History of Texas" the name is given as of doubtful origin. He states, in substance, that some refer the name to the capital village of the Nassonite tribe, others refer it to the Spanish word "teger," to weave, in reference to placing the grass over the cottages; others derive it from "tejas," meaning "cobwebs," the account being that the Spaniards encamped in an expedition into to the country, and one morning the commander seeing many spider webs between himself and the rising sun exclaimed: "Mira ins tejas!" and named the land Texas. The cobweb theory may well be dismissed as legendary.

Florida.

THE origin of the name of Florida is a matter of general agreement among historians. The story of Ponce de Leon sailing to the West in 1512 in search of the fountain of youth, seeing land on Pascua Florida, or "Flowery Easter," and on account of its profusion of flowers named it Florida, is familiar to all.

Oregon.

THE name of Oregon was the first applied to the Columbia River, then to the Territory, and lastly to the State. The origin of the name is conjectural. The earliest printed mention of it is in Carver's travels in 1763. Carver explored the sources of the Mississippi River, and states that by his residence among the Indians, especially the Sioux, he obtained a general knowledge of the situation of the River Oregon, or "the river of the West that falls into the Pacific Ocean at the Straits of Anian." By that which he calls the Oregon, the sources of which he placed not far from the headwaters of the Missouri, he may have referred to some one of the sources of the Missouri or to one of the two rivers which, rising in the Rocky Mountains, formed the principal eastern tributaries of the Oregon. Carver was misled as to the locality of the river of the West, and the supposed sources of it he may have confounded with the sources of the Missouri or one of the tributaries in question. But this much the publication of his travels accomplished—the establishment of a belief in the existence of a great river emptying into the Pacific Ocean. He designated by the name Oregon a great river flowing into the Pacific, and when in after times such a river was discovered the name was ready at hand.

California.

THE name of California appears to have been taken from a Spanish romance, "Las Sergus de Esplandian," in which is described "the great Island of California where a great abundance of gold and precious stones is found." This worthless romance was published in 1510, and generally read. Probably the name of California engaged the fancy of some of the officers of Cortes, and was given by them to the country discovered by him in 1535. It is strange that the name accidently given should have proved so exactly descriptive.

Nevada.

THE State of Nevada takes its name from the Sierra Nevada Mountains, which line its western frontier, the mountains in their turn being named from the Sierra Nevadas of Granada, which they are said to resemble in the serrated line of their summits.

Minnesota.

MINNESOTA is named from the Minnesota or St. Peter's River, the principal tributary of the Mississippi within its limits. The Indian word is Minisotah, signifying "slightly turbid water," or, "as the Minnesota historian more fancifully puts it, "sky tinted water.

Nebraska.

NEBRASKA is named from the Nebraska River. A writer in the North American Review, on "the Missouri Valley," says the name is Indian, and is compounded of nee, "river," and braska, "shallow." **Morgan**, in his article on Indian Migrations, North American Review, says: "The name of the **Platte River** in the Kaw dialect is Ne-blas-ka, signifying 'overspreading flats with shallow water.' "**Dr. Hale** says the name undoubtedly refers to the flatness of the country.

Kansas.

THE State of Kansas is named from its principal river. The latter is named from the tribe of Indians called the **Konzas**, who lived upon its shores. **Mr. Schoolcraft** uses the name Kansas to designate the tribe. De Soto marched southerly to the northern limit of his expedition in search of a rich province called Gayas. This points to the original name of the tribe, the Kaws. The present name has, therefore, an Indian root varied by French orthoepy.

Mississippi.

THE State of Mississippi is named after the great river. **Mr. Atwater**, a member of this society gives the Indian name of the river Meesyscepe ' the great water." That the Indian word signifies the "father of waters" is clearly erroneous. According to **Mr. Gallatin's** "Synopsis of Indian tribes". Messi never means "father" but "all"—"whole." The word "sipi" means in the Chippewa, "river." Thus the words united mean "the whole river, because many streams unite to form it.

Alabama.

IN considering the name of Alabama we go back to the expedition of **De Soto** in 1541. His last battle was at Alibamo, on the Yazoo River. This was the famous fortress of the brave tribe sometimes called the Alibamons, and sometimes the Alabamas. **Le Clerc**, who resided in the Creek Nation twenty years, and wrote a history published in Paris in 1802, says that the Alabamos came to the Yazoo from the north part of Mexico, and that after the battle with **De Soto** they retreated to the river which now bears their name; that they are the same people as the Alibamos, who fought De Soto. **Pickett**, in his 'History of Alabama,' states that "from these people the river and State took their names." **Allen's** 'History of Kentucky' says Alabama is an Indian name signifying "here we rest.' **Mr.**

Schoolcraft says cautiously that the name has been interpreted "here we rest." We have not been able to discover anything very restful in the history of the Alabamos, which is one of migrations. **Mr. Meeks**, a good authority in that State thinks that the word Alaba is only the name Hilaba, the Ulibahallee of De Soto, a theory at variance with that of **Le Clere**, and referring the origin of the name to a different tribe.

Iowa.

THE State of Iowa is named from the river of that name, and the river from the **Ioway Indians**, who after many migrations settled on its banks. In the same article in the Atlantic Monthly to which I have already alluded, it is intimated that the name Ioway is contracted from Ah-hee-oo-ba, meaning "sleepers," which perhaps, explains why the Sioux nearly exterminated them.

Wisconsin.

WISCONSIN was named after its principal river. Until quite a recent period the river was called the Ouisconsin, which is said to mean "westward flowing." Ouis is evidently shortened from the French Ouest." Mr. Schoolcraft says, that "locality was given in the Algonquin by 'ing,' meaning at, in, or by, as Wisconting." The name is probably of mixed origin.

Louisiana.

THE name of Louisiana, now confined to a State of the Union, was originally given to the entire French possessions on the west bank of the Mississippi, by **La Salle**, in 1682, in honor of Louis XIV.

Arkansas.

THE State of Arkansas takes its name from its principal river, the river from the tribe of Indians formerly known in that north. Till quite a recent period the name was that of Arkansas and the tribe the Arkansas Indians. Mr. Schoolcraft says that both the names Arkansas and Kansas are aboriginal roots, but we hear the names as modified by French orthoepy and construction. The same author further relates that there is a species of acacia found in Arkansas, of which the Indians, on the arrival of the French, made for themselves bows. It is light yellow, solid and flexible. "This is thought to have led to the appellation of Arc or Bow Indians. As they belonged to the Kansa race, which had lately separated from them, that term would naturally be adopted by the French as the generic name. In the **"Contributors' Club"** of the Atlantic Monthly, May, 1881, in reference to the name Arkansas, occurs this curious passage: "Does not the name come from the arc-ensang of the early French traders, its likeness to Kansas being accidental? Whether the bloody bow was a special weapon like the medicine-bow that gave its name to a creek, mountain range, and railway station in Wyoming, or the bloody bows were a band like the Saus Arcs, cannot now be determined."

The Naming of New States.

THERE is no State of the Union which bears the na e of Cabot or Coronado, or of De Soto, or of La Salle. And there is **Father Marquette**, whose form rises before us, dazzling and immortal as we open the pages of our early history. Was there no State to feel itself honored to be called after his name? But the wrong may yet be righted. In the naming of the new States which yet remain to be formed from our western domain, the last opportunity will be given to do justice to these **great discoverers**, and it would be a graceful and appropriate office of this society, as cases arise, to exert its influence by correspondence with the local authorities, and by memorial to Congress in favor of rendering to them even at this late day this exalted tribute.

THE PRESIDENCY.

How We Got Along For Several Years Without a President.

FEW people appear to be conscious that the American people passed through the most trying period of our National life without any President at all, the Executive head being Congress when in session and a committee of Congress when that body was not in session, the entire Revolutionary War being conducted without any President—that war practically ending with the surrender of Lord Cornwallis at Yorktown, October 19, 1781, and legally by the Treaty of Paris, which was communicated to the American army April 19, 1783, just eight years after the day on which the conflict was opened by the battle of Lexington. Not only for these eight eventful years were the American people, the American Nation, the United States of America, without any President, but for six years longer the American people managed to worry along without any President at all. After such a long experience without a President it is reasonably certain that if Cleveland had died the same day that Hendricks did the American people would have managed to worry along without any great difficulty or excitement.

When the Revolutionary War ended, in 1783, Washington retired to his country residence at Mt. Vernon, and took no part officially in public affairs until he was chosen by his native State—Virginia—as a delegate to the convention that formulated and proposed for adoption the Constitution of the United States, which assembled at Philadelphia in 1787, when Washington was elected presiding officer of the convention. That Constitution provided for the election of a President and Vice-President, and defined their duties. In the convention the committee had reported that the President should be called "His Excellency"; but that did not suit the plain notions of plain old Ben Franklin, and he squelched it in a bit of sarcasm by immediately proposing as an amendment "And the Vice-President shall be styled 'His Most Superfluous Highness.'" And so it was decided that the President should have no other title than "The President." A North Carolina Democrat applying recently to President Cleveland for a post-office, addressed the President as "His Majesty."

The Constitution did not provide for the election of the Electoral College—"Presidential Electors" as now called—by a direct vote of the people; it left the various Legislatures of the States to provide a method of electing them; and the Legislatures proceeded to elect them by a vote in the Legislature without any popular election There were no political conventions, or nominations made. The theory of the Electoral College was modeled after the Republics of Venice in the Middle Ages, that were governed by an oligarchy, the best and foremost citizens selecting the ruler. So, as many of the foremost citizens of the American Republic as there were Congressmen and Senators were chosen by the various State Legislatures as members of the Electoral College, who, in their wisdom, without being instructed by political conventions, voted for a candidate for President of the United States; but did not vote for a Vice-President—the one having the largest vote, if a majority, was to be the President and the one having the next largest was to be the Vice-President. Every one knows that "George Washington, Esq." was chosen President, and almost every one supposes by the unanimous vote of the people; but the people did not vote

THE AMERICAN MANUAL.

at all, and his support was by no means unanimous in the Electoral College, there being no less than twelve distinguished gentlemen with "Esq." attached to their names who received one or more Electoral votes for the honorable office of President of the United States. The first Congress under the Constitution assembled in New York City, Wednesday, March 4, 1789, and, there being no quorum present, adjourned from day to day until Monday, April 6, 1789, when the Senate elected John Langdon President, "for the sole purpose of opening and counting the vote for President of the United States." In joint session on the same day the vote was announced as follows:

States.	Geo. Washington, Esq.	John Adams, Esq.	Sam'l Huntington, Esq.	John Jay, Esq.	John Hancock, Esq.	Robert H. Harrison, Esq.	George Clinton, Esq.	John Rutledge, Esq.	John Milton, Esq.	James Armstrong, Esq.	Edward Telfair, Esq.	Benjamin Lincoln, Esq.
New Hampshire	5	5										
Massachusetts	10	10										
Connecticut	7	5	2									
New Jersey	6	1		5								
Pennsylvania	10	8			2							
Delaware	3			3								
Maryland	6					6						
Virginia	10	5		1	1		3					
South Carolina	7					1		6				
Georgia	5								2	1	1	
Total	69	34	2	9	4	6	3	6	2	1	1	1

"Whereby it appeared that George Washington, Esq., was elected President, and John Adams, Esq., Vice President of the United States of America." The States of New York, North Carolina, and Rhode Island had not given their consent to the adoption of the Constitution of the United States, and had no voice in the first Presidential election.

THE LADY WHO REJECTED WASHINGTON'S HAND.

Bishop Meade, in his "Old Churches and Families of Virginia," tells the following. The elder sister of **Miss Mary Cary** married George Wm. Fairfax, at whose house she was on a visit, when she captivated **a young man** who paid her his addresses. His affection, however, was not returned, and **the offer of his hand** was rejected by Miss Cary. This young man was afterward known to the world as **George Washington**, the first President of the United States of America. Young Washington **asked permission** of old Mr. Cary to address his daughter, before he ventured to speak to herself. **The reply** of the old gentleman was, "if that is your business here, sir, I wish you to leave the house, for my daughter has been accustomed to riding in her own coach." It has subsequently been said that this answer of Mr. Cary to the stripling Washington produced the **Independence** of the United States, and laid the foundation of the **future** fame of the first of heroes and best of men, **our** immortal Washington; as it was more than probable that, had he obtained the possession of the large fortune which it was known **Miss Cary** would carry to the altar with her, he would have passed the remainder of his life in **inglorious ease**. It was an anecdote of the day that this lady, many years after she had become the wife of **Edward Ambler**, happened to be in Williamsburg when **Gen. Washington** passed through that city at the head of the American army, **crowned** with never fading laurels and adored by his countrymen. Having in their way, among the crowd, his sword would have made her a military salute, whereupon she is said to have fainted. But this was **confirmation**, for her whole life served to show that she never **regretted** the choice she had made. It may be added as a **curious fact** that the lady General Washington afterwards married resembled Miss Cary as much as one twin sister ever did another.

THE PRESIDENTS.

How They Died, Their Last Words and Their Beliefs.

John Adams and **Thomas Jefferson** both died on the same day, and that the 4th of July, 1826. They were friends during their latter years, and Adams' last words were: "**Thomas Jefferson still lives**," but history shows that he was mistaken. Jefferson had died an hour before, exclaiming: "Lord, now lettest thou thy servant depart in peace," and "I resign my soul to God—and my daughter to my Country." **John Quincy Adams** gave his last breath in the Capitol at Washington, saying: "This is the end of earth, I am content," said **General Harrison**, who died in the White House said: "Sir, I wish you to understand the principles of government. I wish them carried out. I ask nothing more.

Garfield's last reported words as he lay racked by his terrible wound, were: "Oh that pain!" But **Lincoln** became unconscious when he was shot, and remained so till he died. **George Washington** was sane during his last hours, and he spent them in calmly arranging his affairs. He told his wife to bring two wills which he had made, and to burn one of them. He then grasped his pulse with one hand and counted the beats until he dropped back dead. Washington died of quinsy, **Polk** of malaria, Andrew Johnson of paralysis and General Harrison of an illness, owing to his exposure during the inaugural ceremonies.

President Jackson was for thirty-one years a diseased man, and the latter part of his life was spent in almost continuous pain. Even on his **death-bed** he was beset by office seekers. "I am dying," said he, "as fast as I can, and they all know it; but they keep swarming about me in crowds, seeking for some intriguing for office." His death-bed scene was a most affecting one. A half an hour before his death his family and friends were standing around his bedside, and his adopted son **Andrew** had taken his hand and whispered in his ear:

"Father, how do you feel? Do you know me?"

"Know you? Yes, I should know you all if I could see. Bring me my spectacles."

These were brought and put on him and he said: "Where is my daughter and Marian? God will take care of you for me. **I am my God's.** I belong to him. I go but a short time before you, and I wish to meet you all, white and black, in heaven.

At this all burst into tears, and the General said: "What is the matter with you, my dear children? **Oh, don't cry.** Be good children and we will all meet in heaven."

These were **Jackson's last words.** A short time after this he passed peacefully away. He died a Christian and a Presbyterian.

Thomas Jefferson was more of a deist than anything else, and when he died he said he would be glad to see a preacher who called "as a **good neighbor**," thereby intimating that he did not care to see him professionally. There was no preacher present at **Washington's** death-bed. He was an Episcopalian and for many years was a vestryman of Christ Church, Alexandria, Va. The **two Adams** believed in Unitarian doctrines, and it is said that **John Quincy Adams,** during his last years, never went to sleep without repeating that little child's prayer:

"Now I lay me down to sleep,
I pray Thee, Lord, my soul to keep;
If I should die before I wake,
I pray Thee, Lord, my soul to take."

There is considerable doubt as to **Lincoln's** christianity, but his best friends believe him to have been a believer. He was certainly a great **Bible-reader,** and understood it thoroughly. **Frank Pierce** was an Episcopalian and a church member. **Generals Grant** and **Hayes** attended the Methodist Church while in the White House, and **Garfield** spent his Sundays at the chapel of the Disciples. **John Tyler** was, I think, a Presbyterian, though his second wife was a Catholic. **Dolly Madison** was an Episcopalian, whatever her husband may have been, and **the old church** which she attended years ago still stands, and in it **President Arthur** worshiped.

A HEROIC FIGURE.

Sergeant Jasper and Some of the Grand Deeds Performed by Him.

IN the history of the State of Georgia one of the most heroic figures is that of a **Sergeant Jasper,** who served in the war of the Revolution in the Second South Carolina Regiment, under **General Moultrie.**

Jasper was a freckled, red-haired, uneducated country lad of singularly-quiet but firm bearing. In the attack made on **Sullivan's Island** by the British, a flag staff, cut by a ball, fell outside of the works. **Jasper** sprang forward, and, under a **shower of bullets,** nailed his own colors to the parapet. For this act of gallantry he was offered promotion, but he **declined it,** saying, "I have not the education nor manners befitting an officer."

General Moultrie then granted him a roving commission and placed six men under him who were known during the war as **"Jasper's Command."** Scarcely a week passed that this troop did not bring in prisoners captured by the most reckless daring.

On one occasion, Jasper, with one comrade, **Newton,** entered the British lines in disguise. In Savannah he overheard a woman, American, with a child in her arms, **bitterly lamenting** the condition of her husband who was held a prisoner in irons for desertion of the royal cause. He was **deeply touched** with her distress and with his comrade resolved to free her husband. They **lay in wait** near a spring about two miles from the town, which the guard with the prisoners in charge had to pass. The **guard,** consisting of two officers and eight privates, arrived about noon, with five prisoners in irons. The day being hot, they **left the prisoners,** as Jasper had expected they would, and hurried to the spring for water, having previously stacked their guns by the roadside **Jasper** and **Newton** crept out from the thicket seized their arms, knocked the irons from the prison.

ers, and **brought the guard** into the American camp.

A few months after this feat, during the attack on **Savannah**, the country lad fell, mortally wounded, while trying to place his **colors** on a redoubt. For one of his many bold exploits a **sword** had been given to Jasper by **Governor Rutledge**. He now unbuckled his sword and gave it to Newton, saying: "Take it to my father, and tell him **I have not dishonored it.**" A county in Georgia is named for this hero.

VAN BUREN A MONARCHIST.

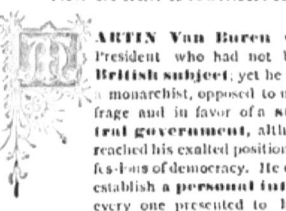

ARTIN Van Buren was the first President who had not been born a **British subject**; yet he was at heart a monarchist, opposed to universal suffrage and in favor of a **strong central government**, although he had reached his exalted position by loud professions of democracy. He endeavored to establish a **personal intimacy** with every one presented to him, and he ostensibly opened his heart for inspection. The **tone of his voice** was that of thorough frankness, accompanied by a pleasant smile, but a **fixed expression** at the corner of his mouth, and the searching look of his keen eye showed that he believed with **Talleyrand** that language was given to conceal thought.

President Van Buren's wife (by birth Miss Hannah Hoes, of Columbia county, New York,) had been dead nineteen years when he took possession of the **White House** accompanied by his four sons, and presided over the official receptions and dinner parties with his **well-known tact** and politeness. In the November following his inauguration, his eldest son and private secretary, **Col. Abraham Van Buren** (who was a graduate of the military academy at West Point, and who had served on the staff of Gen. Worth) was married to **Miss Angeline Singleton**, a wealthy South Carolina lady, who had been educated at Philadelphia, and who had passed the preceding winter at Washington, in the family of her relative, **Senator Preston**. On the New Year's day succeeding the wedding, **Mrs. Van Buren** assisted by the wives of the cabinet officers, received with her father-in-law, the President. Her rare accomplishments, superior education, beauty of face and figure, grace of manner, and vivacity in conversation insured social success. The **White House** was refurnished in the most expensive manner, and a code of etiquette was established which rivaled that of a German principality.—Ben: Perley Poore.

A CONGRESSIONAL DUEL.

MONG other evidences of the bitter and ferocious spirit which **characterized** political contests in those days was the duel between **Mr. Cilley**, of Maine, and **Mr. Graves**, of Kentucky, in which the former fell. Mr. Cilley, in a speech delivered in the House of Representatives, criticised a charge of corruption brought against some unnamed congressman in a letter published in The New York Courier and Enquirer, over the signature of "**A Spy in Washington**," and indorsed in the editorial columns of that paper. **Mr. James Watson Webb**, the editor of The Courier and Enquirer, immediately visited Washington and **sent a challenge** to Mr. Cilley by Mr. Graves, with whom he had but a slight acquaintance. Mr. Cilley declined to receive the **hostile communication** from Mr. Graves, without making any reflections on the personal character of Mr. Webb. Mr. Graves then felt himself bound, by the **unwritten code** of honor, to espouse the cause of Mr. Webb, and challenged Mr. Cilley himself. The challenge was accepted and the preliminaries were arranged between **Mr. Henry A. Wise**, as the second of Mr. Graves, and **Mr. George W. Jones** as the second of Mr. Cilley. Rifles were selected for the weapons, and Mr. Graves found difficulty in obtaining one, but was finally supplied by his friend, **Mr. Rives**, of The Globe. The parties met, the ground was measured, and the **combatants** were placed; on the fourth fire Mr. Cilley fell, shot through the body, and died almost instantly. Mr. Graves, on seeing his antagonist fall, **expressed a desire** to render him some assistance, but was told by Mr. Jones, "**My friend is dead, Sir!**" Mr. Cilley, who left a wife and three young children, was **a popular favorite** and his tragic end caused great excitement all over the country. Mr. Webb was generally **blamed** for having **instigated** the fatal encounter; certainly he did not endeavor to prevent it. Mr. Graves was **never afterward re-elected**—indeed, no man who has killed another in duel has ever been elected to office in Kentucky.—Ben: Perley Poore.

A UNIQUE COMPOSITION.

HIS unique composition was originally published in a Philadelphia paper over a hundred years ago. It may be read three different ways. First, let the whole be read in the order in which it is written; second, read the line downwards on the left of each comma in every line; third, in a like manner on the right of each comma. In the first reading the Revolutionary cause is condemned, and, by the others, encouraged and upheld:

Hark! Hark! the trumpet sounds, the din of war's alarms;
O'er seas and solid grounds, doth call us all to arms.
Who for King George do stand, their honors soon shall shine;
Their ruin is at hand, who with the Congress join.
The acts of Parliament, in them I much delight,
I hate their cursed intent, who for the Congress fight.
The Tories of the day, they are my daily toast;
They soon will sneak away, who Independence boast;
Who non-resistance hold, they have my hand and heart,
May they for slaves be sold, who act a Whiggish part;
On Mansfield, North and Bute, may daily blessings pour;
Confusion and dispute, on Congress evermore;
To North and British lords, may honor still be done.
I wish a block of cord, to General Washington.

AMERICA'S LUCKY DAY.

N Europe and the eastern part of the world **Friday** is generally regarded as an **unlucky day**, and those who are any way superstitious will object to commence any new enterprise or to do anything of importance on that day. Strange to say, **Friday has exercised** the most important and beneficial effects on America, and may be regarded as her **lucky day**. There are many citizens, mostly those of foreign birth, who still abhor Friday, although it is shown that the **most important events** connected with the discoverery of the New World and the independence of the United States all happened on a Friday.

It was on **Friday**, the 3d of August, 1492, that **Christopher Columbus** set sail from the port of Palos on his voyage of discovery. On **Friday**, the 12th of October, of the same year, he sighted land. On **Friday**, the 4th of January, 1493, he set out for Spain to announce his glorious discovery. **He landed** in Andalusia on Friday, the 15th of March, 1593. On **Friday** June 13, 1494, he discovered the **continent of America**. On Friday, March 5, 1497, Henry VII, King of England, sent **Jean Cabot** on a mission which led to the discovery of North America. On **Friday**, November 10, 1565, **Melendez** founded St. Augustine, the oldest city in the United States. On **Friday**, November 10, 1620, the Mayflower landed the

Pilgrim Fathers at Princetown. On **Friday**, December 21, 1620, the immigrants reached Plymouth Rock. On **Friday** Feb. 22, 1732 **Washington** was b.rn. On **Friday** June 27, 1775, the battle of **Bunker Hill** was fought. On **Friday**, October 8, 1778, **Burgoyne** surrendered at Saratoga. **Arnold's** treason plot was discovered on **Friday** September 23, 1780—**Cornwallis** surrendered at Yorktown on **Friday**, in October, 1781.

THE ORIGINAL LAND-OFFICE.

OW many people know that the Surveyor-General's office in Minnesota is **the original office** established in the United States? And yet the original time-worn documents are on file at the State House **establishing that fact**. The office was originally located by authority of Congress and under commission of **George Washington** at Marietta, O., in 1797. As the lands became disposed of and the territory became partitioned off, the office moved gradually westward, halted a brief space at this and that place, until it reached a final resting-place, many years ago at **St. Paul**, where all the records now are. These records are especially interesting to the antiquarians, covering as they do, the **history of land transactions** in this Country for over 100 years. Among them are autograph letters from **Washington** and **Jefferson** and other Presidents, all showing the quaint official phraseology of that bygone day, and winding up with the peculiar signature, "Your honorable and most humble obedient servant." There is also among the records the **first surveyor's chain** used in the West, and accompanying it was a personal letter from the Secretary of the Treasury, under whose jurisdiction the office then was, expressing the belief that "it was a good chain indeed, as the maker had assured him to that effect." Official guileless that seldom exists nowadays.—St. Paul Globe.

AMERICA'S HIGHEST MOUNTAIN.

HE highest mountain in America must now be changed from Mount St. Elias to **Mount Wrangel**, a little to the north. Several of these mountains have been newly measured. **Mount Hood**, once "roughly" estimated at 17,000 feet, then "closely" at 16,000, was brought down by triangulation to 13,000; an aneroid barometer made it 12,000 and a mercurial barometer made it 11,255. **Mount St. Elias** estimated by D'Agelet to be 12,672 feet, is triangulated by **Mr. Baker** to 19,500. It now appears that **Mount Wrangel**, lying to the north, **rises 18,100 feet** above Copper river, which is in turn 2,000 feet above the sea at that point. If this holds true, **Mount Wrangel** is at least **1,000 feet higher** than any other peak in North America. It lies within the United States boundary.—Nature.

ORIGIN OF THE SONG "JOHN BROWN'S BODY."

FOSTER SWEETSER, in his late book on "Boston Harbor and Fort Warren," relates the **origin** of the song of **freedom**. It happened, therefore, that from this happy garrison (Fort Warren, Boston Harbor) proceeded one of the **most powerful influences** which made themselves felt in the National armies during that long and weary war. The famous **song** of the National armies, "John Brown's body lies a mouldering in the grave," was composed and **first sung** at Fort Warren by the glee club of the Second Battalion of Light Infantry in the year 1861. It was adapted to an old **Methodist** camp-meeting tune, somewhat altered in form, and **the brigade band** at the fort was the **first that**

played it. The singers entered the Twelfth Regiment, which marched through Boston, New York and Baltimore, to **this grand chorus** from 1,000 throats and the music ran through the **Army of the Potomac**, nor ceased until grim powdered, blackened choirs had **chanted it in Texas** and **Alabama**, and down the great **Mississippi**, and on all the **flowery** coasts of the **Gulf**, and through the **Carolinas**, and along the streets of conquered **Richmond**. From Fort Warren came the **Marseillaise** of our emancipating revolution. As Admiral Preble says: "Few people aside from those who **kept step to its strains** when leaving home for the battle field and **sang it** round the smoky camp-fires during the long dull nights and days of army life knew the **extent of its popularity** and the deep hold it took upon the soldiers' hearts. It **spread** from regiment to regiment like wild-fire."

ORIGIN OF YANKEE DOODLE.

YANKEE DOODLE.—This popular song was introduced into this Country during the French and Indian War by one **Dr. Shackburg**, of the British army. The origin of the tune can be traced back to the reign of **Charles I.** When the British army was encamped on the shores of the Hudson, recruits from the provinces **came pouring in** in strange dress and equipments. As described by one writer, "Some with long coats, some with short coats, and some with no coats at all, some with cropped hair, and others with flowing wigs." Their **singular appearance** naturally excited mirth among the well-trained British regulars; and Dr. Shackburg wrote out "**Yankee Doodle**," and recommended it to the new officers as one of the **most celebrated airs** of martial music. About a quarter of a century later **Lord Cornwallis** and his troops marched into the American lines to this same tune of "**Yankee Doodle**." A recent writer trying to prove this our national air, quotes the following anecdote related by **John Quincy Adams** to sustain him. "After the Ministers Plenipotentiary of Great Britain and the United States had nearly concluded their pacific labors at **Ghent**, the burghers of the quaint old Dutch city resolved to give an entertainment in their honor, and desired to have **the National airs** of the two treaty-making powers performed as a part of the programme. So the musical director was requested to call upon the **American Ministers** and obtain the music of the National air of the United States. No one knew exactly what to give, and a consultation ensued, at which **Bayard** and **Gallatin** favored 'Hail Columbia,' while **Clay**, **Russell** and **Adams** were decidedly in favor of 'Yankee Doodle.' The director then inquired if any of the gentlemen **had the music**, and receiving a negative reply, suggested that perhaps **one of them** could sing or whistle the air. 'I can't,' said **Mr. Clay**; 'I never whistled or sung a tune in my life. Perhaps **Mr. Bayard** can.' 'Neither can I,' replied Mr. Bayard. 'Perhaps **Mr. Russell** can.' Each confessed his lack of musical ability. 'I have it,' exclaimed Mr. Clay, and ringing the bell he summoned his **colored body-servant**. 'John,' said Mr. Clay, 'whistle "Yankee Doodle" for this gentleman.' John did so, the chief musician took down the notes, and at the entertainment the **Ghent Burghers' Band** played the National air of the United States, with variations, in grand style."

THE WEDGE OF REPUBLICANISM.

BISHOP WARREN, of the Methodist church, is enthusiastic over American progress. He proudly declares that **our Country** is one that in a hundred years has taken a **respectable rank** in literature; that has made fourteen inventions, which have gone wherever **civilization** has gone, while all the rest of the world has not made **half that number** of equal importance; that has revolutionized **land warfare** once and **naval warfare** twice; that has solved social problems which the world has **blundered over** for ages; that has abolished a feudalism and serfdom; that, taking the **Bible declaration** that God has made of **one blood** all the nations, has made **one family** out of representatives of every kindred and tongue and people and nation; that has **founded its institutions** on the rights of man and the laws of God, and that has already driven a wedge of **Republicanism** nearly to the heart of Europe.

A YOUNG HERO.

T the first battle of Bull Run, **John Meigs**, a son of **General Meigs**, and a West Point cadet, seeing no Generals about, assumed and for some time **directed** the movement of the troops, the officers supposing he was an **aid-de-camp**, and that the orders came from the generals. Seeing the enemy massing in the woods to take Green's battery, Meigs ordered **Colonel Mathewson** to move quickly with his regiment to the support of the battery. The movement was promptly executed by the **First California**, and then two other regiments were brought up, I think the Thirty-first and Thirty-second New York. Later in the day the **youthful General**, seeing the field was lost, said to Colonel Mathewson: "You had better fall back toward Centerville." "And by whose authority do you give me such an order as that?" inquired the Colonel. "Well, sir," said young Meigs, "the truth is for the **last two hours** I have been unable to find any generals and have been commanding myself." I saw young Meigs **on the field**, and he was wounded through the knee, but **remained on duty**, although in terrible pain and faint from the loss of blood. He was afterwards killed by the Confederates in the Shenandoah Valley.

The Oldest Structure in Texas.

De Soto took up his line of march into Mexico, leaving only an **old stone fort** in Texas to show to coming dusky generations that the tales of their grandsires were true. A century and more rolled on, when again the **white man** came and passed by, and in scarce thirty years more, lo! two **great nations** claimed the land where stood the old stone fort. Then Spanish rule began, and for 106 years the **flag of Spain** on its wall streamed in the breeze. In 1821 that emblem gave place to the **eagle, snake** and **cactus** of Mexico, which remained until the battle of San Jacinto made Texas a republic and presented a new banner—"**The Lone Star**"—to the world. Then for nine years that flag fluttered, till annexation made **Texas** one of the United States, and the **stars** and **stripes** waved over the hoary walls. But 1861 brought yet another change, and during four short years the ensign of the **Confederacy** greeted the morning sun, until the spring of 1865 once more placed the fort under the **colors of the United States**.— American Magazine.

MEANING OF AMERICA.

HE meaning of the name **Amerigo** has often been discussed, the only thing certain being that it is one of those names of **Teutonic** origin, like **Humberto, Alfonso Grimaldi**, or **Garibaldi**, so common in northern Italy, which testify to the **Gothic** or **Lombard** conquest. Americ, which occurs as early as 744 A. D., is probably a contracted form of the name Amalarie, borne by a king of the **Visigoths**, who died in 531. A **Bishop Emrich** was present at the council of Salisbury in 897, and an **Americus Balisturius** is mentioned in the Close rolls (thirteenth century.)

It has been conjectured that the stem is *ina* from which we get the name Emma. The meaning of this is not known with certainty, though **Ferguson** thinks it may denote "strife" or "noise." Since, however, the name is probably of **Gothic** origin, and since the **Amalungs** were the royal race of the **Ostrogoths**, it is more likely that the stem is *amal*, which was formerly thought to mean "without spot," but is now more plausibly connected with the old Norse **aml**, "labor," "work." The suffix **ric**, cognate with **rex**, **reich**, and **rick**, means "rich" or powerful," and therefore the most probable signification of **Amerigo** is "strong for labor."—Isaac Taylor in Notes and Queries.

THE EVACUATION OF NEW YORK.

NEW YORK does well to celebrate the Anniversary of the Day when the British troops evacuated the City; for it was in truth the birthday of all that we now mean by the City of New York. One hundred and seventy-four years had elapsed since Hendrick Hudson landed upon the shores of Manhattan; but the Town could only boast a population of twenty-three thousand. In ten years the population doubled; in twenty years trebled. Washington Irving was a baby seven months old, at his father's house in William Street, on Evacuation Day, the 25 of November, 1783. On coming of age he found himself the inhabitant of a City containing a population of seventy thousand. When he died, at the age of seventy-five, more than a million of people inhabited the congregation of Cities which form the Metropolis of America.

The beginnings of great things are always interesting to us. New Yorkers, at least, can not read without emotion the plain, matter-of-fact accounts in the old newspapers of the manner in which the City of their pride changed masters. Journalism has altered its modes of procedure since that memorable day. No array of headings in large type called the attention of readers to the details of this great event in the History of their Town, and no editorial article in extra leads commented upon it. The newspapers printed the merest programme of the proceedings, with scarce a comment of their own; and, having done that, they felt that their duty was done, for no subsequent issue contains an allusion to the subject. All will be gratified by a perusal of the account of the Evacuation as given in *Rivington's Gazette* of November 26, 1783.

NEW YORK November 26:—Yesterday in the Morning the American Troops marched from Haerlem to the Bowery-Lane—They remained there until about One o'Clock, when the British Troops left their Posts in the Bowery, and the American Troops marched into and took Possession of the City in the following order, viz.

1. A Corps of Dragoons.
2. Advance Guard of Light Infantry.
3. A Corps of Artillery.
4. Battalion of Light Infantry.
5. Battalion of Massachusetts Troops.
6. Rear Guard.

After the Troops had taken Possession of the City, the GENERAL [Washington] and GOVERNOR [George

Clinton] made their Public Entry in the following Manner:

1. Their Excellencies the General and Governor, with their Suites, on Horseback.

2. The Lieutenant-Governor, and the Members of the Council, for the Temporary Government of the Southern District, four a-breast.

3. Major General Knox, and the Officers of the Army, eight a-breast.

4. Citizens on Horseback, eight a-breast.

5. The Speaker of the Assembly, and Citizens, on Foot, eight a-breast.

Their Excellencies the Governor and Commander in Chief were escorted by a Body of West-Chester Light Horse, under the command of Captain Delavan.

The Procession proceeded down Queen-Street [now Pearl], and through the Broadway, to Cape's Tavern.

The Governor gave a public Dinner at Fraunces's Tavern; at which the Commander in Chief and other General Officers were present.

After Dinner, the following Toasts were drank by the Company:

1. The United States of America.
2. His most Christian Majesty.
3. The United Netherlands.
4. The King of Sweden.
5. The American Army.
6. The Fleet and Armies of France, which have served in America.
7. The Memory of those Heroes, who have fallen for our Freedom.
8. May our Country be grateful to her military children.
9. May Justice support what Courage has gained.
10. The Vindicators of the Rights of Mankind in every Quarter of the Globe.
11. May America be an Asylum to the persecuted of the Earth.
12. May a close Union of the States guard the Temple they have erected to Liberty.
13. May the Remembrance of THIS DAY be a Lesson to Princes.

The arrangement and whole conduct of this march, with the tranquillity which succeeded it, through the day and night, was admirable! and the grateful citizens will ever feel the most affectionate impressions, from that elegant and efficient disposition which prevailed through the whole event.

THE PRESIDENT'S FLAG.

THE United States have existed for more than a hundred years without the President's ever having had a flag to call his own. But the administration of President Arthur made a reputation for observing the proprieties of office. Accordingly a private and peculiar standard was invented for the President. It consists of a blue ground with the arms of the United States in the center, is of the dimensions of the Admiral's flag No. 1, whatever they are, and is to be carried at the main of vessels of war while the President is on board, and in the bow of his boat.

Widows of the Revolutionary Soldiers.

Thirty-eight relicts of **Revolutionary** soldiers were drawing pensions at the beginning of the year 1888, on account of their husbands' services in that historical struggle. The average age of the old ladies is about 85 years. Their husbands have long since **passed over** to the silent majority. It is very probable that the **veterans** married their wives when they themselves were well advanced in years, while the latter were comparatively young women. The list of these **Revolutionary** pensioners, with their ages and addresses, is as follows:

NAME.	AGE.	RESIDENCES.
Margaret T. Brooks	81	Howells Cross Roads, Ga.
Meredy Smith	82	Newman, Ga.
Lucinda Whitmond	81	Marietta, Ga.
Sarah Dabney	87	Barry, Ill.
Jane Harbison	81	Pinckneyville, Ill.
Fanny Chance	79	Winslow, Ind.
Nancy A. Green	64	Versailles, Ind.
Sarah Crutcher	87	Pitts Point, Ky.
Sally Heath	82	Tatesville, Ky.
Susan Curtis	95	Topsham, Maine.
Lovey Aldrich	87	Leslie, Mich.
Olive C. Morton	76	Elva, Mich.
Betsy Wallingford	91	Mankato, Minn.
Sally Mallory	80	Mardsville, Neb.
Jane Dunmore	86	Broadalbin, N. Y.
Asenath Turner	82	Manchester, N. Y.
Elizabeth Boston	91	Valleytown, N. C.
Nancy Gragg	70	Colletville, N. C.
Mahala Hoagland	75	Charlotte, N. C.
Judah Harris	87	Rogers, N. C.
Nancy Weatherman	77	Lineback, N. C.
Elizabeth Davis	84	Morgausville, O.
Elizabeth Betz	84	Harrisburg, Pa.
Sarah Neal	88	Doreville, Pa.
Mary Brown	82	Knoxville, Tenn.
Nancy Jones	73	Jonesboro, Tenn.
Nancy Rains	95	Carter's Furnace, Tenn.
Nancy Robertson	84	Cates Cross Roads, Tenn.
Maria Walker	92	Waco, Texas.
Eleanor Lowe	70	Smith's Creek, Tenn.
Rebecca Mayo	74	Newbern, Tenn.
Mary Snead	71	Accomac Creek, Tenn.
Susan Tulloh	79	Mount Carmel, Va.
Esther S. Damon	73	Plymouth, Vt.
Lucy Morse	76	Barnard, Vt.
Patty Richardson	86	Bethel, Vt.
Nancy Bunton	84	Paris, Tenn.
Mary Carey	79	Sunnyside, O.

IMMIGRATION FOR 1887.

During the year 1887 there arrived at New York about 405,000 immigrants from foreign parts. The various nationalities of these people are shown by the following table, compiled by the Castle Garden authorities:

German Empire	81,864	Armenia	171
Ireland	56,869	Iceland	158
England	45,696	Mexico	151
Italy	44,271	South America	144
Sweden	37,802	Central America	131
Russia	33,203	Portugal	75
Hungary	17,719	China	63
Scotland	14,864	Australia	36
Norway	13,011	Arabia	22
Austria	11,762	Novia Scotia	15
Denmark	8,375	Japan	13
Bohemia	6,449	British East Indies	11
France	5,999	South Africa	11
Netherlands	5,590	New Zealand	11
Wales	5,549	Brazil	9
Switzerland	4,537	India	8
Finland	4,031	Africa	6
Belgium	2,361	Egypt	4
Roumania	834	Sandwich Islands	4
Quebec & Ontario	711	New Brunswick	3
Greece	612	Prince Edward Island	3
Luxembourg	572	British Columbia	2
Spain	485	Java	1
West Indies	460	Morocco	1
Malta	298	St. Helena	1
Syria	175	Peru	1
Burmah	170		
Turkey	160		

HISTORICAL TREES.

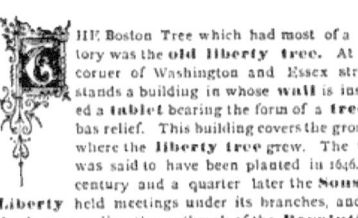THE Boston Tree which had most of a history was the **old liberty tree**. At the corner of Washington and Essex streets stands a building in whose **wall** is inserted a **tablet** bearing the form of a **tree** in bas relief. This building covers the ground where the **liberty tree** grew. The tree was said to have been planted in 1646. A century and a quarter later the **Sons** of **Liberty** held meetings under its branches, and in the days preceding the outbreak of the **Revolution** the ground on which it stood was **a place** of assembly for the men who conspired to throw off the **British yoke**. In 1773 an **anti-tea party** was held beneath it, and it became so obnoxious to the **British** that in 1775 it was **cut down** by a detachment of soldiers of the invading army, one of whom was killed.

The Gates Weeping Willow.

The **poet Pope** had sent to him from Smyrna a drum of figs. In it was a **small twig**, which he stuck in the ground near his Twickenham villa. It **took** root and **grew** rapidly and was the admiration of himself and his friends, and it proved to be the **Salix Babylonica**, or weeping willow, and it was the parent of all its kind in **England and America**. A British officer who came to this Country in 1775 brought with him, wrapped in oiled silk, a **twig** from Pope's willow, intending to plant it himself in **American** soil. The young officer became acquainted with **Custis**, Washington's step-son, and he gave him the willow twig. **Custis** planted it at **Abingdon**, in Virginia, where it grew vigorously. In 1790 **Gen. Gates** brought from Abingdon a shoot of the **Curtis** willow and planted it at the entrance gate to his estate at **Manhattan Island**, and it was known as **Gate's weeping willow**.

The Charter Oak.

The Charter Oak of Hartford, Conn., was estimated to be about **600 years** old when **Hooker** laid the foundation for a common-wealth there. It was at one time known as **Wyllys' tree**, as it stood in front of the house occupied by the **Hon. Samuel Wyllys**. It measured **twenty-six feet** in circumference a foot from the ground. The cavity in which the **charter** was placed on the night of October 31, 1637, was near the root and **large enough** to admit a child. The cavity gradually became smaller, until it would scarcely admit a hand. The **oak** was prostrated in August, 1854, and nearly every particle of it was worked into some **pleasing form** and cherished as a **memento** of a singular incident in **colonial history**.

The Treaty Tree.

The **Treaty Tree** was a **large elm** which stood on the banks of the **Delaware River**, near what is known as **Kensington** precinct, Philadelphia. It was under this tree that **William Penn** formed his treaty with the **Indians** in 1682. **Voltaire** said, "it was the **only treaty** between these nations and the Christians which was never sworn to and never broken." The tree then became an object of **interest** and **veneration**, and when **Penn** contemplated making his permanent home in **Pennsylvania** he tried to purchase the land near the tree, considering it one of the **finest situations** on the river. The **tree** was long protected with care, but was at last **blown down** in a gale on March 3, 1810. It was found to be **283 years old**, and its trunk measured **twenty-three feet** in circumference. The **Penn society** erected a monument, with proper inscriptions upon its site.

PROPERTY RIGHTS OF WIVES.

DOWER is the interest for her lifetime which a widow has in **one-third** of all the real estate owned in possession or right of possession by her husband from the date of the **marriage** till his **death**, and which could by any possibility have been **inherited** by a child of the marriage. It is not necessary, however, that a child should have been born.

Curtesy is the interest for his lifetime which a widower has in all the **real estate** owned in possession by his wife from the **date** of her **marriage** till her **death**. But this right of curtesy does not attach unless a **child** of the **marriage** shall have been born during the life of the mother.

Neither husband nor wife can **deprive** the other of **dower** or **curtesy** by will, or by any conveyance or sale or mortgage on the property. If sold or mortgaged without the signature of wife or husband releasing **dower** or **curtesy**, these rights still **attach** to it and may be **enforced** against the property in the hands of any subsequent owner.

The **community system** as it prevails in some States, briefly stated, preserves to both **husband** and **wife**, as his and her separate property, **all the property**, real and personal, owned by either at **marriage** and all gained by either during the marriage by **inheritance**, **gift**, or through the **will** of any deceased person; and gives no share to the surviving spouse in such **separate property** of the deceased spouse unless he or she die intestate, that is, without a will. But **all property** gained during the marriage by either party in any other way than those named, constitutes the **community** or common property of both, and belongs to **both equally**, and at the death of either party, the **survivor** becomes the absolute owner of the **whole** or of **one-half**, according as the **law** of the particular State may provide.

It may also be mentioned that in States where **curtesy** and **dower** are abolished, **statutes** give to the widow or widower a **certain share** in the estate of the deceased spouse, in case he or she has died intestate. And everywhere different **provision** may be made for the survivor by the **will** of the deceased, but generally a widow must elect to take such **provision**, or to take her **dower** or statutory share. Both cannot be taken unless the will **distinctly shows** such an intention. But the same restriction as to **election** does not seem to prevail concerning widowers in a State where **curtesy** is given.

Whenever children are referred to in the following summary, **grandchildren** of any degree of descent are included in the term.

ABSTRACT OF LAWS OF CURTESY AND DOWER.

1. **Alabama.**—Common law curtesy. Common law dower, but if **husband** dies solvent and childless, dower is one-half interest instead of one-third.

2. **Arizona.**—Community system. Survivor takes the **whole** of the community property if there are no children, **one-half** if there are children.

3. **Arkansas.**—Common law curtesy. Common law dower, but if there are no **children**, one-half instead of one-third.

4. **California.**—Community system. Surviving husband takes the **whole** of the community property; surviving wife **one-half** of it.

5. **Colorado.**—No curtesy or dower.

6. **Connecticut.**—Survivor takes one-third interest for life in **all property** owned by deceased at his or her death.

7. **Dakota.**—No curtesy or dower.

8. **Delaware.**—Common law curtesy. If no child was born, **widower** takes life interest in one-half wife's realty. Common law dower. If one child survives, **widow** takes life interest in one-half of husband's realty, instead of one-third.

9. **District of Columbia.**—Common law dower. Curtesy also in **realty** acquired before 1869; the better opinion seems to be that no **curtesy** has attached to property acquired later.

10. **Florida.**—Common law dower. No curtesy.

11. **Georgia.**—Common law dower. No curtesy.

12. **Idaho.**—Community system. Survivor takes the entire **community** property if there are no children; otherwise, one-half.

13. **Illinois.**—No curtesy. Either survivor takes a **life interest** in one-third of the realty of the deceased, including equitable estates in land.

14. **Indiana.**—No curtesy or dower. Either survivor takes **one-third** of all realty of deceased spouse absolutely—that is, the entire **title**, instead of a life estate merely.

15. **Iowa.**—No curtesy or dower. Either survivor takes **one-third** of all realty of deceased absolutely, including equitable estates in land. If there are no children, the share is **one-half**.

16. **Kansas.**—No curtesy or dower. Either survivor takes **one-half** absolutely of all property of the deceased.

17. **Kentucky.**—Common law curtesy and dower.

18. **Louisiana.**—Community system. Survivor takes **one-half** of the common property.

19. **Maine.**—No curtesy. Either survivor takes **one-third** for life of the land of deceased spouse, if the estate is solvent. If there are no children, the share is **one-half**.

20. **Maryland.**—Common law curtesy and dower, including equitable estates. But it seems that, **by her will**, a wife may deprive her husband of curtesy.

21. **Massachusetts.**—Common law curtesy and dower. If no **child** has been born, so that the husband's right of curtesy does not **accrue**, he is entitled to hold **one-half** of his deceased wife's real estate for his life, and she cannot deprive him of this right by her will. If either husband or wife, leaving no surviving child, the **widow** or **widower** takes the real estate of the deceased to an amount not exceeding $5,000 in value, absolutely; and the widower takes also his curtesy (or other life interest as above described) in his wife's remaining real estate which her husband owned at his death. The statute expressly provides that the **wife** cannot deprive her **husband** of his claim to her real estate by her will; and though it does not so provide in regard to the husband, a recent decision of the Supreme Court declared the right of the wife to elect to take her **statutory share** instead of such share as his will may have given her.

22. **Michigan.**—Common law dower. No curtesy.

23. **Minnesota.**—No curtesy or dower. Either survivor takes **one-third** absolutely of the realty of the deceased spouse.

24. **Mississippi.**—No curtesy or dower.

25. **Missouri.**—Common law curtesy and dower.

26. **Montana.**—Community system. Widower takes the **entire** common property, the widow **one-half** of it.

27. **Nebraska.**—Common law dower. Common law curtesy if no **child** survives. If children only by former husband survive, no curtesy; if children by surviving husband, or by both, husband takes a life **interest** in one third of the inheritance of his own children.

28. **Nevada.**—Community system. Entire common property goes to surviving **husband**. Also a surviving **wife**, if the husband dies without a will or children.

29. **New Hampshire.**—Common law curtesy and dower; but either survivor may elect to take **one-half** absolutely, if no children survive; otherwise, **one-third** absolutely; unless the wife leaves children by a former husband and no child by surviving husband has been born, in which case he takes only a life interest in **one-third** of her realty.

30. **New Jersey.**—Common law curtesy and dower.

31. **New Mexico.**—No curtesy or dower.

32. **New York.**—Common law dower. Curtesy also in land owned by wife at her death, unless otherwise provided by her will.

33. **North Carolina.**—Common law curtesy and dower.

34. **Ohio.**—Either survivor has a life interest in **one-third** of the realty of the deceased, whether in possession, in reversion or remainder, or held by a lease.

35. **Oregon.**—Common law curtesy and dower; but **curtesy** is not dependent on the birth of a child.

36. **Pennsylvania.**—Common law curtesy and dower. But **curtesy** is not dependent on the birth of a child, and dower is lost by sale of land for debt.

37. **Rhode Island.**—Common law curtesy and dower.

38. **South Carolina.**—Common law dower. No curtesy.

39. **Tennessee.**—Common law curtesy and dower.

40. **Texas.**—Community system. Survivor **takes all** the common property if there are no children.

41. **Utah.**—No curtesy or dower.

42. **Vermont.**—Common law curtesy. Also dower in **realty** owned by husband at death.

43. **Virginia.**—Common law curtesy and dower.

44. **Washington.**—Community system. Survivor takes **one-half** of the common property, and if there are no children or will, the **whole** of it.

45. **West Virginia.**—Common law curtesy and dower.

46. **Wisconsin.**—Common law dower. Also, **curtesy** in land of which **wife** dies possessed, unless otherwise disposed of by will, or unless she leaves children by a former husband.

THE FIRST BLOOD OF THE REVOLUTION.

CORRESPONDENT of the Hartford *Times*, who has recently been to East Westminster, Vt., gives the following historical sketch which he derived from Mr. Richmond, a sexton, whom he met in the cemetery at that place:

"Mr. Richmond said that in 1874-'5, the Whigs and Tories were about equally divided, the Judges and juries being appointed by the King. The British authorities attempted to hold a court in the Court-House, then standing about 40 rods north of the cemetery. The colonists were bound that no court should be held—so they armed themselves and attacked and drove the court from the Court-House. In return, the British soldiers attacked the colonists, and a man named William French fell dead from the fire of the soldiers, and Daniel Houghton was fatally wounded. This was the first bloodshed of the Revolution. In 1872 the State of Vermont appropriated $600 for a monument, which now stands about 6 feet from the place where French was buried. A gentleman by the name of William C. Bradley (formerly Congressman from Vermont) a few years ago erected a tomb to tell the exact spot of the grave, and on it is the following inscription:

In memory of William French,
Son of Nathaniel French,
Who was shot at Westminster,

March ye 13th, 1775
by the hands of Cruel Ministerial tools of
George ye 3d
In the Courthouse at 11 O'Clock at Night,
in the 22nd year of his age.

Below this are the following lines:

Here William French his body lies
For murder his blood for Vengeance cries
King George the third his Tory crew
that with a bawl his heart shot threw,
For Liberty and his Countrys Good,
he lost his Life, his Dearest blood.

"The above is an exact copy, capitals and all. As a good many think that the first blood flowed at the battle of Lexington, this may be interesting to them, for it certainly was to me. A building erected in 1770, five years before the battle, is still standing. It was erected as a Congregational church, but is now used as a town-house, and is in good repair."

THE DECLARATION OF INDEPENDENCE IN A NEW LIGHT.

N the 15th of May, 1776, the Second Continental Congress voted to recommend all the Colonies to adopt new forms of government. On the 7th of June Richard Henry Lee, of Virginia, obeying the instructions of that Colony, moved "that these United Colonies are, and of right ought to be, free and independent States; that they are absolved from all allegiance to the British Crown and that all political connection between them and the State of Great Britain is, and ought to be, totally dissolved." Three days later, on the 10th—the day when the first debate on Lee's Resolution was closed—six of the Colonies being unprepared to vote, a postponement was had until the 1st of July, in the expectation that by that time there would be entire unanimity. On the evening of the 1st, John Adams wrote to Samuel Chase that the debate took up most of the day. Jefferson in 1787 stated that the debate lasted "nine hours, until evening, without refreshment and without pause." At the close of the debate, however, no definite action was taken, and the final voting was postponed until the following day. Accordingly, on the 2d of July, the first formal and final vote was taken on independence, all of the Thirteen Colonies voting for it except New York.

A Great Error.

It has been stated by a high authority that the New York delegates, during the entire debate on Lee's Resolution, "remained passive, neither opposing nor helping, as they deemed the whole subject of separation as outside of their instructions." There could be no greater error. To suppose that George Clinton, who had been elected a Delegate to the Continental Congress from New York chiefly on account of his pronounced views against the Crown, or that Robert R. Livingston, one of the five who reported the Declaration, remained "passive," instead of each using all his influence in moulding the sentiments of Congress in the right direction, is to accuse both of those gentlemen of grave inconsistency.

On May 15, 1776, as we have seen, a Resolution was passed by the Continental Congress and ordered to be published. If either Clinton or Livingston was present and voted for it at that time, it could fairly be said that he not only *favored*, but *voted* for independence. One of the phrases of the preamble to the Resolution is, "It is necessary that the exercise of every kind of authority under the said Crown should be totally suppressed, and all the Powers of Government exerted under the authority of the People of the Colonies." John Adams at the time called this Act or Resolution "independence itself." The Colonies were recommended by it to establish popular governments where they had not already done so. Indeed the independence of the Colonies took place in fact, if not in name, before the general independence of the whole was declared. Bancroft says that all the New York Delegates except Alsop were personally ready to vote for independence, and were confident of their constituents. John Adams says that even Duane favored it, and he had been a half Tory all along; how much more, then, must Clinton and Livingston have been for it! The Documentary Declaration was debated in Committee of the Whole before being reported to the House; and there is not much doubt that in such Committee the New-Yorkers voted for it. Wisner, one of the New York Delegates, we know did.

A Disparaging Statement.

But it has been further stated to the disparagement of New York that on the 2d of July, when the vote on Independence was actually taken, New York (the vote was by Colonies, not by individuals,) did not vote, the Delegates from that Colony, over their own signatures, with Clinton at their head, officially reporting as follows: "The important question of independence was agitated yesterday in a Committee of the whole Congress, and this day will be finally determined in the House. We know the line of our conduct on this occasion; we have your instructions, and will faithfully pursue them."

The Proper Course.

But this course was entirely proper, and for the Delegates to have acted otherwise would have been to disobey the express commands of the New York Provincial Congress, which they represented. Upon the passage of the Resolution of May 15 by the Continental Congress the New York Delegates, on June 8, wrote home to ascertain the sentiments of their constituents on the question of independence, which was expected to come up shortly in that Body. Meanwhile, on the 19th of June, a new Provincial Congress was elected by New York for the express purpose of acting on the question of independence, as the previous one, to whom the letter of the Delegates was addressed, did not consider itself authorized so to do. The old Provincial Congress continued to sit for some days after the new one was chosen, but of course can be excused for not authorizing their Delegates in the Continental Congress to vote for independence. They purposely left it to the new Provincial Congress, which met at White Plains July 8, 1776, and which the very next day passed unanimously a Resolution approving the Declaration of Independence.* The fact, therefore, upon which considerable stress has been laid—that the New York Delegates in the Continental Congress were not the voters for the adhesion of New York—is a purely private and local affair between them and their constituents; nor does it in the slightest degree affect the *willingness* of New York to declare itself independent. There was very little Toryism that dared to show itself to the Public at this late day. Most of the leading Loyalists had either left the State or were in hiding; and indeed, as a matter of fact, New York was as nearly unanimous at the time as either New Jersey or Pennsylvania. Finally, when on the 2d of July the vote was taken for formal independence, the New York Delegates, who for local reasons could not act for their State, were probably much better disposed than those of Pennsylvania, who could act, and yet were intending to vote four against independence and three for it; and it was only by great persuasion that two of the four were induced to absent themselves, so as to turn the minority into a majority. Though the *Colony* of New York, for the above reasons, failed to vote, the *State* failed not to act, for liberty and independence.

The Official Record.

The official record of the momentous proceedings of the 2d is in these words:

TUESDAY, July 2, 1776.

"The Congress resumed the consideration of the Resolution from the Committee of the Whole, which was agreed to, as follows:

"*Resolved*, That the United Colonies are, and of right ought ought to be, free and independent States; that they are absolved from all allegiance to the British Crown; and that all political connection between them and the State of Great Britain is, and ought to be, totally dissolved.'

"From the hour when that vote was taken and that record made," says Mr. McKean, very justly in his Centennial Address, "the United States of America assumed among the powers of the earth the separate and equal station to which the laws of Nature and of Nature's God entitle them."

The Second of July Should be Celebrated.

In fact, the *Second* of July and not the *Fourth* should be *the* Day for the celebration of our Independence. That it would be was the opinion of the prominent men of that day. On the morning of the First of July, John Adams, anticipating Independence in that day's vote, wrote from Pennsylvania to Archibald Bullock, "May Heaven prosper the Newborn Republic, and make it more glorious

---

* The Resolution reads as follows: "Resolved, unanimously, that the reason assigned by the Continental Congress for declaring the United Colonies free and independent States are cogent and conclusive; and that while we lament the cruel necessity which has rendered that measure unavoidable we approve the same, and will, at the risk of our lives and fortunes, join with the other Colonies in supporting it."

than any former Republics have been!" and on the 3rd, *after* the adoption of the Resolution of Independence, he wrote to his wife, Mrs. Adams, as follows; "Yesterday the greatest question was decided that was ever debated in America; and a greater, perhaps, never was nor will be decided among men. That will live as Truth among all Americans who know and value the History of their Country." And in the course of the same letter he adds, "The *Second* Day of July 1776, will be the most memorable Epocha in the History of America. I am apt to believe that it will be celebrated by succeeding generations as the *Great Anniversary Festival*; be solemnized with pomp and parade, with shows, games, sports, guns, bonfires, and illuminations from one end of the Continent to the other, from this time forward for evermore. It ought also to be commemorated as the Day of Deliverance by solemn Acts of Devotion to God Almighty . . . Through all the gloom I can see the rays of ravishing light and glory; and Posterity will triumph in this Day's transactions.

At length on the 4th of July, 1776, the Declaration of Independence—the complement of the Act of the 2d—having been drafted by Jefferson, was formally submitted to the Delegates present.

Why the Fourth of July is Commemorated.

If, however, it be asked how has it come to pass that the 4th of July has been substituted as a Day of Celebration for the 2d, the real Date of the Birth of the United States as an Independent Nation, the answer is that the Resolution of the 2d was passed in private Session, and remained unknown to the people generally until it and the Declaration were publicly proclaimed together. "There was nothing in the phrasing of the Resolution to cause it to live in the popular memory, whilst there was everything in the Declaration to give it a vital hold upon the affection of the American People." But there was still another cause for this. It has been well said that "the great importance, the decisive and controlling character of the Resolution of Independence adopted on the 2d of July, 1776, have been obscured to the popular vision by the splendor of Jefferson's immortal Declaration of the Reasons for the adoption of the Resolution. Yet Jefferson himself never allowed the one to overshadow in his estimation the importance of the other. The Declaration in his mind was intended to be an appeal to the tribunal of the World, as a justification of what had already been done. It was intended he says, 'to be an expression of the American mind, and to give that expression the proper tone and spirit called for by the occasion, to place before mankind the common-sense of the subject in terms so plain and firm as to command their assent. Yet the Declaration of Independence *has* dislodged the Resolution of Independence from the place of precedence in the Popular mind, and the Fourth of July has displaced the Second as the Nation's Holiday and the Patriot's High Festival."

We are now prepared to speak of the signing of the Document known as the Declaration of Independence, and which so many of us have seen and examined in Independence Hall, Philadelphia.

In thinking of that Instrument one is apt to call up before him an August Assemblage gravely seated around a table, with the Declaration spread out upon it, and each member of the Continental Congress in turn taking a pen and with great dignity affixing to it his name. Nothing, however, can be further from that which actually took place. Very few of the Delegates, if indeed any, signed the Original Document on the 4th, and none signed the present one now in Independence Hall, for the very good reason that it was not then in existence.

On July 19, Congress voted that the Declaration be engrossed on parchment. Jefferson, however, says that New York signed on July 15. Consequently New York must have signed the Original Copy of the Declaration before it had gone into the hands of the engrosser. On what day the work was done by the copyist is not known. All that is certainly known is that on the 2d of August Congress had the Document as engrossed. This is the Document now in existence in Independence Hall. It is on parchment, or something that the trade calls parchment. On that day (August 2) it was signed by all the Members present. The original Declaration is lost, or rather was purposely destroyed by Congress. All the signatures were made anew. When the business of signing was ended is not known. One, Matthew Thornton, from New Hampshire signed it in November, when he became a Member for the first time; and Thomas McKean, from Delaware, as he says himself, did not sign till January, 1777. Indeed, this signing was, in effect, what at the present day would be called a "test oath." The principles of many of the new Delegates coming into Congress from the different States were not known with certainty —some of them might be Tories in disguise— and thus each one was required on first entering Congress to sign the Declaration. In January, 1777, an authenticated Copy with the names of all the Signers, was sent to each State for signatures—a fact which may have put a stop to the business of signing. It shows, however, the little importance that was attached to this ceremony, that Robert R. Livingston was one of the Committee of five that reported the Declaration, and yet did not sign it, unless his signature is lost with the original Document.

But I am not delving in the field of conjecture. The same questions seem to have occurred as early as 1813, when Thomas Rodney wrote to Governor Thomas McLean—a Delegate from Delaware, and afterward President of Congress and Governor of Pennsylvania—asking why his name was not among the list of the Signers in the Journal of Congress. To this letter Governor McKean replied, under the date of August 22, 1813, as follows;

"Now that I am on this subject, I will tell you something not generally known. In the printed Public Journal of Congress for 1776, Vol. II., it would appear that the Declaration of Independence was signed on the 4th of July by the Members whose names are there inserted. But the fact is not so, *for no person signed it on that day, nor for many days after;* and among the names subscribed one was against it, Mr. Reed, and seven others were not in Congress on that day, viz., Messrs. Morris, Rush, Clymer, Smith, Taylor, and Ross, of Pennsylvania, and Mr. Thornton, of New Hampshire. Nor were the six gentlemen last named at that time Members. The five for Pennsylvania were appointed Delegates by the Convention of that State on the 26th of July; and Mr. Thornton entered Congress for the first time on the 4th of November following' when the names of Henry Wisner, of New York, and Thomas McKean, of Delaware, were not printed as Subscribers, though both were present and voted for Independence."*

The Truth of the Matter.

The truth is, the Declaration of Independence was considered at that time of much less importance than now; nor did the Signers dream of its becoming a shrine almost of worship at the present day. It is a dramatic incident, and naturally concentrates men's attention on it. In the Public mind at the time, Provincial Congresses were more important than the General Congress. The latter was a Body of Agents, and was endowed with no sovereignty except for war purposes. The real Sovereigns were the States.—*Harper's Magazine.*

* The following is the full text of the letter. If Dickinson drafted the Declaration of 1775, as Mr. Moore seems to think, it is singular that he should have voted against the one of 1776, as this letter—most excellent authority—asserts.

PHILADELPHIA, Aug 22, 1813.

"DEAR SIR,—Your favor of the 22d last month with Copy of the **Journal of the Congress** at New York in October, 1765, printed in the Baltimore Register, came safe to hand. Not having heard of this publication, I had the **proceedings** of that Body (not the whole) reprinted here about 2 months ago from a Copy I found in the **1st volume** of American Tracts, contained in four volumes octavo, edited by J. Almon, of London, in 1767. Such an **important transaction** should not be unknown to the future historian.

"I recollect **what passed** in Congress in the beginning of July, 1776, respecting Independence; **It was not as you have conceived**. On Monday the 1st of July, the question was taken in the Committee of the Whole, when the **State of Pennsylvania**, represented by seven gentlemen then present, voted against it; **Delaware**, then having only two Representatives present, was divided; all the **other States** voted in favor of it. Whereupon without delay I sent an express (at my private expense) for your honored uncle, Cæsar Rodney, Esquire, the remaining Member from **Delaware**, whom I met at the Statehouse door in his boots and spurs as the Members were assembling; after a friendly salutation (without a word on the business) we went in the **Hall of Congress** together, and found we were among the latest. Proceedings immediately commenced, and after a few minutes the **great question** was put;when the vote for **Delaware** was called your uncle arose and said, "As I believe the voice of my **constituents** and of all **sensible and honest men** is in favor of Independence, my own judgment concurs with them,I vote for **Independence**," or in words to the same effect. The State of **Pennsylvania** on the 4th of July,there being only five Members present,(Messrs. **Dickinson** and **Morris**, who had, in the Committee of the Whole, voted against Independence, were absent), voted for it, three to two, Messrs **Willing** and **Humphreys** in the negative. Unanimity in the Thirteen States, an **all important point** on so great an occasion, was thus obtained; the dissension of a **single State** might have produced very dangerous consequences.

"Now that I am on this subject," etc.

SALEM WITCHCRAFT AND COTTON MATHER.

THAT there were witches in the time of Cotton Mather was agreed to by every body. The English law provided a punishment for witchcraft, and a famous case, tried by Sir Matthew Hale ("than whom," says Mather, quoting the venerable Baxter, "no man was more backward to condemn a witch without full evidence"), was a weighty precedent with the New England Judges. The witches were condemned and executed.

This whole matter seems to us only a hideous nightmare as we look at it in our lights of to-day—as many of our doings, let us hope, will seem to our posterity. But while it is common enough to talk about witchcraft, perhaps you do not know exactly what a witch was supposed to be.

Cotton Mather believed, and he is the great authority upon witches:

1. That the devils have in their natures a power to work wonders.

2. That to assert this power makes most for the glory of God in preserving man from its effects.

3. That this power is restrained by the Almighty as he pleases.

4. That a witch is one that makes a covenant with the Devil.

5. That by virtue of such covenant she has a power to comission him.

6. That when the Devil is called upon by the witch, though he were before restrained by the Almighty, the desired mischief shall be performed.

7. That to have a familiar spirit is to be able to cause the Devil to take bodily shapes.

This is the account which R. C. gives us of the doctrines of Mather, as laid down in a manuscript which he allowed R. C. to read but not to copy. R. C.'s strong point in all his comments and replies is, that, although witches may be possible, since they are mentioned in the Bible, yet that no sufficient means of determining who is a witch are indicated; and he sees and states very clearly that the course of the Reverend Cotton Mather tends to bring Christianity and pure religion into extreme disrepute.

The whole business is so shallow and sad, that a man at this day can only pity and be humble. In all the accounts of wonders, and all the evidence upon the trials, nothing appears that is not susceptible of the most obvious interpretation. For instance: upon the trial of Susanna Martin, June 29, 1692, Robert Douver testified that this person being some years ago prosecuted at court for a witch, he then said unto her *he believed she was a witch*. Whereat she being dissatisfied said, *that some she-devil would shortly fetch him away;* which words were heard by others as well as himself. The night following, as he lay in his bed, there came in at the window the likeness of a cat, which flew upon him, and took fast hold of his throat, lay on him a considerable while, and almost killed him; at length he remembered what Susanna Martin had threatened the day before, and with much striving he cried out, *Avoid, thou she-devil, in the name of God, the Father, the Son, and the Holy*

Ghost, avoid! where upon it left him, leaped on the floor, and flew out at the window.

Poor Susanna was executed; and upon such grounds as these the lives of the friendless old women in New England were taken, while the Reverend Cotton Mather cried, Amen. The burnings and tortures of the Inquisition were tolerable in comparison, for an ecclesiastical was very likely to prove a political heretic. But the forlorn old women of Salem could be dangerous to nobody in the world. Men also were accused, and children; but the complete list of persons charged with witchcraft includes thirty-five men and two boys, ninety women and seven girls. Of these, twenty were put to death, thirteen women and seven men; and eleven were condemned, but did not suffer, all of whom were women.

These are the chapters of history that should teach us charity. Possibly old Mather, and Noyes, and the Salem magistrates, thought they were doing God service; and they shall have the credit which belongs to honest intention. But the whole history shows us, as we are constantly shown, that the man who invades the sacred natural rights of other people, however honestly he may do it, must pay the penalty of actual punishment, if he is living, and of a public reprobation of his memory, if he be dead, before his guilt is understood. The name of Cotton Mather will be always clouded with the shame of the witchcraft massacres, as the fame of Isabella is disfigured by the Inquisition. To respect the rights of others just as firmly as we insist upon our own, is the only path of peace.

THE AMERICAN UNION AND CONSTITUTION.

Address of Judge Elliot, of Tennessee, to President Cleveland.

MR. PRESIDENT: You have recently participated in a celebration of the one-hundredth anniversary of the formation of the Constitution of the United States, and you beheld the multitudes of our fellow-countrymen flocking from every direction to the spot where that instrument was fashioned, and renewing their vows of fealty at the shrine of that grandest monument of human wisdom. Let me say, sir, that the Southern heart was in full sympathy with that interesting occasion and that nowhere in all this broad land will you find more loyalty to the Constitution of the United States and to the Government created by it than among the people of these Southern States. Differences of opinion as to its true theory and its proper construction in some points existed from its very creation, and controversy has often been angry and bitter. One great and important interest in the progress of things became sectionalized, and out of it arose questions of constitutional interpretation which were regarded by the Southern people as so vital to their rights and interests that they committed their solution to the arbitrament of arms.

The Stern Logic of Events.

But, Mr. President, they have bowed to the stern logic of events, and they have in a frank and manly way accepted the result of the struggle as a final settlement of all the questions in dispute, and they have since labored with rare courage, fortitude, and cheerfulness to accommodate themselves to their new conditions, to reconstruct their broken fortunes, and to contribute as far as possible to the general prosperity and happiness of the whole country. And one practical result accomplished by the conflict, the theory of the right of a State to withdraw from the Federal compact, was overthrown, and the indestructibility of the American Union was established on the firmest foundations.

The Chief Elements of Discord Removed.

The chief element of discord has been removed forever, and though questions will continue to arise about which men may differ, and differ earnestly, it is settled beyond appeal that in all abuses and grievances that may arise from the action of the General Government, the remedy must hereafter be sought within the pale of the Union and under the forms of established law. We have all come to realize that American liberty, the highest type of human freedom, can only be fully enjoyed in the American Union and under the American Constitution. Indeed, the sentiment uttered by Mr. Webster on a memorable occasion may be said to have become imbedded in the constitutional law of America, "Liberty and union, now and forever, one and inseparable." It has seemed to me to be proper that you as President of the United States should hear these sentiments expressed here in the heart of the Southern States and in the presence of this concourse of Southern people. No one of this multitude will repudiate them. All of us, indeed, feel that this Union is our Union, that its bright and starry banner is our flag, and that its destiny for weal or woe is to be our destiny.

This was the last word Judge Elliot spoke. Ten minutes later he was dead.

The Land We Live In.

HE fathers of Massachusetts Bay once decided that population was never likely to be very dense west of **Newton** (a suburb of Boston), and the founders of **Lynn**, after exploring ten or fifteen miles, doubted whether the country was good for anything farther west than that. Until recent times, only less inadequate has been the popular conception of the **Transmissouri region** and the millions destined to inhabit it. Though astonishing comparisons have ceased to astonish, I know of no means more effective or more just by which to present our physical basis of empire.

What, then, should we say of a **Republic** of eighteen States, each as large as Spain; or one of thirty-one States, each as large as Italy; or one of sixty States, each as large as England and Wales? What a **confederation of nations!** Take five of the six first-class Powers of Europe, Great Britain, and Ireland, France, Germany, Austria, and Italy; then add Spain, Portugal, Switzerland, Denmark, and Greece. Let some one greater than **Napoleon** weld them into one mighty empire; and you could **lay it all down** in the United States west of the Hudson River, once and again; and again—three times. Well may **Mr. Gladstone** say that we have "a natural base for the greatest continuous empire ever established by man;" and well may the English Premier add: "And the distinction between **continuous empire** and the empire severed and dispersed over sea is vital." With the exception of Alaska our territory is compact, and though so vast, is unified by railways and an equalled system of rivers and lakes. The latter, occupying a **larger area** than Great Britain and Ireland are said to contain nearly **one-half** of all the fresh water on the globe. We are told that east of the Rocky Mountains we have a river-flow of more than **40,000 miles** (i. e., 80,000 miles of river bank), counting no stream less than a hundred miles in length; while Europe in a larger space has but 17,000. It is estimated that the Mississippi with its affluents, affords **35,000 miles** to navigation. A steamboat may pass up the Mississippi and Missouri 3,900 miles from the Gulf—"as far as from New York to Constantinople." Thus a "**vast system of natural canals**" carries our sea-board into the very heart of the continent,—**our country**.

ORIGIN OF THE TERM "YANKEE."

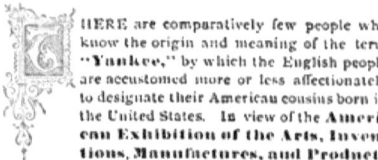

HERE are comparatively few people who know the origin and meaning of the term "**Yankee**," by which the English people are accustomed more or less affectionately to designate their American cousins born in the United States. In view of the **American Exhibition of the Arts, Inventions, Manufactures, and Products** of the United States, held at Earl's Court, Kensington, and which has been nicknamed in some quarters "**The Yankeries**," it may be of interest to readers to know what the word means. When the **Pilgrim Fathers** landed on Plymouth Rock, the friendly Indians asked of what people they were, to which query they replied, "English." But the red man could not twist his tongue around that word, and "**Yengeese**" was as near as he could get to it. It was but a very short time, and by a natural and easy transition, before "Yengeese" became transformed into "**Yankees**." The use of this word also is peculiar. The people of the Southern States call all Northerners, both east and west, "**Yankees**," as will be remembered by those familiar with the great Civil War. The people of the Western States call only those living in the Eastern States, or east of the Hudson River, "**Yankees**," and these are the only people who acknowledge the name, and always so describe themselves. On the other hand, all the English colonists and the people of Great Britain invariably call all citizens of the United States "**Yankees**," and when abroad they cheerfully accept, and are generally proud of the title, which, as we have seen, means, and is only a corruption of the word, "**English**."

Legal Holidays of the States.

Christmas and the Fourth of July Celebrated by all. Curious Combinations.

Kansas stands at the foot of the lists in number of holidays, observing only Christmas, and independence day. To these two **Alabama** and **Mississippi** add new year's, while Delaware adds thanksgiving day instead. **Indiana, Kansas** and **Tennessee** celebrate the four days hitherto named, to which **Iowa** and **Vermont** add decoration day; **Kentucky, Maine, Nebraska, Nevada** and **West Virginia** add Washington's birth day; while **Rhode Island** observes the latter two days, but omits new year's. All the days named thus far are holidays in **Colorado, Illinois, Ohio, South Carolina**, and the **District of Columbia**. As many are kept also by **Florida, Missouri** and **Wisconsin**, which, however, omit decoration day, and make election day a holiday; by **Georgia**, which keeps memorial day and not election day; by **Michigan** and **Virginia**, which omit decoration day in favor of fast day, as **Minnesota** substitutes for it good Friday; and by **New Hampshire**, which keeps fast day and not new year's.

Of states which keep seven holidays in the year, **California** and **New Jersey** add election day to the six principal occasions, **Connecticut** adds fast day instead, **Massachusetts** puts fast day and labor day in place of new year's and election. **Missouri** drops decoration day for good Friday. **Louisiana's** list is more peculiar, consisting of new year's, the battle of New Orleans, Washington's birthday, shrove Tuesday, good Friday, the fourth of July, and Christmas day. **Pennsylvania** observes good Friday, and not election day; and **North Carolina** keeps memorial day; and instead of election day celebrates May 10. **New York, Oregon** and **Texas** are the only states which recognize so many as eight holidays, **New York** adding labor day to the occasions most commonly observed, **Oregon** observing fast day instead, and **Texas** putting the celebration of Texan independence (March 2,) and the battle of San Jacinto (April 21,) in place of labor day and decoration day.

Christmas and the fourth of July are the only holidays everywhere. Thanksgiving comes next—in thirty-five states; then new year's in thirty-four; then Washington's birthday in thirty. There is then a sudden drop to decoration day, which we think readers will wonder to find a holiday only in fourteen states and the **District of Columbia**, helped out, moreover, by only two memorial days in southern states. We suspect some error about this. The figures then trail off to fast day or good Friday in ten states, election day in ten, and labor day in only two. Then succeed the scattering singles.

THE STAR SPANGLED BANNER.

OUR national lyric had its birth during the bombardment of Baltimore by the British fleet, Sep. 13, 1814. Dr. Beans of Upper Marlborough, had been taken prisoner and carried on ship-board by the British when their troops had finished their raid upon Washington. He was universally esteemed, and there was a great desire to obtain his release. It was finally arranged that Mr, Francis S. Key should visit the British vessels and make the request. Mr. Skinner of Baltimore, accompanied Mr. Key. The request was granted, but the three Americans were detained on board because of the coming attack on Baltimore It can be faintly imagined what their feelings were during the furious cannonade of Fort McHenry. The darkness wore on interminably. The roar of guns made the night tremble, and the flashes at their discharge threw a lurid gleam across the water. The fort did not reply, and it could not be told whether the old flag was still flying in its place. The dawn was anxiously awaited. Mr. Key walked up and down the vessel's deck and composed the song which has had a national acceptance. When the light of morning was sufficient it revealed to his eyes the fact that "our flag was still there." The long suspense was passed, and the country had a possession of great value. At the close of the ineffectual bombardment the three friends went ashore, and the British sailed away. Since then, every part of our country has known and sung that

> "The Star Spangled Banner in triumph doth wave
> O'er the land of the free, and the home of the brave."

CONFEDERATE RELICS.

Descriptions of the Great Seal and the Treasury Seal.

 THE archives of the Confederate Government form perhaps the most interesting set of historical relics in the possession of the government. They were taken at Richmond and were handed over to the war department. They have been carefully arranged, and are now packed away from view in two or three rooms of the big state, war, and navy building. They are never shown to strangers and the greatest care is taken in regard to them.

Among these relics is the seal of the Confederate treasury. It is an iron affair with a heavy handle, and its emblem is the palmetto tree of South Carolina.

The die is a little larger around than a trade dollar, and around the outside of it run the words, "Confederate States of America," while inside and just over the palmetto tree reads: "The Treasury Department."

The great seal of the Confederacy was made shortly before its fall, and after that it mysteriously disappeared. One of its authors was Col. A. R. Botelar, now of the attorney general's office who gave the design for the seal. This was sent off to the Confederate minister at London, and the great seal was made of pure silver by Wyatt, the man who has for years made the great seals of England. When the Confederate Government left Richmond this seal was taken along, and I saw a letter from Abbeville, S. C., recently, which states that it was thrown into a well along the way and that the well had since caved in. Whether this be true or not I do not know.

The Confederate Government had very little bullion, and the war department has possession of one of the only 4 silver half-dollars which were coined by it at the Louisiana mint. This mint was turned over to the Confederate Government in February, 1861, and in April Mr. Memminger, Confederate treasurer, sent out asking for designs for silver half-dollars. Several were received, but the one approved bore on one side a representation of the Goddess of Liberty surrounded by thirteen stars, denoting the thirteen states of the confederacy, and on the lower rim the figures "1861." On the other side was a shield with seven stars, representing the seceding states, and above the shield there is a helmet cap, and entwined around it are stalks of sugar cane and cotton. The inscription is "Confederate States of America." After four pieces had been struck, an order was received from the Secretary of the Treasury suspending operations on account of the difficulty of obtaining bullion, and the mint was closed on April 30, 1861. Of these four pieces coined one is in possession of the Government here, one was presented to Prof. Riddle, of the University of Louisiana, one to Dr. E. Ames, of New Orleans, and the other retained by Dr. D F. Taylor, the coiner, who now resides in Louisiana.

As to Confederate paper money the archives contained a great quantity when they were captured. Among them were half a million dollars in Confederate bonds, two large chests and five bags containing millions of dollars of Confederate money, and, in fact, papers giving almost a complete history of the Confederacy. Specimens of this money have been collected into a scrap-book by the clerks of the War Department, and this scrap-book, which is filled with blank orders of the Confederate Government, with money and other curiosities, is now worth more than its weight in gold.

PRAYER OF CARDINAL JAMES GIBBONS.

At The Centennial Of The Constitution, Philadelphia.

WE pray Thee, oh God of might, wisdom, and justice, through Whom authority is rightly administered, laws are enacted, and judgment decreed, assist with Thy holy spirit of counsel and fortitude the President of these United States, that his administration may be conducted in righteousness and be eminently useful to Thy people over whom he presides, by encouraging due respect for virtue and religion, by a faithful execution of the laws in justice and mercy, and by rest aining vice and immorality.

Let the light of Thy divine wisdom direct the deliberations of Congress and shine forth in all their proceedings and laws framed for our rule and government, so that they may tend to the preservation of peace, the promotion of national happiness, the increase of industry, sobriety, and useful knowledge, and may perpetuate to us the blessings of equal liberty.

We pray Thee for all judges, magistrates, and other officers who are appointed to guard our political welfare; that they may be enabled by Thy powerful protection to discharge the duties of their respective stations with honesty and ability.

We pray Thee especially for the judges of our Supreme court, that they may interpret the laws with even-handed justice. May they ever be the faithful guardians of the temple of the constitution whose construction and solemn dedication to our country's liberties we commemorate to-day. May they stand as watchful and incorruptible sentinels at the portals of this temple, shielding it from profanation and hostile invasion.

May this glorious charter of our civil rights be deeply imprinted on the hearts and memories of our people. May it foster in them a spirit of patriotism.

May it weld together and assimilate in national brotherhood the diverse races that come to seek a home among us. May the reverence paid to it conduce to the promotion of social stability and order, and may it hold the ægis of its protection over us and generations yet unborn, so that the temporal blessings which we enjoy may be perpetuated.

Grant, oh Lord, that our republic, unexampled in the history of the world in material prosperity and growth of population, may be also under Thy over-ruling providence a model to all nations in upholding liberty without license, and in wielding authority without despotism.

Finally, we recommend to Thy unbounded mercy all our brethren and fellow-citizens throughout the United States, that they may be blessed in the knowledge and sanctified in the observance of Thy most holy law; that they may be preserved in union and in that peace which the world cannot give, and, after enjoying the blessings of this life, be admitted to those which are eternal.

May the blessing of Almighty God, Father, Son, and Holy Ghost, descend upon our beloved country and upon all her people, and abide with them forever. Amen.

Postal Rates In 1792

NOW that the two-cent postage law has gone into effect, the following provisions of the first law of Congress on the subject will be read with interest:

February 20, 1792, was the date of the first act fixing rates of postage on domestic letters, and established the following rates, to take effect June 1, 1792:

Act February 20, 1792, Section 9, by land: For every single sixty miles, eight cents.

For every single letter over thirty miles and not exceeding sixty miles, eight cents.

For every single letter over sixty miles and not exceeding 100 miles, 10 cents.

For every single letter over 100 miles and not exceeding 150 miles, 12½ cents.

For every single letter over 150 miles and not exceeding 200 miles, 15 cents.

For every single letter over 200 miles and not exceeding 250 miles, 17 cents.

For every single letter over 250 miles and not exceeding 350 miles, 20 cents.

For every single letter over 350 miles and not exceeding 450 miles, 22 cents.

For every single letter over 450 miles, 25 cents.

For every double letter, double the said rates.

For every triple letter, triple the said rates.

For every packet weighing one ounce avoirdupois, to pay at the rate of four single letters for each ounce, and in that proportion for any greater weight.

PHILIP NOLAN.

The Original Agent in the Independence of Texas.

EDWARD EVERETT HALE.

THE settlement of the west began as early as 1775. The city of Lexington Ky., was named by the early settlers who had just heard of the news of the battle of Lexington, in 1775. At this time the adventurous Daniel Boone and his companions were pressing their discoveries in the west and attracting the attention of the continent. It was about this time that Philip Nolan was born in the town of Frankfort, a little town in Kentucky. He grew up to be a spirited, brave young fellow, under the patronage of Wycliffe. When the independence of the United States had been secured he was a boy not old enough to know what had occurred. He took to military adventure early in life. He would tell them, as well as he could, what an adventurous life was. We had gained by treaty the right to the eastern shore of the Mississippi River. Kentucky planters, and Tennessee planters, and Ohio farmers at that time were not inclined to be circumscribed by the route to the sea by the way of the Mississippi, which was denied them by the Spanish government, which held the supremacy in the south. From the beginning of his career Philip Nolan was identified with honest and earnest efforts to secure a passage to the sea, unimpeded by any royal embargo. There were various negotiations and intrigues and interviews set on foot by European governments to maintain their power here.

Philip Nolan first appeared in history in 1791. He was then acting as a merchant, and was thoroughly acquainted with Indian life. He loved the woods, and was well pleased with a life of adventure. He was fond of horses, and traveled far into the wilds of Texas to secure wild horses, which he brought to New Orleans and sold. He longed for a campaign, and was animated by military ardor.

The life of Nolan was mostly spent in the depths of the wilderness west of the Mississippi. He had once been encountered and challenged by a company of Spanish Mexicans, who had halted and then followed him, and this was the beginning of that feeling which resulted finally in the independence of Texas. The language of signs which Nolan greatly relied upon in communicating with the savages was explained. Nolan had said that by this means everything could be expressed but the Declaration of Independence. All bread-and-butter talk could be understood. The earth, the sky, and the rain could be easily expressed. Nolan in his wanderings had obtained considerable influence among the savages, and a traitor in his band had given an exaggerated account of the plan and purposes of his expeditions to the Spanish governor. A company of dragoons numbering 150 men, well armed and equipped were sent against him. Nolan was sleeping in his corral with his little band of 12 men, where he was surprised and surrounded by these dragoons in the night. When daylight came the Spaniards opened fire on the little camp, and the first man that fell was Philip Nolan, who was shot in the head by a musket ball. The little band held out, and finally concluded to retreat. All day long they protected themselves from a force 16 times their number, bearing two wounded men with them.

When night came, a white flag was exhibited by the Americans, and the party surrendered prisoners of war. They were conveyed to Nachitoches and disarmed. There they remained six years, when tardy orders were received from Madrid to decimate the prisoners. They had become, in the meantime, endeared to their captors, and the Spanish officers humanely construed the order to mean that one of them should be shot. One quiet Sabbath morning, Ephraim Blackman, upon whom the lot had fallen, was taken out and executed. At that time the United States was a weak nation. Spain was strong. Twelve American citizens had crossed into Spanish lands under the protection of the Spanish governor, and some of them had lost their lives and all their liberty in so doing. Yet the United States never made the least complaint of that violation of hospitality.

Nothing now remained as a monument to the memory of this brave man, but the river which bore his name. Yet his fame was not forgotten, and it has been proposed to erect a monument to perpetuate his fame, at Washington, so that the deeds of this brave man should not be forgotten.

A HISTORICAL CANE.

The Composition of Mr. Robert Yale's Wonderful Walking Stick.

ROBERT YALE of Norwich, N. Y., has a historical cane which probably is the oddest walking-stick ever built in this or any other country. It contains 2,000 pieces of wood; and each inlaid piece is given an artistic and symbolic form, so that the cane by its various colored woods is given a most artistic look, although no color is used upon it. Sixty of the 2,000 pieces of wood are relics of great value to the relic-hunter, and comprise a piece of wood from the oldest tenantable house in America, the Fairbank residence, built in 1620 and now occupied by the seventh generation. The head of the cane is from the tree at Crown Point to which Gen. Putnam was tied after being condemned to death by burning by the Indians. Set in the cane is a wreath of hair from the head of Rebecca Bates, one of the heroines whose strategy drove the British to their shipping after landing to attack Scituate, Mass. There is a piece of wood from the Charter Oak; another from the house of Hancock, the first signer of the Declaration of Independence; another from the house where witchcraft originated in Salem, and another from the house where the victims of that craze were tried. Set in the cane is a small piece of Plymouth Rock, and also a piece of wood from the Mayflower; also wood from five different forts on Lake Champlain, from Hawthorne's residence at Salem, from the church where Roger Williams preached, and from the tree beneath which Jonathan Edwards preached to the Indians at Stockbridge, Conn.; also a piece from the curbing of the well commemorated by Wadsworth in his poem, "The Old Oaken Bucket," etc. The only foreign relic in the collection is a piece of wood from the Tasso Oak. The cane is a unique and attractive piece of work and is valued at $500 by its owner.

CESSION OF THE NORTHWEST TERRITORY.

THE three centennial celebrations of the first settlement of Ohio which will be held this year at Marietta, Columbus, and Cincinnati have been made the basis of an article in the March number of the *Magazine of American History* by Mr. Douglas Campbell in which he corrects an error that appears not only in school-books but in American histories relative to the cession of the Northwest territory, including the present States of Ohio, Indiana, Illinois, Michigan, and Wisconsin, to the Union, and Kentucky, which was otherwise disposed of.

It has been generally assumed that this cession was made by the State of Virginia. Neither Bancroft nor Hildreth makes any mention of the real facts in the case. Mr. Blaine, in his "Twenty Years of Congress," leaves the reader with this general impression, and Gen. Walker, the Superintendent of the census, in his "Statistical Atlas," published by the Government, also allows Virginia's claim to go unchallenged. Mr. Campbell, however, brings forward an overwhelming array of proofs showing that the cession was made by New York and that the credit which Virginia had enjoyed so long does not belong to her. The question is one of great historical importance, as the cession led to the formation of the confederation and thus to our present Union. A brief statement of Mr. Campbell's evidence will therefore be of as much interest in Illinois as in Ohio, since Illinois was part of the territory conveyed.

In 1780, it was apparent that the Revolutionary War would be successful, and the question of the ownership of the vast area west of the Appalachian Mountains and east of the Mississippi River came up. New York put in her claim for the whole of it, and so did Virginia, while Massachusetts and Connecticut asserted ownership over a strip of the northern portion. The other States, however, protested on the ground that it was common property wrested from the enemy, and the contention became so hot that Maryland refused to join the confederation until some settlement was made, and other States threatened to withdraw.

New York at once came forward and

ceded the whole area to the Government, which pacified Maryland, and she joined the Confederation, thus making the union complete. Virginia, Massachusetts, and Connecticut also proposed deeds of concession, accompanied by certain conditions. The next year all these propositions were referred to a Congressional committee of five members. After a long and careful investigation this committee reported that the territory belonged to New York, advised the acceptance of her offer and the rejection of the others, suggesting, however, that Virginia, Massachusetts, and Connecticut should make releases to the Government so as not to invalidate the title. The report was adopted by Congress and its recommendations carried out. The releases were subsequently made, with these exceptions; that Virginia retained Kentucky, which she subsequently sold, while Connecticut did the same with about 4,000,000 acres in Ohio, now known as the Western Reserve.

Mr. Campbell not only states results but accompanies them with a strong array of proofs. When the Congressional committee was appointed Virginia refused to lay any evidence before it to establish her claim. As a matter of fact she had none, except the charter of 1609 granted by James I., and conveying "a tract of land along the seacoast extending for two hundred miles in each direction north and south from Old Point Comfort, and all that space and circuit of land lying from the seacoast of the precinct aforesaid up into the land throughout from sea to sea, west and northwest"—a description so vague that it would have carried Virginia's ownership to the Pacific Ocean. The description was not only vague but, even if valid, it could not by any rule of legal construction be made to embrace the area of the present Western States. Further than this, the charter was annulled by legal proceeding in 1624, and thenceforward Virginia continued a royal province. More fatal still to her claim is it that when the charter was granted "England did not own the region in dispute, and only gained it afterwards by a title derived through the Province of New York," whose title in turn came through the Six Nations, which were appendant to its government and lived in Central New York. In closing his interesting article Mr. Campbell said:

"How well this report is sustained by the facts is shown in the preceeding pages; its conclusions of law are likewise unassailable. By the Revolution, which severed the connection between the colonies and the mother country, each State succeeded to the title of Great Britain to all public or crown property within its limits. The confederation was simply a league owning nothing and succeeding to no rights. It was the individual State which took to itself the quit rents of the crown, with all the other crown property, such as forts, court-houses, and the unsold or unappropriated lands. In the same way New York succeeded to Great Britain's jurisdiction over the Six Nations and their tributaries, and thereby secured the exclusive privilege of buying or conquering their land, a right which as to the Indians residing in the other States was never questioned. Her title to the soil was not absolute, for it was subject to the occupation of the natives, but it was the only one claimed at that time by the European Powers to any land on this continent, and under it the Indian lands in the West are held by the United States to-day."

It is a little remarkable that so important a matter as the action of Congress upon the deeds of cession, bearing directly upon the formation of the Union, should be passed over without notice by the historians. Mr. Campbell has done good service in supplying their omissions, and the contribution comes at an important time, for it establishes a bond of sisterhood not only between Ohio and New York but also Illinois, Indiana, Michigan and Wisconsin, for the proofs in the one case are the proofs in all.—*The Chicago Tribune.*

THE HISTORY OF THE CIVIL WAR MUST NOT BE IGNORED.

THE RT. REV. SAMUEL FALLOWS, D. D.

LITERATURE is joined with monuments and historical reminiscences as a potent factor in securing needed unity, and this needed literature in our own country the war has given us.

However well intentioned may be the suggestions or the design to eliminate from the history of the United States, as studied in our public schools, the account of the civil war, we cannot afford seriously to entertain a thought in that direction. I know that the desire lying back of the feeler just thrown out in this city speedily as possible a full reconciliation between the North and South. But we cannot conveniently drop out of history, the record of a conflict that shook the globe, and wrought the most momentous social and political changes in our land. The memories of the brave boys who fought against each other are not so treacherous that they can forget what they did on some of the bloodiest battle fields of history. Reconciliation never will come by ignoring, but by accepting the situation. The principles for which the Union armies contended are as permanent as the Republic itself. It would be the most stupendous act of historical hari-kari ever known, for the North and the South to attempt to take out of the national record, in order that the children of the Republic may know nothing of it, the history of the struggle which emancipated four millions of men and demonstrated to the world that we were one nation.

Keep forever before our youth the heroic deeds of the men who served the Republic, and those of the equally heroic deeds of the misguided men who sought to disrupt it. Add, in the successive editions of your common school histories, if you choose, that hundreds of Confederate officers, since the war has closed, have been members of the national Congress. Relate how the gallant heroes who opposed each other in that terrible, decisive battle of '

Gettysburg, have been arm in arm over the fateful field, to find out the exact location of their regiments, brigades and divisions, so that the simple truth relating to the conflict might be told; narrate how, when the appeal was made in Richmond and in New York for a home for disabled Confederate soldiers, Corporal Tanner, the eloquent United States District Attorney for Brooklyn, representing scores of thousands of Union soldiers, stumped about on his wooden legs and made the most glowing effort of his life, in order that the required help might be given. Let it be told, and I hope it may be soon told, that an American Westminister Abbey or Walhalla has been erected to the memory of our distinguished dead, where, ranged within, may be found the sculptured busts and statues of Washington and Franklin, Adams and Jefferson, of Webster and Clay, of Lincoln and Garfield, McPherson and Rawlins, of Thomas and Hooker, of Stonewall Jackson and Polk, of Lee and Stephens; but do not commit the supreme folly of trying to wink out of existence the conflict which has given our country its undisputed nationality, and the world the prophetic assurance of ultimate and universal Freedom.

ENGLAND AND AMERICA.

A Common System of Jurisprudence Must Cement National Friendship.

THE HON. THOMAS A. HENDRICKS.

I DO not know how a free and intelligent people may more emphatically express their respect and regard for another free and intelligent people than by an adoption of their laws.

It is to say you are virtuous, and wise, and strong, and we will trust for our future to the influences that have made you so. National and artificial boundaries may mark political divisions, and standing armies and hostile attitudes may maintain established political relations, but a jurisprudence common to both is an assurance of mutual sympathy and perpetual peace. Both people bow to the authority of the same laws, and if there must come between them trouble, and strife, and bloodshed, it shall be charged to the folly of a vicious diplomacy or to the gratification of a reckless ambition, and not to the pacifying influence of a common jurisprudence. It was in 1807 when this great region of the Northwest was as yet in a territorial condition, that the Territorial Legislature adopted the common law of England, and the general statutes passed in aid thereof prior to the fourth year of James I., excepting three or four statutes, perhaps, of Henry VIII. and Elizabeth, and excepting also certain provisions of the law and statutes as might be in conflict with our Constitution and laws. It may be that this was unnecessary —that we need not have adopted the laws of England, but, lest there might be uncertainty as to the extent of their application in our country, this Territorial Legislature, composed of men not cultured in the laws, representing scattered settlements, adopted them. It may be, and I dare say it would have been so, that these laws would have been ours anyhow, so far as they were suited to our condition and consistent with our institutions; but by their adoption certainty was secured, and such laws as were not suited to our condition were excluded. When the Lord-Chief-Justice, of England visited our country it was not to seek the gratification of curiosity amid scenes and populations to which he is a stranger, but he came here to observe and to contemplate the development of the liberal element of the institutions of his own country upon an area and among a people in the highest degree adapted to such development. He could but be gratified when he saw enormous commerce regulated in a large degree by the usages of the merchants as they existed long before the brilliant policy of Lord Mansfield. He saw that the common law as he administers it at home has overtaken the railroad train, and the rules for the government of the common carrier have become the law of their control. The passenger has the protection of the same rule of law, requiring care and diligence on the part of railroad employees from Edinburg to London and from Chicago to New York. The American who has just arrived in London knows his legal rights quite as well as if he were at home, while the Englishman just landed at New York knows his legal rights as well also as if he were in London. Perhaps one of these parties —I need not say which—is more disposed than the other to stand upon his rights to the very uttermost. If the Chief-Justice of England and the Chief-Justice of the United States should exchange places the judicial machinery of the two great nations would move on without interruption or disturbance.

I have made visits to courts in England, where I heard the same arguments used as here and the same appeals to justice, and I felt that every man I saw was an American, because I heard the language of the law common to both countries. And I heard discussed in the House of Commons the cause of humanity against the power and strength of one high in position, who had murdered a subordinate, and had not been tried for it: and I felt that I might be proud of the country from which my ancestors in part have come.

OUR FOREIGN POPULATION.

REV. GEO. C. LORIMER, D. D.

THE alien on our shores is of the same origin with ourselves, and however one may be disposed to criticize his influence, it has never been as prejudicial to native American interests as has been the native American's and that of their fathers on the destiny of the red man. Few persons are familiar with the facts concerning immigration, and as a consequence there are many faulty generalizations current leading to unwarranted fears on the one hand and to groundless hopes on the other. It is therefore necessary, if these erroneous conclusions are to be questioned, and if we are to form a just estimate of the relations which foreigners sustain to America and to American institutions, that we ascertain with proximate accuracy their numbers and the rate of their increase.

Statistics of Immigration.

No statistics of immigration were kept before 1820; but from those subsequently given to the public we learn that from September 30, 1819, to December 30, 1860, there arrived by sea from other lands a total of 5,062,414 souls, 2,977,603 males, and 2,035,536 females. The author of the census report, C. G. Kennedy, reminds us "that the distribution is materially different from that of a settled population; the females are less than the males in the ratio of two to three; almost precisely one-half of the total passengers are between fifteen and thirty years of age." In alluding to the "disproportion between the rate of gain in the north and south respectively," he says that it is manifestly to some extent caused by the more congenial climate of the former section, combined with the variety of occupations open to the people, and the dignity wherewith respectable employment is there invested. During the stormy period of our history—1861–1865—we gather from the American Almanac that 793,903 persons arrived in the United States; and from the same source, in its issue for the year 1881, we learn that the forthcoming census will show that the total number of alien-born people in this country is 10,138,758, among a population of 50,152,866, of whom the Chinese form the inconsiderable portion of 105,679, and the civilized and taxed Indians even less—some 65,880 souls; that is, the foreign population is about one to every five of the native.

The Rate Of Increase Will Not Diminish.

Nor does this rate of increase promise to diminish. Dr. Boyd, of St. Louis, in a valuable paper on this subject, states that recently "on one day in the single port of New York almost 5,000 immigrants were landed; and that one steamship line has contracted to bring over 80,000 more from Norway and Sweden." He adds that there is a decided tendency on the part of these new comers to settle in the larger towns; that "New York city is the third German city in the world. Vienna is first, Berlin, second; New York, third;" and that "with the Germans of New York a city could be formed whose population would exceed that of Hamburg and Bremen put together." Other great centers of wealth and activity, such as Cincinnati, St. Louis, and Chicago, exhibit a similar state of things; and we have every reason for believing that foreign influence in these centers will not decline for many a day.

The Stability of American Institutions.

Now it is not unnatural in view of this tremendous influx that apprehensions should be felt regarding the stability of American institutions. Many of these strangers are socialists, communists, infidels, many are ignorant and superstitious, and but few are prepared to appreciate the spirit and genius of our government. Can it be, the timid ask, that the United States can endure this strain? Has the country a digestive system of such ostrich-like capacity as to assimilate such a heterogeneous mass? And is it not probable that the invisible destinies mean to reenact the history of the past and permit our civilization to fall before the alien, as the savages were swept before our sires? We shall be *Romanized*, cries one party, we shall be rationalized, cries another; we shall be *Germanized*, responds a third; and that we shall become something unnamably bad these fluttering ones at least very confidently believe. I do not share in this alarm; perhaps as one not native born, it is impossible that I should. But my convictions on this subject are not the result of race prejudice; they have grown with my study of the facts involved, and out of the philosophy of history. LORD MACAULAY says: "Ever since I began to observe I have been seeing nothing but growth, and hearing of nothing but decay."

Such has also been my own experience. In

my boyhood I was told that England with her Chartist riots, and her monster Irish demonstrations, was hastening to destruction; in my youth I was assured that the union and prosperity of these states were drawing to a close; and in manhood I half believed that the utter ruin of France was inevitable, and yet these nations survive and are tolerably vigorous still.

Suspicions of Alarmists.

I have, therefore, become suspicious of alarmists, with their direful prophecies of approaching social and political cataclysms. Nor is there anything I know of in history that imparts to those which are now being uttered the least color of probability. The movement of the ancient Aryans to the banks of the Indus is not analogous to the inflow of foreigners into America, the incursions of the Huns, Goths, and Vandals into Italy were of a tolerably different character; they were warlike invasions, not peaceful migrations; but whenever large bodies of people have emigrated from one country to another, as the Huguenots from France into England, they have uniformly contributed to the prosperity of their adopted land and have gradually been assimilated to its people. Hegel, in his "Philosophy of History," calls attention to the arrival of colonies in ancient Greece; an Egyptian, Cecrops, founding Athens; the Phœnician, Cadmus, founding Thebes, while other individual aliens, such as Danaus and Pelops, were the means of advancing the civilization of that favored country. And wherever similar instances are found, the same beneficial effects may be traced; and, in view of such cases, I shall not despair while I admit the difficulties in the way and the perils to be encountered of the ultimate homogeneousness of the various nationalities which compose our population.

Hopeful View.

There are also facts not generally weighed, but which deserve to be noted, and which in my judgment are fitted to inspire the most skeptical with this feeling of hope.

An eastern paper, The Watchman, of Boston, states in a recent editorial that of the multiplied thousands who seek our shores, not less than 15 per cent. fall out by death or return, and Dr. Boyd, in the paper already alluded to, says: "The last census shows that owing to the large death rate among our foreign population, while the aggregate population of the country increased twelve million during the last period, the addition of the foreign population was but a little more than a million;" and he endorses the statement made by The Watchman, that the ratio or percentage of foreign born to native inhabitants is steadily diminishing. The ravages of mortality, induced probably by change of climate, by strange and exhausting methods of life, and by out-door labors in malarious districts, act as a check on the undue enlargement of the alien element. Thus a providential arrangement seems to shield our institutions, and reproves the alarm which oversensitive nationalists have expressed.

Immigrants Patriotic.

Supt. Kennedy, in the census for 1860, bears this testimony—"the great mass of the immigrants are found to cherish true patriotism for the land of their adoption;" a testimony that has been confirmed by many acts of devotion in peace and war. It would be unnatural for them to feel otherwise. Having escaped from the scepter of rulers unlike the heathen monarch, Demophoon in the tragedy of Euripides, who would not treat his people as barbarians, and who felt himself liable if he did unjustly to suffer justly, they must surely be inspired by sentiments of loyalty to a government that not only offers them an asylum, but admits them to share in its administration. While anarchists among them may fret at the restraints of law and clamor for revolution, the great mass must feel that principles which have done so much for them are sacred, and should be shielded from a profane assault. Moreover, the avenues that are open to their ambition under our democratic forms can hardly fail to increase their attachment. In free America, as in free Athens, where the armorer's son, Demosthenes, rose to commanding power: where the courier, Diodorus, rose to the dignity of embassador; and where the commedian, Aristophanes, exerted marked influence in the affairs of state, all are permitted to contend for the highest offices—with two exceptions—in the gift of the people. No barrier has been reared by class prejudice, no restrictions have been imposed, and persons of any nationality can achieve the place of honors to which their merits entitle them. This is a powerful stimulant to loyalty, and must tend to convert our most tigerish radicals into the most lamb-like conservatives. Nor should it be overlooked, in judging the effect of foreign immigration on American institutions, that we have the records of the past to aid us in shaping our horoscope of the future

Number of Alien Birth in 1860.

In 1860 we had of alien birth among us, 463,704 merchants, 1,529,674 farmers, 815,048 mechanics, 8,652 clergymen, 5,352 lawyers, 14,218 physicians, and a fair porportion of other callings, most of whom lived in northern states. These strangers could have seriously embarrassed the national cause, if not totally impeded it, had they been so minded. Never was a nation more helpless, and never was the time more favorable to plots, counterplots and revolutions. And yet, with the exceptions of a few riots in connection with the draft, our *foreign population* was as *patriotic* and as self-sacrificing as the native. No obligation did they shun, no danger did they shrink from and no exaction did they refuse to bear for the sake of their adopted country. Is it not, therefore, ungenerous to suspect them now of unfriendly intentions towards a government in whose behalf they spent their treasures and shed their blood? And is it not more probable from the course they pursued when the ship of state was tossed on the mad billows of internal strife, that should rebellion, in the name of socialism, communism, or nihilism, ever rear its serpent head they would be among the first to resist its attacks, even though weapons in its defense should be borne by misguided rascals from the old world? Consult the annals of a grateful nation, and observe how foreigners have felt and acted towards her; note the esteem in which they have been held, and then answer whether we should not be slow to challenge the fealty of their kindred to the institutions of America?

Revolutionary Heroes of Foreign Birth.

During the Revolutionary war there were distinguished generals of foreign birth, whose heroism and whose devotion to liberty may be mentioned in the same breath with the names of Washington and Putnam. There was the Welshman, Charles Lee, by some persons credited with the authorship of the celebrated "Letters of Junius," not without blame, but an ardent friend of the colonies; there was the Englishman, Gen. Gates, who received the sword of Burgoyne, and who was publicly honored by congress; there were the Scotchmen, Hugh Mercer, Arthur St. Clair, both distinguished soldiers, and John Paul Jones, the first of our naval heroes, and the last to be forgotten; there were the Irishmen, Commodore Barry and Maj. Gen. Richard Montgomery, the second of whom had fought under Wolfe at Quebec, and incurred the personal spite of England's prime minister on account of his devotion to liberty; there was the Prussian, Baron Steuben, who was with Washington at Valley Forge, and whose vast military knowledge was of eminent service to the Revolutionary army; there was the Polish patriot, Kosciusko, who, after consecrating his genius to the American cause, among other achievements executing the works at West Point, returned to his own country and was wounded when struggling against the tyranny of Russia—

Hope for a season bade the world farewell,
And freedom shrieked as Kosciusko fell;

and there was the Frenchmen, Baron de Kalb, who gloriously fell at the battle of Camden, dying a soldier's death, as he had desired to die, "for the rights of the people," and the immortal Lafayette, who not only with the sword won for himself a place in the affection of our people, but with the pen expressed such sentiments as must endear his name to all future time—for it was he who said: "American interests will always be more dear to me than my own," and in a letter written to his wife, "intimately allied to the happiness of the whole human family is that of America, destined to become the respectable and sure asylum of virtue, honesty, toleration, equality, and of a tranquil liberty."

Loyal Citizens of Foreign Birth.

In days more recent, but less trying to loyalty and valor, we find in positions of grave trust prominent representatives of alien nationalties, who bore themselves nobly in the strife. I need not recall their names—they are familiar to us all. The 24th Illinois volunteers, composed largely of Germans, was heard from on many a field, and they and their gallant commander bear witness to the enduring affection of the foreign citizen for the land of his adoption. Other professions likewise furnish illustrious instances of laborers from the cation on that subject, is to bring about as of Chicago by a member of the board of education old world, through whose enlightenment, energy, enterprise, and sagacity the fortunes of the new have been promoted. It is perhaps impossible to decide how much of our business prosperity and how much of our educational and religious growth are traceable directly to their influence. The Swiss, Louis Agazziz, reflected undying luster on fair Harvard; the Englishman, Dr. Harper, won golden opinions for American science; and as for our naturalized merchants, all that I can say is that when one of the leaders among them, like the lamented Geo. Armour, sinks quietly into the arms of death, the entire community is made conscious of a loss which requires more than ordinary integrity, virtue, common sense and piety to fill.

McClellan's Letter of Acceptance.

ORANGE, NEW JERSEY, Sept. 8th, 1864.

GENTLEMEN:—

I have the honor to acknowledge the **receipt** of your letter, informing me of my nomination by the **Democratic National Convention**, recently held at Chicago, as their **candidate** at the next election for President of the United States.

It is unnecessary for me to say to you that this **nomination** comes to me unsought.

I am happy to know that when the nomination was made, the **record** of my life was kept in view. The **effect** of long and varied service in the **Army**, during war and peace, has been to strengthen and make **indelible** in my mind and heart, the love and reverence for the **Union, Constitution, Laws** and **Flag** of **our country**, impressed upon me in early youth.

These feelings have thus far **guided** the course of my life and must continue to do so to its end. The existence of **more than one Government** over the **region** which once owned our flag is incompatible with the **peace**, the **power** and the **happiness** of the people. The **preservation of our Union** was the sole avowed object for which the **War** was commenced. It should have been conducted for **that object** only and in accordance with those principles which I took occasion to **declare** when in active service. Thus conducted, the **work of reconciliation** would have been easy, and we might have reaped the benefits of our many victories on land and sea. The **Union** was originally formed by the exercise of a spirit of **conciliation** and **compromise**. To restore and preserve it, the same spirit **must prevail** in our Councils and in the hearts of the people.

The **re-establishment** of the Union in all its **integrity**, is, and must continue to be, the indispensable **condition** in any settlement. So soon as it is clear and even probable, that our present adversaries are ready for **peace**, upon the basis of the **Union**, we should exhaust all the resources of Statesmanship practiced by **civilized nations**, and taught by the traditions of the **American people**, consistent with the honor and interests of the Country **to secure** such peace, **establish** the Union, and **guarantee** for the future the **Constitutional rights** of every **State**. The Union is the one condition of peace, we ask no more.

Let me add what I doubt not was, although unexpressed, **the sentiment** of the Convention, as it is of the people they represent, that when any one **State** is willing to return to the **Union**, it should be received at once, with a **full guarantee** of all its Constitutional rights.

If a frank, earnest and persistent **effort** to obtain those objects **should fail**, the responsibility for further consequences **will fall** on those who remain in arms against the Union. But **the Union** must be preserved **at all hazards.**

I could not look in the face of my gallant **comrades** of the army and navy, who have survived so many bloody battles, and tell them that their **labors** and the **sacrifices** of so many of our slain and wounded brethren had been **in vain;** that we had abandoned that **Union** for which we have so often periled our lives.

A **vast majority** of our people, whether in the army and navy or at home, would, as I would, hail with unbounded **joy** the permanent restoration of peace, on the basis of the **Union** under the **Constitution** without the effusion of another drop of blood. But **no peace** can be **permanent** without **Union.**

As to the other subjects presented in the **resolutions** of the Convention, I need only say that I should seek, in the **Constitution** of the United States, and the **laws** framed in accordance therewith, the **rule** of my duty, and the **limitations** of Executive power, endeavor to restore **economy** in public expenditure, re-establish the **supremacy** of law, and by the operation of a more rigorous **nationality**, resume our commanding **position** among the nations of the earth.

The **condition** of our finances, the **depreciation** of our paper money, and the **burdens** thereby imposed on labor and capital, urge upon us the **necessity** of a return to a sound financial **system**, while the rights of **citizens** and the rights of **States**, and the binding **authority** of law over **President, Army** and **People**, are subjects of not less rival importance in **war** than in **peace**.

Believing that the views here expressed are those of the **convention** and the **people** you represent, I accept the nomination. I realize the **weight** of the responsibility **to be borne**, should the people ratify your choice. Conscious of my own **weakness**, I can only seek fervently the **guidance** of the Ruler of the Universe, and **relying** on his all powerful aid, do my best to restore **Union** and **Peace** to a suffering people, and to establish and guard their **liberties** and **rights**.

I am, Gentlemen, Very Respectfully, Your obedient Servant,   GEO. B. McCLELLAN,

HON. HORATIO SEYMOUR and Others, Committee.

QUALIFICATIONS REQUIRED FOR SUFFRAGE IN EACH OF THE 38 STATES.

STATES.	Registration.	Excluded from Voting.
Alabama	Leg. may regulate	Idiots, Indians, convicted of crime.
Arkansas	Prohibited as a bar to suf	Idiots, Indians, convicted of crime.
California	Reg. req'd by law	Idiots, Indians, convicts, Chinese.
Colorado	Required by Constitution	Persons in prison.
Connecticut	Required by law	Those unable to read and convicts.
Delaware	No registration required	Idiots, insane, paupers, criminals.
Florida	Required by Constitution	Idiots, insane, criminals, bettors on elections, duellists.
Georgia	Leg. may regulate, no act	Idiots, insane, criminals and non-tax-payers.
Illinois	Required by law	Convicts.
Indiana	No law for registration	Fraudulent voters and bribers.
Iowa	Required by law	Idiots, insane, criminals.
Kansas	Required in cities only	Idiots, insane, convicts, rebels.
Kentucky	No registration required	Bribery, robbery forgery, &c.
Louisiana	Leg. may regulate	Idiots, insane, criminals.
Maine	Required by law	Paupers, Indians not taxed.
Maryland	Required by Constitution	Lunatics, convicts and guilty of bribery.
Massachusetts	Required by law	Paupers, persons under guardians, non-tax-payers and men unable to read and write.
Michigan	Required by law	Duellists.
Minnesota	Required by law	Idiots, insane, convicts.
Mississippi	Required by Constitution	Idiots, insane, criminals.
Missouri	Required by Constitution in cities only.	Inmates of asylums, poorhouses and prisons, U. S. army.
Nebraska	Required by law	Idiots, convicts, U. S. army.
Nevada	Required by Constitution	Idiots, insane, convicts.
N. Hampshire	Required by law	Paupers.
New Jersey	Req'd in cities of 10,000	Paupers, idiots, insane, convicts.
New York	Req'd in cities of 10,000	Election bettors or bribers, convicts.
North Carolina	Required by Constitution	Convicts.
Ohio	No registration required	Idiots, insane.
Oregon		Idiots, insane, convicts, U. S. army, Chinese.
Pennsylvania	Required by Constitution	Non-taxpayers, political bribers.
Rhode Island	Required by law	Persons without property to value of $134.
South Carolina	Required by Constitution	Insane, inmates of asylums, almshouses and prisons, U. S. army, duellists.
Tennessee	No registration required	Non-payers of poll-tax.
Texas	Prohibited by Constitu'n	Lunatics, idiots, paupers, convicts, U. S. army.
Vermont	Required by law	Bribers.
Virginia	Required by law	Lunatics, idiots, convicts duellists, U. S. army.
West Virginia	Prohibited by Constitu'n	Lunatics, paupers, convicts.
Wisconsin	Required by law	Insane, idiots, conv'ts, bribers, bettors, duellists

NOTE.—All the 38 States limit suffrage to male citizens, but in Colorado, Massachusetts and some other States women may vote at school-district elections.

QUALIFICATIONS REQUIRED FOR SUFFRAGE IN EACH OF THE 38 STATES.

STATES.	Age	Requirement as to Citizenship.	RESIDENCE IN State.	County.	Voting Precinct.
Alabama	21	Citizens or declared intention	1 year	3 months	1 month
Arkansas	21	Citizens or declared intention	1 year	6 months	1 month
California	21	Actual citizens	1 year	90 days	30 days
Colorado	21	Citizens or declared intention	6 months		
Connecticut	21	Actual citizens	1 year	6 months	6 months
Delaware	21	Actual County taxpayers	1 year	1 month	
Florida	21	United States citizens or declared intention	1 year	6 months	
Georgia	21	Actual citizens	1 year	6 months	
Illinois	21	Actual citizens	1 year	90 days	30 days
Indiana	21	Citizens or declared intention	6 months	60 days	30 days
Iowa	21	Actual citizens	6 months	60 days	
Kansas	21	Citizens or declared intention	6 months		30 days
Kentucky	21	Free white male citizens	2 years	1 year	60 days
Louisiana	21	Citizens or declared intention	1 year	6 months	30 days
Maine	21	Actual citizens	3 months		
Maryland	21	Actual citizens	1 year	6 months	
Massachusetts	21	Citizens	1 year		6 months
Michigan	21	Citizens or declared intention	3 months		10 days
Minnesota	21	Citizens or declared intention	4 months		10 days
Mississippi	21	Actual citizens	6 months	1 month	
Missouri	21	Citizens or declared intention	1 year	60 days	
Nebraska	21	Citizens or declared intention	6 months		
Nevada	21	Citizens or declared intention	6 months	30 days	
N. Hampshire	21	Actual citizens			Town 6 mos
New Jersey	21	Actual citizens	1 year	5 months	
New York	21	Actual citizens	1 year	4 months	30 days
North Carolina	21	Actual citizens	12 months	90 days	
Ohio	21	Actual citizens	1 year		
Oregon	21	Citizens or declared intention	6 months		
Pennsylvania	21	Actual citizens	1 year		2 months
Rhode Island	21	Actual tax paying citizens	1 year		Town 6 mos
South Carolina	21	Actual citizens	1 year	60 days	
Tennessee	21	Actual citizens	12 months	6 months	
Texas	21	Citizens or declared intention	1 year	6 months	6 months
Vermont	21	Actual citizens	1 year		
Virginia	21	Actual citizens	12 months		Town 3 mos
West Virginia	21	Actual citizens	1 year	60 days	
Wisconsin	21	Citizens or declared intention	1 year		

NOTE.—All the 38 States limit suffrage to male citizens but in Colorado, Massachusetts and some other states women may vote at school district elections.

THE AMERICAN MANUAL.

OFFENCES FOR WHICH STATES DISFRANCHISE BY THE EXPRESS TERMS OF THEIR CONSTITUTIONS, OR FOR WHICH THEIR LEGISLATURES MAY MAKE DISFRANCHISEMENT A PENALTY.

STATES.	Treason.	Felony.	Bribery.	Perjury.	Forgery.	Murder.	Robbery.	Duelling.
Alabama	Treason	Felony (1)	Bribery					
Arkansas		Felony						
California			Bribery*	Perjury*	Forgery*			Duelling
Colorado								
Connecticut			Bribery	Perjury	Forgery			
Del. w..re (4)		Felony						
Florida		Felony	Bribery	Perjury				Duelling
Georgia	Treason	Felony	Bribery					Duelling
Illinois								
Indiana								
Iowa								
Kansas (3)	Treason	Felony	Bribery					
Kentucky			Bribery	Perjury	Forgery			
Louisiana (2)	Treason	Felony (1)	Bribery	Perjury	Forgery			
Maine			Bribery (6)					
Maryland			Bribery (7)					
Mass.								
Michigan								Duelling
Minnesota	Treason	Felony	Bribery	Perjury				
Mississippi			Bribery	Perjury	Forgery			Duelling (7)
Missouri			Bany					
Nebraska	Treason	Felony (8)						
Nevada	Treason (9)	Felony (9)	Bribery (10)					Duelling
New Hamp.								
New Jersey	Treason (11)		Bribery	Perjury (11)	Forgery (11)	Murder (11)	Robbery (11)	
New York			Bribery					
N. Carolina		Felony						
Ohio			Bribery	Perjury				
Oregon		Felony						
Penn.			Bribery (12)					
Rhode Island			Bribery					
S. Carolina	Treason					Murder	Robbery	Duelling
Tennessee			Bribery (14)					
Texas		Felony (13)	Bribery	Perjury	Forgery			Duelling
Vermont			Bribery (16)					
Virginia	Treason	Felony	Bribery					Duelling
W. Vir. (18)								
Wisconsin	Treason	Felony	Bribery					Duelling (7)

1. A crime punishable by death or imprisonment in a State prison.

2.* The constitution adopted by California in 1879 expressly disfranchises for any infamous crime, embezzlement or misappropriation of public money, and duelling, and says that laws shall be made to exclude from the right of suffrage persons convicted of the above starred crimes.

3. Theft is the term used in the constitution of Connecticut.

4. The legislature may make the forfeiture of the right of suffrage a punishment for crime.

5. No person who has been dishonorably discharged from the service of the United States, or who has voluntarily borne arms against the Government of the United States, is qualified to vote or hold office in Kansas.

6. Since 1876 "the legislature may enact laws excluding from the right of suffrage for a term not exceeding ten years" for this crime.

7. These crimes forever disqualify for voting.

8. "Under the law of the State or of the United States unless restored to civil rights."

9. "In any State or Territory of the United States unless restored to civil rights."

10. The constitution of Nevada, Art. 4, sec. 10, makes ineligible for office persons convicted of embezzlement or defalcation of public funds or bribery, and empowers the legislature to make these crimes punishable as felonies; and by Art. 2, sec. 1, felony disfranchises.

11. The constitution of New Jersey, Art. 2, sec. 1, says that "no person convicted of a crime which now excludes him from being a witness, unless pardoned or restored by law to the right of suffrage, shall enjoy the right of an elector." The laws of the State make persons convicted of the above tabulated crimes incompetent as witnesses, and if the crime is perjury or subornation of perjury a pardon does not remove the incompetency.

12. Disfranchise at such election, as do all corrupt offers to give or receive money or other valuable thing for a vote in both New York and Pennsylvania.

THE AMERICAN MANUAL.

STATES.	Embezzlement of Public Funds. Fraud.	Electoral Misdemeanors.	Infamous Crimes.	Larceny.	Other Offences.
Alabama	Embezzlement of public funds	. . . .	. . . .	Larceny	Malfeasance in office
Arkansas	. . . .	. . . .	. . . .	. . . .	. . . .
California	Embezzlement or misappropriation of pub. moneys (2)	. . . .	Infamous crimes (2)	. . . .	Malfeasance in office or other high crimes*
Colorado	. . . .	. . . .	. . . .	. . . .	. . . .
Connecticut	Fraudulent bankruptcy	. . . .	Infamous crimes (19)	Larceny (3)	. . . .
Delaware (4)	. . . .	. . . .	. . . .	. . . .	. . . .
Florida	. . . .	Election wager	Infamous crimes	Larceny	. . . .
Georgia	Embezzlement of public funds	. . . .	. . . .	. . . .	Malfeasance in office
Illinois	. . . .	. . . .	Infamous crimes	. . . .	. . . .
Indiana	. . . .	. . . .	Infamous crimes	. . . .	. . . .
Iowa	. . . .	. . . .	Infamous crimes	. . . .	. . . .
Kansas (5)	Defrauding U. S. or any of the states thereof	. . . .	. . . .	. . . .	. . . .
Kentucky	. . . .	. . . .	. . . .	. . . .	Other crimes or high misdemeanors
Louisiana (20)	. . . .	. . . .	. . . .	. . . .	. . . .
Maine	. . . .	. . . .	. . . .	. . . .	. . . .
Maryland	. . . .	Illegal voting (7)	Infamous crimes	Larceny	. . . .
Mass.	. . . .	. . . .	. . . .	. . . .	. . . .
Michigan	. . . .	. . . .	. . . .	. . . .	. . . .
Minnesota	. . . .	. . . .	Infamous crimes	. . . .	. . . .
Mississippi	. . . .	. . . .	Infamous crimes	. . . .	Other high crimes and misdemeanors
Missouri	. . . .	Election misdemeanor	Infamous crimes	. . . .	. . . .
Nebraska	. . . .	. . . .	. . . .	. . . .	. . . .
Nevada	Embezzlement or defalcation of public funds (15)	. . . .	. . . .	. . . .	. . . .
New Hamp.	. . . .	. . . .	. . . .	. . . .	. . . .
New Jersey	. . . .	. . . .	. . . .	Larceny	Subornation of perjury, blasphemy, piracy, arson, rape, sodomy, polygamy, conspiracy
New York	. . . .	Election wager (12)	Infamous crimes	. . . .	. . . .
N. Carolina	. . . .	. . . .	Infamous crimes	. . . .	. . . .
Ohio	. . . .	. . . .	Infamous crimes	. . . .	. . . .
Oregon	. . . .	. . . .	. . . .	. . . .	. . . .
Penn.	. . . .	Wilful violation of the Election laws (13)	. . . .	. . . .	. . . .
Rhode Island	. . . .	. . . .	Infamous crimes	. . . .	. . . .
S. Carolina	. . . .	. . . .	. . . .	. . . .	. . . .
Tennessee	. . . .	. . . .	Infamous crimes	. . . .	. . . .
Texas	. . . .	. . . .	. . . .	. . . .	Other high crimes
Vermont	. . . .	. . . .	. . . .	. . . .	. . . .
Virginia	Embezzlement of public funds	. . . .	. . . .	Larc'y (17)	. . . .
W. Vir. (18)	. . . .	. . . .	. . . .	. . . .	. . . .
Wisconsin	. . . .	Election wager (12)	Infamous crimes	Larceny	. . . .

13 Any person convicted of this offense "shall, in addition to any penalties provided by law, be deprived of the right of suffrage absolutely for a term of four years."

14 "Any elector who shall receive any gift or reward for his vote, in meat, drink, money, or otherwise, shall suffer such punishment as the laws shall direct."

15 "Subject to such exceptions as the legislature may make."

16 "Any elector who shall receive any gift or reward for his vote in meat, drink, money, or otherwise, shall forfeit his right to elect at that time, and suffer such other penalty as the law shall direct."

17 "Petit larceny."

18 "No person who is under the conviction of treason, felony, or bribery in an election shall be permitted to vote while such disability continues." (Con. of West Va., art 4 sec. 1.) This phrase "while disability continues" has not received judicial interpretation in West Virginia, but is construed by election officers to mean during imprisonment.

19 "These crimes are treason, felony, and the crimen falsi"—which term includes crimes which involve a charge of such falsehood as may injuriously affect the public administration of justice by the introduction therein of falsehood and fraud, such as forgery, perjury, subornation of perjury, or conspiracy to procure the absence of a witness.

20 And persons "who may be under interdiction."

THE REPUBLICAN AND DEMOCRATIC PARTIES ON PROHIBITION.

ALABAMA.

Republican.—The organization of temperance men in Alabama meets our hearty approval, and we recognize in it the spirit of Him who came among us and taught, "A new command I give." I would that ye love one another. (Adopted by State committee.)

Democratic.—No mention.

ARKANSAS.

Rep.—We recognize the fundamental principles of Government that all power is in the People, and we therefore favor a submission to the people of the State of an amendment to the Constitution, prohibiting the manufacture and sale of alcoholic liquors in the State.

Dem.—No mention.

CALIFORNIA.

Rep.—That the property of our viticultural and horticultural industries is of paramount importance to this State. In order to encourage their rapid improvement and freer extension of trade in domestic and foreign markets, and to prevent unjust discrimination in favor of foreign products, a revision of the internal revenue laws and amendments to the tariff are demanded as of immediate necessity to our People; and the Legislature should by suitable legislation provide for the extermination of fruit pests.

Dem.—That in view of the brilliant future that awaits California, in the development of its wine interests, we most heartily favor the bills now pending in Congress for the release from taxation of spirits used in the fortification of sweet wines, and the protection of our wine industries from the injurious effects of fraud and the unrestricted sale of spurious wines, and we also favor Legislation providing for the protection of the wine industry. That we re-affirm the principles contained in the National Democratic platforms, declaring that the Democratic party is unalterably opposed to all Sumptuary Legislation.

COLORADO.

Rep.—That we shall, in the future as in the past stand firm in our advocacy of temperance and sobriety, and to the advancement of morality and virtue, and pledge ourselves to further the adoption of laws tending to control vice, and lift this People to higher planes of thought and action.

Dem.—No mention.

CONNECTICUT.

Rep.—The traffic in intoxicating liquors is justly chargeable with being a great cause of poverty, ignorance and crime. Our existing local option laws are in accord with the State's ancient theories of local government, and the Republican party is ready, as it always has been, for the enactment of such laws, tending to eradicate the evils of intemperance, as may be demanded by public sentiment.

Dem.—In Legislative enactments the Democratic party pays due regard to the fullest liberty of the individual consistent with law and order. We recognize the fact that no law to prevent the abuse in the use of alcoholic liquors can be enforced against public sentiment; and we adhere to the views heretofore expressed by the Democratic party that a well-regulated License Law, thoroughly executed, will best promote the cause of temperance and good order in society. But a License Law under the control of an exclusively partisan board of County Commissioners, who act for their party rather than the welfare of society, will fail of its primary object.

DELAWARE.
Rep.—No convention.
Dem.—No mention.

FLORIDA.
Rep—No convention.
Dem.—No mention.

GEORGIA.
Rep.—No convention.
Dem.—No mention.

ILLINOIS.
Rep.—No mention.
Dem.—That while we have no purpose to interfere with just laws for the regulation of the traffic in intoxicating liquors and for the prevention or correction of the evils to society, growing out of abuses in their rule, we declare that it is out of the legitimate province of Government to control the habits, tastes, appetites, and liberties of the People so long as they are orderly and peaceable, and do not encroach upon the rights of others or of society. We therefore declare that the Prohibition by Constitution or by general law of the manufacture or sale of vinous, malt, or spiritous liquors, would be in violation of individual and personal rights and contrary to the fundamental principles of free Government.

INDIANA.
Rep.—The domination by the liquor league of political parties and Legislation is a menace to free institutions which must be met and defeated. The traffic in intoxicating liquors has always been under Legislative restraint, and we favor such laws as will permit the People in their several localities to invoke such measures of restriction as they may deem wise to compel the traffic to compensate for the burdens it imposes on society and relieve the oppressions of local taxation.

Dem.—That the Democratic party of Indiana is now, as it has always been, opposed in principle to all Sumptuary Laws and Prohibitory Legislation, but it is in favor of just and proper measures for regulating the traffic in spiritous and intoxicating liquors, under a license system designed to repress the evils of intemperance, and it favors a reasonable increase of the license tax, discriminating between malt liquors and wines and distilled spirits, so as to place the highest license on distilled spirits, the proceeds of such tax to be applied to the support of common schools.

IOWA.
Rep.—Iowa has no compromise to hold with the saloon. We declare in favor of the vigorous and faithful enforcement in all parts of the State, of the Prohibitory Law. The Pharmacy Law and the County Permit Law should be so amended as to prevent the drug store or wholesale liquor store from becoming in any manner the substitute or successor of the saloon.

Dem. We are opposed to all Sumptuary Legislation and in favor of the repeal of the present Prohibitory liquor Law, and substitution in its stead of a local option and carefully guarded License Law with a minimum license fee for better control of the liquor traffic.

KANSAS.
Rep. The People of Kansas have adopted Prohibition as the settled policy of this State, and have deliberately decided that the saloon with its corrupt and demoralizing influences and associations whereby every form of vice, immorality and crime is fostered, must go, and

we are in favor of carrying into effect this verdict of the People by such amendments of the present law as practical experience has shown to be necessary, and by the election of law officers who will so firmly and faithfully enforce it as to render it impossible to sell intoxicating liquors in the State, except for purposes specified in the Prohibition Amendment to the Constitution.

Dem.—That we are in accord with the National Democracy in opposition to all Sumptuary Legislation, either State or National; that we are opposed to the principle of Constitutional Prohibition; and demand the resubmission of the Prohibitory Amendment in this State to a vote of the Electors, so that the question may be finally and intelligently settled and whereby the interests of true temperance may be promoted and the individual liberty and manhood of citizens respected and restored. Instead of Constitutional or Statutory Prohibition, we favor a well-regulated and just License System.

KENTUCKY.

Rep.—No mention.

Dem.—We are opposed to all Sumptuary Laws. We contend that there are already on our statute books sufficient general laws having local application to protect the public morals without infringing on private rights.

LOUISIANA.

Rep.—No mention.
Dem.—No mention.

MAINE.

Rep.—*Resolved*, That the Republicans of Maine now, as heretofore, indorse and approve the Law for the prohibition of the sale of intoxicating liquors. The Law and its several amendments were enacted by Republican Legislators, and this Convention now declares in answer to misrepresentations in many quarters, that the general effect of the Prohibitory Law has been beneficent, and has proved in a marked degree helpful to the cause of temperance in Maine. It has largely reduced the consumption of alcoholic liquors, and has in many ways contributed to the moral and material welfare of the State.

Dem.—No mention.

MARYLAND.

Rep.—No mention.
Dem.—No mention.

MASSACHUSETTS.

Rep.—Recognizing intemperance as the most fruitful source of pauperism, crime, etc., in politics and social degradation, we affirm our belief in the most thorough restriction of the Liquor Traffic and the enforcement of the laws for its suppression. We approve the action of the last Legislature in enacting so many temperance statutes, and demand the continued enactment of progressive temperance measures as the policy of our Party. We repeat the recommendation of last year's Convention, as follows: "Believing, also, that whenever a great public question demands settlement an opportunity should be given the People to express their opinion thereon; We favor the submission to the People of an Amendment to our Constitution prohibiting the manufacture and sale of alcoholic liquors to be used as a beverage. In order to have the matter placed before the People, we call upon all those who are opposed to the political control of the grog-shops to unite with the Republican party in electing Senators and Representatives who will vote for the submission of this Amendment."

Dem.—We, the Democrats of Massachusetts in Convention assembled, renew our adherence to the principles of Democracy declared by the last National Convention, at Chicago.

MICHIGAN.

Rep.—The Republican party has redeemed its promise made in its platform of 1882, and reiterated in subsequent State platforms, by submitting to the People an Amendment to the Constitution prohibiting the manufacture and sale of intoxicating liquors, and the adoption or rejection of the Amendment is now with the people, where it belongs.

Dem.—No mention.

MINNESOTA.

Rep.—The Republican party of Minnesota is in favor of high License, local option and a rigid enforcement of existing laws relating to the Liquor Traffic.

Dem.—The traditions of the Democratic party being in favor of personal liberty, therefore, be it *Resolved*, that this party is opposed to all Class and Sumptuary Legislation.

MISSISSIPPI.

Rep.—No convention.
Dem.—No mention.

MISSOURI.

Rep.—That when a respectable number of the citizens of the State shall petition the Legislature for the submission of any proposition to amend, change or modify the Constitution in any matter which is a proper subject of organic law, their request should be granted.

Dem.—No mention.

NEBRASKA.

Rep.—That the Republican party of Nebraska is in favor of submitting the question of an Amendment to the State Constitution prohibiting the manufacture, sale and importation of any malt, spirituous or vinous liquor in the State.

Dem.—We denounce Prohibition and regard the attempt of the Prohibitory party to force Sumptuary Laws on this State as dangerous to the liberty of the citizen, and hostile to the welfare of the People.

NEVADA.

Rep.—No mention.
Dem.—Heartily endorses the National Democratic Platform.

NEW HAMPSHIRE.

Rep.—We believe that the principle of Prohibition, which has prevailed as the policy of this State for thirty years, has done much to render the Liquor Traffic odious, built up the temperance sentiment of the State and reduced to the minimum the unmitigated evil of the sale and use of intoxicating liquors. To supplant this principle by license would overthrow for a paltry revenue all that has been gained in moral advance and substantial progress in this reform, and we call on all well-wishers of their State and of their fellow-men to join us in preventing the restoration of a License Policy as proclaimed by the Democratic party of New Hampshire, and to the faithful enforcement of the law.

Dem.—We recognize the evils of intemperance, and we profoundly sympathize with all well-directed efforts to eradicate these evils, and, in view of past experience, we are convinced that a judicious License Law, properly enforced, is the best remedy therefor, and will really promote the cause of temperance.

NEW JERSEY.

Rep—The Republican party had its foundation in the belief in the virtue and intelligence of the People; it has always held with its great leader, Abraham Lincoln, that it is a Government of the People, by the People, and for the People; we therefore declare that the Republican party of New Jersey is in favor of the submission of the question of the regulation, control or prohibition of the Liquor Traffic to the votes of the People, at elections specially provided for that purpose.

Dem.—Endorses the National Democratic Platform.

NEW YORK.

Rep.—We heartily endorse the purpose of the Republican majority of the Legislature in passing the bills to limit and restrict the Liquor Traffic, and we condemn the vetoes of the Governor as hostile to that purpose. We recommend comprehensive and efficient Legislation by giving local option by counties, towns and cities, and restriction by taxation in such localities as do not by their option exclude absolutely the Traffic.

Dem.—We favor a revised Excise Law, applicable without unjust discrimination, throughout the State. We oppose all Sumptuary Laws, needlessly interfering with the personal liberties and reasonable habits and customs of any portion of our citizens. We believe that excise revenues, like other proper local revenues, should be applied in lessening local burdens, and to the reduction of local taxation.

NORTH CAROLINA.

Rep.—No mention.
Dem.—No mention.

OHIO.

Rep.—We point with just pride to the enactment of the Dow Law in fulfillment of the promises of the Republican party, and we pledge ourselves to such further Legislation as may be necessary to keep abreast of enlightened public sentiment on this question, to the end that the evils resulting from the Liquor Traffic be restrained to the utmost possible extent in all parts of the State.

Dem.—We declare in favor of the proper regulation of the Liquor Traffic, and believe it to be the duty of all good citizens to aid in reducing to a minimum the evils resulting therefrom, and to this end favor the submission of an Amendment to the Constitution providing for the license of such Traffic.

OREGON.

Rep.—Resolution in favor of submitting the Prohibitory Amendment.

Dem.—That we favor the submission to the voters of the State of Oregon, of the pending Amendment to the Constitution of our State regulating the Liquor Traffic.

PENNSYLVANIA.

Rep.—That they reaffirm their declaration of 1886 in favor of submitting to a vote of the People the Prohibitory Constitutional Amendment.

Dem.—We renew our allegiance to the principles and declaration of the platform adopted at Chicago in 1884.

RHODE ISLAND.

Rep.—We recognize the fact that the adoption of the Fifth Amendment to our State Constitution was not a partisan measure, and that such Amendment has become a part of our Fundamental Law, in obedience to the will of the Constitutional majority. We demand the enactment of Laws adequate to carry this Amendment into effect, and such laws shall be rigidly enforced, recognizing at the same time the right of the People to agitate for the repeal of this or any other Constitutional provision which time may prove to be unwise or ineffectual.

Dem.—No mention.

SOUTH CAROLINA.

Rep.—No convention.
Dem.—No mention.

TENNESSEE.

Rep.—That we, recognizing the sovereignty of the People, do, in response to the demand made through their Representatives in the last Legislature, pronounce in favor of submission to them, for their adoption or rejection, the proposed Constitutional Amendment.

Dem.—Recognizing the sovereignty of the People, and in response to their demands through their Representatives in the last General Assembly, we favor submitting to them for their adoption or rejection, the proposed Constitutional Amendment prohibiting the manufacture and sale of intoxicating liquor as a beverage in Tennessee.

TEXAS.

Rep.—The People in a republic being the source of power, we believe it to be the duty of the Legislature to submit to the People, for their ratification or rejection, such Amendments to our Organic Laws as they may ask, such submission, when petitioned by a sufficient number, being in accordance with the bill of rights.

Dem.—We do not believe that the views of any citizen upon the question of local option should interfere with his standing in the Democratic party; and we declare the question to be one on which every Democrat may indulge his own views without affecting his Democracy.

VERMONT.

Rep.—That we deplore the evils of intemperance. We reaffirm the position of the Republican party in this State upon that question, and declare that in our opinion the Prohibition of the Liquor Traffic, as expressed in our statutes, be and should remain the settled policy of the State; that the influence of the liquor saloon is as debasing in politics as it is baleful in social life. The Republican party should everywhere reject all overtures for open or secret alliance with it.

Dem.—We favor such Legislation as shall control the traffic in intoxicating liquors and increase the revenue rather than the burden of taxation, and, though opposed to Sumptuary Laws, we demand the enforcement of existing laws until repealed, whenever practicable.

VIRGINIA.

Rep.—For a general law providing that every County, city, town and district in this Commonwealth may determine for itself, by a majority of all votes cast, at a special election held for the purpose under due regulations, whether or not the sale of spiritous liquors shall be allowed within its limits.

Dem.—Reaffirming the traditional opposition of the Democratic party to all Sumptuary Laws, or laws unduly interfering with individual liberty, we recommend to the General Assembly to pass such laws as will permit each County or District, at a special election held for that purpose, under proper regulations for ascertaining the popular will, to determine for itself whether the sale of spiritous liquors shall be legally permitted within its limits.

WEST VIRGINIA.

Rep.—A State Conference favored the submission of a Prohibitory Constitutional Amendment.

Dem.—No mention.

WISCONSIN.

Rep.—Recognizing the evils of intemperance, the Republican party desires to adopt the most effective means for its suppression. But we recognize the fact that the statute regulations which are not supported by public opinion are inoperative, and tend to bring all law into disrepute, and we believe that in the present condition of public sentiment the existing laws of this State, which permit communities, according to the sentiment prevailing in them, to prohibit the Traffic in intoxicating liquors or to control it by police regulations and to limit it by High License, offer the best and most practical means of dealing with the evils resulting from the Liquor Traffic.

Dem.—That the intemperate and excessive use of intoxicating liquors is earnestly to be deplored, and we believe that the Liquor Traffic should be regulated by reasonable and liberal laws, whether general or local, designed exclusively for arbitrary regulation of the personal habits of citizens, as an exercise of legislative power, are unwarranted by the Constitution contrary to the fundamental principles of all free governments, and are justified by no practical results yet attained in the experience of mankind.

DEMOCRATIC NATIONAL COMMITTEE.
1888.

WM. H. BARNUM, Chairman,
Lime Rock, Conn.

F. O. PRINCE, Secretary,
Boston, Mass.

CHARLES J. CANDA, Treasurer,
52 Williams St., New York City.

REPUBLICAN NATIONAL COMMITTEE.
1888.

B. F. JONES, Chairman,
and Treasurer, ex-officio,
Pittsburgh, Pa.

SAMUEL FESSENDEN, Secretary,
Stamford, Conn.

Democratic Member	Residence	State	Republican Member	Residence
Henry C. Semple	Montgomery	Alabama	Theo. Youngblood	Union Springs.
S. R. Cockrill, Jr.	Little Rock	Arkansas	Powell Clayton	Eureka Springs.
M. F. Tarpey	East Oakland	California	Horace Davis	San Francisco.
Charles S. Thomas	Denver	Colorado	William A. Hamill	Georgetown.
Wm. H. Barnum	Lime Rock	Connecticut	Samuel Fessenden	Stamford.
Ignatius C. Grubb	Wilmington	Delaware	Daniel J. Layton	Georgetown.
Samuel Pasco	Monticello	Florida	Jesse D. Cole	Monticello.
Patrick Walsh	Augusta	Georgia	F. H. Putner	Hardaway.
S. Corning Judd	Chicago	Illinois	D. T. Littler	Springfield.
Austin H. Brown	Indianapolis	Indiana	John C. New	Indianapolis.
M. M. Ham	Dubuque	Iowa	J. S. Clarkson	Des Moines.
Charles W. Blair	Leavenworth	Kansas	Cyrus Leland Jr.	Troy.
Henry D. McHenry	Hartford	Kentucky	J. B. Moore	Owensboro'.
B. F. Jonas	New Orleans	Louisiana	Frank Morey	Dalton.
		Maine	J. M. Haynes	Augusta.
Arthur P. Gorman	Laurel	Maryland	James A. Gary	Baltimore.
Fred'k O. Prince	Boston	Massachusetts	William W. Crapo	New Bedford.
Don M. Dickinson	Detroit	Michigan	John P. Sanborn	Port Huron.
P. H. Kelly	St. Paul	Minnesota	Robert G. Evans	Minneapolis.
C. A. Johnston	Columbus	Mississippi	John R. Lynch	Natchez.
John G. Prather	St. Louis	Missouri	R. T. Van Horn	Kansas City.
James E. Boyd	Omaha	Nebraska	Church Howe	Auburn.
John H. Denning	Tuscarora	Nevada	Thomas Wren	Eureka.
Alvah W. Sulloway	Franklin	New Hampshire	Edward H. Rollins	Dover.
Miles Ross	New Brunswick	New Jersey	Garret H. Hobart	Paterson.
	New York City	New York	John D. Lawson	New York City.
M. W. Ransom	Weldon	North Carolina	R. W. Humphrey	Goldsboro'.
Wm. W. Armstrong	Cleveland	Ohio	A. L. Conger	Akron.
A. Noltner	Portland	Oregon	J. T. Apperson	Oregon City.
Wm. A. Wallace	Clearfield	Pennsylvania	B. F. Jones	Pittsburgh.
J. B. Barnaby	Providence	Rhode Island	Horace A. Jenks	Woonsocket.
F. W. Dawson	Charleston	South Carolina	E. M. Brayton	Columbia.
R. F. Looney	Memphis	Tennessee	W. P. Brownlow	Jonesboro'.
O. T. Holt	Houston	Texas	N. W. Cuney	Galveston.
Bradley B. Smalley	Burlington	Vermont	George W. Hooker	Brattleboro'.
John S. Barbour	Alexandria	Virginia	Frank S. Blair	Richmond.
Lewis Baker	Wheeling	West Virginia	John W. Mason	Grafton.
William F. Vilas	Madison	Wisconsin	Edward Sanderson	Milwaukee.
W. K. Mead	Tombstone	Arizona	Clark Churchill	Prescott.
M. H. Day	Springfield	Dakota	John E. Bennett	Clark.
William Dickson	Washington	Dist. Columbia	Perry H. Carson	Washington.
John Hailey	Idaho City	Idaho	Sherman M. Coffin	Boise City.
W. J. McCormick	Missoula	Montana	James H. Mills	Deer Lodge.
Geo. W. Fox	Socorro	New Mexico	Stephen B. Elkins	92 B'way, N. Y.
J. B. Rosborough	Salt Lake City	Utah	C. W. Bennett	Salt Lake City.
J. H. Kuhn	Pt. Townsend	Washington	Thomas T. Miner	Pt. Townsend.
M. E. Post	Laramie City	Wyoming	Joseph M. Carey	Cheyenne.

THE AMERICAN MANUAL.

Executive Committee of the National Democratic Committee.

William H. Barnum,
A. P. Gorman,

Wm. A. Wallace,
William F. Vilas,
John S. Barbour,
B. F. Jonas,
P. H. Kelly,
Austin H. Brown,
Henry D. McHenry,

Alvah W. Sulloway,
M. W. Ransom,
M. M. Ham,
Wm. W. Armstrong,
Bradley B. Smalley,
F. W. Dawson,
Miles Ross,
S. Corning Judd,
J. B. Barnaby,
John G. Prather.

Executive Committee of the National Republican Committee.

John C. New,
Stephen B. Elkins,
John W. Mason,

E. H. Rollins,
J. M. Haynes,
W. W. Crapo,
E. Sanderson,
G. A. Hobart,
Geo. W. Hooker,
John W. Lawson,

Frank S. Blair,
R. W. Humphrey,
Powell Clayton,
Frank Morey,
A. L. Conger,
John P. Sanborn,
Church Howe,
Cyrus Leland, Jr.
John R. Lynch,
J. S. Clarkson,
D. J. Layton.

BRIEF HISTORY OF NATIONAL POLITICAL CONVENTIONS.

NATIONAL CONVENTIONS for the nomination of candidates for President and Vice-President are of comparatively recent origin. In the earlier political history of the United States, under the Federal Constitution, candidates for President and Vice-President were nominated by congressional and legislative caucuses. Washington was elected as first President under the Constitution, and re-elected for a second term by a unanimous or nearly unanimous concurrence of the American people; but an opposition party gradually grew up in Congress, which became formidable during its second term, and which ultimately crystalized into what was then called the Republican party. John Adams, of Massachusetts, was prominent among the leading Federalists, while Thomas Jefferson, of Virginia, was pre-eminently the author and oracle of the Republican party, and, by common consent, they were the opposing candidates for the Presidency, on Washington's retirement in 1796-7.

The first Congressional caucus to nominate candidates for President and Vice-President, is said to have been held in Philadelphia, in the year 1800, and to have nominated Mr. Jefferson for the first office and Aaron Burr for the second. These candidates were elected after a desperate struggle, beating John Adams, and Charles C. Pinckney, of South Carolina. In 1804, Mr. Jefferson was re-elected President, with George Clinton, of New York, for Vice, encountering but slight opposition; Messrs. Charles C. Pinckney and Rufus King, the opposing candidates, receiving only 13 out of 176 electoral votes. We have been unable to find any record as to the manner of their nomination.

In January, 1808, when Mr. Jefferson's second term was about to close, a Republican Congressional Caucus was held at Washington to decide as to the relative claims of Madison and Monroe for the succession, the Legislature of Virginia, which had been said to exert a potent influence over such questions, being, on this occasion, unable to agree as to which of her favored sons should have the preference. Ninety-four out of the 136 Republican members of Congress attended this caucus, and declared their preference of Mr. Madison who received 83 votes, the remaining 11 votes being divided between Mr. Monroe and George Clinton. The opposition supported Mr. Pinckney, but Mr. Madison was elected by a large majority.

Toward the close of Mr. Madison's earlier term he was nominated for re-election by a Congressional Caucus, held at Washington in May, 1812. In September of the same year, a convention of the opposition, representing eleven States, was held in the city of New York, which nominated De Witt Clinton, of New York, for President. He was also put in nomination by the Republican Legislature of New York. The ensuing canvass resulted in the re-election of Mr. Madison, who received 128 electoral votes to 89 for DeWitt Clinton.

In 1816, the Republican Congressional Caucus nominated James Monroe, who received in the caucus 65 votes, to 54 for Wm. H. Crawford, of Georgia. The opposition, or Federalists, named Rufus King, of New York, who received only 34 electoral votes out of 217. There was no opposition to the re-election of Mr. Monroe in 1820, a single (Republican) vote being cast against him, and for John Quincy Adams.

In 1824, the Republican party could not be induced to abide by the decision of a Congressional Caucus. A large majority of the Republican members formally refused to participate in such a gathering, or be governed by its decision; still a caucus was called, and attended by the friends of Mr. Crawford alone. Of the 261 members of Congress at this time, 216 were Democrats or Republicans; yet only 66 responded to their names at roll call, 64 of whom voted for Mr. Crawford as the Republican nominee for President. This nomination was very extensively repudiated throughout the country, and three competing Republican candidates were brought into the field through legislative and other machinery, viz.: Andrew Jackson, Henry Clay and John Quincy Adams. The result of this famous "scrub race" for the Presidency, was that no one was elected by the people. Gen. Jackson receiving 99 electoral votes, Mr. Adams 84, Mr. Crawford 41, and Mr. Clay 37. The election then devolved upon the House of Representatives, when Mr. Adams was chosen, receiving the votes of 13 States, against 7 for Gen. Jackson, and 4 for Mr. Crawford. This was the end of "King Caucus."

Gen. Jackson was immediately thereafter put in nomination for the ensuing term by the Legislature of Tennessee, having only Mr. Adams for an opponent in 1828, when he was elected by a decided majority, receiving 178 electoral votes, to 83 for Mr. Adams.

The first political National Convention in this country of which we have any record was held at Philadelphia in September, 1830, styled the United States Anti-Masonic Convention. It was composed of 96 delegates. Francis Granger, of New York, presided, but no business was transacted.

In compliance with its call, a National Anti-Masonic Convention was held at Baltimore in September, 1831, which nominated William Wirt, of Maryland, for President, and Amos Ellmaker, of Pennsylvania, for Vice-President.

The candidates accepted the nomination, and received the electoral vote of Vermont only.

There was no open opposition in the Democratic Party to the nomination of Gen. Jackson for a second term in 1832, but the party was not so well satisfied with Mr. Calhoun, the Vice-President, so a convention was called to meet at Baltimore, in May, 1832, to nominate a candidate for the second office.

Mr. Van Buren received more than two-thirds of all the votes cast, and was declared nominated.

The National Republicans met in convention at Baltimore, December 12, 1831. Seventeen States and the District of Columbia were represented by 157 delegates, who cast a unanimous vote for Henry Clay, of Kentucky, for President.

In May, 1835, a Democratic National Convention, representing twenty-one States, assembled at Baltimore. A rule was adopted that two-thirds of the whole number of votes should be necessary to make a nomination, or to decide any question connected therewith. On the first ballot for President Mr. Van Buren was nominated unanimously, receiving 265 votes.

In 1835, Gen. William H. Harrison was nominated for President, with Francis Granger for Vice-President, by a Whig State Convention at Harrisburg, Pa. Gen. Harrison also received nomination in Maryland, New York, Ohio and other States.

A Whig National Convention, representing twenty-one States, met at Harrisburg, Pa., December 4, 1839. James Barbour, of Virginia, presided, and the result of the first ballot was the nomination of Gen. William H. Harrison, of Ohio, who received 148 votes to go for Henry Clay, and 16 for Gen. Winfield Scott. John Tyler, of Virginia, was unanimously nominated as the Whig candidate for Vice-President.

A Convention of Abolitionists was held at Warsaw, N. Y., on the 13th of November, 1839, and nominated for President James G. Birney, of New York, and for Vice-President, Francis J. Lemoyne, of Pennsylvania. These gentlemen declined the nomination. Nevertheless they received a total of 7,600 votes in various Free States.

A Democratic National Convention met at Baltimore, May 5, 1840, to nominate candidates for President and Vice-President. The Convention then unanimously nominated Mr. Van Buren for re-election as President.

A Whig National Convention assembled in Baltimore on the 1st of May, 1844, at which every State in the Union was represented, and Mr. Clay was nominated for President by acclamation.

A Democratic National Convention assembled at Baltimore on the 27th of May, 1844, adopted the two-thirds rule, and, after a stormy session of three days, James K. Polk, of Tennessee, was nominated for President, and Silas Wright, of New York, for Vice-President. Mr. Wright declined the nomination, and George M. Dallas, of Pennsylvania, was selected.

The Liberty Party National Convention met at Buffalo on the 30th of August, 1843. James G. Birney, of Michigan, was unanimously nominated for President, with Thomas Morris, of Ohio, for Vice-President.

A Whig National Convention met at Philadelphia on the 7th of June, 1848. After a rather stormy session of three days, Gen. Zachary Taylor, of Louisiana, was nominated for President, and Millard Fillmore, of New York, for Vice-President.

The Democratic National Convention for 1848 assembled in Baltimore on the 22d of May. The two-thirds rule was adopted, and Gen. Lewis Cass was nominated for President on the fourth ballot.

On the 9th of August, 1848, a free Democratic or Free Soil Convention was held at Buffalo, which was attended by delegates from seventeen States. Charles Francis Adams, of Massachusetts, presided, and the Convention nominated Messrs. Van Buren and Adams as candidates for President and Vice-President.

The Whig National Convention of 1852 assembled at Baltimore on the 16th of June, and after an exciting session of six days, nominated Gen. Winfield Scott as President on the fifty-third ballot.

The Democratic Convention of 1852 assembled at Baltimore on the 1st of June, and the two-thirds rule was adopted. Gen. Franklin Pierce, of New Hampshire, was nominated for President on the forty-ninth ballot.

The Free Soil Democracy held a National Convention at Pittsburg, on the 11th of August, 1852, Henry Wilson, of Massachusetts, presiding. All the Free States were represented, with Delaware, Virginia, Kentucky and Maryland. John P. Hale, of New Hampshire, was nominated for President, with George W. Julian, of Indiana, for Vice-President.

The Republican National Convention of 1856 met at Philadelphia on the 17th of June. Col. John C. Fremont was unanimously nominated, having received 359 votes on the first ballot against 190 for John McLean.

On February 22d, 1856, the American National Nominating Convention organized at Philadelphia, with 227 delegates in attendance. Millard Fillmore was declared to be the nominee, with Andrew Jackson Donelson, of Tennessee, for Vice-President.

The Democratic National Convention of 1856 met at Cincinnati on the 2d of June, and nominated James Buchanan on the seventeenth ballot. John C. Breckinridge, of Kentucky, was unanimously nominated for Vice-President.

A Republican National Convention assembled at Chicago on May 16, 1860, delegates being in attendance from all the Free States as also from Delaware, Maryland, Virginia, Kentucky and Missouri. Abraham Lincoln was nominated for the Presidency on the third ballot, receiving 354 out of 466 votes; his principal competitors being William H. Seward, Salmon P. Chase, and Edward Bates.

A Democratic National Convention assembled at Charleston, S. C., on the 23d of April, 1860, with full delegations present from every State. Dissensions arising chiefly out of questions of slavery in the Territories, too great to be reconciled, the delegations from seven Southern States withdrew, and the convention adjourned, after fifty-seven individual ballots for a candidate, to meet at Baltimore, June 18. Hon. Stephen A. Douglas was nominated for President, and B. Fitzpatrick for Vice-President. The latter declined, and H. V. Johnson was substituted by the National Committee. The Convention of seceders nominated John C. Breckinridge and Joseph Lane.

A "Constitutional Union" Convention from twenty States met at Baltimore, May ---, and nominated John Bell and Edward Everett for the Presidency and Vice-Presidency.

1864.

The Republican National Convention met at Baltimore, June 7. The renomination of President, of Abraham Lincoln, of Illinois, was made unanimous, he having received the vote of all the States except Missouri.

cast for Gen. Grant. For Vice-President, Andrew Johnson, of Tennessee, was nominated on the second ballot, his principal competitors being D. S. Dickinson and H. Hamlin.

The Democratic National Convention met at Chicago, Ill., August 29. Nominations—President, George B. McClellan, of New Jersey; Vice-President, George H. Pendleton, of Ohio.

1868.

The Republican National Convention met at Chicago, Ill., May 20th. Nominations—President, Ulysses S. Grant, of Illinois; Vice-President, Schuyler Colfax, of Indiana.

The Democratic National Convention met at New York, July 4th. Nominations—President, Horatio Seymour, of New York; Vice-President, Francis P. Blair, Jr., of Missouri.

1872.

The Liberal Republican Convention met at Cincinnati, Ohio, May 1st. Nominations—President, Horace Greeley, of New York, on the sixth ballot, by 482 votes, against 187 for David Davis, of Illinois; Vice-President, B. Gratz Brown, of Missouri, on the second ballot.

The Republican National Convention met at Philadelphia, Pa., June 5th. Nominations—President, Ulysses S. Grant, on the first ballot, unanimously; Vice-President, Henry Wilson, of Massachusetts, receiving 364½ votes against 321½ for Schuyler Colfax.

The Democratic National Convention met at Baltimore, Maryland, July 9th. Nominations—President, Horace Greeley, on the first ballot, receiving 686 votes to 38 scattering; Vice-President, B. Gratz Brown, who received 713 votes.

The Democratic ("Straight Out") Convention met at Louisville, Ky., September 3d. Nominations—President, Charles O'Connor, of New York; Vice-President, John Q. Adams, of Massachusetts. The nominations were declined.

1876.

The Republican National Convention met at Cincinnati, Ohio, June 14. Nominations—President, Rutherford B. Hayes, of Ohio, on the 7th ballot, receiving 384 votes, to 351 for J. G. Blaine, and 21 for B. H. Bristow; Vice-President, William A. Wheeler, of New York.

The Democratic National Convention met at St. Louis, Mo., June 27th. Nominations—President, Samuel J. Tilden, of New York, on the second ballot, receiving 535 votes, against 85 for Hendricks, 54 for Wm. Allen, 58 for W. S. Hancock, and 16 scattering; Vice-President, Thomas A. Hendricks, of Indiana.

A "National Greenback Convention," composed of men opposed to specie resumption and in favor of national paper money to take the place of bank issues, met at Indianapolis, May 17, with nineteen States represented Peter Cooper, of New York, and Samuel F. Cary, of Ohio, were nominated for President and Vice-President.

"A Prohibition Reform Party" Convention met at Cleveland, May 17th, and nominated Green Clay Smith, of Kentucky, and R. T. Stewart, of Ohio.

1880.

The Republican National Convention met at Chicago, June 2, 1880. Nominations—President, James A. Garfield, of Ohio, on the 36th ballot, received 399 votes to 306 for Ulysses S. Grant, 42 for James G. Blaine, 5 for E. B. Washburne, and 3 for John Sherman; Vice-President, Chester A. Arthur, of New York.

The Democratic National Convention met at Cincinnati, Ohio, June 22, 1880. Winfield Scott Hancock was nominated for President.

The National Greenback Convention met at Chicago, June 9, 1880, and nominated General J. B. Weaver, of Iowa, for President, and B. J. Chambers, of Texas, for Vice-President.

The Prohibition Reform Party met at Cleveland, Ohio, June 17, 1880, and Nominated General Neal Dow of Maine, for President, and the Rev. Dr. Thompson, of Ohio, for Vice-President.

The American Party's candidates for 1880, were General John W. Phelps, of Vermont, for President, and Hon. S. C. Pomeroy, of Kansas, for Vice-President.

1884.

The Republican National Convention met at Chicago, June 3, 1884. Nominations—President, James G. Blaine, of Maine, on the 4th ballot received 541 to 207 for Arthur, 40 for Edmunds, 15 for Hawley, 7 for Logan, 2 for Lincoln. Vice-President, John A. Logan, of Illinois.

The Democratic National Convention met at Chicago, July 8, 1884. Nominations—President, Grover Cleveland, of New York, on the second ballot received 683 votes to Bayard 81½, Hendricks 45½, Thurman 4, Randall 4, McDonald 2; Vice-President, Thomas A. Hendricks, of Indiana.

The Prohibition National Convention met at Pittsburg, July 23, 1884. Nominations—President, John P. St. John, of Kansas, on the first ballot, received 60 votes; Vice-President, William Daniel, of Maryland.

The National Greenback Convention met at Indianapolis. Nominations—President, Benj. F. Butler, Vice-President, General A. M. West.

1888.

The Prohibition National Convention met at Indianapolis, May 31, 1888. Nominations—President, Clinton B. Fisk, of New Jersey, and John A. Brooks, of Missouri, for Vice-President.

The Democratic National Convention met at St. Louis, Mo., June 6, 1888. Nominations—President, Grover Cleveland, of New York, on the first ballot, by acclamation, Vice-President, Allen G. Thurman, of Ohio.

The Republican National Convention met at Chicago, June 19, 1888. Nominations—President, Benjamin Harrison, of Indiana, on the eighth ballot received 544 votes to 118 for John Sherman, 100 for Alger, 59 for Gresham, 5 for Blaine, 4 for McKinley; Vice-President, Levi P. Morton, of New York.

HON. LEONARD SWETT,

Political Platforms From 1860 to 1888.

1860.—Constitutional Union Platform.

Baltimore, May 9.

Whereas, Experience has demonstrated that platforms adopted by the partisan conventions of the Country have had the effect to mislead and deceive the people, and at the same time to widen the political divisions of the Country, by the creation and encouragement of geographical and sectional parties; therefore,

Resolved, That it is both the part of patriotism and of duty to *recognize* no political principles other than THE CONSTITUTION OF THE COUNTRY, THE UNION OF THE STATES, AND THE ENFORCEMENT OF THE LAWS; and that as representatives of the Constitutional Union men of the Country, in National Convention assembled, we hereby pledge ourselves to maintain, protect, and defend, separately and unitedly, those great principles of public liberty and national safety against all enemies at home and abroad, believing that thereby peace may once more be restored to the Country, the rights of the people and of the States re-established, and the Government again placed in that condition of justice, fraternity, and equality, which, under the example and constitution of our fathers, has solemnly bound every citizen of the United States to maintain a more perfect union, establish justice, insure domestic tranquility, provide for the common defense, promote the general welfare, and secure the blessings of liberty to ourselves and our posterity.

1860.—Republican Platform.

Chicago, May 17.

Resolved, That we, the delegated representatives of the Republican electors of the United States, in convention assembled, in discharge of the duty we owe to our constituents and our Country, unite in the following declarations:

1. That the history of the Nation, during the last four years, has fully established the propriety and necessity of the organization and perpetuation of the Republican party, and that the causes which called it into existence are permanent in their nature, and now, more than ever before, demand its peaceful and constitutional triumph.

2. That the maintenance of the principles promulgated in the Declaration of Independence and embodied in the Federal Constitution, "That all men are created equal; that they are endowed by their Creator with certain inalienable rights; that among these are life, liberty, and the pursuit of happiness; that to secure these rights, governments are instituted among men, deriving their just powers from the consent of the governed," is essential to the preservation of our Republican institutions; and that the Federal Constitution, the rights of the States, and the union of the States, must and shall be preserved.

3. That to the union of the States this Nation owes its unprecedented increase in population, its surprising development of material resources, its rapid augmentation of wealth, its happiness at home and its honor abroad; and we hold in abhorrence all schemes for disunion, come from whatever source they may; and we

congratulate the Country that no Republican member of Congress has uttered or countenanced the threats of disunion so often made by Democratic members, without rebuke and with applause from their political associates; and we denounce those threats of disunion, in case of a popular overthrow of their ascendency, as denying the vital principles of a free government, and as an avowal of contemplated treason, which it is the imperative duty of an indignant people sternly to rebuke and forever silence.

4. That the maintenance inviolate of the rights of the States, and especially the right of each State to order and control its own domestic institutions according to its own judgment exclusively, is essential to that balance of powers on which the perfection and endurance of our political fabric depends; and we denounce the lawless invasion, by armed force, of the soil of any state or territory, no matter under what pretext, as among the gravest of crimes.

5. That the present Democratic administration has far exceeded our worst apprehensions, in its measureless subserviency to the exactions of a sectional interest, as especially evinced in its desperate exertions to force the infamous Lecompton constitution upon the protesting people of Kansas; in construing the personal relations between master and servant to involve an unqualified property in persons; in its attempted enforcement, everywhere, on land and sea, through the intervention of Congress and of the Federal courts, of the extreme pretensions of a purely local interest; and in its general and unvarying abuse of the power entrusted to it by a confiding people.

6. That the people justly view with alarm the reckless extravagance which pervades every department of the Federal Government; that a return to rigid economy and accountability is indispensable to arrest the systematic plunder of the public treasury by favored partisans; while the recent startling developments of frauds and corruptions at the Federal metropolis, show that an entire change of administration is imperatively demanded.

7. That the new dogma, that the Constitution, of its own force, carries slavery into any or all of the territories of the United States, is a dangerous political heresy, at variance with the explicit provisions of that instrument itself, with contemporaneous exposition, and with legislative and judicial precedent—is revolutionary in its tendency, and subversive of the peace and harmony of the country.

8. That the normal condition of all the territory of the United States is that of freedom; that as our republican fathers, when they had abolished slavery in all our national territory, ordained that "no person shall be deprived of life, liberty, or property, without due process of law," it becomes our duty, by legislation, whenever such legislation is necessary, to maintain this provision of the Constitution against all attempts to violate it; and we deny the authority of Congress, of a territorial legislature, or of any individuals, to give legal existence to slavery in any territory of the United States.

9. That we brand the recent reopening of the African slave trade, under the cover of our national flag, aided by perversions of judicial power, as a crime against humanity and a burning shame to our Country and age; and we call upon Congress to take prompt and efficient measures for the suppression of that execrable traffic.

10. That in the recent vetoes, by their Federal governors, of the acts of the legislatures of Kansas and Nebraska, prohibiting slavery in those territories, we find a practical illustration of the boasted Democratic principle of non-intervention and popular sovereignty, embodied in the Kansas-Nebraska bill, and a demonstration of the deception and fraud involved therein.

11. That Kansas should, of right, be immediately admitted as a state under the constitution recently formed and adopted by her people, and accepted by the House of Representatives.

12. That, while providing revenue for the support of the General Government by duties upon imports, sound policy requires such an adjustment of these imports as to encourage the development of the industrial interest of the whole country; and we commend that policy of national exchanges which secures to the working man liberal wages, to agriculture remunerative prices, to mechanics and manufacturers an adequate reward for their skill, labor, and enterprise, and to the Nation commercial prosperity and independence.

13. That we protest against any sale or alienation to others of the public lands held by actual settlers, and against any view of the homestead policy which regards the settlers as paupers or suppliants for public bounty; and we demand the passage by Congress of the complete and satisfactory homestead measure which has already passed the House.

14. That the Republican party is opposed to any change in our naturalization laws, or any state legislation by which the rights of citizenship hitherto accorded to immigrants from foreign lands shall be abridged or impaired; and in favor of giving a full and efficient protection to the rights of all classes of citizens, whether native or naturalized, both at home and abroad.

15. That appropriations by Congress for river and harbor improvements of a national character, required for the accommodation and security of an existing commerce, are authorized by the Constitution and justified by the obligations of Government to protect the lives and property of its citizens.

16. That a railroad to the Pacific ocean is imperatively demanded by the interest of the whole country; that the Federal Government ought to render immediate and efficient aid in its construction; and that as a preliminary thereto, a daily overland mail should be promptly established.

17. Finally, having thus set forth our distinctive principles and views we invite the co-operation of all citizens however differing on other questions who substantially agree with us in their affirmance and support.

1860.—Democratic (Douglass) Platform.

Charleston, April 23, and Baltimore, June 18.

1. *Resolved,* That we, the Democracy of the Union, in convention assembled, hereby declare our affirmance of the resolutions unanimously adopted and declared as a Platform of principles by the Democratic convention at Cincinnati, in the year 1856, believing that democratic principles are unchangeable in their nature when applied to the same subject-matters; and we recommend, as the only further resolutious, the following:

Inasmuch as differences of opinion exist in the Democratic party as to the nature and extent of a territorial legislature, and as to the powers and duties of Congress, under the Constitution of the United States, over the institution of slavery within the Territories:

2. *Resolved,* That the Democratic party will abide by the decisions of the Supreme Court of the United States on the questions of constitutional law.

3. *Resolved,* That it is the duty of the United States to afford ample and complete protection to all its citizens, whether at home or abroad, and whether native or foreign.

4. *Resolved,* That one of the necessities of the age, in a military, commercial, and postal

point of view, is speedy communication between the Atlantic and Pacific states; and the Democratic party pledge such constitutional government aid as will insure the construction of a railroad to the Pacific coast at the earliest practicable moment.

5. *Resolved,* That the Democratic party are in favor of the acquisition of the island of Cuba, on such terms as shall be honorable to ourselves and just to Spain.

6. *Resolved,* That the enactments of State legislatures to defeat the faithful execution of the Fugitive Slave Law are hostile in character, subversive of the Constitution, and revolutionary in their effect.

7. *Resolved,* That it is in accordance with the true interpretation of the Cincinnati platform, that, during the existence of the territorial governments, the measure of restriction, whatever it may be, imposed by the Federal Constitution on the power of the territorial legislature over the subject of domestic relations, as the same has been, or shall hereafter be, finally determined by the Supreme Court of the United States, shall be respected by all good citizens, and enforced with promptness and fidelity by every branch of the General Government.

1860.—Democratic (Breckinridge) Platform.

Charleston and Baltimore.

Resolved, That the platform adopted by the Democratic party at Cincinnati be affirmed, with the following explanatory resolutions:

1. That the government of a territory, organized by an act of Congress, is provisional and temporary; and, during its existence, all citizens of the United States have an equal right to settle, with their property in the Territory, without their rights, either of person or property, being destroyed or impaired by congressional or territorial legislation.

2. That it is the duty of the Federal Government, in all its departments, to protect, when necessary, the rights of persons and property in the Territories, and wherever else its constitutional authority extends.

3. That when the settlers in a territory having an adequate population form a State constitution in pursuance of law, the right of sovereignty commences, and, being consumated by admission into the Union, they stand on an equal footing with the people of other States, and the State thus organized ought to be admitted into the Federal Union, whether its constitution prohibits or recognizes the institution of slavery.

4. That the Democratic party are in favor of the acquisition of the Island of Cuba, on such terms as shall be honorable to ourselves and just to Spain, at the earliest practicable moment.

5. That the enactments of State legislatures to defeat the faithful execution of the Fugitive Slave Law are hostile in character, subversive of the Constitution, and revolutionary in their effect.

6. That the Democracy of the United States recognize it as the imperative duty of this Government to protect the naturalized citizen in all his rights, whether at home or in foreign lands, to the same extent as its native-born citizens.

Whereas, One of the greatest necessities of the age, in a political, commercial, postal, and military point of view, is a speedy communication between the Pacific and Atlantic coasts; therefore, be it

Resolved, That the Democratic party do hereby pledge themselves to use every means in their power to secure the passage of some bill, to the extent of the constitutional authority of Congress, for the construction of a Pa-

cific railroad from the Mississippi river to the Pacific ocean, at the earliest practicable moment.

1864.—Radical Platform.
Cleveland, May 31.

1. That the Federal Union shall be preserved.
2. That the constitution and laws of the United States must be observed and obeyed.
3. That the Rebellion must be suppressed by force of arms, and without compromise.
4. That the rights of free speech, free press and the *habeas corpus* be held inviolate, save in districts where martial law has been proclaimed.
5. That the Rebellion has destroyed slavery; and the Federal Constitution should be so amended as to prohibit its re-establishment, and to secure to all men absolute equality before the law.
6. That integrity and economy are demanded, at all times in the administration of the government, and that in time of war the want of them is criminal.
7. That the right of asylum, except for crime and subject to law, is a recognized principle of American liberty; and that any violation of it can not be overlooked, and must not go unrebuked.
8. That the National policy known as the "Monroe Doctrine," has become a recognized principle; and that the establishment of an anti-republican government on this continent by any foreign power can not be tolerated.
9. That the gratitude and support of the Nation are due to the faithful soldiers and the earnest leaders of the Union army and navy, for their heroic achievements and deathless valor in defense of our imperiled Country and of civil liberty.
10. That the one-term policy for the presidency, adopted by the people, is strengthened by the force of the existing crisis, and should be maintained by constitutional amendment.
11. That the Constitution should be so amended that the President and Vice President shall be elected by a direct vote of the people.
12. That the question of the reconstruction of the rebellious States belongs to the people, through their representatives in Congress, and not to the Executive.
13. That the confiscation of the lands of the rebels, and their distribution among the soldiers and actual settlers, is a measure of justice.

1864.—Republican Platform.
Baltimore, June 7.

Resolved, That it is the highest duty of every American citizen to maintain, against all their enemies, the integrity of the Union and the paramount authority of the Constitution and laws of the United States; and that, laying aside all differences of political opinions, we pledge ourselves, as Union men, animated by a common sentiment and aiming at a common object, to do everything in our power to aid the Government in quelling, by force of arms, the Rebellion now raging against its authority, and in bringing to the punishment due to their crimes the rebels and traitors arrayed against it.

Resolved, That we approve the determination of the Government of the United States not to compromise with the rebels, nor to offer them any terms of peace, except such as may be based upon an "unconditional surrender" of their hostility and a return to their allegiance to the Constitution and laws of the United States; and that we call upon the Government to maintain this position, and to prosecute the war with the utmost possible vigor to the complete suppression of the Rebellion, in full reliance upon the self-sacrificing patriotism, the heroic valor, and the undying devotion of the American people to the Country and its free institutions.

Resolved, That as slavery was the cause, and now constitutes the strength, of this Rebellion, and as it must be always and everywhere hostile to the principles of republican government, justice and the National safety demand its utter and complete extirpation from the soil of the Republic; and that we uphold and maintain the acts and proclamations by which the Government, in its own defense, has aimed a death-blow at the gigantic evil. We are in favor, futhermore, of such an amendment to the Constitution, to be made by the people in conformity with its provisions, as shall terminate and forever prohibit the existence of slavery within the limits or jurisdiction of the United States.

Resolved, That the thanks of the American people are due to the soldiers and sailors of the army and navy, who have periled their lives in defense of their country and in vindication of the honor of its flag; that the Nation owes to them some permanent recognition of their patriotism and their valor, and ample and permanent provision for those of their survivors who have received disabling and honorable wounds in the service of the Country; and that the memories of those who have fallen in its defense shall be held in grateful and everlasting remembrance.

Resolved, That we approve and applaud the practical wisdom, the unselfish patriotism,and the unswerving fidelity to the Constitution and the principles of American liberty with which Abraham Lincoln has discharged, under circumstances of unparalleled difficulty, the great duties and responsibilities of the presidential office; that we approve and indorse, as demanded by the emergency and essential to the preservation of the Nation, and as within the provisions of the Constitution, the measures and acts which he has adopted to defend the Nation against its open and secret foes; that we approve, especially, the Proclamation of Emancipation, and the employment as Union soldiers, of men heretofore held in slavery;and that we have full confidence in his determination to carry these, and all other constitutional measures essential to the salvation of the Country, into full and complete effect.

Resolved, That we deem it essential to the general welfare that harmony should prevail in the National councils, and we regard as worthy of public confidence and official trust those only who cordially indorse the principles proclaimed in these resolutions, and which should characterize the administration of the Government.

Resolved, That the Government owes to all men employed in its armies, without regard to distinction of color, the full protection of the laws of war; and that any violation of these laws, or of the usages of civilized nations in the time of war, by the rebels now in arms, should be made the subject of prompt and full redress.

Resolved, That foreign immigration, which in the past has added so much to the wealth, development of resources, and increase of power to this Nation—the asylum of the oppressed of all nations-should be fostered and encouraged by a liberal and just policy.

Resolved, That we are in favor of the speedy construction of the railroad to the Pacific coast.

Resolved, That the National faith, pledged for the redemption of the public debt, must be kept inviolate; and that, for this purpose, we recommend economy and rigid responsibility in the public expenditures and a vigorous and just system of taxation; and that it is the duty of every loyal state to sustain the credit and promote the use of the National currency.

Resolved, That we approve the position taken by the Government, that the people of the United States can never regard with indifference the attempt of any European power to overthrow by force, or to supplant by fraud, the institutions of any republican government on the western continent, and that they will view with extreme jealousy, as menacing to the peace and independence of this, our Country, the efforts of any such power to obtain new footholds for monarchical governments, sustained by a foreign military force, in near proximity to the United States.

1864.—Democratic Platform.

Chicago, August, 29.

Resolved, That in the future, as in the past, we will adhere with unswerving fidelity to the Union under the Constitution, as the only solid foundation of our strength, security, and happiness as a people, and as a frame-work of Government equally conducive to the welfare and prosperity of all the States, both northern and southern.

Resolved, That this convention does explicitly declare, as the sense of the American people, that after four years of failure to restore the Union by the experiment of war, during which, under the pretense of a military necessity of a war power higher than the Constitution, the Constitution itself has been disregarded in every part, and public liberty and private right alike trodden down, and the material prosperity of the Country essentially impaired, justice, humanity, liberty, and the public welfare demand that immediate efforts be made for a cessation of hostilities, with a view to an ultimate convention of all the States, or other peaceable means, to the end that, at the earliest practicable moment, peace may be restored on the basis of the federal union of all the States.

Resolved, That the direct interference of the military authority of the United States in the recent elections held in Kentucky, Maryland, Missouri and Delaware, was a shameful violation of the Constitution; and the repetition of such acts in the approaching election will be held as revolutionary, and resisted with all the means and power under our control.

Resolved, That the aim and object of the Democratic party is to preserve the Federal Union and the rights of the States unimpaired; and they hereby declare that they consider the administrative usurpation of extraordinary and dangerous powers not granted by the Constitution, the subversion of the civil by the military law in states not in insurrection, the arbitrary military arrest, imprisonment, trial, and sentence of American citizens in States where civil law exists in full force, the suppression of freedom of speech and of the press, the denial of the right of asylum, the open and avowed disregard of state rights, the employment of unusual test-oaths, and the interference with and denial of the right of the people to bear arms in their defense, as calculated to prevent a restoration of the Union and the perpetuation of a government deriving its just powers from the consent of the governed.

Resolved, That the shameful disregard of the administration of its duty in respect to our fellow-citizens who now are, and long have been, prisoners of war, in a suffering condition, deserves the severest reprobation, on the score alike of public policy and common humanity.

Resolved, That the sympathy of the Democratic party is heartily and earnestly extended to the soldiery of our army and the sailors of our navy, who are and have been in the field and on the sea under the flag of their Country; and, in the event of our attaining power, they will receive all the care and protection, regard and kindness, that the brave soldiers of the Republic have so nobly earned.

1868.—Republican Platform.
Chicago, May 20.

1. We congratulate the Country on the assured success of the reconstruction policy of Congress, as evinced by the adoption, in the majority of the States lately in rebellion, of constitutions securing equal civil and political rights to all; and it is the duty of the Government to sustain those institutions and to prevent the people of such States from being remitted to a state of anarchy.

2. The guarantee by Congress of equal suffrage to all loyal men at the south was demanded by every consideration of public safety, of gratitude, and of justice, and must be maintained; while the question of suffrage in all the loyal States properly belongs to the people of those States.

3. We denounce all forms of repudiation as a National crime; and the National honor requires the payment of the public indebtedness in the uttermost good faith to all creditors at home and abroad, not only according to the letter but the spirit of the laws under which it was contracted.

4. It is due to the labor of the Nation that taxation should be equalized and reduced as rapidly as the National faith will permit.

5. The National debt, contracted as it has been for the preservation of the Union for all time to come, should be extended over a fair period for redemption; and it is the duty of Congress to reduce the rate of interest thereon whenever it can be honestly done.

6. That the best policy to diminish our burden of debts is to so improve our credit that capitalists will seek to loan us money at lower rates of interest than we now pay, and must continue to pay so long as repudiation, partial or total, open or covert, is threatened or suspected.

7. The Government of the United States should be administered with the strictest economy; and the corruptions which have been so shamefully nursed and fostered by Andrew Johnson call loudly for radical reform.

8. We profoundly deplore the tragic death of Abraham Lincoln, and regret the accession to the Presidency of Andrew Johnson, who has acted treacherously to the people who elected him and the cause he was pledged to support; who has usurped high legislative and judicial functions; who has refused to execute the laws; who has used his high office to induce other officers to ignore and violate the laws; who has employed his executive powers to render insecure the property, the peace, liberty, and life of the citizen; who has abused the pardoning power; who has denounced the National legislature as unconstitutional; who has persistently and corruptly resisted, by every means in his power, every proper attempt at the reconstruction of the States lately in rebellion; who has perverted the public patronage into an engine of wholesale corruption; and who has been justly impeached for high crimes and misdemeanors, and properly pronounced guilty thereof by the vote of thirty-five Senators.

9. The doctrine of Great Britain and other European powers, that because a man is once a subject he is always so, must be resisted at every hazard by the United States, as a relic

of feudal times, not authorized by the laws of nations, and at war with our National honor and independence. Naturalized citizens are entitled to protection in all their rights of citizenship as though they were native-born; and no citizen of the United States, native or naturalized, must be liable to arrest and imprisonment by any foreign power for acts done or words spoken in this Country; and, if so arrested and imprisoned, it is the duty of the Government to interfere in his behalf.

10. Of all who were faithful in the trials of the late war, there were none entitled to more special honor than the brave soldiers and seamen who endured the hardships of campaign and cruise, and imperiled their lives in the service of the Country. The bounties and pensions provided by the laws for these brave defenders of the Nation are obligations never to be forgotten; the widows and orphans of the gallant dead are the wards of the people—a sacred legacy bequeathed to the Nation's protecting care.

11. Foreign immigration, which in the past has added so much to the wealth, development, and resources, and increase of power to this Republic, the asylum of the oppressed of all nations, should be fostered and encouraged by a liberal and just policy.

12. This convention declares itself in sympathy with all oppressed people who are struggling for their rights.

13. That we highly commend the spirit of magnanimity and forbearance with which men who have served in the Rebellion, but who now frankly and honestly co-operate with us in restoring the peace of the Country and reconstructing the Southern state governments upon the basis of impartial justice and equal rights, are received back into the communion of the loyal people; and we favor the removal of the disqualifications and restrictions imposed upon the late rebels, in the same measure as the spirit of disloyalty shall die out, and as may be consistent with the safety of the loyal people.

14. That we recognize the great principles laid down in the immortal Declaration of Independence, as the true foundation of democratic government; and we hail with gladness every effort towards making these principles a living reality on every inch of American soil.

1868.—Democratic Platform.

New York, July 4.

The Democratic party, in National convention assembled, reposing its trust in the intelligence, patriotism, and discriminating justice of the people, standing upon the Constitution as the foundation and limitation of the powers of the Government and the guarantee of the liberties of the citizen, and recognizing the questions of slavery and secession as having been settled, for all time to come, by the war or voluntary action of the Southern States in constitutional conventions assembled, and never to be revived or reagitated, do, with the return of peace, demand—

1. Immediate restoration of all the States to their rights in the Union under the Constitution, and of civil government to the American people.

2. Amnesty for all past political offenses, and the regulation of the elective franchise in the States by their citizens.

3. Payment of all the public debt of the United States as rapidly as practicable—all money drawn from the people by taxation, except so much as is requisite for the necessities of the Government, economically administered, being honestly applied to such payment; and where the obligations of the

Government do not expressly state upon their face, or the law under which they were issued does not provide that they shall be paid in coin, they ought, in right and in justice, to be paid in the lawful money of the United States.

4. Equal taxation of every species of property according to its real value, including Government bonds and other public securities.

5. One currency for the Government and the people, the laborer and the office holder, the pensioner and the soldier, the producer and the bondholder.

6. Economy in the administration of the Government; the reduction of the standing army and navy; the abolition of the Freedman's Bureau and all political instrumentalities designed to secure negro supremacy; simplification of the system and discontinuance of inquisitorial modes of assessing and collecting internal revenue; that the burden of taxation may by equalized and lessened, and the credit of the Government and the currency made good; the repeal of all enactments for enrolling the state militia into National forces in time of peace; and a tariff for revenue upon foreign imports, and such equal taxation under the internal revenue laws as will afford incidental protection to domestic manufactures, and as will, without impairing the revenue, impose the least burden upon, and best promote and encourage, the great industrial interests of the Country.

7. Reform of abuses in the administration; the expulsion of corrupt men from office; the abrogation of useless offices; the restoration of rightful authority to, and the independence of, the Executive and Judicial departments of the Government; the subordination of the military to the civil power, to the end that the usurpations of Congress and the despotism of the sword may cease.

8. Equal rights and protection for naturalized and native-born citizens, at home and abroad; the assertion of American nationality which shall command the respect of foreign powers, and furnish an example and encouragement to people struggling for national integrity, constitutional liberty and individual rights; and the maintenance of the rights of naturalized citizens against the absolute doctrine of immutable allegiance and the claims of foreign powers to punish them for alleged crimes committed beyond their jurisdiction.

In demanding these measures and reforms, we arraign the Radical party for its disregard of right and the unparalleled oppression and tyranny which have marked its career. After the most solemn and unanimous pledge of both Houses of Congress to prosecute the war exclusively for the maintenance of the Government and preservation of the Union under the Constitution, it has repeatedly violated the most sacred pledge under which alone was rallied that noble volunteer army which carried our flag to victory. Instead of restoring the Union, it has, so far as in its power, dissolved it, and subjected ten states, in time of profound peace, to military despotism and negro supremacy. It has nullified there the right of trial by jury; it has abolished the *habeas corpus*, that most sacred writ of liberty; it has overthrown the freedom of speech and press; it has substituted arbitrary seizures and arrests, and military trials and secret star-chamber requisitions, for the constitutional tribunals; it has disregarded, in time of peace, the right of the people to be free from searches and seizures; it has entered the post and telegraph offices, and even the private rooms of individuals, and seized their private papers and letters, without any specific charge or notice of affidavit, as required by the organic law. It has converted the American capitol into a bastile; it has established a system of spies and official espionage to which no constitutional monarchy of Europe would now dare to resort. It has abolished the right of appeal, on important constitutional questions, to the supreme judicial tribunals, and threatens to curtail or destroy its original jurisdiction, which is irrevocably vested by the Constitution; while the learned Chief Justice has been subjected to the most atrocious calumnies, merely because he would not prostitute his high office to the support of the false and partisan charges preferred against the President. Its corruption and extravagance have exceeded anything known in history; and, by fraud and monopolies, it has nearly doubled the burden of the debt created by the war. It has stripped the President of his constitutional power of appointment, even of his own cabinet. Under its repeated assaults, the pillars of the Government are rocking on their base; and should it succeed in November next, and inaugurate its President, we will meet, as a subjected and conquered people, amid the ruins of liberty and the scattered fragments of the Constitution.

And we do declare and resolve that ever since the people of the United States threw off all subjection to the British crown, the privilege and trust of suffrage have belonged to the several States, and have been granted, regulated, and controlled exclusively by the political power of each State respectively; and that any attempt by Congress, on any pretext whatever, to deprive any State of this right, or interfere with its exercise, is a flagrant usurpation of power which can find no warrant in the Constitution, and, if sanctioned by the people, will subvert our form of government, and can only end in a single, centralized, and consolidated, government, in which the separate existence of the States will be entirely absorbed, and an unqualified despotism be established in place of a federal union of co-equal States. And that we regard the construction acts (so called) of Congress as usurpations, and unconstitutional, revolutionary, and void.

That our soldiers and sailors, who carried the flag of our Country to victory against the most gallant and determined foe, must ever be gratefully remembered, and all the guarantees given in their favor must be faithfully carried into execution.

That the public lands should be distributed as widely as possible among the people, and should be disposed of either under the pre-emption of homestead lands or sold in reasonable quantities, and to none but actual occupants, at the minimum price established by the Government. When grants of public lands, may be allowed, necessary for the encouragement of important public improvements, the proceeds of the sale of such lands, and not the lands themselves, should be so applied.

That the President of the United States, Andrew Johnson, in exercising the power of his high office in resisting the aggressions of Congress upon the constitutional rights of the States and the people, is entitled to the gratitude of the whole American people; and, on behalf of the Democratic party, we tender him our thanks for his patriotic efforts in that regard.

Upon this platform, the Democratic party appeal to every patriot, including all the conservative element and all who desire to support the Constitution and restore the Union, forgetting all past differences of opinion, to unite with us in the present great struggle for the liberties of the people; and that to all such, to whatever party they may have heretofore belonged, we extend the right hand of fellowship, and hail all such, co-operating with us, as friends and brethren.

Resolved, That this convention sympathizes cordially with the working men of the United States in their efforts to protect the rights and interests of the laboring classes of the Country.

Resolved, That the thanks of the convention are tendered to Chief Justice Salmon P. Chase, for the justice, dignity, and impartiality with which he presided over the court of impeachment on the trial of President Andrew Johnson.

1872.—Labor Reform Platform.
Columbus, February, 21.

We hold that all political power is inherent in the people, and free government founded on their authority and established for their benefit; that all citizens are equal in political rights, entitled to the largest religious and political liberty compatible with the good order of society, as also the use and enjoyment of the fruits of their labor and talents; and no man or set of men is entitled to exclusive separable endowments and privileges or immunities from the Government, but in consideration of public services, and any laws destructive of these fundamental principles are without moral binding force, and should be repealed. And believing that all the evils resulting from unjust legislation now affecting the industrial classes can be removed by the adoption of the principles contained in the following declaration: therefore,

Resolved, That it is the duty of the Government to establish a just standard of distribution of capital and labor, by providing a purely national circulating medium, based on the faith and resources of the Nation, issued directly to the people without the intervention of any system of banking corporations, which money shall be legal tender in the payment of all debts, public and private and interchangeable, at the option of the holder, for government bonds bearing a rate of interest not to exceed 3.65 per cent., subject to future legislation by Congress.

2. That the national debt should be paid in good faith, according to the original contract, at the earliest option of the Government, without mortgaging the property of the people or the future exigencies of labor to enrich a few capitalists at home and abroad.

·3. That justice demands that the burdens of Government should be so adjusted as to bear equally on all classes, and the exemption from taxation of government bonds bearing extravagant rates of interest, is a violation of all just principles of revenue laws.

4. That the Public lands of the United States belong to the people, and should not be sold to individuals nor granted to corporations but should be held as a sacred trust for the benefit of the people, and should be granted to landless settlers only, in amounts not exceeding one hundred and sixty acres of land.

5. That Congress should modify the tariff so as to admit free such articles of common use as we can neither produce nor grow, and lay duties for revenue mainly upon articles of luxury and upon such articles of manufacture as will, we having the raw materials, assist in further developing the resources of the Country.

6. That the presence in our Country of Chinese laborers; imported by capitalists in large numbers for servile use is an evil entailing want and its attendant train of misery and crime on all classes of American people, and should be prohibited by legislation.

7. That we ask for the enactment of a law by which all mechanics and day-laborers employed by, or on behalf of the Government, whether directly or indirectly, through persons, firms, or corporations, contracting with the State shall conform to the reduced standard of eight hours a day, recently adopted by Congress for National employés; and also for an amendment to the acts of incorporation for cities and towns, by which all laborers and mechanics employed at their expense shall conform to the same number of hours.

8. That the enlightened spirit of the age de-

mands the abolition of the system of contract labor in our prisons and other reformatory institutions.

9. That the protection of life, liberty, and property are the three cardinal principles of government, and the first two are more sacred than the latter; therefore, money needed for prosecuting wars, should, as it is required, be assessed and collected from the wealthy of the Country, and not entailed as a burden on posterity.

10. That it is the duty of the Government to exercise its power over railroads and telegraph corporations, that they shall not in any case be privileged to exact such rates of freight, transportation, or charges, by whatever name, as may bear unduly or unequally on the producer or consumer.

11. That there should be such a reform in the civil service of the National Government as will remove it beyond all partisan influence and place it in the charge and under the direction of intelligent and competent business men.

12. That as both history and experience teach us that power ever seeks to perpetuate itself by every and all means, and that its prolonged possession in the hands of one person is always dangerous to the interests of a free people, and believing that the spirit of our organic laws, and stability and safety of our free institutions are best obeyed on the one hand, and secured on the other, by a regular constitutional change in the chief of the Country at each election; therefore, we are in favor of limiting the occupancy of the Presidential chair to one term.

13. That we are in favor of granting general amnesty and restoring the Union at once on the basis of equality of rights and privileges to all, the impartial administration of justice being the only true bond of union to bind the States together and restore the government of the people.

14. That we demand the subjection of the military to the civil authorities, and the confinement of its operations to national purposes alone.

15. That we deem it expedient for Congress to supervise the patent laws so as to give labor more fully the benefit of its own ideas and inventions.

16. That fitness, and not political or personal considerations, should be the only recommendation to public office, either appointive or elective; and any and all laws looking to the establishment of this principle are heartily approved.

1872.—Prohibition Platform.
Columbus, Ohio, February 22.

The preamble recites that protection and allegiance are reciprocal duties; and every citizen who yields obediently to the full commands of Government should be protected in all the enjoyment of personal security, personal liberty, and private property. That the traffic in intoxicating drinks greatly impairs the personal security and personal liberties of a great mass of citizens, and renders private property insecure. That all political parties are hopelessly unwilling to adopt an adequate policy on this question: therefore, as a National Convention, we adopt the following declaration of principles:

That while we acknowledge the true patriotism and profound statesmanship of those patriots who laid the foundation of this Government, securing at once the rights of the States severally in their inseparable union by the federal constitution, we would not merely garnish the sepulchres of our republican fathers, but we do hereby renew our pledges of solemn fealty to the imperishable principles of civil and religious liberty embodied in the Declaration of Independence and our Federal Constitution.

That the traffic in intoxicating beverages is a dishonor to Christian civilization, a political wrong of unequalled enormity, subversive of ordinary objects of government, not capable of being regulated or restrained by any system of license whatever, and imperatively demands, for its suppression, effective legal prohibition, both by State and National legislation.

That there can be no greater peril to a nation than existing party competition for the liquor vote. That any party not opposed to the traffic, experience shows will engage in this competition—will court the favor of criminal classes-will barter away the public morals, the purity of the ballot, and every object of good government, for party success.

That, as prohibitionists, we will individually use all efforts to persuade men from the use of intoxicating liquors; and we invite all persons to assist in this movement.

That competence, honesty, and sobriety are indispensable qualifications for holding office.

That removals from public office for mere political differences of opinion are wrong.

That fixed and moderate salaries of public officers should take the place of fees and perquisites; and that all means should be taken to prevent corruption and encourage economy.

That the President and Vice President should be elected directly by the people.

That we are in favor of a sound National currency, adequate to the demands of business, and convertible into gold and silver at the will of the holder, and the adoption of every measure compatible with justice and public safety to appreciate our present currency to the gold standard.

That the rates of ocean and inland postage, and railroad telegraph lines and water transportation, should be made as low as possible by law.

That we are opposed to all discrimination in favor of capital against labor, as well as all monopoly and class legislation.

That the removal of the burdens imposed in the traffic of intoxicating drinks will emancipate labor, and will practically promote labor reform.

That suffrage should be granted to all persons, without regard to sex.

That the fostering and extension of common schools is a primary duty of the Government.

That a liberal policy should be pursued to promote foreign immigration.

1872.—Liberal Republican Platform.

Cincinnati, May 1.

We, the Liberal Republicans of the United States, in National Convention assembled at Cincinnati, proclaim the following principles as essential to just government.

1. We recognize the equality of all men before the law, and hold that it is the duty of Government, in its dealings with the people, to mete out equal and exact justice to all, of whatever nativity, race, color, or persuasion, religious or political.

2. We pledge ourselves to maintain the Union of these States, emancipation, and enfranchisement, and to oppose any reopening of the questions settled by the thirteenth, fourteenth, and fifteenth amendments of the Constitution.

3. We demand the immediate and absolute removal of all disabilities imposed on account of the Rebellion which was finally subdued seven years ago, believing that universal am-

nesty will result in complete pacification in all sections of the Country.

4. Local self-government, with impartial suffrage, will guard the rights of all citizens more securely than any centralized power. The public welfare requires the supremacy of the civil over the military authority, and the freedom of person under the protection of the *habeas corpus*. We demand for the individual the largest liberty consistent with public order, for the State self-government, and for the Nation a return to the methods of peace and the constitutional limitations of power.

5. The civil service of the Government has become a mere instrument of partisan tyranny and personal ambition, and an object of selfish greed. It is a scandal and reproach upon free institutions, and breeds a demoralization dangerous to the perpetuity of republican government. We, therefore, regard a thorough reform of the civil service as one of the most pressing necessities of the hour; that honesty, capacity, and fidelity constitute the only valid claims to public employment; that the offices of the Government cease to be a matter of arbitrary favoritism and patronage, and that public station shall become again a post of honor. To this end, it is imperatively required that no President shall be a candidate for re-election.

6. We demand a system of federal taxation which shall not unnecessarily interfere with the industry of the people, and which shall provide the means necessary to pay the expenses of the Government, economically administered, the pensions, the interest on the public debt, and a moderate reduction annually of the principal thereof; and recognizing that there are in our midst honest but irreconcilable differences of opinion with regard to the respective systems of protection and free trade, we remit the discussion of the subject to the people in their Congressional districts and the decision of Congress thereon, wholly free from Executive interference or dictation.

7. The public credit must be sacredly maintained, and we denounce repudiation in every form and guise.

8. A speedy return to specie payment is demanded alike by the highest considerations of commercial morality and honest government.

9. We remember with gratitude the heroism and sacrifices of the soldiers and sailors of the Republic; and no act of ours shall ever detract from their justly earned fame or the full rewards of their patriotism.

10. We are opposed to all further grants of lands to railroads or other corporations. The public domain should be held sacred to actual settlers.

11. We hold that it is the duty of the Government, in its intercourse with foreign nations, to cultivate the friendships of peace, by treating all on fair and equal terms, regarding it alike dishonorable either to demand what is not right or submit to what is wrong.

12. For the promotion and success of these vital principles and the support of the candidates nominated by this Convention, we invite and cordially welcome the co-operation of all patriotic citizens, without regard to previous political affiliations.

1872.--Democratic Platform.

Baltimore, July 9.

We, the Democratic electors of the United States, in convention assembled, do present the following principles, already adopted at Cincinnati, as essential to just government:

[Here followed the "Liberal Republican Platform;" which see above.]

1872.—Republican Platform.

Philadelphia, June 5.

The Republican party of the United States, assembled in National Convention in the city of Philadelphia, on the 5th and 6th days of June, 1872; again declares its faith, appeals to its history, and announces its position upon the questions before the country:

1. During eleven years of supremacy it has accepted, with grand courage, the solemn duties of the time. It suppressed a gigantic rebellion, emancipated four millions of slaves, decreed the equal citizenship of all, and established universal suffrage. Exhibiting unparalleled magnanimity, it criminally punished no man for political offences, and warmly welcomed all who proved their loyalty by obeying the laws and dealing justly with their neighbors. It has steadily decreased, with firm hand, the resultant disorders of a great war, and initiated a wise and humane policy toward the Indians. The Pacific railroad and other similar vast enterprises have been generously aided and successfully conducted, the public lands freely given to actual settlers, immigration protected and encouraged, and a full acknowledgment of the naturalized citizen's rights secured from European powers. A uniform National currency has been provided, repudiation frowned down, the National credit sustained under the most extraordinary burdens, and new bonds negotiated at lower rates. The revenues have been carefully collected and honestly applied. Despite annual large reductions of the rates of taxation, the public debt has been reduced during General Grant's presidency at the rate of a hundred millions a year, great financial crises have been avoided, and peace and plenty prevail throughout the land. Menacing foreign difficulties have been peacefully and honorably compromised, and the honor and power of the Nation kept in high respect throughout the world. This glorious record of the past is the party's best pledge for the future. We believe the people will not intrust the Government to any party or combination of men composed chiefly of those who have resisted every step of this beneficent progress.

2. The recent amendments to the National Constitution should be cordially sustained because they are right, not merely tolerated because they are law, and should be carried out according to their spirit by appropriate legislation, the enforcement of which can safely be intrusted only to the party that secured these amendments.

3. Complete liberty and exact equality in the enjoyment of all civil, political, and public rights should be established and effectually maintained throughout the Union by efficient and appropriate State and Federal legislation. Neither the law nor its administration should admit any discrimination in respect to citizens by reason of race, creed, color, or previous condition of servitude.

4. The National Government should seek to maintain honorable peace with all nations, protecting its citizens everywhere, and sympathizing with all peoples who strive for greater liberty.

5. Any system of civil service under which the subordinate positions of the Government are considered rewards for mere party zeal is fatally demoralizing; and we, therefore favor a reform of the system, by laws which shall abolish the evils of patronage, and make honesty, efficiency, and fidelity the essential qualifications for public positions, without practically creating a life tenure of office.

6. We are opposed to further grants of the public lands to corporations and monopolies, and demand that the National domain be set apart for free homes for the people.

7. The annual revenue, after paying current expenditures, pensions, and the interest on the public debt, should furnish a moderate balance for the reduction of the principal; and

that revenue, except so much as may be derived from a tax upon tobacco and liquors, should be raised by duties upon importations, the details of which should be so adjusted as to aid in securing remunerative wages to labor, and promote the industries, prosperity, and growth of the whole Country.

8. We hold in undying honor the soldiers and sailors whose valor saved the Union. Their pensions are a sacred debt of the Nation, and the widows and orphans of those who died for their country are entitled to the care of a generous and grateful people. We favor such additional legislation as will extend the bounty of the Government to all our soldiers and sailors who were honorably discharged, and who in the line of duty became disabled, without regard to the length of service or the cause of such discharge.

9. The doctrine of Great Britain and other European powers concerning allegiance—"once a subject always a subject"—having at last, through the efforts of the Republican party, been abandoned, and the American idea of the individual's right to transfer allegiance having been accepted by European nations, it is the duty of our Government to guard with jealous care the rights of adopted citizens against the assumption of unauthorized claims by their former governments, and we urge continued careful encouragement and protection of voluntary immigration.

10. The franking privilege ought to be abolished, and a way prepared for a speedy reduction in the rates of postage.

11. Among the questions which press for attention is that which concerns the relations of capital and labor; and the Republican party recognizes the duty of so shaping legislation as to secure full protection and the amplest field for capital, and for labor, the creator of capital, the largest opportunities and a just share of the mutual profits of these two great servants of civilization.

12. We hold that Congress and the President have only fulfilled an imperative duty in their measures for the suppression of violence and treasonable organizations in certain lately rebellious regions, and for the protection of the ballot-box; and, therefore, they are entitled to the thanks of the Nation.

13. We denounce repudiation of the public debt, in any form or disguise, as a National crime. We witness with pride the reduction of the principal of the debt, and of the rates of interest upon the balance, and confidently expect that our excellent National currency will be perfected by a speedy resumption of specie payment.

14. The Republican party is mindful of its obligations to the loyal women of America for their noble devotion to the cause of freedom. Their admission to wider fields of usefulness is viewed with satisfaction; and the honest demand of any class of citizens for additional rights should be treated with respectful consideration.

15. We heartily approve the action of Congress in extending amnesty to those lately in rebellion, and rejoice in the growth of peace and fraternal feeling throughout the land.

16. The Republican party proposes to respect the rights reserved by the people to themselves as carefully as the powers delegated by them to the States and to the Federal Government. It disapproves of the resort to unconstitutional laws for the purpose of removing evils, by interference with rights not surrendered by the people to either the State or the National Government.

17. It is the duty of the General Government to adopt such measures as may tend to encourage and restore American commerce and shipbuilding.

18. We believe that the modest patriotism,

the earnest purpose, the sound judgment, the practical wisdom, the incorruptible integrity, and the illustrious services of Ulysses S. Grant have commended him to the heart of the American People; and with him at our head, we start to-day upon a new march to victory.

19. Henry Wilson, nominated for the Vice-Presidency, known to the whole land from the early days of the great struggle for liberty as an indefatigable laborer in all campaigns, an incorruptible legislator and representative man of American institutions, is worthy to associate with our great leader and share the honors which we pledge our best efforts to bestow upon them.

1872.—Democratic (Straight-out) Platform.

Louisville, Kentucky, September 3.

Whereas, A frequent recurrence to first principles and eternal vigilance against abuses are the wisest provisions for liberty, which is the source of progress, and fidelity to our constitutional system is the only protection for either: therefore,

Resolved, That the original basis of our whole political structure is consent in every part thereof. The people of each State voluntarily created their State, and the States voluntarily formed the Union; and each State provided by its written constitution for everything a State could do for the protection of life, liberty, and property within it; and each State, jointly with the others, provided a federal union for foreign and inter-state relations.

Resolved, That all governmental powers, whether State or Federal, are trust powers coming from the people of each State, and that they are limited to the written letter of the Constitution and the laws passed in pursuance of it; which powers must be exercised in the utmost good faith, the Constitution itself stating in what manner they may be altered and amended.

Resolved, That the interests of labor and capital should not be permitted to conflict, but should be harmonized by judicious legislation. While such a conflict continues, labor, which is the parent of wealth, is entitled to paramount consideration.

Resolved, That we proclaim to the world that principle is to be preferred to power; that the Democratic party is held together by the cohesion of time honored principles, which they will never surrender in exchange for all the offices which Presidents can confer. The pangs of the minorities are doubtless excruciating; but we welcome an eternal minority, under the banner inscribed with our principles, rather than an almighty and everlasting majority, purchased by their abandonment.

Resolved, That having been betrayed at Baltimore into a false creed and a false leadership by the Convention, we repudiate both, and appeal to the people to approve our platform, and to rally to the polls and support the true platform and the candidates who embody it.

1875.—The American National Platform.

Adopted in Mass Meeting, Pittsburg, June 9.

We hold:

1. That ours is a Christian and not a heathen nation, and that the God of the Christian Scriptures is the author of civil government.

2. That God requires and man needs a Sabbath.

3. That the prohibition of the importation, manufacture, and sale of intoxicating drinks

as a beverage, is the true policy on the temperance question.

4. The charters of all secret lodges granted by our Federal and State legislatures should be withdrawn, and their oaths prohibited by law.

5. That the civil equality secured to all American citizens by articles 13th, 14th, and 15th of our amended constitution should be preserved inviolate.

6. That arbitration of differences with nations is the most direct and sure method of securing and perpetuating a permanent peace.

7. That to cultivate the intellect without improving the morals of men is to make mere adepts and experts: therefore, the Bible should be associated with books of science and literature in all our educational institutions.

8. That land and other monopolies should be discountenanced.

9. That the Government should furnish the people with an ample and sound currency and a return to specie payment, as soon as practicable.

10. That the maintenance of the public credit, protection to all loyal citizens, and justice to Indians are essential to the honor and safety of our Nation.

11. And, finally, we demand for the American people the abolition of electoral colleges, and a direct vote for President and Vice-President of the United States.

[Their Candidates were James B. Walker, Wheaton, Illinois, for President; and Donald Kirkpatrick, Syracuse, New York, for Vice-President.]

1876.—Prohibition Reform Platform.

Cleveland, Ohio, May 17.

The Prohibition Reform party of the United States, organized in the name of the people, to revive, enforce, and perpetuate in the Government the doctrines of the Declaration of Independence, submit, in this centennial year of the republic, for the suffrages of all good citizens, the following platform of National reforms and measures:

First. The legal prohibition in the District of Columbia, the territories, and in every other place subject to the laws of Congress, of the importation, exportation, manufacture, and traffic of all alcoholic beverages, as high crimes against society; an amendment of the National Constitution, to render these prohibitory measures universal and permanent; and the adoption of treaty stipulations with foreign powers, to prevent the importation and exportation of all alcoholic beverages.

Second. The abolition of class legislation and of special privileges in the Government, and the adoption of equal suffrage and eligibility to office, without distinction of race, religious creed, property, or sex.

Third. The appropriation of the public lands, in limited quantities, to actual settlers only; the reduction of the rates of inland and ocean postage; of telegraphic communication; of railroad and water transportation and travel, to the lowest practical point, by force of laws, wisely and justly framed, with reference, not only to the interest of capital employed, but to the higher claims of the general good.

Fourth. The suppression, by laws, of lotteries and gambling in gold, stocks, produce, and every form of money and property, and the penal inhibition of the use of the public mails for advertising schemes of gambling and lotteries.

Fifth. The abolition of those foul enormities, polygamy and the social evil; and the protection of purity, peace, and happiness of homes, by ample and efficient legislation.

Sixth. The National observance of the Christian Sabbath, established by laws prohibiting ordinary labor and business in all departments of public service and private employment (works of necessity, charity, and religion excepted) on that day.

Seventh. The establishment, by mandatory provisions in National and State constitutions, and by all necessary legislation, of a system of free public schools, for the universal and forced education of all the youth of the land.

Eighth. The free use of the Bible, not as a ground of religious creeds, but as a text-book of the purest morality, the best liberty, and the noblest literature in our public schools, that our children may grow up in its light, and that its spirit and principles may pervade our Nation.

Ninth. The separation of the Government in all its departments and institutions, including the public schools and all funds for their maintenance, from the control of every religious sect or other association, and the protection alike of all sects by equal laws, with entire freedom of religious faith and worship.

Tenth. The introduction into all treaties hereafter negotiated with foreign governments of a provision for the amicable settlement of international difficulties by arbitration.

Eleventh. The abolition of all barbarous modes and instruments of punishment; the recognition of the laws of God and the claims of humanity in the discipline of jails and prisons, and of that higher and wiser civilization worthy of our age and Nation, which regards the reform of criminals as a means for the prevention of crime.

Twelfth. The abolition of executive and legislative patronage, and the election of President, Vice-President, United States Senators, and of all civil officers, so far as practicable, by the direct vote of the people.

Thirteenth. The practice of a friendly and liberal policy to immigrants from all nations, the guaranty to them of ample protection, and of equal rights and privileges.

Fourteenth. The separation of the money of Government from all banking institutions. The National Government, only, should exercise the high prerogative of issuing paper money, and that should be subject to prompt redemption on demand, in gold and silver, the only equal standards of value recognized by the civilized world.

Fifteenth. The reduction of the salaries of public officers in a just ratio with the decline of wages and market prices; the abolition of sinecures, unnecessary offices, and official fees and perquisites; the practice of strict economy in government expenses; and a free and thorough investigation into any and all alleged abuses of public trusts.

1876.—Independent (Greenback) Platform.

Indianapolis, Ind., May 17.

The Independent party is called into existence by the necessities of the people, whose industries are prostrated, whose labor is deprived of its just reward by a ruinous policy which the Republican and Democratic parties refuse to change; and, in view of the failure of these parties to furnish relief to the depressed industries of the Country, thereby disappointing the just hopes and expectations of the suffering people, we declare our principles, and invite all independent and patriotic men to join our ranks in this movement for financial reform and industrial emancipation.

First. We demand the immediate and unconditional repeal of the specie resumption act of January, 14, 1875, and the rescue of our industries from ruin and disaster resulting from its enforcement; and we call upon all patriotic men to organize in every congressional district of the Country, with a view of electing representatives to Congress who will carry out the wishes of the people in this regard and stop the present suicidal and destructive policy of contraction.

Second. We believe that a United States note, issued directly by the Government, and convertible, on demand, into United States obligations, bearing a rate of interest not exceeding one cent a day on each one hundred dollars, and exchangeable for United States notes at par, will afford the best circulating medium ever devised. Such United States notes should be full legal tenders for all purposes, except for the payment of such obligations as are, by existing contracts, especially made payable in coin; and we hold that it is the duty of the Government to provide such a circulating medium, and insist, in the language of Thomas Jefferson, that "bank paper must be suppressed, and the circulation restored to the Nation, to whom it belongs."

Third. It is the paramount duty of the Government, in all its legislation, to keep in view the full development of all legitimate business, agricultural, mining, manufacturing, and commercial.

Fourth. We most earnestly protest against any further issue of gold bonds for sale in foreign markets, by which we would be made, for a long period, "hewers of wood and drawers of water," to foreigners especially as the American people would gladly and promptly take at par all bonds the Government may need to sell, provided they are made payable at the option of the holder, and bearing interest at 3,65 per cent. per annum or even a lower rate.

Fifth. We further protest against the sale of government bonds for the purpose of purchasing silver to be used as a substitute for our more convenient and less fluctuating fractional currency, which, although well calculated to enrich owners of silver mines, yet in operation it will still further oppress, in taxation, an already overburdened people.

1876.—Republican Platform.

Cincinnati, Ohio, June 14.

When, in the economy of Providence, this land was to be purged of human slavery, and when the strength of the Government of the people, by the people, and for the people, was to be demonstrated, the Republican party came into power. Its deeds have passed into history, and we look back to them with pride. Incited by their memories to high aims for the good of our Country and mankind, and looking to the future with unfaltering courage, hope, and purpose, we, the representatives of the party, in National Convention assembled, make the following declaration of principles:

1. The United States of America is a Nation, not a league. By the combined workings of the National and State governments, under their respective constitutions, the rights of every citizen are secured, at home and abroad, and the common welfare promoted.

2. The Republican party has preserved these governments to the hundredth anniversary of the Nation's birth, and they are now embodiments of the great truths spoken at its cradle—"That all men are created equal; that they are endowed by their Creator with certain inalienable rights, among which are life, liberty, and the pursuit of happiness; that for the attainment of these ends governments have been instituted among men, deriving their just powers from the consent of the governed." Until these truths are cheerfully obeyed, or, if need be, vigorously enforced, the work of the Republican party is unfinished.

3. The permanent pacification of the southern section of the Union, and the complete

protection of all its citizens in the free enjoyment of all their rights, is a duty to which the Republican party stands sacredly pledged. The power to provide for the enforcement of the principles embodied in the recent constitutional amendments is vested, by those amendments, in the Congress of the United States; and we declare it to be the solemn obligation of the Legislative and Executive departments of the Government to put into immediate and vigorous exercise all their constitutional powers for removing any just causes of discontent on the part of any class, and for securing to every American citizen complete liberty and exact equality in the exercise of all civil, political, and public rights. To this end we imperatively demand a Congress and a Chief Executive whose courage and fidelity to these duties shall not falter until these results are placed beyond dispute or recall.

4. In the first act of Congress signed by President Grant, the National Government assumed to remove any doubt of its purpose to discharge all just obligations to the public creditors, and "solemnly pledged its faith to make provision at the earliest practicable period for the redemption of the United States notes in coin." Commercial prosperity, public morals, and National credit demand that this promise be fulfilled by a continuous and steady progress to specie payment.

5. Under the Constitution, the President and heads of departments are to make nominations for office, the Senate is to advise and consent to appointments, and the House of Representatives is to accuse and prosecute faithless officers. The best interests of the public service demand that these distinctions be respected; that Senators and Representatives who may be judges and accusers should not dictate appointments to office. The invariable rule in appointments should have reference to the honesty, fidelity, and capacity of the appointees, giving to the party in power those places where harmony and vigor of administration require its policy to be represented, but permitting all others to be filled by persons selected with sole reference to the efficiency of the public service, and the right of all citizens to share in the honor of rendering faithful service to the Country.

6. We rejoice in the quickened conscience of the people concerning political affairs, and will hold all public officers to a rigid responsibility, and engage that the prosecution and punishment of all who betray official trusts shall be swift, thorough, and unsparing.

7. The public school system of the several States is the bulwark of the American Republic; and, with a view to its security and permanence, we recommend an amendment to the Constitution of the United States, forbidding the application of any public funds or property for the benefit of any schools or institutions under sectarian control.

8. The revenue necessary for current expenditures, and the obligations of the public debt, must be largely derived from duties upon importations, which, so far as possible, should be adjusted to promote the interests of American labor and advance the prosperity of the whole Country.

9. We reaffirm our opposition to further grants of public lands to corporations and monopolies, and demand that the National domain be devoted to free homes for the people.

10. It is the imperative duty of the Government, so to modify existing treaties with European governments, that the same protection shall be afforded to the adopted American citizen that is given to the native-born; and that all necessary laws should be passed to protect emigrants in the absence of power in the States for that purpose.

11. It is the immediate duty of Congress to fully investigate the effect of the immigration

and importation of Mongolians upon the moral and material interests of the Country.

12. The Republican party recognizes, with approval, the substantial advances recently made towards the establishment of equal rights for women by the many important amendments effected by Republican legislatures in the laws which concern the personal and property relations of wives, mothers, and widows, and by the appointment and election of women to the superintendence of education, charities and other public trusts. The honest demands of this class of citizens for additional rights, privileges, and immunities, should be treated with respectful consideration.

13. The Constitution confers upon Congress sovereign power over the Territories of the United States for their government; and in the exercise of this power it is the right and duty of Congress to prohibit and extirpate, in the territories, that relic of barbarism—polygamy; and we demand such legislation as shall secure this end and the supremacy of American institutions in all the Territories.

14. The pledges which the Nation has given to her soldiers and sailors must be fulfilled, and a grateful people will always hold those who imperiled their lives for the Country's preservation in the kindest remembrance.

15. We sincerely deprecate all sectional feeling and tendencies. We, therefore, note with deep solicitude that the Democratic party counts, as its chief hope of success, upon the electoral vote of a united South, secured through the efforts of those who were recently arrayed against the Nation; and we invoke the earnest attention of the Country to the grave truth that a success thus achieved would reopen sectional strife, and imperil National honor and human rights.

16. We charge the Democratic party with being the same in character and spirit as when it sympathized with treason; with making its control of the House of Representatives the triumph and opportunity of the Nation's recent foes; with reasserting and applauding, in the National capital, the sentiments of unrepentant rebellion; with sending Union soldiers to the rear, and promoting Confederate soldiers to the front; with deliberately proposing to repudiate the plighted faith of the Government; with being equally false and imbecile upon the overshadowing financial questions; with thwarting the ends of justice by its partisan mismanagement and obstruction of investigation; with proving itself through the period of its ascendency in the lower House of Congress, utterly incompetent to administer the government; and we warn the Country against trusting a party thus alike unworthy, recreant, and incapable.

17. The National administration merits commendation for its honorable work in the management of domestic and foreign affairs, and President Grant deserves the continued hearty gratitude of the American people for his patriotism and his eminent services in war and in peace.

18. We present, as our candidates for President and Vice President of the United States, two distinguished statesmen, of eminent ability and character, and conspicuously fitted for those high offices, and we confidently appeal to the American people to intrust the administration of their public affairs to Rutherford B. Hayes and William A. Wheeler.

1876.—Democratic Platform.
St. Louis Mo., June 27.

We, the delegates of the Democratic party of the United States, in National convention assembled, do hereby declare the administration of the Federal Government to be in urgent need of immediate reform: do hereby enjoin upon the nominees of this convention, and of the Democratic party in each State, a zealous effort and co-operation to this end; and do hereby appeal to our fellow-citizens of every former political connection to undertake with us, this first and most pressing patriotic duty.

For the Democracy of the whole Country, we do here reaffirm our faith in the permanence of the Federal Union, our devotion to the Constitution of the United States, with its amendments universally accepted as a final settlement of the controversies that engendered civil war, and do here record our steadfast confidence in the perpetuity of republican self-government.

In absolute acquiescence in the will of the majority—the vital principle of republics; in the supremacy of the civil over the military authority; in the total separation of church and state, for the sake alike of civil and religious freedom; in the equality of all citizens before just laws of their own enactment; in the liberty of individual conduct, unvexed by sumptuary laws; in the faithful education of the rising generation, that they may preserve, enjoy, and transmit these best conditions of human happiness and hope—we behold the noblest product of a hundred years of changeful history; but while upholding the bond of our Union and great charter of these our rights, it behooves a free people to practice also that eternal vigilance which is the price of liberty.

Reform is necessary to rebuild and establish in the hearts of the whole people the Union, eleven years ago happily rescued from the danger of a secession of States, but now to be saved from a corrupt centralism which, after inflicting upon ten States the rapacity of carpet-bag tyranny, has honey-combed the offices of the Federal Government itself, with incapacity, waste and fraud; infected States and municipalities with the contagion of misrule; and locked fast the prosperity of an industrious people in the paralysis of "hard times."

Reform is necessary to establish a sound currency, restore the public credit, and maintain the National honor.

We denounce the failure, for all these eleven years of peace, to make good the promise of the legal tender notes, which are a changing standard of value in the hands of the people, and the non-payment of which is a disregard of the plighted faith of the Nation.

We denounce the improvidence which, in eleven years of peace, has taken from the people, in Federal taxes, thirteen times the whole amount of the legal-tender notes, and squandered four times their sum in useless expense without accumulating any reserve for their redemption.

We denounce the financial imbecility and immorality of that party which, during eleven years of peace, has made no advance toward resumption, no preparation for resumption, but, instead, has obstructed resumption, by wasting our resources and exhausting all our surplus income; and, while annually professing to intend a speedy return to specie payments, has annually enacted fresh hinderances thereto. As such hinderance we denounce the resumption clause of 1875, and we do demand its repeal.

We demand a judicious system of preparation, by public economies, by official retrenchments, and by wise finance, which shall enable the Nation soon to assure the whole world of its perfect ability and of its perfect readiness to meet any of its promises at the call of the creditor entitled to payment. We believe such a system, well devised, and, above all, intrusted to competent hands for execution, creating, at no time, an artificial scarcity of currency, and at no time alarming the public mind into a withdrawal of the vaster machinery of credit by which ninety-five per cent. of all business transactions are performed.

A system open, public, and inspiring general confidence, would, from the day of its adoption, bring healing on its wings to all our harassed industries—set in motion the wheels of commerce, manufactures, and the mechanic arts—restore employment to labor—and, renew, in all its natural sources, the prosperity of the people.

Reform is necessary in the sum and modes of Federal taxation, to the end that capital may be set free from distrust and labor lightly burdened.

We denounce the present tariff, levied upon nearly four thousand articles, as a masterpiece of injustice, inequality, and false pretense. It yields a dwindling, not a yearly rising revenue. It has impoverished many industries to subsidize a few. It prohibits imports that might purchase the products of American labor. It has degraded American commerce from the first to an inferior rank on the high seas. It has cut down the sales of American manufactures at home and abroad, and depleted the returns of American agriculture—an industry followed by half our people. It costs the people five times more than it produces to the treasury, obstructs the processes of production, and wastes the fruits of labor. It promotes fraud, fosters smuggling, enriches dishonest officials, and bankrupts honest merchants. We demand that all custom house taxation shall be only for revenue.

Reform is necessary in the scale of public expense—Federal, State and municipal. Our Federal taxation has swollen from sixty millions gold, in 1860, to four hundred and fifty millions currency, in 1870; our aggregate taxation from one hundred and fifty-four millions gold, in 1860, to seven hundred and thirty millions currency, in 1870—or, in one decade, from less than five dollars per head to more than eighteen dollars per head. Since the peace, the people have paid to their tax-gatherers more than thrice the sum of the National debt, and more than twice that sum for the Federal Government alone. We demand a rigorous frugality in every department and from every officer of the Government.

Reform is necessary to put a stop to the profligate waste of public lands, and their diversion from actual settlers, by the party in power, which has squandered 200,000,000 of acres upon railroads alone, and, out of more than thrice that aggregate, has disposed of less than one-sixth directly to tillers of the soil.

Reform is necessary to correct the omission of a Republican Congress, and the errors of our treaties and our diplomacy which have stripped our fellow-citizens of foreign birth and kindred race, recrossing the Atlantic, of the shield of American citizenship, and have exposed our brethren of the Pacific coast to the incursions of a race not sprung from the same great parent stock, and in fact now, by law, denied citizenship through naturalization, as being neither accustomed to the traditions of a progressive civilization nor exercised in liberty under equal laws. We denounce the policy which thus discards the liberty-loving German and tolerates a revival of the coolie trade in Mongolian women, imported for immoral purposes, and Mongolian men, held to perform servile labor contracts and demand such modifications of the treaty with the Chinese Empire, or such legislation within constitutional limitations, as shall prevent further importation or immigration of the Mongolian race.

Reform is necessary, and can never be effected but by making it the controlling issue of the elections, and lifting it above the two false issues with which the officeholding class and the party in power seek to smother it.

1. The false issue with which they would enkindle sectarian strife in respect to the public schools, of which the establishment and support belongs exclusively to the several

states, and which the Democratic party has cherished from their foundation, and is resolved to maintain, without prejudice or preference for any class, sect, or creed, and without largesses from the treasury to any.

2. The false issue by which they seek to light anew the dying embers of sectional hate between kindred peoples once estranged, but now reunited in one indivisbile Republic and a common destiny.

Reform is necessary in the civil service. Experience proves that efficient, economical conduct of the governmental business is not possible if its civil service be subject to change at every election, be a prize fought for at the ballot-box, be a brief reward of party zeal, instead of posts of honor assigned for proved competency, and held for fidelity in public employ; that the dispensing of patronage should neither be a tax upon the time of all our public men, nor the instrument of their ambition. Here, again, promises, falsified in the performance, attest that the party in power can work out no practical or salutary reform.

Reform is necessary, even more, in the higher grades of the public service. President, Vice-President, Judges, Senators, Representatives, Cabinet officers—these, and all others in authority—are the people's servants. Their offices are not a private perquisite; they are a public trust. When the annals of this Republic show the disgrace and censure of a Vice-President; a late Speaker of the House of Representatives marketing his rulings as a presiding officer; three Senators profiting secretly by their votes as law-makers; five chairmen of the leading committees of the late House of Representatives exposed in jobbery; a late Secretary of the Treasury forcing balances in public accounts; a late Attorney-General misappropriating public funds; a Secretary of the Navy enriched, or enriching friends, by percentages levied off the profits of contrators with his department; an Ambassador to England concerned in a dishonorable speculation; the President's private secretary barely escaping conviction upon the trial for guilty complicity in frauds upon the revenue; a Secretary of War impeached for high crimes and misdemeanors—the demonstration is complete, that the first step in reform must be the people's choice of honest men from another party, lest the disease of one political organization infect the body politic, and lest by making no change of men or parties we get no change of measures and no real reform.

All these abuses, wrongs and crimes—the product of sixteen years' ascendency of the Republican party—create a necessity for reform, confessed by the Republicans themselves; but their reformers are voted down in convention and displaced from the cabinet. The party's mass of honest voters is powerless to resist the 80,000 office-holders, its leaders and guides.

Reform can only be had by a peaceful civic revolution. We demand a change of system, a change of administration, a change of parties, that we may have a change of measures and of men.

Resolved, That this convention, representing the Democratic party of the United States, do cordially endorse the action of the present House of Representatives, in reducing and curtailing the expenses of the Federal Government, in cutting down salaries and extravagant appropriations, and in abolishing useless offices and places not required by the public necessities; and we shall trust to the firmness of the Democratic members of the House that no committee of conference and no misinterpretation of the rules will be allowed to defeat these wholesome measures of economy demanded by the Country.

Resolved, That the soldiers and sailors of the Republic, and the widows and orphans of those who have fallen in battle, have a just claim upon the care, protection, and gratitude of their fellow-citizens.

1878.—National Platform.
Toledo, Ohio, February 22.

Whereas, Throughout our entire country the value of real estate is depreciated, industry paralyzed, trade depressed, business incomes and wages reduced, unparalleled distress inflicted upon the poorer and middle ranks of our people, the land filled with fraud, embezzlement, bankruptcy, crime, suffering, pauperism, and starvation; and

Whereas, This state of things has been brought about by legislation in the interest of, and dictated by, money-lenders, bankers and bondholders; and

Whereas, While we recognize the fact that the men in Congress connected with the old political parties have stood up manfully for the rights of the people, and met the threats of the money power, and the ridicule of an ignorant and subsidized press, yet neither the Republican nor the Democratic parties, in their policies, propose remedies for the existing evils; and

Whereas, The Independent Greenback party, and other associations more or less effective, have been unable, hitherto, to make a formidable opposition to old party organizations; and

Whereas, The limiting of the legal-tender quality of the greenbacks, the changing of currency bonds into coin bonds, the demonetization of the silver dollar, the exempting of bonds from taxation, the contraction of the circulating medium, the proposed forced resumption of specie payments, and the prodigal waste of the public lands, were crimes against the people; and, as far as possible, the results of these criminal acts must be counteracted by judicious legislation:

Therefore, We assemble in National Convention and make a declaration of our principles, and invite all patriotic citizens to unite in an effort to secure financial reform and industrial emancipation. The organization shall be known as the "National Party," and under this same we will perfect, without delay, National, State, and local associations, to secure the election to office of such men only as will pledge themselves to do all in their power to establish these principles:

First, It is the exclusive function of the General Government to coin and create money and regulate its value. All bank issues designed to circulate as money should be suppressed. The circulating medium, whether of metal or paper, shall be issued by the Government, and made a full legal tender for all debts, duties, and taxes in the United States, at its stamped value.

Second, There shall be no privileged class of creditors. Official salaries, pensions, bonds, and all other debts and obligations, public and private, shall be discharged in the legal-tender money of the United States strictly according to the stipulations of the laws under which they were contracted.

Third, The coinage of silver shall be placed on the same footing as that of gold.

Fourth. Congress shall provide said money adequate to the full employment of labor, the equitable distribution of its products, and the requirement of business, fixing a minimum amount *per capita* of the population as near as may be, and otherwise regulating its value by wise and equitable provisions of law, so that the rate of interest will secure to labor its just reward.

Fifth. It is inconsistent with the genius of

popular government that any species of private property should be exempt from bearing its proper share of the public burdens. Government bonds and money should be taxed precisely as other property, and a graduated income tax should be levied for the support of the Government and the payment of its debts.

Sixth. Public lands are the common property of the whole people, and should not be sold to speculators nor granted to railroads or other corporations, but should be donated to actual settlers, in limited quantities.

Seventh. The Government should, by general enactments, encourage the development of our agricultural, mineral, mechanical, manufacturing, and commercial resources, to the end that labor may be fully and profitably employed; but no monopolies should be legalized.

Eighth. All useless offices should be abolished, the most rigid economy favored in every branch of the public service, and severe punishment inflicted upon officers who betray the trusts reposed in them.

Ninth. As educated labor has devised means for multiplying productions by inventions and discoveries, and as their use requires the exercise of mind as well as body, such legislation should be had that the number of hours of daily toil will be reduced, giving the working classes more leisure for mental improvement and their several enjoyments, and saving them from premature decay and death.

Tenth. The adoption of an American monetary system, as proposed herein, will harmonize all differences with regard to tariff and federal taxation, reduced and equalize the cost of transportation by land and water, distribute equitably the joint earnings of capital and labor, secure to the producers of wealth the results of their labor and skill, and muster out of service the vast army of idlers, who, under the existing system, grow rich upon the earnings of others, that every man and woman may, by their own efforts, secure a competency, so that overgrown fortunes and extreme poverty will be seldom found within the limits of our Republic.

Eleventh. Both National and State Governments should establish bureaus of labor and industrial statistics, clothed with the power of gathering and publishing the same.

Twelfth. That the contract system of employing labor in our prisons and reformatory institutions works great injustice to our mechanics and artisans, and should be prohibited.

Thirteenth. The importation of servile labor into the United States from China is a problem of the most serious importance, and we recommend legislation looking to its suppression.

Fourteenth. We believe in the supremacy of law over and above all perishable material, and in the necessity of a party of united people that will rise above old party lines and prejudices. We will not affiliate in any degree with any of the old parties, but, in all cases and localities, will organize anew, as united National men—nominate for office and official positions only such persons as are clearly believers in and identified with this our sacred cause; and irrespective of creed, color, place of birth, or past condition of political or other servitude, vote only for men who entirely abandon old party lines and organizations.

1879.—National Liberal Platform.
Cincinnati, Ohio, September 14.

1. Total separation of Church and State, to be guaranteed by amendment of the United States Constitution; including the equitable taxation of church property, secularization of the public schools, abrogation of Sabbatarian laws, abolition of chaplaincies, prohibition of

public appropriations for religious purposes, and all measures necessary to the same general end.

2. National protection for National citizens in their equal civil, political, and religious rights to be guaranteed by amendment of the United States Constitution and afforded through the United States courts.

3. Universal education, the basis of universal suffrage in this secular Republic, to be guaranteed by amendment of the United States Constitution, requiring every state to maintain a thoroughly secularized public school system, and to permit no child within its limits to grow up without a good elementary education.

1880.—Independent Republican Principles.

I Independent Republicans adhere to the Republican principles of National supremacy, sound finances, and civil service reform, expressed in the Republican platform of 1876, in the letter of acceptance of President Hayes, and in his message of 1879; and they seek the realization of those principles in practical laws and their efficient administration. This requires,

1. The continuance on the statute-book of laws protecting the rights of voters at National elections. But National supremacy affords no pretext for interference with the local rights of communities; and the development of the South from its present defective civilization can be secured only under constitutional methods, such as those of President Hayes.

2. The passage of laws which shall deprive greenbacks of their legal-tender quality, as a first step toward their ultimate withdrawal and cancellation, and shall maintain all coins made legal-tender at such weight and fineness as will enable them to be used without discount in the commercial transactions of the world.

3. The repeal of the act, which limits the terms of office of certain Government officials to four years; the repeal of the tenure-of-office acts, which limit the power of the Executive to remove for cause; the establishment of a permanent civil service commission, or equivalent measures to ascertain, by open competition, and certify to the President or other appointing power the fitness of applicants for nomination or appointment to all non-political offices.

11. Independent Republicans believe that local issues should be independent of party. The words Republican and Democrat should have no weight in determining whether a school or city shall be administered on business principles by capable men. With a view to this, legislation is asked which shall prescribe for the voting for local and for state officers upon separate ballots.

111. Independent Republicans assert that a political party is a co-operation of voters to secure the practical enactment into legislation of political convictions set forth as its platform. Every voter accepting that platform is a member of that party; any representative of that party opposing the principles or evading the promises of its platform forfeits the support of its voters. No voter should be held by the action or nomination of any caucus or convention of his party against his private judgment. It is his duty to vote against bad measures and unfit men, as the only means of obtaining good ones; if his party no longer represents its professed principles in its practical workings, it is his duty to vote against it.

IV. Independent Republicans seek good nominations through participation in the primaries and through the defeat of bad nominees; they will labor for the defeat of any local Republican candidate, and, in co-operation with those holding like views elsewhere, for the defeat of any general Republican candidate whom they do not deem fit.

1880. Republican Platform.
Chicago, Illinois, June 2.

The Republican party, in National convention assembled, at the end of twenty years since the Federal Government was first committed to its charge, submits to the people of the United States its brief report of its administration:

It suppressed a rebellion which had armed nearly a million of men to subvert the National authority. It reconstructed the Union of the States with freedom, instead of slavery, as its corner-stone. It transformed four million of human beings from the likeness of things to the rank of citizens. It relieved Congress from the infamous work of hunting fugitive slaves and charged it to see that slavery does not exist.

It has raised the value of our paper currency from thirty-eight per cent. to the par of gold. It has restored, upon a solid basis, payment in coin for all the National obligations, and has given us a currency absolutely good and equal in every part of our extended Country. It has lifted the credit of the Nation from the point where six per cent. bonds sold at eighty-six to that where four per cent. bonds are eagerly sought as a premium.

Under its administration railways have increased from 31,000 miles in 1860, to more than 82,000 miles in 1879.

Our foreign trade has increased from $700,000,000 to $1,150,000,000 in the same time; and our exports, which were $20,000,000 less than our imports in 1860, were $264,000,000 more than our imports in 1879.

Without resorting to loans, it has, since the war closed, defrayed the ordinary expenses of the Government, besides the accruing interest on the public debt, and disbursed, annually, over $30,000,000 for soldiers' pensions. It has paid $888,000,000 of the public debt, and, by refunding the balance at lower rates, has reduced the annual interest charge from nearly $151,000,000 to less than $89,000,000.

All the industries of the Country have revived, labor is in demand, wages have increased and throughout the entire country there is evidence of a coming prosperity greater than we have ever enjoyed.

Upon this record, the Republican party asks for the continued confidence and support of the people; and this convention submits for their approval the following statement of the principles and purposes which will continue to guide and inspire its efforts;

1. We affirm that the work of the last twenty years has been such as to commend itself to the favor of the Nation, and that the fruits of the costly victories which we have achieved, through immense difficulties, should be preserved; that the peace we regained should be cherished; that the dissevered Union, now happily restored, should be perpetuated, and that the liberties secured to this generation should be transmitted, undiminished, to future generations; that the order established and the credit acquired should never be impaired; that the pensions promised should be paid; that the debt so much reduced should be extinguished by the full payment of every dollar thereof; that the reviving industries should be further promoted; and that the commerce, already so great, should be steadily encouraged.

2. The Constitution of the United States is a supreme law, and not a mere contract; out of Confederate States it made a sovereign Nation. Some powers are denied to the Nation, while

others are denied to States; but the boundary between the powers delegated and those reserved is to be determined by the National and not the State tribunals.

3. The work of popular education is one left to the care of the several States, but it is the duty of the National Government to aid that work to the extent of its constitutional ability. The intelligence of the Nation is but the aggregate of the intelligence in the several States; and the destiny of the Nation must be guided, not by the genius of any one State, but by the average genius of all.

4. The Constitution wisely forbids Congress to make any law respecting an establishment of religion; but it is idle to hope that the Nation can be protected against the influence of sectarianism while each State is exposed to its domination. We, therefore, recommend that the Constitution be so amended as to lay the same prohibition upon the legislature of each State, to forbid the appropriation of public funds to the support of sectarian schools.

5. We reaffirm the belief, avowed in 1876, that the duties levied for the purpose of revenue should so discriminate as to favor American labor; that no further grant of the public domain should be made to any railways or other corporation; that slavery having perished in the States, its twin barbarity—polygamy—must die in the territories; that everywhere the protection accorded to citizens of American birth must be secured to citizens by American adoption. That we esteem it the duty of Congress to develop and improve our water-courses and harbors, but insist that further subsidies to private persons or corporations must cease. That the obligations of the Republic to the men who preserved its integrity in the day of battle are undiminished by the lapse of fifteen years since their final victory—to do them perpetual honor is, and shall forever be, the grateful privilege and sacred duty of the American people.

6. Since the authority to regulate immigration and intercourse between the United States and foreign nations rests with the Congress of the United States and its treaty-making powers, the Republican party, regarding the unrestricted immigration of the Chinese as an evil of great magnitude, invoke the exercise of that power to restrain and limit that immigration by the enactment of such just, humane, and reasonable provisions as will produce that result.

7. That the purity and patriotism which characterized the early career of Rutherford B. Hayes in peace and war, and which guided the thoughts of our immediate predecessors to select him as a presidential candidate, have continued to inspire him in his career as Chief Executive, and that history will accord to his administration the honors which are due to an efficient, just, and courteous discharge of the public business, and will honor his interposition between the people and proposed partisan laws.

8. We charge upon the Democratic party the habitual sacrifice of patriotism and justice to a supreme and insatiable lust for office and patronage. That to obtain possession of the National and State Governments, and the control of place and position, they have obstructed all efforts to promote the purity and to conserve the freedom of suffrage; have devised fraudulent certifications and returns; have labored to unseat lawfully-elected members of Congress, to secure, at all hazards, the vote of the majority of the States in the House of Representatives; have endeavored to occupy, by force and fraud the places of trust given to others by the people of Maine, and rescued by the courageous action of Maine's patriotic sons; have, by methods vicious in principle and tyrannical in practice, attached partisan legislation to appropriation bills, upon whose

passage the very movements of Government depend; have crushed the rights of the individual; have advocated the principle and sought the favor of rebellion against the Nation, and have endeavored to obliterate the sacred memories of the war, and to overcome its inestimably valuable results of nationalty, personal freedom, and individual equality. Equal, steady, and complete enforcement of the laws, and protection of all our citizens in the enjoyment of all the privileges and immunities guaranteed by the Constitution, are the first duties of the Nation. The danger of a solid South can only be averted by the faithful performance of every promise which the Nation made to the citizen. The execution of the laws, and the punishment of all those who violate them, are the only safe methods by which an enduring peace can be secured, and genuine prosperity established throughout the South. Whatever promises the Nation makes, the Nation must perform; and the Nation can not with safety relegate this duty to the States. The solid South must be divided by the peaceful agencies of the ballot, and all opinions must there find free expression; and to this end honest voters must be protected against terrorism, violence, or fraud. And we affirm it to be the duty and the purpose of the Republican party to use all legitimate means to restore all the States of this Union to the most perfect harmony which may be practicable; and we submit to the practical, sensible people of the United States to say whether it would not be dangerous to the dearest interests of our Country, at this time to surrender the administration of the National Government to a party which seeks to overthrow the existing policy, under which we are so prosperous, and thus bring distrust and confusion where there are now order, confidence, and hope.

9. The Republican party, adhering to a principle affirmed by the last National Convention, of respect for the Constitutional rule covering appointments to office, adopts the declaration of President Hayes, that the reform of the civil service should be thorough, radical and complete. To this end we demand the co-operation of the Legislative and Executive departments of the Government, and that Congress shall so legislate that fitness, ascertained by proper practical tests, shall admit to the public service; and that the power of removal for cause, with due responsibility for the good conduct of subordinates, shall accompany the power of appointment.

National (Greenback) Platform.

Chicago, Illinois, June 9.

The Civil Government should guarantee the divine right of every laborer to the results of his toil, thus enabling the producers of wealth to provide themselves with the means for physical comfort, and facilities for mental, social, and moral culture; and we condemn, as unworthy of our civilization, the barbarism which imposes upon wealth-producers a state of drudgery as the price of a bare animal existence. Notwithstanding the enormous increase of wealth, the task of the laborer is scarcely lightened, the hours of toil are but little shortened, and few producers are lifted from poverty into comfort and pecuniary independence. The associated monopolies, the international syndicates, and other income classes demand dear money, cheap labor, and a strong Government, and, hence, a weak people. Corporate control of the volume of money has been the means of dividing society into hostile classes, of an unjust distribution of the products of labor, and of building up monopolies of associated capital, endowed with power to confiscate private property. It has kept money scarce; and the scarcity of money enforces debt-trade, and public and corporate loans;

debt engenders usury, and usury ends in the bankruptcy of the borrower. Other results are —deranged markets, uncertainty in manufacturing enterprises and agriculture, precarious and intermittent employment for the laborer, industrial war, increasing pauperism and crime, and the consequent intimidation and disfranchisement of the producer, and a rapid declension into corporate feudalism. Therefore we declare—

First. That the right to make and issue money is a sovereign power, to be maintained by the people for their common benefit. The delegation of this right to corporations is a surrender of the central attribute of sovereignty void of Constitutional sanction, and conferring upon a subordinate and irresponsible power an absolute dominion over industry and commerce. All money, whether metallic or paper, should be issued, and its volume controlled, by the Government, and not by or through banking corporations; and, when so issued, should be a full legal tender for all debts, public and private.

Second. That the bonds of the United States should not be refunded, but paid as rapidly as practicable, according to contract. To enable the Government to meet these obligations, legal tender currency should be substituted for the notes of the National banks, the National banking system abolished, and the unlimited coinage of silver, as well as gold, established by law.

Third. That labor should be so protected by National and State authority as to equalize its burdens and insure a just distribution of its results. The eight hour law of Congress should be enforced, the sanitary condition of industrial establishments placed under its rigid control, the competition of contract convict labor abolished, a bureau of labor statistics established, factories, mines, and workshops inspected, the employment of children under fourteen years of age forbidden, and wages paid in cash.

Fourth. Slavery being simply cheap labor, and cheap labor being simply slavery, the importation and presence of Chinese serfs necessarily tend to brutalize and degrade American labor; therefore immediate steps should be taken to abrogate the Burlingame treaty.

Fifth. Railroad land grants forfeited by reason of non-fulfillment of contract should be immediately reclaimed by the Government and, henceforth, the public domain reserved exclusively as homes for actual settlers.

Sixth. It is the duty of Congress to regulate inter-state commerce. All lines of communication and transportation should be brought under such legislative control as shall secure moderate, fair, and uniform rates for passenger and freight traffic.

Seventh. We denounce as destructive to property and dangerous to liberty the action of the old parties in fostering and sustaining gigantic land, railroad, and money corporations, and monopolies invested with and exercising powers belonging to the Government, and yet not responsible to it for the manner of their exercise.

Eighth. That the Constitution, in giving Congress the power to borrow money, to declare war, to raise and support armies, to provide and maintain a navy, never intended that the men who loaned their money for an interest-consideration should be preferred to the soldiers and sailors who imperiled their lives and shed their blood on land and sea in defense of their Country; and we condemn the cruel class legislation of the Republican party, which, while professing great gratitude to the soldier, has most unjustly discriminated against him and in favor of the bondholder.

Ninth. All property should bear its just proportion of taxation, and we demand a graduated income tax.

Tenth. We denounce as dangerous the efforts everywhere manifest to restrict the right of suffrage.

Eleventh. We are opposed to an increase of the standing army in time of peace, and the insidious scheme to establish an enormous military power under the guise of militia laws.

Twelfth. We demand absolute democratic rules for the Government of Congress, placing all representatives of the people upon an equal footing, and taking away from the committees a veto power greater than that of the President.

Thirteenth. We demand a Government of the people, by the people, and for the people instead of a Government of the bondholder, by the bondholder, and for the bondholder; and we denounce every attempt to stir up sectional strife as an effort to conceal monstrous crimes against the people.

Fourteenth. In the furtherance of these ends we ask the co-operation of all fair-minded people. We have no quarrel with individuals, wage no war on classes, but only against vicious institutions. We are not content to endure further discipline from our present actual rulers, who, having dominion over money, over transportation, over land and labor, over the press and the machinery of the Government, wield unwarrantable power over our institutions and over life and property.

1880.—Prohibition Reform Platform.
Cleveland, Ohio, June 17.

The prohibition Reform party of the United States, organized, in the name of the people, to revive, enforce, and perpetuate in the Government, the doctrines of the Declaration of Independence, submit, for the suffrage of all good citizens, the following platform of National reforms and measures:

In the examination and discussion of the temperance question, it has been proven, and is an accepted truth, that alchoholic drinks, whether fermented, brewed, or distilled, are poisonous to the healthy human body, the drinking of which is not only needless but hurtful, necessarily tending to form intemperate habits, increasing greatly the number, severity, and fatal termination of diseases, weakening and deranging the intellect, polluting the affections, hardening the heart and corrupting the morals, depriving many of reason and still more of its heathful exercise, and annually bringing down large numbers to untimely graves, producing, in the children of many who drink, a predisposition to intemperance, insanity, and various bodily and mental diseases, causing diminution of strength, feebleness of vision, fickleness of purpose, and premature old age, and inducing, in all future generations, detorioration of moral and physical character. Alcoholic drinks are thus the implacable foe of man as an individual.

First. The legalized importation, manufacture, and sale of intoxicating drinks minister to their use, and teach the erroneous and destructive sentiment that such use is right, thus tending to produce and perpetuate the above mentioned evils.

Second. To the home it is an enemy—proving itself to be a disturber and destroyer of its peace, prosperity, and happiness; taking from it the earnings of the husband; depriving the dependent wife and children of essential food clothing, and education; bringing into it profanity, abuse and violence; setting at naught the vows of the marriage altar; breaking up the family and sundering the children from the parents, and thus destroying one of the most beneficent institutions of our Creator, and removing the sure foundation of good Government, National prosperity, and welfare.

Third. To the community it is equally an enemy—producing vice, demoralization, and wickedness; its places of sale being resorts of gaming, lewdness, and debauchery, and the hiding place of those who prey upon society; counteracting the efficacy of religious effort, and of all means of intellectual elevation, moral purity, social happiness, and the eternal good of mankind, without rendering any counteracting or compensating benefits: being in its influence and effect evil and only evil, and that continually.

Fourth. To the State it is equally an enemy—legislative inquiries, judicial investigations, and official reports of all penal, reformatory, and dependent institutions, showing that the manufacture and sale of such beverages is the promoting cause of intemperance, crime, and pauperism and of demands upon the public and private charity, imposing the larger part of taxation, paralyzing thrift, industry, manufactures, and commercial life; which, but for it, would be unnecessary; disturbing the peace of streets and highways; filling prisons and poor-houses; corrupting politics, legislation, and the execution of the laws; shortening lives; diminishing health, industry, and productive power in manufactures and art; and is manifestly unjust as well as injurious to the community upon which it is imposed, and is contrary to all just views of civil liberty, as well as a violation of the fundamental maxim of our common law, to use your own property or liberty so as not to injure others.

Fifth. It is neither right nor politic for the State to afford legal protection to any traffic or any system which tends to waste the resources, to corrupt the social habits, and to destroy the health and lives of the people; that the importation, manufacture, and sale of intoxicating beverages is proven to be inimical to the true interests of the individual home, community, and state, and destructive to the order and welfare of society, and ought, therefore, to be classed among crimes to be prohibited.

Sixth. In this time of profound peace at home and abroad, the entire separation of the General Government from the drink-traffic, and its prohibition in the District of Columbia, territories, and in all places and ways over which, under the Constitution, Congress has control and power, is a political issue of the first importance to the peace and prosperity of the Nation. There can be no stable peace and protection to personal liberty, life, and property, until secured by National or State constitutional provisions, enforced by adequate laws.

Seventh. All legitimate industries require deliverance from the taxation and loss which the liquor traffic imposes upon them; and financial or other legislation could not accomplish so much to increase production and cause a demand for labor, and, as a result, for the comforts of living, as the suppression of this traffic would bring to thousands of homes as one of its blessings.

Eighth. The administration of the Government and the execution of the laws are through political parties; and we arraign the Republican party, which has been in continuous power in the Nation for twenty years, as being false to duty, as false to loudly-proclaimed principles of equal justice to all and special favors to none, and of protection to the weak and dependent, insensible to the mischief which the trade in liquor has constantly inflicted upon industry, trade, commerce, and the social happiness of the people; that 5,652 distilleries, 3,830 breweries, and 175,266 places for the sale of these poisonous liquors, involving an annual waste to the Nation of one million five hundred thousand dollars, and the sacrifice of one hundred thousand lives, have, under its legislation, grown up and been fostered as a legitimate source of revenue; that during its history, six Territories have been organized and five States been admitted into the Union, with constitutions provided and approved by Congress, but the prohibition of this debasing and destructive traffic has not been provided, nor even the people given, at the time of admission, power to forbid it in any one of them. Its history further shows, that not in a single instance has an original prohibitory law been passed by any State that was controlled by it, while in four States, so governed, the laws found on its advent to power have been repealed. At its National convention in 1872, it declared, as part of its party faith, that "it disapproves of the resort to unconstitutional laws for the purpose of removing evils, by interference with rights not surrendered by the people to either the State or National Government," which, the author of this plank says, was adopted by the platform committee with the full and implicit understanding that its purpose was the discountenancing of all so-called temperance, prohibitory, and Sunday laws.

Ninth. We arraign, also, the Democratic party as unfaithful and unworthy of reliance on this question; for, although not clothed with power, but occupying the relation of an opposition party during twenty years past, strong in numbers and organization, it has allied itself with liquor-traffickers, and become, in all the States of the Union, their special political defenders, and its National convention in 1876, as an article of its political faith, declared against prohibition and just laws in restraint of the trade in drink, by saying it was opposed to what it was pleased to call "all sumptuary laws." The National party has been dumb on this question.

Tenth. Drink-traffickers, having the history and experience of all ages, climes, and conditions of men, declaring their business destructive of all good—finding no support in the Bible, morals, or reason—appeal to misapplied law for their justification, and intrench themselves behind the evil elements of political party for defense, party tactics and party inertia become battling forces, protecting this evil.

Eleventh. In view of the foregoing facts and history, we cordially invite all voters, without regard to former party affiliations, to unite with us in the use of the ballot for the abolition of the drinking system, under the authority of our National and State Governments. We also demand, as a right, that women, having the privileges of citizens in other respects, be clothed with the ballot for their protection, and as a rightful means for the proper settlement of the liquor question.

Twelfth. To remove the apprehension of some who allege that a loss of public revenue would follow the suppression of the direct trade, we confidently point to the experience of governments abroad and at home, which shows that thrift and revenue from the consumption of legitimate manufactures and commerce have so largely followed the abolition of drink as to fully supply all loss of liquor taxes.

Thirteenth. We recognize the good providence of Almighty God, who has preserved and prospered us as a Nation; and, asking for His Spirit to guide us to ultimate success, we all look for it, relying upon His omnipotent arm.

1880.—Democratic Platform,
Cincinnati, Ohio, June 22.

The Democrats of the United States, in convention assembled, declare:

First. We pledge ourselves anew to the Constitutional doctrines and traditions of the Democratic party, as illustrated by the teachings and examples of a long line of Democratic statesmen and patriots, and embodied in the platform of the last National Convention of the party.

Second. Opposition to centralization, and to the dangerous spirit of encroachment which tends to consolidate the powers of all the departments in one, and thus to create, whatever the form of government, a real despotism; no sumptuary laws; separation of the church and state for the good of each; common schools fostered and protected.

Third. Home rule; honest money, consisting of gold and silver, and paper, convertible into coin on demand; the strict maintenance of the public faith, State and National; and a tariff for revenue only; the subordination of the military to the civil power; and a general and thorough reform of the civil service.

Fourth. The right to a free ballot is a right preservative of all rights; and must and shall be maintained in every part of the United States.

Fifth. The existing administration is the representative of conspiracy only; and its claim of right to surround the ballot boxes with troops and deputy marshals, to intimidate and obstruct the elections, and the unprecedented use of the veto to maintain its corrupt and despotic power, insults the people and imperils their institutions. We execrate the course of this administration in making places in the civil service a reward for political crime; and demand a reform by statute, which shall make it forever impossible for a defeated candidate to bribe his way to the seat of a usurper by billeting villains upon the people.

Sixth. The great fraud of 1876—7, by which, upon a false count of the electoral votes of two States, the candidate defeated at the polls was declared to be President, and, for the first time in American history, the will of the people was set aside under a threat of military violence, struck a deadly blow at our system of Representative Government. The Democratic party, to preserve the Country from the horrors of civil war, submitted for the time, in the firm and patriotic belief that the people would punish the crime in 1880. This issue precedes and dwarfs every other. It imposes a more sacred duty upon the people of the Union than ever addressed the consciences of a Nation of freemen.

Seventh. The resolution of Samuel J. Tilden, not again to be a candidate for the exalted place to which he was elected by a majority of his countrymen, and from which he was excluded by the leaders of the Republican party, is received by the Democrats of the United States with deep sensibility; and they declare their confidence in his wisdom, patriotism, and integrity unshaken by the assaults of the common enemy; and they further assure him that he is followed into the retirement he has chosen for himself by the sympathy and respect of his fellow-citizens, who regard him as one who, by elevating the standard of the public morality, and adorning and purifying the public service, merits the lasting gratitude of his Country and his party.

Eighth. Free ships, and a living chance for American commerce upon the seas; and on the land, no discrimination in favor of transportation lines, corporations, or monopolies.

Ninth. Amendments of the Burlingame treaty; no more Chinese immigration, except for travel, education, and foreign commerce, and, therein, carefully guarded.

Tenth. Public money and public credit for public purposes solely, and public land for actual settlers.

Eleventh. The Democratic party is the friend of labor and the laboring man, and pledges itself to protect him alike against the cormorants and the commune.

Twelfth. We congratulate the Country upon the honesty and thrift of a Democratic Congress, which has reduced the public expenditure $10,000,000 a year; upon the continuation of prosperity at home and the National honor abroad; and, above all, upon the promise of such a change in the administration of the Government as shall insure a genuine and lasting reform in every department of the public service.

Virginia Republican.

[*Adopted August 11.*]

Whereas, It is proper that when the people assemble in Convention they should avow distinctly the principles of Government on which they stand; now, therefore, be it,

Resolved, That we, the Republicans of Virginia, hereby make a declaration of our allegiance and adhesion to the principles of the Republican party of the Country, and our determination to stand squarely by the organization of the Republican party of Virginia, always defending it against the assaults of all persons or parties whatsoever.

Second. That amongst the principles of the Republican party none is of more vital importance to the welfare and interest of the Country in all its parts than that which pertains to the sancity of Government contracts. It therefore becomes the special duty and province of the Republican party of Virginia to guard and protect the credit of our time-honored State, which has been besmirched with repudiation, or received with distrust, by the gross mismanagement of various factions of the Democratic party, which have controlled the legislation of the State.

Third. That the Republican party of Virginia hereby pledges itself to redeem the State from the discredit that now hangs over her, in regard to her just obligations for money loaned her for constructing her internal improvements and charitable institutions, which, permeating every quarter of the State, bring benefits of far greater value than their cost to our whole people, and we in the most solemn form pledge the Republican party of the State to the full payment of the whole debt of the State, less the one-third set aside as justly falling on West Virginia; that the industries of the Country should be fostered through protective laws, so as to develop our own resources, employ our own labor, create a home market, enhance values, and promote the happiness and prosperity of the people.

Fourth. That the public school system of Virginia is the creature of the Republican party, and we demand that every dollar the Constitution dedicates to it shall be sacredly applied thereto as a means of educating the children of the State, without regard to condition or race.

Fifth. That the elective franchise as an equal right should be based on manhood qualification, and that we favor the repeal of the requirements of the prepayment of the capitation tax as a prerequisite to the franchise as opposed to the Constitution of the United States, and in violation of the condition whereby the State was readmitted as a member of our Constitutional Union, as well as against the spirit of the Constitution; but demand the imposition of the capitation tax as a source of revenue for the support of the public schools without its disfranchising effects.

Sixth. That we favor the repeal of the disqualification for the elective franchise by a conviction of petty larceny, and of the infamous laws which place it in the power of a single justice of the peace (oft times being more corrupt than the criminal before him) to disfranchise his fellow-man.

Seventh. Finally, that we urge the repeal of the barbarous law permitting the imposition of stripes as degrading and inhuman, contrary to the genius of a true and enlightened people, and a relic of barbarism.

[The Convention considered it inexpedient to nominate candidates for State officers.]

Virginia Readjuster.

[Adopted June 2]

First. We recognize our obligation to support the institutions for the deaf, dumb, and blind, the lunatic asylums, the public free schools and the Government out of the revenues of the State, and we do deprecate and denounce that policy of bad rule and subordinate sovereignty which for years borrowed money out of the banks at high rates of interest for the discharge of these government trusts, while our revenues were set this year of commercial exchanges available to the state only at the option of speculators and syndicates.

Second. We reassert our purpose to settle and adjust our State obligations on the principles of the "Bill to re-establish public credit, known as the "Riddleberger bill," passed by the last General Assembly and vetoed by the Governor. We maintain that this measure recognizes the just debt of Virginia in that it assumes two-thirds of all the money Virginia borrowed, and sets aside the other third to West Virginia to be dealt with by her on her own way and at her own pleasure; that it gives those of her creditors who have reserved but six per cent. instalments of interest in other years upon an exact equality with those who by certain schemes were installed in the seven and eight per cent. classes of payment; that it agrees to pay such rate of interest on our securities as our will certainly be met out of the revenues of the State, and that it includes all the essential features of equity.

Third. We reassert our allegiance to the Constitutional requirements for the equal and uniform taxation of property, exempting none except that required by law for schools and civil or library for religious, charitable and educational purposes.

Fourth. We reassert that the paramount allegiance of the citizens owes all officers and government is to the people of the State by whose authority they were created, by whose money they were maintained and by whose trust they live, and it is enjoined upon our Representatives and Executive officers to enforce the discharge of that duty; to insure to our people such rules, decisions and concessions as will protect every industry and interest against discrimination; tend to the development of our agricultural and mineral resources, encourage the investment of private capital in manufactures; and the profitable employment of labor in industrial enterprises, grasp for our city and our whole State those advantages to which by their geographical position they are entitled and fulfil all the great public ends for which they were designed.

Fifth. The Readjusters hold the right to a free ballot to be the right preservative of all rights, and that it should be maintained in every State in the Union. We believe the expression has resulted from the suffrage in Virginia to be in conflict with the Fifteenth Amendment to the Constitution of the United States. We believe that it is a violation of that condition of reconstruction wherein the pledge was given not so to amend our State Constitution as to deprive any citizen or class of citizens of a right to vote except as punishment for such crimes as are cited in former law. We believe such a construction of voting to be contrary to the purest and soundest the very foundations of which a representative as intended to institute. We know that it has been a failure as a means for the collection of revenue, the practical reason for its erection in 1876 and we know the bold demoralizing and dangerous use to which it has been prostituted. We know it contributes to the bribery of our citizens, and to corrupting the men who fill the oaths and to weaken the influence of the citizens probably expressed in general laws on tax.

legislation for the collection of this tax, dedicated by the Constitution to the public free schools, and to abolish it as a qualification for and restriction upon suffrage.

Sixth. The Readjusters congratulate the whole people of Virginia on the progress of the last few years in developing mineral resources and promoting manufacturing enterprises in the State, and they declare their purpose to aid these great and growing industries by all proper and essential legislation, State and Federal. To this end they will continue their efforts in behalf of more cordial and fraternal relations between the sections and States and especially for that concord and harmony which will make the Country to know how earnestly and sincerely Virginia invites all men into her borders as visitors or to become citizens without fear of social or political ostracism; that every man, from whatever section of the Country, shall enjoy the fullest freedom of thought, speech, politics, and religion, and that the State which first formulated these principles as fundamental in free Government is yet the citadel for their exercise and protection.

Virginia Democratic.

[*Adopted August 4.*]

The Conservative Democratic party of Virginia—Democratic in its Federal relations and Conservative in its State policy—assembled in convention, in view of the present condition of the Union and of this Commonwealth, for the clear and distinct assertion of its political principles, doth declare that we adopt the following articles of political faith:

First. Equality of right and exact justice to all men, special privileges to none; freedom of religion, freedom of the press, and freedom of the person under the protection of the habeas corpus; of trial by juries impartially selected, and of a pure, upright and non-partisan judiciary; elections by the people, free from force or fraud of citizens or of the military and civil officers of Government; and the selection for public offices of those who are honest and best fitted to fill them; the support of the State Governments in all their rights as the most competent administrations of our domestic concerns and the surest bulwarks against anti-republican tendencies; and the preservation of the General Government in its whole Constitutional vigor as the best sheet-anchor of our peace at home and our safety abroad.

Second. That the maintenance of the public credit of Virginia is an essential means to the promotion of her prosperity. We condemn repudiation in every shape and form as a blot upon her honor, a blow at her permanent welfare, and an obstacle to her progress in wealth, influence and power; and that we will make every effort to secure a settlement of the public debt, with the consent of her creditors, which is consistent with her honor and dictated by justice and sound public policy; that it is eminently desirable and proper that the several classes of the debt now existing should be unified, so that equality, which is equity, may control in the annual payment of interest and the ultimate redemption of the principal; that, with a view of securing such equality, we pledge our party to use all lawful authority to secure a settlement of the State debt so that there shall be but one class of the public debt; that we will use all lawful and Constitutional means in our power to secure a settlement of the State debt upon the basis of a 3 per cent. bond, and that the Conservative-Democratic party pledges itself, as a part of its policy, not to increase the present rate of taxation.

Third. That we will uphold, in its full Constitutional integrity and efficiency, our public-school system for the education of both white and colored children—a system inaugurated by the Constitution of the State and established by the action of the Conservative party years before it was required by the Constitution; and will take the most effectual means for the faithful execution of the same by applying to its support all the revenues set apart for that object by the Constitution or otherwise.

Fourth. Upon this declaration of principles we cordially invite the co-operation of all Conservative Democrats, whatever may have been or now are their views upon the public debt, in the election of the nominees of this Convention and in the maintenance of the supremacy of the Democratic party in this State.

Resolved, further, That any intimation, coming from any quarter, that the Conservative-Democratic party of Virginia has been, is now, or proposes to be, opposed to an honest ballot, and a fair count, is a calumny upon the State of Virginia as unfounded in fact as it is dishonorable to its authors.

That special efforts have been made to foster and encourage the agricultural, mechanical, mining, manufacturing, and other industrial interests of the State.

That, in common with all good citizens of the Union, we reflect with deep abhorrence upon the crime of the man who aimed a blow at the life of the eminent citizen who was called by the Constitutional voice of fifty millions of people to be the President of the United States; and we tender to him and to his friends the sympathy and respect of this Convention and of those we represent, in this great calamity, and our hearty desire for his complete restoration to health and return to the discharge of his important duties, for the welfare and honor of our common Country.

National Conventions.

Republican.	*Democrat.*
1856—Philadelphia.	1856—Cincinnati.
1860—Chicago.	1860—Charleston.
1864—Baltimore.	1864—Chicago.
1868—Chicago.	1868—New York.
1872—Philadelphia.	1872—Cincinnati.
1876—Cincinnati.	1876—St. Louis.
1880—Chicago.	1880—Cincinnati.
1884—Chicago.	1884—Chicago.
1888—Chicago.	1888—St. Louis.

RAILWAY CONSTRUCTION.

NEW LINES FOR 1887—1888.

The *Engineering News* says: The mileage of the new railway lines completed and under way in the States and Territories of the Rocky Mountain region and Pacific coast is summarized in the following table:

States.	Track laid 1886-1887.	In progress of construction.	Located and under way.	Projected.
Wyoming	131,115	...	95	...
Montana	16,616	157	85	150
Idaho	11,440	19	47	80
Washington	171,975	136	315	560
Oregon	4,345	161	245	400
California	274,377	598	715	546
Nevada	...	...	160	...
Utah	6	5	310	200
Colorado	43,948	39	638	865
New Mexico	3,583	71	294	...

1888.—Republican Platform.

Chicago, June 21st.

The Republicans of the United States, assembled by their delegates in National Convention, pause on the threshold of their proceedings to honor the memory of their first great leader, the immortal champion of liberty and the rights of the People—Abraham Lincoln; and to cover also with wreaths of imperishable remembrance and gratitude the heroic names of later leaders, who have been more recently called away from our councils—Grant, Garfield, Arthur, Logan, Conkling. May their memories be faithfully cherished.

We also recall with our greetings and with prayer for his recovery the name of one of our living heroes whose memory will be treasured in the history both of Republicans and of the Republic—the name of that noble soldier and favorite child of victory, Philip H. Sheridan.

In the spirit of those great leaders, and our own devotion to human liberty; and with that hostility to all forms of despotism and oppression which is the fundamental idea of the Republican party, we send fraternal congratulations to our fellow Americans of Brazil upon their great act of emancipation, which completed the abolition of slavery throughout the two American continents. We earnestly hope that we may soon congratulate our fellow-citizens of Irish birth upon the peaceful recovery of home rule for Ireland.

We affirm our unswerving devotion to the National Constitution and to the indissoluble Union of the States; to the autonomy reserved to the States under the Constitution; to the personal rights and liberties of citizens in all the States and Territories in the Union; and especially to the supreme and sovereign right of every lawful citizen, rich or poor, native or foreign born, white or black, to cast one free ballot in public elections, and to have that ballot duly counted. We hold a free and honest popular ballot, and the just and equal representation of all the People, to be the foundation of our Republican Government, and demand effective legislation to secure the integrity and purity of elections, which are the foundation of all public authority. We charge that the present Administration and the Democratic majority in Congress owe their existence to the suppression of the ballot by a criminal nullification of the Constitution and laws of the United States.

We are uncompromisingly in favor of the American system of protection. We protest against its destruction proposed by the President and his party. They serve the interests of Europe: we will support the interests of America. We accept the issue and confidently appeal to the People for their judgment. The protective system must be maintained. Its abandonment has always been followed by general disaster to all interests, except those of the usurer and the sheriff. We denounce the Mills bill as destructive to the general business, the labor and the farming interests of the Country, and we heartily indorse the consistent and patriotic actions of the Republican Representatives in Congress in opposing its passage.

We condemn the proposition of the Democratic party to place wool on the free list, and we insist that the duties thereon shall be adjusted and maintained so as to furnish full and adequate protection to that industry.

The Republican party would affect all needed reduction of the National revenue by repealing the taxes on tobacco, which are an annoyance and burden to agriculture, and the tax upon spirits used in the arts and for mechanical purposes; and by such revision of the tariff laws as will tend to check imports of such articles as are produced by our People, the production of which gives employment to our labor, and release from import duties those articles of foreign production (except luxuries) the like of which can not be produced at home. If there shall still remain a larger revenue than is requisite for the wants of the Government, we favor the entire repeal of internal taxes, rather than the surrender of any part of our protective system at the joint behest of the whisky trusts and the agents of foreign manufacturers.

We declare our hostility to the introduction into this Country of foreign contract labor, and of Chinese labor, alien to our civilization and our Constitution, and we demand the rigid enforcement of the existing laws against it, and favor such immediate Legislation as will exclude such labor from our shores.

We declare our opposition to all combinations of capital organized in trusts or otherwise, to control arbitrarily the condition of trade among our citizens; and we recommend to Congress, and the State Legislatures, in their respective jurisdictions, such Legislation as will prevent the execution of all schemes to oppress the People by undue charges on their supplies, or by unjust rates for the transportation of their products to market. We approve the Legislation by Congress to prevent alike unjust burdens and unfair discriminations between the States.

We reaffirm the policy of appropriating the public lands of the United States to be homesteads for American citizens and settlers, not aliens, which the Republican party established in 1862, against the persistent opposition of the Democrats in Congress, and which has brought our great Western domain into such magnificent development. The restoration of unearned land grants to the public domain for the use of actual settlers, which was begun under the Administration of President Arthur, should be continued. We deny that the Democratic party has ever restored one acre to the People, but declare that by the joint action of Republicans and Democrats about fifty million of acres of unearned lands originally granted for the construction of railroads have been restored to the public domain, in pursuance of the conditions inserted by the Republican party in the original grants. We charge the Democratic Administration with failure to execute the laws securing to settlers titles to their homesteads, and with using appropriations made for that purpose to harass the innocent settlers with spies and prosecutions under false pretense of exposing frauds and vindicating the law.

The Government by Congress of the Territories is based upon necessity only, to the end that they may become States in the Union; therefore, whenever the conditions of population, material resources, public intelligence and morality are such as to secure a stable local Government therein, the People of such Territories should be permitted, as a right inherent in them, to form for themselves constitutions and State Governments and be admitted into the Union. Pending the preparation for Statehood, all officers thereof should be selected from the bona fide residents and citizens of the Territory wherein they are to serve. South Dakota should of right be immediately admitted as a State in the Union, under the Constitution framed and adopted by the People, and we heartily indorse the action of the Republican Senate in twice passing bills for her admission. The refusal of the Democratic House of Representatives, for partisan purposes, to favorably consider these bills, is a willful violation of the sacred American principle of local self-government, and merits the condemnation of all just men. The pending bills in the Senate for acts to enable the People of Washington, North Dakota, and Montana Territories to form Constitutions and establish State Governments should be passed without unnecessary delay. The Republican party pledges itself to do all in its power to facilitate the admission of the Territories of New Mexico, Wyoming, Idaho, and Arizona to the enjoyment of self-government as States, such of them as are now qualified, as soon as possible, and the others as soon as they may become so.

The political power of the Mormon Church in the Territories, as exercised in the past, is a menace to free institutions too dangerous to be long suffered. Therefore, we pledge the Republican party to appropriate Legislation asserting the sovereignty of the Nation in all Territories where the same is questioned, and in furtherance of that end to place upon the statute books Legislation stringent enough to divorce the political from the ecclesiastical power, and thus stamp out the attendant wickedness of polygamy.

The Republican party is in favor of the use of both gold and silver as money, and condemns the policy of the Democratic Administration in its efforts to demonetize silver.

We demand the reduction of letter postage to one cent per ounce.

In a Republic like ours, where the citizen is the sovereign and the official the servant, where no power is exercised except by the will of the People, it is important that the sovereign—the People—should possess intelligence. The free school is the promoter of that intelligence which is to preserve us a free Nation; therefore, the State or Nation, or both combined, should support free institutions of learning, sufficient to afford to every child growing up in the land the opportunity of a good common school education.

We earnestly recommend that prompt action be taken by Congress in the enactment of such Legislation as will best secure the rehabilitation of our American Merchant Marine, and we protest against the passage by Congress of a free ship bill, as calculated to work injustice to labor by lessening the wages of those engaged in preparing the materials, as well as those directly employed in our ship-yards. We demand appropriations for the early rebuilding of our Navy; for the construction of coast fortifications and modern ordnance, and other approved modern means of defense for the protection of our defenseless harbors and cities; for the payment of just pensions to our soldiers; for necessary works of National importance in the improvement of harbors and channels of internal, coastwise, and foreign commerce; for the encouragement of the shipping interests of the Atlantic, Gulf, and Pacific States, as well as for the payment of the maturing public debt. This policy will give employment to our labor, activity to our various industries, increase the security of our Country, promote trade, open new and direct markets for our produce, and cheapen the cost of transportation. We affirm this to be far better for our Country than the Democratic policy of loaning the Government money without interest to "pet banks."

The conduct of foreign affairs by the present Administration has been distinguished by its inefficiency and its cowardice. Having withdrawn from the Senate all pending treaties effected by Republican Administration for the removal of foreign burdens and restrictions upon our commerce and for its extension into better markets, it has neither effected nor proposed any others in their stead. Professing adherence to the Monroe doctrine, it has seen with idle complacency the extension of foreign influence in Central America, and of foreign trade everywhere among our neighbors. It has refused to charter, sanction, or encourage any American organization for constructing the Nicaragua Canal, a work of vital importance to the maintenance of the Monroe doctrine, and of our National influence in Central and South America, and necessary for the development of trade with our Pacific Territory, with South America, and with the Islands and further coasts of the Pacific Ocean.

We arraign the present Democratic Administration for its weak and unpatriotic treatment of the fisheries question, and its pusillanimous surrender of the essential privileges to which our fishing vessels are entitled in Canadian ports under the treaty of 1818, the reciprocal maritime Legislation of 1830, and the comity of Nations, and which Canadian fishing vessels receive in the ports of the United States. We condemn the policy of the present Administration and the Democratic majority in Congress toward our fisheries as unfriendly, and conspicuously unpatriotic, and as tending to destroy a valuable National industry, and an indispensable resource of defense against a foreign enemy.

The name of American applies alike to all citizens of the Republic, and imposes upon all alike the same obligations of obedience to the laws. At the same time that citizenship is and must be the panoply and safeguard of him who wears it, and protect him, whether high or low, rich or poor, in his civil rights. It should and must afford him protection at home, and follow and protect him abroad in whatever land he may be on a lawful errand.

The men who abandoned the Republican party in 1884, and continue to adhere to the Democratic party, have deserted not only the cause of honest Government, of sound finances, of freedom and purity of the ballot, but especially have deserted the cause of reform in the civil service. We will not fail to keep our pledges because they have broken theirs, or because their candidate has broken his. We, therefore, repeat our declaration of 1884, to-wit: "The reform of the civil service, auspiciously begun under the Republican Administration, should be completed by the further extension of the reform system already established by law, to all the grades of the service to which it is applicable. The spirit and purpose of the reform should be observed in all Executive appointments, and all laws at variance with the object of existing reform Legislation should be repealed, to the end that the danger to free institutions which lurk in the power of official patronage may be wisely and effectively avoided."

The gratitude of the Nation to the defenders of the Union can not be measured by laws. The Legislation of Congress should conform to the pledges made by a loyal People, and be so enlarged and extended as to provide against the possibility that any man who honorably wore the Federal uniform shall become an inmate of an almshouse, or dependent upon private charity. In the presence of an overflowing Treasury it would be a public scandal to do less for those whose valorous service preserved the Government. We denounce the hostile spirit shown by President Cleveland in his numerous vetoes of measures for pension relief and the action of the Democratic House of Representatives in refusing even a consideration of general pension Legislation.

In support of the principles herewith enunciated we invite the co-operation of patriotic men of all parties, and especially of all workingmen whose prosperity is seriously threatened by the free-trade policy of the present Administration.

The first concern of all good government is the virtue and sobriety of the People and the purity of the home. The Republican party cordially sympathizes with all wise and well-directed efforts for the promotion of temperance and morality.

1888.—Prohibition Platform.

Indianapolis, May 31.

"*Preamble*: The Prohibition party, in National Convention assembled, acknowledging Almighty God as the source of all power in government, do hereby declare:

"1. That the manufacture, importation, exportation, transportation and sale of alcoholic beverages should be made public crimes, and prohibited as such.

"2. That such Prohibition must be secured through Amendments of our National and State Constitutions, enforced by adequate laws adequately supported by Administrative Authority; and to this end the organization of the Prohibition party is imperatively demanded in State and Nation.

"3. That any form of license, taxation, or regulation of the Liquor Traffic is contrary to good Government; that any party which supports regulation, license, or taxation, enters into alliance with such Traffic and becomes the actual foe of the State's welfare; and that we arraign the Republican and Democratic parties for their persistent attitude in favor of the license iniquity, whereby they oppose the demand of the People for Prohibition, and, through open complicity with the Liquor Crime, defeat the enforcement of law.

"4. For the immediate abolition of the Internal Revenue system, whereby our National Government is deriving support from our greatest National vice.

"5. That an adequate public revenue being necessary, it may properly be raised by import duties by an equitable assessment upon the property and legitimate business of the Country; but import duties should be so reduced that no surplus shall be accumulated in the Treasury, and that the burdens of taxation shall be removed from foods, clothing, and other comforts and necessaries of life.

"6. That the right of suffrage rests on no mere accident of race, color, sex, or nationality; and that where, from any cause, it has been withheld from citizens who are of suitable age and mentally and morally qualified for the exercise of an intelligent ballot, it should be restored by the People through the Legislatures of the several States on such educational basis as they may deem wise.

"7. That Civil Service appointment for all civil offices, chiefly clerical in their duties, should be based upon moral, intellectual and physical qualifications, and not upon any party service or party necessity.

"8. For the abolition of polygamy and the establishment of uniform laws governing marriage and divorce.

"9. For prohibiting all combinations of capital to control and to increase the cost of products for popular consumption.

"10. For the preservation and defense of the Sabbath as a civil institution, without oppression of any who religiously observe the same on any other than the first day of the week.

"11. That arbitration is the Christian, wise and economic method of settling National differences, and the same method should, by judicious Legislation, be applied to the settlement of disputes between large bodies of employes and employers. That the abolition of the saloon would remove burdens, moral, physical, pecuniary and social, which now oppress labor and rob it of its earnings, and would prove to be a wise and successful way of promoting labor reform; and we invite labor and capital to unite with us for the accomplishment thereof. That monopoly in land is a wrong to the People, and the public lands should be reserved for actual settlers; and that men and women should receive equal wages for equal work.

"12. That our immigration laws should be so enforced as to prevent the introduction into our Country of all convicts, inmates of other dependent institutions and all others physically incapacitated for self-support; and that no person should have the ballot in any State who is not a citizen of the United States.

"Recognizing and declaring that Prohibition of the Liquor Traffic has become the dominant issue in National politics, we invite to full party fellowship all who on this one dominant issue are with us agreed in full belief that this party can and will remove sectional differences, and promote National unity, and insure the best welfare of our entire land."

1888.—Democratic Platform.

St. Louis, June 7.

The Democratic party of the United States in National Convention assembled renews the pledge of its fidelity to the Democratic faith and reaffirms the platform adopted by its representatives in the convention of 1884, and indorses the views adopted by President Cleveland in his last earnest message to Congress as the correct interpretation of that platform upon the question of tariff reduction; and also indorses the efforts of our Democratic Representatives in Congress to secure a reduction of excessive taxation.

Chief among its principles of party faith are the maintenance of an indissoluble Union of free and indestructible States, now about to enter upon its second century of unexampled progress and renown; devotion to a plan of government regulated by a written constitution strictly specifying every granted power and expressly reserving to the States or people the entire ungranted residue of power; the encouragement of a jealous popular vigilance directed to all who have been chosen for brief terms to enact and execute the laws and are charged with the duty of preserving the peace, insuring equality, and establishing justice.

The Democratic party welcomes an exacting scrutiny of the administration of the executive power, which four years ago was committed to its trust in the election of Grover Cleveland, President of the United States, and it challenges the most searching inquiry concerning its fidelity and devotion to the pledges which then invited the suffrages of the People. During a most critical period of our financial affairs—resulting from over taxation, the anomalous condition of our currency, and a public debt unmatured-it has by the adoption of a wise and statesmanlike course not only averted disaster, but greatly promoted the prosperity of the People.

It has revised the improvident and unwise policy of the Republican party touching the public domain, and has reclaimed from corporations and syndicates, alien and domestic, and restored to the People nearly 100,000,000 of acres of valuable land, to be sacredly held as homesteads for our citizens.

While carefully guarding the interests of the people, consistent with the principles of justice and equity, it has paid out more for pensions and bounties to the soldiers and sailors of the Republic than was ever paid before during an equal period.

It has adopted and consistently pursued a firm and prudent foreign policy, preserving peace with all nations while scrupulously maintaining all the rights and interests of our own Government and People at home and abroad.

The exclusion from our shores of Chinese laborers has been effectually secured under the provision of a treaty, the operation of which has been postponed by the action of a Republican majority in the Senate.

Honest reform in the civil service has been inaugurated and maintained by President Cleveland, and he has brought the public service to the highest standard of efficiency, not only by rule and precept, but by the example of his own untiring and unselfish administration of public affairs.

In every branch and department of the Government under Democratic control the rights and the welfare of all the People have been guarded and defended; every public interest has been protected, and the equity of all our citizens before the law, without regard to race or color, has been steadfastly maintained.

Upon this record thus exhibited and upon the pledge of a continuance to the People of the benefits of Democracy it invokes a renewal of popular trust by the reelection of a Chief Magistrate who has been faithful, able, and prudent, and invokes in addition to that trust the transfer also to the Democracy of the entire Legislative Power.

The Republican party, controlling the Senate and resisting in both Houses of Congress a reformation of unjust and unequal tax laws—which have outlasted the necessities of war and are now undermining the abundance of a long period of peace—deny to the people equality before the law, and the fairness and the justice which are their right. The cry of American labor for a better share in the rewards of industry is stifled with false pretences, enterprise is fettered and bound down to home markets; capital is discouraged with doubt, and unequal, unjust laws can neither be properly amended nor repealed. The Democratic party will continue, with all the power confided to it, the struggle to reform these laws in accordance with the pledges of its last platform, indorsed at the ballot-box by the suffrages of the people. Of all the industrious freemen of our land, the immense majority, including the tiller of the soil, gain no advantage from excessive tax laws, but the price of nearly everything they buy is increased by the favoritism of an unequal system of tax legislation.

All unnecessary taxation is unjust taxation. It is repugnant to the creed of Democracy that by such taxation the cost of the necessaries of life should be unjustifiably increased to all our people. Judged by the Democratic principles the interests of the People are betrayed when, by unnecessary taxation, trusts and combinations are permitted to exist which, while unduly enriching the few that combine, rob the body of our citizens by depriving them of the benefits of natural competition. Every rule of governmental action is violated when, through unnecessary taxation, a vast sum of money—far beyond the needs of an economical administration—is drawn from the People, the channels of trade, and accumulated as a demoralizing surplus in the National Treasury.

The money now lying idle in the Federal Treasury resulting from superfluous taxation amounts to more than $125,000,000, and the surplus collected is reaching the sum of more than $60,000,000 annually. Debauched by this immense temptation, the remedy of the Republican party is to meet and exhaust by extravagant appropriations and expenses, whether Constitutional or not, the accumulation of extravagant taxation. The Democratic policy is to enforce frugality in public expense and abolish unnecessary taxation.

Our established domestic industries and enterprises should not and need not be endangered by the reduction and correction of the burdens of taxation. On the contrary, a fair and careful revision of our tax laws, with due allowance for the difference between the wages of American and foreign labor, must promote and encourage every branch of such industries and enterprises by giving them assurance of an extended market and continuous operations. In the interests of American labor, which should in no event be neglected, the revision of our tax laws contemplated by the Democratic party should promote the advantage of such labor by cheapening the cost of necessaries of life in the home of every workingman and at the same time secure to him steady and remunerative employment.

Upon this question of tariff reform, so closely concerning every phase of our National life, and upon every question involved in the problem of good government, the Democratic party submits its principles and professions to the intelligent suffrages of the American People.

PRESIDENTIAL TICKETS FOR 1888.

Republican.

President, Benjamin Harrison, of Indiana; Vice President, Levi P. Morton, of New York.

Democrat.

President, Grover Cleveland, of New York; Vice President, Allen G. Thurman, of Ohio.

Prohibition.

President, Clinton B. Fisk, of New Jersey; Vice President, John A. Brooks, of Missouri.

Union Labor.

President, A. J. Streeter, of Illinois; Vice President, Charles E. Cunningham, of Arkansas.

Industrial Reform.

President, Albert E. Redstone, of California; Vice President, John Colvin, of Kansas.

United Labor.

President, Robert H. Cowdry, of Illinois; Vice President, W. H. T. Wakefield, of Kansas.

Woman Suffragists.

President, Belva A. Lockwood, of Washington; Vice President, Albert H. Love, of Pennsylvania.

TITLES OF OUR STATESMEN.

"**Old**" and "**Little**" are two favorite prefixes which admirers use in conferring a **sobriquet** on their hero.

"**Honest Old Abe**" was the plain title that was shouted at the head of **Lincoln's** columns.

Martin Van Buren, who succeeded **Andrew Jackson**, was called "**The Little Magician.**" His enemies dubbed him "**Whisky Van.**"

"**The Little Giant**" is the suggestive, historical, and catching sobriquet that was worn by the great statesman, **Stephen A. Douglas.**

Many of **Polk's** ardent admirers called him "**Young Hickory**" hoping to win for him some of the warm support that "**Old Hickory**" commanded.

Andrew Jackson was called by his friends "**Old Hickory**," because of his sturdy qualities. "**Old Hickory**" is one of the historical nicknames of the world.

"**Log Cabin**" **Harrison** was the way campaign orators used to speak of the "**Tippecanoe**" statesman. "**Hard Cider**" was another appellation of his, while some talked of him as "**Old Tip.**"

General Taylor was not wanting in campaign titles. He was called "**Old Zach**" and "**Old Buena Vista.**" But the title that the people most liked and the one that is historical is "**Rough and Ready.**"

Henry Clay always had flashing nicknames. Three have gone with Clay in history. "**The Gallant Harry of the West**," "**The Young Commoner**," and "**The Millboy of the Slashes**," are titles that the great statesman himself delighted to apply.—*Philadelphia News.*

NATIVITY OF SOLDIERS IN OUR CIVIL WAR.

The nationality of soldiers in the **Federal army** during the War of the Rebellion is as follows:

Native American 1,573,300
British American 53,500
English 45,500
Irish 144,200
German 176,800
Other foreigners 48,400
Nativity unknown, mostly foreign 26,500

Total 2,018,200

The **sum total** does not equal the **number given** by Phisterer's Statistical Record of the **United States army**, as enlisted during the War of the Rebellion. This work, probably the most **correct record** ever completed, makes no attempt to group the soldiers by nationalities. In fact, it could not be **accurately** done, as in many instances the **nationality** was not entered in the record of enlistment. But the above **table** is no doubt **approximately** correct; and the estimate of 75 per cent. rather under than over states the number of **native-born Americans** in our great volunteer Army.

PRESIDENTIAL CANDIDATES.

List of All the Leading Candidates for the Presidency from the Beginning.

Below is a table in which are arranged the **Presidential candidates** of the two great **parties**—the first column of names giving the **successful** candidate, the other his **unsuccessful** opponent. It is a valuable tabulation of facts:

Year	Successful	Unsuccessful
1789	George Washington	No opposition
1792	George Washington	No opposition
1796	John Adams	Thomas Jefferson
1800	Thomas Jefferson	John Adams
1804	Thomas Jefferson	C. C. Pinckney
1808	James Madison	C. C. Pinckney
1812	James Madison	De Witt Clinton
1816	James Monroe	Rufus King
1820	James Monroe	No opposition
1824	John Q. Adams	Andrew Jackson
1828	Andrew Jackson	John Q. Adams
1832	Andrew Jackson	Henry Clay
1836	Martin Van Buren	Wm. H. Harrison
1840	Wm. H. Harrison	Martin Van Buren
1844	James K. Polk	Henry Clay
1848	Zachary Taylor	Lewis Cass
1852	Franklin Pierce	Winfield Scott
1856	James Buchanan	John C. Fremont
1860	Abraham Lincoln	S. A. Douglas
1864	Abraham Lincoln	G. B. McClellan
1868	U. S. Grant	Horatio Seymour
1872	U. S. Grant	Horace Greeley
1876	R. B. Hayes	S. J. Tilden
1880	James A. Garfield	W. S Hancock
1884	Grover Cleveland	James G. Blaine

This **table** is made the subject of a good deal of figuring on **Presidential possibilities.** It is pointed out that three times therein is shown the renomination and success of the **principal candidate** who was defeated at the election next before. This happened in the instances of **Jefferson** in 1800, **Jackson** in 1828, and **Harrison** in 1840. Once, in the instance of **Pinckney**, in 1804, there was such a renomination and a repeated defeat.

On the other hand the fact is equally **patent** that, in seven cases there have been re-elections to the **Presidency** for a second term—in the instances of **Washington, Jefferson, Madison, Monroe, Jackson, Lincoln,** and **Grant.**

LIVES OF REPUBLICAN CANDIDATES.

GENERAL BENJAMIN HARRISON.
The Republican Candidate for President.

Ancestry.

GENERAL Benjamin Harrison is the descendant of one of the historical families of this Country. The head of the family was a Maj. Gen. Harrison, one of Oliver Cromwell's trusted followers and fighters. In the zenith of Cromwell's power it became the duty of this Harrison to participate in the trial of Charles I. and afterwards to sign the death warrant of the King. He subsequently paid for this with his life, by being hanged Oct. 13, 1660. His descendants emigrated to America, and the next of the family that appears in history is Benjamin Harrison of Virginia, great-grandfather of the subject of this sketch and after whom he was named. Benjamin Harrison was a member of the Continental Congress during the years 1774, 1775, and 1776.

He was the brother-in-law of Peyton Randolph, the first President of the American Congress. When Randolph died the Southern Members united upon Harrison to succeed him; but the latter, to secure harmony between the North and the South, withdrew his claims in favor of John Hancock of Massachusetts. Harrison was one of the original signers of the Declaration of Independence and Chairman of the Committee which reported the Declaration to the Continental Congress, was three times elected Governor of Virginia, and was a member of the Convention that ratified the Constitution.

Gen. William Henry Harrison, the son of this distinguished patriot of the Revolution, after a successful career as a soldier during the War of 1812, and with a clean record as a Governor of the enormous Northwest Territory, known then as Indiana, was elected President of the United States in 1846. His career was cut short by death within one month after his inauguration.

John Scott Harrison, the son of William Henry Harrison, and the father of the subject of this sketch, was all his life a farmer in Southern Ohio. He served four years in Congress, from 1852 to 1856, as a member from the Cincinnati district. He died about twelve years ago.

Personal Appearance.

Benjamin Harrison, the Republican party's nominee for President, is a man slightly under the medium hight. His figure, however, is very broad and compact. His large head is set well down between his broad, high shoulders, as his neck is very short. His face is of an almost deadly pallor, although he enjoys excellent health. It is the complexion of a recluse. His eyes are a grayish-blue, deeply set under a very prominent, bulging forehead. His nose is straight, slightly curving outward, and square at the end. His thin-lipped mouth is shaded by a very light, long, curling mustache, while the lower part of his face is hid in a long, sandy, gray beard. The hair upon his head is of the same color, and is combed very smoothly and tight to his head, so as to show plainly the outline of the skull.

BENJAMIN HARRISON.   LEVI P. MORTON.

He always dresses plainly in black. He is a reserved men, and keeps much to himself. He does not appear to have many social traits. He is not in any sense of the word what one would call "a good fellow." He is a man who would prefer any day a quiet corner in his own library to the best company in the world outside of it. He is domestic in his habits, and thoroughly devoted to his handsome, delicate-featured, black-eyed wife, who began with him a struggle for a place and a home in the then Far West when he was only 20 years of age. Those who know Mr. Harrison, however, say that he is a devoted friend, and that underneath his reserve he has a most kindly heart.

His record as a soldier during the War and his life in his Indiana home will bear the closest inspection. He was one of the most conservative members of the Senate; and, while he made no attempts at brilliant display in that body, he built up a solid reputation as a man of positive convictions, with a facility for clearly expressing himself. When he comes to speak, his voice is somewhat too harsh and high-keyed to please strangers, but after one becomes used to his manner, one soon learns to recognize with pleasure his blunt common-sense and the trained manner of a successful lawyer. He is at his best in a personal debate, as he has more than ordinary powers of sarcasm and invective. He has occasionally come into sharp contact with the silver-tongued orator of the Wabash, Dan Voorhees; and the silver-tongued Daniel has in each instance been sorely discomfited. The cold, quiet face of Harrison in such a debate lights up with a flame of almost fierce energy, and for the time being he is entirely transformed.

In the Senate he was third on the Committee on Military affairs, third on the Committee on Indian affairs, and Chairman of the Committee on Territories. He followed in the footsteps of his grandfather in his committee work at least, for William Henry Harrison was a master hand at solving military and Indian problems, while his record as the Gov. of the Territory of Indiana was one of the best. One of the local chronicles of that time alludes to the astonishing fact that some $600,000 had passed through the Governor's hands without a single dollar of his accounts being called in question.

Gen. Harrison is not rich. His law practice is large, but he appears disinclined to set his fees high enough to meet the modern standard. He owns a handsome home where his wife receives much company. They have a married daughter, and a son who is becoming prominent in the politics of Montana Territory. General Harrison is a member of the Indianapolis Literary Club, and occasionally takes part in the debates and exercises. He is also an active member of the First Presbyterian Church, and some years ago taught a Bible class in the Sunday school.

Early Life and Struggles.

General Harrison was born at North Bend, Hamilton County, Ohio, the 20th of August, 1833. His life, up to the time of his graduation from the Miami University, at Oxford, in that State, was the comparatively uneventful one of a country lad belonging to a family of small means. His father was able to give him a good education and nothing more. He graduated from college when he was 18 years of age. His teachers and classmates have borne testimony to the ease with which he held his own in all college contests and his early promise of future success.

Prof. David Swing says that Harrison, while at Oxford, though young, was a studious scholar, and early gave evidence of being foremost in whatever he might undertake. He there acquired the habits of study and mental discipline which have characterized him through life, enabling him to grapple with any subject on short notice, to concentrate his intellectual forces and give his mental energies that sort of direct and effective operation that indicates the trained and disciplined mind.

He became engaged while at college to the daughter of the Rev. Dr. Scott, Principal of a female school at Oxford, Ohio. After graduating he decided to enter upon the study of the law. He went to Cincinnati and studied there in the office of the Hon. Bellamy S. Storer for two years. At the expiration of that time Mr. Harrison received the only inheritance of his life. His aunt, dying, left him a lot in Cincinnati, which was valued at $800. Young Harrison regarded this legacy as a fortune. He decided to be married at once, to take this money and go to some Western town and begin the practice of law—he having been admitted to the bar in this year. There was, however, one difficulty in his way. He was not yet 21, and could not therefore execute a deed of sale for the lot. But he found a Cincinnati friend who was willing to go on a bond to guarantee that he would execute a deed when he reached his majority; and so, with this guarantee, the sale was made.

With $800 in his pocket he started out, with a young wife upon his arm, to fight for a place in the world and a footing in one of the most difficult of the learned professions. He decided to go to Indianapolis, which was even at that time (1854) a town of promise. He met with but little encouragement at first. The work he obtained during the first year amounted to almost nothing. But the $800 carried the young folks over their first year. By the time the second year was reached Harrison began to make enough through collections and trial of cases before Justices of the Peace to support himself and family.

His First Important Case.

About this time he was enabled, through fortunate accident, to have an opportunity to appear before a jury in an important case, which attracted at that time a great deal of attention. It was the trial of a burglar. The Prosecuting Attorney, Maj. J. W. Gordon, was desirous of attending a lecture during the evening of the closing day of the trial, and so he looked about for some one to take his place in making the closing address to the jury. It was evident that this portion of his argument could not be reached before evening. He knew Harrison as as a patient, painstaking, energetic young man, seeking to make his way in the legal profession. He told him early in the day that he should rely upon him for assistance in closing the case, giving him his reasons for his desire to be absent during the evening.

Gov. Wallace, one of the leading lawyers at the bar of Indianapolis at that time, was the counsel for the defense. He was an old friend of Harrison's grandfather, and was by him appointed a cadet at West Point. In the almanacs of 1840 there is a quaint cut illustrating the legend of William Henry Harrison preferring the son of an old friend to his own son. Ben Harrison's father was anxious for a West Point cadetship, but his father appointed Wallace, the son of his friend, instead. Wallace graduated from West Point, but after a time left the army and entered upon the practice of law at Indianapolis.

Young Harrison, when notified of his good fortune in being called in to assist the Prosecuting Attorney, was both dismayed and overjoyed at his opportunity. During the afternoon, when the witnesses were being examined, he eagerly noted every point, writing down with great fullness notes of everything which he thought could be used with advantage in his maiden argument of the evening.

Evening came. The court house was packed. The court room was feebly lighted with tallow candles. When Harrison sat down in the dim, uncertain light of the court-room he observed, greatly to his disgust, that the pencil that he had employed to write with during the day was so hard that his notes, in the uncertain light of the evening, were perfectly illegible. This greatly embarrassed him. At the outset of his speech he made one attempt to use some of the fragments of his paper; but seeing that they were obstacles instead of aids to a free expression of his thought, he, with the energy of despair, threw the notes boldly to one side. With the memory of his wife and baby at home he confronted the jury, grimly determined not to make a failure. The loss of his notes probably saved him. His memory retained enough of the details of the case, without being fretted with the superfluous parts of it. He made such an effective plea to the jury that, when he had completed, Governor Wallace went up to him and patted him upon the shoulder, giving him warm words of encouragement and approval.

The Beginning Of His Political Career.

Governor Wallace had a son who had just established himself in the practice of law in Indianapolis. Ben Harrison's first appearance before a jury and the approval of his address by General Wallace led to the formation of a business partnership between young Wallace and himself. The two young men worked along together, not much more than making a living, until 1860, when Wallace became candidate for Clerk of the Circuit Court, and Harrison for Reporter of the Supreme Court, the salary of which was $2,500 a year. Then he began his first experience as a stump speaker. He canvassed the State thoroughly and was elected by a handsome majority.

The most noticeable incident of the campaign was his famous encounter with Hendricks at Rockville. Harrison was then in his 28th year, and rather boyish in appearance. He was, however, gifted with that fluency of speech which comes to even young lawyers after a few years of moderate success. At Rockville Harrison was advertised to speak at the the court-house. When he arrived there he found that Hendricks, who was then one of the most notable of the Democratic leaders of the State, was billed to speak at nearly the same time and place. The Republicans of Rockville were anxious to counteract the effect of Hendricks' speech. They came to Harrison and asked him if he would undertake a joint discussion with Hendricks. This was a large undertaking for a young campaign speaker; but Harrison pluckily said that he would cheerfully undertake it if it was thought best by the Republicans. The matter was submitted to Hendricks; but he would not dignify his youthful opponent by engaging in a joint discussion with him. He said that he would speak two hours first himself, and then young Mr. Harrison might say what he pleased in the two hours following. The court-house was crowded, and, from the applause and approval which followed nearly every sentence of Hendricks' speech, Harrison at times feared that there was not a single Republican in the building.

The issues of that campaign were largely local ones, with which Harrison was thoroughly familiar. The swamp-land frauds were then subjects of eager inquiry among the people. This was a subject that the young lawyer had carefully studied. He had with him all of the official documents bearing upon these frauds. These papers had been carefully digested by him, and appropriate places marked, so that he had with him an arsenal of ready weapons. He began with such a sharp reply to Hendricks that before he had uttered half a dozen sentences Dan Voorhees, who was seated in the front row of spectators, arose to interrupt him. But the blood of young Harrison was up. He came back at Voorhees so savagely that the silver-tongued orator of the Wabash was quite willing to subside. The cheers and applause which marked this aggressive beginning convinced Harrison that he had plenty of friends in the audience. This inspired him to make an especially vigorous effort. His powers of sarcasm and invective are great. He punished Hendricks with such severity that that gentleman afterwards said to Harrison that he would never again agree to a similar discussion and give Harrison the opportunity of an uninterrupted closing argument.

This episode at Rockville did much to establish Harrison's reputation as a political speaker. From that day to this he has taken part in every campaign in the State, and is regarded as one of the most effective pillars of his party in Indiana.

His Valiant War Record.

When the War broke out Mr. Harrison had just begun keeping house in a home of his own. He had purchased a cottage for $2,900. Upon this house he had made but a small payment, the balance being secured by a deed of trust upon the house. He had then two small children. The pay of his position as Reporter of the Supreme Court, joined to his practice, secured him a modest living, with the promise of saving enough soon to pay for his home. He was working in his library, reading proofs and preparing an index of the first volume of his reports, when he first heard of the fall of Fort Sumter and Lincoln's proclamation calling for 75,000 men. It did not seem possible to him at that time that he could go into the army. There seemed to be no special necessity for a man in his situation, with a young family upon his hands, in an unpaid-for home, to leave them and respond to Lincoln's first call. But in 1862 the situation was altogether different. It was the time of the year when Lincoln had called for 500,000 men. The Rebellion had become formidable. Governor Morton was doing his best to fill out the quota of Indiana. Harrison went one day to call upon Morton with a friend, William Wallace, for the purpose of asking him to appoint a cousin of Wallace to the position of Second Lieutenant in one of the regiments then being recruited to meet Lincoln's call.

They found Morton gloomy and discouraged. He took his visitors into the back room of his office, where, after closing the door, he said: "Gentlemen, there is absolutely no response to Mr. Lincoln's last call for troops. The people do not appear to realize the necessities of the situation. Something must be done to break the spirit of apathy and indifference which now prevails. See here" and he drew them to the window. "Look at those workmen across the way toiling to put up a new building, as if such things could be possible when the Country itself is in danger of destruction."

Mr. Harrison at once responded by saying to the Governor that he felt certain that he could raise a regiment for service and that he would go to work that day to make up the quota of the State.

Morton said: "I feel certain that you can raise a regiment; but I would not ask you to do more than that. I know your situation, and would not think of asking you to go yourself."

To this Harrison said: "Of course I shall go. I would not put myself in the ridiculous position of going out to make war-speeches and to urge my neighbors to go where I would not go myself."

He instantly left the room. What followed shows his decision of character in an emergency. Without consulting his wife, or without asking the judgment of a single friend, he walked straight from the Governor's office to a hat store. Throwing off his black slouch hat he called for a blue military cap. Purchasing it he placed it upon his head, and by this simple change in his head decoration walked out of the hat store a Union soldier who stood by the army of the Union from that day to the close of the War. After purchasing the cap he went out and hired a soul-stirring fifer and a patriotic drummer, and stationed them in front of his law-office, from the windows of which were soon unfurled the Star-Spangled Banner as the sign of a recruiting station.

The fifer piped such shrill blasts of patriotism and the drum rattled such a stirring accompaniment that the town was soon alive with excitement. Harrison's example was speedily followed by many others. Military caps began to appear upon the streets in every direction. Within a brief time Company A of the Seventieth Indiana regiment was raised by Harrison, and in a few weeks a full regiment was organized. He was elected Colonel of this regiment. Within thirty days from the time that Ben Harrison cocked the military cap over his right ear he was at the head of a full regiment of troops at Bowling Green, Kentucky, to assist in the repulse of General Kirby Smith, who had been threatening Southern Indiana with a guerrilla raid.

The Seventieth Indiana was composed of a fine lot of men, but they were all of the rawest material. There was scarcely a man in the regiment who knew how to properly load his gun when they first received their arms at Louisville.

Before leaving Louisville for Bowling Green news had been received of guerrilla raids along the line of the railway. The soldiers of Harrison's regiment were armed with Springfield and Enfield muskets. They were all muzzle-loaders. Colonel Harrison ordered his men to load these guns in the Louisville depot before boarding the train. Then followed a most ridiculous scene, which afforded great amusement for the Confederate symphathizers about the depot. The men, when they first received their guns, began snapping caps upon them like a pack of children with new toys. When the order came to load the greatest awkwardness was shown in carrying out the order. A number of the soldiers did not bite off enough of the paper of the cartridge, and the result was that numerous balls were wedged fast midway in the barrels of the guns. The unfortunate men began hammering their steel ramrods against the walls of the depot to drive the balls home; and it was a great wonder that a number of fatal accidents did not occur then and there.

At Bowling Green this regiment was put into a brigade under the command of General Ward of Kentucky, who was a great favorite of General Thomas. The brigade was under General Rosecrans. Ward was a poor executive man although a brave soldier; and it was largely through his lack of management that the regiment of which Harrison was commander did not see better service, although it was constantly on duty in Kentucky and Tennessee until the march to the sea was planned. The regiment was in repeated small affairs, but its first brilliant record was made upon Sherman's march. Its history in that famous march is one of the best. For a number of months the regiment was almost constantly under fire, and never swerved from its line of courageous duty.

Harrison employed all his time when he first went into the army in mastering military tactics. When he came to move towards the East with Sherman his regiment was one of the best drilled and organized in the army.

His Gallantry in the Field.

It was at Resaca that Col. Harrison's courage as a soldier was tested to its fullest extent. His brigade was under the cover of the woods. Orders were received during the afternoon of one day to break that cover and charge through a stretch of open field to the crest of a hill a quarter of a mile away to take a battery which was being used with terrible effect upon the National forces. Colonel Harrison's regiment was in advance, and he, as the ranking Colonel, was at the head. The orders were peremptory to charge at once. The officers were to dismount and go on foot with the men. Colonel Harrison only asked one question of the aide-de-camp who brought him the order. He said to him: "You are familiar with the field outside. I am not. Will you go ahead with me alone and show me the direction of this battery, for if I were to charge out now I would be as apt to charge flank on to it as any other way." Colonel Harrison walked out of the woods then with this officer. When they had barely left the cover a puff of smoke from a neighboring hill and a screaming projectile emphasized the indication swiftly made by the guide. Harrison instantly waved his sword to his men behind him, shouting, "Come on, boys!" and, with the four regiments yelling at his heels, he ran towards the hill, which now concentrated upon his column a most murderous fire. Between the woods and the crest of the hill the brigade lost one-third of its men in killed and wounded. After a spurt of savage fighting the Union forces succeeded in capturing the outside line of the breastworks; but between them and the battery itself was a line of insurmountable stakes and brushwood. Night fell before the battery itself was taken; but during the night Harrison's men tunneled up through to the guns and captured them, lowering them into the tunnel. At break of day they expected the contest for the crest of the hill to be renewed; but the Confederates had withdrawn in the night, greatly to the disappointment of General Sherman; though not a member of Harrison's brigade was disappointed at the result.

It was at Peachtree Creek that Col. Harrison won the profane and fiery approval of the hot-blooded Fighting Joe Hooker. While waiting with his men in reserve, Harrison saw a detachment of Hood's forces coming towards him. The crest of a hill was between them. Harrison saw instantly that it would not do to wait and receive this attack at the foot of the hill. Without an order he assumed the responsibility of charging his reserves up the hill to meet the Confederates half way. This was done with so much impetuosity and courage that the Confederates were sharply repulsed. It was for this that General Joe Hooker roared out to Harrison, after it was over: "By —, Sir, I will have you made Brigadier General for this."

His word of mouth on the battle-field was supplemented by the following hearty letter of commendation written to the Secretary of War a few months later.

HEADQUARTERS NORTHERN DEPARTMENT, CINCINNATI, O., October 31, 1864.—*The Hon. E. M. Stanton, Secretary of War:* I desire to call the attention of the Department to the claims of Col. Benjamin Harrison of the Seventieth Indiana Volunteers for promotion to the rank of Brigadier-General Volunteers.

Colonel Harrison first joined me in command of a brigade of Ward's division in Lookout Valley preparatory to entering upon what is called the Campaign of Atlanta. My attention was first attracted to this young officer by the superior excellence of his brigade in discipline and instruction, the result of his labor, skill and devotion. With more foresight than I have witnessed in any officer of his experience, he seemed to act upon the principle that success depended upon the thorough preparation in discipline and *espirit* of his command for conflict more than on any influence that could be exerted on the field itself, and when the collision came his command vindicated his wisdom as much as his valor. In the achievements of the Twentieth Corps in that Campaign Colonel Harrison bore a conspicuous part. At Resaca and Peach-Tree Creek the conduct of himself and command was especially distinguished. Colonel Harrison is an officer of superior abilities and of great professional and personal worth. It gives me great favor to commend him favorably to the honorable Secretary with the assurance that his preferment will be a just recognition of his services and martial accomplishments. Respectfully, your obedient servant,

JOSEPH HOOKER, Major-General Commanding.

During the absence of General Harrison in the field the Democratic Supreme Court declared the office of the Supreme Court Reporter vacant and another person was elected to the position. From the time of leaving Indiana with his regiment until the fall of 1864, after the capture of Atlanta, General Harrison had taken no leave absence, but having been nominated by the State Convention of that year for the office from which he had been ousted he took a thirty-day leave of absence, and, under orders from the War Department, reported to Governor Morton for duty. During that thirty-days' leave he again made a brilliant canvass of the State and was elected for another term. After the campaign was over, during the winter of 1864-'65, he was ordered to join Sherman at Savannah. With his wife and two children, accompanied by an orderly, he set out for Savannah by the way of New York. Upon the road he was stricken down with scarlet-fever and forced to get off the train in the snows of midwinter at Narrowsburg, an obscure station upon the New York & Erie Railroad. Fortunately the orderly who was with him was an experienced hospital-nurse. The doctor who attended him had to come seventeen miles over the snow. The man who had escaped death from every variety of Confederate bullet had a hard struggle in the snow-banks of frigid New York. Finally the hospital-nurse himself was attacked by the fever, and Mr. Harrison's children were also taken down. But the pluck of Mrs. Harrison and her untiring care enabled them all to subdue the fever. Harrison lost all the hair off his head and several coats of cuticle. But he rallied rapidly when he once did begin to recover, and reached Sherman in time to participate in the closing incidents of the War. He was with him at the surrender of Johnston, and did not return home until the War was over.

His Political and Personal Career since the War.

In 1868 General Harrison declined a reelection as Reporter and resumed the practice of law. In 1876 he became a candidate for Governor under peculiar circumstances, having been placed on the ticket by the State Central Committee while absent from the State, to fill a vacancy caused by the declination of the regular nominee. He had before the Convention declined to take the nomination, but the action of the Committee was in deference to the popular demand. In tendering it to General Harrison the Committee said: "The nomination was made for no other purpose than to subserve the best interests of the Republican party in Indiana, and in tendering it to you we do so with the assurance that you will receive the earnest and united vote of the entire party."

The nomination was entirely unsought and undesired, but it was accepted in terms that indicated a sense of public duty. Having accepted it, General Harrison threw himself into the campaign with his usual energy. He made a great campaign, canvassing the entire State and addressing immense audiences, but was not elected. The *vis inertiæ* of the Democratic party, strengthened by the candidacy of the most popular Democratic leader in the State, could not be overcome, and, in addition, the corruption fund and tactics of W. H. Barnum were too powerful.

The campaign, though unsuccessful, greatly extended General Harrison's acquaintance and reputation among the People, and from this time he was recognized as the coming man among the Republican leaders of the State. He polled nearly 2,000 more votes than the general average of his ticket. His brilliant campaign had been watched from without the State, and after the October election he was in great demand for speeches in the East, where he added to the high estimate the People had formed of him as a speaker.

In 1880, as usual, he took an active part in the campaign, and when it was found the Republicans had carried the Legislature he became at once the leading candidate for United States Senator. Efforts were made to create diversions in favor of others, but the voice of the party was practically unanimous for the man who had been fighting the party battles for so many years, and had been a conspicuous figure in every campaign since 1856. His nomination was plainly foreshadowed before the Legislature convened, and before the caucus met all other names had been withdrawn. His election gave the greatest satisfaction to Republicans throughout the State.

General Harrison's service of six years in the Senate gave him a National reputation as one of the ablest men, best lawyers, and strongest debaters in that body. During this period he grew rapidly in public estimation and proved himself fully equal to the requirements of the place and the expectations of his friends. His Dakota report and speeches, and his speech on the Edmunds Resolution regarding civil-service reform in general, and on the President's appointments in Indiana are especially remembered.

His Senatorial term expired March 4, 1887, and the Legislature to choose his successor was to be elected in the fall of 1886. The history of that campaign is still fresh in the public mind. It was in a large degree General Harrison's campaign. Though others were good seconds and able assistants he was foremost in the fight. When others wavered, he advanced; when they lost heart he expressed confidence. The result attested General Harrison's wisdom and his work. The Republicans carried the State and came within a hair's breadth of carrying the Legislature, though the apportionment had been gerrymandered so as to give the Democrats at least forty-six majority on joint ballot, and Senator Voorhees said he should feel personally disgraced if that was not the result.

With the expiration of his Senatorial term General Harrison returned to the practice of his profession, being now and for many years past at the head of one of the strongest law firms in the State. As has been said, he is preeminently a lawyer. Politics is a side issue with him, but when he practices politics he practices as he does the law, with all he his might.

In his private life and personal character General Harrison has the good fortune to be unassailable. Neither political opposition nor personal malice has ever dared to attack him in this regard. His character as a citizen, neighbor, and friend is invulnerable.

LEVI P. MORTON.

Candidate for Vice President.

Birth and Parentage.

LEVI P. Morton was born in Shoreman, Vt., May 10th, 1824. On the very threshold of life he was made acquainted with the meaning of the word labor. His parents were of New England stock, and, although they were thrifty, as was the character of the New Englanders, they did not accumulate much wealth. When young Mr. Morton became a clerk in a country store he applied himself so closely to his duties and developed a capacity for business that he soon gained the confidence of his employers and was rapidly advanced in his position.

Business Enterprise.

At the age of 26 Mr. Morton had gained such a business reputation that he was given a partnership in the firm of Beebe, Morgan & Co., of Boston, then a well-known mercantile house. He remained there for four years, and then, seeking a wider field, came to New York and established the firm of Morton & Grinnell. The young and prosperous merchant remained at the head of this firm till 1863, when he founded the banking house of Morton, Bliss & Co., of which he is the senior member. At the same time the house of Morton, Rose & Co. was established in London as the English correspondents of the New York house. From 1873 to 1884 the London firm acted as financial agents of the United States Government. The two firms took a leading position as members of the syndicate that negotiated United States bonds in payment of the Geneva award of $15,000,000 and the Halifax fishery award of $5,500,000.

Political Career.

Mr. Morton has always taken an active interest in politics, and though he has never been known as an office-seeker he has at the call of his fellow-citizens filled with honor several public positions. In 1878 he was appointed Honorary Commissioner to the Paris Exposition, and in the fall of the same year he was nominated and elected by the Republican party to Congress. He was re-elected in 1880. During his service in the House of Representatives Mr. Morton was known as a careful and conservative thinker on all public questions, and his opinions were much respected by his fellow-members. In the Republican National Convention of 1880 Mr. Morton was a staunch ally of Roscoe Conkling, an advocate of the renomination of Gen. Grant for a third term to the Presidency. When the split came and President Garfield was nominated, Mr. Morton was offered the second place on the ticket. He declined the honor, and after the triumphant success of the ticket President Garfield offered him the portfolio of Secretary of the Navy. Mr. Morton also declined the Cabinet offer, saying he preferred to accept the appointment of Minister to France, in which office he was confirmed by the Senate soon after President Garfield was inaugurated.

Mr. Morton's career as representative of the American Government to the French Republic was one of which he may justly feel proud. No American Minister was ever more respected abroad. Through his intercessions the restrictions on the importation of American pork into France were removed and American corporations received a legal status in France. Since the expiration of his term as Minister to France Mr. Morton has had no official position.

Private Life.

Mr. Morton's private life is exemplary. In the winter he occupies a large mansion at No. 85 Fifth Avenue, now the residence of Allen Thorndike Rice. In the summer he resides at his summer seat Emlerslie, at Rhinebeck on the Hudson. His wife, a remarkably beautiful and accomplished woman, is several years his junior. She has always been most popular in society. Levi P. Morton is a typical American and a protectionist to the core.

Lives of Democratic Candidates.

GROVER CLEVELAND.
Democratic Candidate for President.

Grover Cleveland was born in Caldwell, Essex county, New York, March 18, 1837.

He is the son of a Presbyterian minister, and was named in honor of Rev. Stephen Grover, the former occupant of his father's parsonage. When Grover was four years old his father had a call to Fayetteville, near Syracuse, N. Y., where the young boy received an academic education. He afterward served as a clerk in a country store.

The removal of the family to Clinton, Oneida county, gave Grover additional educational advantages in the academy there. He taught school at seventeen and aided his uncle, Lewis T. Allen, in the compilation of a volume of the "American Herd-Book." In 1855 he began the study of the law with the firm of Rogers, Bowen & Rogers, in Buffalo, and was admitted to the bar in 1859, but remained with the firm for three more years, acting as managing clerk at a salary of $1000.

Being the sole support of his sister and widowed mother, he was unable to enlist and fight for his country in her time of need; but he borrowed money to pay a substitute, and it was not until long after the war that he was enabled to repay the loan.

In 1869 he became a partner in the law firm of Lanning, Cleveland & Folsom. He continued a successful practice until 1870, when he was elected sheriff of Erie county, N. Y.

In rapid succession he was elected by a majority of 3,530, Mayor of Buffalo in 1881; Governor of New York in 1882, receiving a majority of 151,742; and President of the United States in 1884. The total popular vote in the United States was 10,067,610, divided as follows:

Cleveland	4,874,986.
Blaine	4,851,981.
Butler	175,370.
St. John	150,369.
Blank, defective and scattering	14,904.
Total	10,067,610.

Cleveland receiving a majority of 37 electoral votes.

Having entered the White House a bachelor, he found solitude too much for him, so, casting his eyes around on the host of his pretty and gentle admirers, they fell upon—Miss Frances Folsom, as the one to be sought, wooed and won. She became Frances Cleveland and the young and handsome mistress of the White House at one and the same time, June 2d, 1886.

She was the daughter of President Cleveland's deceased friend and partner, Oscar Folsom of the Buffalo bar. Except the wife of Madison, Mrs. Cleveland is the youngest of the many mistresses of the White House, having been born in Buffalo, N. Y., in 1864.

Grover Cleveland enjoys the renown of being the first bachelor President, and also, of being the first President married in the White House.

ALLEN G. THURMAN.
Democratic Candidate for Vice-President.

Ex-Senator Allen G. Thurman is a native of Virginia, having been born at Lynchburg, November 13, 1813. In the year 1819 his parents removed West to Ohio. When the lad grew to be a young man he studied law with his uncle, Senator William Allen, who afterward became Governor, and with Noah H. Swayne, subsequently a member of the United States Supreme Court. At the age of 22 he came to the bar, and was elected a member of the Twenty-ninth Congress, which began December 1, 1845, and ended March 3, 1847. He was not re-elected to Congress, and retired to the practice of his profession. In 1851 he was elected a Judge of the State Supreme Court of Ohio, and served one term of four years, the last two years serving as Chief Justice. A long interval ensued between his single term on the bench and his appearance again as a nominee on the Democratic State ticket of Ohio. In 1851 he had led his ticket y about 2,000 which indicated that he was the strong man in his party. On June 8, 1867, he was nominated at Columbus for Governor. The Republicans held their State convention on June 29, and nominated General R. B. Hayes.

The election for State officers was held in October, 1867, and the total vote was 484,603. General Hayes was elected by 2,983 majority over Judge Thurman. The Democratic Legislature of 1868 elected Mr. Thurman to the United States Senate to succeed Senator Ben Wade, for the term beginning in 1869 and ending in 1875, and then he was elected for the term ending 1881. In the year 1876 Mr. Thurman was a candidate in the National Democratic Convention for the nomination for President, but then, as in 1880, the Ohio delegation was not for him. In 1884 he was once more a candidate for the same office, and, like the late Vice President Hendricks, he has been given second place on the Presidential ticket.

Mr. Thurman has distinguished himself as a lawyer and jurist. He rendered valuable services as a member of the judiciary committee of the House of Representatives.

He represented the American Government in the International Congress at Paris in 1881, and afterwards visited France, Switzerland, the Rhine, Belgium and England.

He has been confessedly pure and upright in public life, and in personal character is amiable and lovable.

SENATOR ALLEN G. THURMAN.

LIVES OF PROHIBITION CANDIDATES.

MAJOR-GENERAL CLINTON B. FISK.

THE REV. RICHARD WHEATLEY, D. D.

CLINTON Bowen Fisk, one of the most prominent and influential advocates of the great Temperance Reform, is a winter resident of New York, at No. 175 West 58th street. His home is at Seabright, N. J., where he is a citizen and laborer with God for men.

Born in the town of York, Livingston County, New York, on the 8th day of December, 1828, he derived physical being from the best type of New England ancestry. His earliest American progenitor emigrated hither from the Dano-Saxon county of Lincoln, on the east coast of England, somewhere about the year 1700. Bacon's *Genesis of the New England Churches* conclusively shows that in that section were born the mightiest movements of modern civilization. Lincolnshire is not only the remote parent of the American Republic, but of the great Methodistic revival, which is its strongest conservative force. True to the patriotic and military instincts of his forefathers, the great-grandfather of Clinton B. Fisk entered the Revolutionary army under General Washington, served with great efficiency, and rose to the rank of Major-General. His descendants have distinguished themselves in other fields of warfare than that of the sword. Wilbur Fisk,

the profound theologian, and able President of the Wesleyan University, Middletown, Conn., was a first cousin of Benjamin B., and father of Clinton B. Fisk. The latter married Lydia Aldrich, a New England lady of Lincolnshire descent, and by her became the father of six sons, of whom Clinton B. was the fifth. A manufacturer and contractor by occupation, he was an intimate friend of Governor De Witt Clinton, whom he assisted in building the Erie Canal, and whose patronymic he bestowed upon his fifth child to serve as a given designation. Removing to Michigan in 1830, he there established the town of Clinton, Lenawee County, naming it after his friend and son. There, too, he died in the prime of life —cut off by the malarial fevers incident to the settlement of a new country.

Early Life.

In the struggles and hardships necessary to life in primitive surroundings, Clinton B. grew up to a sturdy and resolute manhood. His parents were of Baptist antecedents, but the training of their children, through the presence and labors of itinerant preachers, was Methodistic. At the early age of nine years he was converted to God, and duly received into the membership of the Methodist Episcopal Church. Educated in the common schools of the neighborhood until he had reached his sixteenth year, he then repaired to Albion Wesleyan Seminary, and there prepared to enter the Sophomore Class of Michigan University. Greek and Latin were studied while engaged in agricultural labors, with such diligence as to threaten the total loss of eyesight. Health failed, and a collegiate career was, therefore, abandoned. Commercial pur-

CLINTON B. FISK. JOHN A. BROOKS.

suits next enlisted his energies. Entering into the employment of L. D. Crippin & Co., proprietors of a country store, mill and bank at Coldwater, Mich., he married Jeannette A., only daughter of the senior partner, on the 20th day of February, 1850, and was also admitted to the firm.

Crippin & Fisk continued in associate relations until 1858, when the firm was dissolved, and the latter removed to St. Louis. There he established a successful insurance and banking business, and was numbered among the rising men of the city at the outbreak of the War for the preservation of the National Union. No series of biographies furnished more impressive illustrations of the biological facts than that of the old New England families. Habits of thought, feeling, and action, organized in the constitution of consecutive generations, and apparently dormant in the piping times of peace, became vigorously active amid the rude clarions of war. The echoes of the guns that fired upon Fort Sumter the 13th of April, 1861, awoke at once the hereditary instinct, and on the day following, Clinton B. Fisk was among the first of Missouri's loyal citizens to enlist as a private in a three months' regiment for services to the United States of America.

Record During the War.

In January, 1862, he was conspicuous among those who led the revolution that created the Union Merchants' Exchange in opposition to the disloyal Chamber of Commerce. His activity as one of the Executive Officers of the new association pointed him out as a fitting commander of the "Merchants' Regiment," better known perhaps as the Thirty-Third Regiment of Missouri Volunteer Infantry. A humorous story is told of the compact between himself and the soldiers, according to which he was to do all the profane swearing for the regiment. This compact seems to have been pretty well observed by general abstinence from a shockingly bad habit, until a teamster, provoked beyond common endurance by irritating stumps, broken wagon poles and kicking mules, fairly made the night air blue with sesquipedalian oaths. Astounded by this explosion, the Colonel reminded the swearer of the compact. But the latter was equal to the occasion. Recounting his grievances, he insisted that as the Colonel was not on hand to do the necessary swearing, he had to do it himself. This story, with variations, was one of President Lincoln's favorites, and was often used "to point a moral, or adorn a tale."

Having raised a brigade of troops, Colonel Fisk received the Commission of Brigadier in November, 1862. Subsequently he commanded a division in the Army of the Tennessee at the memorable siege of Vicksburg. Thence he was sent to take command of the military districts of Missouri and North Missouri. In that capacity he defeated Rice's attempt to capture Jefferson City, the Capital of the State.

Life and Services after the War.

Resigning his position at the close of the Civil War, he found that Mr. Lincoln was unwilling to dispense with his services. Requesting General Fisk's presence at Washington, the martyr President assigned him to duty in Kentucky and Tennessee. He was Commissioner of the Freedmen's Bureau for all the Central South. The conjoint office of Military Commander and Commissioner for Freedmen sought the man, and in the exercise of its functions the incumbent did the noblest work in his life. It was pre-eminently a work of pacification and reconstruction. He was in reality the Military Governor of Kentucky, Tennessee, Eastern Arkansas, and the northern portion of the Gulf States. Under his Administration social order was restored, industry resumed its avocations, goodly fellowship was established, and civil law regained supremacy. Peaceably if possible, but if not, forcibly, these ends were assiduously sought. Peaceably they were accomplished. Church, school-house, and judicial court supplanted the camp and battle-field. All parties were eminently satisfied with the progress of events. People whose wealth was estimated at a hundred million dollars, and who had been largely identified with the Rebellion, petitioned President Johnson to detain General Fisk at his post of duty until the beneficent task of reconstruction was completely done. Since then he has deservedly been one of the most popular and trusted of all men in the regions, and with all the classes, that he served so well. The Methodist Episcopal Church, in particular, justly regards him with friendliest feeling.

He was commissioned as Major-General by the state of Missouri in 1864. In March, 1865, he received a commission as Brevet Major-General in the army of the United States. Resigning all soldierly offices in September, 1866, he again returned to St. Louis, and embarked in business to retrieve the temporal fortunes previously sacrificed on the altar of his Country's unity. Accepting a position as one of the State Railroad Commissioners, he further became identified with the Missouri Pacific and Atlantic & Pacific lines. To these he held the relation of Vice President and Treasurer from 1867 to 1876.

With the educational development of the South, and also of many of the portions of the North, General Fisk has been, and is, most efficiently connected. During his labors in the South he instituted the Fisk School for Colored People. This has since expanded, under the auspices of the American Missionary Association, into the Fisk University at Nashville, Tennessee. It is fairly entitled to the honor of being the first, and perhaps the best, learned institution hitherto founded for the benefit of the Africo-American race. Undoubtedly it is one of the most successful. Its celebrated Jubilee Singers have made it familiar to immense multitudes in two hemispheres. Many of the best colored teachers, preachers, and missionaries have graduated from its halls. Four hundred students, at least, are now in attendance. Well-equipped colleges of liberal arts, science, theology and law justify its claim to the title of University. Jubilee Hall and Livingstone Hall are two of the finest educational edifices in the entire South.

Rarely does it fall to the lot of any citizen to enter so thoroughly into the great philanthropic undertakings of the Age. Appointed by President Grant to the Board of Indian Commissioners in 1874, he was then elected to its Presidency, and still holds that office. Working in harmony with the Department of the Interior, the Board has been singularly effective in the civilization of the Indian tribes. It has secured the organization of Industrial Schools at Hampton, Va.; Carlisle, Pa.; Lawrence, Kan.; Chilocco, in the Indian territory; Genoa, Neb.; and Salem, Oregon. About two thousand Indian children are trained in these institutions. Local schools are also maintained on the reservations of the aborigines. Along the lines indicated by these seminaries lies the way to satisfactory solution of the vexed Indian problem. Ultimate absorption into the American body politic is the most fitting disposition of the original possessors of the soil, and certainly the most Christian. Trustee of Fisk University, Tennessee; of Dickinson College, Pennsylvania; of Pennington Seminary, New Jersey; of Albion College, Michigan; and of Drew Theological Seminary, Madison, N.J., his personal influence touches society at its tenderest and most pervasive points.

In the Methodist Episcopal Church General Fisk holds, or has held, the several offices of Sunday school superintendent, steward, trustee and class leader. License as exhorter or local preacher he has persistently declined, and that from the conviction that laymen—distinctively such—have more power for good outside either office. Of the General Conference of his Church, held quadrennially, he was a lay member from Missouri in 1876, and from New Jersey in 1880 and 1884. In that body he officiated as Chairman of the Committee on the state of the Church, and also of the Committee on the Book Concern. For the past twenty years he has been a member of the Missionary Board of the Methodist Episcopal Church and Chairman of its Committee on missions in Japan and Corea. He is also Chairman of the eastern section of the Book Committee of the Methodist Episcopal Church, under whose supervision its stupendous publishing work is carried on.

Averse to practical politics, and declining personal participation in their procedures, he yet accepted the Prohibitionists' nomination for the Gubernatorial Chair of New Jersey in 1886. Pure sense of duty compelled candidacy. Twenty thousand voters cast their ballots for his election. He failed of the popular choice, as was expected, but was rewarded by an increase of 500 per cent. on any previous vote, and by the strengthening of moral principles in his adopted Commonwealth. All corrupt proffers of aid, or of coalition, were emphatically yet politely refused. Giving five months of time, 5,000 miles of travel, 125 speeches, and money without stint in prosecution of a wholly legitimate canvass, he created no political antagonisms, but said more and better things in behalf of the Republicans than they could say for themselves. Of their great historic party he is one of the founders, and has marched with its leaders from the days of Fremont to those of Garfield. For ten years he pleaded with its guiding minds to take up the burning question of saloon control of politics, and to combine with all genuine philanthropists in the effort to dethrone King Alcohol.

Since 1876 General Fisk has been in the banking and investment business in New York, and naturally commands the confidence and support of a large clientage. But neither pressing financial affairs, nor love of literature, nor participation in great reformatory enterprises, is allowed to deprive him of the luxury of immediate toil for the spiritual and temporal welfare of the masses. As Vice President of the New York City Church Extension and Missionary Society of the Methodist Episcopal Church, his form and voice are familiar, alike in public or private meetings held for the promotion of its interests, and in the garrets and cellars of the poorest of the poor. As an impromptu speaker he is remarkably forceful and felicitous. The whole range of British and American poetry is intimately known to him, and from its choicest products he plucks at will what will most adorn the sentiment on which he lays special stress. Still in the zenith of physical and intellectual power, the cause of total abstinence, of prohibition, and above all of that Christianity in earnest from which each receives its most fitting support, may expect to receive from him, under God, yet more efficient aid in the future.

THE REV. JOHN A. BROOKS, D. D.
Prohibition Candidate for Vice President.

John A. Brooks was born in Mason county, Kentucky, June 8, 1836. His ancestors were of the old Virginia stock, sturdy, self-reliant and honest.

Young Brooks entered Bethany College, Virginia, at a comparatively early age, and graduated from that institution with high honors in 1856.

After graduation he was elected President of Flanningsbury College, Kentucky, which position he occupied two years; then, resigning the position he entered the active ministry. During the civil war Dr. Brooks was identified with the south and struggled bravely for the Confederacy. "Accepting the situation" heartily, he is now an ardent supporter of the stars and stripes.

He has been at the head of the Prohibition Movement in Missouri from its inception, assisting in the orginization of the party at Sedalia, in 1880. He was the Prohibition candidate for Governor of Missouri in 1884, and made a vigorous canvass of the State.

Since 1884 he has been the General Agent of the Prohibition Lecture Bureau and spent much time in its interests in the Southern States. He is a man of powerful physique and possessed of robust health. He is a forceful, earnest speaker, and having "the courage of his convictions," makes a strong impression upon his audiences.

LIVES OF OTHER CANDIDATES.

BELVA ANN LOCKWOOD.
Equal Rights Candidate for President.

The National Convention of the Equal Rights party met at Des Moines, Iowa, May 15, 1888, and nominated Mrs. Belva Ann Bennett Lockwood for President, and Albert H. Love for Vice President.

Mrs. Belva Lockwood was born in Royalton, New York, October 24th, 1820. She was educated in district schools, and taught at the age of fourteen. In 1838 she married Uriah H. McNall, a farmer, who died in 1853, and in 1868 she married Dr. Ezekiel Lockwood, who died in 1877.

She has taught school in New York State and Washington, D. C.

Having early turned her attention and aid to the relief of her oppressed and down-trodden sisters, she secured, in 1870, the passage of a bill "to secure to women employes of the government equal pay with men for equal work."

In 1879 she obtained the passage of a bill "authorizing the admission of properly qualified women to practice in the Supreme and Circuit Courts.

She has been an active advocate of woman suffrage, and in 1884 was nominated by the Woman's National Rights Party in California for the Presidency of the United States.

Mrs. Lockwood graduated in 1857 from the Syracuse University. In 1870 she began the study of law. She was admitted to the bar, and has gained prominence in the lower courts. She is one of the foremost women lawyers in the United States. In 1879 she was permitted to practice before the Supreme Court of the United States and the Court of Claims, and enjoys the distinction of being the only woman ever admitted to practice before the Supreme Court at Washington, D. C.

A. J. STREETER. ROBT. H. COWDRAY.
BELVA A. LOCKWOOD.

A. J. STREETER.
Union Labor Candidate for President.

The Union Labor Party met at Cincinnati, Ohio, February 22, 1887, and nominated A. J. Streeter, of Illinois, for President, and Charles E. Cunningham, of Arkansas, for Vice-President.

A. J. Streeter was born Jan. 18, 1823, in Rensselaer county, New York. He moved with his father to Lee county, Illinois, in 1836.

He helped build the log school house where he received his first lessons in reading, writing and arithmetic. This school he attended two winter terms. At the age of twenty-three he felt the need of an education. Having no means but a pair of hands and an iron constitution and twenty dollars in his pocket, he made his way across the open prairie to Galesburg, Illinois, and entered Knox College. Here he paid for one term's tuition, and worked every spare hour and Saturdays to pay his way. He lived in a garret and cooked his own meals. In this way he lived two years and a half.

Being industrious he soon won success. He now lives in New Windsor, Illinois, where he does a large business in farming and stock raising.

His political life began soon after his location at New Windsor, where he served several terms on the Board of Supervisors. In 1872 he was elected to the Illinois State Legislature. In 1878 he was a candidate for Congress on the Greenback Labor ticket and received a large number of votes. The same party made him their candidate for Governor of Illinois in 1880. He was elected to the State Senate in 1884, and succeeded in having a bill passed to prevent the sale of tobacco to minors.

ROBERT H. COWDREY.
United Labor Candidate for President.

The United Labor party met at Cincinnati, 1888, and nominated Robert H. Cowdrey, of Illinois, for President, and W. H. T. Wakefield, of Kansas, for Vice-President.

Robert H. Cowdrey was born in 1852 at Lafayette, Indiana. He was educated in the village schools, where he soon mastered all that was to be learned there. In 1871 he went to Chicago to seek a wider field. He entered the Chicago Pharmaceutical College from which he graduated in due course of time with honors. He was editor of the Pharmacist and Chemist for seven years.

For a comparatively young man he has superior attainments, marked capabilities, notable as a orator, and stands high in position and estimation among Labor Unions.

TARIFF HISTORY OF THE UNITED STATES.

[*Henry J. Philpott, Esq.*]

In this article I propose to compile the shortest possible complete history of the American tariff sytem. The first tariff was passed the 4th of July, 1789; the last one the 3d of March, 1883. Including these two, there have been fifty-five Tariff acts passed in ninety-nine years. Most of them did not make radical changes in the tariff. The tariffs usually considered the most important by historians, were passed as follows, and they have all been named, also as follows:

Hamilton tariff. . . . . 1789 | Abominations tariff. . . 1828 | Walker tariff. 1846
Calhoun tariff. . . . . . . 1816 | Compromise tariff . . . 1833 | Morrill tariff. 1861
Clay tariff. . . . . . . 1824 | Whig tariff. 1842

The general effects of these various tariffs, and of the modifications made in them between times, may be traced in the following table, which shows the average rate of tax paid on all imports for each year since 1791. There was always a free list—always absolute free trade in many things—but here are the average rates for the year on the things actually taxed:

Year.	Per cent	Year	Per cent	Year	Per cent	Year	Per cent	Year	Per cent
1791	15.34	1811	35.62	1831	47.38	1851	26.63	1871	43.95
1792	11.54	1812	13.07	1832	42.96	1852	27.38	'72	41.35
1793	14.68	1813	69.03	1833	38.25	1853	25.93	'73	38.07
1794	17.10	1814	46.79	1834	40.19	'54	25.61	'74	38.53
1795	11.21	1815	6.84	1835	40.38	'55	26.82	'75	40.68
1796	12.02	1816	27.94	1836	34.94	'56	26.05	'76	44.74
1797	15.60	1817	32.90	1837	29.18	'57	22.45	'77	42.89
1798	19.99	1818	16.78	1838	41.33	'58	22.43	'78	42.75
1799	19.70	1819	29.81	1839	31.77	'59	19.56	'79	44.87
1800	17.42	1820	26.69	1840	34.39	'60	19.67	'80	43.48
1801	16.61	1821	30.99	1841	34.56	'61	18.84	'81	43.20
1802	30.67	1822	27.13	1842	25.81	'62	36.20	'82	42.66
1803	20.52	1823	39.21	1843	29.19	'63	32.62	'83	45.45
1804	22.76	1824	50.21	1844	36.88	'64	36.69	'84	41.61
1805	19.19	1825	50.24	1845	34.45	'65	47.56	'85	45.86
1806	21.22	1826	49.26	1846	33.35	'66	48.35	'86	45.55
1807	20.09	1827	53.76	1847	28.02	'67	46.67	'87	47.10
1808	37.22	1828	47.59	1848	26.28	,68	48.63	Estim'td aver. rate	
1809	18.80	1829	54.18	1849	26.11	'69	47.22	under Mill's	
1810	14.07	1830	61.69	1850	27.14	'70	47.08	bill	40.00

The reader will be surprised to observe that the highest average rate was in 1813 and the lowest in 1815, although there intervened no important change in the law, and that the rate for 1813 was ten times as high as for 1815. Washington never lived to see the tariff as high as 20 per cent—half the rate left by the Mills' bill—though the year before he died, 1798, shaved it pretty close. It was not until 1813, when the Government was 24 years old, and was in the midst of war, that the average rate reached the point proposed in the Mills bill. It has passed that point in only thirty-three of the ninety-nine years of our National life, and twenty-one of these have been collected under the present tariff. The average rate collected in 1887 has been exceeded but thirteen times in our history, and eight of these were before the war. The highest series of rates collected for any term of seven years was from 1824 to 1830, inclusive. It actually averaged for the seven years more than 52 per cent. Numerous other interesting comparisons will occur to the student.

So much for the general average rate collected on all dutiable goods. Now let us tabulate as best we can briefly the history of rates enacted on certain selected articles of common use. This is a herculean task, for the reason that there are two kinds of tariff taxes—specific and ad valorem. A specific tax or duty is so much on the pound, yard, gallon, barrel, or bushel, etc. An ad valorem duty is so much on the dollar's worth. How can we compare these? How can we compare a tax of 10 cents a yard, under one tariff, with a tax of 20 per cent on the cost price, under another tariff? If we knew the foreign cost of the cloth taxed 10 cents a yard, we could do it, but it is only within recent years that the Government has told us that—or even instructed its custom-house officers to find it out. To confuse matters still more, the present tariff often levies both kinds of duties on the same article. Thus on one of the six classes into which women's and children's dress goods are divided, the tax is six cents a square yard (specific) and 35 per cent (ad valorem). But this is not the oddest nor most confusing feature about it, for if the goods weigh over four ounces to the square yard the tax is levied in a still different way, and instead of six or eight cents a yard it is 50 cents a pound, plus the 35 per cent. If past tariffs were as intricate as the present one our task would indeed be hopeless. But in all tariffs there are clauses stating what the taxes shall be on all articles of the several great classes "not otherwise provided for" (n. o. p.). Into these n. o. p. clauses are dumped the articles of each great class which the tax-layers couldn't think of or were afraid they couldn't with sufficient accuracy describe in their proper places. The taxes they laid on these were of necessity simple and usually ad valorem, and furnished a key to the mind of the legislator. If he laid a tax of 20 per cent on cottons "n. o. p.," you may well guess that he thought he was putting about an average of 20 per cent on the cottons he did provide for. In the following table I occasionally make this use of the n. o. p. classes, but always with the letters attached: *See table, page 423.*

The history of the wool tariff needs to be elaborated a little. Down to 1824 wool was free and cotton was taxed. Then wool was divided into two classes, according to value, and if valued at less than 10 cents a pound the tax was 15 per cent, otherwise 20, and afterwards 30. In 1828 the tax on high-grade wool was enormously increased. For eight years it remained at four cents a pound and 40 per cent, and then the compromise tariff began to reduce it a little. The maximum figures I have given from 1828 to 1842 are the highest that could possibly be collected under the complex law, and doubtless far higher than the average actually collected, though that was probably 50 per cent. In 1832 low-grade wool was again made free, and has never since been heavily taxed. Wool is now (since 1867) divided into three classes, "clothing," "combing" and "carpet," and they paid last year 55 per cent, 43 per cent and 25 per cent respectively.

The first tariff was the lightest. It was gradually raised until the war of 1812 broke out, and then it was doubled at a stroke. The genuine high protective system was adopted in 1816, under the influence of Calhoun, who bitterly regretted it. Webster was a free trader when the tariff was raised in 1824, but faced about and helped to raise it again in 1828. This was called the Tariff of Abominations, because the free traders tried to kill it by loading it down with abominations, but to their great surprise it passed with all its sins upon it. It almost led to war, and did lead to the Compromise Tariff of 1833, which proposed a gradual horizontal reduction. In 1842 the Whigs raised the tariff; in 1846 the Democrats reduced it; in 1857 the new Republican party had got control over the Lower House and with Democratic help reduced the tariff again to the lowest point reached since 1816. Four years later they adopted the Morrill, or War Tariff, and gradually raised it until 1867; its extremest features being adopted after the war was over. In 1872 they passed a horizontal reduction of 10 per cent, which they repealed two years later. In 1882 they appointed a tariff commission, and it recommended a reduction which would have left the average rate about 30 per cent on dutiable goods. On the 3d of March 1883, they passed a law which reduced some duties and raised others, among them, as will be seen by the table, those on glass and earthenware, but leaving the general average about the same. All subsequent reduction bills have failed to pass the Lower House until Saturday, July 21, 1888, when the Mills bill, freeing wool, lumber, and some other things, and calculated to reduce the average rate on dutiable imports to 40 per cent, was passed by a vote of 162 to 149.

Tariff act of the year.	Raw cotton per lb.	Cotton goods, per cent.	Raw wool per cent.	Woolen goods	Woolen blank.			Iron manufactures, n. o. p.	Iron in bars	Iron in sheets, plates, n.o.p.	Iron ore, pig & manu.	Earthenware.
1789	free	5	free	5			5	5	5	5	10	10
1790-91		30		free	5		5		5	5	12	10
1792		30	7½	free	7½		free	7½	10	10	15	10
1794-5		30	12½	free	10	10	free	12½	15	15	15	15
1797-1800		30	15	free	12½	12½	free	12½	15	15	20	15
1804-7-5		30	17½	free	20		15	free	15	17½	15	17½
1812-15		60	35	free	30		30	free	30	35	35	30	45	35
1816-19		30	20	free	25		free	30	20	25	20	20
1824-25		30	25		25		free	30	25	25	25	20
1828-30		30	25		35		free	30	25	25	25	20
1832		30	25		25		free	25	25	25	25	20
1833 {1836, 1841}		30	21		24		free	24	24	24	24	20
1842		30	23		23		free	23	23	23	23	20
1846	free	25			25		free	30	30	30	25	30
1857	free	19			15		24	24	24	24	15	24
1861	free	30	5@ 20 lb and 12c ad val	mixed	20		30	30	30	30	30	20@25
1867		35		mixed	20		35	35	45	40	40	25@40
1883	free	35		mixed	20		35	45	45	40	45	25@60

The figures marked with a * are the average rates collected on the next year's imports. All others are the rates embodied in the law.

www.ingramcontent.com/pod-product-compliance
Lightning Source LLC
Chambersburg PA
CBHW022108290426
44112CB00008B/591